FIFTH CANADIAN EDITION

BUSINESS COMMUNICATION

BUILDING CRITICAL SKILLS

Kitty O. Locker

The Ohio State University

Stephen Kyo Kaczmarek

Columbus State Community College

Kathryn Braun

Sheridan Institute of Technology and Advanced Learning

**McGraw-Hill
Ryerson**
Connect. Learn. Succeed.

McGraw-Hill
Ryerson
Connect. Learn. Succeed.

Business Communication: Building Critical Skills
Fifth Canadian Edition

ISBN-13: 978-0-07-105116-3
ISBN-10: 0-07-105116-3

1 2 3 4 5 6 7 8 9 10 TCP 1 9 8 7 6 5 4 3

Printed and bound in Canada.

Publisher: Kim Brewster
Sponsoring Editor: Karen Krahn
Marketing Manager: Margaret Janzen
Developmental Editor: My Editor Inc.
Senior Editorial Associate: Marina Seguin
Supervising Editor: Stephanie Gay
Photo/Permissions Research: Robyn Craig
Proofreader: Judy Sturrup
Production Coordinator: Tammy Mavroudi
Cover Design: Valid Design and Layout / Dave Murphy
Cover Image: © Miguel Navarro/Getty Images; CN Tower: Bruno Muff/Getty Images
Interior Design: Valid Design and Layout / Dave Murphy
Page Layout: Valid Design and Layout / Valerie Van Volkenburg
Printer: Transcontinental Printing Group

Library and Archives Canada Cataloguing in Publication

Locker, Kitty O.
   Business communication : building critical skills / Kitty O. Locker,
Stephen Kyo Kaczmarek, Kathryn Braun. -- 5th Canadian ed.

Includes bibliographical references and index.
ISBN 978-0-07-105116-3

1. Business communication—Textbooks. 2. Business writing—Textbooks. 3. Communication in organizations—Textbooks.
I. Kaczmarek, Stephen Kyo II. Braun, Kathryn, 1947– III. Title.

HF5718.L63 2013   658.4'5   C2012-907223-0

Brief Contents

UNIT 1:

Building Effective Messages 1

MODULE 1: Introducing Business Communications 1
MODULE 2: Adapting Your Messages to Your Audience 18
MODULE 3: Communicating Across Cultures 39
MODULE 4: Planning, Writing, and Revising 61
MODULE 5: Designing Documents, Slides, and Screens 77

UNIT 2:

Composing Letters, Memos, and Emails 93

MODULE 6: Formatting Hardcopy Letters and Memos 93
MODULE 7: Writing Electronic Messages 107
MODULE 8: Composing Informative and Positive Messages 120
MODULE 9: Composing Negative Messages 140
MODULE 10: Composing Persuasive Messages 159

UNIT 3:

Creating Audience-Focused Messages 179

MODULE 11: Communicating Reader Benefits 179
MODULE 12: Communicating with Positive Emphasis 194
MODULE 13: Communicating You-Attitude 208

UNIT 4:

Researching and Reporting 219

MODULE 14: Researching Information 219
MODULE 15: Synthesizing and Documenting Information 235
MODULE 16: Writing Information Reports 248
MODULE 17: Writing Proposals and Analytical Reports 263
MODULE 18: Writing Formal Reports 280
MODULE 19: Using Visuals 302

UNIT 5:

Building Emotional Intelligence: Interpersonal Communication 323

MODULE 20: Listening Actively 323
MODULE 21: Working and Writing in Teams 333
MODULE 22: Planning, Managing, and Recording Meetings 350
MODULE 23: Making Oral Presentations 361

UNIT 6:

Job Hunting 377

MODULE 24: Researching Jobs 377
MODULE 25: Creating Persuasive Resumés 390
MODULE 26: Creating Persuasive Application Letters 413
MODULE 27: Managing the Interview Process 428

Appendix A: Revising Sentences and Paragraphs 447
Appendix B: Editing for Grammar and Punctuation 462
Credits 481
Polishing Your Prose: Answer Key 483
Notes 486
Index 494

Contents

About the Authors   xiii

Preface   xiv

Features of the Fifth Canadian Edition   xviii

Acknowlegements   xxiv

UNIT 1:

Building Effective Messages   1

MODULE 1:   **Introducing Business Communications   1**

Why Do We Communicate?   4

How Is Business Communication Different?   4

What Communications Skills are Essential for Employment?   6

How Much Will I Really Have to Write?   7

How Much Does Correspondence Cost?   8

Poor Writing Costs Everyone   8

Good Writing is Good Business   9

What Makes a Message Effective?   9

How Do Effective Communicators Begin to Analyze Communication Situations?   10

Module Summary   13

Assignments for Module 1   13

Polishing Your Prose: Sentence Fragments   16

MODULE 2:   **Adapting Your Messages to Your Audience   18**

Who Is My Audience?   19

Why Is Audience So Important?   21

Audience and the Communication Process   21

Audience and Business Messages   23

What Do I Need to Know About My Audience?   24

Analyzing Individuals and Members of Groups   24

Analyzing People in Organizations   28

How Do I Use Audience Analysis?   30

Strategy   30

Organization   31

Style   31

Document Design   31

Photographs and Visuals   31

What If My Audiences Have Different Needs?   32

Content and Choice of Details   32

Organization   32

Level of Language   32

Technical Terms and Theory   32

How Do I Reach My Audience?   33

The Advantages of Writing   33

The Disadvantages of Writing   33

The Advantages of Oral Communication   33

The Disadvantages of Oral Communication   34

Use Multiple Channels   34

Module Summary   34

Assignments for Module 2   35

Polishing Your Prose: Comma Splices   38

MODULE 3:   **Communicating Across Cultures   39**

What Is Culture?   40

What Is Canadian Culture?   40

How Does Culture Affect Business Communication?   42

Values, Beliefs, and Practices   43

Non-verbal Communication   45

Body Language   46

Time   48

Other Non-verbal Symbols   48

Oral Communication   49

Writing to International Audiences   50

With So Many Different Cultures, How Can I Communicate Effectively?   51

How Can I Make My Documents Bias-Free?   51

Making Language Non-Sexist   52

Making Language Neutral   54

Talking About People with Disabilities and Illnesses   54

Choosing Bias-Free Photos and Illustrations   55

Module Summary   56

Assignments for Module 3   56

Polishing Your Prose: Subject–Verb Agreement   59

MODULE 4:   Planning, Writing, and Revising   61

What Is the Writing Process?   63

Planning   63

Drafting   64

Rewriting   64

Does It Matter What Process I Use?   65

How Should I Use My Time?   65

What Planning Should I Do to Prepare to Write or Speak?   66

How Can I Jumpstart Ideas?   66

What Else Can Help Me Get Ideas?   66

What Is Revision? How Do I Do It?   67

What Is Editing? How Do I Do It?   68

Editing for Readability   69

Can a Grammar Checker Edit for Me?   69

What Is Proofreading? How Do I Do It?   70

I Use a Spell Checker. Do I Still Need to Proofread?   70

How Can I Get Good Feedback?   71

Can I Use Form Letters?   72

How Can I Get Started?   73

Module Summary   74

Assignments for Module 4   74

Polishing Your Prose: Commas in Lists   76

MODULE 5:   Designing Documents, Slides, and Screens   77

Why Is Design Important?   78

How Do I Begin to Think About Good Design?   80

How Do I Design Paper Pages?   80

Use White Space   80

Use Headings   82

Limit the Use of Words Set in All-Capitals   83

Use No More Than Two Fonts in a Single Document   83

How Do I Decide on a Font?   83

Choose Margins Based On the Situation and the Audience   84

How Do I Design Presentation Slides?   84

How Do I Know If My Design Works?   86

When Should I Think About Design?   87

Module Summary   87

Assignments for Module 5   87

Polishing Your Prose: Active and Passive Voice   91

UNIT 2:

Composing Letters, Memos, and Emails   93

MODULE 6:   Formatting Hardcopy Letters and Memos   93

How Should I Set Up Letters?   94

How Are the Two Formats Similar?   95

How Do I Use Subject Lines?   97

What If My Letter Is More Than a Page?   98

How Do I Show I Am Sending Additional Documents?   98

When Do I Show I Am Sending Copies of My Messages to Other People? 99

What Courtesy Titles Should I Use? 99

When You Know the Reader's Name but Not the Gender 101

When You Know Neither the Reader's Name Nor Gender 101

How Should I Set Up Hardcopy Memos? 101

Module Summary 105

Assignments for Module 6 105

Polishing Your Prose: Making Pronouns Agree with Their Nouns 106

MODULE 7:   Writing Electronic Messages   107

What Do I Need to Know About Communicating Electronically? 108

What Do I Need to Know About Email Messages? 108

How Should I Format Email Messages? 110

How Should I Organize Email Messages? 110

What Kinds of Subject Lines Should I Use for Email Messages? 113

What Should I Know About Content and Tone? 113

When Should I Use Attachments? 115

How Should I Manage Attachments? 115

What "Netiquette" Rules Should I Follow? 116

What Else Do I Need to Know About Communicating Electronically? 116

Module Summary 117

Assignments for Module 7 117

Polishing Your Prose: Correcting Dangling Modifiers 119

MODULE 8:   Composing Informative and Positive Messages   120

What Kinds of Informative and Positive Messages Am I Likely to Write? 121

Confirmations 122

Summaries 122

Instructions 124

Adjustments and Responses to Complaints 124

Thank-You and Congratulatory Notes 125

Why Should I Know How to Organize Messages? 125

How Should I Organize Informative and Positive Messages? 125

When Should I Emphasize How Readers Benefit? 126

What's the Best Subject Line for an Informative or Positive Message? 127

Making Subject Lines Specific 128

Making Subject Lines Concise 128

Making Subject Lines Appropriate for the Pattern of Organization 128

How Can PAIBOC Analysis Help Me Write Informative and Positive Messages? 129

A PAIBOC Problem for Analysis 129

Discussion of the Sample Solutions 130

Module Summary 133

Assignments for Module 8 133

Polishing Your Prose: Applying Parallel Structure 138

MODULE 9:   Composing Negative Messages   140

What Kinds of Negative Messages Am I Likely to Write? 141

Rejections and Refusals 141

How Should I Organize Negative Messages? 142

Giving Bad News to Customers and Other People Outside Your Organization 143

The Buffer 144

Reasons 145

Refusals 146

Alternatives 146

Endings 148

Giving Bad News to Superiors   148

Giving Bad News to Peers and
Subordinates   148

What's the Best Subject Line for a Negative
Message?   149

How Can PAIBOC Help Me Write Negative
Messages?   150

Problem   150

Discussion of the Sample Solutions   152

Module Summary   154

Assignments for Module 9   154

Polishing Your Prose: Finding Your Narrative
Voice   157

**MODULE 10:   Composing Persuasive
Messages   159**

What Are Persuasive Appeals?   160

What Purposes Do Persuasive Messages
Serve?   160

What Kinds of Persuasive Messages Am I Likely to
Write?   161

Orders   161

Collection Letters   161

How Should I Organize Persuasive
Messages?   163

Writing Direct Requests   163

Organizing Indirect Request Messages.   164

How Do I Identify and Overcome
Objections?   164

What's the Best Subject Line for a
Persuasive Message?   169

How Can PAIBOC Help Me Write
Persuasive Messages?   169

Problem   170

Discussion of the Sample Solutions   171

Module Summary   174

Assignments for Module 10   174

Polishing Your Prose: Correcting Run-On
Sentences   177

UNIT 3:

Creating Audience-Focused
Messages   179

**MODULE 11:   Communicating Reader
Benefits   179**

How Do Reader Benefits Work?   180

How Do I Identify Reader Benefits?   181

1. Consider Your Readers' Needs   183

2. Translate Features into Benefits   184

How Do I Decide Which Benefits to Use?   185

1. Use at Least One Benefit for Each Subgroup
in Your Audience   185

2. Use Intrinsic Benefits   185

3. Use the Benefits You Can Develop Most
Fully   188

What Else Do Reader Benefits Need?   189

Module Summary   189

Assignments for Module 11   190

Polishing Your Prose: Plurals and
Possessives   193

**MODULE 12:   Communicating with Positive
Emphasis   194**

What's the Point of Positive Emphasis?   195

What Should I Do If My Message Is
Bad News?   196

How Do I Create Positive Emphasis?   196

Avoid Negative Words and Words with
Negative Connotations   198

Focus on What the Reader Can Do Rather Than
on Limitations   200

Justify Negative Information by Giving a Reason
or Linking It to a Reader Benefit   200

Omit the Negative If It Is Truly
Unimportant   201

Place the Negative Information Strategically,
and Present It Compactly   202

Why Do I Need to Think About Tone, Politeness,
and Power?   202

What's the Best Way to Apologize?   204

   Module Summary   205

   Assignments for Module 12   205

   Polishing Your Prose: Using the Apostrophe to
   Show Ownership   207

MODULE 13: **Communicating You-Attitude   208**

What Is You-Attitude in Writing?   209

How Do I Create Reader-Focused,
You-Attitude?   211

   1. Talk About the Reader, Not Yourself. Readers
      Want to Know How They Benefit.   211

   2. Avoid Talking About Feelings, Except to
      Congratulate or Offer Sympathy.   211

   3. Use *You* More Often Than *I* in Positive
      Situations.   212

   4. Avoid *You* in Negative Situations.   212

Does You-Attitude Mean Using the
Word *You*?   213

I've Revised My Sentences. Do I Need to
Do Anything Else?   213

   Module Summary   216

   Assignments for Module 13   216

   Polishing Your Prose: Using the Apostrophe
   for Contractions and It's/Its   218

UNIT 4:
Researching and Reporting   219

MODULE 14: **Researching Information   219**

How Do I Begin My Research?   220

How Can I Find Information?   221

   How Can I Search Efficiently?   222

How Should I Analyze Information I Find?   224

   Where Else Can I Find Information?   225

How Do I Decide Whom to Survey or
Interview?   225

How Do I Create Surveys and Write Questions for
Interviews?   226

   How Should I Design the Questionnaire?   228

How Should I Analyze the Data I Collect?   228

   Checking Your Logic   228

   Module Summary   230

   Assignments for Module 14   230

   Polishing Your Prose: Combining Sentences   233

MODULE 15: **Synthesizing and Documenting
Information   235**

How Do I Summarize Information?   236

   Summarizing Documents   236

   Summarizing Oral Communications   237

   Paraphrasing   238

How Do I Use My Research Effectively?   239

   Using Précis   241

   Using Quotations   241

Why Must I Document My Sources?   242

How Should I Document My Sources?   242

   Module Summary   244

   Assignments for Module 15   245

   Polishing Your Prose: Using APA and MLA
   Style   247

MODULE 16: **Writing Information Reports   248**

What Is a Report?   249

   What Do Reports Have in Common?   249

What Should I Do Before I Write Any Report?   251

   Writing Purpose Statements   251

What Types of Short Reports Will I Write?   252

   Information and Closure Reports   253

   Conference and Trip Reports   255

   Incident Reports   256

   Progress Reports   257

   Chronological Progress Reports   258

   Task Progress Reports   259

   Recommendation Progress Reports   260

   Module Summary   260

   Assignments for Module 16   261

   Polishing Your Prose: *Who/Whom* and *I/Me*   262

MODULE 17: Writing Proposals and Analytical Reports   263

What Other Kinds of Reports Will I Be Asked to Write?   264

　Feasibility Reports   264

　Justification Reports   265

What Should Go into a Proposal?   266

　Sales Proposals, Requests for Proposal (RFPs), and Grants   268

　Proposals for Class Reports   270

How Should I Organize Reports?   273

　1. General-to-Particular or Particular-to-General   273

　2. Chronological   274

　3. Comparison or Contrast   274

　4. Problem–Solution   274

　5. Elimination of Alternatives   275

　6. Geographic or Spatial   275

　7. Functional   275

　Module Summary   277

　Assignments for Module 17   277

　Polishing Your Prose: Writing Subject Lines and Headings   278

MODULE 18: Writing Formal Reports   280

What Does a Formal Report Look Like?   281

How Should I Organize My Time?   282

How Do I Draft the Report?   283

　Report Body   283

　The Report Ending   285

　The Report Beginning   286

How Should I Submit the Report?   287

　Module Summary   298

　Assignments for Module 18   298

　Polishing Your Prose: Improving Paragraphs   300

MODULE 19: Using Visuals   302

Why Use Visuals?   303

What Are Stories, and How Do I Find Them?   304

Does It Matter What Kind of Visual I Use?   306

　Tables   308

　Pie Graphs   308

　Bar Graphs   308

　Line Graphs   309

What Design Conventions Should I Follow?   309

　Tell Your Story Effectively   309

　Provide the Context   310

Can I Use Colour and Clip Art?   310

　Clip Art   311

What Else Do I Need to Check For?   312

Can I Use the Same Visual in My Document and in My Presentation?   312

　Module Summary   313

　Assignments for Module 19   313

　Polishing Your Prose: Being Concise   321

UNIT 5:

Building Emotional Intelligence: Interpersonal Communication   323

MODULE 20: Listening Actively   323

What Do Good Listeners Do?   324

　1. Good Listeners Pay Attention   324

　2. Good Listeners Focus on the Other Speaker(s) in a Generous Way   325

　3. Good Listeners Avoid Making Assumptions   325

　4. Good Listeners Listen for Feelings and Facts   326

What Is the Difference between Good Listening and Active Listening?   326

How Do I Show People That I'm Listening to Them?   328

Can I Use These Techniques If I Really Disagree with Someone?   328

Module Summary 330

Assignments for Module 20 330

Polishing Your Prose: Using Colons and
Semicolons 332

MODULE 21: Working and Writing in Teams 333

What Kinds of Communication Happen
in Groups? 335

What Roles Do People Play in Groups? 336

Leadership in Groups 337

Characteristics of Successful Student
Groups 337

Peer Pressure and Groupthink 338

How Can Team Members Handle Conflict? 339

Steps in Conflict Resolution 339

Responding to Criticism 341

Paraphrasing 341

Checking for Feelings 341

Checking for Inferences 342

Buying Time with Limited Agreement 342

You-Attitude in Conflict Resolution 342

How Can Teams Co-author Good Documents? 343

Planning the Work and the Document 343

Composing the Drafts 344

Revising the Document 345

Editing and Proofreading the Document 345

Making the Group Process Work 345

Module Summary 346

Assignments for Module 21 346

Polishing Your Prose: Delivering Criticism 349

**MODULE 22: Planning, Managing, and
Recording Meetings 350**

What Planning Should Precede a Meeting? 352

Identify Your Purpose 352

Create an Agenda 353

When I'm in Charge, How Do I Keep the Meeting
on Track? 354

What Decision-Making Strategies Work Well in
Meetings? 354

How Can I Be an Effective Meeting
Participant? 356

What Should Be in Meeting Minutes? 356

What Should I Know About Virtual Meetings? 357

Module Summary 358

Assignments for Module 22 358

Polishing Your Prose: Using Hyphens and
Dashes 360

MODULE 23: Making Oral Presentations 361

What Kinds of Presentations Are There? 362

What Decisions Do I Need to Make as I Plan a
Presentation? 363

Choosing the Kind of Presentation 364

How Should I Organize a Presentation? 365

How Do I Adapt My Ideas to the Audience? 366

How Can I Create a Strong Opening and
Close? 366

Begin With… 366

Close With… 367

How Should I Use Visuals? 368

What About PowerPoint? 368

What Are the Keys to Delivering an Effective
Presentation? 371

Putting Your Nervousness to Work 371

Using Eye Contact 371

Standing and Gesturing 372

Using Notes and Visuals 372

How Should I Handle Questions from
the Audience? 372

What Are the Guidelines for Group
Presentations? 373

Module Summary 374

Assignments for Module 23 374

Polishing Your Prose: Choosing Levels of
Formality 376

UNIT 6:

Job Hunting   377

MODULE 24: Researching Jobs   377

What Do I Need to Know About Myself to Job-Hunt?   378

What Do I Need to Know About Companies That Might Hire Me?   379

How Should I Use Social Networking Sites?   381

What Is the Information Interview?   381

What Is the "Hidden Job Market"? How Do I Tap into It?   383

How Do I Present My Non-traditional Experiences?   384

"All My Experience Is in My Family's Business"   384

"I've Been out of the Job Market for a While"   384

"I Want to Change Fields"   385

"I Was Fired"   386

"I Don't Have Any Experience"   386

"I'm a Lot Older Than the Other Employees"   387

Module Summary   387

Assignments for Module 24   387

Polishing Your Prose: Using Details   388

MODULE 25: Creating Persuasive Resumés   390

How Do Employers Read Resumés?   392

How Can I Encourage the Employer to Pay Attention to My Resumé?   392

What Kind of Resumé Should I Use?   393

How Do Resumé Formats Differ?   398

Chronological Resumés   399

Functional Resumés   401

Combination and Skills Resumés   401

What Parts of Resumé Formats Are the Same?   403

Career Objective   403

Career Achievements   403

Education   404

Honours and Awards   405

References   405

What Should I Do If the Standard Categories Don't Fit?   406

Should I Limit My Resumé Length?   406

How Do I Create a Scannable Resumé?   406

How Should I Prepare an Online Resumé?   409

Module Summary   409

Assignments for Module 25   410

Polishing Your Prose: Proofreading   411

MODULE 26: Creating Persuasive Application Letters   413

What Kind of Letter Should I Use?   415

How Are the Two Letters Different?   415

Prospecting Letters   417

The First Paragraph of a Solicited Letter   419

First Paragraphs of Prospecting Letters   419

Last Paragraphs   420

What Parts of the Two Letters Are the Same?   420

Showing Knowledge of the Position and the Company   420

Separating Yourself from Other Applicants   421

How Long Should My Letter Be?   421

How Do I Create the Right Tone?   421

You-Attitude   421

Positive Emphasis   423

How Should I Write an Email Application?   423

Module Summary   424

Assignments for Module 26   424

Polishing Your Prose: Using *You* and *I*   426

MODULE 27: Managing the Interview Process   428

What's the Best Interview Strategy?   429

What Details Should I Think About?   430

What to Wear   430

How to Get There   431

What to Take to the Interview   431

What Notes to Take   431

What Should I Practise Before the Interview?   431

How to Act   432

Parts of the Interview   432

How Should I Answer Traditional Interview
Questions?   433

How Can I Prepare for Behavioural and Situational
Interviews?   437

How Can I Prepare for Phone or Skype
Interviews?   438

How Should I Follow Up the Interview?   439

What If My First Offer Isn't for the Job I Most
Want?   442

Module Summary   443

Assignments for Module 27   444

Polishing Your Prose: Matters on Which Experts
Disagree   446

**APPENDIX A: Revising Sentences and
Paragraphs   447**

What is Good Business Writing Style?   448

What Style Rules Should I Follow?   449

What Should I Look For When I Revise
Sentences?   449

Use Active Verbs Whenever Possible   449

Use Strong Action Verbs to Carry the Weight of
Your Sentence   451

Make Your Writing Concise   451

Vary Sentence Length and Sentence
Structure   453

Use Parallel Structure   456

Put Your Readers in Your Sentences   456

What Should I Look For When I Revise
Paragraphs?   457

Begin Most Paragraphs with Topic Sentences   457

Use Transitions to Link Ideas   458

How Does Corporate Culture Affect Style?   458

Revising Exercises and Problems   459

**APPENDIX B: Editing for Grammar and
Punctuation   462**

What Grammatical Errors should I Focus On?   462

Agreement   463

Case   464

Dangling Modifier (DM)   465

Misplaced Modifier (MM)   466

Parallelism   466

Predication Errors   466

How Can I Fix Sentence Errors?   466

Comma Splices (CS)   467

Run-on Sentences (RO)   468

Sentence Fragments (Frag)   468

When Should I Use Commas?   469

What Punctuation Should I Use Inside
Sentences?   469

Apstrophes   469

Colons   470

Commas   471

Dashes   472

Hyphens   472

Parentheses   473

Periods   473

Semicolons   474

What Do I Use When I Quote Sources?   474

Quotation Marks   474

Square Brackets   475

Elipses   475

Italics versus Underlining   475

How Should I Write Numbers and Dates?   476

How Do I Mark Errors I Find When
Proofreading?   471

Editing Exercises and Problems   478

Credits   481

Polishing Your Prose: Answer Key   483

Notes   486

Index   494

About the Authors

Kitty O. Locker was an Associate Professor of English at The Ohio State University, where she taught courses in workplace discourse and research methods. She had taught as Assistant Professor at Texas A&M University and the University of Illinois at Urbana. She received her BA from DePauw University and her MA and PhD from the University of Illinois at Urbana. Her consulting clients included Abbott Laboratories, AT&T, and the American Medical Association. She developed a complete writing improvement program for Joseph T. Ryerson, the largest steel materials service centre in the USA. In 1994–95, she served as President of the Association for Business Communication (ABC). From 1997–2000, she edited *The Journal of Business Communication* for ABC. She received ABC's Outstanding Researcher Award in 1992 and ABC's Media Gibbs Outstanding Teacher Award in 1998. Kitty Locker passed away in 2005.

Stephen Kyo Kaczmarek is an Associate Professor at Columbus State Community College and a Lecturer at Ohio State University. He teaches courses in business communication, composition, creative writing, freshman experience, film and literature, globalization and culture, and public relations. He has also taught public relations at Ohio Dominican University. Steve received an MA in English and BAs in journalism and English from Ohio State. He has presented papers at conferences of the Association for Business Communication (ABC), College English Association of Ohio (CEAO), and Conference on College Composition and Communication. His consulting clients include Nationwide Insurance, Red Capital Mortgage Group, and United Energy Systems. He also advises individual clients on job search and interviewing techniques.

Kathryn Braun is a Professor of English and Communications, and a professional writer, editor, and training facilitator specializing in business communications and interpersonal leadership skills. Kathryn teaches critical thinking and rhetoric and composition at Sheridan Institute of Technology. She also trains adults in business and technical report writing, proposal writing, Web writing, revising and editing techniques, active listening strategies, influencing others, interpersonal skills, negotiating and reducing conflict, communicating non-verbally, power reading strategies, and designing and delivering persuasive presentations. Kathryn has an MA in English and is Myers-Briggs-certified.

Preface

The fifth Canadian edition of *Business Communication: Building Critical Skills* provides a practical, plain-language approach to building communication competencies.

This edition builds on the outstanding features of the previous four editions:

- The **PAIBOC** ("payback") **model** emphasizes the rhetorical analysis necessary for all successful communication. PAIBOC prompts students to consider **P**urpose, **A**udiences, **I**nformation, **B**enefits, **O**bjections, and **C**ontext to create audience-centred messages. Effective communicators use PAIBOC analyses to think, listen, read, speak, and write for intended results.
- Each module relates text material and examples to specific **Conference Board of Canada** Employability Skills 2000+.
- **Current examples of Canadian experiences** demonstrate communication theory in action.
- The **modular format** offers teaching/learning flexibility: easily tailored to any course length or organization, the modules can be taught in any order.

Our Audience

Context creates meaning: people learn best when the context is familiar and relevant. This edition provides contemporary Canadian illustrations, references, examples, and stories, with emphasis on communication strategies for techno-savants.

Responding to Teacher and Student Needs

This fifth Canadian edition of *Business Communication: Building Critical Skills* reflects the suggestions of teachers across Canada. I am indebted to these reviewers; their constructive comments inform both the form and the content of the revised text.

As a result of reviewer suggestions

- The text design, plain language, and conciseness improve readability
- Updated exercises encourage student interactivity and focus on communicating successfully in a technology-driven world
- New "Question of Ethics" situations challenge students to analyze their cultural assumptions
- Revised content order increases clarity and coherence
- Information on revising for audience-focused messages (previously Unit 2) now follows the new Unit 3 module on composing strategies
- Information on building interpersonal skills (previously Unit 4) now follows the new Unit 5 module devoted to report writing
- Icons embedded in each module refer users to relevant exercises

Ex.
1.7
1.8

The Fifth Canadian Edition

Module 1: Introducing Business Communications

- Introduces the skills valued in our "conceptual age"
- Demonstrates the interdependence of communication competencies and workplace success
- Describes the conventions of business communications
- Challenges students to apply their knowledge and understanding by comparing academic and business writing

Module 2: Adapting Your Messages to Your Audience

- Describes how context and culture create meaning
- Provides a variety of strategies for audience analysis

Module 3: Communicating Across Cultures

- Expands the sections on intercultural communication to include generational differences
- Describes the values of high-context versus low-context cultures

Module 4: Planning, Writing, and Revising

- Provides revising, editing and proofreading techniques
- Expands information on overcoming writer's block
- Challenges students to use both right- and left-brain techniques in creating notes

Module 5: Designing Documents, Slides, and Screens

- Asks students to analyze the rhetorical purposes of design choices
- Provides relevant examples of how design shapes meaning
- Challenges students to develop their own design criteria based on **PAIBOC** analysis

Module 6: Formatting Hardcopy Letters and Memos

- Provides numerous document models, including hardcopy and electronic letters, memos, and short reports
- Challenges students to apply **PAIBOC** analysis to their hardcopy and electronic communications

Module 7: Writing Electronic Messages

- Discusses email users' ethical and legal responsibilities
- Describes current email usage
- Challenges students to think critically about their electronic communications

Module 8: Composing Informative and Positive Messages

- Illustrates common informative messages
- Describes the organizational pattern for informative/positive messages
- Provides a **PAIBOC** problem for analysis

Module 9: Composing Negative Messages

- Illustrates common negative messages
- Describes the organizational pattern for negative messages
- Provides a **PAIBOC** problem for analysis

Module 10: Composing Persuasive Messages

- Illustrates a variety of persuasive messages
- Analyzes the language of persuasion

- Describes the organizational pattern for persuasive messages
- Provides a **PAIBOC** problem for analysis

Module 11: Communicating Reader Benefits

- Describes how to source reader benefits
- Demonstrates how to translate features into benefits
- Challenges students to analyze benefits from a cultural perspective

Module 12: Communicating with Positive Emphasis

- Discusses the rhetorical purposes of positive emphasis
- Describes how to revise for positive emphasis through layout, organization, and language
- Focuses on ethical considerations of positive emphasis

Module 13: Communicating You-Attitude

- Discusses the rhetorical purposes of you-attitude
- Describes how to revise for you-attitude through layout, organization, and language
- Challenges students to analyze the impact of technology on effective communications

Module 14: Researching Information

- Describes primary and secondary sources
- Explains how to research using primary and secondary sources
- Details the process of preparing to take notes
- Challenges students to analyze and evaluate electronic resources

Module 15: Synthesizing and Documenting Information

- Describes how to paraphrase, summarize, and précis information
- Explains the legal and ethical reasons for accurate documentation
- Describes how to document sources fully
- Models APA in-text citations throughout

Module 16: Writing Information Reports

- Describes types of reports in the context of **PAIBOC** analysis
- Describes how to create purpose statements
- Describes common information reports

Module 17: Writing Proposals and Analytical Reports

- Describes common analytical reports
- Describes report organizational patterns
- Describes how to revise for readability

Module 18: Writing Formal Reports

- Describes formal reports
- Illustrates the writer's approach to managing the report project
- Provides a formal report sample

Module 19: Using Visuals

- Describes the rhetorical purposes of visuals
- Discusses the ethics of using visual representations, with relevant examples

Module 20: Listening Actively

- Describes how to develop active listening skills
- Defines the differences between good listening and active listening

Module 21: Working and Writing in Teams

- Describes the task and maintenance roles of team members
- Describes behaviours of successful team members
- Provides proven negotiating and conflict-reducing communications
- Illustrates the process and activities of collaborative writing

Module 22: Planning, Managing, and Recording Meetings

- Describes productive meeting management
- Challenges students to identify and analyze communication behaviours necessary in virtual meetings

Module 23: Making Oral Presentations

- Describes how to create and deliver successful presentations
- Challenges students to analyze Monroe's Motivated Sequence as a presentation guide
- Challenges students to create presentations supported by alternative media

Module 24: Researching Jobs

- Describes a variety of networking strategies and opportunities
- Asks students to apply their knowledge by gathering industry, organization, and career information

Module 25: Creating Persuasive Resumés

- Explains and models current resumé formats
- Challenges students to identify their accomplishments, reframing these as achievement statements
- Describes proofreading strategies

Module 26: Creating Persuasive Application Letters

- Models contemporary application letters
- Explains how to tailor job application materials to a specific organization
- Describes how to write an email application
- Challenges students to create job application materials that differentiate them from the competition

Module 27: Managing the Interview Process

- Explains how to prepare an interview strategy
- Describes the communication behaviours of successful interviewees
- Provides common interview questions and answers
- Describes how to prepare for behavioural, situational, phone, and video interviews
- Describes how to follow up the interview

Revising and Editing Resources

- Provides specifics on how to create clear, concise, comprehensive, and correct prose
- Identifies the common errors of adult writers and describes how to correct them
- Offers numerous exercises that allow students to apply their learning

Features of the Fifth Canadian Edition

Conference Board of Canada's Employability Skills 2000+

Module 1 introduces students to the Conference Board of Canada Employability Skills 2000+, a grouping of critical skills and aptitudes needed for success in the workplace. Each subsequent module begins with an Employability Skills 2000+ checklist, which students can use to focus their learning.

Employability Skills

Employability Skills 2000+ Checklist

You will need these skills to enter and excel in the world of work—whether you work on your own or as a part of a team. Indeed, job postings consistently list "excellent verbal and written communication skills, strong analytical and decision-making abilities, and the ability to work well with others" at the top of their position requirements.[1]

You can apply and build these skills in every personal and professional situation.

Fundamental Skills: The skills needed as a base for further development

You will be better prepared to progress in the world of work when you can

Communicate
- Read and understand information presented in a variety of forms (e.g., words, graphs, charts, diagrams)
- Write and speak so others pay attention and understand
- Listen and ask questions to understand and appreciate the points of view of others
- Share information using a range of information and communications technologies (e.g., voice, email, computers)
- Use relevant scientific, technological, and mathematical knowledge and skills to explain or clarify ideas

Manage Information
- Locate, gather, and organize information using appropriate technology and information systems
- Access, analyze, and apply knowledge and skills from various disciplines (e.g., the arts, languages, science, technology, mathematics, social sciences, the humanities)

Use Numbers
- Decide what needs to be measured or calculated
- Observe and record data using appropriate methods, tools, and technology
- Make estimates and verify calculations

Think and Solve Problems
- Assess situations and identify problems
- Seek different points of view and evaluate them based on facts
- Recognize the human, interpersonal, technical, scientific, and mathematical dimensions of a problem
- Identify the root cause of a problem
- Be creative and innovative in exploring possible solutions
- Readily use science, technology, and mathematics as ways to think, gain and share knowledge, solve problems, and make decisions
- Evaluate solutions to make recommendations or decisions
- Implement solutions
- Check to see if a solution works, and act on opportunities for improvement

Employability Skills 2000+ Icons

These icons indicate which material is directly relevant to the workplace. Highlighting employability skills ensures that students understand how text content is important for achieving their employment goals.

Oral Communication

Effective oral communication also requires cultural awareness. Both the purpose and content of business communication differ across cultures and genders. Deborah Tannen uses the term *conversational style* to denote our conversational patterns and the meanings we give to them: the way we show interest, courtesy, social decorum.[32]

Your answers to the following questions reveal your own conversational style:

- How long a pause tells you that it's your turn to speak?
- Do you see interruption as rude? Or do you say things while other people are still talking to show that you're interested and to encourage them to say more?
- Do you show interest by asking many questions? Or do you see questions as intrusive and wait for people to volunteer whatever they have to say?

No conversational style is better or worse than any another, but people with different styles may feel uncomfortable without knowing why. A boss who speaks slowly may frustrate a subordinate who talks quickly. People who talk more slowly may feel shut out of a conversation with people who talk more quickly. Someone who has learned to make requests directly ("Please pass the salt") may be annoyed by someone who uses indirect requests ("This casserole needs some salt").

In the workplace, conflicts may arise because of differences in conversational style. GenXers often use a rising inflection on statements as well as questions. They see this style as gentler and more polite. But Boomer bosses may see this speech pattern as hesitant, as if the speaker wants advice—which they then proceed to deliver.[33]

Many middle-aged professionals consider certain speech patterns—"you know," "like," "basically," "right?"—to be eye-rolling irritants. According to University of Toronto sociolinguistics professor Sali Tagliamonte, however, our speech patterns reflect our age and our cultural values. People under 40 "are much more likely to use 'like' when narrating a story, than those over 40." ("And I'm like, OK, I'm all over that.") Tagliamonte believes the use of "like" is a demographic identifier; migrating from California, it has become a fashionable "way to voice a speaker's inner experience."[34]

Daniel N. Maltz and Ruth A. Borker believe that differences in conversational style might be responsible for the miscommunication that sometimes occurs in male–female conversations. For example, researchers have found that women are much more likely to nod and to say yes or say "mm-hmm" than men are. Maltz and Borker hypothesize that to women, these symbols mean simply, "I'm listening; go on." Men, on the other hand, may decode these symbols as "I agree" or at least "I follow what you're saying so far." A man who receives nods and "mm"s from a woman might feel she is inconsistent and unpredictable if she then disagrees with him. A woman might feel that a man who doesn't provide any feedback isn't listening to her.[35]

Sample Documents

More than 50 sample documents provide examples for students. Annotations call students' attention to exemplary approaches as well as areas for improvement.

FIGURE 26.2   **A Solicited Letter (1)**

210 Steeles Avenue West
Brampton, ON L6Y 2K3

Phone: 905.555.3828
Email: mshafe@bell.live

February 1, 2013

Region of Peel
1126 Fewster Drive
Mississauga, ON L4W 2A4

Attention Human Resources

Subject: Job/95423-134317
HHW Facility Operator (Co-op)

As a second-year Chemical Engineering Technology Co-op student at Sheridan Institute, I have the skills and knowledge to contribute to the operation of your Hazardous Waste facility. Through practical application, I understand the Occupational Health and Safety Act WHMIS. Furthermore, in my summer jobs I learned how to handle and store hazardous materials.

At Sheridan I have also developed excellent written and oral communication skills which enable me to communicate information about hazardous waste and depot services to the public clearly and helpfully.

I have my Class G driver's license, a clean driving record, and my own vehicle. I am very flexible and am able to work rotating shifts and weekends. I am used to hard physical shift work. For the past two summers, I worked rotating shifts at an auto parts factory to pay my college tuition. You can count on me to be at work on time and complete tasks to the best of my ability. I take initiative and work well in a team environment.

My Grade Point Average of 3.96 (out of 4.0) illustrates that I am diligent and a quick learner. I will quickly adapt to the Region of Peel's system of receiving, categorizing, storing, and co-coordinating waste shipment.

Please contact me to arrange an interview to further discuss how I can contribute to your organization.

Sincerely

Mohammed Shafer

Mohammed Shafer

Encl.

Annotations: Open punctuation · Letter uses short sentences, clear language and language of the industry and job posting throughout · Letter asks for the interview

FIGURE 26.3   **A Solicited Letter (2)**

638 Changery Court
Lethbridge, AB T1J 2A5
May 21, 2012

Shelley Aquina
Human Resources Manager
Home Outfitters
425 18 Avenue Northwest
Calgary, AB T2N 2G6

Dear Shelley Aquina:
RE: File # 7664566-F

Please consider me for the position of sales manager, advertised in the *Calgary Sun*, Saturday, May 20. I possess the educational background, work experience, and exceptional organizational and communication skills for which you have advertised.

In June I will graduate with a business administration diploma from Mount Royal University, Calgary, Alberta. Throughout my college career I worked with peers on a variety of projects, including sales proposals, formal reports, and sales presentations. In my third year I was chosen team captain for our marketing project, a year-long analysis, and oral and written report of possible marketing initiatives for a Calgary client, MediaWaves. My responsibilities included identifying time lines, delegating tasks, negotiating conflicts among group members, reporting to the client and our Marketing professor, and revising and editing the final 30-page report. Our team project not only secured the top grade in the class, but the client also accepted our recommendations, resulting in an immediate 10 percent sales increase for MediaWaves.

Since Grade 11, I have worked part-time and summers at Canadian Tire in Lethbridge, Alberta. Starting as a stock clerk, I worked my way up to sales associate. My supervisor has commented on my excellent sales skills, particularly my product knowledge and ability to up-sell. During my employment with Canadian Tire—a high-energy, fast-paced environment—I learned to focus calmly on clients' concerns and to communicate confidently. As a result of my performance, I was promoted to assistant manager. While working part-time, attending school, and participating in varsity basketball, I learned to juggle multiple priorities, to manage my time, and to problem-solve.

Please see my résumé for further details.

The market for home decorations and furnishings has become increasingly competitive, and with the entry of American big-box stores like Heritage Homes, it promises to become even more so. I would welcome an opportunity to apply my skills to increase your market share. Please call me at 403-555-4339 to arrange an interview time and date at your convenience.

Sincerely,
Carlos DeLeon
Carlos DeLeon
ENC: Résumé

Annotations: Addresses reader as ad indicates · Repeats words of the ad · Specifics directly connect the experience with the resultant skill · Demonstrates research and industry awareness · Quotes file number as ad requests · Thesis or controlling paragraph tells the reader what's going to be proven in the letter · Jargon of the marketing industry · Skills would have been identified in the ad as necessary for the position · Asks for the interview

Expanding a Critical Skill Boxes

Expanding a Critical Skill boxes focus on how a particular skill works in the workplace and suggest ways students can develop these skills.

EXPANDING A CRITICAL SKILL

Building an Online Community

People spend more time meeting virtually than on any other Internet activity. Social media sites are now "the number one platform for creating and sharing content";[6] and as blogs and Wikis become even more sophisticated digital applications, users' demand for participation in online communities will increase. And for employee communication, that's a good thing.

Organizations can use digital media to build an online community of interdependent teams. As is true of all team building, however, success depends on careful planning. The project managers must consider their purposes, and prospective audiences, content, and culture. When they have decided why they want to encourage virtual networking, companies have to consider how to encourage employees to engage, what content will keep people coming back, what guidelines will communicate appropriate behaviours, who will manage the technological and staffing logistics, and how they will measure success.

Online communities can truly democratize the workplace, facilitate interdisciplinary knowledge sharing, and foster team building. But the community can only be as good as its blueprint and its members.

Sources: Jason Falls, Seven questions to ask before starting an online community; Dave Wilkins and Drew Darnbrough, Developing an online community; Michael Wilson, Best practices for building successful online communities, *IABC CW Bulletin*, 7(4) (April 2009). Retrieved September 18, 2009 from http://www.iabc.com/cwb/archive/2009/0409/#feature1.

A Question of Ethics Boxes

A Question of Ethics boxes contain ethics questions based on business, technology, and media concerns relevant to students' lives.

> **A Question of Ethics: COMEDY OR RACISM?**
>
> CBC's *Little Mosque on the Prairie* continues to attract a global audience, despite its detractors. What ethical concerns might a viewer have about this TV show?

Language Focus Boxes

Language Focus boxes explain the finer points of the English language, and help native English speakers and ESL learners troubleshoot tricky grammar areas.

> **Language FOCUS**
>
> When taking notes, it is best to record them in the language they are given in. If the lecturer is using English, record your notes in English. Do not try to translate into your own language while taking notes, as this might lead to mistakes later when you are studying or writing a report. For example, if you have incorrectly translated a word during a lecture or in a meeting, it will affect the accuracy of your report when you are writing it later and not able to double-check on your translation accuracy.

Cultural Focus Boxes

Cultural Focus boxes explore North Americans' approach to communication, often in juxtaposition with how other regions in the world communicate in business.

> **Cultural FOCUS**
>
> In some cultures, perhaps your own, repeating word for word what a scholar has said is considered the best way to show you have understood and agree with certain points. It is also considered the best way to show respect for that scholar. However, for documents to be acceptable in North America (and many other Western cultures), you have to cite the source and also integrate the points into your own writing. This is how respect for the original writer or thinker is shown; it also demonstrates your own understanding of the ideas. By following the expected rules here, you are showing respect for and understanding of the cultural norms, just as you would expect others to show the same respect while working in your culture.

Checkpoint Boxes

Checkpoint boxes reinforce key concepts presented in the module.

> **Checkpoint**
>
> A **chronological resumé** summarizes what you did in a timeline, starting with the most recent events and going backward (**reverse chronology**). Use a chronological resumé when your education and experience
>
> - Are logical preparations for the position for which you're applying
> - Show a steady progression leading to the present
>
> Use a **functional** or **combination resumé** in these cases:
>
> - Your education and experience are not the usual route to the position.
> - You're changing fields.
> - You want to combine experience from paid jobs, activities, volunteer work, and courses.
> - Your recent work history might create the wrong impression.

Module Summary

Module Summaries provide a concise recap of the key concepts presented in each module.

MODULE SUMMARY

- **Primary research** gathers new information: personal observations, interviews, and surveys are common methods for gathering new information for business documents.
- **Secondary research** retrieves information that someone else has gathered. Library research and online searches are well-known kinds of secondary research.
- Begin your research by narrowing your focus. What are you looking for, and why?
- Draft a **working purpose statement** to clarify your objectives. This purpose statement
- Narrows your research parameters
  - Structures your document or presentation
  - Becomes part of your document or presentation introduction
- Next, ask your reference librarian about the free resources available in your library.
- To research efficiently online, use
  - Keyword and Boolean searches
  - Suggested topics searches
  - Advanced searches
  - A variety of search engines
  - RSS feeds
  - Online tools, topics, and tutorials to navigate, and narrow your quest
- A **survey** questions a large group of people, called **respondents** or **subjects. A questionnaire** is a written list of questions people fill out. An **interview** is a

structured conversation with someone who can give you useful information.
- When creating a questionnaire or interview questions, define your terms, and phrase questions clearly. Use words that mean the same thing to your respondents as they do to you. Use concrete, quantitative, measurable language.
- Closed questions limit answers to yes or no. Open questions encourage more information. Branching questions direct different respondents to different parts of the questionnaire based on their answers to earlier questions.
- To find credible information sources
  - Check the source: look for an author.
  - Look for credentials.
  - Look for the date.
  - Is the information adapted from other sources? If so, try to get the original.
  - Compare the information with other sources. Internet sources should complement print sources. When facts are correct, you'll likely find them recorded elsewhere.
- To take and create good notes, prepare beforehand:
  - Define your purpose.
  - Listen actively.
  - Pre-read materials.
  - Focus on the material you want to record.

Assignments

Each module contains a variety of problems and exercises for in-class activities or homework.

ASSIGNMENTS FOR MODULE 14

Questions for Critical Thinking

14.1 What two variables must your working statement contain? Why?

14.2 Why look for alternative explanations for your research findings?

14.3 Why should you know the exact way a question was phrased before using results from the study as evidence?

14.4 How should users assess the credibility of a website? What methods would you use for critical evaluation?

14.5 How do you review and evaluate what you learn through your research? What systems or practices do you apply to assess how useful the information is?

Student Resources

McGraw-Hill Connect™ www.mcgrawhillconnect.ca

Connect provides students with a powerful tool for improving academic performance and truly mastering course material, plus 24/7 online access to an interactive and searchable eBook. Connect allows students to practise important skills at their own pace and on their own schedule. Importantly, students' assessment results and instructors' feedback are all saved online—so students can continually review their progress and plot their course to success. Additional student resources available within Connect include:

- Practice Quizzes
- Model Documents
- Grammar Practice
- Additional Exercises
- Videos
- Writing Tutors

Instructor Resources

McGraw-Hill Connect™ www.mcgrawhillconnect.ca

McGraw-Hill Connect™ is a web-based assignment and assessment platform that gives students the means to better connect with their coursework, with their instructors, and with the important concepts that they will need to know for success now and in the future.

With Connect, instructors can deliver assignments, quizzes and tests online Instructors can edit existing questions and author entirely new problems. Track individual student performance—by question, assignment or in relation to the class overall—with detailed grade reports. Integrate grade reports easily with Learning Management Systems (LMS) such as WebCT and Blackboard. And much more.

By choosing Connect, instructors are providing their students with a powerful tool for improving academic performance and truly mastering course material. Connect allows students to practice important skills at their own pace and on their own schedule. Importantly, students' assessment results and instructors' feedback are all saved online—so students can continually review their progress and plot their course to success.

Connect also provides 24/7 online access to an eBook—an online edition of the text—to aid them in successfully completing their work, wherever and whenever they choose.

The Connect Instructor Library and Assignment Bank provide all the critical resources instructors will need to build their courses, including a Test Bank, Instructor's Manual, ready-made PowerPoint® presentations, Homework Activities and Custom Assignments.

The Instructor's Manual includes overviews and a listing of learning objectives for each module, key lecture points supported by teaching tips, in-class exercises, answers to textbook assignments, and answers to even-numbered Polishing Your Prose exercises.

The Test Bank contains multiple-choice, true-false, and short answer questions, each categorized according to learning objective, and text page reference.

PowerPoint® Slides present key points for each module.

Pre-Built Homework Activities Bank includes Internet Exercises and Case Study Quizzes. These activities can be assigned separately or in combination with the Test Bank or your own material for interactive assignments and quizzes.

Superior Learning Solutions and Support

The McGraw-Hill Ryerson team is ready to help you assess and integrate any of our products, technology, and services into your course for optimal teaching and learning performance. Whether it's helping your students improve their grades, or putting your entire course online, the McGraw-Hill Ryerson team is here to help you do it. Contact your iLearning Sales Specialist today to learn how to maximize all of McGraw-Hill Ryerson's resources!

For more information on the latest technology and Learning Solutions offered by McGraw-Hill Ryerson and its partners, please visit us online: www.mcgrawhill.ca/he/solutions.

Acknowledgments

This fifth Canadian edition is the result of my ongoing collaboration with the McGraw-Hill Ryerson team: Karen Krahn, Sponsoring Editor; Robyn Craig, Permissions Editor; and Katherine Goodes, Developmental Editor.

Reviewers' comments and suggestions also contributed to creating this edition. Thank you so much for your generous ideas and expertise:

Pat Alix, *Saskatchewan Institute of Applied Science and Technology*
Clay Armstrong, *Vancouver Island University*
Kendra Carmichael, *Conestoga College*
Gail Clenman, *Seneca College*
Valerie Creelman, *Saint Mary's University*
Marissa Fleming, *Georgian College*
Gerta Grieve, *Northern Alberta Institute of Technology*
Karen Kilbride, *Saint Clair College*
Kim Lambrecht, *SAIT Polytechnic*
Janet Legault, *Saskatchewan Institute of Applied Science and Technology*
Chris Legebow, *St. Clair College*
Kathleen Moran, *Conestoga College*
Samantha Pattridge, *University of the Fraser Valley*
Paula Pedwell, *Georgian College*
Sonia Perna, *SAIT Polytechnic*
Susan Ronchka, *Sheridan College*
Carolyn Speakman, *Lethbridge College*
Binod Sundararajan, *Dalhousie University*
Bill Thompson, *Trillium College*
Jacqui Woods-Powell, *Georgian College*

I am particularly indebted to the interviewees, writers, students, and colleagues who continue to teach me so much.

Kathryn Braun

Introducing Business Communications

Learning Objectives

After reading and applying the information in Module 1, you'll be able to demonstrate

Knowledge of

LO1 Why we communicate

LO2 What business communication accomplishes

LO3 What communication and interpersonal skills employers seek

LO4 How to begin to analyze communication situations

Skills to

LO5 Identify the characteristics of effective business messages

LO6 Begin to analyze communication situations

MODULE OUTLINE

- Why do we communicate?
- How is business communication different?
- What communications skills are vital for career success?
- How much will I really have to write?
- How much does correspondence cost?
- What makes a message effective?
- How do effective communicators begin to analyze communications situations?

Module Summary

Assignments for Module 1

Polishing Your Prose: Sentence Fragments

Employability Skills 2000+ Checklist

You will need these skills to enter and excel in the world of work—whether you work on your own or as a part of a team. Indeed, job postings consistently list "excellent verbal and written communication skills, strong analytical and decision-making abilities, and the ability to work well with others" at the top of their position requirements.[1]

You can apply and build these skills in every personal and professional situation.

Fundamental Skills: The skills needed as a base for further development

You will be better prepared to progress in the world of work when you can

Communicate

○ Read and understand information presented in a variety of forms (e.g., words, graphs, charts, diagrams)
○ Write and speak so others pay attention and understand
○ Listen and ask questions to understand and appreciate the points of view of others

○ Share information using a range of information and communications technologies (e.g., voice, email, computers)
○ Use relevant scientific, technological, and mathematical knowledge and skills to explain or clarify ideas

Manage Information

○ Locate, gather, and organize information using appropriate technology and information systems

○ Access, analyze, and apply knowledge and skills from various disciplines (e.g., the arts, languages, science, technology, mathematics, social sciences, the humanities)

Use Numbers

○ Decide what needs to be measured or calculated
○ Observe and record data using appropriate methods, tools, and technology

○ Make estimates and verify calculations

Think and Solve Problems

○ Assess situations and identify problems
○ Seek different points of view and evaluate them based on facts
○ Recognize the human, interpersonal, technical, scientific, and mathematical dimensions of a problem
○ Identify the root cause of a problem
○ Be creative and innovative in exploring possible solutions

○ Readily use science, technology, and mathematics as ways to think, gain and share knowledge, solve problems, and make decisions
○ Evaluate solutions to make recommendations or decisions
○ Implement solutions
○ Check to see if a solution works, and act on opportunities for improvement

Personal Management Skills: **The personal skills, attitudes, and behaviours that expand your potential for growth**

You will be able to offer yourself greater possibilities for achievement when you can

Demonstrate Positive Attitudes and Behaviours

- ○ Feel good about yourself and be confident
- ○ Deal with people, problems, and situations with honesty, integrity, and personal ethics
- ○ Recognize your own and other people's good efforts
- ○ Take care of your personal health
- ○ Show interest, initiative, and effort

Be Responsible

- ○ Set goals and priorities balancing work and personal life
- ○ Plan and manage time, money, and other resources to achieve goals
- ○ Assess, weigh, and manage risk
- ○ Be accountable for your actions and the actions of your group
- ○ Be socially responsible and contribute to your community

Be Adaptable

- ○ Work independently or as a part of a team
- ○ Carry out multiple tasks or projects
- ○ Be innovative and resourceful: identify and suggest alternative ways to achieve goals and get the job done
- ○ Be open and respond constructively to change
- ○ Learn from your mistakes and accept feedback
- ○ Cope with uncertainty

Learn Continuously

- ○ Be willing to learn and grow continuously
- ○ Assess personal strengths and areas for development
- ○ Set your own learning goals
- ○ Identify and access learning sources and opportunities
- ○ Plan for and achieve your learning goals

Work Safely

- ○ Be aware of, and act in accordance with personal and group health and safety practices and procedures

Teamwork Skills: **The skills and attributes needed to contribute productively**

You will be better prepared to add value to the outcomes of a task, project, or team when you can

Work with Others

- ○ Understand and work within the dynamics of a group
- ○ Ensure that a team's purpose and objectives are clear
- ○ Be flexible: respect, be open to, and be supportive of the thoughts, opinions, and contributions of others in a group
- ○ Recognize and respect people's diversity, individual differences, and perspectives
- ○ Accept and provide feedback in a constructive and considerate manner
- ○ Contribute to a team by sharing information and expertise
- ○ Lead or support when appropriate, motivating a group for high performance
- ○ Understand the role of conflict in a group to reach solutions
- ○ Manage and resolve conflict when appropriate

Participate in Projects and Tasks

- ○ Plan, design, or carry out a project or task from start to finish with well-defined objectives and outcomes
- ○ Develop a plan, seek feedback, test, revise, and implement
- ○ Work to agreed quality standards and specifications
- ○ Select and use appropriate tools and technology for a task or project
- ○ Adapt to changing requirements and information
- ○ Continuously monitor the success of a project or task and identify ways to improve

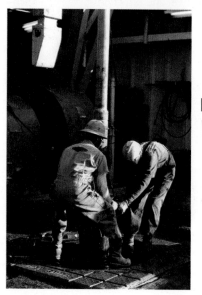

LO1 Why Do We Communicate?

We communicate to connect.

We communicate because of our innate need to make meaning. We communicate to identify and express ourselves, to get work done, to gain recognition, and to make our lives meaningful. And the more skilful communicators we are, the more we are valued, and the more we will advance in our chosen careers.[2]

We communicate most successfully when we (1) take the time to consider what results we want and (2) adapt our message content, tone, and style to meet the needs of our audience, so we can achieve those results. Successful communication usually includes elements of persuasion: we cannot get what we want, unless and until we understand and meet the other person's wants.

LO2 How Is Business Communication Different?

Ex.
1.3
1.4

Business communication uses specific conventions to get the job done.

Effective business communication conforms to your audience's expectations—of medium, format, style, and tone—to meet audience needs as efficiently as possible.

Most successful organizations doing business in North America value time as a commodity. For people in these businesses, "time is money"; their primary need is to get the message, clearly and completely, the first time.

FIGURE 1.1 **Business Communication Conventions, North American Style**

	Medium	**Format**	**Style**	**Tone**
Oral, Nonverbal	– Face to face – Telephone – Electronic and in-person meetings	Space, time, and behaviours defined by participants' individual and organizational cultures	Emphasis is on multitude of symbols: language and paralanguage, eye contact, facial expressions, and body language	Friendly and polite, first-name basis; however, people in positions of power—the boss or the client—establish the tone
Written	– Email memos and letters – Hard copy memos and letters	Defined by organization/ software app	Salutation, simple, concrete language, short sentences and paragraphs, white space and bullets/ numbers for emphasis, headings to guide the reader, direct or indirect method of development, close	Polite but neutral; memos go to internal audiences, letters to external audiences; however, people in positions of power—the boss or the client— establish the tone

Cultural FOCUS

In North America, and in northern Europe, people feel that time can be measured and is valuable, and all activities are scheduled accordingly. (Even children's playtime is scheduled.) Not only do we believe time is money, but we also believe we can "spend time," "waste time," and "save time." Because of this, North Americans believe business communication needs to be clear and concise—to avoid the waste of valuable time.

Business communications—oral, nonverbal, and written—reach both internal and external audiences. Internal audiences (Figure 1.2) are other people in the same organization: subordinates, superiors, and peers. External audiences (Figure 1.4) are people outside the organization: customers, suppliers, unions, stockholders, potential employees, government agencies, the press, and the public.

FIGURE 1.2   **Internal Audiences of a Small Information Technology Business**

FIGURE 1.3   **Example of Business Communication, Internal Audience**

FIGURE 1.4   **Potential External Audiences**

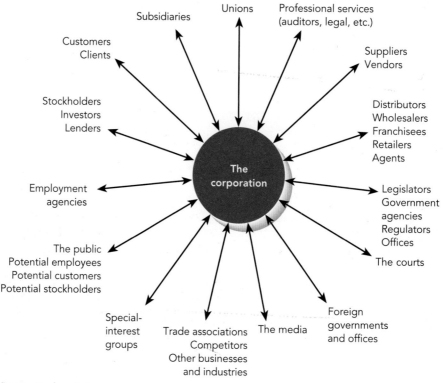

Source: Daphne A. Jameson.

Today's employees have to be able to use a wide variety of media and strategies to communicate effectively with internal and external audiences. Employers expect that even those in entry-level positions will know how to interpret comments from informal channels, such as the company grapevine, to speak effectively to customers and colleagues, to work well in small groups, and to write well.

Checkpoint

Business communication serves three purposes: to inform, to request or persuade, and to build goodwill. Most communication has more than one purpose.

What Communications Skills are Essential for Employment?

LO3 *Effective listening, reading, speaking, interpersonal, and writing skills are vital.*

Listening, reading, speaking, writing, and working in groups are part of doing business. In every job, you need to listen to others to find out what you are supposed to do, to learn about the organization's culture and values, and to establish and maintain work relationships.

You need to read a variety of informal and formal documents, including text messages, emails, blogs, industry journals, newspapers, magazines, instructions, and reports in order to keep current and keep learning.

Your interpersonal communications skills connect you to the grapevine, an informal source of organizational information. Moreover, networking and working with others—inside and outside your workplace—are crucial to developing positive relationships and to your personal and professional growth.

Business, government, and not-for-profit organizations—in fact, all organizations—also depend on written messages. People in organizations produce written documents for the record, to inform, request, or persuade. When you write to inform, you tell or explain something to your readers; when you write to request or persuade, you want your readers to do something. However, the primary purpose of business messages is to build goodwill with the reader: to create a positive image of yourself, and of your organization, so readers will want to do business with you.

How Much Will I Really Have to Write?

You will have to write a lot. Luckily, you already do.

People in organizations have always written to create a record, to convey complex information, to make things convenient for readers, to save money, to make themselves visible, and to express their ideas more effectively. Now, however, people write more than ever before because advances in technology have transformed workers' roles and responsibilities.

Almost every entry-level professional or managerial job requires employees to write memos and email messages, and to work productively in small groups. Tradespeople and technicians also have to write incident reports and instructions.

Businesses today expect their junior engineers to manage projects and write reports. In response to industry complaints about graduates' poor communications skills, universities across Canada now emphasize writing and leadership

On his site, The Business of Fashion, Calgarian Imran Amed combined his business training and fashion interest to herald fashion trends. Imran now lives and works in London while The Business of Fashion continues to be a must-read for anyone in the fashion industry.

A Question of Ethics: THE POLITICS OF FUNDRAISING

Quebec filmmaker Léa Pool based her documentary *Pink Ribbons, Inc.*—which focuses on the politics of certain kinds of fundraising—on Queen's University professor Samantha King's book of the same name. Advertisers and fundraisers encourage us to buy pink products to support breast cancer research. What ethical concerns do the pink ribbon and other "pink" campaigns raise?

Sources: Linda Barnard (2011, September 9), Seeing red over 'pinkwashing' of cancer fundraising, *Toronto Star*, www.toronto.com/article/697879--seeing-red-over-pinkwashing-of-cancer-fundraising; Selby Jordan (2011, September 2), Film based on "Queen's University professor's book to show at TIFF", *Kingston Herald*, http://kingstonherald.com/release/pink-ribbons-inc-premier-tiff-201036218.

People communicate to influence others; to plan; to create products and services; to hire, train, and motivate workers; to coordinate manufacturing and delivery; to persuade customers to buy; and to bill for the sale.

courses in their undergraduate engineering faculties. According to Gabriel Desjardins, a Queen's University computer engineering graduate working in California's Silicon Valley, "Engineers with excellent writing skills are often promoted over people with superior technical skills."[3]

International literacy surveys consistently find a "clear link" between literacy and employment, with "document literacy" proficiency (the ability to read and write well) corresponding most strongly to higher employment rates and higher salaries.[4] To remain competitive in the global market, according to employers, Canadian professionals need business basics that include "communications, team building, report writing and preparing presentations."[5]

Ex.
1.7
1.8

Fortunately, you already write a lot—to a variety of audiences—in texts, tweets, websites, and blogs. These media provide plenty of writing practice, and when audience-centred, can build careers.

How Much Does Correspondence Cost?

Business correspondence is very expensive and even more costly when it doesn't work.

Writing costs money. Canadian communications expert and professional speaker Helen Wilkie maintains that written correspondence—emails, letters, reports, memos—is an "integral part of doing business. If a $40,000-a-year employee spends just two hours a day reading, writing and managing email, that's a $9,000 annual cost." Moreover, as Wilkie and other experts point out, two hours a day is a very conservative estimate of the amount of time employees spend composing, revising, and reading written documents.[6]

In many organizations, all external documents have to be approved before they go out. A document might cycle from writer to superior, back to writer, then to another superior, and back to writer again three, four, or even eleven times before it is finally approved. The cycling process increases the cost of correspondence.

Poor correspondence costs even more. When writing isn't clear, complete, and correct, you and your organization pay in wasted time, wasted effort, and lost customers.

Poor Writing Costs Everyone

- Poor writing takes more time to read and interpret.
- It requires more time for revisions.
- It confuses and irritates the reader.
- It delays action while the reader requests more information or tries to figure out the meaning.

Quite simply, ineffective messages get negative results. A reader who has to guess what the writer means may guess wrongly. A reader who finds a letter or memo unconvincing or insulting won't do what the writer asks.

Whatever the literal content of the words, every letter, memo, and report serves either to enhance or to damage the image the reader has of the writer. Poor messages damage business relationships. Good communication is worth every minute it takes and every penny it costs. In a survey conducted by the International Association of Business Communicators, CEOs said that communication yielded a 235 percent return on investment.[7] Consulting firm Watson Wyatt Worldwide's research corroborates these results. Their most recent study confirmed that organizations that communicate effectively profit dramatically over those that do not. Effective communication translated into a 19.4 percent higher market premium, over 57 percent higher shareholder returns, and reports of higher morale and higher employee retention.[8]

Good Writing Is Good Business

- **Good writing**
  - ✔ **Saves time**, because well-written correspondence is easy to read and respond to.
  - ✔ **Saves money**, because effective writing increases the number of requests answered positively and promptly the first time, and presents your point of view—to other people in your organization, to clients, customers, and suppliers, to government agencies, and to the public—more persuasively.
  - ✔ **Saves energy**, because effective messages reduce the misunderstandings that occur when the reader has to supply missing or unclear information, and because good writing clarifies the issues so that disagreements can surface and be resolved more quickly.
  - ✔ **Builds goodwill**, because it projects a positive image of your organization and an image of the writer as a knowledgeable, intelligent, capable person.

LO5 What Makes a Message Effective?

Successful messages build goodwill by focusing on the reader.

An effective, reader-centred business message meets five criteria:

1. The message is **clear**: the writer chooses the facts—and the structure and language to convey those facts—that enable the reader to get the meaning that the writer intended.
2. The message is **concise**: the writer conveys maximum meaning using as few words as possible.
3. The message is **comprehensive**: the style, organization, and visual impact of the message help the reader to read, understand, and act.
4. The message is **complete**: the reader has enough information to evaluate the message and act on it.
5. The message is **correct**: the information in the message is accurate and is free of errors in punctuation, spelling, grammar, word order, and sentence structure.

An effective message initiates or builds a positive relationship between the writer and the reader (see Figure 1.9).

Checkpoint

Effective business and administrative writing is **clear, concise, comprehensive, complete,** and **correct**. The best messages save the reader time and build goodwill. Whether a message meets these criteria depends on the **interactions among the writer, the audience, the purposes of the message,** and **the situation**. No single set of words will work in all situations.

LO4 How Do Effective Communicators Begin to Analyze Communication Situations?

Ex.
1.1
1.5–
1.6

They consider the context!

Before you write—or listen, speak, or read—you need to analyze and understand the situation. What do you really want to happen as a result of your communication? How can you get the results you want?

Communication has consequences. To get the results you want, consider these questions:

- **What's the point?** What information am I reading, imparting, or listening to, and why is it relevant?
- **What's my purpose?** What is the intended result? What do I want to happen as a result of this communication? How can I make a favourable impression? Do I want to inform or to confirm plans? Do I want to change attitudes and behaviours? What do I really want as a result?
- **Who's my audience?** What do they already know? What do they need to know to make a decision? What are their wants and needs? What do they value? What's in it for them?

EXPANDING A CRITICAL SKILL

Thinking Creatively

Since change is the only constant in today's workplace, the ability to bring a fresh perspective to situations is essential for career success. For example, more and more companies are relying on innovative interviewing and hiring practices, such as behavioural and speed interviewing, to find suitable employees. Some recruiters ask prospects to submit taped presentations; young, entrepreneurial companies such as 1-800-Got-Junk interview several candidates together and choose the most impressive people for further interviews.

Innovative solutions come out of preparedness: you generate insights best by immersing yourself in the situation. But, like any skill, creative, right-brain, or lateral thinking can be learned with practice. Improve your flexible thinking by approaching even mundane tasks in new ways: brush your teeth with your non-dominant hand, for example. In writing, assess problems creatively using brainstorming and mind-mapping techniques.

IBM's tips for creativity are even more diverse:

- Have an argument.
- Brainstorm with someone 10 years older and someone 10 years younger.

Ex-Torontonian Christian Lander, an Internet copywriter in Los Angeles, originated the blog Stuff White People Like in January 2008. The satiric postings attracted thousands of hits and comments, and proved so popular that two months later Random House paid Landers over $300,000 to write a book based on his blog.

- Clean your desk.
- Come in early and enjoy the quiet.
- Leave the office. Sit with a pencil and a pad of paper. See what happens.

Sources: Mathew Ingram (2008, March 26), Stuff white people like, the book, *Globe and Mail*, http://v1.theglobeandmail.com/servlet/story/RTGAM.20080326.WBmingram20080326111531/WBStory/WBmingram/; Mathew Ingram, (2008, March 14), Stuff white people in Toronto like, *Torontoist*, http://torontoist.com/2008/03/stuff_white_peo.php; Allan Salkin (2008, April 6), Why blog? Reason no. 92: Book deal, *New York Times*, www.nytimes.com/2008/03/30/fashion/30web.html?ref=style.

Language FOCUS

You **brainstorm** when you generate every possible idea on a topic, no matter how silly or far-fetched. Critical analysis begins only after you have expressed every solution you can think of. **Mind-mappers** use visuals to outline or cluster, and solve problems, as illustrated in Module 4, Figure 4.2.

- **Where will the communication happen?** Do I have best possible environment for maximum meaning transfer? If I am trying to resolve a conflict, am I speaking face-to-face with my audience? When reading complicated material, have I found a quiet space? If my message is confidential, have I ensured maximum privacy?
- **When will the communication happen?** What time of day and what length of time have I chosen to deliver the message? When will the audience really be able to pay attention to my message? If I am reading difficult material, when am I most alert to absorb it? What is the best time of day for my team to meet for highest productivity?

In every communication situation, your success depends on thinking strategically. You must think both critically and creatively to get the results you want. Use the PAIBOC (payback) questions (Figure 1.5) to analyze the communication context and to consider your message from your audience's point of view. Then get creative: brainstorm solutions that might resolve the situation and meet the psychological needs of the people involved.

LO6 **FIGURE 1.5   PAIBOC Questions for Analysis**

Use the PAIBOC (pronounced "payback") questions to analyze business communication problems:
P   What are your **purposes** in writing?
A   Who is your **audience**? How do members of your audience differ? What audience characteristics are relevant to this particular message?
I   What **information** must your message include?
B   What reasons or reader **benefits** can you use to support your position?
O   What **objections** can you expect your readers to have? What negative elements of your message must you de-emphasize or overcome?
C   How will the **context** affect the reader's response? Think about your relationship to the reader, the morale in the organization, the economy, the time of year, and any special circumstances.

P   What are your **purposes** in writing or speaking?

What must this message do to solve the problem? What must it do to meet your own needs? What do you want your audience to do, to think, or to feel? List all your purposes, major and minor. Specify exactly what you want your reader to know or think or do. Specify exactly the images of you and your organization you want to project. Answer this question: "What do I want to happen as a result of this message?"

Even a simple message might have several related purposes: to announce a new policy, to make readers aware of the policy's provisions and requirements, to convince readers that the policy is a good one, to tell readers that the organization cares about its employees, and to show readers that you are a competent writer.

A   Who is your **audience**? How are readers going to feel about your message? What do they care about? What do they value? What's in the message that will appeal to them?

How much does your audience know about your topic? How will audience members respond to your message? Some characteristics of your readers will be irrelevant; focus on ones that matter for this message. Whenever you write to several people or to a group (like a memo or blog to all employees), try to identify the economic, cultural, or situational differences that may affect how various subgroups will respond to what you have to say.

I   What **information** must your message include?

Make a list of the points that must be included; check your draft to make sure you include them all. If you're not sure whether a particular fact must be included, ask your instructor or your boss.

To include information without emphasizing it, put it in the middle of a paragraph or document, and present it as briefly as possible.

B   What reasons or reader **benefits** can you use to support your position?

Brainstorm to develop reasons for your decision, the logic behind your argument, and possible benefits to readers if they do as you ask. Reasons and reader benefits do not have to be monetary. Making the reader's job easier or more pleasant is a good reader benefit. For an informative or persuasive message, identify at least five reader benefits. In your message, use those that you can develop most easily and most effectively.

Be sure that the benefits are adapted to your reader. Many people do not identify closely with their companies; the fact that the company benefits from a policy will help the reader only if the saving or profit is passed on directly to the employees. That is rarely the case: savings and profits are often eaten up by returns to stockholders, bonuses to executives, and investments in plants and equipment or in research and development.

O   What **objections** can you expect your reader(s) to have? What negative elements of your message must you de-emphasize or overcome?

Some negative elements can only be de-emphasized. Others can be overcome. Be creative: is there any advantage associated with (even though not caused by) the negative? Can you rephrase or redefine the negative to make the reader see it differently?

C   How will the **context** affect the reader's response? Think about your relationship to the reader, the morale in the organization, the economy, the time of year, and any special circumstances.

Readers might like you or resent you. You might be younger or older than the people you're writing to. The organization might be prosperous or going through hard times; it might have just been reorganized or it might be stable. All these different situations will affect what you say and how you say it.

Consider the news, interest rates, the economy, and the weather. Think about the general business and regulatory climates, especially as they affect the organization specified in the problem. Use the real world as much as possible. Is the industry in which the problem is set doing well? Is the government agency in which the problem is set enjoying general support? Think about the time of year. If it's fall when you write, is your business in a seasonal slowdown after a busy summer? Gearing up for the holiday shopping rush? Going along at a steady pace unaffected by seasons?

To answer these questions, draw on your experience, your courses, and your research. Talk to other students, read newspapers and magazines, search the Internet, and look at a company's annual report. You may want to phone a local businessperson to get information. For instance, if you need more information on reader benefits for a problem set in a bank, call a local bank representative to research services and loan rates.

The remaining modules in this book will show you how to use PAIBOC analysis to create business messages that meet your needs, the needs of the audience, and the needs of the organization.

Language FOCUS

PAIBOC is an **acronym**—a word formed from the initials of other words. Acronyms help people remember information.

MODULE SUMMARY

- Although technology has transformed our expectations about *where*, *when*, and *how* we communicate, we still communicate because of our innate need to make meaning.

- Business communication creates, promotes, sells, and delivers products, services, and information.

- In a business context, people write for the record, and to communicate with global audiences simultaneously and instantly.

- Business communication uses specific conventions of formatting, style, and medium.

- The most successful communicators make conscious, informed choices, based on their analysis of purpose and audience: they know that they can only get what they want when they understand and acknowledge what their audience wants.

- PAIBOC analysis helps you to make conscious rhetorical choices about *what*, *when*, and *how* you communicate to achieve your purposes and build positive relationships with your audiences.

ASSIGNMENTS FOR MODULE 1

Questions for Critical Thinking

1.1 Why are most of us such poor communicators? Identify four reasons we often fail to communicate successfully.

1.2 How valuable is a person's time in various cultures? Find a business message (written or visual) that demonstrates that the writer's culture values courtesy or consensus over time.

1.3 How is "school" writing different from business writing? Identify three major differences between school and business writing.

Exercises and Problems

1.4 Business Communications Analysis

How do business messages differ from the communication methods you have learned in school? Together with three of your classmates, analyze a minimum of four business messages (memos, emails, slide shows, advertisements, proposals, flyers, brochures), using the following criteria:

- Purposes
- Audiences
- Information (content, length)
- Organization
- Style (wording, sentence length, paragraph length)
- Layout
- Visuals

Create a table comparing academic writing with the business messages you have chosen. Be prepared to present and explain your results.

1.5 Emails for Discussion—Landscape Plants

Your nursery sells plants, not only in your store but also online. Today you've received an email from Pat Sykes, complaining that the plants (in a $572 order) did not arrive in satisfactory condition. "All of them were dry and wilted. One came out by the roots when I took it out of the box. Please send me a replacement shipment immediately."

The following email letters are possible approaches to answering this complaint. How well does each message meet the needs of the reader, the writer, and the organization? Is the message clear, complete, and correct? Does it save the reader time? Does it favourably influence the reader? Will it keep the reader as a customer?

1. Dear Sir:

    I checked to see what could have caused the defective shipment you received. After ruling out problems in transit, I discovered that your order was packed by a new worker who didn't understand the need to water plants thoroughly before they are shipped. We have fired the worker, so you can be assured that this will not happen again.

    Although it will cost our company several hundred dollars, we will send you a replacement shipment.

    Let me know if the new shipment arrives safely. We trust that you will not complain again.

2.   Dear Pat:

Sorry we messed up that order. Sending plants across country is a risky business. Some of them just can't take the strain. (Some days I can't take the strain myself!) We'll credit your account for $572.

3.   Dear Mr. Smith:

I'm sorry you aren't happy with your plants, but it isn't our fault. The box clearly says, "Open and water immediately." If you had done that, the plants would have been fine. And anybody who is going to buy plants should know that a little care is needed. If you pull by the leaves, you will pull the roots out. Always lift by the stem! Since you don't know how to handle plants, I'm sending you a copy of our brochure, "How to Care for Your Plants." Please read it carefully so that you will know how to avoid disappointment in the future.

We look forward to your future orders.

4.   Dear Ms. Sikes:

Your letter of the 5th has come to the attention of the undersigned.

According to your letter, your invoice #47420 arrived in an unsatisfactory condition. Please be advised that it is our policy to make adjustments as per the Terms and Conditions listed on the reverse side of our Acknowledgment of Order. If you will read that document, you will find the following:

"...if you intend to assert any claim against us on this account, you shall make an exception on your receipt to the carrier and shall, within 30 days after the receipt of any such goods, furnish us detailed written information as to any damage."

Your letter of the 5th does not describe the alleged damage in sufficient detail. Furthermore, the delivery receipt contains no indication of any exception. If you expect to receive an adjustment, you must comply with our terms and see that the necessary documents reach the undersigned by the close of the business day on the 20th of the month.

5.   Dear Pat Sykes:

Next week you'll receive a replacement shipment of the perennials you ordered.

Your plants were watered carefully before shipment and packed in specially designed cardboard containers. But if the weather is unusually warm, or if the truck is delayed, small root balls may dry out.

Perhaps this happened with your plants. Plants with small root balls are easier to transplant, so they do better in your yard.

The violas, digitalis, aquilegias, and hostas you ordered are long-blooming perennials that will get even prettier each year. Enjoy your garden!

1.6   Memos for Discussion—Announcing a Web Page

The Acme Corporation has just revised its website. Ed Zeplin in Management Information Systems (MIS) created the page and wants employees to know about it.

The following memos are possible approaches. How well does each message meet the needs of the reader, the writer, and the organization? Is the message clear, complete, and correct? Does it save the reader time? Does it build goodwill?

1.   Subject: It's Ready!

I am happy to tell you that my work is done. Two months ago the CEO finally agreed to fund a revised web presence for Acme, and now the work of designing and coding is done.

I wanted all of you to know about Acme's page. (Actually, it's more than 40 pages.) Now maybe the computerphobes out there will realize that you really do need to learn how to use this stuff. Sign up for the next training session! The job you save may be my own.

If you have questions, please do not hesitate to contact me.

L. Ed Zeplin, MIS

2.   Subject: Web Page

Check out the company web page at

www.server.acme.com/homepage.html

3.   Subject: Visit Our Web Page

Our revised web pages are finally operational. The 43 pages take 460 MB on the server and were created using HoTMetaL, a program designed to support HTML creation. Though the graphics are sizable and complex, interlacing and code specifying the pixel size serve to minimize download time. Standard HTML coding is enhanced with forms, Java animation, automatic counters, and tracking packages to ascertain who visits our site.

The site content revision was determined by conducting a survey of other corporate websites to become cognizant of the pages made available by our competitors and other companies. The address of our web page is www.server.acme.com/homepage.html. It is believed that this site will support and enhance our marketing and advertising efforts, improving our outreach to desirable demographic and psychographic marketing groups.

L. Ed Zeplin, MIS

Voice: 713-555-2879; Fax: 713-555-2880; Email: zeplin.1@acme.com

"Only the wired life is worth living." —Anonymous

4. Subject: Web Page Shows Acme Products to the World, Offers Tips to Consumers, and Tells Prospective Employees about Job Possibilities

Since last Friday, a new Acme's been on the World Wide Web. Check out the page at www.server.acme.com/homepage.html. You can't view the page if you don't have a computer.

I have included pages on our products, tips for consumers, and job openings at Acme in the hope of making our page useful and interesting. Content is the number one thing that brings people back, but I've included some snazzy graphics, too.

When I asked people for ideas for the company pages, almost nobody responded. But if seeing the page inspires you, let me know what else you'd like. I'll try to fit it into my busy schedule.

So check it out. But don't spend too much time on the web: you need to get your work done, too!

L. Ed Zeplin, MIS

zeplin.1@acme.com

Today's Joke

Fun Links

5. Subject: Acme's Revised Website

Tell your customers that Acme is new on the web:

www.server.acme.com/homepage.html

Web pages offer another way for us to bring our story to the public. Our major competitors have updated web pages; now we do, too. Our advertisements and

packaging will feature our web shopping. And people who check out our web page can learn even more about our commitment to selling quality products, protecting the environment, and meeting customer needs.

If you'd like to learn more about how to create Intranet pages for your unit, sign up for one of our workshops. For details and online registration, see www.server.acme.com/training.

If you have comments on Acme's web pages or suggestions for making them even better, just let me know.

L. Ed Zeplin

zeplin.1@acme.com

1.7 Discussing Strengths

Introduce yourself to a small group of students. Identify three of your strengths that might interest an employer. These might be experience, knowledge, or personality traits (such as enthusiasm).

1.8 Introducing Yourself to Your Instructor

Write a memo (at least 1.5 pages long) introducing yourself to your instructor. Include the following topics:

- *Background:* Where did you grow up? What have you done in terms of school, extracurricular activities, jobs, and family life?
- *Interests:* What are you interested in? What do you like to do? What do you like to think about and talk about?
- *Achievements:* What achievements have given you the greatest personal satisfaction? List at least five. Include achievements that gave you a real sense of accomplishment and pride, whether or not you'd list them on a resumé.
- *Goals:* What do you hope to accomplish this term? Where would you like to be professionally and personally five years from now?

Use a memo format with appropriate headings. Your teacher will provide you with an overview of the memo format. (See Modules 6 and 7 for examples of memo format.) Use a conversational writing style; check your draft to polish the style and edit for mechanical and grammatical correctness. A good memo will enable your instructor to see you as an individual. Use specific details to make your memo vivid and interesting. Remember that one of your purposes is to interest your reader!

1.9   Describing Your Experiences In and Goals For Writing

Write a blog (at least three paragraphs) to your classmates and instructor describing the experiences you've had writing and what you'd like to learn about writing during this course. Use any of the following questions to prompt you:

- What would you most like to learn in a writing course? What topics would motivate your interest in writing?
- What memories do you have of writing? What made writing fun or miserable in the past?
- What have you been taught about writing? List the topics, rules, and advice you remember.
- What kinds of writing have you done in school? How long have the papers been?
- How has your school writing been evaluated?
  - Did the instructor mark or comment on mechanics and grammar? Style? Organization? Logic? Content? Audience analysis and adaptation? Have you received extended comments on your papers? Have instructors in different classes had the same standards, or have you changed aspects of your writing for different classes?

- What voluntary writing have you done—journals, poems, stories, essays? Has this writing been just for you, or has some of it been shared or published?
- Have you ever written as part of a job, or a student or volunteer organization? Have you ever edited or typed other people's writing? What have these experiences led you to think about business writing?
- What do you see as your current strengths and weaknesses in writing skills? What skills do you think you'll need in the future? What kinds of writing do you expect to do after you graduate?

If you need help setting up your blog, go to www.blogger.com for step-by-step instructions. Then visit Seth's Blog at http://sethgodin.typepad.com/seths_blog/2008/04/write-like-a-bl.html to review tips for writing effectively. Edit your final draft for mechanical and grammatical correctness.

Read and respond to three other students' blogs. Prepare a five-minute presentation summarizing students' most positive writing experiences.

POLISHING YOUR PROSE

Sentence Fragments

A sentence has a subject and a verb, and expresses a complete thought. If the subject or the verb is missing, or the idea is unfinished, the result is a sentence fragment.

> **Going to be in Burnaby April 30.**

> **And buy a hybrid car. Maybe a Saturn.**

To fix the fragment, add a subject or a verb to express a complete thought.

> **When I am in Burnaby April 30, I may buy a Saturn hybrid.**

Sentence fragments also occur when there's a subject and a verb but the thought is incomplete.

> **Although I often wait to make client calls until after 4 p.m.**

> **Because she saved her work.**

> **When he upgrades his computer.**

The words *although*, *because*, and *when* begin *dependent clauses*, which means the idea cannot stand alone. It depends on a main, *or independent clause* (idea) for completion.

> **Although I often wait to make client calls until after 4 p.m., I still get voicemail instead of a real person.**

> **Because she had saved her work, Paula was able to restore it after the crash.**

> **When he upgrades his computer, he will be able to use the new software.**

Words that make clauses dependent include

after	**if**
although, though	**when, whenever**
because, since	**while, as**
before, until	

Sometimes fragments work. For instance, fragments are used in text messages, resumés, advertisements, and some sales and fundraising letters. However, fragments are inappropriate for most business documents. Because they are incomplete, they can confuse or mislead readers.

The biggest problem with grammatical errors like sentence fragments is that readers sometimes assume that people who make errors are unprofessional or illiterate. Of course, using "incorrect" grammar has nothing to do with intelligence; nevertheless, many people use grammar as a yardstick. People who cannot measure up to that yardstick may be stuck in low-level jobs.

Exercises

Find and complete the sentence fragments in the following paragraphs:

1. Because people are constantly fiddling with their smartphones, even during meetings and training sessions. We need to establish some ground rules about checking and rechecking smartphones. Surfing the web on their laptops. Leaving meetings to look at email and listen to voicemail messages. I am not convinced that our preoccupation with technology is really saving us time and money. Or contributing to productivity.

2. Since it's only a matter of time before government mandates it, I would appreciate your suggestions for going greener in the office. And in the building itself. While many of you have already taken responsibility for turning off lights, unplugging PCs and the like. We can make even greater, cost-effective changes. And the benefits? Thereby improving morale and employee health. And possibly qualifying for municipal grants.

Check your answers to the odd-numbered exercises in the Polishing Your Prose Answer Key.

McGraw Hill connect™

Practise and learn online with Connect. Connect allows you to practise important skills at your own pace and on your own schedule, with 24/7 online access to an eBook, practise quizzes, interactives, videos, study tools, and additional resources.

Adapting Your Messages to Your Audience

MODULE OUTLINE

- Who is my audience?
- Why is audience so important?
- What do I need to know about my audience?
- How do I use audience analysis?
- What if my audiences have different needs?
- How do I reach my audience?

Module Summary

Assignments for Module 2

Polishing Your Prose: Comma Splices

Learning Objectives

After reading and applying the information in Module 2, you'll be able to demonstrate

Knowledge of

LO1 The audiences who may evaluate your business messages

LO2 The variables of the communication process

LO3 The importance of adapting your message to your audience

LO4 Audience analysis

Skills to

LO5 Analyze your audience when composing messages

LO6 Begin to shape the content, organization, and form of your messages to meet audience needs

Employability Skills 2000+ Checklist

Module content builds these Conference Board of Canada Employability Skills 2000+

Communicate

Be Adaptable

Think and Solve Problems

Learn Continuously

Demonstrate Positive Attitudes and Behaviours

Work with Others

Audience analysis is fundamental to the success of any message: to capture and hold an audience's attention, and to motivate readers and listeners, you must shape your message to meet the audience's interests, and needs.

LO1 Who is My Audience?

Your audience may include many people.

In an organizational setting, a message may have five audiences.

1. The **initial audience**—your supervisor or the client, for example—receives the message first and routes it to other audiences. Sometimes the initial audience also tells you to write the message.
2. The **primary audience**—your supervisor, or the client, or your peers—will decide whether or not to act on your message.

FIGURE 2.1   **The Audiences for a Marketing Plan**

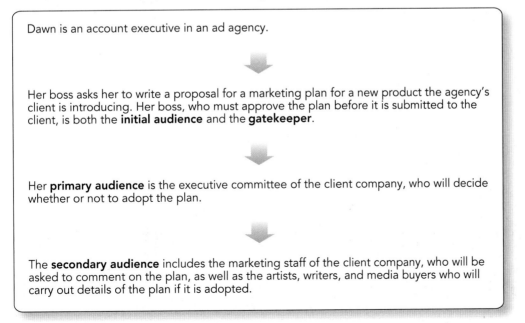

Dawn is an account executive in an ad agency.

Her boss asks her to write a proposal for a marketing plan for a new product the agency's client is introducing. Her boss, who must approve the plan before it is submitted to the client, is both the **initial audience** and the **gatekeeper**.

Her **primary audience** is the executive committee of the client company, who will decide whether or not to adopt the plan.

The **secondary audience** includes the marketing staff of the client company, who will be asked to comment on the plan, as well as the artists, writers, and media buyers who will carry out details of the plan if it is adopted.

FIGURE 2.2   The Audiences for a Consulting Report

Jim and Hiro work for a consulting think tank.

Their company has been hired by a consortium of manufacturers of a consumer product to investigate how proposed federal regulations would affect manufacturing, safety, and cost. The consortium is both the consultants' **initial audience** and a **gatekeeper**. If the consortium doesn't like the report, it won't send the report to the federal government.

The federal government agency that regulates this consumer product is the **primary audience**. It will set new regulations, based in part (the manufacturers hope) on Jim's and Hiro's report. Within this audience are economists, engineers, and policymakers.

Secondary audiences include the public, other manufacturers of the product, and competitors and potential clients of the consulting company.

During the revision process, industry reviewers emerge as a **watchdog audience**. They read drafts of the report and comment on it. Although they have no direct power over this report, their goodwill is important for the consulting company's image—and its future contracts. Their comments are the ones that the authors consider most seriously as they revise their drafts.

Source: Based on Vincent J. Brown (1994), Facing multiple audiences in engineering and R&D writing: The social context of a technical report, *Journal of Technical Writing and Communication*, 24(1), 67-75.

3. The **secondary audience** may be asked to comment on your message or to implement your ideas after they've been approved. Secondary audiences can also include lawyers and researchers who may use your message—perhaps years later—as evidence of your organization's culture and practices.

4. A **gatekeeper** has the power to stop your message before it gets to the primary audience. The supervisor or executive assistant who decides whether or not you can speak to the boss is a gatekeeper. Occasionally, gatekeepers exist outside the organization. For example, regulatory boards are gatekeepers.

5. A **watchdog audience**—the media, boards of directors, and members of program advisory committees—has political, social, or economic power. The watchdog pays close attention to the communication between you and the primary audience and may base future actions on its evaluation of your message.

As Figures 2.1 and 2.2 show, one person or group can be part of two audiences. Frequently, a supervisor is both the initial audience and the gatekeeper. The initial audience can also be the primary audience who will act on the message.

Language FOCUS

A **think tank** is a group of people, usually experts in their field, who work together to provide advice. People in the think tank often work for business or government to help solve a problem, such as how new laws will affect a company.

Why Is Audience So Important?

When people know what's in it for them, they're more likely to pay attention and favourably respond to your message. Successful communicators analyze, identify, and meet the audience's needs.

Audience focus is central to both the communication process and message analysis (PAIBOC).

Ex. 2.5 2.6

LO2 Audience and the Communication Process

True communication involves an exchange of meaning. This meaning transfer is a complex process because each of us is unique and believes his or her own perceptions of reality (meaning) are true; therefore, misunderstandings can occur during any part of the process. Understanding what your audience needs and expects, and adapting your messages accordingly, greatly increase your chances of communicating successfully.

The communication process is the most complex of human activities, and audience is central to that process. We communicate unceasingly. Our audiences interpret our communication symbols unceasingly. Our words, tone, volume and rate of speech, posture, stance and gait, height and weight, hairstyle and hair colour, choice of clothing styles, materials, and colours, cell phone, iPod, and social media use—the thousands of symbols we use, intentionally and unintentionally, are perceived and translated according to our audience's perceptions, shaped by age, gender, culture, intelligence, and the experiences unique to every individual.

Throughout the process, both sender and receiver construct meaning together. Genuine communication occurs when both parties agree on the meaning and significance of the symbols they are exchanging.

For example, suppose you and your friend Mediha are having a cup of coffee together, and you realize you need help studying for the upcoming economics exam. You decide to ask Mediha. You choose to **encode** your request in symbols. What kinds of symbols will you use to convey your meaning? Why?

FIGURE 2.3   The Communication Process

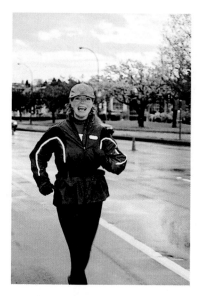

Walking coach Lee Scott, president of WOW Company, uses newspaper ads, email newsletters, her company website, and word of mouth to attract clients from all over Ontario. WOW's walkers—men and women of all cultures, ages, and incomes—have finished first in charity events around the world.

Once you have chosen your symbols, you must **transmit** your **message** to Mediha via a **channel**. Channels include cell phones, memos, smartphones, iPods, billboards, telephones, television, and radio, to name just a few. What channel will you use for this particular message, and why?

Mediha must **perceive** the message in order to **receive** it. That is, Mediha must have the physical ability to hear your request. Then she **decodes** your words: she makes meaning from your symbols. Then she interprets the message, chooses a response, and encodes it. Her response is **feedback**. Feedback may be direct and immediate, or indirect and delayed. What kinds of feedback could Mediha use to answer you? What symbols could she use?

Meanwhile, **noise** influences every part of the process. Noise can be physical or psychological. You're talking to Mediha in the cafeteria; the windows are open. What are the many physical noises that could interfere with your message?

Psychological noise, including emotional, intellectual, or psychological interference, also distorts communication. What psychological noise could interfere with message transfer?

What can you do as an effective communicator, to reduce or eliminate physical and psychological noise?

Channel overload occurs when the channel cannot handle all the messages being sent. Two people may be speaking to you simultaneously, or a small business may have only two phone lines so no one else can get through when both lines are in use.

Information overload occurs when more messages are transmitted than the human receiver can handle. Because of technology, information overload seems to be a constant modern complaint. Some receivers process information on a "first come, first served" basis. Some may try to select the most important messages and ignore others. Some depend on abstracts or summaries prepared by other people. None of these ways is completely satisfactory.

At every stage, both Mediha and you can misperceive, misinterpret, choose badly, encode poorly, or choose inappropriate channels. Miscommunication also frequently occurs because every individual makes meaning using **different frames of reference**. We always interpret messages in the light of our perceptions, based on personal experiences, our cultures and subcultures, and the time in which we live.

Ex.
2.3
2.5
2.6

Successful communication depends on identifying and establishing common ground between you and your audience. Choose information that your audience needs and will find interesting. Encode your message in words and other symbols the audience will understand. Transmit the message along channels that your audience pays attention to.

Correctly identifying your audience and choosing audience-appropriate symbols (words, gestures, illustrations) guarantee a more accurate meaning transfer. Moreover, choosing audience-appropriate symbols and channels means your message will attract and hold your audience's attention.

Cultural FOCUS

Not all cultures communicate the same way. Because culture is an unconscious part of who we are, we are not always able to determine whether miscommunication occurs because of **what** we said or **how** we said it. Study other cultures and try to determine the most effective way to communicate; however, try to avoid stereotypes. For example, many women in North America prefer to be addressed as *Ms.* rather than *Mrs.* or *Miss.* But this is not always the case, so it is best to understand the common standards for a culture and also try to determine individual preferences. This understanding will help you learn to communicate effectively in another culture.

LO3 Audience and Business Messages

Consider the PAIBOC questions introduced in Module 1. Five of the six questions relate to audience, **because successful communication is always audience-focused**. You must know and understand your audiences to identify the information that will attract and hold their attention and motivate them to comply with your message.

A Communication Problem for Analysis

You work in a small, not-for-profit agency that supports disadvantaged youth (ages 13 to 19) in your city. Your organization's purpose is to raise public awareness and resources (funding, housing, job training, counselling services, bursaries, scholarships, and jobs) for these young people. Your agency's mandate includes encouraging and educating these youth to 1) assume personal responsibility for their lives and career goals, and 2) give back to the community through modelling leadership skills for and mentoring others.

Your director has decided that the agency will introduce a wellness program to educate your clients about healthy living practices and to encourage them to find ways to adopt these practices. You and your team members must prepare a message—or series of messages—to explain the new wellness program to your youth clients and to build support and acceptance.

Ex. 2.5 2.9

FIGURE 2.4 PAIBOC Questions for Analysis

P What are your **purposes** in communicating?

Your purposes come from you and your organization. Your audience determines how you achieve those purposes.

A Who is your **audience**? What audience characteristics are relevant to this particular message?

These questions ask directly about your audience.

I What **information** must your message include?

The information you need to give depends on your audience. You need to add relevant facts when the topic is new to your audience. If your audience is familiar with specific facts, concentrate more on clarifying new information.

B What reasons or reader **benefits** can you use to support your position?

Regardless of your own needs, a good reason or benefit depends on your audience's perception. For some audiences, personal experience counts as a good reason. Other audiences are persuaded more by scientific studies or by experts.

Module 11 gives more information on developing reader benefits.

O What **objections** can you expect your readers to have? What elements of your message will your audience perceive as negative? How can you arrange the message to overcome audience objections or de-emphasize negative elements?

Module 10 on persuasion gives more information on overcoming objections.

C How will the **context** affect reader response? Consider your relationship to the reader, the reader's values and expectations, the economy, the time of year, the place and time of day, and any special circumstances surrounding the message exchange.

People, information, and organizations exist in a context. How well your audience knows you, how they feel about you and your organization, how well the economy is doing, even what's been in the news recently: all influence audience response to your message.

LO4 LO5 What Do I Need To Know About My Audience?

You need to know everything that's relevant to what you're writing or talking about.

Almost everything about your audience is relevant to some message, but for any particular message, only a few facts about your audience will be relevant. These facts will vary depending on each communication situation (see Table 2.1).

Employability Skills

In general, you need to use empathy and critical-thinking tools. **Empathy** is the ability to put yourself in someone else's shoes, to feel with that person. Empathy requires being audience-centred because the audience is *not* just like you.

Ex. 2.7

Critical thinking involves gathering as much information as you can about someone or something, and then making decisions based on that information. You need to use your research and your knowledge about people and about organizations to predict likely responses.

Analyzing Individuals and Members of Groups

When you write or speak to people in your own organization, and in other organizations you work with, you may be able to analyze your audience as individuals. You may already know your audience; it might be easy to get additional information by talking to members of your audience, talking to people who know your audience, and observing your audience.

In other organizational situations, however, you'll analyze your audience as members of a group: "taxpayers who must be notified that they owe more income tax," "customers living in the northeast end of the city," or "employees with small children."

TABLE 2.1   Identifying Key Audience Characteristics for Messages Ex. 2.7 2.8

Message, Medium, and Purpose	Audience	Relevant factors
Intranet and corporate blog announcing that the company will reimburse employees for tuition if they take work-related college or university courses	All employees	1. Attitudes toward formal education (some people find courses enjoyable; others might be intimidated) 2. Time available (some might be too busy) 3. Interest in being promoted or in receiving cross-training 4. Attitude toward company (those committed to its success will be more interested in the program)
Tweet, Facebook announcement offering special financing on a new or used car	Postsecondary students	1. Income 2. Expectations of future income (and ability to repay loan) 3. Interest in having a new car 4. Attitude toward cars offered by that dealership 5. Attitude about environmental concerns 6. Knowledge about fuel efficiency and hybrid cars 7. Knowledge of interest rates 8. Access to other kinds of financing
Municipal website and pamphlet describing new methods of waste sorting and collecting	Municipal homeowners	1. Education 2. Attitudes about home ownership 3. Awareness of environment 4. Feelings about neighbourhood and community

Since audience analysis is central to the success of your message, you'll need to consider the following pertinent information about your audience:

- Their knowledge about your topic
- Their demographic factors, such as age, gender, education, income, class, marital status, number of children, home ownership, location
- Their personality
- Their attitudes, values, and beliefs
- Their past behaviour

Prior Knowledge
Even people in your own organization won't share all your knowledge. Many salespeople in the automotive industry, for example, don't know the technical language of their service mechanics.

Most of the time, you won't know exactly what your audience knows. Moreover, even if you've told readers before, they might not remember the old information when they read the new message. In any case, avoid mind-numbing details. If, however, you want to remind readers of *relevant facts* tactfully,

- Preface statements with "As you know," "As you may know," "As we've discussed," or a similar phrase.
- Always spell out acronyms the first time you use them: "Employee Stock Ownership Plan (ESOP)."
- Provide brief definitions in the text: "the principal (the money you have invested)."

Demographic Factors
Demographic characteristics can be objectively quantified, or measured, and include age, gender, religion, education level, income, location, and so on.

Businesses and governments use a variety of demographic data to forecast people's behaviours, and to design their strategies accordingly. For example, in his *Boom, Bust and Echo*

EXPANDING A CRITICAL SKILL

Understanding What Your Organization Wants

Every workplace has rules about what "counts," and the best communicators ferret these out fast. These rules make up the corporate culture (Module 3); your awareness of the norms of your organizational culture is essential to work–life success.

Even in the same industry, different organizations and different supervisors may care about different things. One boss circles misspelled words and posts the offending message on a bulletin board for everyone to see. Other people are more tolerant of errors. One company values original ideas, while another workplace tells employees just to do what they're told. One supervisor likes technology and always buys the latest hardware and software; another is technophobic and has to be persuaded to get needed upgrades. Private-sector clients value short proposals and reports,

preferably in PowerPoint™; many governments prefer longer, more detailed paper documents.

To find out what counts in your organization,

Ex. 2.8 2.9

- Ask your boss, "What parts of my job are most important? What's the biggest thing I could do to improve my work?"
- Listen to the stories colleagues tell about people who have succeeded and those who have failed. When you see patterns, check for confirmation: "So his real problem was that he didn't socialize with co-workers?" This gives your colleagues a chance to provide feedback: "Well, it was more than never coming to the company picnic. He didn't really seem to care about the company."
- Observe. See who is praised, and who is promoted.

books, University of Toronto economics professor David Foot uses his analysis of Canada's changing population demographics to identify economic and social trends. This audience analysis affects decisions about every part of our lives, from social policy and urban design to store lighting and aisle width.

Foot's forecasts proved accurate. Canada's census results reflect an increasing number of foreign-born and aging workers: immigrants account for over 20 percent, and people 55 years and older for 15 percent of today's workers. Many Boomers intend to keep on working, and those who leave paid work will do so for self-employment opportunities.[1]

Sometimes demographic information is irrelevant; sometimes it's important. Does age matter? Almost always, since people's perspectives and priorities change as they grow older. If you were explaining a change in your company's pension plan, for example, you would expect older workers to pay much closer attention than younger workers. And you would need to shape your explanation to appeal to both audiences.

Demographic data has certainly determined the sharp increase in small business start-ups devoted to personal services. For example, the North American concierge industry—providing services from animal care and house-sitting to running errands—thrives because it provides time for busy people. And in the hospitality, real estate, accounting, financial, and personal services industries, businesses that cater to specific populations and ethnic groups flourish.

Business and nonprofit organizations get demographic data by surveying their customers, clients, and donors, by using Statistics Canada data or by purchasing demographic data from marketing companies. For many messages, simply identifying subsets of your audience is enough. For example, a school board trying to win support for a tax increase knows that not everyone living in the district will have children in school. It isn't necessary to know the exact percentages to realize that successful messages need to contain appeals not only to parents but also to voters who won't directly benefit from the improvements that the tax increase will fund.

Personality
Understanding and adapting to your primary audience's personality can also help make your message more effective.

Personality and learning style assessment instruments can provide you with useful insights into your own and others' behaviours. In his bestsellers, *Secrets of Powerful Presentations* and *Leadership from Within*, business consultant Peter Urs Bender says that knowing your audience is key to communication success. Bender describes four personality types, and offers a free online assessment for readers to identify their type.[2] Another popular assessment tool, the Myers-Briggs Type Indicator, uses four dimensions (introvert–extrovert, sensing–intuitive, thinking–feeling, judging–perceiving) to identify personality preferences:[3]

1. **Introvert–extrovert**: The source of one's energy. Introverts get their energy from within; extroverts are energized by interacting with other people.
2. **Sensing–intuitive**: How someone gathers information. Sensing types gather information systematically through their senses. Intuitive types see relationships among ideas.
3. **Thinking–feeling**: How someone makes decisions. Thinking types use objective logic to reach decisions. Feeling types make decisions that "feel right."

Cultural FOCUS

North Americans place value in understanding personality **types**. Many companies use assessments such as the Myers-Briggs to help decide whether an employee will fit in with the corporate culture. Many such personality assessment tools are available online.

4. **Judging–perceiving**: The degree of certainty someone needs. Judging types like organization, and prefer to finish one task before starting another. Perceptive types like possibilities, like to keep their options open, and may interrupt their work on one task to start another.

Table 2.2 suggests how you can use this information to adapt a message to your audience.

You'll be most persuasive if you play to your audience's strengths. Indeed, many of the general principles of business communications reflect the types most common among managers. Putting the main point up front satisfies the needs of judging types, and some 75 percent of managers are judging. Giving logical reasons satisfies the needs of the nearly 80 percent of managers who are thinking types.[4]

Values and Beliefs **Psychographic characteristics** are qualitative rather than quantitative and include values, beliefs, goals, and lifestyles. Knowing what your audience finds important allows you to organize information in a way that seems natural to your audience, and to choose appeals that audience members will find persuasive.

Looking at values enables a company to identify customer segments. The Canadian-based Tim Hortons chain introduced a more diverse menu (croissants, muffins, soup, and sandwiches) to attract new fast-food clients and to appeal to its original, increasingly weight-conscious

TABLE 2.2   Using "Type" Analysis for Persuasive Messages

If Your Audience Is:	Use This Strategy	For This Reason
An introvert	Write a memo and let the reader think about your proposal before responding.	Introverts prefer to think before they speak. Written documents give them the time they need to think through a proposal carefully.
An extrovert	Try out your idea orally, in an informal setting.	Extroverts like to think on their feet. They are energized by people; they'd rather talk than write.
A sensing type	Present your reasoning step by step. Get all your facts exactly right.	Sensing types usually reach conclusions systematically. They want to know why something is important, but they trust their own experience more than someone else's say-so. They're good at facts and expect others to be, too.
An intuitive type	Present the big picture first. Stress the innovative, creative aspects of your proposal.	Intuitive types like solving problems and being creative. They can be impatient with details.
A thinking type	Use logic, not emotion, to persuade. Show that your proposal is fair, even if some people may be hurt by it.	Thinking types make decisions based on logic and abstract principles. They are often uncomfortable with emotion.
A feeling type	Show that your proposal meets the emotional needs of people as well as the dollars-and-cents needs of the organization.	Feeling types are very aware of other people and their feelings. They are sympathetic and like harmony.
A perceiving type	Show that you've considered all the alternatives. Ask for a decision by a specific date.	Perceiving types want to be sure they've considered all the options. They may postpone making a decision, or finishing a project.
A judging type	Present your request quickly.	Judging types are comfortable making quick decisions. They like to settle so they can move on to something else.

Discourse communities create meaning and connection through verbal and non-verbal symbols, including uniforms, safety wear, food choices, use of space, observances of religion, time, and levels of courtesy and formality.

customers. Ranked as Canada's "best-managed brand," based on customer service, Tim Hortons continues to expand in Canada and internationally.[5]

Canadian Tire, another national top brand, also remains competitive in a very crowded market through audience analysis. Although still selling automotive and home repair products and services, Canadian Tire has expanded its lines of gardening, landscaping, lighting, and decorating products in response to Canadians' increasing investment (both emotional and financial) in their homes. And the company catalogue—in print since 1928—is now only online, "an environmentally responsible" move that also appeals to an increasing consumer base.[6]

Marketers also use **geodemographic data** to analyze and appeal to audiences according to where they live and what they buy. Postal-code clusters identify current and potential customers based on two assumptions: 1) people are what they buy, and 2) birds of a feather flock together. In other words, "Our shopping habits are shaped by environment and our desire to belong." [7]

Analyzing Canadians' shopping habits is a $550 million industry, and technological innovation continues to refine research methods. International marketing firms use "global ethnography" to study the impact of culture on consumerism. And researchers increasingly take advantage of the speed and convenience of the Internet to analyze audiences through online surveys and focus groups.[8]

Past Behaviour   Experts in human behaviour believe that we can analyze and predict people's future actions based on their past behaviours: the more recent the behaviour, the more accurate the prediction. On this premise, employers are using behavioural-based interviews ("Tell me about a situation in which you ran into conflict. What happened and how did you deal with it?") to assess a candidate's potential.[9] (See Module 27 on interviewing skills.)

Analyzing People in Organizations

Ex. 2.8– 2.11

Audience reaction is also strongly influenced by the perceptions and expectations of the groups to which they belong. These groups are **personal, social, religious, political,** and **class associations**. These groups are known as discourse communities because their members create their affiliation, rules, and norms through accepted verbal and non-verbal symbols (discourse).

These groups include family, peers, professional associations, clubs, and the workplace—all communities with which members of your audience identify. Members communicate through symbols (language, non-verbals) that may or may not be exclusive to their group, but which identify them as members of that group. For example, the uniform of a sports team symbolizes association, and the team's name reflects the culture and values members hold. Therefore, a discourse community is a group of people who share assumptions about their particular culture and values: what to wear; how to behave; what topics to discuss and how to discuss them; what channels, formats, and styles to use; and what constitutes evidence. Each person is part of several discourse communities, which may or may not overlap.

Ex. 2.1

Checkpoint

A **discourse community** is a group of people who share assumptions about what channels, formats, and styles to use, what topics to discuss and how to discuss them, and what constitutes evidence.

For example, the Internet hosts thousands and thousands of discourse communities, where the audience might, potentially, be the whole world. Social websites such as BallHype, Facebook, Twitter, LinkedIn, IndianPad, and Free IQ are their own discourse communities with their own set of rules; each reflects the values, norms, and expectations of its users. On Twitter, for example, you may use only 140 characters per message. This limitation defines the kind of discourse, conversation, or meaning members can exchange. And violating the conventions can get you plenty of negative feedback.

Consider your discourse communities: perhaps you wear jeans to signify your membership in the student community; your hairstyle or piercing indicates your membership in a subculture; your iPod holds music that reflects your affiliation to another group. When you go for a job interview, you might get a haircut and put on more formal clothes to reflect the norms of the organization's discourse community that you want to join.

When analyzing an organization's discourse community, consider both non-verbal and verbal clues:

In response to traditional expectations, some people invent their own. University of Manitoba student Jesse Hamonic did not appreciate the red tape he had to go through to volunteer for a local charity. So he started his own charities. Student Harvest relies on university students across Canada for donations and volunteer work. Hamonic has started two other not-for-profits dependent on student volunteers and is in the process of establishing his fourth charity organization, one that will use high school volunteers.

- What does the physical environment say about who and what are valued? What departments and services are front and centre? Where is the reception area located? What messages do the decor and furnishings send? How are visitors welcomed? Is the company mission statement prominent? What does the office space layout indicate about the organization's values? Where are the library, training rooms, gymnasium, and cafeteria located? How well are they resourced?
- Where do the managers work? Do bosses dress differently from other employees?
- How are employees treated? How are new hires oriented? How is employee performance recognized? What's featured in the company newsletter? How do people in the organization get important information?
- How do people in the organization communicate? What channels, formats, and styles are preferred for communication? Do they text, send an email, or walk down the hall to talk to someone? How formal or informal are people expected to be—in their dress, on the telephone, in meetings?
- What do people talk about? What is not discussed?
- What kind of and how much evidence is needed to be convincing? Is personal evidence convincing? Do people need to supply statistics and formal research to be convincing?

An organization's **culture** is expressed through its values, attitudes, and philosophies. Once established, **organizational** or **corporate** culture can shape members' attitudes and behaviours, and become very difficult to change. Organizational or corporate culture reveals itself verbally in the organization's myths, stories, and heroes, and non-verbally in the allocation of space, money, and power (Module 3).

Checkpoint

An organization's **culture** is its values, attitudes, and philosophies. **Organizational culture** (or **corporate culture**, as it is also called) is revealed verbally in the organization's myths, stories, and heroes, and non-verbally in the allocation of space, money, and power.

Employability Skills
2000+

Ex. 2.9–2.11

The following questions will help you analyze an organization's culture:

- What are the organization's goals? Making money? Serving customers and clients? Advancing knowledge? Contributing to the community?
- What does the organization value? Diversity or homogeneity? Independence or being a team player? Creativity or following orders?

- How do people get ahead? Are rewards based on seniority, education, being well liked, making technical discoveries, or serving customers? Are rewards available to only a few top people, or is everyone expected to succeed?
- How formal are behaviour, language, and dress?
- What behavioural expectations predominate? How do employees treat one another? Do employees speak in "I," "we," or "them and us" language? How do employees get organizational information?

Two companies in the same business may express very different cultures. Their company websites can offer some clues about what those cultures value, and how they want to project their brand. Royal Bank's standing as Canada's oldest bank is reflected in its corporate website colours: conservative dark blue and gold. TD Canada Trust's green and white site—implying a fresh approach—offers photos of young, happy people, apparently delighted by the products and services the bank provides.[10]

Many companies describe their cultures as part of the section on employment. Job candidates who research the corporate culture to identify how their skills match with the company have a significant advantage in an interview. (See Unit 6.) Researcher Jennifer Chatman found that new hires who "fit" a company's culture were more likely to stay with the job, be more productive, and be more satisfied than those who did not fit the culture.[11]

Organizations also contain several subcultures. For example, manufacturing and marketing may represent different subcultures in the same organization: workers may dress differently and espouse different values. In a union environment, management and union representatives traditionally employ adversarial language to advance their own subculture's perspective while undermining the other's point of view.

You can learn about organizational culture by paying attention to communication clues and cues. In particular, read the organizational publications (newsletters and blogs), observe people, and listen to their stories. Every discourse community and every culture creates and perpetuates meaning and membership through the stories their members share.

The Sleeman Breweries story, for example, is that the quality of its beer is the result of family recipes handed down through five generations—even though that family no longer owns the company. And McCain Foods continues to present itself as a "family business" culture, despite its founding brothers' feuding, its 20,000 employees, and its multinational, global presence. Meanwhile, Google's cultural story boasts of a "fun and inspiring workspace" where free meals, "healthy, yummy, and made with love," casual dress, "shoreline running trails…and plenty of snacks…get you through the day."[12]

Your awareness of an organization's spoken and unspoken messages can provide you with important information on its values and norms.

LO6 How Do I Use Audience Analysis?

Use audience analysis to plan strategy, organization, style, document design, and visuals.

Ex.
2.7
2.10

Take the time to analyze your audience, then adapt your strategy, style, and organizational pattern to your audience's needs. For paper or electronic documents, you can also adapt the document's design and the photos or illustrations you choose. Always revise your message with your audience in mind.

Employability Skills

Strategy

- Choose appeals and reader benefits that work for the specific audience (Module 11).
- Use details and language that reflect your knowledge of, and respect for the specific audience, the organizational culture, and the discourse community.

- Make it easy for the audience to respond positively.
- Include only necessary information.
- Anticipate and overcome objections (Modules 8–13 show you how to emphasize positive aspects, decide how much information to include, and overcome obstacles).

Organization

- Analyze your audience's reaction to the meaning of the message. When your message is positive, you can make your point right away. However, many business messages cause negative reader reaction: messages demanding payment, attempting to sell a product or service, or informing readers of a rate increase or of changes that may inconvenience them. When you must persuade a reluctant reader, and when your audience would see the message negatively, organize the message to break the news gradually (Modules 8–10).
- Anticipate and meet the audience's expectations of format: make the organizational pattern clear to the audience. (Modules 6 and 16–18 show you how to use headings and overviews. Module 23 shows how to use overviews and signposts in oral presentations.)

Style

Many North Americans value "saving" time, and boast of multi-tasking and of their busyness. Because we've been trained by technology, we expect immediate gratification. Therefore, most business audiences today expect messages that are short and clear.

- Strive for clarity and accessibility: use simple words, a mixture of sentence lengths (average today: 14 words), and short paragraphs with topic sentences (refer to the Revising and Editing Resources at the end of this book).
- Use natural, conversational, personable, tactful language: avoid negative, defensive, arrogant, and "red-flag" words—*unfortunately*, *fundamentalist*, *crazy*, *incompetent*, *dishonest*—that may generate a negative reaction.
- Use the language that appeals to your audience. In parts of Canada, including Quebec and some areas of Ontario, Manitoba, and New Brunswick, bilingual messages in English and in French, with French first, are the norm.
- Use natural, conversational language.

Document Design

- Use headings, bulleted lists, and a mix of paragraph lengths to create white space.
- Choose the format, footnotes, and visuals expected by the organizational culture or the discourse community. (Module 5 discusses effective document design.)

Photographs and Visuals

- Carefully consider the difference between cartoons and photos of "high art." Photos and visuals can make a document look more informal or more formal.
- Use bias-free photographs. Unintentional cultural, gender, religious, and economic assumptions can offend readers and cost you business.

Language FOCUS

Multi-tasking means working on many tasks at the same time. For example, a manager might be overseeing two or three projects, completing a report for a project, and planning an upcoming meeting all at the same time. How often do you study, use the Internet, and listen to music all at once? This is considered multi-tasking as well.

- Choose photographs and illustrations that project positive cultural meanings for your audience. Middle Eastern readers, for example, find pictures of bare-legged and bare-armed women offensive and may object to pictures of clean-shaven men.
- Do your research and audience analysis: some cultures (e.g., France and Japan) use evocative photographs that bear little direct relationship to the text. North American audiences expect photos to relate to the text.

LO6 What If My Audiences Have Different Needs?

Focus on gatekeepers and decision makers.

When the members of your audience share the same interests and the same level of knowledge, you can use these principles for individual readers or for members of homogenous groups. But sometimes, different members of the audience have different needs.

When you are writing or speaking to pluralistic audiences, meet the needs of gatekeepers and primary audiences first.

Content and Choice of Details

- Always provide an overview—the introductory paragraph or topic sentence—for reader orientation.
- In the body of the document, provide enough evidence to prove your point.

Organization

- Organize your message based on the primary audience's attitudes toward it: give good news up front; provide the explanation before you deliver the bad news. (See Modules 8–10.)

  - Organize documents to make reading easy: provide a table of contents for documents more than five pages long so that your readers can turn to the portions that interest them.
  - Use headings as signposts: use headings to tell readers what they're about to read and to connect ideas throughout your document. This strategy reinforces your credibility through unity and coherence. If the primary audience doesn't need details that other audiences will want, provide those details in attachments or appendices.

Level of Language

- Contemporary business communication uses conversational, semiformal language. Use *I* and *you*, and address your reader by name. Do research, however, to discover if your reader prefers a title: *Mr., Mrs., Ms., Dr.*
- When both internal and external audiences will read the document, use a slightly more formal style and the third person; avoid *I*.
- Use a more formal style when you write to international audiences.

Technical Terms and Theory

Best Buy and Future Shop have the same parent company and offer similar products. Their customer demographic, however, differs. Future Shop is designed to attract the more upscale customer.

- Know what your reader knows, then provide only the necessary information. Use technical terms only if these will increase reader comprehension (refer to the Revising and Editing Resources at the end of this book).

- Put background information and theory under separate headings. Readers can use the headings to read or skip these sections, as their knowledge dictates.
- If primary audiences will have more knowledge than other audiences, provide a glossary of terms. Early in the document, let readers know that the glossary exists.

LO3 LO6 How Do I Reach My Audience?

Employability Skills 2000+

Ex. 2.5

Effective messages make use of multiple channels.

Communication channels include verbal and non-verbal symbols (in-person, electronic, speaking, gesturing, writing, colour, use of space and time). These vary in

- Transmission speed
- Transmission accuracy
- Cost
- Efficiency
- The number of people reached
- Audience impact
- Positive influence

Your purpose, the audience, and the situation—known as the *communication context*—determine which and how many channels you choose (refer to the PAIBOC questions in Figure 2.4). However, given the potential for miscommunication, the more channels you use, the better.

The Advantages of Writing

A written message is primarily for the record. Writing makes it easier to do several things:

- Present many specific details of a law, policy, or procedure
- Present extensive or complex financial data
- Minimize undesirable emotions

The Disadvantages of Writing

Writing, however, often requires more time than speaking face-to-face. Furthermore, once you mail the letter, or hit "send," your documents, including your email messages, are permanent and potentially available to everyone.

When you do decide to write, use the channel that best meets the expectations and needs of your audience. Text messaging may work for family and friends. Email messages are appropriate for routine business messages to people you already know. Paper may be better for someone to whom you're writing for the first time.

The Advantages of Oral Communication

Speaking is easier and more efficient when you need to do any of the following:

- Answer questions, resolve conflicts, and build consensus
- Use emotion to help persuade the audience
- Provoke an immediate action or response
- Focus the audience's attention on specific points
- Modify a proposal that may not be acceptable in its original form

Scheduled meetings and oral presentations are more formal than phone calls or stopping someone in the hall. Important messages should use more channels and more formal channels, whether they're oral or written.

The Disadvantages of Oral Communication

Meaning and morale can be jeopardized, however, when people choose efficiency and formality over real communication. For example, some organizations regularly use "town hall meetings"—large-auditorium gatherings—to tell employees about new strategies, policies and procedures, and/or new initiatives. The manager employs only one channel (voice), and even when the presentation includes slides, the message is often all one-way: top-down. In this "command and control" corporate culture, employees often feel too intimidated or too disaffected to provide feedback. True communication does not occur.

Use Multiple Channels

When sending and receiving both oral and written messages, you maximize success when you

1. Adapt the message to the specific audience.
2. Show the audience members how they benefit from the idea, policy, service, or product (Module 11).
3. Anticipate and overcome any objections the audience may have.
4. Adopt a good attitude and use positive emphasis (Modules 12–13).
5. Use visuals to clarify or emphasize material (Module 19).
6. Specify exactly what the audience should do.

Even when everyone in an organization has access to the same channels, different discourse communities often prefer different channels. When a university updated its employee benefits manual, the computer scientists and librarians wanted the information online. Faculty wanted to be able to read the information on paper. Maintenance workers and carpenters wanted to get answers on voicemail.[13]

The bigger your audience, the more complicated channel choice becomes, because few channels reach everyone. When possible, use multiple channels. Always use multiple channels for very important messages. For example, talk to key players about a written document before the meeting where the document will be discussed. Or, in the case of town hall meetings, make sure everyone has a chance to preview the announcements (via email and bulletin boards), and generate feedback through focus groups or team meetings.

MODULE SUMMARY

- Communication is the transfer of meaning: both sender and receiver, using multiple symbols, reach agreement on the meaning intended.

- The communication process includes a **sender**, **receiver**, **message**, **channel(s)**, and **noise**. True communication is transactional: both parties provide **feedback** for meaning clarification. Noise is ever-present; any physical, emotional, or psychological interference affects meaning exchange.

- Audience focus is the key to communication success. Empathy and critical thinking are crucial to valid audience analysis. Analyzing your audience's needs and expectations lets you shape messages accordingly, with positive results.

- Business messages may include five audiences: the **initial audience** first receives the message, or tells you to send the message; the decision maker, or **primary audience**, makes the decision or acts on the basis of your message; the **secondary audience** may comment on your message, or implement your ideas after they've been approved; the **gatekeeper** manages your message flow—this person has the power to stop your message before it reaches the primary audience; the **watchdog audience** has the political, social, or economic power to evaluate your message.

- You need to know everything about your audience that's relevant to your purposes for communicating. Use demographic factors, personality characteristics, values and beliefs, past behaviours, and your own observations and experiences to analyze your audience.

- Audience reaction is also strongly influenced by the perceptions and expectations of the groups to which they belong. These groups, or **discourse communities**, create group norms through verbal and non-verbal symbols. Each of us belongs to a number of very different discourse communities (family, religious affiliation, Facebook, varsity team).

- When you want to understand people in organizations, you need to observe the organizational, or **corporate culture**. People create their corporate culture—values, attitudes, and philosophies—and express these through discourse—their stories and behaviours.

- Channel choice is shaped by the organizational culture. However, effective messages use multiple channels, and encourage feedback.

ASSIGNMENTS FOR MODULE 2

Questions for Critical Thinking

2.1 Who might be the audiences for your Facebook comments?

2.2 Emphasizing the importance of audience, salespeople often say, "The customer is king," or "The customer is always right," or "The customer is in control." To what extent do you feel in control as a customer, a citizen, or a student? How do you use technology to increase your feelings of control?

2.3 If you are employed, which aspects of your organization's culture match your own values? Describe the culture you would most like to work in.

Exercises and Problems

2.4 Identifying Audiences

In each of the following situations, label the audiences as initial, gatekeeper, primary, secondary, or watchdog.

1. Cheechoo is seeking venture capital so that he can expand his business of offering soccer camps to youngsters. He's met an investment banker whose clients regularly hear presentations from businesspeople seeking capital. The investment banker decides who will get a slot on the program, based on a comprehensive audit of each company's records and business plan.

2. Maria is marketing auto loans. She knows that many car buyers choose one of the financing options presented by the car dealership, so she wants to persuade dealers to include her financial institution in the options they offer.

3. Paul works for the mayor's office in a big city. As part of a citywide cost-cutting measure, a panel has recommended requiring employees who work more than 40 hours in a week to take compensatory time off rather than be paid overtime. The only exceptions will be the police and fire departments. The mayor asks Paul to prepare a proposal for the city council, which will vote on whether to implement the change. Before they vote, council members will hear from 1) citizens, who will have an opportunity to read the proposal and communicate their opinions to the city council; 2) mayors' offices in other cities, who may be asked about their experiences; 3) union representatives, who may be concerned about the reduction in income that will result if the proposal is implemented; 4) department heads, whose ability to schedule work might be limited if the proposal passes; and 5) panel members and government lobbying groups. Council members come up for re-election in six months.

2.5 Choosing a Channel to Reach a Specific Audience

Suppose that your business, government agency, or non-profit group has a product, service, or program targeted for each of the following audiences. What would be the best channel(s) to reach people in that group in your city? Would that channel reach all group members?

1. Renters
2. Small business owners
3. People who use wheelchairs
4. Teenagers who work part-time while attending school
5. Competitive athletes
6. Parents whose children play soccer
7. People willing to work part-time
8. Financial planners
9. Hunters
10. New immigrants

2.6 Persuading Your Organization to Adopt Flextime

Flextime is a system that allows employees to set their own starting and stopping times. It is especially appealing to organizations that have a hard time keeping good employees or cannot easily raise salaries, and companies with the philosophy of giving workers as much independence as possible. Most employees prefer flextime. However, in some organizations, the system creates conflict between workers who get the schedules they want and those who have to work traditional hours to cover the phones. Some firms are afraid that the quality of work may suffer if employees and supervisors aren't on the job at the same time. Record keeping may be more complicated.

Identify the major argument that you could use to persuade each of the following organizations to use flextime, and the major objection you anticipate. Which of the organizations would be fairly easy to convince? Which would be harder to persuade?

1. A large, successful insurance company
2. A branch bank
3. A small catering service
4. The admissions office on your campus
5. A church, synagogue, temple, or mosque with a staff of two clergy, a director of music, two secretaries, and a custodian
6. A government agency
7. The business where you work part-time

2.7 Analyzing the Other Students in Your College or University

Analyze the students in your college or university. (If your college or university is large, analyze the students in your program of study.) Is there a "typical" student?

If all students are quite different, how are they different? Consider the following kinds of information in your analysis:

- Demographic data
- Age (average; high and low)
- Gender (What proportion are men? What proportion are women?)
- Ethnic background (What groups are represented? How many of each?)
- Languages
- Marital status
- Number of children
- Parents' income/personal or family income
- Full- or part-time
- Outside jobs (What kinds? How many hours a week?)
- Membership in campus organizations
- Religious affiliations
- Political preferences
- Proportion going on for further education after graduation
- Psychographics

What values, beliefs, goals, and lifestyles do students have? Which are common? Which are less common?

What's the relationship between the students' values and their choice of major or program?

What do students hope to gain from the classes they're taking? What motivates them to do their best work in class?

Additional Information

What are students' attitudes toward current campus problems? Current political problems?

What is the job market like for students in your school or major? Will students find it difficult to get jobs after graduation? How much will they be making? Where will they be working?

After you answer these questions, identify the factors that would be most relevant in each of the following situations:

1. You want to persuade students to participate in an internship program.
2. You want to persuade students to join a not-for-profit charity organization.
3. You want to persuade students to adopt "green habits," including carpooling, taking the bus rather than driving, avoiding products that are packaged or sold in plastic or Styrofoam, and eating locally.
4. You want to know whether the campus placement office is providing adequate services to students.
5. You want to hire students to staff a business that you're starting.

2.8 Analyzing People in Your Organization

1. Analyze your supervisor:
   - Does he or she like short or long explanations?
   - Does he or she want to hear about all the problems in a unit or only the major ones?
   - How important are punctuality and deadlines?
   - How well informed about a project does he or she want to be?
   - Is he or she more approachable in the morning or the afternoon?
   - What are your supervisor's major concerns?

2. Analyze other workers in your organization:
   - Is work "just a job" or do most people really care about the organization's goals?
   - How do workers feel about clients or customers?
   - What are your co-workers' major concerns?

3. Analyze your customers or clients:
   - What attitudes do they have toward the organization and its products or services?
   - How are their attitudes affected by education, age, or other factors?
   - What are their major concerns?

As your instructor directs,

a. Write a memo to your instructor summarizing your analysis.
b. Discuss your analysis with a small group of students.
c. Present your analysis orally to the class.
d. Combine your information with classmates' information to present a collaborative report comparing and contrasting your audiences at work.

2.9 Analyzing a Discourse Community

Analyze the way one of your discourse communities uses language. Possible groups are

- Family
- Peers
- YouTube, Facebook, or any social media site to which you belong
- Work teams
- Work blogs
- Wikipedia
- Sports teams
- Associations, organizations, and other service or social groups
- Churches, synagogues, temples, and mosques
- Geographic or ethnic group

Questions to ask include the following:

- What specialized terms might not be known to outsiders?
- What topics do members talk or write about? What topics are considered unimportant or improper?
- What channels do members use to convey messages?
- What forms of language do members use to build goodwill? To demonstrate competence or superiority?
- What strategies or kinds of proof are convincing to members?
- What formats, conventions, or rules do members expect messages to follow?

As your instructor directs,

a. Share your results orally with a small group of students.
b. Present your results in an oral presentation to the class.
c. Present your results in a memo to your instructor.
d. Share your results in an email message to the class.

e. Share your results with a small group of students, and write a joint memo reporting the similarities and differences you found.

2.10 Analyzing Corporate Culture on the Web

Use three organizations' websites and/or blogs to analyze their corporate cultures.

1. What assumptions can you make about the corporate culture, based on your analysis of these media?
2. What inconsistencies do you find?
3. What aspects of each culture do you like best? What, if anything, do you not like? What questions do you have about the organizational culture that the web pages or blogs don't answer?

As your instructor directs,

a. Share your results orally with a small group of students.
b. Present your results orally to the class.
c. Present your results in a memo to your instructor.
d. Share your results in an email message to the class.
e. Share your results with a small group of students, and write a joint memo reporting the similarities and differences you found.

2.11 Analyzing an Organization's Culture

Interview several people about the culture of their organization. (This exercise provides a great opportunity to become known in a company where you would like to work. See Module 24.)

Possible organizations are

- Work teams
- Sports teams
- Associations, organizations, and other service or social groups
- Churches, synagogues, temples, and mosques
- Geographic or ethnic groups
- Groups of friends

Questions to ask include those in this module and the following:

1. Tell me about someone in this organization whom you admire. Why is he or she successful?
2. Tell me about someone who failed in this organization. What did he or she do wrong?
3. What ceremonies and rituals does this organization have? Why are they important?
4. Why would someone join this group rather than joining a competitor?

As your instructor directs,

a. Share your results orally with a small group of students.

b. Present your results orally to the class.

c. Present your results in a memo to your instructor.

d. Share your results in an email message to the class.

e. Share your results with a small group of students, and write a joint memo reporting the similarities and differences you found.

POLISHING YOUR PROSE

Comma Splices

In filmmaking, editors splice, or connect, two segments of film to create one segment. A *comma splice* occurs when writers try to create one sentence by connecting two sentences, or independent clauses, with only a comma.

Incorrect: We shipped the order on Tuesday, it arrived on Wednesday.

Comma splices are inappropriate in business communication. (Poetry and fiction sometimes use comma splices to speed up action or simulate dialect; some sales letters and advertisements use comma splices for the same effect, though not always successfully.)

You can fix a comma splice in four ways:

- If the ideas in the sentences are closely related, use a semicolon: We shipped the order on Tuesday; it arrived on Wednesday.
- Add a coordinating conjunction (*and, yet, but, or, for, nor*): We shipped the order on Tuesday, and it arrived on Wednesday.
- Make the incorrect sentence into two correct ones: We shipped the order on Tuesday. It arrived on Wednesday.
- Make one of the clauses subordinate, or dependent on the other for meaning: Since we shipped the order on Tuesday, it arrived on Wednesday.

Exercises

Fix the comma splices in the following sentences.

1. The conference call came at 1 p.m., we took it immediately.
2. We interviewed two people for the accounting position, we made a job offer to one.
3. Janelle drafted her problem-solving report, she sent a copy to each committee member for review.
4. The director of purchasing went to our Main Street warehouse to inspect the inventory, Chum called him later to ask how things had gone.
5. Katy called the hotel in Montreal for a reservation, the desk staff booked a room for her immediately.
6. Mr. Margulies gave an audiovisual presentation at our September sales meeting in Whistler, it went very well.
7. I'll have Tina call the main office, you ask Polsun to set up an appointment for the four of us tomorrow.
8. You know, many countries forbid talking on your cellphone while driving, Canadian provinces are adopting legislation to do the same, even non-handheld devices are going to be banned.
9. I like to make oral presentations, they're fun.
10. Sunil is our most experienced employee, he joined the department in 2009.

Check your answers to the odd-numbered exercises in the Polishing Your Prose Answer Key.

Communicating Across Cultures

Learning Objectives

After reading and applying the information in Module 3, you'll be able to demonstrate

Knowledge of

LO1 The components of culture

LO2 Workplace diversity

LO3 The importance and variety of non-verbal communication symbols

LO4 Bias-free language

Skills to

LO5 Consider diversity as part of your audience analysis

LO6 Apply your awareness of others' values to your spoken and written messages

LO7 Use bias-free language and photos

MODULE OUTLINE

- What is culture?
- What is Canadian culture?
- How does culture affect business communication?
- With so many different cultures, how can I communicate effectively?
- How can I make my documents bias-free?

Module Summary

Assignments for Module 3

Polishing Your Prose: Subject–Verb Agreement

Employability Skills 2000+ Checklist

Module content builds these Conference Board of Canada Employability Skills 2000+

Communicate

Work with Others

Manage Information

Learn Continuously

Think and Solve Problems

Participate in Projects and Tasks

Our culture shapes the way we "see" reality. Often we are unaware of our cultural biases until we encounter people whose cultural assumptions differ from our own. If we come from a culture where cows and pigs are raised to be food, for example, that may seem normal until we meet people who consider these animals sacred, or unclean, or people who consider raising any animal for consumption to be cruel and barbaric.

Regardless of our cultural convictions, our ability to communicate flexibly and sensitively with others is necessary for our personal and professional success. Cultural awareness makes sound economic, ethical, and legal sense.

LO1 What Is Culture?

Our culture is a learned set of assumptions that shape our perceptions of the world, and of appropriate values, norms, attitudes, and behaviours.

We learn our concepts of gender, age, and social class, as we do our ideas about

- Race
- Ethnicity
- Religious practices
- Sexual orientation
- Physical appearance and ability
- Regional and national characteristics

Communication difficulties arise because we take our cultural behaviours for granted, and we assume they are "normal." Culturally sophisticated communicators know better. They know that people's expectations of behaviours vary from culture to culture, and even within cultures.

LO2 What Is Canadian Culture?

Canada is a country of multiple cultures.

Our cultural diversity is very much a part of the Canadian identity. Indeed, Canada is becoming the most culturally diverse country in the world, home to more than 200 different ethnic groups,[1] and with a foreign-born population second only to Australia's.[2] Almost a quarter of a million people from all over the world choose to immigrate to Canada every year.

Ethnic Diversity

Because two out of three of these immigrants settle in our largest cities, Toronto is "the most ethnically diverse city in the world... home to more than 80 ethnic groups speaking 100 languages."[3] And this diversity is growing. According to Statistics Canada, if Canada's attraction for immigrants continues, by 2017 over 22 percent of Canada's population will be foreign-born, one-fifth of whom (over seven million) will be members of a visible minority. Presently, Chinese and South Asian immigrants form the two largest of Canada's visible-minority populations. West Asian, Korean, and Arab populations will expand rapidly by 2017.[4]

Canada is home to a multitude of cultural realities.

Without our immigrant population, Canada would not have had the labour force necessary to prosper during the boom times of the late 20th and early 21st centuries: "skilled immigrants who arrived in the past ten years accounted for 70 percent of the growth in Canada's labour force during the same period."[5]

Moreover, as the workforce continues to age (North America's Boomers are 57 or older), skilled worker shortages will be filled by new Canadians.[6]

Age Diversity

Diversity at work also includes Canada's aging population. In 2006, the ratio of potential young workers (15 to 24 years) to potential retirees (55 to 64 years) was about 1.2, half what it was in 1976.[7] According to population projections, by 2013, 55-to-64-year-olds will outnumber 15-to-24-year-olds.[8]

Ex. 3.2 3.3 3.7

Current research suggests age-related behavioural differences are a source of potential workplace conflict. In addition to Boomers, GenXers, and GenYs, Echos, or Millennials, the Canadian population apparently now includes Zoomers: "Boomers with Zip! The 14.5 million Canadians 45-plus."[9] "Zip" notwithstanding, supposedly most people over 30 are "immigrants" to the "new, instant satisfaction" Millennial culture (those born between 1979 and 1994). Although they can learn to adapt, people born before 1979 can never be "natives" like the Millennials, who are "a huge generation of impatient, experiential learners, digital natives, multitaskers, and gamers who...expect nomadic connectivity, 24x7."[10]

Millennial multi-tasking includes answering cell phones at a business lunch, in meetings, and even in the middle of a conversation. Regardless of age or culture, many people consider this behaviour blatantly rude. As a result, more and more workplaces and public spaces have rules regulating cell phone use. However, University of Toronto economics professor David Foot, author of *Boom, Bust and Echo*, claims that "regardless of the generation, age-based tensions have always existed in the workplace." These tensions arise from different perspectives ("older employees tend to forget what they were like as 20-year-olds").[11]

For both financial and psychological reasons, many of these older employees will remain in the workforce long after they turn 65, so you will be working with and for people older than your grandparents. These older people will be an important audience demographic for you (Module 2), as their values (and expectations) continue to shape what is considered appropriate business communication and culture.

Cultural diversity includes differing generational perspectives and values

Therefore, cultural sensitivity is not only emotionally intelligent (see this chapter's Expanding a Critical Skill box), but also financially smart: people you work with and for are *not* just like you; being aware of others' norms and values enables you to shape your messages for positive results.

Cultural Sensitivity is Legally and Financially Responsible Behaviour

Recognition of and respect for the diverse views of others is also legally responsible behaviour. Legal support for the heterogeneous population in Canadian workplaces is articulated in the *Canadian Charter of Rights and Freedoms* (1982), the *Canadian Human Rights Act* (1985), the *Multiculturalism Act* (1985), the *Official Languages Act* (1988), the *Pay Equity Act* (1990), and the *Employment Equity Act* (1995). "Provinces and territories also have laws, human rights commissions and programs that promote diversity."[12]

Furthermore, the rapidity of change and the economic effects of globalization demand effective intercultural communication. Foreign trade is essential to the growth of both individual businesses and Canada's economy. Although the United States is our primary trading partner, the North American Free Trade Agreement (NAFTA) and the interests of countries worldwide, especially those of China and India, are the future for Canadian businesses.

How Does Culture Affect Business Communication?

LO5 *Cultural assumptions and expectations determine both the form and the content of every business transaction.*

Cultural assumptions and expectations determine both the form and the content of every business interaction.

Culture influences every single aspect of our personal and professional communication: how to dress; how to demonstrate politeness and respect; how much information to give; how to motivate people; when, how much, and how loudly to talk and laugh; and how to organize a letter, what medium to use to send it, and even what size paper to print it on.

Cultural anthropologist E. T. Hall theorized that people's cultural values and beliefs determine their communication style. Hall characterized these communication behaviours as high context and low context:

- In **high-context cultures**, most of the information is inferred from the context of a message; little is "spelled out." Chinese, Japanese, Arabic, North American Aboriginal, and Latin American cultures might be considered high context.
  - In **low-context cultures**, context is less important; most information is explicitly spelled out. German, Scandinavian, and the dominant North American cultures might be considered low context.

Ex. 3.8 3.14

High-context and low-context cultures value different kinds of communication and have different attitudes toward oral and written channels.[13] As Table 3.1 shows, low-context cultures favour direct approaches, and see indirectness as dishonest or manipulative. The written word is seen as more important than spoken agreements, so contracts are binding but promises may be broken. Details, logic, and time constraints matter. North American and some European communication practices reflect these low-context preferences.

TABLE 3.1 **Views of Communication in High-Context and Low-Context Cultures**

Key elements of "face"	Individualistic/low-context	Collectivistic/high-context
Identity	Emphasis on "I" identity	Emphasis on "we" identity
Concern	Self-face concern	Other-face concern
Need	Negative face need	Positive face need
Supra-strategy	Self-positive and self-negative facework	Other-positive and other-negative facework
Mode	Direct Mode	Indirect mode
Style	Controlling, confrontational, solution-oriented style	Obliging, avoiding, affective-oriented style
Speech acts	Direct speech acts	Indirect speech acts
Non-verbal acts	Individualistic non-verbal acts, direct emotional expressions	Contextualistic (role-oriented), non-verbal acts, indirect emotional expressions

Source: Lee, J., & Lee, K. (2009). Facilitating dynamics of focus group interviews in East Asia: Evidence and tools by cross-cultural study. *International Journal of Design* [Online] 3:1. Retrieved from: www.ijdesign.org/ojs/index.php/IJDesign/article/view/351

Communication is also influenced by the organizational culture and by personal culture, such as gender, race and ethnicity, social class, and so forth. As Figure 3.1 suggests, these cultures intersect to determine the communication needed in a given situation. Often one kind of cultural assumption dominates another cultural assumption. For example, in a study of aerospace engineers in Europe, Asia, and the United States, researchers John Webb and Michael Keene found that the similarities of the professional discourse community (one kind of culture) (Module 2) outweighed differences in national cultures.[14]

Technology also changes cultural assumptions. A Toronto university student faced expulsion for running a Facebook study group that the university said was a threat to academic integrity. The student and members of the study group argued that theirs was no different from any other collaborative learning group—which the university encourages—except that the online information exchange made sense for their wired generation. Ultimately, the student was disciplined because the professor had stipulated that students were to work independently.[15] Technological innovation and accessibility will continue to challenge our cultural assumptions about everything, from how we learn to what constitutes private space.

Values, Beliefs, and Practices

Values and beliefs, often unconscious, affect our response to people and situations. Most Canadians, for example, value "fairness." "You're not playing fair" is a sharp criticism calling for changed behaviour. In some countries, however, people expect certain groups to receive preferential treatment. Most North Americans accept competition and believe that it produces better performance. The Japanese, however, believe that competition leads to disharmony. U.S. businesspeople believe that success is based on individual achievement and is open to anyone who excels. Many Canadians prefer co-operation to blatant competition. In England and in France, success is more obviously linked to social class. And in some countries, the law prohibits people of some castes or races from participating fully in society.

Many North Americans value individualism. Other countries rely on group consensus for decision making. In Japan, for example, groups routinely work together to solve problems. In the dominant North American culture, quiet is a sign that people are working. In Latin American, Mediterranean, Middle Eastern, and Asian countries, people talk to get the work done.[16] Conversely, the extroverted behaviours rewarded in the classrooms and boardrooms of North America are considered rude and crazy in Japanese culture.

Cultural assumptions also affect people's spiritual, religious, and political beliefs, and these, in turn, shape personal and professional communications.

Employability Skills

Ex. 3.4

FIGURE 3.1

National Culture, Organizational Culture, and Personal Culture Overlap

Source: Adapted from Farid Elashmawi and Philip R. Harris (1998), *Multicultural management 2000: Essential cultural insights for global business success* (p. 169). Houston: Gulf.

Ex. 3.8 3.14

Employability Skills

Ex.
3.4
3.9
3.10

For example, Christianity coexists with a view of the individual as proactive. In some Muslim and Asian countries, however, it is seen as presumptuous to predict the future by promising action by a certain date. Some Mennonite and Jewish communities live and work in strict adherence to traditional customs. Meanwhile, the Puritan work ethic, embraced as a cultural value throughout the northeastern United States regardless of race or religion, legitimizes wealth by seeing it as a sign of divine favour. In other cultures, a simpler lifestyle is considered closer to God.

Of course, these differences in values, beliefs, and practices lead to different behaviours. Professor Emeritus and researcher Geert Hofstede, an expert in culture influences in the workplace, uses five **cultural dimensions** (Table 3.2) to describe these behaviours in high-context versus low-context cultures.

TABLE 3.2   Hofstede's Five Cultural Dimensions

Value Dimension	Value Description	High Score	Low Score
Power Distance Index (PDI)	The degree of equality, or inequality, between people in the country's society	Indicates that inequalities of power and wealth have been allowed to grow within the society. These societies are more likely to follow a caste system that does not allow significant upward mobility for its citizens.	Indicates the society de-emphasizes the differences between the citizen's power and wealth. In these societies equality and opportunity for everyone is stressed.
Individualism (IDV)	Degree to which a society reinforces individual or collective achievement and interpersonal relationships.	Indicates that individuality and individual rights are paramount within the society. Individuals may tend to form a larger number of looser relationships.	Typifies societies of a more collectivist nature with close ties between individuals. Reinforces extended families and collectives where everyone takes responsibility for fellow members of their group.
Masculinity (MAS)	Degree to which a society reinforces, or does not reinforce, the traditional masculine work role model of male achievement, control, and power.	Indicates the country experiences a high degree of gender differentiation. Males dominate a significant portion of the society and power structure, with females being controlled by male domination.	Indicates the country has a low level of differentiation and discrimination between genders. Females are treated equally to males in all aspects of the society.
Uncertainty Avoidance Index (UAI)	Level of tolerance for uncertainty and ambiguity within the society, i.e., unstructured situations.	Indicates the country has a low tolerance for uncertainty and ambiguity. Creates a rule-oriented society that institutes laws, rules, regulations, and controls in order to reduce the amount of uncertainty.	Indicates the country has less concern about ambiguity and uncertainty and has more tolerance for a variety of opinions. Reflected in a society that is less rule-oriented, more readily accepts change, and takes more and greater risks.
Long-Term Orientation (LTO)	Degree to which a society embraces, or does not embrace, long-term devotion to traditional, forward-thinking values.	Indicates the country subscribes to the values of long-term commitments and respect for tradition. This is thought to support a strong work ethic where long-term rewards are expected as a result of today's hard work. However, businesses may take longer to develop in this society, particularly for an "outsider."	Indicates the country does not reinforce the concept of long-term, traditional orientation. In this culture, change can occur more rapidly as long-term traditions and commitments do not become impediments to change.

Source: Geert Hofstede, Gert Jan Hofsteade, Michael Minkov (2010). *Cultures and Organizations, Software of the Mind* (3rd Rev. ed.). McGraw-Hill. 2010, ISBN: 0-07-166418-1. c Geert Hofstede B.V. Quoted with permission.

Cultural FOCUS

Mennonites are a Christian religious group who live mostly in Southern Ontario and Manitoba. Some live without electricity and do not drive cars, using a horse and buggy for transportation instead.

The **Puritan work ethic** refers to the belief that hard work and success are important in order to be a good Christian, and that if you are successful it means God is happy with you.

LO3 Non-Verbal Communication

Non-verbal communication—communication that makes meaning without words—permeates our lives. Facial expressions, gestures, our use of time and space—even our pauses and vocal intonations—all communicate pleasure or anger, friendliness or distance, power and status.

Non-verbal communication is older and more powerful than spoken language. And its symbols can be misinterpreted just as easily as can verbal symbols (words). For example, a woman brought a new idea to her boss, who glared at her, brows together in a frown, as she explained her proposal. The stare and lowered brows symbolized anger to her, and she assumed that he was rejecting her idea. Several months later, she learned that her boss always "frowned" when he was concentrating. The facial expression she had interpreted as anger really conveyed thinking.

Misunderstandings are even more common in communication across cultures, since non-verbal signals are culturally defined. An Arab student assumed that his North

EXPANDING A CRITICAL SKILL

Building Emotional Intelligence

In his bestselling book *Emotional Intelligence*, Daniel Goleman claims that we can develop intrapersonal and interpersonal communication skills that can transform our lives. Goleman's emotional intelligence (EQ) consists of knowing and managing your emotions, motivating yourself, recognizing the emotions of other people, and managing relationships productively. A strong EQ, audience awareness, and cultural sensitivity are interdependent.

The concept that we can build and apply emotional competencies to better understand and manage our own feelings and relationships has gained considerable currency. Indeed, studies show that having high EQ is a better predictor of personal, academic, and professional success than is having a high IQ. The best managers and top-performing employees all demonstrate a number of high-EQ competencies; many organizations use EQ tests to identify and nurture people with strong emotional competencies, since these people outperform employees with average or low EQ; organizations that train employees in EQ consistently outperform their competitors.

Strengthening your emotional intelligence is vital for survival in our wired world. You must consider carefully before you push "send," for, as social media expert Joan Vinall-Cox points out, whatever words or visuals you choose to post "are out there forever, for everyone, anywhere." Failing to consider your audience (and to check your privacy box) leads to failure, period. Fortunately, plentiful print and electronic resources exist to help you assess and develop your EQ.

Sources: Daniel Goleman (1995). *Emotional intelligence*, New York: Bantam Books Joan Vinall Cox, statement to Kathryn Braun, April 9, 2009; R.E. Boyatzis & A. Howard, *Career success through emotional intelligence: Developing EI competencies*. Retrieved from www.careertrainer.com; Cary Chernis, *The business case for emotional intelligence*. Retrieved from www.eiconsortium.org/reports/business_case_for_ei.html; Michael E. Rock, *The 90% factor: EQ (emotional intelligence) and the new workplace*. Retrieved from www.canadaone.com/magazine/eq050198.html; Emotional intelligence may be good predictor of success in computing studies. *Science Daily*, October 5, 2005. Retrieved from www.sciencedaily.com/releases/2005/10/051005072152.htm

Our cultural assumptions shape our perceptions of the world and of appropriate values, norms, attitudes, and behaviours.

American roommate disliked him intensely because the roommate sat around the room with his feet up on the furniture, soles toward the Arab roommate. Arab culture sees the foot in general and the sole in particular as unclean; showing the sole of the foot is an insult.[17]

Employability Skills 2000+

As is true of every communication situation, knowledge is power: learning about non-verbal symbols gives you the information you need to project the image you want, and makes you more conscious of the signals you are interpreting. Since most of our communication is based on non-verbal symbols, your awareness and correct interpretation of non-verbal communication is vital to your personal and professional development. Remember, however, that non-verbal communication is also culturally learned. Always check your perceptions before making assumptions about the non-verbal signals of others.

Body Language

Posture and **body language** show self-concept, energy, and openness. North American **open body positions** include leaning forward with uncrossed arms and legs, with the arms away from the body. **Closed or defensive body positions** include leaning back, arms and legs crossed or close together, or hands in pockets. As the labels imply, "open" positions suggest that people are accepting and open to new ideas. "Closed" positions suggest that people are physically or psychologically uncomfortable, that they are defending themselves and shutting other people out.

People who cross their arms or legs claim that they do so only because the position is more comfortable. Certainly crossing one's legs is one way to be more comfortable in a chair that is the wrong height. Canadian women used to be taught to adopt a "ladylike" posture: arms close to their bodies and knees and ankles together. But notice your own body the next time you're in a perfectly comfortable discussion with a good friend. You'll probably find that you naturally assume open body positions. The fact that so many people in organizational settings adopt closed positions may indicate that many people feel at least slightly uncomfortable in school and on the job.

People of Eastern cultures value the ability to sit quietly. They may see the North American tendency to fidget and shift as an indication of a lack of mental or spiritual balance. Even Canadian interviewers and audiences usually respond negatively to nervous gestures, such as fidgeting with a tie or hair or jewellery, tapping a pencil, or swinging a foot.

Eye Contact
Canadians of European background see eye contact as a sign of honesty. But in many cultures, dropped eyes are a sign of appropriate deference to a superior. Puerto Rican children are taught not to meet the eyes of adults.[18] The Japanese are taught to look at the neck.[19] In Korea, prolonged eye contact is considered rude. The lower-ranking person is expected to look down first.[20] In Muslim countries, women and men are not supposed to make eye contact. These differences can lead to miscommunication in the multicultural workplace. Supervisors may infer from their eye contact that employees are being disrespectful, when, in fact, the employee is behaving appropriately according to the norms of his or her culture.

Gestures
Canadians sometimes assume that, if language fails, they can depend on gestures to communicate with non-English-speaking people. But Birdwhistell reported that "although we have been searching for 15 years (1950–1965), we have found no gesture or body motion

which has the same meaning in all societies."[21] Gestures that mean approval in Canada may have very different meanings in other countries. The "thumbs up" sign that means "good work" or "go ahead" in Canada, the United States, and most of Western Europe is a vulgar insult in Greece. The circle formed with the thumb and first finger that means OK in Canada is obscene in Southern Italy and Brazil, and it can mean "You're worth nothing" in France and Belgium.[22]

Space   Concepts of space are also culturally understood. **Personal space** is the distance people want between themselves and other people in ordinary, non-intimate interchanges. Most North Americans, North Europeans, and Asians want a bigger personal space than do Latin Americans, French, Italians, and Arabs. People who are accustomed to lots of personal space and are forced to accept close contact on a crowded elevator or subway react in predictable and ritualistic ways: they stand stiffly and avoid eye contact with others. Even within a culture, some people like more personal space than do others. One study found that men took up more personal space than women did. In many cultures, people who are of the same age and sex take less personal space than do mixed-age or mixed-sex groups. Latin Americans stand closer to people of the same sex than North Americans do, but North Americans stand closer to people of the opposite sex.

Touch   Humans crave touch. Babies need to be touched to grow and thrive, and older people are healthier both mentally and physically if they are touched. But some people are more comfortable with touch than others. Some people shake hands in greeting but otherwise don't like to be touched at all, except by family members or lovers. Other people, having grown up in families that touch a lot, hug as part of a greeting and touch even casual friends. Each kind of person may misinterpret the other. A person who dislikes touch may seem unfriendly to someone who's used to touching. A toucher may seem overly familiar to someone who dislikes touch.

In general, North Americans are much more casual about touch than Easterners and Middle-Easterners. Studies indicate that in North American culture, touch can be interpreted as power: people who are more powerful touch people who are less powerful. When the toucher has higher status than the recipient, both men and women liked being touched.[23] In Iran and Iraq, handshakes between men and women are seen as improper.[24] Handshakes between men and women are beginning to be accepted in India's larger cities because of their expanding young, urban, middle-class workers.[25]

Most parts of North America allow opposite-sex couples to hold hands or walk arm in arm in public, but frown on the same behaviour in same-sex couples. People in Asia, the Middle East, and South America have the opposite expectation: male friends or female friends can hold hands or walk arm in arm, but it is slightly shocking for an opposite-sex couple to touch in public.

Spatial Arrangements   In North America, the size, placement, and privacy of a person's office indicate status. Large corner offices have the highest status. An individual office with a door that closes suggests more status than a desk in a common area.

People who don't know each other well may feel more comfortable with each other if a piece of furniture separates them. For example, in most Canadian interviews, a desk, which both people perceive as part of the interviewer's space, separates the interviewer and the applicant. It's considered inappropriate for the applicant to place his or her property (notebook, purse) on a desk or to lean on the desk. In some situations, a group might work better sitting around a table than just sitting in a circle. In North America, a person sitting at the head of a table is generally assumed the group's leader. However, one experiment showed that when a woman sat at the head of a mixed-sex group, observers assumed that one of the men in the group was the leader.[26]

In low-context cultural settings, the size, placement, and privacy of a person's office connote status.

Time

Canadian organizations—businesses, government, and schools—keep time by the calendar and the clock. Being "on time" is seen as a sign of dependability. Other cultures may keep time by the seasons and the moon, the sun, internal "body clocks," or a personal feeling that "the time is right."

Canadians who believe "time is money" are often frustrated in negotiations with people who take a much more leisurely approach. Part of the miscommunication stems from a major perception difference: people in many other cultures want to take the time to establish a personal relationship before they decide whether to do business with each other.

Miscommunication occurs because various cultures perceive time differently. Many Canadians measure time in five-minute blocks. Someone five minutes late to an appointment or a job interview feels called upon to apologize. If the executive or interviewer is running half an hour late, the caller expects to be told about the likely delay when he or she arrives. Some people won't be able to wait that long and will need to reschedule their appointments. But in Latin American and other cultures, 15 minutes or half an hour may be the smallest block of time. To someone who mentally measures time in 15-minute blocks, being 45 minutes late is no worse than being 15 minutes late.

Further, Edward T. Hall distinguishes between **monochronic cultures**, where people do only one important activity at a time, and **polychronic cultures**, where people do several things at once.

Canada and the United States are predominantly monochronic cultures. When North American managers feel offended because a Latin American manager also sees other people during "their" appointments, the two kinds of time are in conflict. However, people who eat breakfast while they drive are doing more than one thing at a time. In a few organizations, it is even acceptable to do other work during a meeting. Such "multi-tasking" may indicate that some North American companies are evolving from a monochronic culture to a somewhat polychronic culture.

According to some scholars, Europeans schedule fewer events in a comparable period than North Americans. Perhaps as a result, Germans and German Swiss see North Americans as too time-conscious.[27]

Other Non-Verbal Symbols

Many other symbols—clothing, colours, age, and height, to name a few—carry non-verbal meanings. In Canada, certain styles and colours of clothing are considered more "professional" and more "credible." Certain fabrics—silk and linen, for example—carry non-verbal messages of success, prestige, and competence. In Japan, clothing denotes not only status but also occupational group. All students in junior and senior high school wear school uniforms. Company badges indicate rank within the organization. Workers wear different clothes when they are on strike than they do when they are working.[28]

Colours can also carry cultural meanings. In Canada, mourners wear black to funerals, while brides wear white at their wedding. In pre-Communist China and in some South American tribes, white is the colour of mourning. Purple flowers are given to the dead in Mexico.[29] In Korea, red ink is used to record deaths but never to write about living people.[30]

North American culture values youth. More and more individuals choose to colour their hair and have surgery to look as youthful as possible. In Japan, younger people defer to older people. North Americans attempting to negotiate in Japan are usually taken more seriously if at least one member of the team is noticeably grey-haired.

Our clothing choices reflect our cultural assumptions.

A Question of Ethics: COMEDY OR RACISM?

CBC's *Little Mosque on the Prairie* continues to attract a global audience, despite its detractors. What ethical concerns might a viewer have about this TV show?

Height connotes status in many parts of the world. Executive offices are usually on the top floors; the underlings work below. Even being tall can help a person succeed. Studies have shown that employers are more willing to hire men who are over 1.85 metres tall than shorter men with the same credentials. Studies of real-world executives and graduates have shown that taller men make more money. In one study, every extra inch of height brought in an extra $600 a year.[31] But being too big can be a disadvantage. A tall, brawny football player complained that people found him intimidating off the field and assumed that he was stupid.

Oral Communication

Effective oral communication also requires cultural awareness. Both the purpose and content of business communication differ across cultures and genders. Deborah Tannen uses the term *conversational style* to denote our conversational patterns and the meanings we give to them: the way we show interest, courtesy, social decorum.[32]

Employability Skills

Your answers to the following questions reveal your own conversational style:

- How long a pause tells you that it's your turn to speak?
- Do you see interruption as rude? Or do you say things while other people are still talking to show that you're interested and to encourage them to say more?
- Do you show interest by asking many questions? Or do you see questions as intrusive and wait for people to volunteer whatever they have to say?

No conversational style is better or worse than any another, but people with different styles may feel uncomfortable without knowing why. A boss who speaks slowly may frustrate a subordinate who talks quickly. People who talk more slowly may feel shut out of a conversation with people who talk more quickly. Someone who has learned to make requests directly ("Please pass the salt") may be annoyed by someone who uses indirect requests ("This casserole needs some salt").

In the workplace, conflicts may arise because of differences in conversational style. GenXers often use a rising inflection on statements as well as questions. They see this style as gentler and more polite. But Boomer bosses may see this speech pattern as hesitant, as if the speaker wants advice—which they then proceed to deliver.[33]

Ex.
3.2
3.4

Many middle-aged professionals consider certain speech patterns—"you know," "like," "basically," "right?"—to be eye-rolling irritants. According to University of Toronto sociolinguistics professor Sali Tagliamonte, however, our speech patterns reflect our age and our cultural values. People under 40 "are much more likely to use 'like' when narrating a story, than those over 40." ("And I'm like, OK, I'm all over that.") Tagliamonte believes the use of "like" is a demographic identifier; migrating from California, it has become a fashionable "way to voice a speaker's inner experience."[34]

Daniel N. Maltz and Ruth A. Borker believe that differences in conversational style might be responsible for the miscommunication that sometimes occurs in male–female conversations. For example, researchers have found that women are much more likely to nod and to say yes or say "mm-hmm" than men are. Maltz and Borker hypothesize that to women, these symbols mean simply, "I'm listening; go on." Men, on the other hand, may decode these symbols as "I agree" or at least "I follow what you're saying so far." A man who receives nods and "mm"s from a woman might feel she is inconsistent and unpredictable if she then disagrees with him. A woman might feel that a man who doesn't provide any feedback isn't listening to her.[35]

To decrease conflict due to differences in conversational style, talk less and listen more—always a successful communication strategy—and try to mirror the speaker's pace (Module 20).

Understatement and Exaggeration   Closely related to conversational style is the issue of understatement and overstatement. The British have a reputation for understatement. Someone good enough to play at Wimbledon may say he or she "plays a little tennis." Or ask a Canadian how the meeting yesterday or last night's game went, and the answer will be "Not bad!" even if the event was a roaring success. On the other hand, many people in the United States exaggerate. A U.S. businessperson negotiating with a German said, "I know it's impossible, but can we do it?" The German saw the statement as nonsensical: by definition, something that is impossible cannot be done at all. The American saw "impossible" as merely a strong way of saying "difficult," and assumed that with enough resources and commitment, the job could, in fact, be done.[36]

Compliments   The kinds of statements that people interpret as compliments and the socially correct way to respond to compliments also vary among cultures. The statement "You must be really tired" is a compliment in Japan, since it recognizes the other person has worked hard. The correct response is "Thank you, but I'm OK." A Canadian complimented on giving a good oral presentation will probably say, "Thank you." A Chinese or Japanese person, in contrast, will apologize: "No, it wasn't very good."[37]

Statements that seem complimentary in one context may be inappropriate in another. For example, businesswomen may feel uncomfortable if male colleagues or superiors compliment them on their appearance: the comments suggest that the women are being treated as visual decoration rather than contributing workers.

Silence   Silence also has different meanings in different cultures and subcultures. North Americans have difficulty doing business in Japan, because they do not realize that silence usually means that the Japanese do not like the ideas.

Different understandings of silence can prolong problems with sexual harassment in the workplace. Women sometimes use silence to respond to comments they find offensive, hoping that silence will signal their lack of appreciation. But some men may think that silence means appreciation, or at least neutrality.

Writing to International Audiences

Most cultures are more formal than that of North America. When you write to international audiences, use titles, not first names. Avoid contractions, slang, and sports metaphors.

The patterns of organization that work for Canadian audiences might not work for international correspondence beyond the United States. You will need to adapt your style, structure, and strategy when writing to international readers. For most cultures, buffer negative messages (Module 9), and make requests (Module 10) more indirect. Avoid phrases your audience might interpret as arrogant or uncaring. Cultural mistakes made orally may float away on the air; those made in writing are permanent.

> ## Checkpoint
>
> **Culture** is a learned set of assumptions about the norms and values that we internalize and accept as true. Our culture shapes our perceptions of the world around us and influences our communication styles and content.

LO6 With So Many Different Cultures, How Can I Communicate Effectively?

Focus on being aware and flexible.

The first step in understanding people of another culture is to realize that they may do things very differently, and that they value their way as much as you do yours. Realize, too, that people within a single culture differ. To get a sense of the kinds of things that differ from one culture to another, research and ask. If you work with people from other cultures, or if you plan to travel to a specific country, read about that country or culture and learn a little of the language. Also, talk to people; that's really the only way to learn whether someone is wearing black as a sign of mourning, as a fashion statement, or as a colour that slenderizes and doesn't show dirt.

As Brenda Arbeláez suggests,[38] the successful international communicator is

- Aware that his or her preferred values and behaviours are influenced by culture and are not necessarily "right"
- Flexible and open to change
- Sensitive to verbal and non-verbal behaviour
- Aware of the values, beliefs, and practices in other cultures
- Sensitive to differences among individuals within a culture

Use the PAIBOC questions shown in Figure 3.2 to prepare to communicate interculturally.

FIGURE 3.2   PAIBOC Questions for Analysis

P	What are your **purposes** in communicating?
A	Who is your **audience**? What are their values and expectations? How will they react to the content of your message? What form will make your message accessible to your audience? How should you frame your message to your audience's expectations?
I	What **information** will meet the needs of your audience and your purposes?
B	What reasons or audience **benefits** can you use to support your position?
O	What **objections** can you expect from your audience? What negative content must you de-emphasize or overcome?
C	What is the **context** of the message, and how will the context affect your audience's response? What is your relationship with your audience? What time of day are you delivering your message? What cultural differences should you be sensitive to? What special circumstances should shape the form and content of your message?

How Can I Make My Documents Bias-Free?

Start by using non-sexist, non-racist, and non-ageist language.

Bias-free language avoids discriminating against people based on sex, physical condition, race, age, or any other category. Bias-free language is fair and friendly; it complies with the law. It includes all readers; it helps to sustain goodwill. When you produce newsletters or other documents with photos and illustrations, choose a sampling of the whole population, not just part of it.

Ex.
3.2
3.5
3.6

LO4 Making Language Non-Sexist

Non-sexist language treats both sexes neutrally. Check to be sure that your writing is free from sexism in four areas: words and phrases, job titles, pronouns, and courtesy titles. Courtesy titles are discussed in Module 6 on format. Words and phrases, job titles, and pronouns are discussed in this module.

Words and Phrases
If you find any of the terms in the first column in Table 3.3 in your writing or your company's documents, replace them with terms from the second column.

Not every word containing *man* is sexist. For example, *manager* is not sexist. The word comes from the Latin *manus*, meaning *hand*; it has nothing to do with maleness.

Job Titles
Use neutral titles that imply that a person of either gender could hold the job. Many job titles are already neutral: *accountant, banker, doctor, engineer, inspector, manager, nurse, pilot, secretary, technician,* to name a few. Other titles reflect gender stereotypes and need to be changed. (See Table 3.3 for examples.)

Pronouns
When you write about a specific person, use gender-appropriate pronouns:

In his speech, John Jones said that…

In her speech, Judy Jones said that…

TABLE 3.3   Eliminating Sexist Terms and Phrases

Instead of:	Use:	For this Reason
The girl at the front desk	The woman's name or job title: Ms. Browning, Rosa, the receptionist	Call female employees women just as you call male employees men. When you talk about a specific woman, use her name, just as you use a man's name to talk about a specific man.
The ladies on our staff	The women on our staff	Use parallel terms for males and females. Therefore, use "ladies" only if you refer to the males on your staff as "gentlemen." Few businesses do, since social distinctions are rarely at issue.
Manpower Man-hours Manning	Personnel Hours or worker hours Staffing	The power in business today comes from both women and men. Use non-sexist alternatives.
Managers and their wives	Managers and their guests	Managers may be female; not everyone is married.
Businessman	A specific title: executive, accountant, department head, owner of a small business, men and women in business, businessperson	Gender-neutral title
Chairman	Chair, chairperson, moderator	Gender-neutral title
Foreman	Supervisor	Gender-neutral title
Salesman	Salesperson, sales representative	Gender-neutral title
Waitress	Server	Gender-neutral title
Woman lawyer	Lawyer	Gender-neutral title; you would not describe a man as a "male lawyer"
Workman	Worker, employee, or use a specific title: crane operator, bricklayer	Gender-neutral title

When you are not writing about a specific person, but about anyone who may be in a given job or position, avoid using traditional-gender pronouns.

Sexist: a. Each supervisor must certify that the time sheet for his department is correct.

Sexist: b. When the nurse fills out the accident report form, she should send one copy to the Central Division Office.

Business writing offers four alternatives to sexist generic pronouns: use plurals, use second person (*you*), revise the sentence to omit the pronoun, and use pronoun pairs. Whenever you have a choice of two or more ways to make a phrase or sentence non-sexist, choose the alternative that is smoothest and least conspicuous.

The following examples use these methods to revise sentences (a) and (b) above.

1. Use plural nouns and pronouns.

   Non-sexist: a. Supervisors must certify that the time sheets for their departments are correct.

Note: When you use plural nouns and pronouns, other words in the sentence may need to be made plural too. In the example above, plural supervisors have plural time sheets and plural departments.

Avoid mixing singular nouns and plural pronouns.

   Non-sexist,   a. Each supervisor must certify that the time sheet for their department is
   but lacks   correct.
   agreement:

Since *supervisor* is singular, it is incorrect to use the plural *they* to refer to it. The resulting lack of agreement is acceptable orally, but not yet acceptable to many readers in writing. Instead, use one of the four grammatically correct ways to make the sentence non-sexist.

2. Use *you*.

   Non-sexist: a. You must certify that the time sheet for your department is correct.

   Non-sexist: b. When you fill out an accident report form, send one copy to the Central Division Office.

You is particularly good for instructions and statements of the responsibilities of someone in a given position. Using *you* frequently shortens sentences, because you write "Send one copy" instead of "You should send one copy." It also makes your writing more direct.

3. Substitute an article (*a*, *an*, or *the*) for the pronoun, or revise the sentence so that the pronoun is unnecessary.

   Non-sexist: a. The supervisor must certify that the time sheet for the department is correct.

   Non-sexist: b. The nurse will

                          1. Fill out the accident report form

                          2. Send one copy of the form to the Central Division Office

4. When you must focus on the action of an individual, use pronoun pairs.

   Non-sexist: a. The supervisor must certify that the time sheet for his or her department is correct.

   Non-sexist: b. When the nurse fills out the accident report form, he or she should send one copy to the Central Division Office.

Making Language Neutral

Language is as neutral as possible when it treats all races and ages fairly, avoiding negative stereotypes of any group. Use these guidelines to check for bias in documents you write or edit:

- *Avoid terms that assume everyone is married or is heterosexual.*

   Biased: You and your husband or wife are cordially invited to the dinner.

   Better: You and your guest are cordially invited to the dinner.

- *Give someone's race or age only if it is relevant to your story.* When you do mention these characteristics, give them for everyone in your story—not just the non-Caucasian, non-young-to-middle-aged adults you mention.

- *Refer to a group by the term it prefers. As preferences change, change your usage.* Sixty years ago, *negro* was preferred as a more dignified term than *coloured* for North Americans of African origin. As times changed, *black person* and *African American* replaced it in the United States. In Canada, *black person* is generally preferred to *African Canadian*, which is more often used for recent immigrants from Africa and thus might not include, for example, black Canadians from Caribbean nations, or black Canadians who came to Nova Scotia as Loyalists in the late 18th century.

   Asian is preferred to *Oriental*, which may be considered offensive.

   East Indian is frequently misused to include people of non-Indian origin, such as new Canadians from Pakistan, Sri Lanka, and Bangladesh. *South Asian* is more accurate, and *Pakistani, Sri Lankan,* and *Bangladeshi* are preferred.

   Eskimo is a negative label. The correct term is *Inuit,* which means "the people".

   The term *Aboriginal peoples* is generally used to refer to Canada's indigenous peoples: *First Nations, Inuit,* and *Métis.* But usage will vary according to the preference of the individual or group referred to. For example, most Aboriginal peoples consider *Indian* offensive or at least a source of confusion with people from India. Where possible, consider referring to the specific band or nation of the individual (e.g., *Métis, Mohawk, Cree, Haida*).

   Older people and *mature customers* are more generally accepted terms than *senior citizens* or *golden agers.*

- *Avoid terms that suggest competent people are unusual in a group.* The statement "She is an intelligent Métis woman" suggests that the writer expects most Métis women to be unintelligent. "He is a credit to his race" suggests that excellence in the "race" is rare. "He is a spry 70-year-old" suggests that the writer is amazed that anyone that old can still move.

Talking About People with Disabilities and Illnesses

A disability is a physical, mental, sensory, or emotional impairment that interferes with the major tasks of daily living. In 2006, approximately four-and-a-half "million (one in seven) Canadians…reported having a disability." The number of people with disabilities will rise as social acceptance of reporting increases, and as the population ages.[39]

Cultural FOCUS

First Nations has replaced *Indian* in Canada, and **Inuit** has replaced *Eskimo*. **Métis** are also Aboriginal people in North America; their First Nations ancestors married Europeans.

- *People-first language* focuses on the person, not the condition. Avoid outdated adjectives used as nouns that imply that the condition defines the person, like *asthmatic* or *schizophrenic*.
- *Avoid negative terms, unless the audience prefers them.* Preference takes precedence over positive emphasis: use the term a group prefers. People who lost their hearing as infants, children, or young adults often prefer to be called *deaf*. But people who lose their hearing as older adults often prefer to be called *hard of hearing*, even when their hearing loss is just as great as someone who identifies as part of deaf culture.

Just as people in a single ethnic group may prefer different labels based on generational or cultural divides, so differences exist within the disability community (see Table 3.4). Using the right term requires keeping up with changing preferences. If your target audience is smaller than the whole group, use the term preferred by that audience, even if the group as a whole prefers another term.

Some negative terms, however, are never appropriate: *afflicted*, *suffering from*, *the victim of*, and *struck down by* suggest an outdated view of illness.

TABLE 3.4   **Eliminating the Use of Terms and Phrases to Define Persons with Disabilities**

Instead of:	Use:
The mentally retarded	People with developmental delays
The blind	People with vision impairments
Cancer patients	People being treated for cancer

LO7 Choosing Bias-Free Photos and Illustrations

Ex.
3.1

When you produce a document with photographs or illustrations, check the visuals for possible bias. Do they show people of both sexes and all races? Is there representation of various kinds of people (younger and older, people using wheelchairs, etc.)? It is acceptable to have individual pictures of just one sex or one race; the photos as a whole do not need to show exactly 50 percent men and 50 percent women. But the general impression should suggest that diversity is welcome and normal.

Check relationships and authority figures as well as numbers. If all the men appear in business suits and all the women in maids' uniforms, the pictures are sexist even if an equal number of men and women are pictured. If the only black people and Filipinos pictured are factory workers, the photos support racism even when equal numbers of people from each race are shown.

Don't use biased clip art or stock photos: look for alternatives, or create your own bias-free illustrations.

Checkpoint

The successful international communicator is

- Aware that his or her preferred values and behaviours are influenced by culture and are not necessarily "right"
- Flexible and open to change
- Sensitive to verbal and non-verbal behaviour
- Aware of the values, beliefs, and practices in other cultures
- Sensitive to differences among individuals within a culture

MODULE SUMMARY

- Culture is a learned set of assumptions that shape our perception of reality. No culture exits wherein all members adhere to one notion of reality, and in urban Canada, cultural diversity is the norm.

- Each of us belongs to a number of cultures, whose expectations are communicated through symbols, including language. Cultural assumptions and expectations shape the form and content of our communication.

- In high-context cultures, most of the meaning is inferred from the context of the message; little is explicitly conveyed. In low-context cultures, most information is explicitly stated.

- No gesture has a universal meaning across cultures, and non-verbal symbols can be misinterpreted as easily as verbal symbols (words).

- North Americans, who believe "time is money," are often frustrated in negotiations with people from cultures with different values. In polychronic cultures, people want to establish a personal relationship before they decide whether to do business with each other, and may measure time in 15- or 30-minute increments rather than the 5-minute increments North Americans are used to.

- Conversational style reflects our cultural patterns, and the way we display age, interest, politeness, and appropriateness.

- Generational differences may affect perceptions, and lead to conflict in the workplace. Use empathy to try to see other points of view, and adapt accordingly.

- In today's global marketplace, cultural awareness is vital to communication success. Analyzing your audience members allows you to be sensitive to their cultural norms, and flexible about adapting to those norms. The most effective communicator mirrors others in form and content.

ASSIGNMENTS FOR MODULE 3

Questions for Critical Thinking

3.1 Review the photos in this module. Which show bias, and what is the bias?

3.2 Suppose you know your audience is sexist, ageist, racist, or otherwise prejudiced. How should you adapt your message to your audience? What are the ethical implications of such an adaptation?

3.3 Based on your own experience, identify one area of business communication that could be a source of intergenerational conflict. What could the younger person do to avoid or defuse the conflict? What could the older person do?

3.4 What cultures do you work with? Describe one example of a communication practice of that culture that you see as markedly different from your own.

Exercises and Problems

3.5 Revising Sexist Job Titles

Suggest non-sexist alternatives for each of the following:

cleaning lady	mailman
alderman	night watchman
garbage man	repairman
male nurse	salesman
mail boy	waitress
actress	stewardess

3.6 Eliminating Biased Language

Explain the source of bias in each of the following and revise to remove the bias.

1. We recommend hiring Jim Renker and Elizabeth Shuman. Both were very successful summer interns. Jim drafted the report on using rap music in ads, and Elizabeth really improved the look of the office.
2. All sales associates and their wives are invited to the picnic.
3. Although he is blind, Mr. Morin is an excellent group leader.

4. Unlike many Caribbean Canadians, Yvonne has extensive experience designing web pages.

5. Chris Gottlieb
   Pacific Perspective
   6300 West 12th Avenue
   Vancouver, BC

Gentlemen:

6. Enrique Torres is very intuitive for a man.

7. Twenty-First-Century Parenting shows you how to persuade your husband to do his share of childcare chores.

8. Mr. Paez, Mr. O'Connor, and Tonya will represent our office at the convention.

9. Sue Corcoran celebrates her 50th birthday today. Stop by her cubicle at noon to get a piece of cake and to help us sing "The Old Grey Mare She Ain't What She Used to Be."

10. Because older customers tend to be really picky, we will need to give a lot of details in our ads.

3.7 Dealing with Discrimination

Despite Canada's reputation for tolerance, courtesy, and fair play, many of its citizens frequently experience discriminatory behaviour. Some believe that prejudice is systemic—that bias against visible minorities, women, people with disabilities, and seniors is built into our legal and judicial systems and demonstrated daily in our assumptions and attitudes.

Media attention has focused on such culturally sensitive issues as racism among members of the police force, and discriminatory hiring and promotion practices in Canadian postsecondary institutions.

Find a specific, relevant news story of cultural bias or discrimination. Or use your own experience to identify a serious miscommunication based on cultural assumptions. Write a summary of the news story or of your experience. Using what you have learned in Modules 1 and 2, write a memo to your classmates and your professor, providing specific ideas about how to deal positively with such a situation.

3.8 Identifying Sources of Miscommunication

In each of the following situations, identify one or more ways in which cultural differences may be leading to miscommunication.

a. Alan is a Canadian sales representative in Mexico. He makes appointments and is careful to be on time. But the person he's calling on is frequently late. To save time, Alan tries to get right to business. But his host wants to talk about sightseeing and his family. Even worse, his appointments are interrupted constantly, not only by business phone calls, but also by long conversations with other people and even the customer's children who come into the office. Alan's first progress report is very negative. He hasn't yet made a sale. Perhaps Mexico just isn't the right place to sell his company's products.

b. To help her company establish a presence in Japan, Susan wants to hire a local interpreter who can advise her on business customs. Kana Tomari has superb qualifications on paper. But when Susan tries to probe about her experience, Kana just says, "I will do my best. I will try very hard." She never gives details about any of the previous positions she's held. Susan begins to wonder whether Kana's resumé is inflated.

c. Stan wants to negotiate a joint venture with a Chinese company. He asks Tung-Sen Lee if the Chinese people have enough discretionary income to afford his product. Mr. Lee is silent for a time, and then says, "Your product is good. People in the West must like it." Stan smiles, pleased that Mr. Lee recognizes the quality of his product, and he gives Mr. Lee a contract to sign. Weeks later, Stan still hasn't heard anything. If China is going to be so inefficient, he wonders if he really should try to do business there.

d. Elspeth is very proud of her participatory management style. On assignment in India, she is careful not to give orders but to ask for suggestions. But people rarely suggest anything. Even a formal suggestion system doesn't work. And to make matters worse, she doesn't sense the respect and camaraderie of the plant she managed in Canada. Perhaps, she decides gloomily, people in India just aren't ready for a female boss.

3.9 Analyzing Cultural Preferences: Business Introductions

What are some differences between high-context and low-context cultures in business introductions? Research a high-context culture you are interested in, and compare this culture's norms for business introductions with your own. Use the following criteria for your comparison: purpose of the introduction, image of the individual introducing him/herself, information provided, level of language (formal, informal, slang) and values (harmony, competition, respect, individualism, openness, directness, etc.).

Prepare a comparison chart of the culture you chose and your own culture, based on the criteria. Attach the chart to a memo to your instructor. In your memo, describe one intercultural communication difference you found interesting.

3.10 Analyzing Cultural Preferences: Business Correspondence

What values and norms shape the business writing of high-context cultures? Research a high-context culture you are interested in, and, with reference to Table 3.1, compare this culture's norms for business writing with your own. Using a short request letter from each culture (your own and that of the high-context culture) and compare the letters based on the following criteria: salutation or greeting, close, organizational pattern (direct or indirect), level of language (formal, informal), emphasis (positive, neutral, friendly, polite, reader-centred, writer-centred).

Prepare a comparison chart of the culture you chose and your own culture, based on the criteria. Attach the chart to a memo to your instructor. In your memo, describe one intercultural communication difference you found interesting.

3.11 Asking About Travel Arrangements

The CEO is planning a trip to visit colleagues in another country (you pick the country). As executive assistant to the CEO of your organization, it's your job to make travel plans. At this stage, you don't know anything except dates and flights. (The CEO will arrive in the country at 7 a.m. local time on the 28th of next month, and stay for three days.) It's your job to find out what the plans are and communicate any of the CEO's requirements. Write an email message to your contact.

Hints:

- Pick a business, non-profit organization, or government agency you know something about, making assumptions about the kinds of things its executive would want to do during an international visit.
- How much international travelling does your CEO do? Has he or she ever been to this country before? What questions will he or she want answered?

3.12 Sending a Draft to Japan

You've drafted instructions for a product that will be sold in Japan. Before the text is translated, you want to find out whether the pictures will be clear. So you send an email to your Japanese counterpart, Takashi Haneda, asking for a response within a week. Write an email message; assume that you will send the pictures as an attachment.

3.13 Creating a Web Page

Create a web page for managers who must communicate across cultures. Assume that this page can be accessed from the organization's intranet. Offer at least seven links. (More

are better.) You may offer information as well as links to other pages with information. At the top of the page, offer an overview of what the page covers. At the bottom of the page, put the dates of creation and update your name and email address.

As your instructor directs,

- a. Turn in two printed copies of your page(s). On another page, give the URLs for each link.
- b. Write a memo to your instructor identifying the audience for whom the page is designed and explaining (1) what search strategies you used to find material on this topic, (2) why you chose the pages and information you've included, and (3) why you chose the layout and graphics you've used. Include your web page URL.
- c. Post your memo in an email message to the class.
- d. Present your page orally to the class.

Hints:

- Limit your page to just one culture or country.
- Try to cover as many topics as possible: history, politics, notable people, arts, conversational style, customs, and so forth. For a culture in another country, also include money, living accommodations, geography, transport, weather, business practices, and so forth.
- Chunk your links into small groups under headings.
- See Module 5 on web page design.

3.14 Requesting Information About a Country

Use one or more of the following ways to get information about a country. You might focus on

- Business opportunities
- History and geography
- Principal exports and imports
- Dominant religions
- Holidays
- School system
- Political system

1. Visit the Canadian government's Canada Business Network website for information on international markets at http://www.canadabusiness.ca/eng/page/2825/ and click on Country Information—Export Development Canada or Market reports—Canadian Trade Commissioner
2. Check the country's trade office, if there is one in your city.
3. Interview someone from that country or someone who has lived there.
4. Read about the country.

As your instructor directs

a. Share your findings orally with a small group of students.
b. Summarize your findings in a memo to your instructor.
c. Present your findings to the class.
d. Email your findings to the class.
e. Join with a group of classmates to write a group report on the country.

3.15 Answering an Inquiry About Photos

You've just been named vice-president for diversity, the first person in your organization to hold this position. Today, you receive the following memo from Sheila Lathan, who edits the employee newsletter:

Subject: Photos in the Employee Newsletter

Please tell me what to do about photos in the monthly employee newsletter. I'm concerned that almost no single issue represents the diversity of employees we have here.

As you know, our layout allows two visuals each month. One of those is always the employee of the month (EM). In the last year, most of those have been male and all but two have been white. What makes it worse is that people want photos that make them look good. You may remember that Ron Olmos was the EM two months ago; in the photo he wanted me to use, you can't tell that he's in a wheelchair. Often the EM is the only photo; the other visual is a graph of sales or something relating to quality.

Even if the second visual is another photo, it may not look balanced in terms of gender and race. After all, 62 percent of our employees are women, and 70 percent are non-white. Should the pictures try to represent those percentages? The leadership positions (both in management and in the union) are heavily male and white. Should we run pictures of people doing important things and risk continuing the imbalance?

I guess I could use more visuals, but then there wouldn't be room for as many stories—and people really like to see their names in print. Plus, giving people information about company activities and sales is important to maintaining goodwill. A bigger newsletter would be one way to have more visuals and keep the content, but with the cost-cutting measures we're under, that doesn't look likely.

What should I do?

As your instructor directs

a. Work in a small group with students to come up with a recommendation for Sheila.
b. Write a memo responding to Sheila.
c. Write an article for the employee newsletter about the photo policy you recommend and how it relates to the company's concern for diversity.

POLISHING YOUR PROSE

Subject–Verb Agreement

The subjects and verbs in your sentences must agree in number: singular subjects take singular verbs; plural subjects take plural verbs. Remember that singular subjects (laser, chair, etc) and the pronouns he, she, and it require a singular verb, that, in the present tense, ends in "s."

Correct: The laser printer no longer works.

Correct: The broken laser printers are in the storeroom.

Often, subject–verb errors occur when other words come between the subject and verb. Learn to correct errors by looking for the subject—who or what is doing the principal action—and the verb—the action itself:

Incorrect: A team of marketing researchers are reviewing our promotional campaign.

Correct: A team of marketing researchers is reviewing our promotional campaign.

Incorrect: The idea of tax rebates do not solve the growing gap between rich and poor.

Correct: The idea of tax rebates does not solve the growing gap between rich and poor.

Canadian and American usage treats company names and the words company and government as singular nouns. In England and countries adopting the British system, these nouns are plural:

Correct (Canada): Clarica is headquartered in Waterloo, Ontario.

Correct (U.S.): National Insurance is headquartered in Columbus, Ohio.

Correct (U.K.): Lloyds of London are headquartered in London.

Use a plural verb when two or more singular subjects are joined by and.

Correct: Mr. Simmens, Ms. Lopez, and Mr. Yee were in Seoul for a meeting last week.

Use a singular verb when two or more singular subjects are joined by *or*, *nor*, or *but*.

Correct: Neither Dr. Hroscoe nor Mr. Jamieson is in today.

When the sentence begins with *There* or *Here*, make the verb agree with the subject that follows the verb:

Correct: There were blank pages in the fax we received.

Correct: Here is the information on the job candidate you requested.

Some words that end in *s* are considered singular and require singular verbs:

Correct: The World Series features advertisements of our product in the stadium.

When you encounter situations that don't seem to fit the rule, or when following the rules produces an awkward sentence, rewrite the sentence to avoid the problem:

Problematic: The grant coordinator in addition to the awarding agency (is, are?) happy with the latest proposal we submitted.

Better: The grant coordinator and the awarding agency are happy with the latest proposal we submitted.

Exercises

Choose the correct verb or rewrite the sentence.

1. Each of us (is, are) entitled to company healthcare benefits.
2. KPMG, a leading management consulting firm, (operate, operates) in nine Canadian provinces.
3. The price of our stocks (is, are) increasing.
4. Every project team (train, trains) for at least 90 days before projects (is, are) started.
5. We (order, orders) a dozen new toner cartridges each month.
6. A series of meetings (is, are) devoted to concerns about our office air quality.
7. Marina Schiff and her assistant (is, are) attending the conference in Halifax.
8. Make it a point to (has, have) your report ready by Monday.
9. Professor Beauparlant, Mr. Kincaid, and Ms. Carolla (is, are) on the guest list and (plan, plans) to sit at the same table.
10. The offices in Buenos Aries (report, reports) a 19 percent increase in employee turnover for the past year.

Check your answers to the odd-numbered exercises in the Answer Key at the back of the text.

Planning, Writing, and Revising

Learning Objectives

After reading and applying the information in Module 4, you'll be able to demonstrate

Knowledge of

LO1 The activities in the writing process

LO2 The process application

Skills to

LO3 Begin to apply the activities in the writing process

LO4 Begin to identify and analyze your own strategies

LO5 Begin to use revision and editing techniques

LO6 Get started writing

MODULE OUTLINE

- What is the writing process?
- Does it matter what process I use?
- How should I use my time?
- What planning should I do to prepare to write or speak?
- What is revision? How do I do it?
- What is editing? How do I do it?
- Can a grammar checker edit for me?
- What is proofreading? How do I do it?
- I use a spell checker. Do I still need to proofread?
- How can I get good feedback?
- Can I use form letters?
- How can I get started?

Module Summary

Assignments for Module 4

Polishing Your Prose: Commas in Lists

Employability Skills 2000+ Checklist

Module content builds these Conference Board of Canada Employability Skills 2000+

Communicate   **Be Adaptable**

Think and Solve Problems   **Learn Continuously**

**Demonstrate Positive Attitudes and
Behaviours**

Writing is rewriting. Writing is a process that includes jotting down ideas, drafting, revising, editing, and proofing. Competent writers do not necessarily follow the process steps in order. However, all business writers agree that writing is a learned skill that requires regular practice and plenty of feedback from others. Figures 4.1a and 4.1b show two versions of an email, a draft and a revised version. Although many people send draft emails only, revising before you send ensures a better result.

FIGURE 4.1a   Writing Is Rewriting: Draft Email

November 10, 2013

To: Bartenders, servers, and bussing staff

From: Omar

Re: Christmas

While we're planning our Christmas party we should also be thinking about what we're going to do about who's going to be responsible for cleaning up and locking up after the party, if we start partying after closing time at 1 on the 21, and party until 3 or 4, that's fine with the managers, and some staff have already said they will taxi people home but we need people to stay to clean up and set up for the next day's lunch crowd. Also, somebody has to take the day's receipts and money for safekeeping, and bank it the next day.

Party includes free food and you can bring a guest. You need to bring your own booze

Can you let me know who will volunteer to do that? Thx

FIGURE 4.1b   Writing Is Rewriting: Revised Email

November 10, 2013

To: Bartenders, servers, and bussing staff

From: Omar

Re: After-Hours Christmas Party and Cleanup

Our employee celebration starts at 1 a.m. on December 21. Food is on the house. Please BYOB, and a guest. We have volunteer designated drivers.

Frank is not concerned about our end time. However, we are responsible for cleanup, and lunch setup for business on December 22. I will also need a volunteer to take the day's count and receipts, and to bank them the next day.

Please let me know your duty preference by filling in the attached to-do list, and emailing it to me by end of today. If I don't hear from you, I'll assign you where you're needed.

Thank you.

Subject line sums up memo

Paragraphs increase readability

To and From content depends on the relationship between writer and reader

Most important info to the reader put in first and last paragraphs

Language FOCUS

BYOB stands for "Bring Your Own Beverage" or "Bring Your Own Booze" (which means alcoholic beverages). Being asked to bring your own beverage to a party is common practice in Canada.

LO1 What Is the Writing Process?

The process includes planning, drafting, and rewriting.

Planning

- Analyze the situation: what has the initial audience (Module 2) requested? Specifically, what is the task?
- Define your purposes, and analyze your audience needs: use PAIBOC to understand the situation.
- Think about the information: What "proof" meets your purposes, and matters to your audience? Where can you find it?
- Gather the information: through your own and others' observations and experiences, from the Internet, from articles.
- Make notes, create outlines (See Figure 4.2 **Clustering Helps Generate Ideas**).
  - ✔ Consider how to format the information: Are you writing in an academic or a business context? What are the reader's expectations?
  - ✔ Consider how to organize the information: What do your audiences already know? What do they need to know? How can you organize your information for maximum effect on your audience? (See Modules 8 and 9, and "How Should I Organize Reports?" in Module 17.)

FIGURE 4.2   Clustering Helps Generate Ideas

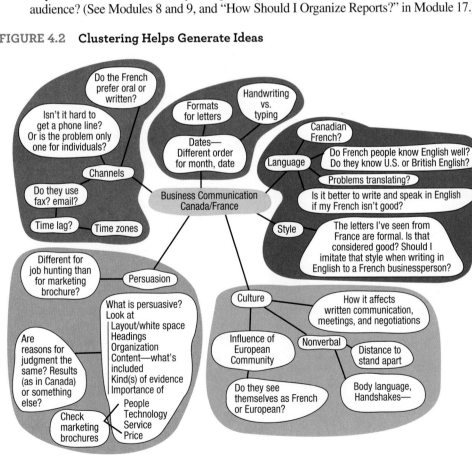

Drafting

Put notes on paper or on the screen. Drafting can include

- Purpose statements
- Visuals (See Figure 4.2 **Clustering Helps Generate Ideas**)
- Lists
- Brainstorms
- Dot jots
- Stream-of-consciousness thoughts
- Formal draft

Language FOCUS

Dot jots means *jotting* or writing thoughts down in point form; *stream of consciousness* writing is like freewriting: write down everything that occurs to you without censuring or critiquing.

Employability Skills
2⚬⚬+

Rewriting

Revising

Ex. 4.3 4.5 4.6

- Assess the writing **from your audience's point of view**. Focus on the **meaning** of the writing.
- Get feedback as soon and as often as you can. Ask peers and colleagues to comment on the **content**: What questions do they have about the message? What content or words cause them confusion? How well do they understand the message?
- Compare your draft to the answers to your PAIBOC questions: what are your purposes in writing, and who is your audience?
- Read your drafts from the reader's point of view: Is the meaning clear? Complete? Convincing? Tactful?
- Rewrite based on your analysis and feedback: delete, add, substitute, rearrange; change sections of the document, or revise sentences or single words.

Editing

Ex. 4.5– 4.7

- Focus on the surface of the writing.
- Edit the draft for grammar, usage, and punctuation. Spellchecking is not enough: check for typos.
- Ask a peer to read your document for surface errors.

Proofreading

- Focus on the mechanics of the document.
- Proof the final copy to ensure it is error-free.
- Ask a peer to read your document for errors.

We may text friends and family our first and only draft. Depending on your purposes and your audiences, however, you may revise and edit a message—even one sent from your smartphone—several times before you hit send.

The writing process can include many critical thinking strategies.

LO2 LO3 LO4 Does It Matter What Process I Use?

Know what the experts do, and use what works best for you.

Although there is no one *right* way to write, all writers agree that they write best when they know their topic and understand the audience reading their work. Thinking about the processes you currently use and trying out experts' strategies can help you become a better writer.

Experienced writers tend to

- Focus on their purpose and audience
- Identify a story, thesis, theme, or central idea related to their purpose and audience
- Assume that the first draft will be revised
- Break big writing jobs into a series of steps
- Read daily
- Write daily
- Work to acquire a large vocabulary of concrete nouns and action verbs
- Discuss their writing with others
- Ask for and apply feedback
- Use a reader for revising, editing, and proofing
- Use whatever rules work for them[1]

Practised writers spend more time identifying and analyzing the initial problem, understanding the task more broadly and deeply, drawing from a wider repertoire of strategies, and seeing patterns more clearly. Practised writers compose more slowly than novices and spend more time evaluating their work.[2]

LO2 How Should I Use My Time?

Make notes on your research and thinking. Save plenty of time for rewriting.

To get the best results,

- Try to use only one-third of your time composing your first draft: spend at least one-third of your time analyzing your purpose(s) and audience(s), gathering your information, and organizing what you want to say.
- Keep notes (electronic and hardcopy) on all your information. These jottings can stimulate your thinking and serve as your rough draft.
- Spend another third of your time revising and editing: assess your draft based on your analysis of purpose and audience; revise; get feedback, and revise again; edit for correct grammar and mechanics; proofread your final copy.

Ex.
4.3
4.5
4.6

Different projects have different lead times. When you get an assignment, consider the steps you'll need to go through so you can timeline the project (Module 18).

Language FOCUS

Good writers do not rely on direct translations from dictionaries. If English is not your first language, it is important to use words and phrases as they are used in North America. Instead of directly translating from your first language, pay close attention to the way native speakers use the language and try to copy it.

What Planning Should I Do to Prepare to Write or Speak?

Do as much planning as you can, and keep a record.

Spend at least one-third of your time gathering ideas, researching, planning, and making notes. The more familiar you are with your ideas, the fewer drafts you'll need to produce a good document.

Start by using PAIBOC to identify purpose and audience. Use the strategies described in Module 2 to analyze your audience and to identify what **audience needs** your talk or your document can meet. Gather information you can use for your document.

LO3 How Can I Jumpstart Ideas?

To encourage ideas, try the following techniques:

- **Brainstorm.** Write down all your ideas without judging them. Consciously try to get at least a dozen different ideas before you stop.
- **Freewrite.**[3] Make yourself write, without stopping, for 10 minutes or so, even if you have to write "I will think of something soon." At the end of 10 minutes, read what you've written and identify the best point in the draft. Get a clean paper or screen and write for another 10 uninterrupted minutes. Read this draft, marking anything that's good and should be kept, and then write again for another 10 minutes. By the third session, you will probably produce several sections worth keeping—maybe even a complete draft that's ready to be revised.
- **Cluster.**[4] Write your topic in the middle of the page and circle it. Write down the ideas the topic suggests, circling them, too. (The circles are designed to tap into the non-linear half of your brain.) When you've filled the page, look for patterns or repeated ideas. Use different-coloured pens to group related ideas (Modules 14 and 15). Then use these ideas to develop reader benefits in a memo, questions for a survey, or content for the body of a report. Figure 4.2 presents the clusters that one writer created about business communication in Canada and France.
- **Talk to your audiences.** Talking to internal and external audiences is invaluable. Talking to real audiences helps writers involve readers in the planning process, understand social and political relationships among readers, and negotiate conflicts orally rather than depending solely on the document. These writers are then able to think about content as well as about organization and style, appeal to common ground (such as reducing waste or increasing productivity) that several readers share, and reduce the number of revisions needed before documents are approved.[5]

LO2

What Else Can Help Me Get Ideas?

Thinking and talking to others about the content, layout, or structure of your document can also give you ideas. For long documents, *write out the headings you'll use*. For anything that's shorter than five pages, less formal notes will probably work. You may want to jot down ideas that you can use as the basis for a draft.

For an oral presentation, a meeting, or a document with lots of visuals, use your presentation software to create a storyboard, or make your own paper storyboard with a rectangle representing each page or unit. Draw a box with a visual for each main point. Below the box, write a short caption or label.

Letters and memos will go faster if you can visualize a basic organizational pattern before you start. Modules 7 through 10 give detailed patterns of organization for the most common kinds of letters and memos. You may want to customize those patterns with a **planning guide**[6] to help you keep the big picture in mind as you write. Figure 4.3 shows planning guides developed for specific kinds of documents.

FIGURE 4.3   **Examples of Planning Guides for Specific Documents**

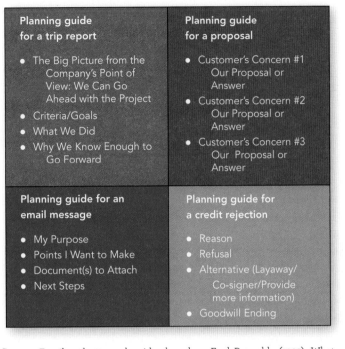

Source: Email and proposal guides based on Fred Reynolds (1995), What adult work-world writers have taught me about adult work-world writing, *Professional writing in context: Lessons from teaching and consulting in worlds of work* (Hillsdale, NJ: Lawrence Erlbaum Associates), 18, 20.

LO5 What Is Revision? How Do I Do It?

Revision means seeing the document anew, from the reader's point of view.

Writers improve their messages by "reading out": that is, by reading their documents from the reader's point of view. Revision means taking an aerial or wide-angled view of the document: you assume the perspective of the reader, with the reader's needs (which is, above all, to understand, quickly, what the writer wants). Further, many writers revise more quickly and accurately when they work on hard copy. Check the revision tips in Figure 4.4.

FIGURE 4.4   **Revision Tips**

1. Ask a colleague (friend, parent) to read your writing and give you feedback (using the criteria outlined in Figure 4.5).

2. Read the message with fresh eyes: when you can, leave the draft for a few hours or overnight. Then start revising.

3. As you revise, be sure to read the document through from start to finish.

4. Plan to revise the draft at least three times when you're writing to a new audience or solving a particularly difficult problem. The first time, look for content and clarity. The second time, check the organization and layout. Finally, check style and tone, using the information in the Revising and Editing Resources at the end of this book.

5. Wait to edit until after you have revised: it's a waste of your time to fix a grammatical error in a sentence that you may cut when you clarify your meaning or tighten your style.

If you're short on time, do at least a light revision (see Figure 4.6). The quality of the final document might not be as high as with a thorough revision, but even a light revision is better than nothing.

FIGURE 4.5   Checklist for Revision

Organization and Layout

❑ Does the design of the document make it easy for readers to find the information they need? Is the document visually inviting?

❑ Are transitions between ideas smooth? Do ideas within paragraphs flow smoothly?

❑ Are the most important points emphasized?

❑ Are the first and last paragraphs effective?

Content and Clarity

❑ Does your document meet the needs of the organization and of the reader—and make you look good?

❑ Have you given readers all the information they need to understand and act on your message?

❑ Have you organized your message for optimum positive audience impact? (Modules 2 and 11)

❑ Is all the information accurate?

❑ Is each sentence clear? Is the message free from apparently contradictory statements?

❑ Are statements supported with details/explanations/examples?

❑ Is the message free from biased/sexist language?

Style and Tone

❑ How does the message build goodwill?

❑ Is the message easy to read? How so?

❑ Does the message reflect you-attitude (Module 13) and positive emphasis (Module 12)?

FIGURE 4.6   Checklist for Light Revision

❑ How does the design of the document make it easy for readers to find the information they need?

❑ How effective are the first and last paragraphs?

❑ Where have I told the reader what to do?

LO5 What Is Editing? How Do I Do It?

Editing is making surface-level changes that make the document grammatically correct.

To edit, you need to know the rules of grammar and punctuation. Most writers make a small number of errors repeatedly. If you know that you have trouble with dangling modifiers or subject–verb agreement, for example, specifically look for them in your draft. Also look for any errors that especially bother your boss and correct them. See Figure 4.7 for more editing tips.

Then check for correct word use, correct spelling—including spelling of names—and numbers accuracy.

FIGURE 4.7   Editing Tips

1. Ask a colleague (friend, parent) who knows grammar rules to edit for you, as you watch.
2. Learn and check for the most common grammar mistakes of adult writers:
   ❏ Sentence structure
   ❏ Subject–verb and noun–pronoun agreement
   ❏ Dangling or misplaced modifiers
   ❏ Parallelism
   ❏ Punctuation
   ❏ Passive verbs

Editing for Readability

Grammar checkers frequently include an option for checking the readability of a selected passage. Word's grammar checker will indicate readability based on the Flesch-Kincaid Grade Level (corresponding to years of education required to comprehend the material) and a Flesch Reading Ease score (assessing the difficulty level based on the average number of words per sentence and the average number of syllables per word). Table 4.1 sets out guidelines for interpreting these results.

Most business writers strive for a readability score of Grade 8 to 10, because clear and concise documents make it easier for the audience to read and understand the message. Saving the reader time and trouble has a positive impact (Modules 12 and 13), increasing the chances of you getting the results you want.

TABLE 4.1   Interpreting Flesch Readability Scores

Flesch Reading Ease	Difficulty	Flesch-Kincaid Grade Level	Example
0–29	Very difficult	Postgraduate	
30–49	Difficult	College	32: *Harvard Law Review* 40–50: Standard score for insurance documents required by law in several U.S. states
50–59	Fairly difficult	High school	52: *Time*
60–69	Standard	Grade 8 to 9	60: "Plain English" (20 words per sentence, 1.5 syllables per word) 65: *Reader's Digest*
70–79	Fairly easy	Grade 7	
80–89	Easy	Grade 5 to 6	
90–100	Very easy	Grade 4 to 5	

Source: OXFORD COMPANION TO THE ENGLISH LANGUAGE edited by McArthur (1992). Adapted "Interpreting Flesch Readability Scores" p.407. By permission of Oxford University Press.

Can a Grammar Checker Edit for Me?

No. You have to decide on each change.

Grammar checkers are good at finding missing halves. For example, if you open a parenthesis and forget to close it, a grammar checker will note that you need a second one. Of course, *you* have to decide where it goes. In terms of other errors, all a grammar checker can do is ask you about what you have done. A grammar checker can tell you that you've used a passive construction (refer to the Revising and Editing Resources at the end of this book) and ask whether you want to change it. But

Employability Skills
2+

you have to decide whether the passive is justified. If it finds the word *well*, the grammar checker can tell you that *good* and *well* are sometimes confused. But you have to decide which word fits your meaning. You still need to know the rules so you can decide which changes to make.

What Is Proofreading? How Do I Do It?

Proofreading means checking to be sure the document is free from typographical errors.

Proofreading is hard, because writers tend to see what they expect to be there rather than what is really on the page or screen. Since it's always easier to proof something you haven't written, you may want to swap papers with a proofing buddy. (Be sure the person looks for typos, not for content.)

Wait until the final draft to proofread your document, and print out a hard copy to do so. Finding spelling errors and typos may be easier and faster on hard copy. Use the proofreading tips listed in Figure 4.8.

FIGURE 4.8   **Proofreading Tips**

- ❑ Read the document aloud, listening for poor or incorrect phrasing.
- ❑ Read the document from last word to first word to catch spelling errors.
- ❑ Read the document in stages—first page, second page, third page—with plenty of time in between so you are fresh for each page.
- ❑ Read pages out of sequence so you can concentrate on the characters on the page rather than the meaning.
- ❑ Ask a friend to read the document aloud, with punctuation, while you follow along with the original.
- ❑ Double-check numbers, dates, and people's names.

I Use a Spell Checker. Do I Still Need to Proofread?

Yes.

Proofread every document both with a spell checker and by eye to catch the errors a spell checker can't find.

Spell checkers can't think; they cannot recognize words that are out of context. If you write "two" instead of "too," or "there" instead of "their" or "they're," the spell checker will not identify a problem. Similarly, if you misspell your client's name, or write down the wrong date, the spell checker won't notice or care. But your reader will.

> ## Checkpoint
>
> **Writing** is a complex, time-consuming process that includes **planning, researching, composing, assessing, getting feedback, revising, editing,** and **proofreading**. Writers do not follow these activities in order, although the most successful writers focus their time on **planning, researching, revising,** and **proofreading**.

How Can I Get Good Feedback?

Ask for the kind of feedback you need.

Being asked to revise documents is standard in businesses, government, and non-profit organizations.

To improve the quality of the feedback you get, and of your revisions, tell people which aspects you'd especially like comments about. For example, when you give a reader the outline or planning draft,[7] you might want to know whether the general approach is appropriate. After your second draft, you might want to know whether reader benefits are well developed. When you reach the polishing draft, you'll be ready for feedback on style and grammar. Figure 4.9 lists questions to ask.

To get a fresh perspective, writers talk to others about their work.

FIGURE 4.9   **Questions to Ask Readers**

Outline or Planning Draft

❑ Does the plan seem to be on the right track?

❑ What topics should be added? Should any be cut?

❑ Do you have any other general suggestions?

Revised Draft

❑ Does the message satisfy all its purposes?

❑ Is the message adapted to the audience(s)?

❑ Is the organization effective?

❑ Are any parts unclear?

❑ What ideas need further development?

❑ Do you have any other suggestions?

Polished Draft

❑ Are there any problems with word choice or sentence structure?

❑ Did you find any inconsistencies?

❑ Did you find any typos?

❑ Is the document's design effective?

It's easy to feel defensive when someone criticizes your work. If the feedback stings, put it aside until you can read it without feeling defensive. Even if you think the reader has misunderstood what you were trying to say, the fact that the reader commented means the section could be improved.

Your supervisor's comments on a draft can help you improve that document, help you write better drafts the next time, and teach you about the culture of your organization. Look for patterns in the feedback you receive. Are you asked to use language that is more formal or to make the document more conversational? Does your boss want to see an overview before details? Does your company prefer information presented in bulleted lists rather than in paragraphs? When the feedback is honest, even harsh criticism can be beneficial. Pay attention to the meaning of the criticism, rather than how it is delivered. You can choose to use any feedback as a source of valuable information.

Can I Use Form Letters?

Yes, but make sure they're appropriate in form and content.

Employability Skills
2   0   +

A **form letter** or **template** is a prewritten, fill-in-the-blanks document designed for routine situations. Some form letters have different paragraphs that can be inserted, depending on the situation. For example, a form letter admitting students to university might add additional paragraphs for students receiving financial aid.

Boilerplate is language—sentences, paragraphs, even pages—from a previous document that a writer includes in a new document. In academic papers, material written by others must be quoted and documented. However, because businesses own the documents their employees write, text from these documents may be included without attribution.

Many organizations encourage their employees to use templates and boilerplate to save time and energy, and to use language that has already been approved by the organization's legal staff. However, using templates and old text creates problems:[8]

- The template pattern may be outdated or inappropriate to the content you are adding. For example, many organizations continue to send letters that place the subject above the salutation:

Re: Basement Flood Repairs

Dear Ms. Tuwawi:

- Unrevised boilerplate can be outdated, or can create a document with incompatible styles and tones. The salutations *Dear Sir/Madam* and *To Whom It May Concern* are examples of unacceptable boilerplate language.
- Form letters and boilerplate can encourage writers to see situations and audiences as identical when, in fact, they differ.

Before you use a form letter, make sure that it is well written, uses contemporary language and tone, and applies to the current situation.

EXPANDING A CRITICAL SKILL

Revising After Feedback

When you get feedback that you understand and agree with, make the change.

If you get feedback you don't understand, ask for clarification.

- Paraphrase: "So you're saying I need to give more information?"
- Ask for more information: "Can you suggest a way to do that?"
- Test your inference: "Would it help if I did this?"

Sometimes you may get feedback you don't agree with.

- If it's to do with grammar or usage, check this book or online (sometimes even smart people get things wrong).

- If it's about the content, recognize that something about the draft could be improved; something is leading the reader to respond negatively.
- If the reader thinks a fact is wrong (and you know it's right), show in your text where the fact came from: "According to…"
- If the reader suggests a change in wording you don't like, try another option.
- If the reader seems to have misunderstood or misread, think of ways to make the meaning clearer.
- If the reader says "This isn't true" and you know that the statement is true, try rephrasing the statement, giving more information or examples, or documenting the source.

L06 How Can I Get Started?

Talk, participate, and practise. Reward yourself for activities that encourage writing.

According to psychologist Robert Boice, a combination of actions works to get people writing.[9]

- **Participate actively in the organization and the community.** The more you talk to people, the more you communicate with some of your audiences, the more you learn about the company, culture, and context (Module 2), the easier it will be to write—and the better your writing will be.
- **Practise writing regularly, and in moderation.**
- **Learn as many strategies as you can.** Good writers have a repertoire of strategies they draw on. They try a variety of techniques in each new situation. Research these strategies and patterns, and try them to see what works for you.
- **Talk positively to yourself.** "I can do this." "I'll write for 15 minutes, and see what happens." "It doesn't have to be perfect; I can make it better later."
- **Talk about writing with other people.** Talk to peers, colleagues, and supervisors about writing. Value the feedback you get. Ask your supervisor for models of good examples of writing. Talking to other people expands your repertoire of strategies, and helps you understand what is valued in the discourse communities (Module 2) in which you write.

To avoid procrastinating, modify your behaviour by rewarding yourself for activities that *lead* to writing:

- **Set a regular time to write.** Sit down and stay there for the time you planned, even if you write nothing usable.
- **Develop a ritual for writing.** Choose tools—laptop, pen and paper, chair—that you find comfortable. Use the same tools in the same place every time you write.
- **Freewrite.** Write for 10 minutes without stopping.
- **Write down your thoughts and fears as you write.** If your thoughts are negative, try to reframe them more positively: "I can do this." "I'll keep going and evaluate it later." "If I keep working, I'll produce something that's okay."
- **Identify the problem that keeps you from writing.** Deal with the problem; then go back to your writing.
- **Set modest goals** (a paragraph, not the whole essay or report) **and reward yourself for reaching them.**

MODULE SUMMARY

- Planning, writing, and revising can include analyzing, collecting information, composing, assessing, getting feedback, revising, editing, and proofreading.

- **Revising** means *re-seeing* the document from the reader's point of view; you revise to maximize positive audience impact while satisfying your purposes.

- **Editing** means making surface-level changes for correct grammar, punctuation, and usage.

- **Proofreading** means checking to ensure the document is free from typographical errors.

- Practised writers expect to revise the first draft, read and write regularly, have clear goals, know many different strategies, wait to edit until the first draft is complete, and regularly ask for feedback.

- Writers use processes that work for them: these include expecting to revise, writing regularly, having clear goals, modifying the task if it's too easy or too hard, knowing many different strategies, using rules as guidelines, and waiting to edit until after the draft is complete. To think of ideas, try **brainstorming**, **freewriting** (writing without stopping for 10 minutes or more), and **clustering** (brainstorming using visuals).

- You can improve the quality of feedback you get by telling people which aspects of the draft you'd like comments about. Look for patterns in the feedback you get.

- If the writing task is new or difficult, plan to revise at least three times. The first time, look for clarity and content. The second time, check the layout and organization. Finally, check style and tone.

- **Form letters** are prewritten, fill-in-the-blanks documents designed for routine situations. **Boilerplate** is language from a previous document that writers include in new documents. Using templates (or form letters) and boilerplate indiscriminately can create documents that are inconsistent, outdated, or incompatible in tone and style.

- **To get started** writing
  1. Participate actively in the organization, and the community.
  2. Follow a routine: practise writing regularly.
  3. Learn as many strategies as you can.
  4. Talk about your writing tasks with other people.

ASSIGNMENTS FOR MODULE 4

Questions for Critical Thinking

4.1 How important is it for you to revise and proof your text messages? How do you decide?

4.2 Of the people who have seen your writing, who has given you the most useful feedback? What makes it useful?

Exercises and Problems

4.3 Analyzing Your Own Writing Processes

Save your notes and drafts from several assignments to answer the following questions:

- Which of the activities in the writing process do you use? How often?
- How much time do you spend on each of the activities?
- What kinds of revisions do you make most often?
- Which practices of good writers do you follow?
- What parts of your process seem most successful? What would you like to change? Why?
- What relation do you see between the process(es) you use and the quality of the final document?

Using the answers to these questions, and as your instructor directs

a. Draft a memo to your instructor describing your process(es) for composing a work-related memo or school-related document (memo, email, essay).

b. Exchange your draft with another student, so that you and s/he can give feedback on each other's writing.

c. Read that student's memo, and assess it based on the Checklist for Revision questions in Figure 4.5. Write down your comments and questions. Be constructive and specific.

d. Give feedback to your writing partner, and listen to and note the feedback s/he gives you.

e. Exchange your draft with a second student, and repeat steps c and d.

f. Based on your analysis of the feedback your peers provided, revise your original draft.

g. Exchange papers with a third student, this time for editing. This student is to circle any grammar, usage, and punctuation errors s/he finds in your revised copy, while you do the same for him/her.

h. Correct the errors your peer identified, and write your third draft.

i. Print your memo and proofread it using the strategies described in Figure 4.8. If you find errors, correct them.

j. Print your polished copy and hand in to your instructor.

4.4   Clustering or Mind-Mapping a Lecture

Use clustering to mind-map (see Figure 4.2) a classroom lecture or organizational meeting. Then convert your visuals into a summary of the lecture or meeting. To maximize your results, compare them with those of peers or colleagues. Where are the similarities? Where are the differences? As a form of note taking, how well does clustering work for you?

4.5   Writing, Revising, and Editing a Volunteer Letter

Choose a local organization (academic, athletic, community, seniors, social, youth) that you are interested in, and write a letter (hard copy or electronic attachment) volunteering your time. In the body of the letter 1) describe what you think you can offer the organization, 2) ask what the greatest need is, and 3) ask when and for what length of time you would be of most use.

As your instructor directs

a. Form a group of three people

b. Exchange drafts

c. Read your group member's letter for clarity, positive emphasis (Module 12), thorough content/details, and courtesy

d. Suggest revisions, in writing (on the letter itself, or on a separate note

e. Return letters to their writers

f. Make the revisions

g. Exchange papers again

h. Read the revised letter for mechanical errors and usage

i. Indicate necessary corrections

j. Return letters to their writers

k. Edit and print

l. Proofread your letter, make any necessary corrections, and hand in to your instructor

4.6   Writing a Cell Phone Usage Policy for Your Classroom or Place of Business.

Draft a one-page policy statement about appropriate cell phone use among staff where you work, or among students and teachers in one of your classes. What kinds of problems do indiscriminate calling, texting, and receiving cause? As you write, keep the needs of your boss and customers (or, in the case of classrooms, students and teachers) in mind.

As you instructor directs

a. Form a group of three people

b. Exchange drafts

c. Read each group member's policy draft for clarity, positive emphasis (Module 12), thorough content/details, and courtesy

d. Together as a team, discuss the policy ideas you find most useful

e. Together as a team, choose the policy format you find most useful

f. Together as a team, revise one policy statement, in the best format, to include the best ideas

g. Attach the team policy to a memo to your instructor

4.7   Checking Spell Checkers and Grammar Checkers

Each of the following paragraphs contains errors in grammar, spelling, and punctuation. Which errors does your spelling or grammar checker catch? Which errors does it miss? Does it flag as errors any words that are correct?

1. Answer to an Inquiry
   Enclosed are the tow copies you requested of our pamphlet, "Using the Internet to market Your products. The pamphlet walks you through the steps of planning the Home Page (The first page of the web cite, shows examples of other web pages we have designed, and provide a questionnaire that you can use to analyze audience the audience and purposes).

2. Performance Appraisal
   Most staff accountants complete three audits a month. Ellen has completed 21 audits in this past six months she is our most productive staff accountant. Her technical skills our very good however some clients feel that she could be more tactful in suggesting ways that the clients accounting practices could be improved.

3. Brochure
   Are you finding that being your own boss crates it's own problems? Take the hassle out of working at home with a VoiceMail Answering System. Its almost as good as having your own secretary.

POLISHING YOUR PROSE

Commas in Lists

Use commas in lists to separate items:

> At the office supply store I bought pens, stationery, and three-ring binders.

Commas show distinctions between items in a list. Technically, the comma before the coordinating conjunction *and* is optional, but the additional comma always adds clarity. Use commas consistently throughout your document. Missing or improperly placed commas confuse readers:

> We bought the following items for the staff lounge: television cabinet computer desk refrigerator and microwave oven.

Does television describe cabinet or is it a separate item? Is computer desk one item? Or are computer and desk two separate things? Inserting commas makes the distinction clear:

> We bought the following items for the staff kitchen: television, cabinet, computer, desk, refrigerator, and microwave oven.

Semicolons replace commas in lists in which the items themselves contain commas:

> Our company has plants in Moncton, New Brunswick; Flin Flon, Manitoba; and Lethbridge, Alberta.

Exercises

Use commas to make these lists clearer.

1. Please send the "fruit of the month" in April May June and July.
2. At the weekly staff meeting we will be joined by Mr. Loomis Ms. Handelman Ms. Lang and Mr. Kim.
3. The special parts division is opening offices in Brampton Ontario Fredericton New Brunswick and Big Salmon Yukon.
4. Buy small medium and large paper clips at the office supply store.
5. I need to telephone Mary Frank and Paul to finish my report and mail copies of it to Ted Sam and Latanya.
6. Applicants should send copies of their resumés to Mr. Arthur Bramberger human resource director Ms. Tina Ramos vice-president of marketing and Ms. Ellen Choi administrative assistant in marketing.
7. The weather affects our offices in Montreal New York City and Philadelphia.
8. Interns will be rotated through the receiving claims adjustment customer service and shipping departments.
9. Elizabeth Tyrone Mark and Sara presented the team's recommendations.
10. We are open until 9 p.m. on Mondays Wednesdays Fridays and Saturdays.

Check your answers to the odd-numbered exercises in the Answer Key at the end of the text.

Designing Documents, Slides, and Screens

Learning Objectives

After reading and applying the information in Module 5, you'll be able to demonstrate

Knowledge of

LO1 The importance of document appearance, layout, and design

LO2 Essential design principles

LO3 The interdependence of readability, legibility, and your credibility

Skills to

LO4 Apply design principles to paper pages, presentation slides, and web pages

LO5 Use computer software to increase document readability

MODULE OUTLINE

- Why is design important?
- How do I begin to think about good design?
- How do I design paper pages?
- How do I design presentation slides?
- How do I know if my design works?
- When should I think about design?

Module Summary

Assignments for Module 5

Polishing Your Prose: Active and Passive Voice

Employability Skills 2000+ Checklist

Module content builds these Conference Board of Canada Employability Skills 2000+

Communicate

Think and Solve Problems

Manage Information

Work with Others

Participate in Projects and Tasks

LO1 Why Is Design Important?

Design is essential to making meaning.

Readers "see" document design and layout first. A well-designed document invites reading. And good document design saves time and money, builds goodwill, and reduces legal problems. Effective design also puts ideas together visually, making the document content and organization more obvious and easier to understand.

Poor design causes problems. For example, look at Figure 5.1a, then answer these PAIBOC questions:

1. What is the purpose of the form?
2. Who is the audience?

FIGURE 5.1a   Design Is an Essential Communication Tool: Before

```
┌─────────────────────────────────────────────────────────────────┐
│      GAME PRODUCTION ANIMAL REGISTRATION CERTIFICATE              │
│      ─────────────────────────────────────────────────           │
│                          ELK                                      │
│      ─────────────────────────────────────────────────           │
│  Registration Number:      ABBB9999     Sex:        F             │
│                                                                   │
│  Genetic Status:           ELK          Birth Year:  93           │
│                                                                   │
│  Plastic Ear Tag Number:   9999C        Tag Colour:  Purple       │
│                                                                   │
│  Sire Registration Number: TBIR045W                               │
│                                                                   │
│  Dam Registration Number:  TALL011                                │
│                                                                   │
│  Present Owner (please print): _____           │
│                                                                   │
│  Present Owner Signature:      _____           │
│                                                                   │
│  Located at Licensed Farm No.: 028                                │
│                                                                   │
│  Farm Licensee:                John Carson                        │
│                                                                   │
│  Licensee Signature:           _____           │
│                                                                   │
│  Date of Issue:                21-April-93                        │
│  - - - - - - - - - - - - - - - - - - - - - - - - - - - - - -      │
│             APPLICATION TO TRANSFER OWNERSHIP                     │
│  Registration Number:      ABBB9999     Sex:        F             │
│  Plastic Ear Tag Number:   9999C        Tag Colour:  Purple       │
│                                                                   │
│  Present Farm Licence No.: 028          Licensee: Carson          │
│                                                                   │
│  Present Owner (print):_____  Signature:_____    │
│                                                                   │
│  New Farm Licence No.:      ____         Licensee: _____    │
│                                                                   │
│  New Owner (print):     _____  Signature:_____    │
│                                                                   │
│  Date of Actual Transfer: _____                      │
└─────────────────────────────────────────────────────────────────┘
```

3. What is the required information?
4. What objections might the reader have to responding?

Now look at the redesigned document (Figure 5.1b) and answer the same questions. What design changes have increased your understanding of the document purpose and audience?

FIGURE 5.1b   Design Is an Essential Communication Tool: After

Elk and Deer Registration Certificate

Information about the animal

Animal registration number   Dangle ear tag number

Species of animal   Sex of animal   Purebred or hybrid

Birth date (dd/mm/yy)   Origin

Sire's registration number   Dam's registration number

Location and ownership of animal

Licensed farm where animal is located   Owner's name and address (if different from owner of licensed farm)

Farm licence number   Date issued

When this animal is sold, give the certificate to the new owner. The new owner must complete and mail the Notice to Change Registration on the back of this certificate. If the animal dies, is slaughtered, or escapes, you must complete the back of this certificate and mail it to us.

Alberta
AGRICULTURE, FOOD AND RURAL DEVELOPMENT

AG0499 Rev. 10/94

Notice to Change Registration

Please fill out the section below that applies to you, then date and sign this notice. Mail it to the address below.

This animal (check ✓ one):
Sold to a new owner ❏

Licensed farm where animal is located	New owner's name and address (if different from owner of licensed farm)
Farm licence number	Date of sale

Moved to new location ❏

Licensed farm to where animal was moved	Farm licence number
	Date moved

Exported or sent to slaughter ❏   **Escaped** ❏   **Died** ❏

Date sent	Date of escape	Date of death

Signature of farm operator	Date

You must send this notice to the address below within 30 days of the sale, move, death, loss, or escape of the animal.

Send this notice to:
Animal Industry Division
Alberta Agriculture, Food and Rural Development
#204, 7000 - 113 Street
Edmonton, AB T6H 5T6
Tel: (403) 427-5083
Fax: (403) 427-1057

Alberta
AGRICULTURE, FOOD AND RURAL DEVELOPMENT

AG0499 Rev. 10/94

Source: Adapted from Elk and Deer Inventory Certificates with permission of Alberta Agriculture and Rural Development.

When the Alberta government redesigned this form to meet its audience's needs, 70 percent more game farmers registered.

LO3 How Do I Begin to Think About Good Design?

Use PAIBOC analysis to create reader-friendly design.

FIGURE 5.2   **PAIBOC Questions for Analysis**

P	What are your **purposes** for writing, or for creating slides or screens?
A	Who will be reading your document, slide, or screen? What physical, psychological, and emotional expectations does your **audience** bring to your document, slide, or screen? What slide colours and backgrounds are meaningful to your audience?
I	What **information** must your message include? What does your audience already know? What does your audience need to know? How can you design your message to meet your audience's needs? What design will emphasize the vital information? What design will make your message most attractive and accessible to your audience?
B	How can you use your design to emphasize reasons or reader **benefits**?
O	How can you use design to de-emphasize or eliminate potential reader **objections**?
C	How will the **context** of the information affect reader response? What time of day will your presentation take place? What is the room size, and what is the lighting like? What economic, environmental, cultural, and organizational realities will affect reader response to your message? How can you use design principles to attract and hold audience interest?

LO2 How Do I Design Paper Pages?

Follow these guidelines.

To create visually attractive documents

- Use white space to separate and emphasize points.
- Use headings and sub-headings to signal readers, and to group points.
- Limit the use of words set in all-capitals.
- Use no more than two typefaces in a single document.
- Decide on margins based on the situation and your audience.

Use White Space

Ex. 5.4

White space—the empty space on the page—emphasizes the material that it separates from the rest of the text. This emphasis makes the material easier to read.

Creating white space is also known as "menu writing," because the visual design principle—brief text highlighted by space—is the same as you find on restaurant menus.

A Question of Ethics: FROSH WEEK FUN?

Incoming students at the Université de Montréal business school blackened their faces and dressed as Jamaican runners for a frosh-week Olympic-themed event. Another business student recorded their performance on his BlackBerry and posted it on YouTube. What ethical concerns are raised by the behaviour of the students and the recording and posting of the video?

You can create white space in several ways:

- Use headings and subheadings.
- Use a mix of paragraph lengths (maximum six to seven typed lines).
- Use lists.
- Use tabs or indents—not spacing—to align items vertically.
- Use numbered lists when the number or sequence of items is exact.
- Use bullets (large dots or squares like those in this list) when the number and sequence are equal.

When you create a list, use parallelism: begin each item on the list with the same part of speech. If you begin your list with a verb, for example, begin every following item on the list with a verb. This parallel structure meets the reader's subconscious expectation. *And meeting reader expectations is the most important aspect of business writing.*

Not parallel: The following suggestions can help employers avoid bias in job interviews:
1. Base questions on the job description.
2. Questioning techniques
3. Selection and training of interviewers

Parallel: The following suggestions can help employers avoid bias in job interviews:
1. Base questions on the job description.
2. Ask the same questions of all applicants.
3. Select and train interviewers carefully.

Also parallel: Employers can avoid bias in job interviews by
1. Basing questions on the job description
2. Asking the same questions of all applicants
3. Selecting and training interviewers carefully

In Figure 5.3, Roysner, a legal firm, describes what happens to consumers who fail to pay their bills. Figure 5.4 illustrates how the same information becomes clearer and more reader-friendly by using shorter paragraphs, lists, and headings. However, these devices take space. When saving space is essential, it is better to cut the text and keep white space and headings.

FIGURE 5.3   A Document with Poor Visual Impact

Full capital letters make title hard to read

Long paragraph is visually uninviting

Important information is hard to find

MONEY DEDUCTED FROM YOUR WAGES TO PAY CREDITORS

When you buy goods on credit, the store will sometimes ask you to sign a Wage Assignment form allowing it to deduct money from your wages if you do not pay your bill. When you buy on credit, you sign a contract agreeing to pay a certain amount each week or month until you have paid all you owe. The Wage Assignment form is separate. It must contain the name of your present employer, your social insurance number, the amount of money loaned, the rate of interest, the date when payments are due, and your signature. The words "Wage Assignment" must be printed at the top of the form and also near the line for your signature. Even if you have signed a Wage Assignment agreement, Roysner will not withhold part of your wages unless all of the following conditions are met: 1. You have to be more than forty days late in payment of what you owe; 2. Roysner has to receive a correct statement of the amount you are in default and a copy of the Wage Assignment form; and 3. You and Roysner must receive a notice from the creditor at least twenty days in advance stating that the creditor plans to make a demand on your wages. This twenty-day notice gives you a chance to correct the problems yourself. If these conditions are all met, Roysner must withhold 15 percent of each paycheque until your bill is paid and give this money to your creditor.

If you think you are not late or that you do not owe the amount stated, you can argue against it by filing a legal document called a "defence." Once you file a defence, Roysner will not withhold any money from you. However, be sure you are right before you file a defence. If you are wrong, you have to pay not only what you owe but also all legal costs for both yourself and the creditor. If you are right, the creditor has to pay all these costs.

Use Headings

Headings are words or short phrases that identify or sum up the text below them, and divide your letter, memo, or report into sections. Headings should "talk": that is, your headings should "say" in a phrase or question what the information underneath explains. Headings and sub-headings increase readability because they summarize what the reader is about to read, and they increase white space.

- Use first-level and second-level (sub-headings) to emphasize organization.
- Make each heading cover all the material until the next heading.

FIGURE 5.4   A Document Revised to Improve Visual Impact

This letter is in full block format

First letter of each main word capitalized—title split onto two lines

Money Deducted from Your Wages to Pay Creditors

When you buy goods on credit, the store will sometimes ask you to sign a Wage Assignment form allowing it to deduct money from your wages if you do not pay your bill.

Headings divide document into chunks

Have You Signed a Wage Assignment Form?

When you buy on credit, you sign a contract agreeing to pay a certain amount each week or month until you have paid all you owe. The Wage Assignment form is separate. It must contain the following:

- The name of your present employer
- Your social insurance number
- The amount of insurance
- The rate of interest
- The date when payments are due
- Your signature

List with bullets where order of items doesn't matter

The words "Wage Assignment" must be printed at the top of the form and also near the line for your signature.

When Would Money Be Deducted from Your Wages to Pay a Creditor?

Headings should be parallel. Here, all are questions.

Even if you have signed a Wage Assignment agreement, Roysner will not withhold part of your wages unless all of the following conditions are met:

Numbered list where number, order of items matter

1. You have to be more than 40 days late in payment of what you owe.
2. Roysner has to receive a correct statement of the amount you are in default and a copy of the Wage Assignment form.
3. You and Roysner must receive a notice from the creditor at least 20 days in advance stating that the creditor plans to make a demand on your wages. This 20-day notice gives you a chance to correct the problem yourself.

White space between items emphasizes them

If these conditions are all met, Roysner must withhold fifteen percent (15 percent) of each paycheque and give this money to your creditor until your bill is paid.

What Should You Do If You Think the Wage Assignment Is Incorrect?

Important information emphasized

If you think you are not late or that you do not owe the amount stated, you can argue against it by filing a legal document called a "defence." Once you file a defence, Roysner will not withhold any money from you. However, be sure you are right before you file a defence. If you are wrong, you have to pay not only what you owe but also all legal costs for both yourself and the creditor. If you are right, the creditor has to pay these costs.

- Use sub-headings to signal the reader that you are about to give more specific information.
- Use even more levels of headings in long documents.
- Keep headings at any one level parallel: all nouns, all complete sentences, or all questions.

This text uses talking headings, sub-headings, and sub-sub-headings throughout.

In a letter or memo, type main headings flush with the left-hand margin in bold. Capitalize the first letters of the first word and other major words; use lowercase for all other words. (See Figure 5.4 for an example.) In single-spaced text, triple-space between the previous text and the heading; double-space between the heading and the text that follows.

Limit the Use of Words Set in All-Capitals

We recognize words by their shapes.[1] (For example, try reading each line in Figure 5.5.) With all-capitals, words look rectangular; letters lose the descenders and ascenders that make reading easier and faster. Use full capitals sparingly. Instead, bold text to emphasize it.

FIGURE 5.5   Full Capitals Hide the Shape of a Word

| Full | capitals | hide | the | shape | of | a | word | and | slow | reading | 19%. |

| FULL | CAPITALS | HIDE | THE | SHAPE | OF | A | WORD | AND | SLOW | READING | 19%. |

Use No More Than Two Fonts in a Single Document

Each font comes in several sizes and usually in several styles (bold, italic, etc.). Most computer fonts are **proportional**: wider letters (such as *w*) take more space than narrower letters (such as *i*). Times Roman, Palatino, Helvetica, Geneva, and Arial are proportional fonts. Fonts such as Courier and Prestige Elite, designed for typewriters and still offered as computer fonts, are **fixed**. Every letter takes the same space, so that an *i* takes the same space as a *w*.

How Do I Decide on a Font?

Choose your font style and size based on your purposes, audiences, and medium.

Serif fonts have little extensions, called *serifs*, from the main strokes. (In Figure 5.6, look at the feet on the *T* in Times Roman and the little flicks on the ends of the top bar of the *T*.) In hardcopy documents, serif fonts are easier to read, because the serifs help the eyes move from

FIGURE 5.6   Examples of Different Fonts

This sentence is set in 12-point Times Roman.

This sentence is set in 12-point Arial.

This sentence is set in 12-point New Courier.

This sentence is set in 12-point Lucinda Calligraphy.

This sentence is set in 12-point Broadway.

This sentence is set in 12-point Technical.

letter to letter. Courier, Times Roman, Palatino, and Lucinda Calligraphy are serif fonts. Helvetica, Geneva, and Arial are called **sans serif** fonts because they lack serifs (*sans* is French for "without"). Sans serif fonts are good for titles, tables, and narrow columns.

In magnified text, and electronic messages, sans serif fonts are easier to read; therefore, use sans serif fonts for your PowerPoint presentations.

Most business documents use just one font—usually Times Roman, Palatino, Helvetica, or Arial in 11-point or 12-point. In a complex document, use bigger type for main headings and slightly smaller type for subheadings and text. If you combine two fonts in one document, choose one serif and one sans serif typeface.

Employability Skills

Ex. 5.4– 5.9

Choose Margins Based On the Situation and the Audience

Margins that line up to the left (see Figure 5.4) are left justified, with **ragged right margins**. Lines end in different places because words are of different lengths. Left justification with ragged right margins are common in current business usage. However, computers allow you to use **full justification**, so that type on the both sides of the page is evenly lined up. Books, like this one, usually use full justification.

Use ragged right margins when you

- Do not have proportional typefaces
- Want a less formal look
- Want to be able to revise an individual page without reprinting the whole document
- Use very short line lengths

Use justified margins when you

- Can use proportional typefaces
- Want a more formal look
- Want to use as few pages as possible

LO4 How Do I Design Presentation Slides?

Keep slides simple, relevant, and interesting.

As you design slides for PowerPoint and other presentation programs, keep these guidelines in mind:

- Create slides that reinforce or illustrate your key ideas.
- Emphasize visuals. Pictures, charts, and graphs have much greater impact than text: they appeal to the right, or creative, side of the brain; they are more easily accessible than text; and they are more memorable.
- Use audience-relevant photos or illustrations to keep memorable images in your listeners' minds.
- Keep the text to an absolute minimum; give your audience slide handouts on which to write notes.
- Use bullet-point phrases with concrete words.
- Contrast background and text: the rule is light on dark or dark on light.

- Use a big font: 44-point or 50-point for titles, 32-point for subheads, and 28-point for examples.
- Customize your slides with the company logo, charts, and scanned-in photos and drawings.
- Place illustrations at the top right of the slide for a stronger and longer impression.

Avoid PowerPoint pass-out: Use no more than one slide per minute of your talk, and keep words to a minimum.

Use relevant animation, video, and/or sound files in your presentations only if these contribute to audience understanding, and meet your objectives. Use clip art only if the art is appropriate to your points and only if you are able to find non-sexist and non-racist images.

Choose a consistent template, or background design, for the entire presentation. Make sure that the template is appropriate for your subject matter. PowerPoint's templates may bore people who see many presentations. Whenever possible, create your own template.

Choose a light background if the lights are off during the presentation and a dark background if the lights are on. Slides will be easier to read if you use high contrast between the words and background. Figure 5.7 shows examples of effective and ineffective colour combinations.

FIGURE 5.7   **Effective and Ineffective Colours for Presentation Slides**

Cultural FOCUS

Pay close attention to the colours you use for presentations. Certain colour combinations may not be acceptable to North American audiences. For example, orange and brown were used together in the 1970s in fast-food restaurants in order to encourage customers to hurry in and out, as most people considered this colour combination unpleasant. Today, however, some businesses are using these colours in order to be "retro" and portray a 70s image. As another example, few businesses will use purple and orange together, as this is not a pleasing colour combination. Pay close attention to the slides your instructors use and examine Figure 5.7 carefully so that you understand the colour rules that North American businesses follow. You can also go online and learn about colour psychology on various websites.

How Do I Know If My Design Works?

Test it.

A design that looks fine to you may not work for your audience. To know whether your design is functional, test it with your audience:

- Watch someone as he or she uses the document to do a task. Where does the reader pause, reread, or seem confused? How long does it take? Does the document enable the reader to complete the task accurately?
- Ask the reader to "think aloud" while completing the task: interrupt the reader at key points to ask what he or she is thinking, or ask the reader to describe his or her thought processes after completing the document and the task. Exploring the reader's thought processes is important, since a reader may get the right answer for the wrong reasons. You can thus identify where and how the design needs work.
- Test the document with the people most likely to have trouble with it: very young readers, people with little education, people who read English as a second language, and people who have little experience with web pages.

EXPANDING A CRITICAL SKILL

LO5 Using Computer Software to Create Good Design

Standard word-processing programs such as Word help you create well-designed documents. Different versions of each program handle commands differently. Look up the bolded terms below in a manual, a book about the program, or the online Help menu of your computer program to find out how to use each feature.

Letters and Memos

- Choose a businesslike **font** in 11-point or 12-point type. Times Roman, Palatino, Helvetica, and Arial are the most commonly used business fonts.
- Use **bold** headings. Avoid having a heading all by itself at the bottom of the page. If you can't have at least one line of text under it, move the heading to the next page. You can check this by eye or set your program to avoid **widows** and **orphans (single lines at the top and bottom of the page)**.
- Use **tabs** or **indents** to line up the return address and signature blocks in modified block format (Module 6), the To/From/Subject line section of a memo, or the items in a list.
- Change your **tab settings** to create good visual impact. A setting at 0.6 inches (1.5 centimetres) works well for the Date/To/From/Subject line section of memos. Use 0.4 inches (1 centimetre) for paragraphs and 0.6 inches (1.5 centimetres) for the start of bulleted lists. For lists with 10 or more items, the setting will need to be a bit farther to the right—about 0.65 inches (1.65 centimetres).
- Choose the design for **bullets** under **Insert** or **Format**. Word will create bulleted or numbered lists automatically.

- Use a **header** (in the **Insert** or **View** menu) with automatic **page numbering** (pull down **Format Page Numbers**) for second and subsequent pages. That way, when you delete a paragraph or expand your reader benefits, you don't have to move the header manually. You can either delay the header until page two or create it on page two. For best visual impact, make your header one point size smaller than the body type.
- For a two-page document, change the top **margin** of the second page to 0.5 inches (1.25 centimetres) so the header is close to the top of the page.
- Use the same-size margins as your letterhead. If you aren't using letterhead, use 1-inch (2.5 centimetre) side margins.
- On a two-page document, make sure the second page has at least four to six lines of text for letters and at least 10 lines of text for memos. If you have less, either (1) add details, (2) start the message further down on page one so that there is more text on page two, or (3) make the text fit on just one page by (a) tightening your prose, (b) using full justification to save space, or (c) using less white space.
- Word-processing programs have a **quick correct** or **auto correct** feature that changes *hte* to *the*, (c) to ©, and so forth. Go into the **Tools** or **Format** menus to find these features and edit them so they make only the changes you want.
- Hyphenation may be under **Format** or **Language** in **Tools**.
- Before you print, centre your document on the page like a picture in a frame. Go to **File**, **Page Setup**, **Layout**, **Vertical Alignment**, **Centre**.

Cultural FOCUS

Statistics predict that, in Canada, the number of immigrants will continue to rise. Therefore, documents will need to be easy to read for all audiences. Make sure your design is accessible to the majority of people, not just you. Also, if you are creating documents for a specific cultural group, make sure you examine samples before you create your own. This way, you will ensure your documents meet the cultural expectations of that group.

When Should I Think About Design?

Ex. 5.6– 5.8

Think about design at each stage of the writing process.

Because layout and design make the first impression on readers, document design is a vital component of persuasion. Indeed, you create the best documents when you think about design at each stage of your writing process:

Employability Skills

- As you plan, apply your PAIBOC audience analysis. Are your audience members skilled readers? Are they busy? Will they read the document straight through or skip around in it? Design the document to meet readers' needs and expectations.
- As you write, incorporate lists and headings. Use visuals to convey numerical data clearly and forcefully.
- Get feedback from people who will be using your document. What parts of the document do they find hard to understand? What additional information do they need?
- As you revise, check your draft against the guidelines in this module.

MODULE SUMMARY

- Your audience makes meaning primarily from the design of your message. Business audiences expect documents and slides to be easy to read and understand.

- An attractive document is inviting and easy to read. Visual grouping of ideas also makes the document easier to read.

- Good document design saves time, money, and legal problems.

- To create visually inviting documents
  - Use white space
  - Use headings
  - Limit the use of words in all capital letters
  - Limit the number of fonts in a single document
  - Decide on whether to justify margins based on your audience and situation analysis

- Keep presentation slides simple and relevant.
- To avoid slide overkill
  - Use a large, sans-serif font
  - Use bullets
  - Use clear, concise language
  - Make only three to five points on a slide
  - Customize your slides to your audience

- To test a document, observe readers, ask them to "think aloud" while completing the task, interrupt them at key points to ask them what they are thinking, or ask them to describe their thought processes after completing the document and the task.

- You create the best documents when you consider design throughout the writing process, and get feedback from people who will be using your document.

ASSIGNMENTS FOR MODULE 5

Questions for Critical Thinking

5.1 Identify three specific functions of document design.

5.2 Royal College is preparing a brochure to persuade prospective students to consider taking classes. The

school doesn't want to invest a lot of money in full-scale document testing. What free or almost-free things could it do to make the document as effective as possible?

5.3 Design choices have ethical implications. Indicate whether you consider each of the following actions ethical, unethical, or a grey area. Which of the actions would you do? Which would you feel uncomfortable doing? Which would you refuse to do? Why?

a. Putting the advantages of a proposal in a bulleted list, while discussing the disadvantages in a paragraph

b. Using a bigger type size so that a resumé fills a whole page

c. Putting the services not covered by your health plan in full capitals to make it less likely people will read the page

Exercises and Problems

5.4   Evaluating Page Designs

Use the guidelines in this module to evaluate each of the following page designs. What are their strong points? What might be improved?

Source: D. Burns and S. Venit (October 13, 1987), What's wrong with this paper? *PC Magazine 17:* 174–75.

5.5   Evaluating PowerPoint Slides

Gar Reynolds offers "10 slide design tips for producing powerful and effective presentations" at www.techrepublic.com/article/10-slide-design-tips-for-producing-powerful-and-effective-presentations/6117178

Using these tips, and your experience, evaluate the following drafts of PowerPoint slides for

- Background relevance to topic
- Content complexity
- Font size
- Art relevance
- Errors

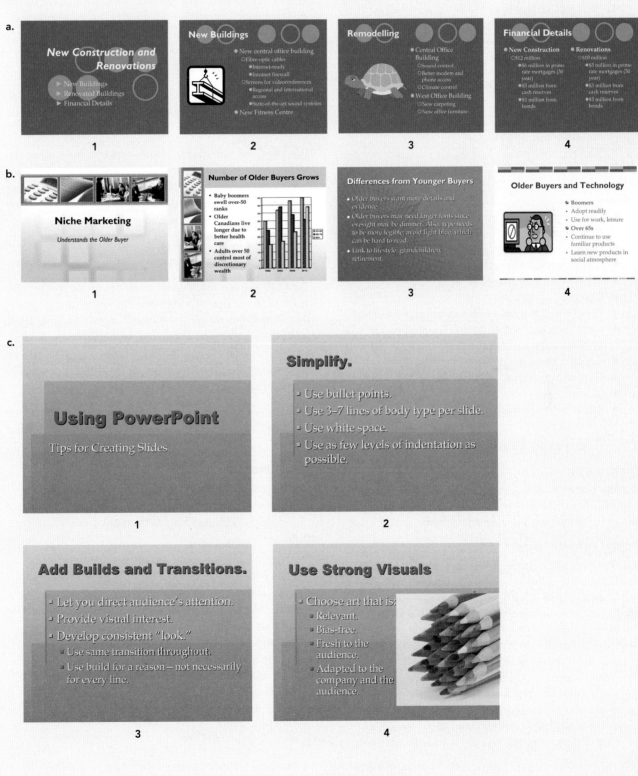

5.6 Using Headings

Reorganize the items in each of the following lists, using appropriate headings. Use bulleted or numbered lists as appropriate.

a. Rules and Procedures for a Tuition Reimbursement Plan

 1. You are eligible to be reimbursed if you have been a full-time employee for at least three months.
 2. You must apply before the first class meeting.
 3. You must earn a C or better in the course.
 4. You must submit a copy of the approved application, an official grade report, and a receipt for tuition paid to be reimbursed.
 5. You can be reimbursed for courses related to your current position or another position in the company, or for courses that are part of a degree related to a current or possible job.
 6. Your supervisor must sign the application form.
 7. Courses may be at any appropriate level (high school, college or university, or graduate school).

b. Activities in Starting a New Business
 - Getting a loan or venture capital
 - Getting any necessary city or provincial licences
 - Determining what you will make, do, or sell
 - Identifying the market for your products or services
 - Pricing your products or services
 - Choosing a location
 - Checking zoning laws that may affect the location
 - Identifying government and university programs for small business development
 - Figuring cash flow
 - Ordering equipment and supplies
 - Selling
 - Advertising and marketing

5.7 Analyzing Websites

Review several organizational websites that are available to you as a worker, student, or consumer. Using the guidelines in Module 5, your research, and your experience, create your own set of criteria to evaluate each of them.

As your instructor directs

a. Form a group of three or four students.
b. Compare your design evaluation criteria.
c. Choose criteria you can all agree on.
d. Evaluate the websites using the group's criteria.
e. Write a memo to your instructor evaluating three or more of the sites. Include URLs or screenshots of the sites in an appendix to your memo.
f. Write a memo to your supervisor recommending ways the organization can improve its documents.
g. In an oral presentation to the class, explain what makes one website good and another one weak. Show the sites, so classmates can see them as you evaluate them.

5.8 Analyzing a Document

Your municipal and provincial governments may offer internships and co-operative placements to postsecondary students. Research (visit, telephone, email, find someone who knows someone) the placement possibilities through your college/university co-op placement office or contact the government department directly. Request a copy of the application or information documents for these positions. Write an analysis of the document's layout and page design.

5.9 Revising a Financial Aid Form

You've just joined the Financial Aid office at your school. The director gives you the accompanying form and asks you to redesign it.

"We need this form to see whether parents have other students in college or university besides the one requesting aid. Parents are supposed to list all family members that they support—themselves, the person here, any other kids in college or university, and any younger dependent kids.

"Half of these forms are filled out incorrectly. Most people just list the student going here; they leave out everyone else.

"If something is missing, the computer sends out a letter and a second copy of this form. The whole process starts over. Sometimes we send this form back two or three times before it's right. In the meantime, students' financial aid is delayed—maybe for months. Sometimes things are so late that they can't register for classes, or they have to pay tuition themselves and get reimbursed later.

"If so many people are filling out the form wrong, the form itself must be the problem. See what you can do with it. But keep it to a page."

As your instructor directs

a. Analyze the current form and identify its problems.
b. Revise the form. Add necessary information; reorder information; change the chart to make it easier to fill out.

Hints:

- Where are people supposed to send the form? What is the phone number of the financial aid office? Should they need to call the office if the form is clear?
- Does the definition of *half-time* apply to all students or just those taking courses beyond high school?
- Should capital or lowercase letters be used?
- Are the lines big enough to write in?
- What headings or subdivisions within the form would remind people to list all family members whom they support?
- How can you encourage people to return the form promptly?

Please complete the chart below by listing all family members for whom you (the parents) will provide more than half support during the academic year (July 1 through June 30). Include yourselves (the parents), the student, and your dependent children, even if they are not attending college or university.

EDUCATIONAL INFORMATION, 2006–2007						
FULL NAME OF FAMILY MEMBER	AGE	RELATIONSHIP OF FAMILY MEMBERS TO STUDENT	NAME OF SCHOOL, COLLEGE, OR UNIVERSITY SCHOOL YEAR	FULL-TIME	HALF-TIME* OR MORE	LESS THAN HALF-TIME
STUDENT APPLICANT						

*Half-time is defined as 6 credit hours or 12 clock hours a term.

When the information requested is received by our office, processing of your financial aid application will resume.

Please sign and mail this form to the above address as soon as possible. Your signature certifies that this information and the information on the FAF is true and complete to the best of your knowledge. If you have any questions, please contact a member of the needs analysis staff.

_____   _____
Signature of Parent(s)   Data

POLISHING YOUR PROSE

Active and Passive Voice

The verb is the most important word in a sentence. Verbs tell who or what is doing the action. When whoever is acting is the subject of the sentence, the verb is active; when the subject is not doing the action, the verb is passive.

Active: The man bought grapes at the store.

Passive: The grapes were bought at the store by the man.

In the active voice, the subject "the man," is doing the action—"bought." In the second sentence, "The grapes" is the subject; the grapes are not doing the action. When the verb is passive, it is harder for the reader to follow who or what is doing the action. In addition, it takes more words to convey the same idea.

Contemporary communication prefers verbs in the active voice, because the resulting sentence is clearer and shorter. When writers want to avoid or downplay responsibility, they use the passive voice.

To change a passive verb into the active, start by identifying who or what is doing the action. A passive verb is usually accompanied by a copula verb, such as *is*, *are*, or *were*.

Rewrite the sentence by putting the actor in the role of subject and changing the verb:

Passive: The plan was approved by our clients.

Active: Our clients approved the plan.

Passive: PowerPoint slides have been created.

Active: Susan created the PowerPoint slides.

Passive: It is desired that you back up your work daily.

Active: Back up your work daily.

In business communication, active voice is usually better. However, passives are better in three situations:

1. Use passives to emphasize the object receiving the action, not the agent.

   My mother was taken to hospital last night.

   It does not really matter who took her.

2. Use passives to provide coherence within a paragraph. A sentence is easier to read if "old" information comes at the beginning of a sentence. When you have been discussing a topic, use the word again as your subject even if that requires a passive verb.

The bank made several risky loans in the early 2000s. These loans were written off as "uncollectible" in 2008.

Using "loans" as the subject of the second sentence provides a link between the two sentences, making the paragraph as a whole easier to read.

3. Use passives to avoid assigning blame.

The order was damaged during shipment.

An active verb would require the writer to specify who damaged the order. The passive here is more tactful.

Exercises

Identify whether the passives in the following sentences are acceptable, or whether the verb should be changed to active.

1. The contract was signed by the vice-president of finance.
2. New employees Ms. Taleroski, Mr. Franklin, and Ms. Holbreck were introduced at last week's staff meeting.
3. Two visitors are expected to arrive at headquarters tomorrow.
4. Outgoing correspondence was collected by the mailroom staff.
5. The proposal was turned in late.

Turn these passive-voice constructions into active-voice ones:

6. Correspondence was collected by the mailroom staff.
7. Phone calls were returned by the human resources administrator.
8. In April, budgets were amortized and files created for the project.
9. Phone calls need to be returned within 24 hours.
10. Packages are to be sent to the mailroom for delivery.

Check your answers to the odd-numbered exercises in the Answer Key at the back of the text.

Formatting Hardcopy Letters and Memos

Learning Objectives

After reading and applying the information in Module 6, you'll be able to demonstrate

Knowledge of

LO1 The basic design formula: form follows function

LO2 How to use PAIBOC to decide on your format

LO3 Basic business formats

Skills to

LO4 Use PAIBOC to choose appropriate formats

LO5 Use non-sexist courtesy titles

LO6 Create an appropriate business image

MODULE OUTLINE

- How should I set up letters?
- What courtesy titles should I use?
- How should I set up hardcopy memos?

Module Summary

Assignments for Module 6

Polishing Your Prose: Making Pronouns Agree with Their Nouns

Employability Skills 2000+ Checklist

Module content builds these Conference Board of Canada Employability Skills 2000+

Communicate	Think and Solve Problems
Manage Information	Participate in Projects and Tasks

LO1 Business letters, memos, and emails are similar in formality, length, style, and organization. **Letters** go to people outside the organization, whereas **memos** are messages sent to people within your organization. Because they have different **audiences**, letters and memos differ in format, signalling readers that they are getting an external or internal message.

Format includes the parts of a document and the way they are arranged on the page. Short reports use letter or memo format (Modules 16 and 17). Long reports can use the format described in Module 18. If your organization has its own formats for letters and memos, use them. Otherwise, choose one of the formats in this module.

When you are considering how best to deliver your message, remember the principle of all good design: *form follows function*. This design principle is essential to communication success: when you shape your message (format) to meet the needs of your audience and your purposes (function), you get the results you want.

Ex. 6.1

Use PAIBOC analysis (Figure 6.1) to choose the right format and medium for your message.

LO3 How Should I Set Up Letters?

Letters are written in block and modified block.

The two most common letter formats are block, sometimes called **full block**, and **modified block** or **semi-block**.

FIGURE 6.1   **PAIBOC Questions for Analysis**

<table>
<tr><td>LO2
LO4</td><td>P</td><td>What is the purpose of your communication? What do you hope to achieve? What results do you want?</td></tr>
<tr><td></td><td>A</td><td>Who is your audience? Are they inside or outside your organization? What are their expectations? What do they care about? What do they value? What do they know? What do they need to know? How will they feel about your message? How does your audience expect to receive messages—hard copy or electronic? Is texting acceptable for your purpose, the audience, and the content of the message?</td></tr>
<tr><td></td><td>I</td><td>Based on your purpose and audience analysis, what information must your message include?</td></tr>
<tr><td></td><td>B</td><td>Based on your purpose and audience analysis, what benefits can you use to meet your audience's needs and achieve your purpose?</td></tr>
<tr><td></td><td>O</td><td>Based on your audience and purpose analysis, what objections can you expect from your audience? What negative aspects of your message must you de-emphasize, or overcome?</td></tr>
<tr><td></td><td>C</td><td>How does the context affect audience response? What circumstances—economic, environmental, legal, and/or organizational—might influence how your audience will perceive the message?</td></tr>
</table>

FIGURE 6.2   **Block Format on Letterhead (mixed punctuation, collection letter)**

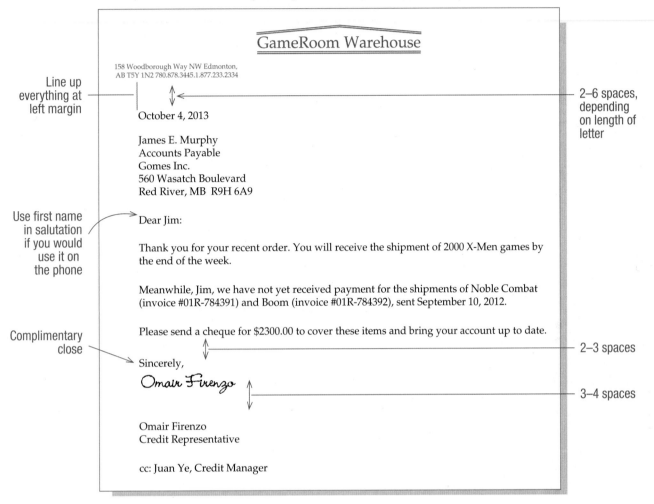

Line up
everything at
left margin

2–6 spaces,
depending
on length of
letter

Use first name
in salutation
if you would
use it on
the phone

Complimentary
close

2–3 spaces

3–4 spaces

How Are the Two Formats Similar?

Block and modified-block business letters share many elements:

- Organizations include their return address in their **letterhead**.
- Written documentation is for the record, so the **date** is essential.
- Readers are addressed by name in the **salutation**.
- Subject and reference lines direct readers' attention to your purpose.
- A standard **complimentary close** (*Sincerely*, *Best*, *Regards*) comes before your signature.
- Correct punctuation is essential for credibility.
- Continuation (subsequent) pages maintain coherence.
- "Enclosure" tells the reader that you have included additional material, like a duplicated document or a resumé.

Choose the level of formality in the **salutation** based on your relationship with the person: *Dear Ahmed* if you're on a first-name basis and *Dear Mr. Guten* if you don't know the reader well enough to use a first name. When you are responding to a letter or memo, use a salutation that mirrors the original sender's signature, which reflects how the person wants to be addressed.

Sincerely, Cordially, and *Regards* are standard complimentary closes.

FIGURE 6.3   Indented Format on Letterhead (mixed punctuation, employee evaluation letter)

Capital Information Systems

151 Bayview Road
Ottawa, ON K1S 2C5

2–6 spaces

September 14, 2013

Line up date with signature block 1/2 or 2/3 of the way over to the right

2–4 spaces

Ms. Mary E. Arcas
Personnel Director
Cyclops Communication Technologies
1050 Bonita Avenue
Moncton, NB E1C 4M6

Postal code on same line

Salutation — Dear Ms. Arcas:

Colon in mixed punctuation

Indenting ¶ is optional in modified block

Let me respond to your request for an evaluation of Colleen Kangas. Colleen was hired as a clerk-typist by Capital Information Systems on April 4, 2011, and was promoted to administrative assistant on August 1, 2011. At her review in September, I recommended that she be promoted again. She is an intelligent young woman with excellent work habits and a strong knowledge of computer software.

Single-space paragraphs

As an administrative assistant, Colleen not only handles routine duties such as processing time cards, ordering supplies, and entering data, but also screens calls for two marketing specialists, answers basic questions about Capital Information Systems, compiles the statistics I need for my monthly reports, and investigates special assignments for me. In the past eight months, she has investigated freight charges, inventory department hardware, and microfiche files. I need only give her general directions: she has a knack for tracking down information quickly and summarizing it accurately.

Double-space between paragraphs

Although our workload has increased during the year, Colleen manages her time so that everything gets done on schedule. She is consistently poised and friendly under pressure. Her willingness to work overtime on occasion is particularly remarkable considering that she has been going to college part-time ever since she joined our firm.

At Capital Information Systems, Colleen uses Word and Access software. She tells me that she has also used PowerPoint in her community college classes.

If Colleen were staying in Ottawa, we would want to keep her. She has the potential either to become an executive secretary or to move into line or staff work, especially once she completes her degree. I recommend her highly.

2–3 spaces

Headings are optional in letters

Comma in mixed punctuation

Sincerely,

Jeanne Cederlind

Jeanne Cederlind
Vice President, Marketing

Line up signature block with date

2–4 spaces

Encl.: Evaluation Form for Colleen Kangas

3–4 spaces

Leave at least 3–6 spaces at bottom of page—more if letter is short

In two-point or **mixed punctuation**, a colon follows the salutation and a comma follows the close. Today, many people use a comma after the salutation to make the letter look more personal.

In **open punctuation**, omit all punctuation after the salutation and the close. A few organizations use open punctuation because it's faster to type.

How Do I Use Subject Lines?

A **subject line** tells readers what they are about to read. Subject lines are required in hardcopy memos, and all emails; however, they are optional in letters. Use a subject line in your hardcopy and electronic letters when you want to focus the audience's attention on specific content in the message.

Good subject lines are specific, concise, and appropriate for your purposes and the response you expect from your reader:

- When you have good news, put it in the subject line. (Module 8)
- When your information is neutral, summarize it concisely in the subject line. (Module 8)
- When your information is negative, use a negative subject line. (Module 9)
  - if the reader may not read the message
  - the reader needs the information to act
  - if the negative is your error
- When you have a request that will be easy for the reader to grant, put either the subject of the request or a direct question in the subject line.
- When you must persuade a reluctant reader, use common ground, a reader benefit, or a directed subject line (Module 10) that makes your position clear.

Modules 7 to 9 cover subject lines in detail.

When you do use a subject line in your letter

1. Write it last, so that it covers the message or explicit content to suit your purpose and meet the audience's needs.

2. Place it after the salutation.

A **reference line** refers the reader to the number used on previous correspondence, or the order or invoice number that this letter is about. Government organizations, such as Revenue Canada, use numbers on every piece of correspondence they send out, so they can quickly find the earlier document to which an incoming letter refers.

Both block and modified block formats use headings, lists, and indented sections (known as *telegraphing*, *highlighting*, *bulleting,* or *dot jotting*) for emphasis.

Each format has advantages. Block is the format most frequently used for business letters; readers expect it and it can be typed quickly, since everything lines up at the left margin. Speed-readers say it is easier to read. *Modified* block format creates a visually attractive page by moving the date and signature block into what would otherwise be empty white space. Table 6.1 compares the two formats.

TABLE 6.1 **Differences Between Letter Formats**

	Block	**Modified Block**
Date and signature block	Lined up at left margin	Lined up 1/2 or 2/3 over to the right
Paragraph indentation	None	Optional
Subject line	Optional	Rare

Letterhead is pre-printed stationery with the organization's name, logo, address, and phone number. Figure 6.4 shows how to set up modified block format without letterhead. You can also use block format without letterhead.

Ex. 6.5

What If My Letter Is More Than a Page?

When your letter runs two or more pages, use a heading on the second page to identify it. Putting the reader's name helps the writer, who may be printing out many letters at a time, to make sure the right second page gets in the envelope.

Reader's Name
Date
Page Number

or

Reader's Name   Page Number   Date

When a letter runs to two or more pages, use the letterhead only for page 1. (See Figure 6.5) For the remaining pages, use plain paper that matches your first page in weight, texture, and colour.

How Do I Show I Am Sending Additional Documents?

Many letters are accompanied by other documents. Whatever these documents may be—a multi-page report or a two-line note—in hardcopy letters, they are called **enclosures**, since they are enclosed in the envelope. The writer should refer to the enclosures in the body of the letter: "As you can see from my resumé…" The enclosure line is usually abbreviated: *Encl.* (see Figure 6.5). The abbreviation reminds the person who seals the letter to include the enclosure(s).

FIGURE 6.4   Modified Block Letter (open punctuation, subject line)

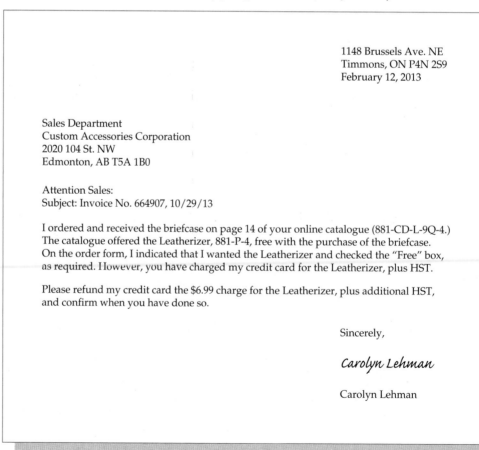

1148 Brussels Ave. NE
Timmons, ON P4N 2S9
February 12, 2013

Sales Department
Custom Accessories Corporation
2020 104 St. NW
Edmonton, AB T5A 1B0

Attention Sales:
Subject: Invoice No. 664907, 10/29/13

I ordered and received the briefcase on page 14 of your online catalogue (881-CD-L-9Q-4.) The catalogue offered the Leatherizer, 881-P-4, free with the purchase of the briefcase. On the order form, I indicated that I wanted the Leatherizer and checked the "Free" box, as required. However, you have charged my credit card for the Leatherizer, plus HST.

Please refund my credit card the $6.99 charge for the Leatherizer, plus additional HST, and confirm when you have done so.

Sincerely,

Carolyn Lehman

Carolyn Lehman

A Question of Ethics

You work for a national retail pharmacy chain. You receive a memo from your supervisor instructing you to post a sign at the cash counter advertising an in-store cosmetic special. The memo and sign contain multiple grammar and spelling errors.

What should you do? Is this an ethical issue? Why or why not?

When Do I Show I Am Sending Copies of My Messages to Other People?

Sometimes you write to one person and send copies of your letter to other people. To let the reader know that other people are getting copies, list their names on the last page. The abbreviation *cc* originally meant "carbon copy" but now means "computer copy." Other acceptable abbreviations include *pc* for "photocopy" or simply *c* for "copy."

You can also send copies to other people without telling the reader. These **blind copies** are not mentioned on the original; they are listed on the copy that you save for the organization's file, with the abbreviation *bcc* preceding the names of people getting these copies.

Saving a copy of a message for your own files is standard business practice. However, sending blind copies of your messages to other people is not. Module 7 discusses the ethical concerns of blind copying your electronic messages to others.

LO5 What Courtesy Titles Should I Use?

Research your reader's preference.

Today, most salutations use "Dear *first name last name*." Using *Dear* is a courteous, standard business convention and in no way implies a personal relationship with the recipient.

Some people and many cultures prefer their professional titles: Director Chadraba, President Mauricio. Use *Ms.*, *Mr.*, or *Mrs.* when your audience has signed his or her correspondence that way.

1. Use professional titles when they're relevant.

> Dr. Kristen Sorenson is our new company physician.
> The Rev. Robert Townsley gave the invocation.

2. If a woman prefers to be addressed as *Mrs.* or *Miss*, rather than *Ms.*, use the title she prefers. You-attitude (Module 13) takes precedence over non-sexist language: address the reader as she—or he—prefers to be addressed. To find out whether a woman prefers a traditional title:
   a. Check the signature block in previous correspondence. If a woman types her name as *(Miss) Elaine Anderson* or *(Mrs.) Kay Royster*, use the title she designates.
   b. Notice the title a woman uses in introducing herself on the phone. If she says, "This is Robin Stine," use *Dear Robin Stine* when you write to her. If she says, "I'm Mrs. Stine," use the title she specifies.
   c. Check your company directory. In some organizations, women who prefer traditional titles list them with their names.
   d. When you're writing job letters or other crucial correspondence, call the company and ask the receptionist which title your reader prefers.

Ms. is particularly useful when you do not know a woman's marital status. However, when you know that a woman is married or single, use courtesy titles only when your audience requests them.

In addition to using parallel courtesy titles, use parallel forms for names (Table 6.2).

FIGURE 6.5   Two-Page Letter, Block Format (mixed or two-point punctuation; informative)

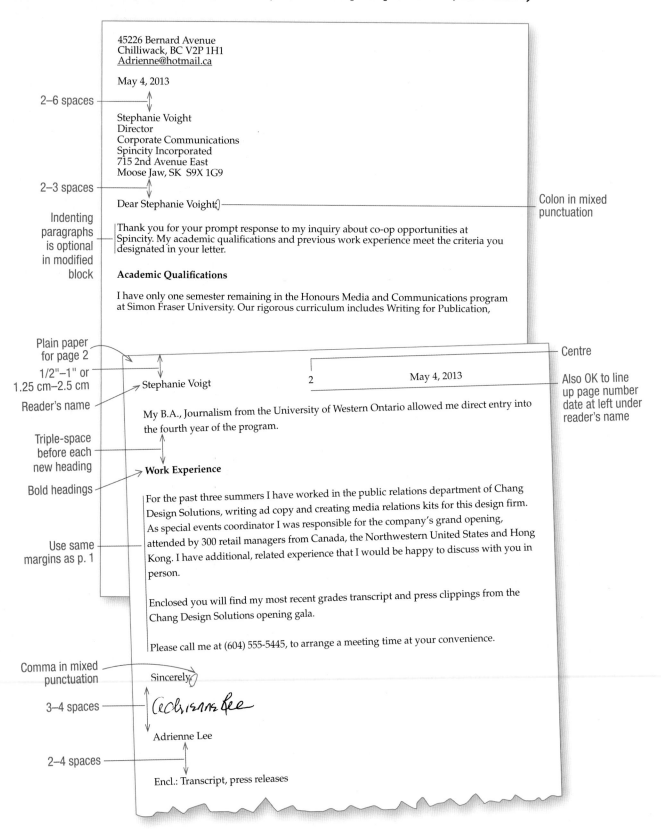

45226 Bernard Avenue
Chilliwack, BC V2P 1H1
Adrienne@hotmail.ca

May 4, 2013

2–6 spaces

Stephanie Voight
Director
Corporate Communications
Spincity Incorporated
715 2nd Avenue East
Moose Jaw, SK S9X 1G9

2–3 spaces

Dear Stephanie Voight: ———— Colon in mixed punctuation

Indenting paragraphs is optional in modified block

Thank you for your prompt response to my inquiry about co-op opportunities at Spincity. My academic qualifications and previous work experience meet the criteria you designated in your letter.

Academic Qualifications

I have only one semester remaining in the Honours Media and Communications program at Simon Fraser University. Our rigorous curriculum includes Writing for Publication,

Plain paper for page 2
1/2"–1" or 1.25 cm–2.5 cm
Reader's name

Stephanie Voigt

2   May 4, 2013 ———— Centre

Also OK to line up page number date at left under reader's name

My B.A., Journalism from the University of Western Ontario allowed me direct entry into the fourth year of the program.

Triple-space before each new heading

Bold headings

Work Experience

For the past three summers I have worked in the public relations department of Chang Design Solutions, writing ad copy and creating media relations kits for this design firm. As special events coordinator I was responsible for the company's grand opening, attended by 300 retail managers from Canada, the Northwestern United States and Hong Kong. I have additional, related experience that I would be happy to discuss with you in person.

Use same margins as p. 1

Enclosed you will find my most recent grades transcript and press clippings from the Chang Design Solutions opening gala.

Please call me at (604) 555-5445, to arrange a meeting time at your convenience.

Comma in mixed punctuation

Sincerely,

3–4 spaces

Adrienne Lee

2–4 spaces

Encl.: Transcript, press releases

TABLE 6.2 **Use Parallel Forms for Names**

Not Parallel	Parallel
Members of the committee will be Mr. Jones, Mr. Yacone, and Lisa	Members of the committee will be Mr. Jones, Mr. Yacone, and Ms. Melton *or* Members of the committee will be Irving, Ted, and Lisa

When You Know the Reader's Name but Not the Gender

Never assume a person's gender by his/her name. When you know your reader's name but not the gender, you can do two things:

1. Call the company and ask the receptionist.

2. Use the reader's full name in the salutation.

Dear Chris Crowell:
Dear J. C. Meath:

When You Know Neither the Reader's Name nor Gender

When you know neither the reader's name nor gender, you have four options:

1. Use an attention line:

Attention Customer Service:
Attention Human Resources:

2. Use the reader's position or job title:

Dear Loan Officer:
Attention Registrar:

3. Use a general group to which your reader belongs:

Dear Investor:
Attention Admissions Committee:

4. Omit the salutation and use a subject line in its place:

Subject: Recommendation for Ben Wandell

Using bolded attention and subject lines is acceptable.

LO3 How Should I Set Up Hardcopy Memos?

The standard memo uses block format but has no salutation, close, or signature.

Hardcopy and electronic memos are messages sent **within** an organization.

LO1   FIGURE 6.6   **Simple Request Memo**

May 4, 2013

To: Noushad

From: Shantel   *SW*

Subject: Forgotten Password

Please accept my apologies: I have forgotten my new password to get into client files. Please reset, and call me (extension 5340) with the temporary password.

Thank you, Noushad.

LO1   FIGURE 6.7   **Memo Format (analytical proposal/short report)**

Everything lined up at left

2–4 spaces

Double-space

October 8, 2013

To: Annette T. Califero

From: Kyle B. Abrams   *KBA*

Subject: A Low-Cost Way to Reduce Energy Use

Plain paper

Line up

Writer's initials added in ink

Capitalize first letter of each major word in subject line

No heading for ¶ 1

As you requested, I've investigated low-cost ways to reduce our energy use. Reducing the building temperature on weekends is a change that we could make immediately, that would cost nothing, and that would cut our energy use by about 6 percent.

Triple-space before each new heading

The Energy Savings from a Lower Weekend Temperature

Bold headings

Single-space paragraphs; double-space between paragraphs

Lowering the temperature from 20°C to 15.5°C from 8 p.m. Friday evening to 4 a.m. Monday morning could cut our total consumption by 6 percent. It is not feasible to lower the temperature on weeknights because many staff members work late; the cleaning crew is also on duty from 6 p.m. to midnight. Turning the temperature down for only four hours would not result in a significant saving.

Turning the heat back up at 4 a.m. on Mondays will allow the building temperature to be back to 20°C by 9 a.m. Our furnace already has computerized controls that can be set to automatically lower and raise the temperature.

Triple-space

How a Lower Temperature Would Affect Employees

Capitalize first letter of each major word of heading

A survey of employees shows that only seven people use the building every weekend or almost every weekend. Eighteen percent of our staff have worked at least one weekend day in the last two months; 52 percent say they "occasionally" come in on weekends.

Paragraphs left justified

People who come in for an hour or less on weekends could cope with the lower temperature just by wearing warm clothes. However, most people would find 15.5°C too cool for extended work. Employees who work regularly on weekends might want to install space heaters.

Action Needed to Implement the Change

Would you also like me to check into the cost of buying a dozen portable space heaters? Providing them would allow us to choose units that our wiring can handle and would be a nice gesture toward employees who give up their weekends to work. I could have a report to you in two weeks.

We can begin saving energy immediately. Just authorize the lower temperature, and I'll see that the controls are reset for this weekend.

No signature

Hardcopy memos

- Omit the salutation and the close
- Use left justification
- Require subject lines

The simple request memo in Figure 6.6 uses a standard format.

FIGURE 6.8   Memo Format (memo letterhead, good news)

Line up horizontally with printed Date/To/From/Subject

Margin lined up with items in To/From/Subject block to save typing time

Kimball, Walls, and Morganstern

Date: March 15, 2013

To: Annette T. Califero

From: Kyle B. Abrams   *KBA*

Subject: The Effectiveness of Reducing Building Temperatures on Weekends

Writer's initials added in ink

Capitalize first letter of each major word in subject line

Triple-space

Reducing the building temperature to 20°C on weekends has cut energy use by 4 percent compared to last year's use from December to February and has saved our firm $22 000.

This saving is particularly remarkable when you consider that this winter has been colder than last year's, so more heat would have been needed to maintain the same temperature.

Fewer people have worked weekends during the past three months than during the preceding three months, but snow and bad driving conditions may have had more to do with keeping people home than the fear of being cold. Five of the 12 space heaters we bought have been checked out on an average weekend. On one weekend, all 12 were in use, and some people shared their offices so that everyone could be in a room with a space heater.

Fully 92 percent of our employees support the lower temperature. I recommend that we continue turning down the heat on weekends through the remainder of the heating season and that we resume the practice when the heat is turned on next fall.

Figures 6.7 and 6.8 illustrate the standard memo format. Note that the first letters of the reader's name, the writer's name, and the subject phrase are lined up vertically. Note also that memos are usually initialled beside the To/From block. Initialling tells the reader that the memo's writer takes responsibility for the document.

Some organizations have special letterhead for hardcopy memos, with the *Date/To/From/ Subject* already printed on the form (see Figure 6.8).

Checkpoint

Letters are business messages written to readers outside the company. Letters use **block** or **modified semi-block** format.

Memos are business messages sent between people in the same company. Memos begin with a **Date** line, a **To** line, a **From** line, and a **Subject** line.

If the memo is long, consider breaking the text up with headings (Module 5, Modules 16 and 17) (see Figure 6.7). Designing and formatting your messages so that it's easy for your audience to read, understand, and respond makes it much more likely that they will.

LO6 EXPANDING A CRITICAL SKILL

Creating a Business Image

The way you and your documents look affects the way people respond to you and to them. All discourse communities and organizations (Module 2) have a dress code. One young man was upset when an older man told him he should wear better shoes. He was wearing leather shoes but not the kind that said "I'm promotable" in that workplace. Dress codes are rarely spelled out; the older worker was doing the young man a favour by being direct.

If you have a mentor in the organization, ask him or her if there are other ways you can make your appearance even more professional. If you don't have a mentor, look at the people who rank above you. Notice clothing, jewellery, and hairstyles. If you're on a budget, go to stores that sell expensive clothing to check the kind of buttons, the texture and colours of fabric, the width of lapels and belts. Then go to stores in your price range and choose garments that imitate the details of expensive clothing.

Some urban, multicultural workplaces welcome clothing choices that reflect a person's ethnic background and/or religious beliefs, and accept personal artifacts, including tattoos and piercing. However, such choices may evoke

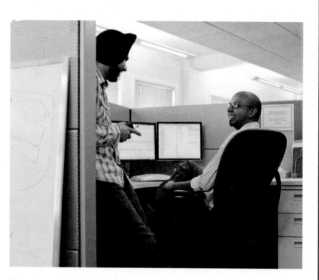

The dress codes of some organizations are less formal than those of others.

negative assumptions; it's up to you to research the apparel choices considered appropriately professional in your organization.

MODULE SUMMARY

- Letters are written to people outside the organization; memos are documents written to people inside your organization.

- Block and modified block are the two standard letter formats.

- Use the courtesy titles people prefer. If you don't know a person's gender or title preference, ask.

- In a list of several people, use parallel forms for names. Use courtesy titles and last names for everyone, or use first names for everyone.

- Traditional hardcopy memos omit both the salutation and the close. Memos never indent paragraphs. Memos require subject lines; headings are optional. Each heading must cover all the information until the next paragraph. Never use a separate heading for the first paragraph.

ASSIGNMENTS FOR MODULE 6

Questions for Critical Thinking

6.1 Since everybody uses email now, why should you learn about hard copy letters and memos?

6.2 Word offers dozens of templates for business documents. How would you decide what template to use? What are the advantages of using Word templates? What are the disadvantages?

6.3 How do you decide how to address your recipient when you write?

Exercises and Problems

6.4   Formatting a Message

Correct the format errors in the following hardcopy memo.

March 3,2013

To: Professor Hughes
From: Adele Cameron
Subject: My Writing Progress

Overview

Dear Professor Hughes. Thank you for the opportunity to review my writing progress so far. Because I have been using a reader to provide specific feedback, my writing has improved since the beginning of the semester.

Writing Strategies

When you encouraged us to find someone to read and respond to our writing, I asked my older brother, a recent university graduate, to do so. He and I sit together while he reads the first drafts of my writing assignments. He gives me specific feedback on my organization, content, word choice, and transitions.

Initially I felt very awkward and defensive when Daniel was reading my papers. He often stopped reading to ask me to clarify an argument, or to explain the meaning of a sentence that seemed pretty obvious to me. After a few such meetings, however, I found that my brother's feedback was forcing me to examine my writing in a new way. I was learning to move from the role of writer to the role of reader, in order to assess whether what I was trying to say made sense from the reader's point of view. Now I reread my papers from the reader's perspective.

Editing Strategies

Daniel also critiqued my grammar and punctuation, which have never been strong. After watching and listening to him, I was able to make some of these corrections myself. Although by no means an expert, I am learning how to edit and proofread my own work.

Thank you very much for the suggestion about using a reader. This practice and my patient brother's assistance have helped me to improve my writing skills.

Sincerely,

Adele Cameron

6.5   Analyzing and Revising Message Formats

As consumers, employees, and/or students, we all receive hardcopy letters regularly. Bring in two hardcopy letters you have received recently.

As your instructor directs,

  a. Share your examples with a small group of students.
  b. Identify the formats the writers are using.
  c. Identify any format errors.
  d. Be prepared to present your results to the rest of the class.

POLISHING YOUR PROSE

Making Pronouns Agree with Their Nouns

Pronouns stand in for nouns, and must agree with the nouns they refer to, so that your meaning is clear to your reader.

For the sake of clarity, make your pronouns agree in person (first, second, third) and number (singular, plural) with the nouns they replace.

	Singular	Plural
First person	I, my, mine, me, myself	we, our, us, ourselves
Second person	you, your, yourself	you, your, yourselves
Third person	he, she, it, him, her, his, hers	they, their, them, themselves

Incorrect:	In my internship, I learned that you have to manage your time wisely.
Correct:	In my internship, I learned to manage my time wisely.
Incorrect:	The sales team reached their goal.
Correct:	The sales team reached its goal. (*Team* is a collective or group noun, and takes a singular verb and pronoun.)

In Canada and the United States, company names and the words *company* and *government* are singular nouns. In Great Britain, these nouns are plural and require plural pronouns:

Correct (Canadian):	Clarica trains its agents well.
Correct (U.S.):	Nationwide Insurance trains its agents well.
Correct (U.K.):	Lloyd's of London train their agents well.

Exercises

Identify and correct any errors. Note that some sentences do not contain errors.

1. An administrative assistant should help their boss work efficiently.
2. The mayor should give themselves credit for doing a good job.
3. The company announces their quarterly profits today.
4. Most new employees find that they need to learn a new culture.
5. A CEO's pay is often based on the performance of their company.
6. The union votes today on whether they will go on strike.
7. In my first month of work, I learned that you need to check email at least three times a day.
8. One of the features of my corporate culture is a willingness to share ideas.
9. The team will present its recommendations to the Executive Committee.
10. Every employee is interested in improving their technical skills.

Check your answers to the odd-numbered exercises in the Answer Key at the back of the text.

connect™

Practise and learn online with Connect. Connect allows you to practise important skills at your own pace and on your own schedule, with 24/7 online access to an eBook, practise quizzes, interactives, videos, study tools, and additional resources.

Writing Electronic Messages

Learning Objectives

After reading and applying the information in Module 7, you'll be able to demonstrate

Knowledge of

LO1 Electronic communication basics

Skills to

LO2 Write business emails for the results you want

LO3 Consider the best medium for your message

MODULE OUTLINE

- What do I need to know about communicating electronically?
- What do I need to know about email messages?
- How should I format email messages?
- How should I organize email messages?
- What kinds of subject lines should I use for email messages?
- What should I know about content and tone?
- When should I use attachments?
- What "netiquette" rules should I follow?
- What else do I need to know about communicating electronically?

Module Summary

Assignments for Module 7

Polishing Your Prose: Correcting Dangling Modifiers

Employability Skills 2000+ Checklist

Module content builds these Conference Board of Canada Employability Skills 2000+

Communicate

Manage Information

Work with Others

Use Numbers

Think and Solve Problems

Participate in Projects and Tasks

Electronic messaging may feel as informal and spontaneous as speaking. However, electronic messages lack all the subtle symbols—facial expressions, gestures, tone, posture, use of space—we use to exchange meaning. Communicating effectively by email, therefore, demands the same analytical thinking (PAIBOC), and the same writing processes (composing, revising, editing) as any other document.

LO1 What Do I Need to Know About Communicating Electronically?

Be discreet: you leave an electronic trail.

Electronic privacy does not exist. Your text messages, tweets, Facebook posts—all your electronic messages—are retrievable, virtually forever. Even personal electronic conversations are in the public domain, as the court case between CIBC and Genuity Capital Markets Technology demonstrated. CIBC was able to trace BlackBerry users' private, PIN-to-PIN messages to use as evidence.[1] Potential employers, police, and courts around the world can follow your every tweet and post.

LO2 What Do I Need to Know About Email Messages?

While electronic communication continues to evolve, one reality is constant: When you post, you're published.

As you write email and text messages, keep these guidelines in mind:

- Texts and emails are neither private nor informal, as a conversation may be. Governments, law enforcement agencies, and employers may legally check your messages. And any emails you send can be printed out or forwarded to others without your knowledge or consent.
- Unless you are communicating with friends or family, you must apply all the principles of good business writing to your electronic messages. And because they are so easily misinterpreted, composing emails requires a heightened awareness of audience.

- Because email seems to be as instantaneous as text messaging, some writers pay less attention to grammar, punctuation, and spelling. However, business emails should be as correct as paper documents. Use a spell checker; check for grammar and punctuation. Whenever you can, ask a peer to proof your message.
- If your subject line and first paragraph are not interesting, readers will hit Delete. Use your subject line effectively. Take special care when writing to people who do not report to you, or to people outside your organization or unit.

Use the PAIBOC model to analyze business communication situations—and to identify the best possible medium and content to resolve the situation satisfactorily.

FIGURE 7.1 PAIBOC Questions for Analysis

P	Why are you communicating? What is your **purpose**? What do you want to accomplish? Are you texting a friend to verify an address? Emailing a colleague about work? Writing to a client to arrange a meeting? What results do you want?
A	Who is your **audience**? What is your relationship with your audience? Are you close friends? Acquaintances? Are you communicating with your supervisor? With a subordinate? How will your audience feel about your message? Happy? Neutral? Angry? What medium does your audience consider appropriate for your communication?
I	What does your audience already know? What do they need to know? Will you need to persuade your audience? Based on your audience and purpose analysis, what **information** must you include?
B	What reasons or reader **benefits** support your ideas? What will motivate your audience to do as you request? What's in it for them?
O	What **objections** can you expect your audience to have to your message content, to the medium you have chosen, or to you? What negatives must you de-emphasize or overcome?
C	How will the **context** affect your message? What cultural, organizational, economic, environmental, and/or seasonal circumstances will affect your content and medium and your audience response to your message? For example, your organization might encourage employees to text each other on work matters, but consider it inappropriate for you to text a client. This cultural expectation is the context that determines when you use texting and when you send emails.

FIGURE 7.2 Outlook Express Email Memo Template

LO2 How Should I Format Email Messages?

Follow organizational formats, or use a software template.

Many organizations use boilerplate formats for their electronic and hardcopy documents. If you are unsure about how to format a document, ask co-workers. Other resources include software and email programs that provide formats you can customize.

Although the email screen has a To line (as do memos), most of us prefer a salutation: *Hi* or *Hello* (*Name*), *Good Morning* (*Name*). Omitting the salutation sounds brusque, even rude. A salutation is particularly important for readers of cultures whose members value courtesy and formality.

The writer in Figure 7.3 ends the message with all his contact information, but you can choose to type only your name. Text messages between colleagues often omit salutations and signatures. These conventions depend on your relationship with the reader and the assumptions and expectations of your company's culture. When in doubt, always err on the side of courtesy, since your respect for the reader builds respect for your organization and for you.

When you hit Reply, the email program automatically uses *Re:* (Latin for "about") and the previous subject. Revise the subject line to make it appropriate for your message. When you change the subject line, you can include the original one in parentheses for the reader who sorts messages by thread. When you create a new subject line, delete the *Re:*.

FIGURE 7.3   A Basic Email Message

The writer can type in the email address directly.

System puts in writer's name and email address.

```
         To:  larenzor@artemis.com
       From:  Sacha Zevchik <zevchik.2@acme.com>
    Subject:  Please Protect Computers
         Cc:
        Bcc:
   Attached:
   _____

   Roger--

   Just a reminder: when your workers install the ceiling insulation next
   week, be sure to have them put plastic sheeting over the desks and
   computers to protect them from sawdust, insulation, and debris.

   Thanks!

   Sacha Zevchik
   Administrative Assistant
   Voice: 630-555-1000 ext. 117
   Fax: 630-555-2391
   Email:  zevchik.2@acme.com
```

Some writers use an informal salutation to personalize the message.

No need to indent paragraphs.

The writer creates the signature block once and can use it automatically. Some email programs permit you to store several signature blocks with different levels of formality.

Employability Skills

LO2 How Should I Organize Email Messages?

Organize to meet readers' expectations. Deliver good news directly; give bad news indirectly.

Ex.
7.5
7.6

Because they have to deal with so many electronic messages daily, people need to be able to read and respond to emails rapidly. Your responsibility as a writer is to meet that need.

Write with intention, and make conscious choices:

- Use PAIBOC analysis to plan: identify why you are writing—what results you want—and how your audience will feel about your message.
- Give all the necessary information your reader needs to make a decision and act on your request.
- Organize to meet readers' needs: use the indirect pattern when your message is bad news for your reader—that is, your message will inconvenience or cost the reader time or money—or you have to say no to the reader (Modules 9 and 10).
- Revise for clarity and conciseness: choose concrete nouns and action verbs; keep sentences and paragraphs short; eliminate unnecessary words.

FIGURE 7.4   Email Letter/Sales Letter

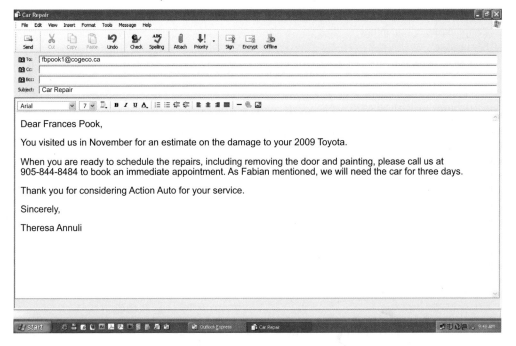

FIGURE 7.5   Email Letter Request for Adjustment

- Compose your subject line last. The ideal subject line sums up your email, but you don't know what you're going to say until you've said it; furthermore, you may be revising to discover exactly what it is you do want to say. Why write a subject line that you'll have to change?
- Make time to proofread, just as you would with paper messages; it's easier to catch errors in hard copy, so if you can, print your messages out to edit and proofread

Note the differences between the two emails—the draft and revised copies—below. In Figure 7.7, the writer uses PAIBOC analysis to revise for clarity and conciseness.

Modules 8, 9 and 10 further describe how best to organize messages to meet your audience's needs.

FIGURE 7.6   Email Message with Attachment (direct request, draft copy)

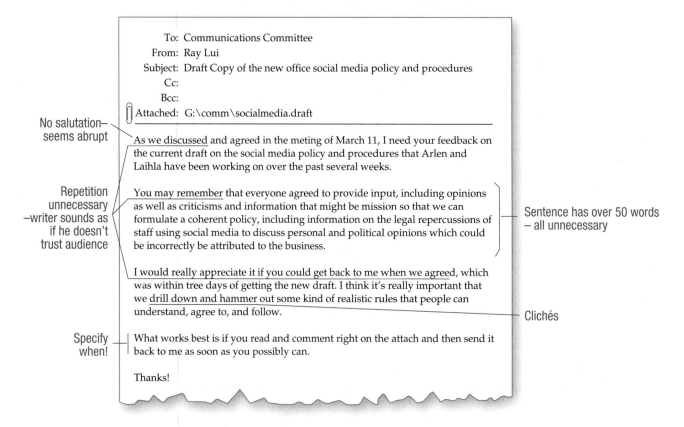

To: Communications Committee
From: Ray Lui
Subject: Draft Copy of the new office social media policy and procedures
Cc:
Bcc:
Attached: G:\comm\socialmedia.draft

No salutation—seems abrupt

As we discussed and agreed in the meting of March 11, I need your feedback on the current draft on the social media policy and procedures that Arlen and Laihla have been working on over the past several weeks.

Repetition unnecessary —writer sounds as if he doesn't trust audience

You may remember that everyone agreed to provide input, including opinions as well as criticisms and information that might be mission so that we can formulate a coherent policy, including information on the legal repercussions of staff using social media to discuss personal and political opinions which could be incorrectly be attributed to the business.

Sentence has over 50 words – all unnecessary

I would really appreciate it if you could get back to me when we agreed, which was within tree days of getting the new draft. I think it's really important that we drill down and hammer out some kind of realistic rules that people can understand, agree to, and follow.

Clichés

Specify when!

What works best is if you read and comment right on the attach and then send it back to me as soon as you possibly can.

Thanks!

FIGURE 7.7   Email Message with Attachment (direct request, revised)

To: Communications Committee
From: Ray Lui
Subject: Please Comment on New Draft
Cc:
Bcc:
Attached: G:\comm\socialmediapolicy.draft

Hi everyone,

Here is the latest draft of our social media policy.

Please send me any changes by 10 a.m. Thursday. I'll collate them and bring them to our Thursday afternoon meeting.

LO2 What Kinds of Subject Lines Should I Use for Email Messages?

Use subject lines that are specific, concise, and catchy.

Subject lines in emails are even more important than those in letters and memos, because it's so easy for the recipient to hit the Delete key. Subject lines must be specific, concise, and catchy. Many email users get so many messages that they don't bother reading them if they don't recognize the sender or if the subject doesn't catch their interest.

When you send emails just for information, put "FYI" at the end of the subject line.

Dilbert © 1998 Scott Adams. Used by permission of UNIVERSAL UCLICK. All rights reserved.

If your message is very short, you may be able to put it in the subject line. "EOM" (end of message) tells your reader there is no additional information in the body of the message.

Subject: Will Attend 3:00 p.m. Meeting EOM

Checkpoint

Keep your subject line short. If that's difficult, put the most important part into the first few words, because some email programs show only the first 28 characters of the subject line.

What Should I Know About Content and Tone?

Use PAIBOC analysis: Write to meet your audience's needs and your purposes.

York University professor Heather Lotherington, a multi-technological literacy expert, claims that as soon as people could chat in real time (what Lotherington calls "synchronous messages"), they developed a code to convey meaning instantaneously. This systematic email code includes such symbols as sound-based abbreviations ("c u ltr"), emoticons, sentence fragments, full caps (for shouting), and cyber names.[2] These symbols may work fine for like-minded audiences (family, friends, colleagues with whom you have an informal relationship). However, many of your readers will expect traditional business language even in electronic communications. It's your job as a writer to find out your readers' preferences.

Because electronic messages lack the thousands of symbols that characterize face to face communication, you have to consider your audience very carefully. Humour, sarcasm, jokes, and chain letters do not travel well, especially in a global workplace: recipients find them incomprehensible, rude, and a waste of time and resources. Many people feel overwhelmed by the amount of email they receive daily; any part of your message that readers perceive as frivolous will negatively affect your purpose.

Remember to

- *Deliver sensitive messages in person whenever possible.* Because of the limitations of electronic media, negative and persuasive messages (reprimands, negotiations) are more efficiently delivered face to face. The important nuances added through non-verbal communication speak volumes and can save time and energy. If you must deliver negative information electronically, write so that it's easy for readers to understand and act on the information quickly.
- *Be clear, courteous, and concise.* Unless your reader's expectations, your corporate culture, or your purposes dictate otherwise, compose and revise your messages to convey necessary information as politely, clearly, and briefly as possible. This reader-focus is not only good business, it is also legally responsible behaviour.
- *Format and name attachments appropriately.* Attached documents (letter, resumés, reports, invoices, etc.) use standard paper formats (Module 6).
- *Compose and copy with discretion.* In email memos, *cc* denotes computer copies; your recipient can see the names of other people getting the message. *Bcc* denotes blind computer copies, usually used for mailing lists or for sending yourself electronic copies; the recipient

EXPANDING A CRITICAL SKILL

Using the Best Medium for your Message

To get the results you want, you need to use PAIBOC analysis to identify the best possible medium for your message. Often we do this analysis subconsciously: when texting family and good friends, for example, we default to informal cryptic messages because we share a communications history with these audiences. Because of that history, we depend more on a mutual understanding than on language. In fact, electronic media often work best for simple, direct, and emotionally neutral conversations.

However, no technology or app can replace personal contact for establishing and building relationships. People want to hire and work with people they feel they know.

Those all-important personal connections that lead to business success depend on face time, as entrepreneur and business founder Candice Holmstrom can attest. Attending the annual meeting of the Toronto-based Canadian Council for Aboriginal Business, Holmstrom, whose company "is one of 100 businesses affiliated with the…CCAB," found herself seated "one person away

Source: Richard Lautens, Torstar Syndication Services.

from Nick [Javor]"—Tim Hortons' senior vice president of corporate affairs." Holmstrom, owner of retail design business CH Designs Incorporated, introduced herself and her company during a break. The result of this proximity and her introduction: Holmstrom's company is helping redesign the decor of Tim Hortons' North America. Holmstrom's client list includes a number of Canadian retail giants, including Loblaw's and Holt Renfrew—a testament to her facility with the interpersonal communication.

Source: Reprinted with permission—Torstar Syndication Services.

Cultural FOCUS

Many writers feel that ending a message with an **end-date** (when you want a response by) might seem pushy. However, this is not the case. Readers often appreciate knowing a deadline so they can plan accordingly.

does not see the names of these people. Copying your supervisor and/or other people unnecessarily is inflammatory and unethical.

- *Count to ten before you Send.* When you write, you are on the record. Emails sent in anger, to the wrong person, or to everyone on a list can damage your relationships, your reputation, and your future.

You'll find more information on how to structure informative, positive, negative, and persuasive messages, and how to write subject lines in Modules 8, 9, and 10.

LO1 When Should I Use Attachments?

Send attachments when your PAIBOC analysis tells you that they meet the needs of your audience.

Any text document can be copied and pasted into the body of your email message. However, sending attachments makes sense when your reader needs any of the following:

- A business letter or report
- A long text document
- A text document with extensive formatting
- A non-text file (e.g., PowerPoint slides, HTML file, spreadsheet)

How Should I Manage Attachments?

When you send an attachment, remember that

- Word-processing programs can generally open documents created in earlier versions of such programs but not later ones; Word 2003 can open documents created in Word 98 but not in Word 2007.
- Attachments require a cover email drawing the reader's attention to them—*Here is, I have attached, You'll see*—just as in a hard-copy letter *(Enclosure).*
- All files, including attachments, require appropriate names so that 1) you can find the file easily and 2) the reader understands the attachment's purpose and contents.

Viruses can infect files that are attached to email messages or that you download. You can do several things to stay virus-free:[3]

- Install an antivirus program on your computer, and keep it up to date.

Language FOCUS

Netiquette is the short form for "Internet etiquette." Netiquette describes the rules that you should follow when using the Internet for email, blogs, and discussion boards. Following these rules will help you be a good **netizen** (citizen of the Internet, or virtual world).

- Ask people who send you attachments to include their names in the document titles; virus titles aren't that specific.
- If you're in doubt about an attachment, don't open it.
- Forward email messages only when you're sure of the source and contents.

LO1 LO3 What Netiquette Rules Should I Follow?

Follow these guidelines to be a good netizen.

- *Never send angry messages by email.* If you have a conflict with someone, work it out face to face, not electronically.
- *Send people only messages they need.* Send copies to supervisors/bosses only if they have asked you to.
- *Avoid clichés* such as "Enclosed please find" and "Please don't hesitate to call," as you would when composing hardcopy documents.
- *Send cards, rather than emails, to express condolences and appreciation for hospitality.* Use the appropriate medium for your message. When you respond to a message, mirror the sender's choice of medium, format, and language.
- *Before you hit Send, assume your email will appear on the front pages of the national newspaper*, because it very well could.
- *Avoid using full caps; use mixed case in subject lines and full caps only if you have to emphasize a word or two.* Putting the whole message in full caps is considered shouting.
- *Find out how your recipient's system works, and adapt your messages to it.* Most people would rather get a separate short message on each of several topics, so that the messages can be stored in different mailboxes. But people who pay a fee to download each message might prefer longer messages that deal with several topics.

LO1 What Else Do I Need to Know About Communicating Electronically?

Be discreet: You are leaving an electronic trail.

Evolving technology means that electronic capabilities will continue to grow in number and sophistication. However, new features will demand an ongoing learning curve for users. Many people are concerned about cell phone etiquette, as they are offended by interruptions and loud or inappropriate conversations in such spaces as theatres, classrooms, and even restrooms.

Many people routinely use their smartphones for text messages. As with a telephone conversation, messaging requires you to respond quickly but also to think carefully about what you are going to say. Whatever you send electronically is retrievable by others and can be permanent.

MODULE SUMMARY

- Use good writing principles for all your electronic communications. Use PAIBOC analysis to write for the results you want. Because emails omit the thousands of non-verbal nuances present in face to face communication, humour, sarcasm, and sensitive interpersonal negotiations are not appropriate in emails.

- Create emails that are clear, concise, and courteous. Make sure you write messages that people can read and act on quickly.

- Compose important messages offline to give yourself time for thought and revision.

- Organize email messages as you would paper documents: give good news directly and bad news indirectly.

- Write your subject lines last: make them specific, concise, and catchy.

- Be discreet when you post or hit Send. All electronic communications can be shared without your permission, and all is retrievable by others.

ASSIGNMENTS FOR MODULE 7

Questions for Critical Thinking

7.1 Because electronic communication is so accessible, people often misuse it. Have you ever received an angry/rude/threatening email at work? How did you deal with it? What did you do?

7.2 When is it unethical to send blind copies of your emails to other people? Why? When is it acceptable to send blind copies to others?

7.3 Why should you compose important email messages offline?

7.4 How do you decide on the best medium to convey your message? What criteria do you use?

Exercises and Problems

7.5 Telling an Employee That a Workshop Is Full

As director of human resources, you sponsor a variety of workshops for employees. You received this email message today:

> Subject: Re: Oral Presentations Workshop
>
> Please register me for the workshop on giving oral presentations next week. My supervisor has told me I should attend this.

The workshop is full, however, and you already have three people on a waiting list to fill vacancies if anyone should cancel. You will repeat the workshop only if you have guarantees for at least 15 participants.

Write the message.

7.6 Saying No to the Boss

Today, you received this email from your boss:

> Subject: Oversee United Way
>
> I'm appointing you as company representative to oversee our United Way campaign. You've done a good job the last three years, so this year should be a piece of cake.

It's true that you know exactly what to do. The job wouldn't be hard for you. But that's just the problem. You wouldn't learn anything, either. You'd rather have an assignment that would stretch you, teach you new skills, or enable you to interact with new people. Continuing to grow helps ensure your continued employability and mobility. Three upcoming projects in your division might offer growth: creating DVDs for a "town meeting" for all employees to be held at the beginning of next quarter, creating a plain language policy for the company, or serving on the diversity committee. Any of these would be time-consuming, but no more time-consuming than running the United Way campaign.

Respond to your boss, asking for something more challenging to do.

7.7 Persuading the CEO to Attend Orientation

As the director of education and training of your organization, you run orientation sessions for new hires. You're planning next quarter's session (new quarters start in January, April, July, and October) for a big group of new college graduates. You'd really like the organization's president and CEO to come in and talk to the group for at least 15 minutes. Probably most of the employees have seen the CEO, but they haven't had any direct contact. The CEO could come any time during the three-day session. Speaking just before or after lunch would be ideal, because then the CEO could also come to lunch and talk informally with at least a few people. Next best would be speaking just before or after a mid-morning or mid-afternoon break. But the CEO is busy, and you'll take what you can get.

As your instructor directs

a. Assume that your instructor is your CEO, and send an email message persuading him or her to come to the orientation.

b. Send an email message to your instructor asking him or her to address new members of a campus organization.

c. Address the CEO of your university, college, or workplace, asking him or her to speak to new employees.

7.8 Asking for More Time or Resources

Today, this message showed up in your email inbox from your boss:

Subject: Re: Want Culture Report

This request has come down from the CEO. I'm delegating it to you. See me a couple of days before the board meeting—the first Monday of next month—so we can go over your presentation.

I want a report on the culture for underrepresented groups in our organization. A presentation at the last board of directors' meeting showed that although we do a good job of hiring women and minorities, few of them rise to the top. The directors suspect that our culture may not be supportive and want information on it. Please prepare a presentation for the next meeting. You'll have 15 minutes to speak.

Making a presentation to the company's board of directors might really help your career. But preparing a good presentation and report will take time. You can look at exit reports filed by Human Resources when people leave the company, but you'll also need to interview people—many people. You're already working 60 hours a week on three major projects, and one of them is behind schedule. Can one of the projects wait? Can someone else take one of the projects? Can you get some help? Should you do just enough to get by? Ask your boss for advice—in a way that makes you look like a committed employee, not a slacker.

7.9 Asking for Volunteers

You have an executive position with a major employer in town. (Pick a business, non-profit organization, or government office you know something about.) Two years ago, your company "adopted" a local school. You've provided computers and paid for Internet access; a small number of workers have signed up to be mentors. Today you got a call from the school's principal,

a friend of yours. "I'd like to talk to you about the mentoring program. You're providing some mentors, and we're grateful for them, but we need ten times that number."

(You wince. This program has not been one of your successes.) You reply: "I know that part of the program hasn't worked out as well as we hoped it would. But people are really busy here. Not all that many people have two or three hours a week to spend with a kid."

Principal: "So you think the time it takes is really the problem?"

(Maybe your friend will appreciate that you can't force people to do this.) You say: "Pretty much."

Principal: "Do you think people would be willing to be mentors if we could find a way for it to take less time?"

"Maybe," you say. (You sense a hook is coming, and you're wary.)

Principal: "Your people spend a lot of time on email, don't they?"

"Yes. Two to three hours a day, for most of them."

Principal: "What if we created a new mentoring structure in which people just emailed their mentees instead of meeting with them? That way they could still provide advice and support, but they could do it at any time of the day. And it wouldn't have to take long."

(That sounds interesting.) You reply: "So people would just have email conversations. That would be a lot easier, and we'd get more people. But can they really have a relationship if they don't meet the kids?"

Principal: "Maybe we could have a picnic or go to a game a couple of times a year so people could meet face to face."

"And all the kids have computers?" you ask.

Principal: "Not necessarily at home. But they all have access to email at school. Writing email to professionals will also give them more practice and more confidence. People like to get email."

"Not when they get 200 messages a day, they don't."

Principal: "Well, our kids aren't in that category. What do you say?"

"I think it will work. Let's try it."

Principal: "Great. Just send me a list of the people who are willing to do this, and we'll match them up with the kids. We'd like to get this started as soon as possible."

Write an email message to all employees asking them to volunteer.

7.10 Asking for Something Different for Administrative Professionals' Week

Your clerical job gives you the flexibility you need while you're in school. Administrative Professionals' (formerly Secretaries') Week is approaching, and you really don't want flowers or a free lunch. You'd much rather have a bonus or at least time off

to attend an educational seminar (resourced by the company). You're interested in learning advanced features of a computer program or assertive behaviour techniques.

Write an email to the person who supervises clerical workers in your unit, asking that Administrative Professionals' Week give you something useful.

Hints:

- Assume that you work in an organization you know something about.

- Specify one or more seminars you'd like to attend.
- Some seminars may cost a lot more than flowers or lunch; some may cost less. How much financial flexibility does the organization have?
- Are there other clerical workers? Would they also like bonuses or seminars, or do some prefer flowers or lunch?
- How well does the person who will make the decision know you? How positively does he or she view you and any other clerical workers?

POLISHING YOUR PROSE

Correcting Dangling Modifiers

Modifiers are words or phrases that give more information about parts of a sentence. For instance, an adjective is a modifier that usually describes a noun (*top* performer), and an adverb modifies a verb (performs *brilliantly*).

Dangling modifiers confuse readers, because the word they modify is not in the sentence. If you diagrammed the sentence, the modifier would not be attached to anything; it would dangle.

Dangling: Confirming our conversation, your Hot Springs Hot Tub Spa is scheduled for delivery April 12. (This sentence seems to imply that the spa is doing the confirming.)

Correct a dangling modifier in either of these ways:

1. Rewrite the modifier as a subordinate clause.

   Correct: As we agreed yesterday, your Hot Springs Hot Tub Spa is scheduled for delivery April 12.

2. Rewrite the main clause so its subject or object can be modified correctly.

   Correct: Talking on the phone, we confirmed that your Hot Springs Hot Tub Spa is scheduled for delivery April 12.

Exercises

Correct the dangling modifiers in these sentences.

1. After working here a year, dental insurance covers you.
2. Using the fax machine, new orders are processed quickly.
3. At the age of 10, I bought my daughter her first share of stock.
4. Working in teams, projects can be completed quickly.
5. Calling ahead of time, the reservations can be made efficiently.
6. Before joining our company, your resumé shows a good deal of experience with computer software.
7. Posting risqué material on Facebook potential employers can access even years later.
8. A simple notebook filled with thoughts and ideas, you can keep a journal of your business experiences.
9. Sharing files with our legal department, our attorneys can work better with you.
10. As a new employee, your supervisor can answer your questions.

Check the Answer Key for odd-numbered exercises.

MODULE

8

Composing Informative and Positive Messages

MODULE OUTLINE

- What kinds of informative and positive messages am I likely to write?
- Why should I know how to organize messages?
- How should I organize informative and positive messages?
- When should I emphasize how readers benefit?
- What's the best subject line for an informative or positive message?
- How can PAIBOC analysis help me write informative and positive messages?

Module Summary

Assignments for Module 8

Polishing Your Prose: Applying Parallel Structure

Learning Objectives

After reading and applying the information in Module 8, you'll be able to demonstrate

Knowledge of

LO1 The criteria that define positive messages

LO2 The "good news" message structure

LO3 The persuasive element of all effective messages

LO4 The ethical implications of organizational patterns

Skills to

LO5 Further analyze business communication situations

LO6 Begin to organize and write informative and positive messages

Employability Skills 2000+ Checklist

Module content builds these Conference Board of Canada Employability Skills 2000+

Communicate

Manage Information

Think and Solve Problems

Use Numbers

Work with Others

LO1 Direct messages provide information that you expect will please the audience or that you expect the audience will respond to neutrally. These informative or "good news" messages usually have both primary and underlying purposes.

Primary purposes:

- To give information or good news to the reader, or to reassure the reader
- To have the reader "hear" the message, understand it, and view the information positively
- To de-emphasize any negative elements
- To reduce or eliminate future correspondence on the same subject

Underlying purposes:

- To build a good image of the writer
- To build a good image of the writer's organization
- To initiate or build a good relationship between the writer and reader

LO3 Because you want to build positive attitudes about yourself and the information you are presenting, even informative messages have persuasive elements, including clarity, brevity, and courtesy.

> ### Checkpoint
>
> You want to build positive attitudes toward the information you are presenting, so in that sense, even an informative message has a persuasive element.

LO1 What Kinds of Informative and Positive Messages Am I Likely to Write?

You will likely write acceptances, confirmations, summaries, instructions, adjustments, and thank-you notes.

Ex.
8.4
8.17

- Readers may feel neutral about assembly, safety, and fire drill instructions (unless, of course, these are badly written and therefore hard to understand and follow; then readers may feel irritated or frustrated).
- A transmittal can be positive when you're sending glowing sales figures or persuasive when you want the reader to act on the information.
- A collection letter is persuasive; it becomes negative in the last stage when you threaten legal action.

Confirmations

Many informative messages are for the record: they go to the other party in the conversation to summarize the conversation. These messages should be brief, and give only the information shared orally, as in Figure 8.1. Start the message by indicating that it is a confirmation, not a new message:

> As we discussed on the phone today…
>
> As I told you yesterday…
>
> Attached is the meeting schedule we discussed earlier today.

FIGURE 8.1 **A Confirmation Email**

Dear Dennis Baronski,

Thank you for shopping at goodbooks.ca. The item(s) listed below have been shipped from your order, OR141133149. Any item(s) remaining in your order will ship as they become available. If you paid for your order by credit card we are now processing a charge to your card for the shipped item(s).

To check your order's status, sign in to your Online Account and reference your Order History.

ITEM(S) SHIPPED
1. Bob Dylan: In His Own Words - 1 @ 29.88
2. Down the Highway: The Life of Bob Dylan - 1 @ 49.35

Item(s) Subtotal: $79.23
Shipping: $0.00
HST: $3.96

—————————————
—————————————

TOTAL: $83.19

Summaries

You may summarize a team meeting, a dialogue with a client, or a conversation, document, or outside meeting for colleagues or superiors. (Minutes of an internal meeting are usually more detailed. See Module 22 for advice on writing minutes of meetings.)

In a summary of a conversation for internal use, apply PAIBOC analysis: to meet your needs, and the needs of your audience, identify

- Who was present
- What was discussed
- What was decided
- Who does what next

Language FOCUS

All business messages have both a **primary purpose** and an **underlying** (or **secondary**) **purpose**. In order to be an effective writer, you must always think about both purposes and address them in your message.

FIGURE 8.2   Informative Email Letter Summarizing Meeting

From:	www.tutoringtalent.ca
To:	dtravers@metroluge.ca
Cc:	jholmes@metroluge.ca
Sent:	Friday, July 12, 2013 12:50 p.m.
Subject:	Coaching Debra Travers

Dear Janice and Debra:

Thank you for our conversation yesterday.

Debra, as we discussed, I can begin your coaching sessions on July 17, 2013. The three-hour session will include SMART goal setting, so you can identify specifically what objectives you want to meet and how you will demonstrate that you have met them. Then we can meet once a week, for five more weeks, three hours a session, customizing the coaching content each week.

Janice, please send me a copy of the contract at your convenience.

Again, thank you for your time. Debra, I look forward to working with you.

Sincerely,

Martha

Martha Dulmage
TutoringTalent Inc.
www.tutoringtalent.ca
905-847-3395

To summarize a document

- Start with the main point
- Give supporting evidence and details
- Evaluate the document, if your audience asks for evaluation

Identify the actions that your organization should take based on the document. Should others in the company read this blog? Should someone in the company write a letter to the editor responding to this newspaper article? Should your company try to meet with someone in the organization who is the subject of the story?

Ex. 8.8 8.14 8.18

Instructions

Information on new procedures may generate hostility, since most of us are reluctant to change. You can use placement, language, and font size for effective emphasis. Instructions for complicated procedures (electronic application, machine assembly) require diagrams right beside the text.

FIGURE 8.3   Instructions on Safety Procedures (memo)

Date: May 11, 2013
Memo to: All chefs, sous-chefs, wait staff, staff
From: Franco
Re: Procedures for Spills

To comply with Health and Safety legislation, and to protect your own safety and the safety of all employees and patrons, please ensure that you read, understand, and comply with the following instructions for dealing with spills:

1. STOP! whatever you are doing immediately.

2. Alert the person closest to you.
    Indicate to that person
    a. The exact location of the spill
    b. The nature of the spill (e.g., grease, juice, water, gravy, sauce, etc.)

3. WHILE THAT PERSON WAITS IN PLACE, get the yellow warning sign, and a pail and mop from cupboard #3.

4. Place the sign and clean the spill immediately.

5. Ensure the floor/area is completely clean.

6. Ensure the floor/area is completely dry.

7. Return the sign, mop, and pail to cupboard #3.

Your cooperation is essential for the safety, security, and comfort of us all.

Adjustments and Responses to Complaints

A study showed that when people had gripes about a company but didn't complain, only 9 percent would buy from the company again. But when people did complain—and their problems were resolved quickly—82 percent would buy again.[1]

When you grant a customer's request for an adjusted price, discount, replacement, or other benefit to resolve a complaint, do so in the very first sentence:

> Your Visa bill for a night's lodging has been adjusted to $63. Next month, a credit of $37 will appear on your bill to reimburse you for the extra amount you originally paid.

Language FOCUS

To **gripe** is an informal way of saying that someone is complaining continually. Often, when we say people are griping, we mean they are complaining about something to friends and colleagues, but they are not complaining to the correct person. For example, someone may have been unhappy about the service at a local restaurant. However, instead of complaining to the restaurant manager, who is the proper person to complain to, the person goes to work the following day and complains to everyone there about the terrible service.

Readers are not interested in your own process in making the decision. Give the reason for the original mistake only if it reflects credit on the company. (In most cases, it doesn't, so omit it.)

Thank-You and Congratulatory Notes

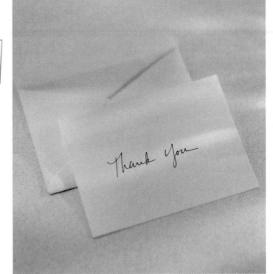

Sending a **thank-you note** recognizes and acknowledges a person's contribution (see Maslow's Hierarchy of Needs in Module 11). And when you recognize others, those people are more willing to help you again in the future.

Thank-you letters are prompt and short. They need to be specific to sound sincere. Most of us appreciate any sincere thank-you; when you put it in writing, however, you demonstrate that you feel grateful enough to take the time to write, and you give the recipient a record of your appreciation. Congratulating someone sincerely and respectfully can build good feelings between you and the reader, and enhance your own visibility.

Ex.
8.6
8.7
8.16

[LO3] Why Should I Know How to Organize Messages?

Form follows function: The way you organize your message shapes how your audience reacts to it.

Knowing the appropriate organizational pattern can help you compose messages more quickly and create a more effective final product. How you organize your messages affects how your audience responds to the information.

The organization patterns described in this module and Modules 9 and 10 work in most business writing situations. Be sure you understand the rationale behind each pattern so that you can modify the pattern if necessary. (For example, when you write instructions, any warnings should go up front, in a place of emphasis, as in Figure 8.3.)

[LO2] [LO5] [LO6] How Should I Organize Informative and Positive Messages?

Consider your audience's needs: Put the good news and a summary of the information first.

Putting good news up front meets your audience's needs for recognition and respect (Module 11).

Present informative and positive messages in the following order:

1. *Give any good news and summarize the main points.* Share good news immediately. Include details such as the date that policies begin and the percent of a discount. If the reader has already raised the issue, make it clear that you're responding.
2. *Give details, clarification, and background.* Don't repeat information from the first paragraph. Do answer all the questions your reader is likely to have; provide all the information necessary to achieve your purposes. Present details in *the order of importance to the reader.*

Ex.
8.4
8.6

8.7
8.13
8.16

FIGURE 8.4
How to Organize an Informative or Positive Message

- Main Point
- Details
- Negatives
- Reader Benefits
- Goodwill Ending

3. *Present any negative elements as positively as possible.* A policy might have limits, information might be incomplete, or the reader might have to satisfy requirements to get a discount or benefit. Make these negatives clear, but present them as positively as possible.

4. *Explain any reader benefits.* Most informative memos need reader benefits. Show that the policy or procedure helps readers, not just the company. Give enough detail to make the benefits clear and convincing. In letters, you may want to give the benefits of dealing with your company as well as the benefits of the product or policy (Module 11). In a good news message, it's often possible to combine a short reader benefit with a *goodwill ending* in the last paragraph.

5. *Use a goodwill ending that's positive, personal, and forward-looking.* Shifting your emphasis away from the message to the reader suggests that serving the reader is your real concern.

Figure 8.4 summarizes the pattern. Figures 8.1 and 8.5 illustrate two ways to apply the pattern.

Ex. 8.9– 8.12

8.15 8.18

When Should I Emphasize How Readers Benefit?

Use reader benefits when you want readers to view your policies and your organization positively.

Not all informative and positive messages need reader benefits (See Module 11). Use reader benefits when you want readers to view your policies and your organization positively.

You don't need reader benefits when

- You're presenting factual information only
- The reader's attitude toward the information doesn't matter
- Stressing benefits may make the reader sound selfish
- The benefits are so obvious that to restate them insults the reader's intelligence

You do need reader benefits when

- You are presenting policies
- You want to shape readers' attitudes toward the information or toward your organization
- The benefits frame readers' motives positively
- The benefits may not be obvious to readers

Search engine DuckDuckGo emphasizes users' privacy as its primary benefit over Google.

Checkpoint

Organizing Informative and Positive Messages

1. Give any good news and summarize the main points.
2. Give details, clarification, background.
3. Present any negative elements—as positively as possible.
4. Explain any reader benefits.
5. Use a goodwill ending that's positive, personal, and forward-looking.

A Question of Ethics

LO4 Banks and credit card companies use the direct or good news organizational pattern to let consumers know that they have qualified for a credit card. The congratulations message at the beginning is often in 14-point or higher font; the interest rate on unpaid balances is stated in small print towards the end of the document. What ethical considerations might this organizational pattern and font size raise?

FIGURE 8.5   An Informative, Good News Memo with Benefits

Good news in subject line and first paragraph

Headings prepare the reader and provide good visual impact

Negatives presented as positively as possible

Goodwill ending and benefit for people not yet eligible to participate

Date: December 15, 2013
To: All Family Centre Therapy Employees
From: Sundra Owusu
Subject: New Tuition Reimbursement Program

SO

Starting February 1, full-time employees with more than three months of service can be reimbursed up to $2500 a year for tuition and fees for career-related courses.

These include

- courses related to your current position, including licence updating
- courses to prepare you for advancement at Family Therapy Centre
- courses required for a job-related degree program

You may take the courses at any level, from high school to graduate school.

Reimbursement

You'll receive reimbursement if you earn a C grade or better. If you are eligible for other financial aid (scholarships, grants) you will be reimbursed up to $2500 per calendar year for tuition and fees not covered by that aid.

Program Application

Please pick up an application form in the Human Resources office, fill it out, and have it signed by your supervisor. Return it to Human Resources at least two weeks before your classes start. Your application must be approved as part of the program requirements.

Details about the program and necessary documentation for reimbursement are attached to the program application.

Please note that the courses you choose do not have to relate to counselling and psychology. Management, interpersonal, teamwork, advanced computer courses: any of these would contribute to our collective productivity.

This program gives us the opportunity to build on our strengths as we help people face the challenges in their lives.

LO5 What's the Best Subject Line for an Informative or Positive Message?

The best subject line contains the basic information or good news.

A **subject line** should give readers a preview of your document. Good subject lines should

- Help in filing and retrieving the document
- Tell readers why they need to read the document, and
- Provide a framework or context for what you're about to say

Try composing the subject line **after** writing the message. Because you now know what you want to say, you can compose a subject line that sums up and previews the message content for the reader.

Subject lines are standard in memos, but not in letters (Module 6). However, since a subject line saves the reader's time (and builds the writer's credibility), many businesspeople consider a subject line in a letter to be very important. A good subject line meets three criteria: it is specific, concise, and appropriate to the kind of message (positive, negative, persuasive).

Making Subject Lines Specific

The subject line needs to be specific enough to differentiate that message from others on the same subject, but broad enough to cover everything in the message.

Too general:	Training Sessions
Better:	Technical Training Sessions Dates
Or:	Evaluation of Training Sessions on Conducting Interviews
Or:	Should We Schedule a Short Course on Proposal Writing?

Making Subject Lines Concise

Most subject lines are relatively short—usually no more than 10 words, often only three to seven words.[2]

Wordy:	Survey of Student Preferences in Regard to Various Pizza Factors
Better:	Student Pizza Preferences
Or:	The Feasibility of a Pizza Pizza Branch on Campus
Or:	What Students Like and Dislike About Pizza Pizza

If you can't make the subject line both specific and short, be specific.

Making Subject Lines Appropriate for the Pattern of Organization

In general, make sure that the subject line delivers the same message as that expressed in the first paragraph. When you have good news for the reader, build goodwill by **highlighting** it in the subject line. When your information is neutral, summarize it concisely for the subject line.

Subject: Discount on Rental Cars Effective January 2

Starting January 2, as an employee of Amalgamated Industries you can get a 15 percent discount on cars you rent for business or personal use from Roadway Rent-a-Car.

Subject: Update on Arrangements for Videoconference with Montreal

In the last month, we have chosen the participants and developed a tentative agenda for the videoconference with our Montreal office scheduled for March 21.

The checklist in Figure 8.6 summarizes the points to remember when writing informative and positive messages.

FIGURE 8.6   Checklist for Informative and Positive Messages

- ❏ In positive messages, does the subject line give the good news? Whether the message is positive or negative, is the subject line specific enough to differentiate this message from others on the same subject?
- ❏ Does the first paragraph summarize the information or good news? If the information is too complex to fit into a single paragraph, does the paragraph list the basic parts of the policy or information in the order in which the memo discusses them?
- ❏ Is all the information given in the message? (The information needed will vary depending on the message, but information about dates, places, times, and anything related to money usually needs to be included. When in doubt, ask!)
- ❏ In messages announcing policies, is there at least one reader benefit for each segment of the audience? Do all reader benefits seem likely to occur in this organization?
- ❏ Is each reader benefit developed, showing how the benefit will come from the policy and why the benefit matters to this organization? Do the benefits build on the job duties of people in this organization and on the specific circumstances of the organization?
- ❏ Does the message end with a positive paragraph—preferably one specific to the readers, not a general one that might fit any organization or policy?

Originality in a positive or informative message may come from

- ❏ Creating good headings, lists, and visual impact
- ❏ Developing reader benefits
- ❏ Thinking about readers and giving details that answer their questions and make it easier for them to understand and follow the policy

And, for all messages, not just informative and positive ones

- ❏ Does the message use you-attitude and positive emphasis?
- ❏ Is the style easy to read and friendly?
- ❏ Is the visual design of the message inviting?
- ❏ Is the format correct?
- ❏ Does the message use standard grammar? Is it free from typos?

LO6 How Can PAIBOC Analysis Help Me Write Informative and Positive Messages?

Ex. 8.1 8.4

PAIBOC analysis helps you identify a reader-centred organizational pattern and the information you should include.

Before you tackle the assignments for this module, examine the following problem. See how the PAIBOC questions probe the basic points required for a solution. Study the two sample solutions to see what makes one unacceptable and the other one good. Note the recommendations for revision that might make the good solution excellent.[3] The checklist in Figure 8.6 can help you evaluate a draft.

A PAIBOC Problem for Analysis

Employability Skills

CanWest Insurance's payments and billings system is computerized. Often there's a time lag between receiving a payment from a customer and recording it on the computer. Sometimes, while the payment is in line to be processed, the computer sends out additional notices: past-due notices, collection letters, even threats to sue. Customers are frightened or angry and write asking for an explanation. In most cases, if customers just waited a little longer, the situation would be straightened out. But policyholders are afraid that they'll be without insurance because the company thinks the bill has not been paid.

CanWest doesn't have the time to check every individual situation to see if the cheque did arrive and has been processed. It wants you to write a letter that will persuade customers to wait. If something is wrong and the payment never reaches CanWest, the company sends a legal notice to that effect, saying that the policy will be cancelled by a certain date (which the notice would specify) at least 30 days after the date on the original premium bill. Continuing customers always get this legal notice as a third chance (after the original bill and the past-due notice).

Prepare a form letter that can go out to every policyholder who claims to have paid a premium for automobile insurance and resents getting a past-due notice. The letter should reassure readers and build goodwill for CanWest.

The insurance business is highly competitive—other companies offer similar rates and policies. The customer might be able to get a similar policy for about the same money from someone else. Most people find that money is tight, so they want to keep insurance costs low. On the other hand, the fact that prices are steady or rising means that the value of what they own is higher—they need insurance more than ever.

Many insurance companies are refusing to renew policies (car, liability, malpractice insurance). These refusals to renew have received lots of publicity, and many people have heard horror stories about companies and individuals whose insurance has been cancelled or not renewed after a small number of claims. Readers don't feel very kindly toward insurance companies.

FIGURE 8.7   PAIBOC Analysis of the Problem

P	What are your **purposes** in writing or speaking?
	To reassure readers: they're covered for 30 days; to inform them they can assume everything is OK unless they receive a second notice; to avoid further correspondence on this subject; to build goodwill for CanWest: (a) we don't want to suggest CanWest is error-prone or too cheap to hire enough people to do the necessary work; (b) we don't want readers to switch companies; (c) we do want readers to buy from CanWest when they're ready for more insurance.
A	Who is your **audience**? How do the members of your audience differ from one another? What audience characteristics are relevant to this particular message?
	The audience is automobile insurance customers who say they've paid but still received a past-due notice. They're afraid they're no longer insured. Since it's a form letter, different readers will have different situations: in some cases payment arrived late, in some cases the company made a mistake, in some the reader never paid (cheque lost in mail, unsigned, bounced, etc.).
I	What **information** must your message include?
	Readers are still insured. We cannot say whether their cheques have now been processed (company doesn't want to check individual accounts). Their insurance will be cancelled only if they do not pay after receiving the second past-due notice (the legal notice).
B	What reasons or reader **benefits** can you use to support your position?
	Computers help us provide personal service to policyholders. We offer policies to meet all their needs. Both of these points would need specifics to be interesting and convincing.
O	What **objections** can you expect your readers to have? What negative elements of your message must you de-emphasize or overcome?
	Computers appear to cause errors. We don't know whether the cheques have been processed. We will cancel policies if their cheques don't arrive.
C	How will the **context** affect the reader's response? Think about your relationship to the reader, the morale in the organization, the economy, the time of year, and any special circumstances.
	Insurance is very expensive. In Canada, drivers are legally required to have car insurance. If their insurance policies are cancelled because of a computer error, drivers have a legitimate worry.

Discussion of the Sample Solutions

The solution in Figure 8.8 is unacceptable. The marginal comments show problem spots. Since this is a form letter, we cannot tell customers we have their cheques; in some cases, we may not. The letter is far too negative. The explanation in paragraph two makes CanWest look irresponsible and uncaring. Paragraph 3 is far too negative. Paragraph 4 is too vague; there are no reader benefits; the ending sounds selfish.

FIGURE 8.8   An Unacceptable Solution to the Sample Problem

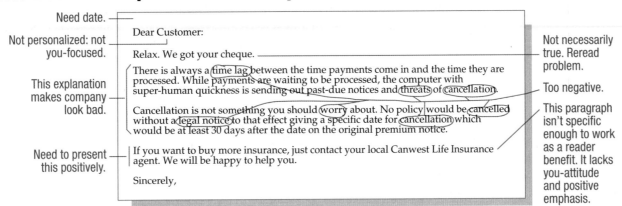

Need date.

Not personalized: not you-focused.

This explanation makes company look bad.

Need to present this positively.

Dear Customer:

Relax. We got your cheque. —

There is always a time lag between the time payments come in and the time they are processed. While payments are waiting to be processed, the computer with super-human quickness is sending out past-due notices and threats of cancellation.

Cancellation is not something you should worry about. No policy would be cancelled without a legal notice to that effect giving a specific date for cancellation which would be at least 30 days after the date on the original premium notice.

If you want to buy more insurance, just contact your local Canwest Life Insurance agent. We will be happy to help you.

Sincerely,

Not necessarily true. Reread problem.

Too negative.

This paragraph isn't specific enough to work as a reader benefit. It lacks you-attitude and positive emphasis.

A major weakness with the solution is that it lifts phrases straight out of the problem; the writer does not seem to have thought about the problem or about the words he or she is using. Measuring the draft against the answers to the questions for analysis suggests that this writer should start over.

The solution in Figure 8.9 is much better. The marginal comments show the letter's strong points. The message opens with the good news that is true for all readers. (Whenever possible, one should use the good-news pattern of organization.) Paragraph two explains CanWest's policy. It avoids assigning blame and ends on a positive note. The negative information is buried in paragraph three and is presented positively: the notice is information, not a threat; the 30-day extension is a grace period. Telling the reader what to do if a second notice arrives eliminates the need for a second exchange of letters. Paragraph four offers benefits for using computers, since some readers may blame the notice on computers, and offers benefits for being insured by CanWest. Paragraph five promotes other policies the company sells and prepares for the last paragraph.

FIGURE 8.9   A Good Solution to the Sample Problem

Need date

Good paragraph #1; true for all readers

Good to treat notice as information, tell reader what to do if it arrives

Benefits of using computers

Dear Amjit Sunder:

Re: Auto Insurance Policy ATP10004395

Your auto insurance is still in effect.

Past-due notices are mailed out if the payment has not been processed within three days after the due date. This may happen if a cheque is delayed in the mail or arrives without a signature or account number. When your cheque arrives with all the necessary information, it is promptly credited to your account.

Even if a cheque is lost in the mail and never reaches us, you still have a 30-day grace period. If you do get a second notice, you'll know that we still have not received your cheque. To keep your insurance in place, just stop payment on the first cheque and send a second one.

Computer processing of your account guarantees that you get any discounts you're eligible for: multicar, accident-free record, good student. If you have a claim, your agent uses computer tracking to find matching parts quickly, no matter what kind of car you drive. You get a cheque quickly—usually within three working days—without having to visit dealer after dealer for time-consuming estimates.

Today, your home and possessions are worth more than ever. You can protect them with Canwest Insurance's homeowners' and renters' policies. Let your local agent show you how easy it is to give yourself full protection. If you need a special rider to insure a personal computer, a coin or stamp collection, or a fine antique, you can get that from Canwest, too.

Whatever your insurance needs—auto, home, life, or health—one call to Canwest can do it all.

Sincerely,

Use computer to personalize. Put in name and address of a specific reader.

Good you-attitude

Good specifics

Acceptable ending

As the red circle indicates, this good solution might be improved by including the name and number of the local agent. Computers could make both of those insertions easily. This good letter can become an excellent letter by revising paragraph 4 to include more reader benefits. For instance, do computers help agents advise clients of the best policies for them? Does CanWest offer good service—quick, friendly, non-pressured—that might be emphasized? Are agents well trained? All these might yield ideas for additional reader benefits.

EXPANDING A CRITICAL SKILL

Writing a Goodwill Ending

Goodwill endings focus on establishing or building business relationships. When you write to one person, tailor the last paragraph to that person specifically. When you write to someone who represents an organization, the last paragraph can refer to your company's relationship with the reader's organization. When you write to a group (e.g., to "All Employees") your ending should apply to the whole group.

Possibilities include complimenting the reader for a job well done, describing a reader benefit, or looking forward to something positive that relates to the subject of the message. For example, consider possible endings for a response to an information query about tours of Wikwemikong Indian reserve on Manitoulin Island. The People of the Three Fires community offer group tours tailored to special interests.

Weak closing paragraph: Should you have any questions regarding this matter, please feel free to call me.

Goodwill ending: Upon request, the People of the Three Fires Tours can develop custom tours for educational institutions and corporate retreats. Please contact us at threefirestours@rogers.ca for further information.

Some writers end every message with a standard invitation:

If you have questions, please do not hesitate to ask.

This sentence lacks positive emphasis (Module 10). But saying "feel free to call"—though more positive—is rarely a good idea. Most of the time, the writer should omit the sentence. Don't make more work for yourself by inviting calls to clarify simple messages. And avoid clichés.

One of the reasons you write is to save the time needed to tell everyone individually. People in business aren't shrinking violets; they will call if they need help. Do make sure your phone number is in the letterhead or is typed below your name. You can also add your email address below your name.

MODULE SUMMARY

- You decide how to organize your message based on your purpose and audience analysis.
- Use PAIBOC analysis to identify what you want your message to achieve, how your audience will feel about your message, and what information you should include.
- If your audience will feel neutral or pleased about your message, use the direct or good news organizational pattern:
  1. Give the good news, and summarize the main points
  2. Give details
  3. Give any reader benefits
  4. End positively

- Use reader benefits in informative and positive messages when
  ○ You are presenting policies
  ○ You want to influence readers' attitudes toward the information or your organization
  ○ Stressing benefits presents readers' motives positively
  ○ Some of the benefits may not be obvious to readers
- For informative and positive documents, use a subject line that highlights the good news and/or concisely summarizes the information.

ASSIGNMENTS FOR MODULE 8

Questions for Critical Thinking

8.1 Why do even simple informative messages need to be persuasive? What persuasive elements can writers add?

8.2 What specific benefits would help to convince you to accept a new organizational policy that now charges you for something that was previously free (parking,

coffee, refreshments during meetings and training sessions)?

8.3 Would certain benefits appeal to some cultures and not to others? Give a specific example to prove your answer.

Exercises and Problems

8.4   Revising a Letter

Your colleague emails you the following draft letter asking for your feedback before she sends it:

Dear Ms. Hebbar:

I received your request to send a speaker to participate in "Career Day" at King Elementary School next month. I am pleased to be able to send Audrey Lindstrom to speak at your school about her job at the childcare centre.

Audrey has been working in the childcare centre for over five years. She trains contracted centre personnel on policies and procedures of the department.

Another commitment later that day will make it impossible for her to spend the whole day at your school. She will be happy to spend two hours with your class participating in the event.

Call Audrey to coordinate the time of the program, the expected content, and the age group of the audience.

Your students will see the importance of trained daycare providers in our neighbourhoods.

Thank you for asking our agency to be part of your school's special event. Our future lies in the hands of today's students.

Sincerely,

This draft definitely needs some work. It lacks you-attitude and positive emphasis, it isn't well organized, and it doesn't have enough details. "Ms. Lindstrom" would be more professional than "Audrey." And more information is needed. Exactly when should she show up? Will she be giving a speech (how long?), speaking as a member of a panel, or sitting at a table to answer questions? Will all grade levels be together, or will she be speaking to specific grades? Will all students hear each speaker, or will there be several concurrent speakers from which to choose?

As your instructor directs

a. Write an email to your colleague, explaining what revisions are necessary.

b. Revise the letter.

8.5 Responding to a Supervisor's Request

You've received this email from your supervisor. Answer the message, describing something that you or others in your unit do well.

> Subject: Need "Best Practices"
>
> Our organization is putting together something on "Best Practices" so that good ideas can be shared as widely as possible. Please describe something our unit does well—ideally something that could be copied by or at least applied to other units.
>
> Be specific. For example, don't just say "serve customers"—explain exactly what you do and how you do it to be effective. Anecdotes and examples would be helpful.
>
> Also, indicate whether a document, a videotape, or some other format would be the best way to share your practice. It may be possible to use more than one format, depending on the response.
>
> I need your answer ASAP so that I can send it on to my boss.

8.6 Accepting Suggestions

Your municipal government encourages money-saving suggestions to help balance the city budget. The suggestion committee, which you chair, has voted to adopt five suggestions:

1. Direct-deposit paycheques to save distribution and printing costs. Suggested by Poh-Kim Lee, in Recreation and Parks.
2. Buy supplies in bulk. Suggested by Jolene Zigmund, in Maintenance.
3. Charge nearby towns and suburbs a fee for sending their firefighters through the city fire academy. Suggested by Charles Boxell, in Fire Safety.
4. Set up an honour system for employees to reimburse the city for personal photocopies or phone calls. Suggested by Maria Echeverria, in Police.
5. Install lock boxes so meter readers don't have to turn off water valves when people move. This causes wear and tear, and broken valves must be dug up and replaced. Suggested by Travis Gratton, in Water Line Maintenance.

Each suggester gets $100. The Accounting Department will cut cheques the first of next month; cheques should reach people in interoffice mail a few days later.

As your instructor directs

a. Write to one of the suggesters, giving the good news.
b. Write to all employees, announcing the award winners.

8.7 Giving Good News

Write to a customer or client, to a vendor or supplier, or to your boss announcing good news. Possibilities include a product improvement, a price cut or special, an addition to your management team, a new contract.

8.8 Easing New Hires' Transition into Your Unit

Prepare an orientation document to help new hires adjust quickly to your unit. You may want to focus solely on work procedures; you may also want to discuss aspects of the corporate culture.

8.9 Announcing a Change in Group Life Insurance Rates

Your organization provides group life insurance to your salaried employees, worth 2.5 times the employee's annual salary. Hourly employees who worked 30 hours or more a week in the last year receive life insurance equal to what the person was paid in the last year. The premium that the organization pays has been considered taxable income. The exact value is listed on the pay stub in the box labelled "Employer-Paid Benefits." Now, the Ministry of Finance has announced a reduction in the rates used to calculate the taxable value of this employer-provided life insurance. As a result, the value of the insurance will be slightly lower, and all the taxes based on pay will be slightly lower: federal, provincial, city, provincial hospitalization insurance, and school district taxes. These changes will be effective in the paycheque issued at the end of this month for employees paid monthly and in the paycheque issued 10 days from now for employees paid biweekly.

Write a memo to all employees explaining the change.

8.10 Introducing a Wellness Program

Your company has decided to launch a wellness program in an effort to get employees to adopt healthier lifestyles. Studies show that people who smoke, who are moderate or heavy drinkers, who are overweight, and who do not exercise regularly have higher rates of absence due to illness. They visit doctors more often, need more prescription drugs, and are hospitalized more often and for longer periods.

You'll give a $100 rebate (annually) to each employee who doesn't smoke or use chewing tobacco. Employees who don't drink to excess (more than an average of 170 millilitres of beer, 85 of wine, or 42 of hard liquor a day) and who don't use illegal drugs can also get $100, as can those whose cholesterol isn't over 150. Employees who exercise at least 30 minutes a day, three times a week, will get rebates of $50. Exercise doesn't have to be difficult: walking and gardening count. Another rebate of $50 is available for a waist-to-hip ratio under 0.8 for women or 0.95 for men.

As part of the wellness program, the company cafeteria will focus on serving healthier foods and the company will offer twice-yearly health fairs with free routine immunizations and flu shots for employees and dependants. These parts of the program will begin next month.

Write to all employees informing them about the wellness program.

Hints:

- Choose an organization you know something about to use for this message.
- If the organization saves money through reduced absenteeism, will employees benefit?
- Why don't people already follow healthy practices? What can you do to overcome these objections?
- Saving money may not motivate everyone. Offer intrinsic benefits as well.
- Use the analysis that you developed for Exercise 2.6 in Module 2.

8.11 Explaining Packing Material

Your organization ships thousands of boxes to fill orders from catalogues and from your website. To cushion items, you fill the empty spaces around the items with plastic "popcorn." Some customers have written to complain about the plastic, which is not biodegradable. Some have asked you to use real popcorn, paper, or starch (which will degrade when wet). However, these materials do not cushion as well as plastic does (so more items are damaged during shipment) and weigh more (so shipping costs are higher). In addition, popcorn is subject to Canadian Food Inspection Agency regulations, which you do not want to monitor; paper fill creates dust and thus is a health hazard for packers; and starch doesn't work in very humid or very dry climates. You want to use one packing material for all boxes, wherever they are going.

Customers could save and reuse the plastic packaging material. If they can't reuse it, they may be able to recycle it. They can call their local solid waste department to find out. Or they could check The Internet Consumer Recycling Guide at www.obviously.com/recycle/guides/hard.html.

As your instructor directs

   a. Write to one customer who has complained showing why you are continuing to use plastic fill.

   b. Prepare a one-page insert to be included in every package, explaining your decision about packaging.

8.12 Reminding Guests About the Time Change

Twice a year the switch to and from daylight saving time affects people in Canada. The time change can be disruptive for hotel guests, who may lose track of the date, forget to change the clocks in their rooms, and miss appointments as a result.

Prepare a form letter to leave in each hotel room reminding guests of the impending time change. What should guests do?

Write the letter.

Hints:

- Use an attention-getting page layout so readers don't ignore the message.
- Pick a specific hotel or motel chain you know something about.
- Use the message to build goodwill for your hotel or motel chain. Use specific references to services or features the hotel offers, focusing not on what the hotel does for the reader, but on what the reader can do at the hotel.

8.13 Confirming a Reservation

You work in reservations at Basin Hot Springs Lodge in Banff National Park. Most travellers phone 13 months in advance to reserve a room and once you process the credit card payment for the first night you write to them to confirm the reservation.

The confirmation contains the amount charged to the credit card, the date on which the reservation was made, the confirmation number, the kind of room (Lakefront Retreat or Mountainview Retreat), and the dates the guest will be arriving and leaving.

In addition, the letter needs to give several pieces of general information. The amount of the deposit and the amount quoted per night are the rates for the current calendar year. However, room rates change annually; in general, rates increase by about 4 to 5 percent, per year. Guests need to know that they will pay the new rate for each additional night after the first night.

Anyone who wants a refund must cancel the reservation in writing four days before the scheduled arrival date. Cancellations may be faxed: the fax number is on the letterhead the letter will be printed on.

Parking is limited. People who bring big motor homes, boats, or camp trailers may have to park in the main parking area rather than right by their cabins.

All the rooms are cabin style with three to four rooms in each building. There are no rooms in a main lodge. People will need to walk from their cabins to the restaurants, unless they do their own cooking.

Both Lakefront and Mountainview Retreats have kitchenettes with microwaves, but guests have to bring their own cooking utensils, dishes, supplies, and food. The bedroom area (with a king-size bed in the Lakefront Retreats and a queen-size bed in the Mountainview Retreats) has a sliding divider that can separate it from the sitting area, which has a sofa bed.

Since the deposit pays for the first night, the room will be held regardless of the time of arrival. Check-in time is 3 p.m.; earlier room availability cannot be guaranteed. Checkout time is 11 a.m.

All cabins are non-smoking. Smoking is permitted on the decks of the Lakefront Retreats or the porches of the Mountainview Retreats.

The guest should present the confirmation letter when checking in.

As your instructor directs

a. Write a form letter that can be used for one type of room (either Lakefront or Mountainview Retreat). Indicate with square brackets material that would need to be filled in for each guest: for instance, arriving [date of arrival] and departing [date of departure].

b. Write a letter to Stephanie Lafleur, who has reserved a Lakefront Retreat room arriving September 18 and departing September 20. Her credit card is being billed for $183.75 ($175 plus GST). Her address is 3122 Rue Laurier, Quebec City, QC, G1R 3M7.

8.14 Lining Up a Consultant to Teach Short Courses in Presentations

As director of education and training, you oversee all in-house training programs. Five weeks ago, Runata Hartley, vice-president of human resources, asked you to set up a training course on oral presentations. After making some phone calls, you tracked down Brian Barreau, a professor of communications at a nearby college.

"Yes, I do short courses on oral presentations," he told you on the phone. "I would want at least a day and a half with participants—two full days would be better. They need time to practise the skills they'll be learning. I'm free Thursdays and Fridays.

"I'm willing to work with up to 20 people at a time. Tell me what kind of presentations they make, whether they use PowerPoint, and what kinds of things you want me to emphasize. I'll need a digital video camera to record each

participant's presentations and a DVD for each person. My fee is $3,500 a day."

You told him you thought a two-day session would be feasible, but you'd have to get back to him after you got budget approval. You wrote a quick memo to Runata explaining the situation and asking about what the session should cover.

Two weeks ago, you received this memo:

> I've asked for budget approval of $7,000 for a two-day session plus no more than $500 for all expenses. I don't think there will be a problem.
>
> We need some of the basics: how to plan a presentation, how to deal with nervousness. Adapting to the audience is a big issue: our people give presentations to varied audiences with very different levels of technical knowledge and interest. Most of our people have PowerPoint on their computers, but the slide shows I've seen have been pretty amateurish.
>
> I don't want someone to lecture. We need practical exercises that can help us practise skills that we can put into effect immediately.
>
> Attached is a list of 18 people who can attend a session Thursday and Friday of the second week of next month. Note that we've got a good mix of people. If the session goes well, I may want you to schedule additional sessions.

Today, you got approval from the vice-president to schedule the session, pay Professor Barreau's fee, and reimburse him for expenses to a maximum of $500. He will have to keep all receipts and turn in an itemized list of expenses to be reimbursed; you cannot reimburse him if he does not have receipts.

You also need to explain the mechanics of the session. You'll meet in the conference room, which has a screen and flip charts. You have an overhead projector, a laptop, a digital video camera, and a monitor, but you need to reserve these if he wants to use them. Will he bring his own laptop computer, or does he want you to provide the computer?

Write to Professor Barreau. You don't have to persuade him to come since he's already informally agreed, but you do want him to look forward to the job and to do his best work.

Hints:

- Choose an organization you know something about.
- What audiences do people speak to? How formal are these talks? What are their purposes?
- Is this session designed to hone the skills of people who are competent or is it designed to help people who are very weak, perhaps even paralyzed with fright?
- What role do presentations play in the success of the organization and of individuals in it?
- Check the calendar to get the dates. If there's any ambiguity about what "the second week of next month" is, call Runata to check.

8.15 Answering an International Inquiry

Your business, government, or non-profit organization has received the following inquiries from international correspondents. (You choose the country the inquiry originated from.)

1. Please tell us about a new product, service, or trend so that we can decide whether we want to buy, license, or imitate it in our country.
2. We have heard about a problem (technical, social, political, or ethical) that occurred in your organization. Please tell us what really happened, and estimate how likely it is to affect the long-term success of the organization.
3. Please tell us about college or university programs in this field. We are interested in sending some of our managers to your country to complete a degree.
4. We are considering setting up a plant in your city. We have already received adequate business information. However, we would also like to know how comfortable our nationals would feel. Do people in your city speak our language? How many? What opportunities exist for our nationals to improve their English? Does your town already have people from a wide mix of nations? Which are the largest groups?
5. Our organization would like to subscribe to an English-language trade journal. Which one would you recommend? Why? How much does it cost? How can we order it?

As your instructor directs

a. Answer one or more of the inquiries. Assume that your reader either reads English or can have your message translated.
b. Write a memo to your instructor explaining how you've adapted the message for your audience.

Hints:

- Even though you can write in English, English may not be your reader's native language. Write a letter that can be translated easily.
- In some cases, you may need to spell out background information that might not be clear to someone from another country.

8.16 Writing a Thank-You Message

Write a thank-you message to someone who has helped you achieve your goals.

As your instructor directs

a. Turn in a copy of the letter.
b. Mail the letter to the person who helped you.
c. Write a memo to your instructor explaining the choices you made in writing the thank-you letter.

8.17 Evaluating Web Pages

Today you received this email from your boss:

> Subject: Evaluating Our Web Page
>
> Our CEO wants to know how our Web page compares to those of our competitors. I'd like you to do this in two steps. First, send me a list of your criteria. Then give me an evaluation of two of our competitors' pages and of our own pages. I'll combine your memo with others on other Web pages to put together a comprehensive evaluation for the next executive meeting.

As your instructor directs

a. List the generic criteria for evaluating a Web page. Think about the various audiences for the page and the content that will keep them coming back, page organization and navigation, the visual design, and details such as a creation or update date.
b. List criteria for pages of specific kinds of organizations. For example, a non-profit organization might want information for potential and current donors, volunteers, and clients. A financial institution might want to project an image of both trustworthiness and optimism.
c. Evaluate three Web pages of similar organizations. Which is best? Why?

Hint:

- Review the information on Web page design in Module 5.

8.18 Creating a Human Resources Web Page

As firms attempt to help employees balance work and family life (and as employers become aware that personal and family stresses affect performance at work), human resource departments sponsor an array of programs and provide information on myriad subjects. However, some people might be uncomfortable asking for help, either because the problem is embarrassing (who wants to admit needing help to deal with drug or spousal abuse, or addiction to gambling?) or because they feel that focusing on non-work issues (e.g., childcare) might lead others to think they aren't serious about their jobs. The Internet allows organizations to post information that employees can access privately—even from home.

Create a Web page that could be posted by human resources to help employees with one of the challenges they face. Possible topics include

- Appreciating an ethnic heritage
- Buying a house

- Caring for dependants: childcare, helping a child learn to read, living with teenagers, elder care, and so forth
- Dealing with a health issue: exercising, having a healthy diet, and so on
- Dealing with an environmental situation: energy prices, conserving resources, recycling and/or reusing items
- Dealing with a health problem: alcoholism, cancer, diabetes, heart disease, obesity, and so on
- Dressing for success or dressing for casual days
- Managing finances: basic budgeting, deciding how much to save, choosing investments, and so on
- Nourishing the spirit: meditation, religion, mindfulness
- Planning for retirement
- Planning vacations
- Reducing stress
- Resolving conflicts on the job or in families

Assume that this page can be accessed from another of the organization's pages. Offer at least seven links. (More are better.) You may offer information as well as links to other pages with information. At the top of the page, offer an overview of what the page covers. At the bottom of the page, put the creation and update date and your name and email address.

As your instructor directs

a. Turn in two printed copies of your page(s). On another page, give the URLs for each link.

b. Turn in one printed copy of your page(s) and a disk with the HTML code and gif files.

c. Write a memo to your instructor identifying the audience for which the page is designed and explaining (1) how you found material on this topic, (2) why you chose the pages and information you've included, and (3) why you chose the layout and graphics you've used.

d. Present your page orally to the class.

Hints:

- Pick a topic you know something about.
- Realize that audience members will have different needs. You could explain the basics of choosing daycare or stocks, but don't recommend a specific daycare centre or a specific stock.
- If you have more than nine links, chunk them in small groups under headings.
- Create a good image of the organization.
- Review the information on Web page design in Module 5.

POLISHING YOUR PROSE

Applying Parallel Structure

Use parallel structure in lists, headings, and subheadings by using the same grammatical form for ideas that have the same relationship in your sentence.

Not parallel: Good reports are factual, logical, and demonstrate clarity.

It may be easier to see faulty parallelism by listing parts that need to be parallel. Check to make sure each component fits with the words that introduce the list.

Not parallel: Good reports are

    Factual

    Logical

    Demonstrate clarity

Parallel: Good reports are

    Factual

    Logical

    Clear

Make sure the entire list is horizontal or vertical. Don't start a list horizontally and finish it vertically.

Incorrect: As department manager, I supervised eight employees.

- Wrote the department budget
- Presented our sales strategy to the board of directors

Correct: As department manager, I supervised eight employees, wrote the department budget, and presented our sales strategy to the board of directors.

Also correct: As department manager, I

- Supervised eight employees
- Wrote the department budget
- Presented our sales strategy to the board of directors

Headings have to be parallel throughout the document, but subheads need only be parallel to other subheads in the same section.

Not parallel: Should Ogden Industries Purchase Blue Chip International in 2013?

- Short-Term Costs

- What Are the Long-Term Gains?

Parallel: Should Ogden Industries Purchase Blue Chip International in 2013?

- Short-Term Costs

- Long-Term Gains

In addition to grammatical parallelism, also check your sentences for logical parallelism.

Incorrect: The group ranges from males and females to people in their 20s, 30s, and 40s.

Better: We interviewed men and women ranging in age from 20 to 50.

Gender is one category; age is another.

Exercises

Rewrite the following sentences or headings to make them parallel.

1. Last week, Alain and Rochelle flew to Toronto, Montreal, Quebec City, and the capital of the province of Nova Scotia.
2. Ask Ms. Liken, Mr. Fitzgerald, Bill Anderson, and Professor Timmons to join us for the meeting.
3. To ship a package

   1. Fill out an address form.
   2. Specify on the form how the package should be sent.
   3. If you want to send a package by overnight mail, your supervisor must initial the appropriate box on the address form.

4. Make sure benefits announcements are routed to managers, supervisors, and the folks in the Human Resources Department.
5. Appointments can be scheduled in 5-minute, 10-minute, quarter-hour, or 20-minute intervals.
6. The project's fixed costs include material, salaries, advertising, bonus packages for anyone who goes above and beyond the call of duty, and the cost of travel to different cities.
7. This report discusses Why We Should Upgrade Capital Equipment, Why We Should Increase Staff by 25 percent, The Benefits of Decreasing Employee Turnover, and The Importance of Identifying New Product Markets.
8. The selection committee reviews each job applicant based on education, experience, extracurricular activities, the awards the employee has received, and the strength of the applicant's personal statement.
9. Use the telephone to answer customer questions, email to send order confirmations, and take orders using our Web page.
10. Each agency should estimate Annual Costs, Costs per Month, Salaries, New Equipment Costs, and How Much You Need in a Reserve Fund for Unexpected Expenses.

Check the Answer Key for odd-numbered exercises.

McGraw Hill **connect**

MODULE
9

Composing Negative Messages

MODULE OUTLINE

- What kinds of negative messages am I likely to write?
- How should I organize negative messages?
- What's the best subject line for a negative message?
- How can PAIBOC help me write negative messages?

Module Summary

Assignments for Module 9

Polishing Your Prose: Finding Your Narrative Voice

Learning Objectives

After reading and applying the information in Module 9, you'll be able to demonstrate

Knowledge of

LO1 The criteria that define negative messages

LO2 The "bad news" message structure

LO3 The legal and ethical implications of your messages

Skills to

LO4 Organize negative messages

LO5 Give bad news while retaining goodwill

LO6 Write common kinds of negative messages

LO7 Further analyze business communication situations

Employability Skills

Employability Skills 2000+ Checklist

Module content builds these Conference Board of Canada Employability Skills 2000+

Communicate

Think and Solve Problems

Manage Information

Work with Others

Use Numbers

LO1 Negative or bad news messages contain information that will cost the reader comfort, time, money, esteem, or resources. Few people like to give bad news—and fewer still like to get it. However, negative messages are common in business. How we present negatives, and what we write or say can affect how audiences respond to our messages, and how they see our organization and us.

Negative or "bad news" messages have both primary and secondary purposes:

Primary purposes

- To give the reader the bad news, and have the reader read, understand, and accept the message
- To maintain as much goodwill as possible

Secondary purposes

Although readers may be unhappy with the news, we still want readers to feel several positive things:

- They have been taken seriously
- Your decision is fair and reasonable
- If they were in your shoes, they would make the same decision

Therefore, our messages should also serve

- To build a good image of the writer
- To build a good image of the writer's organization
- To reduce or eliminate future correspondence on the same subject so the message doesn't create more work for the writer

LO6 What Kinds of Negative Messages Am I Likely to Write?

You will likely write rejections and refusals, announcements of policy changes that do not appear to benefit readers, requests that readers will see as bothersome, insulting, or intrusive, and messages that focus on problems.

Rejections and Refusals

Ex. 9.4 9.7

When you refuse requests, try to use a buffer. Give an alternative if one is available. For example, if you are denying credit, it might still be possible for the reader to put an item on layaway.

Politeness and length help. An experiment using a denial of additional insurance found that subjects preferred a rejection letter that was longer, more tactful, and more personal. The preferred letter started with a buffer, used a good reason for the refusal, and offered a sales promotion in the last paragraph.[1]

Since many Canadians, especially those of high-context cultures (Module 3), value courtesy, they prefer this organizational pattern.[2]

When you refuse requests within your organization, use your knowledge of the culture and of the specific individual to craft your message. In some organizations, it may be appropriate to use company slogans, offer whatever help established departments can give, and refer to the individual's good work. In less personal organizations, a simple negative without embellishment might be more appropriate.

LO2 LO4 How Should I Organize Negative Messages?

It depends on your purposes and audiences.

Use PAIBOC analysis (and **Maslow's hierarchy of needs**, Module 11) to identify your audience's needs. Whether saying no to a request, notifying a client about a price increase, or emailing colleagues about extra work they must do, you want to give the necessary information

FIGURE 9.1   **A Refusal with Alternative**

AlbertaFilmInstitute

8th floor Commerce Place 10155 102 Street Edmonton AB T5J 4L6
T: 780.415.0200 F. 780.415.0201 E. stephanblackbird@gov.ab.ca

November 22, 2013

Mr. Marco Novelli
319 Sweetwater Bay
Winnipeg, MB R2J 3G4

Dear Mr. Novelli:
Subject: Submission, Original Screenplay *Doubtful*

Buffer: Beginning clause — Although your script is highly original and well crafted, we have found that film noir — **Explanation** themes do not attract a large box office. Therefore we cannot use your story for next — **Refusal** year's festival.

With your permission, however, we would like to send your treatment on to Jessie Prynne, chair of the Alberta Arts Foundation. Foundation members are always looking — **Alternative** for original works to present.

If this is agreeable to you, please let me know by email, letter, or phone.

Meanwhile, please keep writing, and please continue to send us your work. — **Positive, forward-looking ending**

Sincerely,

Stephan Blackbird

Stephan Blackbird
Script Supervisor

while maintaining goodwill. Otherwise, you'll waste time and money in lost customers and disruptive work relationships.

Choose your pattern of organization based on the situation.

LO5 • Letters to people outside your organization should be indirect to build goodwill.
• When you write to supervisors, propose solutions when you report a problem.
• When you write to peers and subordinates, ask for their input in dealing with negative situations.

Giving Bad News to Customers and Other People Outside Your Organization

The following pattern helps writers maintain goodwill:

1. *Start with a neutral statement or buffer.* These opening statements are meant to prepare readers for news that they are not going to like. Whether writing or speaking, the best buffers begin with areas that both you and your audience can agree on. Buffer statements such as "Thank you for your letter," in response to a complaint or query, acknowledge that you have read, understood, and are responding to your reader's concern.

FIGURE 9.2   **A Claim Letter**

Nature's Lifesource Inc
111 Pleasant Street
Stephan, NB E3L 1B4

May 8, 2013

Alyssa Scarangella
72 Rue Windermere
Montreal, PQ H9A 2C4

Dear Alyssa Scarangella:
Subject: **Shipments # 3101-3105 inclusive**

Buffer: Neutral statement — Thank you for the information you provided yesterday.

Explanation: Reasons — As we discussed, the last three shipments have arrived with product damage. Both our transportation service suppliers and warehouse personnel have expressed concerns about the security of the loading. The quality of the pallets supporting the products and of the equipment fastenings could lead to load shifts, creating dangerous highway conditions.

Explanation: Proof — As you requested, I am enclosing photographs of the damage to shipments # 3103, 3104, and 3105. These photographs show the condition of the pallets and the manner in which the load was secured. Since our research indicates that these two factors led to the damage, I would appreciate your help in recouping our costs for the damaged products. — **Bad News: Reimbursement owed**

Positive ending — Thank you for your assurance that the quality of the pallets and the fastenings of all future shipments will provide a safe, secure load.

When you have reviewed the photographs, please let me know what additional information you will need.

Sincerely,

Leovee Yang

Leovee Yang

Enclosure

2. *Give the reason for the refusal before the refusal itself* when you have a reason that readers will understand and accept. A good reason prepares the reader to expect the refusal.

3. *Give the negative just once, clearly.* Inconspicuous refusals can be missed, making it necessary to say no a second time.

4. *Always present an alternative or compromise, if one is available.* An alternative gives readers another way to get what they want; it also suggests that you care about the readers and want to help them solve their problems.

5. *End with a positive, forward-looking statement.*

Figure 9.1, on page 142, includes the buffer, the reason, and the refusal in the first paragraph. Figure 9.2, a message asking for costs due to the shipper's negligence, follows the bad news pattern: buffer + rationale + the bad news + friendly close.

LO5 The Buffer

A **buffer** is a neutral or positive statement that allows you to delay the negative. You'll want to begin messages with a neutral statement or buffer when the reader (individually or culturally) values harmony, or when the buffer serves another purpose. For example, when you have to thank the reader somewhere in the letter, putting the thank-you in the first paragraph allows you to start on a positive note.

To be effective, a buffer must put the reader in a good frame of mind—not give the bad news but not imply a positive answer either—and provide a natural transition to the body of the letter. The kinds of statements most often used as buffers are good news, facts, and chronologies of events, references to enclosures, thanks, and statements of principle, as the examples below illustrate.

1. Start with any good news or positive elements the letter contains.

> Starting Thursday, June 26, you'll have access to your money 24 hours a day at TD Canada Trust.

Letter announcing that the drive-up windows will be closed for two days while new automatic teller machines are installed

2. State a fact or provide a chronology of events.

> A new, graduated dues schedule, determined by delegate assembly vote last December, has been endorsed by the executive council. Members are now asked to establish their own dues rate and to calculate the total amount of their remittance.

Announcement of a new dues structure that will raise most members' dues

3. Refer to enclosures in the letter.

> Enclosed is a new sticker for your car. You may pick up additional ones in the office if needed. Please destroy old stickers bearing the signature of "L. S. LaVoie."

Letter announcing an increase in parking rental rates

4. Thank the reader for something he or she has done.

> Thank you for scheduling appointments for me with so many senior people at the Bank of Montreal. My visit there March 14 was very informative.

Letter refusing a job offer

5. State a general principle.

> Good drivers should pay substantially less for their auto insurance. The Good Driver Plan was created to reward good drivers (those with five-year accident-free records) with our lowest available rates. A change in the plan, effective January 1, will help keep those rates low.

Letter announcing that the company will now count traffic tickets, not just accidents, in calculating insurance rates—a change that will raise many people's premiums

FIGURE 9.3   How to Organize a Negative Message

> Buffer
>
> Explanation
>
> Negative
>
> Alternative
>
> Goodwill Ending

Buffers are hard to write. Even if you think the reader would prefer to be let down easily, use a buffer only when you can write a good one.

It's better *not* to use a buffer (1) if the reader might ignore a letter with a bland first paragraph, (2) if the reader or the organization prefers "bottom-line-first messages," (3) if the reader is suspicious of the writer, or (4) if the reader "won't take no for an answer."

Checkpoint

To be effective, a **buffer** has to put the reader in a good frame of mind, not give the bad news but not imply a positive answer either, and provide a natural transition to the body of the letter.

LO5 Reasons

Make the reason for the refusal clear and convincing in terms of the audience's needs and wants (Modules 3 and 11). The following reason is inadequate.

Weak reason: The goal of the ValuDrug CHARGE-ALL Centre is to provide our customers with faster, more personalized service. Since you now live outside the Halifax ValuDrug CHARGE-ALL service area, we can no longer offer you the advantages of a local CHARGE-ALL Centre.

If the reader says, "I don't care if my bills are slow and impersonal," will the company let the reader keep the card? No. The real reason for the negative is that the drugstore's franchise allows it to have cardholders only in a given geographical region.

Better reason: Each local CHARGE-ALL Centre offers accounts to customers in a specific regional area. The Nova Scotia ValuDrug CHARGE-ALL Centre serves customers east of Quebec. Your current card is good until it expires. When that happens, please open an account with a CHARGE-ALL Centre that serves Quebec.

Don't hide behind "company policy": readers will assume the policy is designed to benefit you at their expense. If possible, show how the readers benefit from the policy. If they do not benefit, don't mention policy.

Weak reason: I cannot write an insurance policy for you because company policy does not allow me to do so.

Better reason: General Insurance insures cars only when they are normally garaged at night. Standard insurance policies cover a wider variety of risks and charge higher fees. Limiting policies gives General's customers the lowest possible rates for auto insurance.

Avoid saying that you *cannot* do something. Most negative messages exist because the writer or company has chosen certain policies or cut-off points. In the example above, the company could choose to insure a wider variety of customers if it wanted to do so.

Often you will enforce policies that you did not design. Don't pass the buck by saying, "This is a terrible policy." Carelessly criticizing your superiors is never a good idea. If you really think a policy is bad, try to persuade your superiors to change it. If you can't think of convincing reasons to change the policy, maybe it isn't so bad after all.

If you have several reasons for saying no, use only those that are strong and watertight. If you give five reasons and readers dismiss two of them, readers may feel that they've won and should get the request.

> **Weak reason:**   You cannot store large bulky items in the dormitory over the summer: moving them into and out of storage would tie up the stairs and the elevators right at the busiest times when people are moving in and out.

> **Way to dismiss the reason:**   We'll move large items before or after the two days when most people are moving in or out.

If you do not have a good reason, omit the reason rather than use a weak one. Even if you have a strong reason, omit it if it reflects poorly on your organization.

> **Reason that reflects poorly on company:**   Our company is not hiring now because profits are down. In fact, the downturn has prompted top management to reduce the salaried staff by 5 percent just this month, with perhaps more reductions to come.

> **Better:**   Our company does not have any openings now.

Checkpoint

Organizing Negative Letters to Customers

1. Provide a buffer, if possible.
2. Give the reason for the refusal before the refusal itself when you have a reason that readers will understand and accept.
3. Give the negative just once, clearly.
4. Present an alternative or compromise, if one is available.
5. End with a positive, forward-looking statement.

Refusals

De-emphasize the refusal by putting it in the same paragraph as the reason, rather than in a paragraph by itself. Sometimes you may be able to imply the refusal rather than stating it directly.

> **Direct refusal:**   You cannot get insurance for just one month.

> **Implied refusal:**   The shortest term for an insurance policy is six months.

Be sure that the implication is clear. Any message can be misunderstood, but an optimistic or desperate reader is particularly likely to misunderstand a negative message. One of your purposes in a negative message is to close the door on the subject. You do not want to have to write a second letter saying that the real answer is no.

Ex.
9.7
9.10–
9.12

Alternatives

Employability Skills

Giving the reader an alternative or a compromise, if one is available, does several things:

- It offers the reader another way to get what he or she wants.
- It suggests that you really care about the reader, and about meeting his or her needs.

- It enables the reader to re-establish the psychological freedom you limited when you said no.
- It allows you to end on a positive note and to present yourself and your organization as positive, friendly, and helpful.

Psychological reactance in action.

When you give an alternative, give readers all the information they need to act on it, but let readers decide whether to try the alternative.

Negative messages limit the reader's freedom. People may respond to a limitation of freedom by asserting their freedom in some other arena. University of Kansas psychology professor Jack W. Brehm calls this phenomenon **psychological reactance**.[3] Psychological reactance is at work when a customer who has been denied credit no longer buys even on a cash basis, or a subordinate who has been passed over for a promotion gets back at the company by deliberately doing a poor job.

An alternative allows the reader to react in a way that doesn't hurt you. By letting readers decide for themselves whether they want the alternative, you allow them to re-establish their sense of psychological freedom.

The specific alternative will vary depending on the circumstances. In Figure 9.1, the script supervisor of the Alberta Film Institute refuses to accept *Doubtful*, but tells the screenwriter he is sending his script on to someone who might use it.

LO3 EXPANDING A CRITICAL SKILL

Thinking About the Legal and Ethical Implications of What You Say

Any message that is recorded—on paper (even a napkin), on a disk or hard drive, on a cell phone, or in voicemail—can be used in a legal case, as former CIBC employees found to their chagrin after discovering that messages sent from their BlackBerries were not totally confidential. Even an erased electronic message can be recovered by experts. In any message you write, however informal or hurried, you need to be sure to say exactly what you mean. The Supreme Court of Canada and provincial defamation legislation protect individuals' dignity, right to privacy, and reputation. Libel and slander liability can include everyone who participates in disseminating injurious material.

Thinking about the legal implications of what you say is particularly important in negative messages. In an effort to cushion bad news, writers sometimes give reasons that create legal liabilities. For example, as Elizabeth McCord has shown, the statement that a plant is "too noisy and dangerous" for a group tour could be used as evidence against the company in a worker's compensation claim. In another case, a writer telling a job candidate that the firm had hired someone else said that he thought she was the best candidate. She sued and won.

Although you may choose the direct or indirect bad news pattern—depending on your audience's expectations—you also need to think about the ethical implications of your messages. People prefer to do business with someone they trust; therefore, it's good business to deliver negative messages honestly and sensitively.

Acting ethically means acting out of enlightened self-interest: treating others as you want to be treated. You need to assume your audience's point of view to figure out what to say—or not to say. Think about how a reasonable person might interpret your words. If that interpretation isn't what you mean, revise the passage so that it says what you mean, in a way you would find acceptable.

Sources: Sinclair Stewart and Richard Bloom (7 July 2005), BlackBerry battle chills Bay St. gossips, *Globe and Mail*, www.blackberryforums.com/blackberry-news/2169-2005-01-07-blackberry-battle-chills-bay-st-gossips.html; Javad Heydary (26 May 2005), Is your boss monitoring your BlackBerry? *E-Commerce Times*, www.ecommercetimes.com/story/43376.html; Elizabeth A. McCord (1991), The business writer, the law, and routine business communication: A legal and rhetorical analysis, *Journal of Business and Technical Communication* 5(2), 173–199.

Endings

If you have a good alternative, refer to it in your ending: "We are offering 10% off all treatments in March."

The best endings look to the future, as in this example of refusing to continue a charge account for a customer who has moved:

> Wherever you have your account, you'll continue to get all the service you've learned to expect from CHARGE-ALL and the convenience of charging items at more than a thousand ValuDrugs stores in Canada—and in Halifax, too, whenever you come back to visit!

To maintain goodwill and retain a positive business relationship, end sincerely:

> Please call me at 403-555-7700 if you need further clarification.

Avoid endings that seem insincere or clichéd:

> We are happy to have been of service, and should we be able to assist you in the future, please do not hesitate to contact us.

This ending lacks you-attitude and would not be good even in a positive message. In a situation where the company has just refused to help, it sounds sarcastic.

Giving Bad News to Superiors

Your superior expects you to solve minor problems by yourself. But sometimes, solving a problem requires more authority or resources than you have. When you give bad news to a superior, try to recommend a way to deal with the problem. Turn the negative message into a persuasive one.

1. *Describe the problem.* Say what's wrong, clearly and unemotionally.
2. *Tell how it happened.* Provide the background. What underlying factors led to this specific problem?
3. *Describe the options for fixing it.* If one option is clearly best, you may need to discuss only one. But if the reader will think of other options, or if different people will judge the options differently, describe all the options, giving their advantages and disadvantages.
4. *Recommend a solution and ask for action.* Ask for approval so that you can go ahead to make the necessary changes to fix the problem.

> ### Checkpoint
>
> **Organizing Bad News to Superiors**
> 1. Describe the problem
> 2. Tell how it happened
> 3. Describe the options for fixing it
> 4. Recommend a solution and ask for action

Giving Bad News to Peers and Subordinates

When giving serious bad news to peers and subordinates, use a variation of the pattern to superiors:

1. *Describe the problem.* Say what's wrong, clearly and unemotionally.
2. *Present an alternative or compromise, if one is available.* An alternative gives readers another way to get what they want and suggests that you care about the readers and want to help them meet their needs.
3. *If possible, ask for input or action.* People in the audience may be able to suggest solutions. And workers who help make a decision are far more likely to accept the consequences.

When the bad news is less serious, as in Figure 9.4, use the bad news organizational pattern (buffer, explanation, bad news, positive ending) unless your knowledge of the reader suggests that another pattern will be more effective.

Whatever the medium, the context of communication is crucial. The reader's reaction is influenced by the answers to these questions:

- Do you and the reader have a good relationship?
- Does the organization treat people well?
- Have readers been warned of possible negatives?
- Have readers "bought into" the criteria for the decision?
- Do communications following the negative build goodwill?

Checkpoint

Organizing Bad News to Peers and Subordinates

1. Describe the problem
2. Present an alternative or compromise, if one is available
3. If possible, ask for input or action

LO4 LO5 What's the Best Subject Line for a Negative Message?

Only use negative subject lines if you think the reader might otherwise ignore the message.

Letters don't require subject lines (Module 6). Omit a subject line in negative letters unless you think readers might ignore what they think is a routine message. (See, for example, Figure 9.2.)

FIGURE 9.4   **A Bad News Memo to Subordinates**

Memo

Brampton Corporate Trade
Peel County, Brampton, ON

Date: January 10, 2013
To: All Employees
From: Floyd E. Loer, Dorothy A. Walters, and Stewart Mattson
Subject: Accounting for Work Missed Because of Bad Weather

Buffer and explanation

Our office is always open for our customers, whatever the weather. Employees who missed work during the snowstorm last week may count the absence as vacation, sick day(s), or personal day(s).

Bad news: Workday/hours missed because of bad weather must be counted as a vacation, sick, or personal day

Hourly workers who missed less than a day have the option of taking the missed time as vacation, sick, or personal hours or of being paid only for the hours they worked.

Small positive

Approval of vacation or personal days will be automatic; the normal requirement of giving at least 24 hours' notice is waived.

Goodwill ending

Thanks for all the efforts you have made to continue giving our customers the best possible service during one of the snowiest winters on record.

When you give bad news, use a subject line that focuses on solutions, not problems:

Subject: Improving Our Subscription Letter

Or you can put the topic (but not your action on it) in the subject line:

Subject: Status of Conversion Table Program

Because of heavy demands on our time, we have not yet been able to write programs for the conversion tables you asked for.

Employability Skills

LO7 How Can PAIBOC Help Me Write Negative Messages?

The PAIBOC questions help you examine the points your message should include.

Before you tackle the assignments for this module, examine the following problem. As in Module 8, the PAIBOC questions probe the basic points required for a solution. Study the two sample solutions to see what makes one unacceptable and the other one good.[4] The checklist in Figure 9.9 can help you evaluate a draft.

Problem

You're director of employee benefits for a Fortune 500 company. Today, you received the following memo:

From: Michelle Jagtiani

Subject: Getting My Retirement Benefits

Next Friday will be my last day here. I am leaving (name of company) to take a position at another firm.

Please process a cheque for my retirement benefits, including both the deductions from my salary and the company's contributions for the last three and a half years. I would like to receive the cheque by next Friday if possible.

You have bad news for Michelle. Although the company does contribute an amount to the retirement fund equal to the amount deducted for retirement from the employee's paycheque, employees who leave with fewer than five years of employment receive only their own contributions. Michelle will get back only the money that has been deducted from her own pay, plus 4 percent interest compounded quarterly. Her payments and interest come to just over $17,200; the amount might be higher depending on the amount of her last paycheque, which will include compensation for any unused vacation days and sick leave. Furthermore, since the amounts deducted were not considered taxable income, she will have to pay income tax on the money she receives.

You cannot process the cheque until after her resignation is effective, so you will mail it to her. You have her home address on file; if she's moving, she needs to let you know where to send the cheque. Processing the cheque may take two to three weeks.

Write a memo to Michelle using PAIBOC analysis.

FIGURE 9.5 **Allocating Time for Writing a Bad News Memo (memo denying matching funds; time may vary)**

	Total Time: 3 hours
Planning	1 hour
Understand the situation.	
Answer the PAIBOC questions (Module 1).	
Think about document design (Module 5).	
Organize the message.	
Writing	1/2 hour
Draft the memo.	
Revising	11/2 hours
Reread draft.	
Measure draft against PAIBOC questions and checklist for negative messages (Figure 9.9).	
Revise draft.	
Ask for feedback.	
Revise draft based on feedback.	
Edit to catch grammatical errors.	
Run spell check.	
Proofread.	
Initial memo.	
Put in interoffice mail.	

FIGURE 9.6 **PAIBOC Analysis of the Problem**

P	What are your **purposes** in writing or speaking?
	• To tell Michelle that she will receive only her own contributions, plus 4 percent interest compounded quarterly; that the cheque will be mailed to her home address two to three weeks after her last day on the job; and that the money will be taxable as income
	• To build goodwill so that she feels that she has been treated fairly and consistently; to minimize negative feelings she may have
	• To close the door on this subject
A	Who is your **audience**? How do the members of your audience differ from each other? What audience characteristics are relevant to this particular message?
	The audience is Michelle Jagtiani. Unless she's a personal friend, you probably wouldn't know why she's leaving and where she's going.
	There's a lot you don't know. She may or may not know much about taxes; she may or may not be able to take advantage of tax-reduction strategies. You can't assume the answers, because you wouldn't have them in real life.
I	What **information** must your message include?
	Your message must tell Michelle when the cheque will arrive; the facts that the cheque will be based on her contributions, not her employer's, and that the money will be taxable income; how lump-sum retirement benefits are calculated; and the fact that you have her current address on file but need a new address if she's moving.
B	What reasons or reader **benefits** can you use to support your position?
	Stating the amount currently in her account might make Michelle feel that she is getting a significant sum of money. Suggesting someone who can give free tax advice (if the company offers this as a fringe benefit) reminds her of the benefits of working with the company. Wishing her luck with her new job is a nice touch.
O	What **objections** can you expect your readers to have? What negative elements of your message must you de-emphasize or overcome?
	Michelle is getting about half the amount she expected, since she won't receive any matching funds.
	She might have been able to earn more than 4 percent interest if she had invested the money herself. Depending on her personal tax situation, she may pay more tax on the money as a lump sum than would have been due had she paid it each year as she earned the money.
C	How will the **context** affect the reader's response? Think about your relationship to the reader, the morale in the organization, the economy, the time of year, and any special circumstances.
	The stock market has not been doing well; 4 percent interest is looking good.

Discussion of the Sample Solutions

The solution in Figure 9.7 is not acceptable. The subject line gives a negative with no reason or alternative. The first sentence has a condescending tone that is particularly offensive in negative messages. The last sentence focuses on what is being taken away rather than what remains. Paragraph 2 lacks you-attitude and is vague. The memo ends with a negative. There is nothing anywhere in the memo to build goodwill.

FIGURE 9.7   An Unacceptable Solution to the Sample Problem

April 20, 2013

To: Michelle Jagtiani

From: Lisa Niaz   *LN*

Subject: Denial of Matching Funds ——————————————————— Negative!

Give reason before refusal.

You cannot receive a cheque the last day of work and you will get only your own contributions, not a matching sum from the company, because you have not worked for the company for at least five full years.

Better to be specific.

This is lifted straight from the problem. The language in problems is often negative and stuffy; information is disorganized.

Your payments and interest come to just over $17 200; the amount could be higher depending on the amount of your last paycheque, which will include compensation for any unused vacation days and sick leave. Furthermore, since the amounts deducted were not considered taxable income, you will have to pay income tax on the money you receive.

How will reader know what you have on file? Better to give current address as you have it.

Think about the situation and use your own words to create a satisfactory message.

The cheque will be sent to your home address. If the address we have on file is incorrect, please correct it so that your cheque is not delayed.

Negative

The solution in Figure 9.8, in contrast, is very good. The policy serves as a buffer and explanation. The negative is stated clearly but is buried in the paragraph to avoid overemphasizing it. The paragraph ends on a positive note by specifying the amount in the account and the fact that the sum might be even higher.

Paragraph 3 contains the additional negative information that the amount will be taxable, but offers the alternative that it might be possible to reduce taxes. The writer builds goodwill by suggesting a specific person the reader might contact.

Paragraph 4 tells the reader what address is in the company files (Michelle might not know whether the files are up to date), asks that she update it if necessary, and ends with the reader's concern: getting her cheque promptly.

The final paragraph ends on a positive note. This generalized goodwill is appropriate when the writer does not know the reader well.

FIGURE 9.8   A Good Solution to the Sample Problem

April 20, 2013

To: Michelle Jagtiani

From: Lisa Niaz *LN*

Subject: Receiving Employee Contributions from Retirement Accounts ———— Neutral

Good to state reason in third person to deemphasize negative.

Employees who leave the company with at least five full years of employment are entitled both to the company contributions and to the retirement benefit paycheque deductions contributed to retirement accounts. Those employees who leave the company with fewer than five years of employment will receive the employee paycheque contributions made to their retirement accounts.

Good to be specific.

You now have $17 240.62 in your account, which includes 4% interest compounded quarterly. The amount you receive could be even higher since you will also receive payment for any unused sick leave and vacation days.

Good to show how company can help.

Because you now have access to the account, the amount you receive will be considered taxable income. Beth Jordan in Employee Financial Services can give you information about possible tax deductions and financial investments that can reduce your income taxes.

Good to be specific.

The cheque will be sent to your home address on May 16. The address we have on file is 2724 Merriman Road, Kingston, ON K7L 3N7. If your address changes, please let us know so you can receive your cheque promptly. ———— Positive

Forward-looking

Good luck with your new job!

FIGURE 9.9   Checklist for Negative Messages

- ❏ Is the subject line appropriate?
- ❏ If a buffer is used, does it invite a neutral or affirmative response?
- ❏ Is the reason presented before the refusal? Is the reason clear and relevant to the reader?
- ❏ Is the negative information clear and concise?
- ❏ Is an alternative given, if a good one is available? Does the message provide all the information needed to act on the alternative, but leave the choice up to the reader?
- ❏ Is the last paragraph forward-looking?
- ❏ Is the tone appropriate—positive, confident, and respectful?

Checklist for All Effective Messages

- ❏ Does the message use you-attitude and positive emphasis?
- ❏ Is the style easy to read and friendly?
- ❏ Is the visual design of the message inviting?
- ❏ Is the format correct?
- ❏ Does the message use standard grammar? Is it free from typos?

Add Originality in a Negative Message

- ❏ Use an effective buffer, if one is appropriate.
- ❏ Include a clear, complete statement of the reason for the refusal.
- ❏ Offer a good, clear alternative showing that you're thinking about what the reader really needs.
- ❏ Add details that show you're thinking about a specific organization and the specific people in that organization.

MODULE SUMMARY

- Organize negative messages in this way
  1. Begin with a buffer or neutral statement when possible.
  2. Explain the refusal
  3. Give the negative once, clearly
  4. End with a positive, forward-looking statement
- Use a buffer when the reader values harmony or when the buffer serves a purpose in addition to simply delaying the negative.
- Organize negative messages to superiors this way
  ○ Describe the problem.
  ○ Explain how it happened.
  ○ Describe options for fixing it.
  ○ Recommend a solution, and ask for action.
- When giving bad news to peers or subordinates
  ○ Describe the problem.
  ○ Present an alternative or compromise, if one is available.
  ○ If possible, ask for input.

- Make sure your reason for refusing is valid. Omit the reason if it is weak, or makes your organization look bad.
- Giving an alternative or compromise
  ○ Offers the audience another way of getting what they want
  ○ Suggests you care about the audience and helping to meet their needs
  ○ Enables the reader to re-establish the psychological freedom limited when you said no
  ○ Lets you end on a positive note and to present your organization and yourself as positive, friendly, and helpful
- Use PAIBOC analysis and Maslow's hierarchy to analyze how best to compose negative messages that meet your purposes and your audience's needs.

ASSIGNMENTS FOR MODULE 9

Questions for Critical Thinking

9.1 Different cultures may choose different organizational patterns to convey bad news. What organizational pattern is common in your culture, and why?

9.2 Different cultures choose different words to give bad news. What words does your culture use to deliver bad news, and why?

Exercises and Problems

9.3   Scripting Bad News Messages

Think of a negative or bad news message you have had to deliver in your personal or professional life.

As your instructor directs

a. Write down the negative or bad news, and the audience.
b. Exchange your suggested bad news message and audience with another student.
c. Using the other student's "bad news" message, prepare an oral presentation to deliver to the designated audience.
d. Present your bad news script to the class.
e. Be prepared to explain your choice of organizational pattern.

9.4   Rejecting Employees' Suggestions

For years, businesses have had suggestion programs, rewarding employees for money-saving ideas. Now your city government has adopted such a program, but not all the suggestions are adopted. Today, you need to send messages to the following people. Because their suggestions are being rejected, they will not get any cash award.

1. *Diane Hilgers, secretary, mayor's office.* Suggestion: Charge for 911 calls. Reason for rejection: "This would be a public relations disaster. People call because they have emergencies. We already charge for ambulance or paramedic trips; to charge just for the call will offend people. And it might not save money. It's a lot cheaper to prevent a burglary or murder than to track down the person afterward—to say nothing of the trauma of the loss or death. Bad idea."

2. *Steve Rieneke, building and grounds supervisor.* Suggestion: Fire the city's public relations specialists. Reason for rejection: "Positive attitudes toward city workers and policies make the public more willing to support public programs and taxes. In the long run, we think this is money well spent."

3. *Jose Rivera, accountant.* Suggestion: Schedule city council meetings during the day to save on light bills and staff overtime. Reason for rejection: "Having the meetings in the evening enables more citizens to attend. People have to be able to comment. Open meetings are essential so that citizens don't feel that policies and taxes are being railroaded through." Write the messages.

9.5   Telling the Boss About a Problem

In any organization, things sometimes go wrong. Tell your supervisor about a personnel, procedural, or technical problem in your organization, and suggest what should be done.

As your instructor directs

a. Prepare notes for a meeting with your supervisor.
b. Write an email to your supervisor.
c. Give an oral presentation on the problem.
d. Write an email to your instructor explaining the problem, the corporate culture, and the reasons for your solution.

9.6   Telling Customers that Prices Are Going Up

Periodically, organizations raise prices or impose separate fees for services that were previously free. Think of an increase in the prices your customers pay.

As your instructor directs

a. Write an email to customers, telling them about the new fees or higher prices.
b. Examine your organization's files for messages sent out the last time prices were raised. Are the messages effective? Why or why not? Include copies of the messages with your analysis of them.

9.7   Refusing a Gift

As the head of a charitable organization, you spend a lot of your time asking for money. But today, you're turning down a gift: a timeshare condominium in Florida. Timeshares are so difficult to sell that regular real-estate agents do not list them. Places that list timeshares frequently charge an upfront fee (not just a commission, which is paid only when the unit sells). If you accepted the gift, your organization would have to pay maintenance fees charged by the home-owners' association and taxes until the unit sold (if it sold).

And you'd probably have to hire someone to check on the property occasionally, since the maintenance fee covers general building maintenance, not repairs for a specific unit. You don't want the expense and hassle of something that might not ever yield funds for your organization, so you're going to refuse the gift.

Write a letter to the would-be donors, Benjamin and Sarah Mellon, refusing the gift.

As your instructor directs

Write letters for one or more of the following situations.

a. Yours is a well-known national charity. You have never met the Mellons, but your records show that they have given small gifts (under $100) in three of the last five years.
b. Yours is a local religious organization; the Mellons are prominent members. They don't give much money, but they're active and faithful.
c. Yours is a local charitable organization that struggles to stay open. The Mellons are major contributors. Sarah Mellon served on your board of directors in a term ending three years ago.
d. Yours is a national charity. No one in the office has ever heard of the Mellons. They haven't contributed in the last three years—your records don't go back further.

Hints:

- Choose a charitable organization you know something about.
- Give the real reason for the refusal. You would accept real estate that seemed easy to sell.
- In situations (a) to (c) above, thank the Mellons for their past support. Be specific about what they've done.
- Use a salutation and complimentary close appropriate to the situation.
- In all the situations, encourage the donor to give other (more liquid) gifts to you in the future. Tell about upcoming opportunities for giving.

9.8   Refusing to Participate on a Panel

As a prominent speaker, you get many requests to appear before various groups. Today, you've received a request to participate in a panel of three to five professionals who will talk about "Investing in the Real World." The session will run from 2 to 5 p.m. on the second Sunday of next month.

You're trying to cut back on outside commitments. Work continues to take much of your time, you have major obligations in a volunteer organization, and you want some time for yourself and your family. This request does not fit your priorities. Decline the invitation.

As your instructor directs

Assume that the request is from one of the following:

a. A university business honour society that expects 250 students at the session

b. The youth group at the church, synagogue, temple, or mosque you attend

c. The Chinese Student Association at the local college or university

9.9 Announcing Cost-Saving Measures

Your company has to cut costs but would prefer to avoid laying off workers. Therefore, you have adopted the following money-saving ideas. Some can be implemented immediately; some will be implemented at renewal dates. The company will no longer pay for

- Flowers at the receptionist's desk and in executive offices
- Skyboxes for professional sporting events
- Employees' dues for professional and trade organizations
- Liquor at business meals

Only essential business travel will be approved. The company will pay only for the lowest cost of air travel (coach, reservation 7 to 14 days in advance, stay over Saturday night).

The company will no longer buy tables or blocks of tickets for charitable events and will not make any cash donations to charity until money is less tight.

Counters will be put on the photocopiers. People must have access numbers to make photocopies; personal photocopies will cost $0.10 a page.

As the chief financial officer, write an email to all employees, explaining the changes.

9.10 Closing Bill-Payment Offices

For many years, Chilliwack Public Utilities Commission had five office locations where people could take their payments. On the first of the month following next month, you're closing these offices. On that date, 100 local merchants, such as grocers, will begin to accept utility payments. Closing the freestanding offices will save the municipality almost $1 million a year. Customers will still be able to mail in payments or have them deducted automatically from their bank accounts.

Write a notice that can be inserted in utility bills this month and next month.

9.11 Giving a Customer Less Credit than She Wants

Yang-Ming Lee applied for your VISA card, asking for a credit limit of $15,000 and a separate card for her husband, Chad

Hoang. You've checked the credit references, and they're good enough to merit granting a credit card. But you generally give new customers only a $7,500 limit, even when the family income is very high, as it is in this case. You might make an exception if your bank had a previous relationship with the client, but no such relationship exists here. Although you have no set policy for reviewing and raising credit limits, normally you would expect at least six months of paying the minimum amount promptly.

Write a letter to Ms. Lee, granting her a credit card with a $7,500 limit.

9.12 Rejecting a Member's Request

All non-supervisory public service workers in your province are union members. As a paid staff person for the union, you spend about a third of your time writing and editing the monthly magazine, *Public (Your Province) Employee*. You receive this letter:

> Dear Editor:
>
> Every month, we get two copies of the union magazine—one addressed to me, one to my husband. We have different last names, so your computer might not realize that we're connected, but we are, and we don't need two copies. Sending just one will save printing and postage costs and reduce environmental waste. My name is Dorothy Livingston; my husband is Eric Beamer. Please combine our listings to send just one copy.
>
> Sincerely,
>
> Dorothy Livingston

As it happens, a couple of years ago you investigated the possible savings of sending just one mailing to couples who both work for the province. Sophisticated computerized merge/purge programs to eliminate duplicates are far too expensive for the union's tight budget. Your information comes directly from the province, which updates your list for you every year. Ms. Livingston's suggestion is a good one, but going through the mailing list manually each year to locate and change duplications would cost more than would be saved in postage. Printing costs wouldn't necessarily drop either, since the cost per copy is lower the higher the print run.

But you want to build goodwill—both with this writer and for the union in general. Extra copies of the magazine (whether a double mailing or simply a copy someone is finished with) might be given to a non-member, or taken to a doctor's or dentist's waiting room or a barber or beauty shop. Such sharing would help spread public support for the union and provincial government workers.

Write an email to Ms. Livingston, explaining why you can't combine mailings.

POLISHING YOUR PROSE

Finding Your Narrative Voice

Narrative voice refers to the "personality" of the writer. Words, phrases, expressions, and tone convey narrative voice. Just as fiction and composition do, business communication uses narrative voice. The "voice" in memos, letters, and reports can be friendly, assertive, bureaucratic, threatening, or confident, to name just a few possibilities. You'll get the results you want, however, if you *speak* to your reader the way you would want to be spoken to.

Consider the following email message from a student to his instructor. If you were the instructor, how persuasive would you judge this memo?

> To: Kathryn
>
> From: Dave
>
> Subject: report
>
> i am sending my final report. i cant remember when its do but here it is.iknow ive missed alot of classes but i have to work. im going to keep on sending this message until you tell me you got it. Whats my final grade.

Narrative voice is as individual as personality. However, we have control over narrative voice, because we can choose the language we use to make meaning. Knowing your own voice can help you to understand the "personality" it demonstrates.

Exercises

How would you characterize the narrative voice in each of the following messages? Which voices appeal to you as appropriate for business communication? How could you communicate the same message in a more appropriate voice?

1. Employees will clock in at their designated hour. Employees will follow their assigned schedules to the letter. There will be NO EXCEPTION to these rules.

2. Hi, Mr. Mills! Just stop in to pick up your order when you get a chance. Give us a ring if you want delivery. Thanks!

3. Attention *Balance and Wellness Magazine* Subscriber:

   Thank you for your interest in our magazine. I hope you have enjoyed your two free issues. As you can read in November's Letters to the Editor, subscribers have responded enthusiastically to October's article on the health benefits of keeping a journal.

   Perhaps you have already sent your annual subscription fee of $29.98 (plus HST). If so, please accept my thanks. If not, please take a few minutes to enclose your cheque in the postage-paid envelope to enjoy a whole year of healthful reading.

   Sincerely,

   Joe Malone, Editor-in-chief

4. Please find enclosed my resumé, which speaks to my superlative and most relevant qualities as a candidate for the advertised position of account executive with your illustrious organization.

5. Dear Homeowner,

   It has been brought to our attention that your hydro meter is obstructed by dense shrubbery. This makes it difficult for our technician to read your hydro meter and represents a potential safety hazard.

   We would ask that you cut back or remove the obstructing shrubbery to allow ease of access.

6. Dear Client,

   I am now spending up to four hours a day responding to emails, telephone calls, faxes, tax assessments, etc. As I'm sure you can appreciate, this correspondence contributes to an already overly long day. Please be advised, therefore, that effective immediately, your annual accounting fee will include a correspondence fee of $150.00 plus HST every six months ($28.25 per month).

   Alternatively, I can measure actual time spent and bill accordingly (expensive and time-consuming)

   I enclose a self-addressed envelope.

   Sincerely,

   George Estrada, CA

7. Pertaining to the party of the first part, hereafter called "party first," and excepting any and all objections from the party of the second part, hereafter called "party second," this amendment shall be considered null and void with proper written notice three (3) days prior to the execution of the original agreement.

8. Congratulations on your recent promotion to district manager, Rita. All of us in accounting look forward to working with you.

9. Martina,

I've spent at least three hours looking for the invoice, which is a complete waste of my time. Where would you suggest I look NOW??!!

10. In the event of catastrophic LAN failure, users will
  1. Perform SYS/MD-3 shutdown for affected systems
  2. Engage standard recovery matrix (SRM), per #4105.1 in SYS/MD Manual (2000: H3-H12)
  3. Record time and date, RE: LAN Failure, in compliance log, cc. MEISNER
  4. Notify Data Services at ext. 5547, ATTN: J.J. MEISNER

11. Nope. This idea won't work. It's not very good. I'm not sure the project is even worth our time anymore. I'm definitely not interested in having a meeting to discuss it. Don't call me unless you guys have something better.

Check the Answer Key for odd-numbered exercises.

McGraw Hill **connect**™

Composing Persuasive Messages

Learning Objectives

After reading and applying the information in Module 10, you'll be able to demonstrate

Knowledge of

LO1 Persuasive appeals

LO2 Persuasive patterns of organization

Skills to

LO3 Choose and use persuasive strategies

LO4 Organize persuasive messages

LO5 Identify and overcome objections

LO6 Write common kinds of persuasive messages

LO7 Write effective subject lines for persuasive messages

LO8 Further analyze business communication situations

MODULE OUTLINE

- What are persuasive appeals?
- What purposes do persuasive messages serve?
- What kinds of persuasive messages am I likely to write?
- How should I organize persuasive messages?
- How do I identify and overcome objections?
- What's the best subject line for a persuasive message?
- How can PAIBOC help me write persuasive messages?

Module Summary

Assignments for Module 10

Polishing Your Prose: Correcting Run-On Sentences

Employability Skills 2000+ Checklist

Module content builds these Conference Board of Canada Employability Skills 2000+

Communicate

Manage Information

Think and Solve Problems

Be Responsible

Be Adaptable

Participate in Projects and Tasks

All successful communication contains a persuasive element. Even attracting and holding your audience's attention long enough for you to make your pitch depends on your understanding of persuasion.

LO1 What Are Persuasive Appeals?

People are persuaded by their perceptions of (1) the trustworthiness of the messenger, and (2) the emotional and logical resonances of the message.

Credibility, emotion, and logic: this is the alchemy of persuasion.

Audiences pay attention to people whom they see as trustworthy or credible. In fact, perceptions trump facts, as we know from experience: attractive media models who peddle everything from painkillers to pizza are really selling a story about how buying the product will transform us.

We respond most strongly to stories in which facts and their presentation appeal to our deepest values and beliefs. For example, the drama of trapped Chilean miners made them celebrities and held worldwide attention for days; media attention ensured that we were emotionally invested in the story of their rescue.

Ex.
10.4
10.8–
10.10

Persuasive appeals permeate all parts of our lives—from the personal to the political. In business, people depend on persuasion to build relationships and to get quality work done, as illustrated in Figure 10.1.

LO8 What Purposes Do Persuasive Messages Serve?

Ex.
10.4
10.7

10.10
10.13
10.14

Persuasive messages have both primary and secondary purposes.

Primary purposes

- To have the reader act and to overcome any objections that might prevent or delay action
- To provide enough information so that the reader knows exactly what to do

Secondary purposes

- To establish a good impression of the writer
- To build a good image of the writer's organization
- To build a good relationship between the writer and reader
- To reduce or eliminate future correspondence on the same subject

FIGURE 10.1   **Small Business Marketing Brochure Tells a Story**

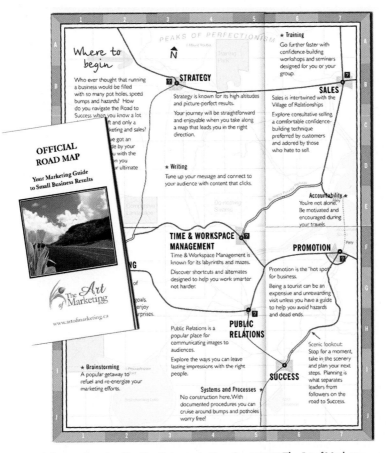

Source: Imagine Creative Communications Inc. © 2008 *The Art of Marketing.*

LO6 What Kinds of Persuasive Messages Am I Likely to Write?

You will likely write orders and requests, collection letters, job application letters and resumés (Unit 6), and reports.

Orders

Orders may be written on forms, phoned in, or made by clicking boxes on the Internet. When you write an order, be sure to do three things:

- Be specific. Give model or page numbers, colours, finishes, and so forth.
- Tell the company what you want if that model number is no longer available.
- Double-check your arithmetic, and add tax and shipping charges.

Collection Letters

Ex.
10.7
10.12

Most businesses find that phoning rather than writing results in faster payment. But if you receive no response to repeated voicemail messages, you may need to write a series of collection letters.

FIGURE 10.2   **An Initial Collection Letter**

Saki's

October 23, 2013

Eva Pavlinic
532 Heath Street East
Toronto, ON M5W 3M1

Card Number: 503 913 248 1
Balance: $36.28
Payment Required: $33.00

Dear Eva Pavlinic

Perhaps you missed making your recent payment because the balance on your account is so small. It is not difficult to do, and many of us overlook small account balances.

However, we would appreciate it if you would take a few minutes to mail us your cheque for $33.00.

If your payment has already been made, thank you.

Credit Department
Tel: 416-555-4567

Request topic in subject line.

Courteous opening saves reader's face.

Ask for actions. Make action easy.

Positive, friendly close.

Collection letters ask customers to pay (as they have already agreed to do) for the goods and services they have already received. Good credit departments send a series of letters. Letters in the series should be only a week or two apart. Waiting a month between letters implies that you're prepared to wait a long time—and the reader will be happy to oblige you.

Early letters are gentle, assuming that the reader intends to pay but has met with temporary problems or has forgotten. However, the request should assume that the cheque has been mailed but did not arrive. A student who had not yet been reimbursed by a company for a visit to the company's office put the second request in the P.S. of a letter refusing a job offer:

> P.S. The cheque to cover my expenses when I visited your office in March hasn't come yet. Could you please check to see whether you can find a record of it? The amount was $690 (airfare, $490; hotel room, $185; taxi, $15).

Unless you have firm evidence to the contrary, assume that readers have some legitimate reason for not paying yet. Even people who do not have enough money to pay all their bills, or who put payment off as long as possible, will respond more quickly if you do not accuse them. If a reader is offended by your assumption that he or she is dishonest, that anger can become an excuse to continue delaying payment.

Late letters threaten legal action if the bill is not paid. However, the writer cannot threaten legal action unless he or she actually intends to sue. Other regulations also spell out what a writer may and may not do in a late letter.

Many small businesses find that establishing personal relationships with customers is the best way to speed payment.

How Should I Organize Persuasive Messages?

Use PAIBOC analysis to analyze and identify your audience's reaction. When you do not anticipate objections, start with the request. When you expect resistance from the reader, start with an objective description of the situation.

Start with the request only when you anticipate ready agreement, when you fear that a busy reader may not read a message whose relevance isn't clear, or when your organization's culture prefers direct requests.

Ex.
10.4
10.5

Writing Direct Requests

When you expect quick agreement, save the reader's time by presenting the request directly, as in Figure 10.3.

1. *Consider asking immediately for the information or service you want.* Delay the request if it seems too abrupt or if you have several purposes in the message.
2. *Give readers all the information and details they will need to act on your request.* Number your questions or set them off with bullets so the reader can check to see that all of them have been answered.

    In a claim (in which a product is under warranty or a shipment was defective), explain the circumstances so that the reader knows what happened. Be sure to include all the relevant details: date of purchase, model or invoice number, and so on.

    In more complicated direct requests, anticipate possible responses. Suppose you're asking for information about equipment meeting certain specifications. Explain which criteria are most important so that the reader can recommend an alternative if no single product meets all your needs. You may also want to tell the reader what your price constraints are and ask if the item is in stock or must be special-ordered.
3. *Ask for the action you want.* Do you want a cheque? A replacement? A catalogue? Answers to your questions? If you need an answer by a certain time, say so. If possible, show the reader why the time limit is necessary.

FIGURE 10.3 A Direct Request

Request topic in subject line —

To: mantonucci@bcs.com

Subject: Suggestion # 97204

Good morning, Michael, —————— Request in para. 1

Please evaluate the attached suggestion by May 29. —————— Specifics/ explanation

Appeals to recognition, esteem needs

- Should BCS adopt it? Why or why not?
- Will the company save money? If so, how much annually?
- If we adopt the suggestion, what kind of award should we give?

Ask for action; make action easy

Please send your responses and brief reasons to me by May 29 for the committee meeting May 30.

Thanks!

Note that direct requests do not contain reader benefits (Module 11) and do not need to overcome objections: they simply ask for what is needed.

Direct requests should be direct. Don't make the reader guess what you want.

> **Indirect request**: Is there a newer version of the 2013 *Accounting Reference Manual*?

> **Direct request**:   If there is a newer version of the 2013 *Accounting Reference Manual*, please send it to me.

In some direct requests, your combination of purposes may suggest a different pattern. For example, in a letter asking a prospective employer to reimburse you for expenses after a job interview, you'd want to thank your hosts for their hospitality and reinforce the good impression you made at the interview. To do that, you'd spend the first two paragraphs talking about the trip and the interview. Only in the last third of the letter (or even in the postscript) would you make your request for reimbursement.

Similarly, in a letter asking about a graduate program, a major purpose might be to build a good image of yourself so that your application for financial aid will be viewed positively. To achieve that goal, you would provide information about your qualifications and interest in the field before you ask questions.

Organizing Indirect Request Messages.

Use indirect (inductive or bad news) organization when you expect resistance from the reader, but you can show that doing what you suggest will resolve the situation or solve the problem.

This pattern allows you to anticipate and overcome objections; you describe all the reasons in favour of your position before you give your readers a chance to say no.

1. *Describe the situation you share (or the problem that your request will solve).* Because you're interested in solving the problem, describe the situation objectively: it's a waste of time and ink to assign blame or mention personalities.
2. *Detail the results of the situation as they affect your reader.* Be specific about the cost in money, time, lost goodwill, inconvenience, and so on. Persuade your readers that *something* has to be done before you convince them that your solution is the best one.
3. *Explain your solution.* If you know that the reader will favour another solution, start with that solution and show why it won't work before you present your solution. Present your solution, focusing on practicality, workability, and desirability without using the words *I* or *my*. Appeal to the reader's wallet or sense of enlightened self-interest.
4. *Prove that any negative elements (cost, time, concerns, disruptions) are outweighed by the advantages.*
5. *Summarize any additional benefits of the solution.* You can present the main benefit—solving the problem—briefly, since you have described the problem in detail. However, if there are any additional benefits, mention them.
6. *Ask for the action you want.* Often your reader will authorize or approve something; other people will implement the action. Give your reader a reason to act promptly, perhaps offering a new reader benefit. ("By buying now, we can avoid the next quarter's price hikes.")

FIGURE 10.4 How to Organize an Indirect Persuasive Message

- Shared Problem
- Details
- Solution
- Negatives
- Reader Benefits
- Request for Action

Figure 10.4 summarizes the pattern. Figure 10.5 uses the pattern. Reader benefits (Module 11) can be brief in this kind of message, because the biggest benefit is solving the problem.

LO3 LO5 How Do I Identify and Overcome Objections?

Know your audience. Talk to your audience. Then try these strategies.

The easiest way to learn about objections your audience may have is to ask knowledgeable people in your network or organization.

- *Use open questions and phrase your questions neutrally* so that people feel encouraged to express their opinions openly: "What concerns would you have about a proposal to do X?"

FIGURE 10.5   **A Bad News Persuasive Message**

COMMUNITY LIVING

Memorandum

To: All Employees

CC:

From: Janice Hofbauer

Date: February 15, 2013

Re: New Sign-Out System ————————————————————————————————— Directed subject line

Buffer: common ground — Our clients enjoy the times they get to go to the mall or out to lunch, instead of being here all day. And their daily interaction with the community is very important. Recently, however, clients have been taken out on activities without staff members' knowing where the client is, or whom the client is with.

Shared problem

Specific example — We need to know where clients are at all times, because social workers, psychologists, and relatives constantly stop by unannounced. Last week, a client's parent came by to pick her up for an appointment. Not only was the client not here, but no one knew where she was, or with whom. Not knowing where our clients are, and with whom, damages the reputation of our program and our staff.

Solution — Starting Monday, March 23, a sign-out board will be located at Magali's desk. Please write down where the client and you are going, and when you expect to return. When signing out, help clients sign out. We can make this a learning experience for our clients. Then when

Reader benefit — visitors stop by to see someone who isn't here, we can simply look at the sign-out board to tell where the client is, and when he or she will return.

Please help preserve the superb reputation you have helped WestRiver earn as a quality centre for adults with handicaps. Sign clients and yourself out at all times.

Ask for action

"Who makes a decision about Y?" "What do you like best about (the supplier or practice you want to change)?"

- *Ask follow-up questions* to be sure you understand: "Would you be likely to stay with your current supplier if you could get a lower price from someone else? Why?"

LO5 People are most aware of and willing to share objective constraints such as time and money. We are all less willing to acknowledge emotional anxieties. We have a **vested interest** in something when we benefit directly from keeping things as they are. For example, during his summer job, an engineering student saw how his company's waste treatment system could be redesigned to save the company more than $200,000 a year. He wrote a report recommending the change and gave it to his boss. Nothing happened. Why not? His supervisor wasn't about to send up a report that would require him to explain why *he'd* been wasting more than $200,000 a year of the company's money.[1] The supervisor's emotional investment in keeping the old system overrode any logical considerations.

To avoid situations such as these, you need to probe to find out the real reasons for your audience's objections.

The best way to deal with an objection is to eliminate it. To sell Jeep Cherokees in Japan, Mitsuru Sato convinced Chrysler to make a right-hand-drive version, to make an extra pre-shipment quality check, and to rewrite the instruction booklet in Japanese style with big diagrams and cartoons.[2]

If an objection is false or based on misinformation

- Give the response to the objection without naming the objection, or
- Present responses in a "question/answer" format, or
- State the objection neutrally, and then respond: "Some people wonder…"; "Some clients are concerned that…"

If real objections remain, try one or more of the following strategies to counter objections:

1. Specify how much time or money is required—it may not be as much as the reader fears.

   Distributing flyers to each house or apartment in your neighbourhood will probably take two afternoons.

2. Put the time or money in the context of the benefits they bring.

   The additional $152,500 will (1) allow the Open Shelter to remain open 24 rather than 16 hours a day, (2) pay for three social workers to help men find work and homes, and (3) keep the neighbourhood bank open, so that men don't have to cash welfare cheques in bars, and so they can save the $800 they need to have up front to rent an apartment.

3. Show that money spent now will save money in the long run.

   By replacing the boiler now, we'll no longer have to release steam that the overflow tank can't hold. Depending on how severe the winter is, we will save $100 to $750 a year in energy costs. If energy costs rise, we'll save even more.

4. Show that doing as you ask will benefit a group or cause the reader supports, although the action may not help the reader directly.

   By being a Big Brother or a Big Sister, you'll give a child the attention he or she needs to become a well-adjusted, productive adult.

5. Show the reader that the sacrifice is necessary to achieve a larger, more important goal to which he or she is committed.

   These changes will mean more work for all of us. But we have to cut our costs 25 percent to keep the plant open and to keep our jobs.

6. Show that the advantages as a group outnumber or outweigh the disadvantages as a group.

   None of the locations is perfect. But the Quebec City location gives us the most advantages and the fewest disadvantages.

To persuade, be prepared to appeal to emotions as well as to logic.

7. Turn a disadvantage into an opportunity.

> With the hiring freeze, every department will need more lead time to complete its own work. By hiring a freelance worker, the Planning Department could provide that lead time.

LO5 **Finding common ground** builds emotional appeal. To find common ground, you must understand your audience's needs. And you must identify with your audience to help them identify with you. Finding this common ground is based on a respect for your audience's position.

People are highly sensitive to manipulative emotional appeals. No matter how much you disagree, you must respect your audience's intelligence in order to understand why they believe or do something, and why they may object to your position. When you can understand your readers' point of view, you'll be more effective. And you won't alienate your readers by talking down to them.

The best common grounds are specific and focus on something the reader cares about.

| **Weak common ground:** | We all want the business to be profitable. |
| **Improved common ground:** | We lost about $186,000 in profits last summer due to a 17% drop in productivity. |

In your common ground, emphasize the parts of your idea that fit with what your audience already believes or knows. For example, an employee of 3M wanted to develop laser disks. He realized that 3M's previous successful products were thin and flat: Scotch Tape, Post-it Notes™, magnetic tape. When he made his presentation to the group that chose new products for development, he held his prototype disk horizontally, so his audience saw a flat, thin object rather than a large, round, record-like object. Making his project fit with the audience's previous experience was a subtle and effective emotional tool to make it easier for the audience to say yes.

Stories and psychological description are also effective ways to build emotional appeal. Even when you need to provide statistics or numbers to convince the careful reader that your anecdote is a representative example, telling a story first makes your message more persuasive. For example, many charities send out letters describing how a person's life has changed because of donors' generosity. These stories motivate people to give.

The language you use creates the tone of your request. When you ask for action, you have several choices. Orders ("Get me the Ervin file") and questions ("Do we have the third-quarter

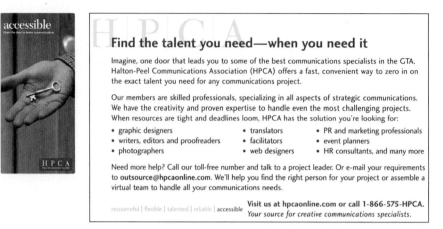

Both picture and text tell a story that makes this marketing postcard memorable.

numbers yet?") might work; however, you'll get better results with courtesy. You may need to be firm, but you must always be polite.

Avoiding messages that sound parental or preachy is a matter of tone. Saying *please* is important, especially to people on your level or outside the organization. Tone works better when you give reasons for your request.

Parental: Everyone is expected to comply with these regulations. I'm sure you can see that they are common-sense rules needed for our business.

Better: Even on casual days, visitors expect us to look professional. So please let's leave the gym clothes at home.

Writing to superiors is trickier. You may want to tone down your request by using language that shows you aren't taking a yes for granted.

Arrogant: Based on this evidence, I expect you to give me a new computer.

Better: If department funds permit, I would like a new computer.

Give a reason to act promptly because the longer people delay, the less likely they are to carry through. Request action by a specific date. Always give people at least a week or two: they have other things to do besides respond to your requests.

Set deadlines in the middle of the month, if possible. If you say, "Please return this by March 1," people will think, "I don't need to do this until March." Ask for the response by February 28 instead. If you can use a response even after the deadline, say so. Otherwise, people who can't make the deadline may not respond at all.

To help pay his way through UBC, Brian Scudamore persuaded people to pay him to take out the trash. The CEO and founder of 1-800-GOT-JUNK began an industry and now runs an international franchise worth millions.

Show why you need a quick response:

- *Show that the time limit is real.* Perhaps you need information quickly to use in a report that has a due date. Perhaps a decision must be made by a certain date to catch the start of the school year, the holiday selling season, or an election campaign. Perhaps you need to be ready for a visit from out-of-town or international colleagues.
- *Show that acting now will save time or money.* If business is slow and your industry isn't doing well, your company needs to act now (to economize, to better serve customers) in order to be competitive. If business is booming and everyone is making a profit, then your company needs to act now to get its fair share of the available profits.
- *Show the cost of delaying action.* Will labour or material costs be higher in the future? Will delay mean more money spent on repairing something that will still need to be replaced?

LO7 What's the Best Subject Line for a Persuasive Message?

For direct requests, use the request, the topic, or a question. For messages, use a directed subject line or a reader benefit.

In a direct request, put the request, the topic of the request, or a question in the subject line.

Direct request subject line:	Subject: Request for Updated Software
	My copy of HomeNet does not accept the aliases for Magnus accounts.
Direct request subject line:	Subject: Status of Account #3548-003
	Please send me the following information about account #3548-003.
Direct request subject line:	Subject: Additional Training Session in October
	The two training sessions scheduled for October will accommodate 40 people. Last month, you said that 57 new staff accountants had been hired. Should we schedule an additional training session in October? Or can the new hires wait until the next regularly scheduled session in February?

When you have a reluctant reader, putting the request in the subject line just gets a quick no before you've had a chance to give all your arguments. One option is to use a directed subject line that makes your stance on the issue clear. In the following examples, the first is the most neutral. The remaining two increasingly reveal the writer's preference.

Directed subject line:	Subject: A Proposal to Change the Formula for Calculating Retirees' Benefits
Directed subject line:	Subject: Arguments for Expanding the Bramalea Plant
Directed subject line:	Subject: Why Cassano's Should Close Its West-Side Store

Another option is to use common ground or a reader benefit—something that shows readers that this message will help them.

Reader benefit subject line:	Subject: Reducing Energy Costs in the Office
	Energy costs in our office have risen 12 percent in the past three years, although the cost of gas has risen only 8 percent and the cost of electricity has risen only 5 percent.

Although your first paragraph may be negative in a problem-solving message, your subject line should be neutral or positive, to show that you are solving a problem, not just reporting one.

Both directed subject lines and benefit subject lines can also be used as report titles.

LO8 How Can PAIBOC Help Me Write Persuasive Messages?

The PAIBOC questions help you examine the points your message should include.

Before you tackle the assignments for this module, examine the following problem. As in Modules 8 and 9, the PAIBOC questions probe the basic points required for a solution. Study the two sample solutions to see what makes one unacceptable and the other one good.[4] The checklists in Figures 10.9 and 10.10 can help you evaluate your draft.

Problem

In one room in the production department of Golden Electronics Company, employees work on computer monitors in conditions that are scarcely bearable because of the heat. Even when the temperature outside is only 23°C, it is more than 30°C in the monitor room. In June, July, and August, 24 out of 36 workers quit because they couldn't stand the heat. This turnover happens every summer.

In a far corner of the room sits a quality control inspector in front of a small fan (the only one in the room). The production workers, in contrast, are carrying 10-kilogram monitors. As production supervisor, you tried to get air conditioning two years ago, before Golden acquired the company, but management was horrified at the idea of spending $500,000 to insulate and air condition the warehouse (it is impractical to air condition the monitor room alone).

You're losing money every summer. Write a memo to Jennifer M. Kirkland, operations vice-president, renewing your request. Review the PAIBOC analysis in Figure 10.6 to help you get started.

FIGURE 10.6　PAIBOC Analysis of the Problem

P	What are your **purposes** in writing or speaking?
	You need to persuade Kirkland to authorize insulation and air conditioning, and you want to build a good image.
A	Who is your **audience**? How do members of your audience differ? What audience characteristics are relevant to this particular message?
	The operations vice-president will be concerned about keeping costs low and keeping production running smoothly. Kirkland may know that the request was denied two years ago, but another person was vice-president then; Kirkland wasn't the one who said no.
I	What **information** must your message include?
	You need to include the cost of the proposal and the effects of the present situation.
B	What reasons or reader **benefits** can you use to support your position?
	Cutting turnover may save money and keep the assembly line running smoothly. Experienced employees may produce higher-quality parts. Putting in air conditioning would relieve one of the workers' main complaints; it might make the union happier.
O	What **objections** can you expect your readers to have? What negative elements of your message must you de-emphasize or overcome?
	The cost, including the cost of the time that operations will be shut down while installation is taking place, will be the main objection.
C	How will the **context** affect reader response? Think about your relationship to the reader, the morale in the organization, the economy, the time of year, and any special circumstances.
	Prices on computer components are falling; interest rates are low. Nonetheless, the company will be reluctant to make a major expenditure. Although people are looking for jobs, filling vacancies in the monitor room is hard; we are getting a reputation as a bad place to work. Summer is over, but the problem will recur next year.

Discussion of the Sample Solutions

Solution 1, shown in Figure 10.7 is unacceptable. By making the request in the subject line and the first paragraph, the writer invites a no before giving all the arguments.

The writer does nothing to counter the objections that any manager will have to spending a great deal of money. By presenting the issue in terms of fairness, the writer attempts a manipulative emotional appeal. The writer doesn't use details or find common ground to show that the problem is indeed serious. The writer asks for fast action but doesn't show why the reader should act now to solve a problem that won't occur again for eight months.

FIGURE 10.7   An Unacceptable Solution to the Sample Problem

Inappropriate emphasis on writer.

Memo sounds arrogant. Logic isn't developed. This attacks reader instead of enlisting reader's support.

Request in subject line stiffens resistance when reader is reluctant.

Attacks reader.

Cost sounds enormous without a context.

> Date: October 13, 2013
>
> To: Jennifer M. Kirkland, Operations Vice-President
>
> From: Arnold M. Morgan, Production Supervisor *AMM*
>
> Subject: Request for Air Conditioning in the Monitor Room
>
> Please put air conditioning in the monitor room. This past summer, 2/3 of our employees quit because it was so hot. It's not fair that they should work in unbearable temperatures when management sits in air-conditioned comfort.
>
> I propose that we solve this problem by air conditioning the monitor room to bring down the temperature to 26°C.
>
> Insulating and air conditioning the monitor room would cost $500 000.
>
> Please approve this request promptly.

Solution 2, shown in Figure 10.8, is an effective persuasive message. The writer chooses a positive subject line. The opening sentence catches the reader's attention by focusing on a problem the reader and writer share. The paragraph makes it clear that the memo offers a solution to the problem. The problem is spelled out in detail. The writer creates emotional impact by taking the reader through the day as the temperature rises. The solution is presented impersonally. There are no *I*'s in the memo.

The memo stresses reader benefits: the savings that will result once the investment is recovered. The last paragraph tells the reader exactly what to do and links prompt action to a reader benefit. The memo ends with a positive picture of the problem solved.

Figures 10.9 and 10.10 provide checklists for direct requests and problem-solving persuasive messages.

FIGURE 10.8   A Good Solution to the Sample Problem

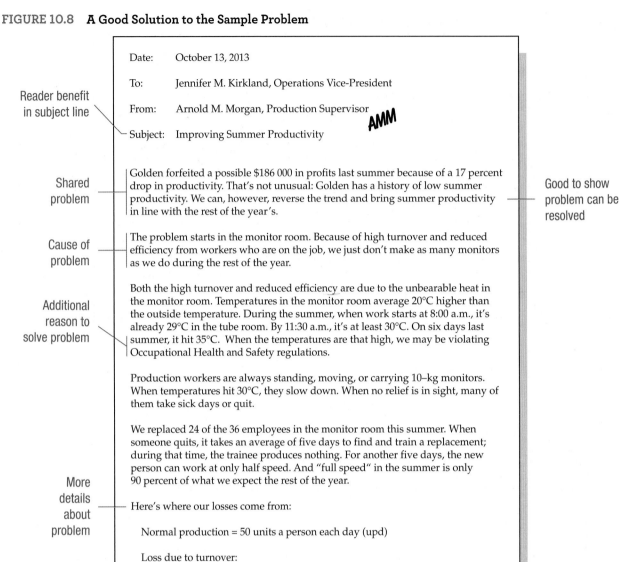

Reader benefit in subject line

Shared problem

Cause of problem

Additional reason to solve problem

More details about problem

Good to show problem can be resolved

Shows detail— set up like an arithmetic problem

Date: October 13, 2013

To: Jennifer M. Kirkland, Operations Vice-President

From: Arnold M. Morgan, Production Supervisor   AMM

Subject: Improving Summer Productivity

Golden forfeited a possible $186 000 in profits last summer because of a 17 percent drop in productivity. That's not unusual: Golden has a history of low summer productivity. We can, however, reverse the trend and bring summer productivity in line with the rest of the year's.

The problem starts in the monitor room. Because of high turnover and reduced efficiency from workers who are on the job, we just don't make as many monitors as we do during the rest of the year.

Both the high turnover and reduced efficiency are due to the unbearable heat in the monitor room. Temperatures in the monitor room average 20°C higher than the outside temperature. During the summer, when work starts at 8:00 a.m., it's already 29°C in the tube room. By 11:30 a.m., it's at least 30°C. On six days last summer, it hit 35°C. When the temperatures are that high, we may be violating Occupational Health and Safety regulations.

Production workers are always standing, moving, or carrying 10–kg monitors. When temperatures hit 30°C, they slow down. When no relief is in sight, many of them take sick days or quit.

We replaced 24 of the 36 employees in the monitor room this summer. When someone quits, it takes an average of five days to find and train a replacement; during that time, the trainee produces nothing. For another five days, the new person can work at only half speed. And "full speed" in the summer is only 90 percent of what we expect the rest of the year.

Here's where our losses come from:

    Normal production = 50 units a person each day (upd)

    Loss due to turnover:
        loss of 24 workers for 5 days =   6 000 units
        24 at 1/2 pace for 5 days =   3 000 units
            Total loss due to turnover =   9 000 units

    Loss due to reduced efficiency:
        loss of 5 upd × 12 workers × 10 days =   600 units
        loss of 5 upd × 36 × 50 days =   9 000 units
            Total loss due to reduced efficiency =   9 600 units

    Total loss =   18 600 units

FIGURE 10.8   A Good Solution to the Sample Problem (continued)

Jennifer M. Kirkland   2   October 13, 2013

Shows where numbers in para. 1 come from

According to the accounting department, Golden makes a net profit of $10 on every monitor we sell. And, as you know, we sell every monitor we make. Those 18 600 units we don't produce are costing us $186 000 a year.

Additional benefit

Bringing down the temperature to 25°C (the minimum allowed under provincial guidelines) from the present summer average of 30°C will require an investment of $500 000 to insulate and air-condition the warehouse. Extra energy costs for the air conditioning will run about $30 000 a year. We'll get our investment back in less than three years. Once the investment is recouped, we'll be making an additional $150 000 a year—all without buying additional equipment or hiring additional workers.

Tells reader what to do

Ends on positive note of problem solved, reader enjoying benefit

By installing the insulation and air conditioning this fall, we can take advantage of lower off-season rates. Please authorize the Purchasing Department to request bids for the system. Then, next summer, our productivity can be at an all-time high.

Reason to act promptly

FIGURE 10.9   Checklist for Direct Requests

- ❏ If the message is a memo, does the subject line indicate the request? Is the subject line specific enough to differentiate this message from others on the same subject?
- ❏ Does the first paragraph summarize the request or the specific topic of the message?
- ❏ Does the message give all the relevant information? Is there enough detail?
- ❏ Does the message answer questions or overcome objections that readers may have without introducing unnecessary negatives?
- ❏ Does the last paragraph ask for action? Does it give a deadline if one exists and a reason for acting promptly?

Checklist for All Messages, Not Just Direct Requests

- ❏ Does the message use you-attitude and positive emphasis?
- ❏ Is the style easy to read and friendly?
- ❏ Is the visual design of the message inviting?
- ❏ Is the format correct?
- ❏ Does the message use standard grammar? Is it free from typos?

Add Originality to a Direct Request

- ❏ Provide good lists and visual impact.
- ❏ Think about readers and give details that answer their questions, overcome any objections, and make it easier for them to do as you ask.
- ❏ Add details that show you're thinking of a specific organization and the specific people in that organization.

FIGURE 10.10   **Checklist for Indirect Persuasive Messages**

❏ If the message is a memo, does the subject line indicate the writer's purpose or offer a reader benefit? Does the subject line avoid making the request?
❏ Is the problem presented as a joint problem both writer and reader have an interest in solving, rather than as something the reader is being asked to do for the writer?
❏ Does the message give all the relevant information? Is there enough detail?
❏ Does the message overcome objections that readers may have?
❏ Does the message avoid phrases that sound dictatorial, condescending, or arrogant?
❏ Does the last paragraph ask for action? Does it give a deadline if one exists and a reason for acting promptly?

Checklist for All Messages, Not Just Persuasive Ones
❏ Does the message use you-attitude and positive emphasis?
❏ Is the style easy to read and friendly?
❏ Is the visual design of the message inviting?
❏ Is the format correct?
❏ Does the message use standard grammar? Is it free from typos?

Add Originality to a Problem-Solving Persuasive Message
❏ Use a good subject line and common ground.
❏ Include a clear and convincing description of the problem.
❏ Be sure the content reflects readers' interests, gives details that answer their questions, overcomes objections, and makes it easier for them to do as you ask.
❏ Include details that show you're thinking of a specific organization and the specific people in that organization.

MODULE SUMMARY

- All successful communication contains an element of persuasion: you can only get what you need and want when you recognize and try to meet your audience's needs and wants.
  - Use your PAIBOC analysis when considering how to organize your messages for best results.
- The direct approach works well when you anticipate that your audience will feel positively or neutrally about you and/or your message.
- The indirect, problem-solving approach works best when you anticipate your audience will be resistant to you and/or the message.

- People have a **vested interest** in something if they benefit directly from keeping things as they are.
- Analyze your audience members to understand their positions better, and to establish common ground.
- To counter objections, use sound logical and emotional appeals.
- To encourage readers to act promptly, give a deadline. Show that the time limit is real and that acting now will save time or money.

ASSIGNMENTS FOR MODULE 10

Questions for Critical Thinking

10.1 Different cultures value different types of appeals. What specific appeals do people in your culture find most persuasive?

10.2 Based on your own experiences and observations, conversations with friends and/or media advertising, what appeals might Canadians find most compelling? How do age, class, ethnicity, and/or geography

affect persuasive appeals? What other factors might impact what a person finds persuasive?

10.3 What specific persuasive appeals do infomercials make? Choose an example of an infomercial and identify the persuasion tactics. What story does the infomercial tell?

Exercises and Problems

10.4 Revising a Form Memo

You've been hired as a staff accountant; one of your major duties will be processing expense reimbursements. Going through the files, you find this form memo:

> Subject: Reimbursements
>
> Enclosed are either receipts that we could not match with the items in your request for reimbursement, or a list of items for which we found no receipts, or both. Please be advised that the Accounting Department issues reimbursement cheques only with full documentation. You cannot be reimbursed until you give us a receipt for each item for which you desire reimbursement. We must ask that you provide this information. This process may be easier if you use the Expense Report Form, available in your department.
>
> Thank you for your attention to this matter. Please do not hesitate to contact us with questions.

You know this is not a persuasive memo. In addition to wordiness, poor tone, and a vague subject line, the document design and organization of information bury the request.

Create a new memo that could be sent to people who do not provide all the documentation needed for them to be reimbursed.

10.5 Recommending a Co-worker for a Bonus or Award

Recommend someone at your workplace for a bonus or award. The award can be something bestowed by the organization itself (Employee of the Month, Dealership of the Year, and so forth), or it can be a community or campus award (Business Person of the Year, Volunteer of the Year, Order of Canada, an honorary degree, and so forth).

As your instructor directs

a. Create a document or presentation to achieve the goal.
b. Write a memo to your instructor describing the situation at your workplace and explaining your rhetorical choices (medium, strategy, tone, wording, organization, graphics or document design, and so forth).

10.6 Handling a Sticky Recommendation

As a supervisor in a not-for-profit provincial agency, you have a dilemma. You received this email message today:

> From: John Inoye, Director of Personnel, Communications
> Subject: Need Recommendation for Peggy Chafez
>
> Peggy Chafez has applied for a position in the Communications Department. Based on her application and interview, she is the leading candidate. However, before I offer the job to her, I need a letter of recommendation from her current supervisor.
>
> Could you please let me have your evaluation within a week? We want to fill the position as quickly as possible.

Peggy has worked in your office for 10 years. She designs, writes, and edits your office's monthly newsletter; she designed and maintains the department website. Her designs are creative; she's a very hard worker; she seems to know a lot about computers.

However, Peggy is in many ways an unsatisfactory staff member. Her standards are so high that most people find her intimidating. Some find her abrasive. People have complained to you that she's only interested in her own work; she seems to resent requests to help other people with projects. And yet both the newsletter and the website are projects that need frequent interaction. She's out of the office a lot. Some of that is required by her job, but some people don't like the fact that she's out of the office so much. They also complain that she doesn't return voicemail and email messages.

You think that managing your office would be a lot smoother if Peggy weren't there. You can't fire her: employees' jobs are secure once they get past the initial six-month probationary period. Because of budget constraints, you can hire new employees only if vacancies are created by resignations. You feel that it would be easy to find someone better.

If you recommended that John Inoye hire Peggy, you would be able to hire someone you want. If you recommended that John hire someone else, you might be stuck with Peggy for a long time.

As your instructor directs

a. Write an email message to John Inoye.
b. Write an email to your instructor listing the choices you've made and justifying your approach.

Hints:

- What are your options? Consciously look for more than two.
- Is it possible to select facts or to use connotations so that you are truthful but still encourage John to hire Peggy? Is it ethical? Is it certain that John would find Peggy's work as unsatisfactory as you do? If you write a strong recommendation and Peggy doesn't do well at the new job, will your credibility suffer? Why is your credibility important?

10.7 Writing Collection Letters

You have a small desktop publishing firm. Today, you've set aside some time to work on overdue bills.

As your instructor directs

Write letters for one or more of the following situations:

a. A $750 bill for producing three monthly newsletters for a veterinarian to mail to her clients. The agreement was that you'd bill her $250 each month. But somehow you haven't sent out bills for the last two months, so they'll go on this month's bill. You'd like payment for the whole bill, and you want to continue this predictable income of $250 a month.

b. A $200 bill for creating flyers for a local rock band to post. You've called twice and left messages on an answering machine, but nothing has happened. The bill is only three weeks overdue, but the band doesn't seem very stable. You want to be paid now.

c. A $3,750 bill, three weeks past due, for designing and printing a series of brochures for Creative Interiors, a local interior decorating shop. When you billed Creative Interiors, you got a note saying that the design was not acceptable and that you would not be paid until you redesigned it (at no extra charge) to the owner's satisfaction. The owner had approved the preliminary design on which the brochures were based; he did not explain in the note what was wrong with the final product. He's never free when you are; indeed, when you call to try to schedule an appointment, you're told the owner will call you back—but he never does. At this point, the delay is not your fault; you want to be paid.

10.8 Getting Permission from Parents for a School Project

As part of a community cleanup program, all public school students will spend the afternoon of the second Friday of April picking up trash. Younger students will pick up trash on school grounds, in parks, and in parking lots; older students will pick up trash downtown. Teachers will supervise the students; where necessary, school buses will transport them. After students are finished, they'll return to their school's playground, where they'll be supervised until the end of the school day. Each school will maintain a study hall for any students whose parents do not give them permission to participate. Trash bags and snacks have been donated by local merchants.

Write a one-page cover letter that students can take home to their parents telling them about the project and persuading them to sign the necessary permission form. You do not need to create the permission form but do refer to it in your letter.

Hints:

● What objections may parents have? How can you overcome these?

● Where should parents who drive their kids to school pick them up?

● Should students wear their normal school clothing?

● When must the form be returned? Who gets it? Whom can parents call if they have questions before they sign the form?

10.9 Asking an Instructor for a Letter of Recommendation

You're ready for the job market or for transfer to a college or university, and you need letters of recommendation.

As your instructor directs

a. Assume that you've asked an instructor for a recommendation, and he or she has agreed to write one. "Why don't you write up something to remind me of what you've done in the class? Tell me what else you've done, too. And tell me what they're looking for. Be sure to tell me when the letter needs to be in and whom it goes to."

b. Assume that you've been unable to talk with the instructor whose recommendation you want. When you call, no one answers the phone; you stopped by once and no one was in. Write asking for a letter of recommendation.

c. Assume that the instructor is no longer on campus. Write him or her a letter asking for a recommendation.

Hints:

● Detail the points you'd like the instructor to mention.

● How well will this instructor remember you? How much detail about your performance in his or her class do you need to provide?

● Specify the name and address of the person to whom the letter should be written; specify when the letter is due. If there's an intermediate due date (e.g., if you must sign the outside of the envelope to submit the recommendation), say so.

10.10 Recommending Investments*

Recommend whether your instructor should invest in a specific stock, piece of real estate, or other investment. As your instructor directs, assume that your instructor has $1,000, $10,000, or $100,000 to invest.

Hints:

● Pick a stock, property, or other investment you can research easily.

● What are your instructor's goals? Is he or she saving for a house? For retirement? For the kids' post-secondary education expenses? To pay off his or her own student loans? When will the money from the investment be needed?

● How much risk is your instructor comfortable with?

● Is your instructor willing to put time into the investment (as managing a rental house would require)?

*Based on an assignment created by Cathy Ryan, Ohio State University.

10.11 Retrieving Your Image

As director of business communication, you get this letter from Sharon Davis, a member of your college advisory board and a major donor:

> My bank received this email from one of your soon-to-be-graduates. It seems as though a closer look at writing skills is warranted.
>
> To Whom It May Concern:
>
> This is in reference to the loan soliciation that I received in the mail. This is the second offer that I am now inquiring about. The first offer sent to my previous address I did not respond. But after some careful though and consideration I think it

wise to consolidate my bills. Therefore I hope the information provided is sufficient to complete a successful application. I think the main purpose of this loan is to enable me to repair my credit history. I have problems in the past because of job status as part-time and being a student. I will be graduating in June and now I do have a full-time job. I think I just need a chance to mend the past credit problems that I have had.

As your instructor directs

a. Write to the faculty who teach business communications, reminding them that the quality of student writing may affect fundraising efforts.

b. Write to Ms. Davis, convincing her that, indeed, your school does make every effort to graduate students who can write.

10.12 Persuading Tenants to Pay the Rent

As the new manager of an apartment complex, you find this message in the files:

> ATTENTION!
>
> DERELICTS
>
> If you are a rent derelict (and you know if you are) this communiqué is directed to you!
>
> RENT IS DUE THE 5TH OF EACH MONTH AT THE LATEST!
>
> LEASE HAS A 5-DAY GRACE PERIOD UNTIL THE 5TH OF THE MONTH NOT THE 15TH.
>
> If rent is not paid in total by the 5th, you will pay the $25 late charge. You will pay the $25 late charge when you pay your late rent or your rent will not be accepted.
>
> Half of you people don't even know how much you pay a month. Please read your lease instead of calling up to waste our time finding out what you owe per month! Let's get with the program so I can spend my time streamlining and organizing maintenance requests. My job is maintenance only.
>
> RENT PAYMENT IS YOUR JOB!
>
> If you can show up for a test on time, why can't you make it to the rental office on time or just mail it?
>
> P.S. We don't take cash any longer due to a major theft.

This message is terrible. It lacks respect, and may even encourage people who are now paying on the 1st to wait until the 5th.

Write a message to go to people who have been slow to pay in the past.

10.13 Writing a Performance Appraisal for a Member of a Collaborative Group

During your collaborative writing group meetings, keep a log of events. Record the specifics of both effective and ineffective behaviours of group members. Then evaluate the performance of the other members in your group. (If there are two or more other people, write a separate appraisal for each of them.)

In your first paragraph, summarize your evaluation. Then, in the body of your memo, give the specific details that lead to your evaluation by answering the following questions:

- What specifically did the person do in terms of the task? Brainstorm ideas? Analyze the information? Draft the text? Suggest revisions in parts drafted by others? Format the document or create visuals? Revise? Edit? Proofread? (In most cases, several people will have done each of these activities together. Don't overstate what any one person did.) What was the quality of the person's work?

- What did the person contribute to the group process? Did he or she help schedule the work? Raise or resolve conflicts? Make other group members feel valued and included? Promote group cohesion? *What roles did the person play in the group?* (See What Roles Do People Play in Groups? in Module 21.)

Support your generalizations with specific observations. The more observations you have and the more detailed they are, the better your appraisal will be.

As your instructor directs

a. Write a midterm performance appraisal for one or more members of your collaborative group. In each appraisal, identify the two or three things the person could try to improve during the second half of the term.

b. Write a performance appraisal for one or more members of your collaborative group at the end of the term. Identify and justify the grade you think each person should receive for the portion of the grade-based group process.

c. Give a copy of your appraisal to the person about whom it is written.

POLISHING YOUR PROSE

Correcting Run-On Sentences

A sentence with too many ideas, strung together by coordinating conjunctions that lack the required comma, is a run-on. (Remember that coordinating conjunctions such as *and*, *or*, *for*, *yet*, and *but* need a comma to connect independent clauses.)

Although most run-on sentences are long, length is not the real problem. Don't confuse run-ons with grammatically

correct long sentences whose ideas are still clear to readers. Run-ons confound readers, because there are too many ideas competing for attention, and because the missing commas make the ideas harder to follow. The effect is similar to listening to a speaker who does not pause between sentences: Where does one point begin and another end?

Test for run-ons by looking for more than two main ideas in a sentence and a lack of commas with coordinating conjunctions:

> We installed the new computers this morning and they are running fine but there aren't enough computers for everyone so we are going to purchase more on Wednesday and we will install them and then the department will be fully operational.

Count the number of things going on in this sentence. Where are the commas?

Fix a run-on in one of three ways:

1. For short run-ons, add the missing commas:

    Incorrect: The purchasing department sent order forms but we received too few so we are requesting more.

    Correct: The purchasing department sent order forms, but we received too few, so we are requesting more.

2. Rewrite the sentence using subordination:

    Correct: Because we received too few order forms, we are requesting more from the purchasing department.

3. For longer run-ons, break the run-on into two or more sentences, add missing commas, and subordinate where appropriate.

    Correct: We installed the new computers this morning. They are running fine, but because there aren't enough computers for everyone, we are going to purchase more on Wednesday. We will install them, and then the department will be fully operational.

Exercises

Fix the following run-on errors:

1. The marketing department ordered new brochures that are really nice and the brochures are in four-colour.
2. All expense accounts should be itemized based on type and cost so remember to include the appropriate shipping confirmation number.
3. Work into your schedule some time to meet next week and we can talk about your promotion so you can transition easily into the new job.
4. We will take a final product inventory on December 1 and managers will report any lost stock so employees should make sure any broken items are reported and managers should record this information in their computer databases.
5. Employees may request benefits changes during the annual enrolment period and supervisors should pass out the required forms and employees should have them completed by the deadline on the form.
6. Ian leaves his computer on overnight but Aaron turns his off and Marilyn leaves hers on, too, and so does Tashi.
7. Mohammed should make sure he specifies 50-lb. rather than 40-lb. paper stock and Jenna should call the print shop and ask them whether they need anything and Bruce needs to tell Ms. Winans we appreciate her letting us know we originally ordered the wrong stock.
8. The Halifax office is planning a new marketing campaign so the St. John's office will help with the promotion but the Fredericton office is coordinating the product show.
9. A few customers are concerned about the shipping date but the mailroom is sure we can ship overnight and I think there's no reason to be concerned.
10. Last week I went to Montreal and Haj went to Miami and this week Tony took a trip too so our travel budget is almost gone.

Check the Answer Key for odd-numbered exercises.

Communicating Reader Benefits

Learning Objectives

After reading and applying the information in Module 11, you'll be able to demonstrate

Knowledge of

LO1 People's motivations and needs

LO2 The importance of identifying audience benefits

LO3 Elements of psychological description

Skills to

LO4 Use audience analysis to identify and choose reader benefits

LO5 Develop reader benefits with logic and detail

LO6 Match the benefit to the audience

MODULE OUTLINE

- How do reader benefits work?
- How do I identify reader benefits?
- How do I decide which benefits to use?
- What else do reader benefits need?

Module Summary

Assignments for Module 11

Polishing Your Prose: Plurals and Possessives

Employability Skills 2000+ Checklist

Module content builds these Conference Board of Canada Employability Skills 2000+

Communicate

Manage Information

Think and Solve Problems

Demonstrate Positive Attitudes and Behaviours

Learn Continuously

Staples' brand reinforces the basic benefit of shopping at Staples: it makes life easy for the customer.

Reader benefits are benefits or advantages the reader receives when

Ex. 11.1

- Using your services
- Buying your products
- Following your policies
- Adopting your ideas

How Do Reader Benefits Work?

Reader benefits appeal to the audience's attitudes and actions.

LO1 Reader benefits appeal to both the attitudes and the behaviours of your audience. When you describe benefits that focus on readers' needs and wants, people feel more positive about you and your request. Providing reader benefits makes it easier for you to accomplish your goals. Most people try to do their best only when they believe that they can succeed and when they want the rewards that success brings. Indeed, studies reveal that how we think about a task determines our feelings about the task "and ultimately our willingness to put our heads down and work."[1]

Ex. 11.7 11.11

LO2 Reader benefits convince readers that they can do the job successfully and that they will be rewarded.[2] Reader benefits help overcome two problems that reduce motivation: people may not think of all the possible benefits, and they may not understand the relationships among effort, performance, and reward.[3]

Checkpoint

Reader benefits are benefits or advantages that the reader gains when using your services, buying your products, following your policies, or adopting your ideas.

FIGURE 11.1   **A Persuasive Memo with Benefits**

Buy Right Groceries

Memo

To: Stan Jerzynski, Store Manager

CC:

From: Mitsui Kaido, Cashier   MK

Date: October 18, 2013

Re: Bottled Water at Checkouts

Staff presents supervisor with mutual problem & solution —

The store's new policy banning bottled water at cashiers' checkouts will be costly to enforce and could become a health and safety issue. However, modifying the policy costs nothing and would maintain staff morale.

Explanation of problem & results stated in terms of importance to audience —

The new policy will be expensive to enforce because some cashiers will need frequent reliefs to go to the staffroom for water breaks. More than the standard 15 minutes per shift means the store must hire and train at least two more part-timers to relieve potentially eight cashiers per shift.

Also, not having water readily available could become a health and safety issue if any cashier(s) cared to complain to the health and safety committee about unhealthy working conditions.

However, a small modification to the policy would cost nothing and would ensure that 1) cashiers' bottled water would not be obvious to customers, and 2) staff morale would not suffer.

— Three benefits
1) extrinsic
2) solves the problem
3) intrinsic

Instead of banning bottled water outright, why not ask cashiers to store their water containers in the cupboard beneath the counter where customers checking out cannot see them? Cashiers should not drink water while cashing people out, but if they get thirsty they could take sips between customers.

Another possible benefit —

The store could even encourage cashiers to buy our Kleen Canteen water bottles to drink from, which might promote a store product.

I would appreciate discussing these modifications with you further, at your convenience.

LO4 How Do I Identify Reader Benefits?

Use PAIBOC: Analyze your reader, and brainstorm.

Sometimes reader benefits are obvious and easy to describe. When they are harder to identify, brainstorm in two steps:

1. Think of the feelings, values, needs, and fears that may motivate your reader. Then identify features of your service, product, or policy that meet those values or needs.
2. Identify the obvious features of your product or policy. Then think how these features might benefit the audience.

Employability Skills

FIGURE 11.2   **PAIBOC Questions for Analysis**

P	Why are you communicating? What are your **purposes**? What results do you want?
A	Who is your **audience**? How will they respond to your message? Is it good or bad news for them? What does your audience need? What do they value? What will they find objectionable about your message? What's in it for them?
I	What **information** must your message include? What does your audience already know? What do they need to know? What organizational pattern will emphasize the positive parts of your message? What organizational pattern will de-emphasize the downside?
B	What reasons or reader **benefits** can you use to support your position? How do these benefits meet your audience's needs, match their values, and/or answer, "What's in it for me?"
O	What **objections** can you expect your audience to have? What information will eliminate or reduce these objections?
C	How will the **context** affect audience response? Consider your relationship with the audience, and economic, political, social and cultural, and organizational factors that may influence audience perception.

Try to brainstorm three to five possible benefits for every informative message and five to seven benefits for every persuasive message. The more benefits you think of, the easier it will be to choose ones that will directly appeal to your audience.

For example, supposing you want to start your own business: a window-washing service. What benefits does your service offer? Your brainstorming notes might look like those in Table 11.1.

TABLE 11.1   **Brainstorming to Identify Audience Benefits of a Window-Washing Service**

Customer Feelings, Values, Needs	Service Offers	Service Features	Customer Benefits
Cleaning windows takes a lot of time.	We spend the time.	We do the work and guarantee results.	Save time for other activities.
Takes a lot of energy.	We do the work.	We do the work and guarantee results.	Use energy on other projects.
It's a dirty job.	We get dirty.	We do the work and guarantee results.	Customer can forget about this dirty job, and does not have any mess to clean up.
Uses many products.	We use our own cleaning products.	Materials are all environmentally friendly.	Save money on buying these products; save storage space; feel good about not harming environment.
Leaves streaks.	Trained employees do streak-free job.	We guarantee results.	Satisfaction.
Have to get the ladder out; have to climb up ladder.	We bring and climb ladder.	Customer safety.	Worry- and hassle-free job done for you.
Window-cleaning service costs money.	We offer competitive prices.	Money spent offers peace of mind and quality work.	Good value: freedom from low-level chore = time to spend on more interesting, fun projects.

LO1   I. Consider Your Readers' Needs

One of the best-known analyses of needs is Abraham H. Maslow's hierarchy of needs.[4] Maslow's model (Figure 11.3) is a good starting point to identify the feelings, fears, and needs that may motivate your audience. Physical needs are the most basic, followed by needs for safety and security, for love and a sense of belonging, for esteem and recognition, and finally for self-actualization or self-fulfilment.

But we do not experience these needs sequentially, the way they are illustrated. Instead, we all go back and forth between higher-level and lower-level needs. Whenever lower-level needs make themselves felt, they take priority. When we're hungry for lunch, for example, that low-level need takes up our attention: we are much less motivated then to pay attention to a lecture.

Compare the PAIBOC model with Maslow's hierarchy. Notice that you must define and refine your message **purpose(s)**, **information**, **benefits, anticipated objections**, and **context** according to the needs of your **audience**.

Often a product or idea can meet needs on several levels. Focus on the ones that your audience analysis suggests are most relevant for your audience. But remember, even the best analysis

FIGURE 11.3   Organizational Motivations for Maslow's Hierarchy of Needs

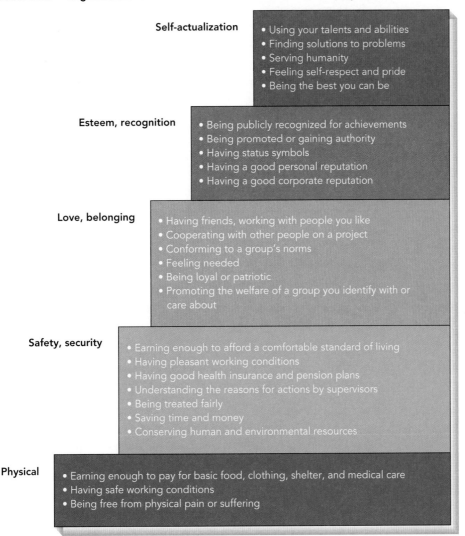

Self-actualization
- Using your talents and abilities
- Finding solutions to problems
- Serving humanity
- Feeling self-respect and pride
- Being the best you can be

Esteem, recognition
- Being publicly recognized for achievements
- Being promoted or gaining authority
- Having status symbols
- Having a good personal reputation
- Having a good corporate reputation

Love, belonging
- Having friends, working with people you like
- Cooperating with other people on a project
- Conforming to a group's norms
- Feeling needed
- Being loyal or patriotic
- Promoting the welfare of a group you identify with or care about

Safety, security
- Earning enough to afford a comfortable standard of living
- Having pleasant working conditions
- Having good health insurance and pension plans
- Understanding the reasons for actions by supervisors
- Being treated fairly
- Saving time and money
- Conserving human and environmental resources

Physical
- Earning enough to pay for basic food, clothing, shelter, and medical care
- Having safe working conditions
- Being free from physical pain or suffering

may not reveal the most pressing of your reader's needs. For example, a well-paid manager may be worried about security if her spouse has lost his job or if the couple is supporting children in college or an elderly parent.

Furthermore, age and culture influence motivation (Module 3). For example, Millennials (people born between 1980 and 2000) value inclusiveness and flexibility. In the workplace, "they want to make a meaningful contribution immediately, and they want their input to be taken seriously." Therefore, challenging work motivates them more than pay or security.[5]

2. Translate Features into Benefits

A feature by itself is not a benefit. A **feature** is a part of the product or service itself, while a **benefit** results from using the feature. For example, a feature of a door-to-door dry cleaning service is that the service picks up your dirty clothes and delivers your clean clothes. The **benefit** to you is saving time and gas. (A benefit you'll pay for, by the way, in higher dry-cleaning costs!)

Often, a feature has several possible benefits.

Feature: Lowering office air conditioning and lighting

Benefits: Saves energy
Reduces overhead costs
Is easy to do
Could reduce monitor glare
Encourages awareness
Encourages people to feel they can contribute

Feature: Carpooling

Benefits: Saves fuel costs and vehicle wear and tear

Reduces greenhouse gas emissions

Enables carpoolers to use fastest highway lane: people can wake up later and get to work sooner

Reduces driving anxiety

Is easy to do

Encourages awareness

Encourages people to feel they can contribute

Feature: Flextime

Benefits: Enables workers to accommodate personal needs

Helps organizations recruit, retain workers

Makes more workers available in early morning and in evening

Enables office to stay open longer—more service to clients, customers

Enables workers to communicate with colleagues in different time zones more easily

Different features may benefit different subgroups in your audience. Depending on the features a restaurant offers, you might appeal to one or more of the subgroups shown in Table 11.2. To develop your benefits, think about the details of each one. If your selling point is your relaxing atmosphere, think about the specific details that make the restaurant relaxing. If your strong point is elegant dining, consider all the details that contribute to that elegance. Sometimes you may offer features that do not meet any particular need but are still good benefits. In a sales letter for a restaurant, you might also want to mention your free coatroom, your convenient location, free parking or a drive-up window, and speedy service.

TABLE 11.2 Audience Subgroups

Subgroup	Features to Meet the Subgroup's Needs
People who work outside the home	A quick lunch; a relaxing place to take clients or colleagues
Parents with small children	High chairs, child-sized portions, and activities to keep the kids entertained while they wait for their order
People who eat out a lot	Variety both in food and decor
People on tight budgets	Economical food; a place where they don't need to tip (cafeteria or fast food)
People on special diets	Low-sodium and low-calorie dishes; vegetarian food; kosher food
People for whom eating out is part of an evening's entertainment	Music or a floor show; elegant surroundings; reservations so people can get to a show or event after dinner; late hours so they can come to dinner after a show or game

Whenever you're writing to customers or clients about features that are not unique to your organization, present both the benefits of the features themselves *and* the benefits of dealing with your company. If you talk about the benefits of dining in a relaxed atmosphere but don't mention your own restaurant, people may go somewhere else!

LO6 How Do I Decide Which Benefits to Use?

Use the following three guidelines to decide.

Three principles guide your choice of reader benefits:

1. Use at least one benefit for each subgroup in your audience.
2. Use intrinsic benefits.
3. Use the benefits you can develop most fully.

1. Use at Least One Benefit for Each Subgroup in Your Audience

Most messages go to multiple audiences. In a memo announcing a company-subsidized day-care program, you want to describe benefits not only for parents who might use the service, but also for people who don't have children or whose children are older. Reader benefits for these last two audiences help convince them that spending money on daycare is a good use of scarce company funds.

In a letter to "consumers" or "voters," different people will have different concerns. The more of these concerns you address, the more persuasive you'll be.

LO1 2. Use Intrinsic Benefits

Intrinsic benefits are natural outcomes of doing something, or using a product. Such benefits appeal to our need to feel good about ourselves. For example, an intrinsic benefit of helping a friend in need is feeling kind. An intrinsic benefit of getting an A on an assignment is feeling recognized. The Beer Store survey appeal (see Figure 11.4) offers intrinsic benefits to meet such high-level needs as feeling needed, co-operative, loyal, and recognized.

LO3 LO5   EXPANDING A CRITICAL SKILL

Creating Audience-Focused Benefits

Develop reader benefits by linking features to readers' needs—and provide details to make the benefit clear!

Use concrete, vivid details. Paint a mental picture.

You may need several sentences to give enough details about a reader benefit. If you develop two or three reader benefits fully, you can use just a sentence or two for less important benefits.

Weak: We have placemats with riddles.

Better: Answering all the riddles on Caesar's special placemats will keep the kids happy until your pizza comes. If they don't have time to finish (and they may not, since your pizza is ready so quickly), just take the riddles home—or answer them on your next visit.

Make your reader benefits specific.

Weak: You get quick service.

Better: If you only have an hour for lunch, try our Business Buffet. Within minutes, you can choose from a variety of main dishes, vegetables, and a make-your-own-sandwich-and-salad bar. You can put together a lunch that's as light or filling as you want, with time to enjoy it—and still be back to the office on time.

Psychological description is a technique you can use to develop vivid, specific reader benefits. Psychological description means creating a scenario rich with sense impressions—what the reader sees, hears, smells, tastes, feels—so readers can picture themselves using your product or service and enjoying its benefits. You can also use psychological description to describe the problem your product will solve. Psychological description works best early in the message to catch readers' attention.

Feature: Snooze alarm

Benefit: When you press the snooze button, the alarm goes off and comes on again nine minutes later.

Psychological description: Some mornings, you really want to stay in bed just a few more minutes. With the Sleepytime Snooze Alarm, you can snuggle under the covers for a few extra winks, secure in the knowledge that the alarm will come on again to get you up for that breakfast meeting with an important client. If you want to sleep in, you can keep hitting the snooze alarm for up to an additional 63 minutes of sleep. With Sleepytime, you're in control of your mornings.

Feature: Tilt windows

Benefit: Easier to clean

Psychological description: No wonder so many cleaners "don't do windows." Balancing precariously on a rickety ladder to clean upper-story windows…shivering outside in the winter winds and broiling in the summer sun as you scrub away…running inside, then outside, then inside again to try to get the spot that always seems to be on the other side. Cleaning traditional windows really is a chore.

You'll find cleaning a breeze with Tilt-in Windows. Just pull the inner window down and pull the bottom toward you. The whole window lifts out! Repeat for the outer window. Clean inside in comfort (sitting down or even watching TV if you choose). Then replace the top of the outer window in its track, slide up, and repeat with the inner window. Presto! Clean windows!

With psychological description, you're putting your reader in a picture. If the reader doesn't feel that the picture fits, the technique backfires. To prevent this, psychological description often uses subjunctive verbs ("If you like…" "If you were…") or the words *maybe* and *perhaps*.

You're exhausted after a long day. You're hungry but too tired to cook. Perhaps you are having guests for dinner. Or it's your turn to bring Mom and Dad a meal. Or you only have a half-hour for lunch. Whatever the situation, foodathome.com cooks delicious, nutritious meals and delivers them to your door.

If you want homemade, we have it. If you want plenty of choice, we have it. If you want free delivery, we have it. And the price is right.

So why not make the convenient, budget-wise choice for your next dining dilemma: order online at foodathome.com

FIGURE 11.4   A Promotional Handout with Intrinsic and Extrinsic Appeals

This survey request offers both intrinsic and extrinsic benefits.

Extrinsic benefits are "added on"; they do not necessarily come from using the product, or doing the action. The Beer Store appeal offers 50 chances to win a prize for completing the online survey. You may not win; chances are that you won't, given the number of people who may choose to participate in the survey. But the extrinsic benefit is the added inducement of the chance to win.

Table 11.3 gives examples of extrinsic and intrinsic rewards for three activities.

Intrinsic rewards or benefits are better than extrinsic benefits for two reasons:

1. There just aren't enough extrinsic rewards for everything you want people to do. You can't give a prize to every customer every time he or she places an order or a promotion to every subordinate who does what he or she is supposed to do.
2. Research suggests that you'll motivate people more effectively by stressing the intrinsic benefits of following policies and adopting proposals. People prefer recognition and respect to more tangible rewards.

TABLE 11.3   Extrinsic and Intrinsic Rewards

Activity	Intrinsic Reward	Extrinsic Reward
Making a sale	Pleasure in convincing someone; pride in using your talents to create a strategy and execute it	Getting a commission
Turning in a suggestion to a company suggestion system	Solving a problem at work; making the work environment a little pleasanter; feeling pride in a job well done	Getting a monetary reward when the suggestion is implemented
Writing a report that solves an organizational problem	Pleasure in having an effect on an organization; pride in using your skills to solve problems; pleasure in solving the problem itself	Getting praise, a good performance appraisal, and maybe a raise

Indeed, in a groundbreaking study of professional employees, Frederick Herzberg found that the things people said they liked about their jobs were all intrinsic rewards—pride in achievement, an enjoyment of the work itself, responsibility. Extrinsic features—pay, company policy—were sometimes mentioned as things people disliked, but they were never cited as things that motivated or satisfied them. People who made a lot of money still did not mention salary as a good point about the job or the organization.[6]

Language FOCUS

Turnover refers to how quickly employees come and go at a company. A company with high turnover incurs many additional expenses, such as placing ads in newspapers or online for new candidates, spending time and money interviewing new people, and training new hires. Most companies try to keep turnover low.

Many family-friendly companies have discovered that a culture of care keeps turnover low. The higher salary that a competitor might pay doesn't overcome the advantage of working at a supportive, flexible company that values its employees.[7] In the current job market, different candidates want different things. But many accept lower salaries to get flextime, stock options, interesting work, or people they want to work with.[8]

Checkpoint

Good reader benefits are

- Adapted to the audience
- Based on intrinsic advantages
- Supported clearly and comprehensively
- Phrased using you-attitude

Employability Skills
2 **+**

LO5 3. Use the Benefits You Can Develop Most Fully

An audience benefit is a reward for the reader if he or she does something. Convincing the audience, therefore, requires two steps: ensuring that the benefit appeals to your reader and really will happen, and explaining it to the reader. One-sentence benefits don't do much. Develop benefits in three to five sentences or more.

Your benefit(s) have to be relevant and real. If the logic behind a claimed reader benefit is faulty or inaccurate, there's no way to make that particular reader benefit convincing. Revise the benefit to make it logical.

Faulty logic:	Using a computer will enable you to write letters, memos, and reports much more quickly.
Analysis:	If you've never used a computer, in the short run it will take you *longer* to create a document using a computer than it would to type it. Even after you know how to a computer and its software, the real-time savings come when a document incorporates parts of previous documents or goes through several revisions. Creating a first draft from scratch still takes planning and careful composing; the time savings may or may not be significant.
Revised reader benefit:	Using a computer allows you to revise and edit a document more easily. It eliminates retyping as a separate step and reduces the time needed to proofread revisions. It allows you to move the text around on the page to create the best layout.

If the logic is sound, making that logic evident to the reader is a matter of providing enough evidence and showing how the evidence proves the benefit claim. Always provide enough detail to be vivid and concrete. (See this chapter's Expanding a Critical Skill box.)

You'll need more detail in the following situations:

- The reader may not have thought of the benefit before.
- The benefit depends on the difference between the long run and the short run.

- The reader will be hard to persuade, and you need detail to make the benefit vivid and emotionally convincing.

Does the following statement have enough detail?

You'll save money by using our shop-at-home service.

Audiences always believe their own experience. People who have never used a shop-at-home service may think, "If somebody else does my shopping for me, I'll have to pay that person. I'll save money by doing it myself." They might not think of the savings in gas and parking, in travel time, and in less car wear and tear.

Readers who already use shop-at-home services may believe you if they compare your items and services with another company's to see that your cost is lower. Even then, you could make saving money seem more forceful and more vivid by telling readers how much they could save and mentioning some of the ways they might use your service.

What Else Do Reader Benefits Need?

Check for audience focus.

If reader benefits aren't stated in audience-focused terms, they'll sound egocentric and won't be as effective as they could be. It doesn't matter how you phrase audience benefits while you're brainstorming and developing them, but in your final draft, edit for audience focus.

Lacks audience focus:	We have the lowest prices in town.
Audience focus:	At Abbotsford Honda, you get the best deal in town.

The Beer Store survey request (Figure 11.4) uses audience-focused language throughout. Both the intrinsic appeal ([You] *Please take a few minutes…your feedback…*) and the extrinsic benefit (*you could WIN…*) are emphatically reader-based.

MODULE SUMMARY

- Reader benefits are advantages the reader gains from using your services, buying your products, following your policies, or adopting your ideas. Reader benefits assure readers that they can do the job and their success will be rewarded.

- Good reader benefits are adapted to the audience, based on innate, intrinsic, esteem, and recognition advantages, supported by clear logic, detailed, and presented with you-attitude. There are not enough extrinsic (external) benefits to reward every desired behaviour; furthermore, extrinsic benefits reduce the high-level satisfaction in doing something for its own sake.

- To create reader benefits:
  - Identify the feelings, needs, and fears that may motivate your reader.
  - Describe how readers can meet their needs with the features of your service, product, or policy.

- Psychological description creates rich sense impressions—what the reader can see, hear, smell, taste, feel—so readers can picture themselves using your product and service and enjoying its benefits.

- Brainstorm twice as many reader benefits you think you'll need for a message. Use the benefits you can develop most fully.

- Make sure you communicate reader benefits with audience focus.

ASSIGNMENTS FOR MODULE 11

Questions for Critical Thinking

11.1 Different cultures value different benefits. What specific benefits would motivate people in your culture?

11.2 What three intrinsic benefits motivate you most strongly? Which of these, if any, are related to your age? Which are related to your culture?

11.3 Identify three ways you can apply your knowledge of Maslow's hierarchy of needs to improving your professional and/or interpersonal communications.

Exercises and Problems

11.4 Identifying and Developing Reader Benefits

Listed here are five things an organization might like its employees to do:

1. Use less paper
2. Attend a brown-bag lunch to discuss ways to improve products or services
3. Become more physically fit
4. Volunteer for community organizations
5. Ease a new hire's transition into the unit

As your instructor directs,

a. Identify the motives or needs that might be met by each of the activities.
b. Develop each need or motive as a reader benefit in a full paragraph. Use additional paragraphs for the other needs met by the activity.

11.5 Identifying Objections and Reader Benefits

Think of an organization you know something about, and answer the following questions for it:

1. Your organization is thinking of creating a training video. What objections might people have? What benefits could videos offer your organization? Which people would be easiest to convince?
2. The advisory council of Nunavut Arctic College recommends that business faculty complete three-month internships with local organizations as a learning experience. What objections might people in your organization have to bringing in faculty interns? What benefits might your organization receive? Which people would be easiest to convince?
3. Your organization wants to start a workplace social networking site. How could the organization benefit? How could employees benefit? What objections might employees have?

As your instructor directs

a. Share your answers orally with a small group of students.
b. Present your answers in an oral presentation to the class.
c. Email your answers to class members.
d. Write a paragraph developing the best reader benefit you identified. Remember to use you-attitude.

11.6 Identifying and Developing Reader Benefits for Different Audiences

You want to encourage people to do one of the activities listed below. What objections do you anticipate your audiences might have? What benefits can you offer that would overcome these objections?

1. Hire a personal trainer

   Audiences: Professional athletes
   Busy managers
   Someone trying to lose weight
   Someone making a major lifestyle change after a heart attack

2. Buy a cell phone

   Audiences: People who do a lot of driving
   Older people
   People who drive in rural areas
   People who do a lot of flying

3. Get advice about interior decorating

   Audiences: Young people with little money to spend
   Parents with small children
   People upgrading or adding to their furnishings
   Older people moving from single-family homes into apartments or condominiums
   Builders furnishing model homes

4. Get advice on investment strategies

Audiences: New college or university graduates

People earning more than $100,000 annually

People responsible for investing funds for a church, synagogue, temple, or mosque

Parents with small children

People within 10 years of retirement

5. Gardening

Audiences: People with small children

People in apartments

People concerned about reducing pesticides

People on tight budgets

Retirees

Teenagers

6. Buy voice-activated computer software

Audiences: College and university students

Financial planners who visit clients at home

Sales representatives who travel constantly

People who make PowerPoint presentations

Older people

7. Teach adults to read

Audiences: Retired workers

Businesspeople

Students who want to become teachers

High school, college, and university students

People concerned about poverty

8. Vacation at a luxury hotel

Audiences: Stressed-out people who want to relax

Tourists who like to sightsee and absorb the local culture

Businesspeople who want to stay in touch with the office even on vacation

Parents with small children

Weekend athletes who want to have fun

As your instructor directs

a. Identify needs that you could meet for the audiences listed here. In addition to needs that several audiences share, identify at least one need that would be particularly important to each group.

b. Identify a product or service that could meet each need.

c. Write a paragraph or two of reader benefits for each product or service. Remember to use you-attitude.

d. Develop one or more of the benefits using psychological description.

Hints:

- For this assignment, you can combine benefits or programs as if a single source offered them all.
- Add specific details about particular sports, cities, tourist attractions, activities, and so on, as material for your description.
- Be sure to move beyond reader benefits to vivid details and sense impressions.
- Phrase your benefits using you-attitude.

11.7 Asking for a Raise or Reclassification

Do you deserve a raise? Should your job be reclassified to reflect your increased responsibilities (with more pay, of course!)? If so, write a memo to the person with the authority to determine pay and job titles, arguing for what you want.

As your instructor directs

a. Create a document or presentation to achieve the goal.

b. Write a memo to your instructor describing the situation at your workplace and explaining your rhetorical choices (medium, strategy, tone, wording, organization, graphics or document design, and so forth).

11.8 Persuading Guests to Allow Extra Time for Check-Out

Your hotel has been the headquarters for a convention, and on Sunday morning, you're expecting 1,000 people to check out before noon. You're staffing the checkout desk to capacity, but if everyone waits until 11:30 a.m. to check out, things will be a disaster.

You want to encourage people to allow extra time. And they don't have to stand in line at all: by 4:00 a.m., you'll put a statement of current charges under each guest's door. If that statement is correct and the guest is leaving the bill on the credit card used at check-in, the guest can just leave the key in the room and go. You'll mail a copy of the final bill, together with any morning charges, by the end of the week.

Write a one-page message that can be put on pillows when the rooms are made up Friday and Saturday night.

11.9 Persuading an Organization to Expand Flextime

Municipal government offices are open from 9:00 a.m. to 5:00 p.m. Employees have limited flextime: they can come in and leave half an hour early or half an hour late. But employees want much more flexible hours. Some people want to start at 6:00 a.m. so they can leave at 2:00 p.m.; others want to work from 11:00 a.m. to 7:00 p.m. When the idea was proposed, supervisors were very negative. "How will we hold staff meetings? How can we supervise people if everyone works different hours? We have to be here for the public, and we won't be if people work whatever hours they please."

But conversations with co-workers and a bit of research show that there are solutions. Many firms that use flextime require everyone to be at work (or at lunch) between 10:00 a.m. and 2:00 p.m. or 11:00 a.m. and 2:00 p.m., so that staff meetings can be scheduled. Right now, when clients call, a representative is frequently on the phone and has to call back. Voicemail and better message forms might solve the problem. And flextime might actually let offices stay open longer hours—say 8:00 a.m. to 6:00 p.m., which would be helpful for taxpayers who themselves work 9:00 a.m. to 5:00 p.m. and now can come in only on their own lunch hours. Write a memo to the mayor and municipal council, persuading them to approve a change in work hours.

Hints:

- Assume that this situation is happening in your own municipal government. What services does the municipality offer?
- Use any facts about your municipality that are helpful (e.g., being especially busy right now, having high turnover, dealing with tax issues).
- Use what you know about managing to allay managers' fears.
- Use the analysis that you developed for Exercise 2.7.

11.10 Persuading Disability Services to Increase the Handivan's Hours

The local community college has a "Handivan" that takes students who use wheelchairs from their residences or apartments to campus locations and back again. But the van stops at 6:00 p.m. (even though there are evening classes, lectures, and events). And it doesn't take people to off-campus restaurants, movies, grocery stores, or shopping centres. Write to the director of disability services, urging that the Handivan's services be increased.

11.11 Persuading Employees to Join the Company Volleyball Team

Your company has decided to start a company volleyball team to play in the city recreation league. Now you need to get people to sign up for the team. Ideally, you'd like to have several teams to involve as many people as possible and build company loyalty. If you have enough teams, they can play each other once a week in a round-robin company tournament.

Write a memo to all employees persuading them to sign up.

Hints:

- How young and how athletic are your employees? How busy are they? Will this be an easy or a difficult thing to persuade them to do?
- Some people may be reluctant to join because their skills are rusty. How can you persuade people that you want everyone to participate even if they're not athletic?
- Will the people who sign up have to pay anything or buy uniforms?
- How do people sign up? Is there a deadline?
- What other perks or positives might team members enjoy?

11.12 Informing Employees about a New Policy or a Policy Change

- Organizational policies—like paying for coffee or personal photocopying—are a reaction to changing circumstances—such as an economic downturn or an increase in personnel. Think of a situation at your workplace that requires a policy or a change in policy. What is the situation, and what are the results? What should people be doing instead, and what would be the benefits?

As your instructor directs

a. Draft the new policy or the policy change.
b. Write a memo to your supervisor describing the situation at your workplace and explaining your new/revised policy (and the benefits).
c. Write a memo to your fellow employees describing the situation at your workplace and explaining your new/revised policy (and the benefits).

POLISHING YOUR PROSE

Plurals and Possessives

Possessives and plurals usually sound the same but don't mean the same to your readers. And they are spelled differently. You add an apostrophe to show possession or ownership. You make nouns plural by adding *s*; when the noun ends in *y*, you drop the *y* and replace with *ies*. However, you almost never add an apostrophe to pluralize a noun.

Right:	No cameras allowed in the theatre.
Wrong:	No camera's allowed in the theatre.
Wrong:	No cameras' allowed in the theatre.

Singular Possessive	Plural Possessive	Plural
company's	companies'	companies
computer's	computers'	computers
family's	families'	families
job's	jobs'	jobs
manager's	managers'	managers
team's	teams'	teams

When possessive nouns and plurals sound the same, you have to look at the logic of your sentence to choose the right punctuation.

Exercises

Choose the right word in each set of parentheses.

1. Canadian (companies, company's) are competing effectively in the global market.

2. We can move your (families, family's) furniture safely and efficiently.

3. (Managers, Manager's, Managers') ability to listen is more important than their technical knowledge.

4. A (memos, memo's) appearance, word choice, paragraph length, and subject heading can positively or negatively influence the reader.

5. The community (social workers, social worker's) tell clients about services available in their neighbourhoods.

6. Savvy employees check the (companies, company's, companies') benefit plan periodically to make sure it continues to serve their needs.

7. Information about the new community makes the (families, family's) move easier.

8. The (managers, manager's) all have open-door policies.

9. (Memos, Memo's) are internal documents, sent to other workers in the same organization. (Letters', Letters, Letter's) are for external readers.

10. Burnout affects an (employees', employees, employee's) productivity and morale.

Check your answers to the odd-numbered exercises in the Polishing Your Prose Answer Key.

Communicating with Positive Emphasis

MODULE OUTLINE

- What's the point of positive emphasis?
- What should I do if my message is bad news?
- How do I create positive emphasis?
- Why do I need to think about tone, politeness, and power?
- What's the best way to apologize?

Module Summary

Assignments for Module 12

Polishing Your Prose: Using the Apostrophe to Show Ownership

Learning Objectives

After reading and applying the information in Module 12, you'll be able to demonstrate

Knowledge of

LO1 Methods to reframe information positively

LO2 The legal and practical advantages of doing business ethically

LO3 Techniques to convey appropriate tone in your messages

Skills to

LO4 Continue to build your persuasion skills

LO5 Emphasize the positive

LO6 Use positive emphasis ethically

LO7 Choose an appropriate tone

Employability Skills 2000+ Checklist

Module content builds these Conference Board of Canada Employability Skills 2000+

Communicate

Think and Solve Problems

Manage Information

Be Adaptable

Positive emphasis is a way of presenting or framing a situation. Framing a position positively—through conscious choices in layout (Module 5), medium, format and organization (Modules 8–10), and word choice—can affect people's perceptions and, therefore, their behaviour.[1] And positive emphasis is persuasive. Projecting the positive can favourably influence your audience's opinion of you and your message. Even when delivering negative messages, doing so clearly, briefly, and honestly—as Toyota did in a variety of media throughout the recall crisis that started in 2009[2]—can positively influence your audiences.

LO1 LO4 What's the Point of Positive Emphasis?

Positive emphasis is part of creating goodwill.

A positive work environment is essential to recruit, retain, and motivate employees.[3] And, according to VanCity Savings Credit Union CEO Dave Mowat, a positive workplace is more productive: "…you can draw a direct, straight-line relationship to the financial success of

Ex. 12.8

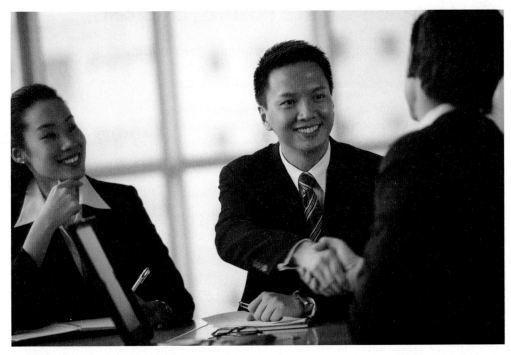

Positive emphasis is part of successful communication.

your company. It is just a fact that the higher the morale of your organization, the more money you make."[4] Positive emphasis is characteristic of successful entrepreneurs, since they perceive opportunities and are undaunted by failure.[5] Furthermore, people who choose to communicate positively tend to live longer and healthier lives.[6] Positive emphasis is part of successful communication.

LO2 What Should I Do If My Message Is Bad News?

Deliver the news responsibly: be clear and sensitive.

It is important, for both legal and practical reasons, to deliver negative information sensitively. Straightforward negatives build credibility when you have bad news to give the reader, such as announcements of layoffs, product defects and recalls, or price increases. Being honest about the drawbacks of a job situation increases motivation, morale, and the likelihood that employees will stay. Furthermore, negatives may help people take a problem seriously. Wall Data improved the reliability of its computer programs when it eliminated the term *bugs* and used the term *failures* instead.

In some messages, such as negative performance appraisals, the purpose is to deliver a rebuke with no alternative. In these situations, the supervisor or boss is legally responsible for ensuring that his/her language conforms to organizational and governmental regulations (in a union environment, to the rules in the collective agreement; in every workplace situation, to the province's *Employment Standards Act/Code* and to the Human Rights Commission mandates concerning issues of harassment and discrimination). In most situations, however, it's better to be positive. People respond more favourably to positive than to negative language, and are more likely to act on a positively worded request.[7]

LO1 LO5 How Do I Create Positive Emphasis?

De-emphasize or omit negative words and information.

The following five techniques de-emphasize negative information:

1. Avoid negative words and words with negative connotations.
2. Focus on what the reader can do rather than on limitations.
3. Justify negative information by giving a reason or linking it to a reader benefit (Modules 9 and 11).
4. Omit the negative if it is unimportant (Module 9).
5. Put the negative information in the middle and present it compactly.

Figures 12.1 and 12.2 show the difference you can make by de-emphasizing the negative. You can choose words and organizational patterns that de-emphasize the negative while achieving your purposes and meeting the needs of your audience.

FIGURE 12.1   Draft Email with Negative Emphasis

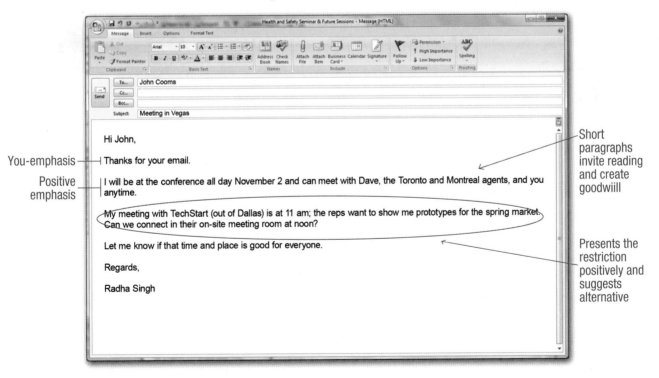

Takes writer 12 words to get to the point

Negative word

Negative — the reader doesn't need to know this

Negative

Phrased as a negative

No close

FIGURE 12.2   Revised Email with Positive Emphasis

You-emphasis

Positive emphasis

Short paragraphs invite reading and create goodwiill

Presents the restriction positively and suggests alternative

TABLE 12.1   Negative Words to Avoid

Negative Words			Some *dis-* Words	Some *mis-* Words
afraid	fail	objection	disapprove	misfortune
anxious	fault	problem	dishonest	missing
avoid	fear	reject	dissatisfied	mistake
bad	hesitate	reluctant		
careless	ignorant	sorry	**Many *in-* Words**	**Many *un-* Words**
damage	ignore	terrible	inadequate	unclear
delay	impossible	trivial	incomplete	unfair
delinquent	lacking	trouble	inconvenient	unfortunate
deny	loss	wait	injury	unfortunately
difficulty	neglect	weakness	insincere	unpleasant
eliminate	never	worry		unreasonable
error	no	wrong		unreliable
except	not			unsure

LO3 LO5   Avoid Negative Words and Words with Negative Connotations

Table 12.1 lists some common negative words. If you find one of these words in a draft, substitute a more positive word. When you must use a negative, use the *least negative* term that will convey your meaning.

The following examples show how to replace negative words with positive words.

Negative: We have failed to finish taking inventory.

Better: We haven't finished taking inventory.

Still better: We will be finished taking inventory on Friday.

Negative: If you can't understand this explanation, feel free to call me.

Better: If you have further questions, please call me.

Still better: (Omit the sentence.)

If a sentence has two negatives, substitute one positive term.

Negative: Do not forget to back up your disks.

Better: Always back up your disks.

When you must use a negative term, use the least negative word that is accurate.

Negative: Your balance of $835 is delinquent.

Better: Your balance of $835 is past due.

Sentences with three or more negatives are very hard to understand.[8] Getting rid of negatives has the added benefit of making what you write easier to understand.

Language FOCUS

Connotation means an associated meaning for a word, not the literal meaning. For example, if you think of the word "dog," you may think of caring and loyalty if you like dogs, but if you are afraid of dogs, the connotation is negative. Words have many connotations in different cultures, so it important to be aware of these as well as the literal meaning of words. If you are using a translation dictionary while composing, be sure to use a good English dictionary to check for both literal and connotative meanings.

Beware of **hidden negatives**: words that are not negative in themselves but become negative in context. *But* and *however* indicate a shift; so, after a positive statement, they are negative. *I hope* and *I trust that* suggest you aren't sure. *Patience* may sound like a virtue, but it is a necessary virtue only when things are slow. Even positives about a service or product may backfire if they suggest that in the past the service or product was bad.

Negative:	I hope this is the information you wanted. (Implication: I'm not sure.)
Better:	Enclosed is a brochure about road repairs scheduled for 2013–2014.
Still better:	The brochure contains a list of all roads and bridges scheduled for repair during 2013–2014. Call Gwen Wong at 604-555-3245 for specific dates when work will start and stop and for alternative routes.
Negative:	Please be patient as we switch to the automated system. (Implication: You can expect problems.)
Better:	If you have questions during our transition to the automated system, call Melissa Morgan.
Still better:	You'll be able to get information instantly about any house on the market when the automated system is in place. If you have questions during the transition, call Melissa Morgan.
Negative:	Now Crispy Krisp tastes better. (Implication: It used to taste terrible.)
Better:	Now Crispy Krisp tastes even better.

Removing negatives does not mean being arrogant or pushy.

Negative:	I hope that you are satisfied enough to place future orders.
Arrogant:	I look forward to receiving all of your future business.
Better:	Call Mercury whenever you need transistors.

When you eliminate negative words, be sure to maintain accuracy. Words that are exact opposites will usually not be accurate. Instead, use specifics to be both positive and accurate.

Negative:	The exercycle is not guaranteed for life.
Not true:	The exercycle is guaranteed for life.
True:	The exercycle is guaranteed for 10 years.
Negative:	Customers under 25 are not eligible for the Prime Time discount.

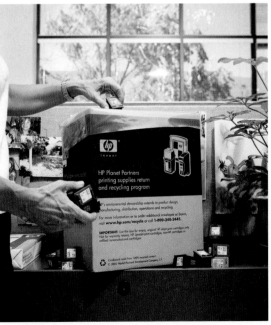

Hewlett-Packard's free recycling envelope positively emphasizes free and easy environmental awareness while reinforcing its brand.

Not true:	You must be over 25 to be eligible for the Prime Time discount.
True:	If you're 25 or older, you can save 10 percent on all your purchases with RightWay's Prime Time discount.

Legal phrases also have negative connotations for most readers and should be avoided whenever possible. The idea will sound more positive if you use everyday English.

Negative:	If your account is still delinquent, a second, legal notice will be sent to you informing you that cancellation of your policy will occur 30 days after the date of the legal notice if we do not receive your cheque.
Better:	Even if your cheque is lost in the mail and never reaches us, you still have a 30-day grace period. If you do get a second notice, you will know that your payment hasn't reached us. To keep your account in good standing, stop payment on the first cheque and send a second one.

LO3 LO5 Focus on What the Reader Can Do Rather Than on Limitations

Sometimes, positive emphasis is a matter of the way you present something: Is the glass half empty or half full? Sometimes it's a matter of eliminating double negatives. When there are limits, or some options are closed, focus on the alternatives that remain.

Negative:	We will not allow you to charge more than $1,500 on your Visa account.
Better:	You can charge $1,500 on your new Visa card.
Or:	Your new Visa card gives you $1,500 in credit that you can use at thousands of stores nationwide.

As you focus on what will happen, check for you-attitude (Module 13). In the last example, "We will allow you to charge $1,500" is positive, but it lacks you-attitude.

When you have a benefit, and a requirement the reader must meet to get the benefit, the sentence is usually more positive if you put the benefit first.

Negative:	You will not qualify for the student membership rate of $25 a year unless you are enrolled for at least 10 hours.
Better:	You get all the benefits of membership for only $25 a year if you're enrolled for 10 hours or more.

LO3 LO5 Justify Negative Information by Giving a Reason or Linking It to a Reader Benefit

A reason can help your reader see that the information is necessary; a benefit can suggest that the negative aspect is outweighed by positive factors. Be careful, however, to make the logic behind your reason clear and to leave no loopholes.

Negative:	We cannot sell computer disks in lots of fewer than 10.
Loophole:	To keep down packaging costs and to help you save on shipping and handling costs, we sell computer disks in lots of 10 or more.

Suppose the customer says, "I'll pay the extra shipping and handling. Send me seven." If you can't or won't sell in lots of fewer than 10, you need to write:

Better:	To keep down packaging costs and to help customers save on shipping and handling costs, we sell computer disks only in lots of 10 or more.

If you link the negative element to a benefit, be sure that it is an audience-based benefit.

Avoid telling people that you're doing things "for their own good." They may have a different notion of what their own good is. You may think you're doing customers a favour by limiting their credit so they don't get in over their heads. They may feel they'd be better off with more credit so they could expand in hopes of making more sales and more profits.

LO3 LO5 Omit the Negative If It Is Truly Unimportant

Omit negatives entirely only in three instances:

- The reader does not need the information to make a decision.
- You have already given the reader the information, and he or she has access to the previous communication.
- The information is trivial.

The following examples suggest the kind of negatives you can omit:

Negative: A one-year subscription to *Canada Business* is $49.97. That rate is not as low as the rates charged for some magazines.

Better: A one-year subscription to *Canada Business* is $49.97.

Still better: A one-year subscription to *Canada Business* is $49.97. You save 43 percent off the newsstand price of $87.78.

Negative: If you are dissatisfied with Sun Life Insurance, do not renew your policy.

Better: (Omit the sentence.)

LO6 EXPANDING A CRITICAL SKILL

Using Positive Emphasis Ethically

Several of the methods to achieve positive emphasis can be misused. Consider omission.

A bank notified customers that chequing account fees were being "revised" but omitted the amounts. Customers had to go into the bank and copy down the new (higher) fees themselves.

In another case, a condominium resort offered an "all-terrain vehicle" as a prize for visiting. (Winners had to pay $29.95 for "handling, processing, and insurance.") The actual "prize" was a lawn chair with four wheels that converted into a wheeled cart. The company claims it told the truth: "It is a vehicle. It's a four-wheel cart you can take anywhere—to the beach, to the pool. It may not be motorized, but [we] didn't say it was motorized."

In both cases, full disclosure might have affected decisions: some customers might have chosen to change banks; some customers would have declined the condominium visit. It isn't ethical to omit information that people need to make decisions. Presenting information compactly can also go too far. A credit card company mailed out a letter with the good news that the minimum monthly payment was going down. But a separate small flyer explained that interest rates (on the charges not repaid) were going up. The print was far too small to read: 67 lines of type were crowded into five vertical inches of text.

Ethicist Chris MacDonald suggests that making ethical choices, regardless of our motivation, leads to positive results. Even when businesses act ethically because doing so "is good for the bottom line," everyone benefits. An organization that treats its employees, clients, and shareholders ethically enhances its reputation and builds its business. Furthermore, even when it originates out of self-interest, ethical behaviour can be habit-forming.

Sources: Chris MacDonald (2004, August 4), Why act ethically? And does the answer a company gives matter?, http://businessethicsblog.com/; Carmella M. Padilla (1987, July 17), It's a … a … a … all-terrain vehicle, yeah, that's it, that's the ticket, *The Wall Street Journal*, p. 17; Donna S. Kienzler (1997), Visual ethics, *Journal of Business Communication* 34, 175–76.

LO3 LO5 Place the Negative Information Strategically, and Present It Compactly

To de-emphasize a negative, put it in the middle of a paragraph rather than in the first or last sentence, or in the middle of the message rather than in the first or last paragraphs.

The beginning and end of a message are always positions of emphasis. Put negatives there only if you want to emphasize the negative, as you may in a negative message (Module 9).

When a letter or memo runs several pages, remember that the bottom of the first page is also a position of emphasis, even if it is in the middle of a paragraph, because of the extra white space of the bottom margin. (The first page gets more attention since it is on top, and the reader's eye may catch some lines of the message even when he or she isn't consciously reading it; the tops and bottoms of subsequent pages don't get this extra attention.) If possible, avoid placing negative information at the bottom of the first page.

Giving a topic plenty of space emphasizes it. You can de-emphasize negative information by giving it as little space as possible. Give negative information only once in your message. Don't list negatives vertically on the page, since lists take space and emphasize material.

LO1 LO7 Why Do I Need to Think About Tone, Politeness, and Power?

Think about these factors so that your attitude is always respectful.

No one likes to deal with people who seem condescending or rude. Poorly chosen words can create that sense, whether the sender "meant" to be rude or not. Tone is the implied attitude of the writer toward the reader. Tone is tricky, because it interacts with power: the words that might seem friendly from a superior to a subordinate may seem discourteous if used by the subordinate to the superior. Furthermore, courtesy norms are cultural and generational. Language that is acceptable within one group may be unacceptable if used by someone outside the group (Module 3).

Ex. 12.4 12.6

Cultures that value group cohesiveness put much more emphasis on courtesy than the dominant North American culture does. Politeness spares others' feelings, and "saves face" for both message sender and receiver. A direct "no" response is rude in Pakistani and Chinese culture, for example, and such discourtesy might cost you a deal.

The desirable tone for business writing is businesslike but not stiff, friendly but not phoney, confident but not arrogant, polite but not grovelling. The following guidelines will help you achieve the tone you want:

- *Use courtesy titles for people outside your organization whom you don't know well.* Canadian organizations use first names for everyone, whatever their age or rank. But many people don't like being called by their first names by people they don't know or by someone

Cultural FOCUS

In Canadian schools, students are trained to look at the first sentence of a paragraph and to try to guess what the rest of the paragraph will be about. If they are told to *skim* a document, they will read the first and last paragraph to determine what the essay or paper is about. Therefore, when people are looking at a business document, they will often look at the beginning and end to *scan* for the information they need. This is why negative news is placed in the middle. Customers will see the neutral information first and then continue to read on.

Cultural FOCUS

In North America, many women use *Ms.*, not *Mrs. or Miss.* If you are unsure which to use, *Ms.* is best.

much younger. When you talk or write to people outside your organization, use first names only if you've established a personal relationship. If you don't know someone well, use a courtesy title (Module 6):

Dear Mr. Reynolds:

Dear Ms. Lee:

● *Be aware of the power implications of the words you use.* "Thank you for your co-operation" is generous coming from a superior to a subordinate; it's not appropriate in a message to your superior.

Different ways of asking for action carry different levels of politeness, as Table 12.2 shows.[9]

You need to be more courteous if you're asking for something that will inconvenience the reader *and* help *you* more than the person who does the action. Generally, you might be less polite when you're asking for something small, routine, or to the reader's benefit. Most readers and some cultures, however, prefer that even small requests be made politely.

Lower politeness: To start the scheduling process, please describe your availability for meetings during the second week of the month.

Higher politeness: Could you please let me know what times you'd be free for a meeting the second week of the month?

Higher levels of politeness may be unclear. In some cases, a question may seem like a request for information to which it's acceptable to answer, "No, I can't." In other cases, it will be an order, simply phrased in polite terms.

Generally, requests sound friendliest when they are framed in conversational language.

Poor tone: Return the draft with any changes by next Tuesday.

Better tone: Let me know by Tuesday whether you'd like any changes in the draft.

Poor tone: Distribution of the low-fat plain granola may be limited in your area. May we suggest that you discuss this matter with your store manager?

Better tone: Our low-fat granola is so popular that there isn't enough to go around. We're expanding production to meet the demand. Ask your store manager to keep putting in orders, so that your grocery is on the list of stores that will receive supplies when they become available.

TABLE 12.2 **Forms of Request and Their Levels of Politeness**

Form of Request	Level of Politeness	Example
Order	Lowest politeness	Turn in your time card by Monday.
Polite order	Mid-level politeness	Please turn in your time card by Monday.
Indirect request	Higher politeness	Time cards should be turned in by Monday.
Question	Highest politeness	Would you be able to turn in your time card by Monday?

Or: Store managers decide what to stock. If your store has stopped carrying our low-fat granola, the store manager has stopped ordering it. Talk to the manager. Managers try to meet customer needs, so if you say something, you're more likely to get what you want.

When you must give bad news, consider hedging your statement. Linguistic experts John Hagge and Charles Kostelnick have shown that auditors' suggestion letters rarely say directly that firms are using unacceptable accounting practices. Instead, they use three strategies to be more diplomatic: specifying the time ("Currently, the records are quite informal"), limiting statements ("It appears," "It seems"), and using impersonal statements that do not specify who caused a problem or who will perform an action.[10]

LO3 LO4 What's the Best Way to Apologize?

Apologies may have legal implications, so some organizations prefer that their employees do not offer apologies to customers.

When you are at fault, you build goodwill by admitting that fact promptly. However, apologizing to customers is tricky territory. If you are in an entry position, ask your manager/supervisor how to deal with a situation where you feel an apology is needed. Even people in senior management positions may have to consult legal counsel in high-risk situations.

When you have done everything you can for your customer, and when a delay or problem is due to circumstances you have no control over, you aren't at fault and don't need to apologize. It may be appropriate to include an explanation so the reader knows you weren't negligent. If the news is bad, put the explanation first. If you have good news for the reader, put it before your explanation.

Negative: I'm sorry that I could not answer your question sooner. I had to wait until the sales figures for the second quarter were in.

Better (neutral or bad news):   We needed the sales figures for the second quarter to answer your question. Now that they're in, I can tell you that…

Better (good news):   The new advertising campaign is a success. The sales figures for the second quarter are in, and they show that…

If the delay or problem is long or large, it is respectful to ask the reader whether he or she wants to confirm the original plan or make different arrangements.

Negative: I'm sorry that the chairs will not be ready by August 25 as promised.

Better: Because of a strike at the manufacturer, the desk chairs you ordered will not be ready until November. Do you want to keep the ones you originally chose on back order, or would you like to look at the models available from other suppliers?

When an apology is appropriate, do so early, briefly, and sincerely. Apologize only once, early in the message. Let the reader move on to other, more positive information.

Even if major trouble or inconvenience has resulted from your error, you don't need to go on about all the horrible things that happened. The reader already knows this negative information, and you can omit it. Instead, focus on what you have done to correct the situation. If you don't know whether any inconvenience has resulted, don't raise the issue at all. Why draw attention to a negative your reader may not have thought of?

Negative: I'm sorry I didn't answer your letter sooner. I hope that my delay has not inconvenienced you.

Better: I'm sorry I didn't answer your letter sooner.

MODULE SUMMARY

- Beware of **hidden negatives**: words not negative in themselves that become negative in context.

- The best business communication tone is businesslike but not stiff, friendly not phoney, confident but not arrogant, polite but not grovelling.
  - Use courtesy titles for people outside your organization whom you don't know well.
  - Be aware of the power implications of the words you use.
  - When the stakes are low, be straightforward.
  - When you must give bad news, consider hedging your statement.

- Don't apologize if the error is small and if you are correcting the mistake. Don't apologize if you are not at fault. If the delay is long, or the problem large, it is good you-attitude to ask your reader whether he/she wants to make different arrangements.

- When you do apologize, do it early, briefly, and sincerely. However, apologies may have legal implications, so some organizations prefer that their employees do not apologize to customers or the public.

ASSIGNMENTS FOR MODULE 12

Questions for Critical Thinking

12.1 How do people say "no" in your culture? In what circumstances is a direct refusal acceptable?

12.2 In several provinces, hand-held cell use while driving carries a hefty fine. And despite many media reports of car accidents and fatalities due to drivers talking or texting on their phones, people continue to call and drive.

What positive messages could governments and the media use to get people to choose to drive phone free?

12.3 When could positive emphasis backfire or be inappropriate? What strategies would be most likely to meet the audience's needs in those situations?

Exercises and Problems

12.4 Revising a Memo to Improve Positive Emphasis

Revise the following memo to improve positive emphasis.

> Subject: Status of Building Renovations
>
> The renovation of the lobby is not behind schedule. By Monday, October 7, we hope to be ready to open the west end of the lobby to limited traffic.
>
> The final phase of the renovation will be placing a new marble floor in front of the elevators. This work will not be finished until the end of the month.
>
> Insofar as is possible, the crew will attempt to schedule most of the work during the evenings so that normal business is not disrupted.
>
> Please exercise caution when moving through the construction area. The floor will be uneven and steps will be at unusual heights. Watch your step to avoid accidentally tripping or falling.

12.5 Identifying Positive Emphasis in Ads and Documents

Look at print and online advertisements and at documents you receive from your college or university, from your workplace, and from organizations to which you belong. Identify

five sentences that either (a) use positive emphasis or (b) should be revised to be more positive.

As your instructor directs,

a. Share your examples with a small group of students.

b. Write a memo to your instructor discussing your examples.

c. Post an email message to the class discussing your examples.

d. Present two or three of your examples to the class in a short presentation.

e. In a small group, write a collaborative short report to your instructor about the patterns you see.

12.6 Analyzing Your Discourse Community for Tone, Courtesy, and Power

Analyze the cultural norms for tone, levels of courtesy, and use of power in your organization. Choose a discourse community of which you are a member—you can use a club; social, ethnic, religious, or academic organization; or your place of work.

Identify a minimum of three oral and three written messages that exemplify the norms and attitudes toward power in the organization. Write a memo to your instructor and classmates about your findings.

12.7 Evaluating the Ethics of Positive Emphasis

The first word in each line at the right is negative; the second is a positive term that is sometimes substituted for it. Which of the positive terms seem ethical? Which seem unethical? Briefly explain your choices.

junk bonds	high-yield bonds
second mortgage	home-equity loan
tax	user fee
tax increase	revenue enhancement
nervousness	adrenaline
problem	challenge
price increase	price change

12.8 Focusing on the Positive

Revise each of the following sentences to focus on the options that remain, not those that are closed off.

1. As a first-year employee, you are not eligible for dental insurance.
2. I will be out of the country October 25 until November 10 and will not be able to meet with you until I return.
3. You will not get your first magazine for at least four weeks.
4. I'm sorry I'm away from my desk and cannot answer your call.

12.9 Identifying Hidden Negatives

Identify the hidden negatives in the following sentences and revise to eliminate them. In some cases, you may need to add information to revise the sentence effectively.

1. This publication is designed to explain how your company can start a recycling program.
2. I hope you find the information in this brochure beneficial and a valuable reference as you plan your move.
3. In thinking about your role in our group, I remember two occasions where you contributed something.

12.10 Revising Sentences to Improve Positive Emphasis

Revise the following sentences to improve positive emphasis. In some cases, you may need to add or omit information to revise effectively.

1. It will be necessary for you to submit Form PR-47 before you can be reimbursed for your travel expenses.
2. If you have further questions, please do not hesitate to contact me.

3. I'm sorry you were worried about your health insurance. It is not too late to sign up for a flexible spending account.
4. You cannot return this item for a full refund if you keep it more than 30 days.
5. When you write a report, do not make claims that you cannot support with evidence.
6. Although I was only an intern and didn't actually make presentations to major clients, I was required to prepare slides for the meetings and to answer some of the clients' questions.
7. You will pay $30 more if you wait until after October 1 to register for the conference.
8. To reduce unnecessary delays in processing your order, please check the form at the end of this letter to see that nothing is omitted or incorrect before you sign the form and return it.
9. The figures for budget changes made at the meeting may be wrong, as I got lost during John's presentation. Please check the figures and let me know if they need correction.
10. We cannot process your application to graduate, because you did not supply all of the necessary information.

12.11 Revising Sentences to Improve Positive Emphasis

Revise the following sentences to improve positive emphasis. In some cases, you may need to add or omit information to revise effectively.

1. No subcontractor shall be employed without the previous consent of the director.
2. To avoid unnecessary delays, call for an appointment before coming in to the office.
3. I realize that Wednesday at 10 a.m. is not a convenient time for everyone, but I was unable to arrange a time that is good for everyone.
4. I'm sorry you were worried about the resumé you emailed us. We did not have any problems scanning it into our system.
5. I am anxious to talk with you about the job.
6. People who come to work late may be perceived as unreliable.
7. I hope that you receive the April spreadsheet (three pages) that follows and that the fax quality isn't too poor.
8. I was treasurer of the accounting club. Of course, we didn't have much money so I didn't have much responsibility, but I was able to put into practice principles I learned in the classroom.
9. If you have any problems using your email account, I will try to explain it so that you can understand.
10. If you submitted a travel request, as you claim, we have failed to receive it.

POLISHING YOUR PROSE

Using the Apostrophe to Show Ownership

The apostrophe usually indicates ownership or possession:

Sidwat's idea; Veronica's textbook; Verdun's report

When the noun (company, student, neighbour) doing the owning does not end in s, the apostrophe goes between the noun and the s:

company's flagship (flagship of the company)

student's text (text of the student)

neighbour's complaint (complaint of the neighbour)

When the noun is a plural ending in s, put the apostrophe after the s:

companies' customers (customers of companies)

students' texts (texts of students)

neighbours' complaints (complaints of neighbours)

In names that end with s or an s sound, stylebooks permit either form:

Thomas'

Thomas's

Linux'

Linux's

Look at the logic of your sentence to choose the right place for the apostrophe. Or turn the ownership phrase around to determine if the noun ends in an s:

We welcome our employees opinions

becomes

We welcome the opinions of our employees.

The noun *employees* ends in s, so the apostrophe comes after the s:

We welcome our employees' opinions.

Exercises

Choose the correct word in each set of parentheses:

1. Research indicates that most Canadians feel responsible for the (world's/worlds') global warming.
2. The winter holiday season can account for one-quarter to one-half of a (store's/stores') annual profits.
3. (Canadian's/Canadians') views of the economy reflect their confidence in the stock market.
4. To sell in another country, you need to understand its (people's/peoples') culture.
5. We meet the municipal, provincial, and federal (government's/governments') standards for quality control.
6. Skirt's/Skirts' lengths reflect the state of the economy: the maxi becomes popular during economic downturns.
7. The (committee's/committees') duties will be completed after it announces its decision.
8. Employees who have worked as Big Sisters have enjoyed seeing the (girl's/girls') progress.
9. We'll decide whether to have more computer training sessions based on (employee's/employees') feedback.
10. The (company's/companies') benefit plan is excellent.

Check your answers to the odd-numbered exercises in the Polishing Your Prose Answer Key.

McGraw Hill **connect**™

Practise and learn online with Connect. Connect allows you to practise important skills at your own pace and on your own schedule, with 24/7 online access to an eBook, practise quizzes, interactives, videos, study tools, and additional resources.

MODULE
13

Communicating You-Attitude

MODULE OUTLINE

- What is you-attitude in writing?
- How do I create reader-focused, you-attitude?
- Does you-attitude mean using the word *you*?
- I've revised my sentences. Do I need to do anything else?

Module Summary

Assignments for Module 13

Polishing Your Prose: Using the Apostrophe for Contractions and *It's/Its*

Learning Objectives

After reading and applying the information in Module 13, you'll be able to demonstrate

Knowledge of

LO1 The importance of audience-focused messages

LO2 Strategies to revise for audience-focused messages

Skills to

LO3 Adapt your message to the audience

LO4 Use persuasion strategies

LO5 Emphasize what the reader wants to know

LO6 Assess your messages for audience focus

Employability Skills 2000+ Checklist

Module content builds these Conference Board of Canada Employability Skills 2000+

Communicate

Be Responsible

Think and Solve Problems

Work with Others

LO1 Audience-focus or you-attitude is a way of communicating that demonstrates your ability to see another point of view. It means empathizing—"putting yourself in the other person's shoes."

 Whether in text messages, emails, letters, or presentations, you-attitude

Kirk Layton's online porter products and services provide client recognition.

- Looks at the situation from the audience's point of view
- Treats the audience with courtesy
- Respects the audience's intelligence
- Protects the audience's ego
- Emphasizes what the audience wants to know

Communicating with you-attitude pays with positive results. For example, entrepreneur Kirk Layton, founder and president of Eservus.com Online Services Ltd., uses you-attitude to differentiate his service in a highly competitive industry.

Layton's online concierge services are accessible and easy to use. His audience—property managers and building tenants across Canada—get exclusive access to "discounted sports, theatre and movie tickets, flower…[and] travel services and a variety of other things usually associated with traditional in-house concierges at high-end properties." Layton markets his services by getting clients to register online; registrants' "weekly permission-based email newsletter" generates services sales and builds Eservus' client base. Layton has translated his you-attitude focus into a $3 million enterprise.[1]

LO2 What Is You-Attitude in Writing?

You-attitude messages focus politely and positively on the audience.

Writers create you-attitude through conscious communication choices. Appearance, layout, visuals, content, and language all contribute to reader-centred documents, as Figure 13.1 demonstrates.[2]

Language FOCUS

To be **condescending** means that you are speaking to someone as if he/she were younger or not as smart as you are. It is often referred to as "talking down to" someone. When writing, if you are unsure if your tone is condescending, ask one of your classmates for feedback.

FIGURE 13.1   Reader-Centred Christmas Appeal from the Salvation Army

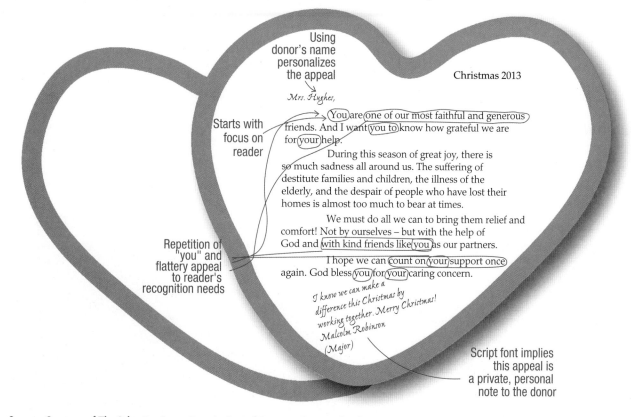

Using donor's name personalizes the appeal

Christmas 2013

Mrs. Hughes,

Starts with focus on reader

You are one of our most faithful and generous friends. And I want you to know how grateful we are for your help.

During this season of great joy, there is so much sadness all around us. The suffering of destitute families and children, the illness of the elderly, and the despair of people who have lost their homes is almost too much to bear at times.

We must do all we can to bring them relief and comfort! Not by ourselves – but with the help of God and with kind friends like you as our partners.

Repetition of "you" and flattery appeal to reader's recognition needs

I hope we can count on your support once again. God bless you for your caring concern.

I know we can make a difference this Christmas by working together. Merry Christmas!
Malcolm Robinson
(Major)

Script font implies this appeal is a private, personal note to the donor

Source: Courtesy of The Salvation Army, Ontario Central Division. Reprinted with permission.

Compare the reader-focused language in Figure 13.1 with the language the writer uses in Figure 13.2. This writer-centred memo refers to the author throughout, and the last paragraph sounds condescending: no colleague or supervisor would appreciate being spoken to this way.

FIGURE 13.2   Writer-Centred Memo, Negative, Without You-Attitude

No salutation and no close: unfriendly, brusque, rude

All you-based language negative and critical

Subject: J & B Label Design

Lucas,

I guess from the look of your design that you were in a hurry or you don't have any idea who the client is. The label is for J & B winery, their new ice wine, and your design doesn't tell the buyer anything about the product quality, etc.

I would be very embarrassed to present the design to the client. Please advise.

Pat

Both paras start with the writer

No solution suggested to the problem—which is really a shared problem

LO2 LO3 How Do I Create Reader-Focused, You-Attitude?

Talk about the reader—except in negative situations.

To create you-attitude,

1. Talk about the reader, not about yourself.
2. Avoid talking about feelings, except to congratulate or offer sympathy.
3. Use *you* more often than *I* in positive situations. Use *we* when it includes the reader.
4. Avoid the blaming *you* in negative situations.

1. Talk about the reader, not yourself. Readers want to know how they benefit.

Lacks you-attitude:	I have negotiated an agreement with Apex Rent-a-Car that gives you a discount on rental cars.
You-attitude:	As a Sun Life employee, you now get a 20 percent discount when you rent a car from Apex.
Lacks you-attitude:	We are shipping your order of September 21 this afternoon.
You-attitude:	The two dozen print cartridges you ordered will be shipped this afternoon and should reach you by September 28.

The reader is more interested in *when* the order will arrive than when you shipped it.

2. Avoid talking about feelings, except to congratulate or offer sympathy.

Lacks you-attitude:	We are happy to extend you a credit line of $5,000.
You-attitude:	You can now charge up to $5,000 on your Bank of Montreal card.

The reader doesn't care whether you're happy or bored stiff. *All the reader cares about is the situation from his or her point of view.*

Don't talk about the reader's feelings, either. It can be offensive to have someone else tell us how we feel—especially if the writer is wrong.

Lacks you-attitude:	You'll be happy to hear that Open Grip Walkway Channels meet Occupational Health and Safety requirements.
You-attitude:	Open Grip Walkway Channels meet Occupational Health and Safety requirements.

When you have good news for the reader, simply give the good news.

Lacks you-attitude:	You'll be happy to hear that your scholarship has been renewed.
You-attitude:	Congratulations! Your scholarship has been renewed.

It is appropriate to talk about your own emotions in a message of congratulations or condolences.

You-attitude:	Congratulations on your promotion to district manager! I was really pleased to read about it.
You-attitude:	I was sorry to hear that your father died.

Of course, you-attitude also includes choosing the appropriate medium for your message. People prefer to get handwritten cards—not emails or text messages—on important occasions (births, deaths, marriages). Negotiations and conflict-resolution situations demand face-to-face dialogue.

> ### Checkpoint
>
> **You-attitude** is a style of writing that
> - Looks at things from the reader's point of view
> - Respects the reader's intelligence
> - Protects the reader's ego
> - Emphasizes what the reader wants to know

3. Use *you* more often than *I* in positive situations.

Use *we* when it includes the reader.

Talk about the reader, not you or your company.

Lacks you-attitude:	We provide dental coverage to all employees.
You-attitude:	You receive dental coverage as a full-time Clairtone employee.

Depending on your audience, you may certainly use *I* in email messages, letters, and memos. However, avoid beginning the first sentence of any written message with *I*.

Edit external messages to ensure *I* is used rarely. *I* suggests that you're concerned about personal issues, not about the organization's problems, needs, and opportunities. *We* works well when it includes the reader. Avoid *we* if it excludes the reader (as it would in a letter to a customer or supplier, or as it might in a memo about what *we* in management want *you* to do).

LO5 4. Avoid *you* in negative situations.

To avoid blaming the reader, use an impersonal expression or a passive verb.

Lacks you-attitude:	You failed to sign your cheque.
You-attitude (impersonal):	Your cheque arrived without a signature.
You-attitude (passive)	The cheque was not signed.
Impersonal constructions	omit people and talk only about things.

Passive verbs describe the action performed on something, without necessarily saying who did it. (See Polishing Your Prose in Module 5 on active and passive voice. See the Revising and Editing Resources at the end of this book for a full discussion of passive verbs.)

Normally, writing is most lively when it's about people, and most interesting to readers when it's about them. When you have to report a mistake or bad news, however, you can protect the reader's ego by using an impersonal construction—one in which things, not people, do the acting.

Lacks you-attitude:	You made no allowance for inflation in your estimate.
You-attitude (passive):	No allowance for inflation has been made in this estimate.
You-attitude (impersonal):	This estimate does not allow for inflation.

When you restrict the reader's freedom, talk about the group to which the reader belongs rather than about the reader as an individual.

Despite the perception that North Americans prefer openness and informality, people of all cultures (see Module 3) expect a respectful tone in business communication.

Lacks you-attitude: You must get approval from the communications department before you speak with any media agency.

You-attitude: Conversations with the media require approval from the communications department.

When you have negatives, third person (*she, he, it*) is better you-attitude than second person (*you*), because third person shows that everyone is being treated the same way.

Checkpoint

Four Ways to Create You-Attitude

1. Talk about the reader, not about yourself.
2. Avoid talking about feelings, except to congratulate or offer sympathy.
3. In positive situations, use *you* more often than *I*. Use *we* when it includes the reader.
4. Avoid *you* in negative situations.

Employability Skills

LO4 Does You-Attitude Mean Using the Word *You?*

Communicating you-attitude means making deliberate choices in layout, content, language, and organization—choices that influence your audience to pay attention to and act on your message.

All reader-centred messages use you-attitude, but the words that achieve it change depending on the situation.

- In a positive message, focus on what the reader can do. "We give you" lacks you-attitude, because the sentence focuses on what *we* are doing.
- Avoid *you* when it criticizes the reader or limits the reader's freedom.
- In a job application letter, create you-attitude by showing how you can help meet the reader's needs, but keep the word *I* to a minimum (Module 26).

LO5 I've Revised My Sentences. Do I Need to Do Anything Else?

Emphasize what the reader wants to know.

Good messages apply you-attitude beyond the sentence level by using *content* and *organization* as well as style to build goodwill.

Consider the email letter in Figure 13.3. As the marginal notes indicate, many individual sentences in this letter lack you-attitude. The last sentence in paragraph one sounds both high-handed and defensive. The language is stiff, harsh, repetitive, and filled with outdated jargon.

Perhaps the most serious problem is that the fact most interesting to the reader is surrounded by negative-sounding statements. Since we have good news for the reader, we should put that information first, as the writer does in her revision, Figure 13.4. (See Module 8.)

FIGURE 13.3   **Email Lacking You-Attitude**

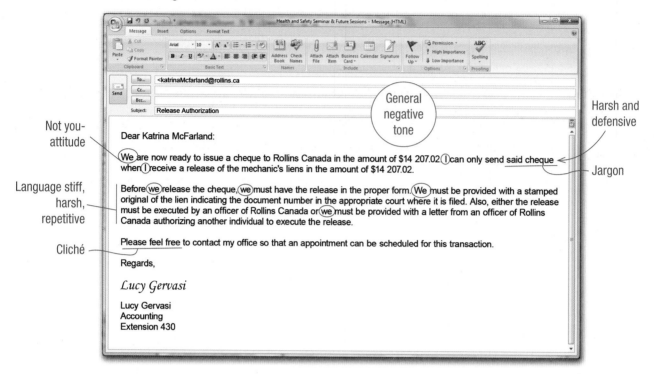

Not you-attitude

Language stiff, harsh, repetitive

Cliché

General negative tone

Harsh and defensive

Jargon

FIGURE 13.4   **Email Revised to Improve You-Attitude**

Positive emphasis on reader and shared problem

Positive placed first with emphasis on reader benefit

List emphasizes choices; clear language encourages reader to act

To create goodwill with *content*,

- Be concise and complete: give the reader the necessary information and *only* the necessary information to get the results you want.
- Consider using an appendix or attachment for information that the reader may want to see but that does not directly support your purpose.
- Anticipate and answer questions or objections the reader is likely to have.
- Show why information that the reader did not ask for, but that you've included, is important.
- Explain to readers how the subject of your message affects them.

To build goodwill with *organization*,

- Put the information that readers are most interested in first.
- Arrange the information to meet your reader's needs, not yours.
- Use headings and lists so that the reader can find key points quickly.

Use the checklist in Figure 13.5 to assess your messages for the content, organization, and language that influences audiences positively.

LO6 FIGURE 13.5   **Persuasive, Audience-Focused Message Checklist**

1. **The message is clear:**
   - ❏ Signals to the reader that it's a business message
   - ❏ Defines the purpose of the message
   - ❏ Organized so that form follows function
   - ❏ Uses business language
   - ❏ Provides specific details in concrete language

2. **The message is concise:**
   - ❏ Provides all relevant information using the fewest possible words

3. **The message is comprehensive:**
   - ❏ Uses a format appropriate to the purpose, the audience, and the situation
   - ❏ Has a beginning, middle, and end
   - ❏ Uses a thesis to establish unity and coherence
   - ❏ Establishes rapport; is reader-centred
   - ❏ Demonstrates that the writer knows, understands, and respects the audience
   - ❏ Uses transitional words and phrases to lead the reader from one idea to the next
   - ❏ Tells the audience what's in it for them

4. **The message is complete:**
   - ❏ Gives all necessary proof, explanations, and examples
   - ❏ Anticipates the audience's questions, concerns, and objections
   - ❏ Tells the audience what to do next or what's going to happen next

5. **The message is correct:**
   - ❏ Is error-free
   - ❏ Demonstrates revision, editing, and proofreading

EXPANDING A CRITICAL SKILL

Seeing Another Point of View

Imagine the job competition in the most populated country in the world: How would you differentiate yourself? For the Chinese, market differentiation lies in knowing how to speak English well, which translates into more job opportunities and an "estimated 70% higher" salary. Given the motivation, and the numbers of eager students, how would you proceed?

Canadian entrepreneur Michael Kraft (Lingo Media Corporation) designed the ideal solution: fun and free interactive English lessons at Speak2Me.cn.

Learners hold conversations with Lucy, the virtual language teacher; speech recognition software encourages learners to refine their English pronunciation. The site uses social networking software to target a potential 40 million post-secondary students.

The initial projection of 600,000 Speak2Me.cn users may be low. Research shows at least 250 million people want

to learn conversational English, and China's ESL market is worth over $2 billion.

How will Kraft make money from his venture? Again, audience analysis is key. Companies pay to place their products in a conversation scenario (e.g., buying a coffee), and have over 300 such scenarios to choose from. The advertiser is targeting a potential client base of millions.

PAIBOC analysis with a focus on you-attitude provided Michael Kraft with a perspective on how to encourage people to master a difficult skill: make it fun and free. That same analysis will pay back millions.

Sources: Fabrice Taylor (2010, November 17), How to make money teaching english for free, Report on Business, *Globe and Mail*, www.theglobeandmail.com/report-on-business/how-to-make-money-teaching-english-for-free/article4344887/. Lingo Media, October 2012, www.lingomedia.com

MODULE SUMMARY

- Communicating with you-attitude means consciously writing and speaking in a way that
  - Looks at the situation from the audience's point of view
  - Treats the audience with courtesy
  - Respects the audience's intelligence
  - Protects the audience's ego
  - Emphasizes what the audience wants to know
- You convey you-attitude when you choose organization, content, layout, and style to build goodwill with your audience.

- You apply you-attitude in sentences when you
  - Talk about the reader/audience, not about yourself
  - Refer specifically to the audience's request or order
  - Don't talk about feelings, except to congratulate or offer sympathy
- In positive situations, use *you* more often than *I*. Use *we* when it includes the reader.
- Avoid the blaming *you* in negative situations.

ASSIGNMENTS FOR MODULE 13

Questions for Critical Thinking

13.1 How does technology influence you-attitude in communications? When texting and/or creating voicemail messages, what strategies do you use to create audience-focused messages?

13.2 In what situation(s) might you consider you-attitude messages manipulative? Consider print and Internet advertising, and the tactics of telemarketers, or people canvassing or selling something door to door.

When have you felt uncomfortable or exploited by you-attitude messages?

13.3 Consider the you-attitude of an organization where you have worked. What strategies does this organization use to project a customer-service attitude? What could the organization do better to convey customer-service focus?

Exercises and Problems

13.4 Analyzing the Salvation Army Appeal Letter

Consider the Salvation Army Christmas letter (Figure 13.1). What is the purpose of the letter, and who is the audience? What is the context? Specifically, what strategies does the message use to communicate you-attitude? What persuasive appeals does the message use? How effective is the letter?

As your instructor directs,

a. Write an email to your instructor describing the purpose, audience, and context of the appeal letter, and the persuasive strategies the writer uses.

b. Describe two specific ways you think the letter could be improved.

13.5 Revising a Form Letter for You-Attitude

You've taken a part-time job at a store that sells fine jewellery. In orientation, the manager tells you that the store photographs the jewellery it sells or appraises and mails the photo as a goodwill gesture after the transaction. However, when you see the form letter, you know that it doesn't build much goodwill—and you say so. The manager says, "Well, you're in postsecondary. Suppose you rewrite it."

Rewrite the letter. Use square brackets for material (such as the customer's name) that would have to be inserted in the form letter to vary it for a specific customer. Add information that would help build goodwill.

> Dear Customer:
>
> We are most happy to enclose a photo of the jewellery that we recently sold you or appraised for you. We feel that this added service, which we are happy to extend to our fine customers, will be useful should you want to insure your jewellery.
>
> We trust you will enjoy this additional service. We thank you for the confidence you have shown by coming to our store.
>
> Sincerely,
>
> Your Sales Associate

13.6 Using Passives and Impersonal Constructions to Improve You-Attitude

Revise each of these sentences to improve you-attitude, first using a passive verb, then using an impersonal construction (one in which things, not people, do the action). Are both revisions equally good? Why or why not?

1. You did not send us your cheque.

2. You did not include all the necessary information in your letter.

3. By failing to build a fence around your pool, you have created a safety hazard.

4. Because your section is always late, we miss the deadline and lose marks.

5. You didn't look at the itinerary so you aren't prepared.

6. Your driving a Hummer is neither cost-effective nor environmentally friendly.

13.7 Improving You-Attitude

Revise these sentences to improve you-attitude. Eliminate any awkward phrasing. In some cases, you may need to add information to revise the sentence effectively.

1. We are pleased to offer you the ability to sign up for dental coverage online on our intranet.

2. You will be happy to know that you can use your new cell phone anywhere in Canada.

3. After hours of hard work, I have negotiated a new employee benefit for you.

4. I urge you to attend a meeting about the new benefits package so that we can inform you about your rights and responsibilities.

5. You will be happy to learn that additional cards for your spouse or child are free.

6. We have added another employee benefit for you.

7. Today, we shipped the book you ordered.

8. In your report, you forgot to tell how many people you surveyed.

9. I hope that it is obvious to you that we want to give you the very best prices on furniture.

10. You didn't order enough doughnuts for the meeting.

13.8 Improving You-Attitude

Revise these sentences to improve you-attitude. Eliminate any awkward phrasing. In some cases, you may need to add information to revise the sentence effectively.

1. Starting next month, the company will offer you a choice of three different health plans.

2. We provide dental coverage to all full-time employees.

3. At the meeting, we'll tell you about the team responsibilities and how we expect you to behave.

4. I have ordered a new computer for you. I expect it to arrive by the 15th, and I'll get it ready for you to use as soon as my schedule permits.

5. We are happy to enrol you in our stock-purchase plan.

6. You will be happy to learn that you can transfer credits from our business diploma programs to a university commerce degree.

7. We give you the following benefits when you join our Frequent Flier program.

8. We are pleased to send you a copy of "Investing in Stocks," which you requested.

9. Your audit papers did not convert U.S. revenue into Canadian dollars.

10. Of course we want to give you every possible service that you might need or want.

13.9 Evaluating You-Attitude in Documents That Cross Your Desk

Identify three sentences that use (or should use) you-attitude in documents you see as a student, consumer, or worker. If the sentences are good, write them down or attach a copy of the document(s) marking the sentence(s) in the margin. If the sentences need work, provide both the original sentence and a possible revision.

As your instructor directs,

a. Share your examples with a small group of students.

b. Write a memo to your instructor discussing your examples.

c. Post an email message or blog to the class discussing your examples.

d. Present two or three of your examples to the class orally.

e. In a small group, write a collaborative short report to your instructor about the patterns you see.

POLISHING YOUR PROSE

Using the Apostrophe for Contractions and It's/Its

The apostrophe replaces the missing letter(s) in a contraction:

it is → it's

I have → I've

you will → you'll

we are → we're

you are → you're

they are → they're

With an apostrophe, *it's* is a contraction meaning *it is.* Without an apostrophe, *its* is a possessive pronoun meaning *belonging to it.*

Since *it's* and *its* sound the same, you have to look at the logic of your sentence to choose the right word: if you can substitute *it is*, and the sentence makes sense, use *it's.*

Exercises

Choose the right word in the set of parentheses.

1. (It's/Its) too bad that the team hasn't finished (it's/its) presentation.

2. The company projected that (it's/its) profits would rise during the next quarter.

3. (It's/Its) going to require overtime, because the data centre needs (it's/its) reports quickly.

4. I don't want responsibility for the project unless (it's/its) important.

5. The company will announce (it's/its) new name at a press conference.

6. I'm not sure whether (it's/its) a good idea to offer a conference.

7. (It's/Its) a good idea to keep your travel receipts in a separate file.

8. (It's/Its) good that our computer automatically backs up (it's/its) files.

9. The Saskatoon office will share (it's/its) findings with the other branch offices.

10. (It's/Its) cash reserves protected the company from a hostile takeover.

Check your answers to the odd-numbered exercises in the Polishing Your Prose Answer Key.

McGraw Hill **connect**

Researching Information

Learning Objectives

After reading and applying the information in Module 14, you'll be able to demonstrate

Knowledge of

LO1 How and where to get information

LO2 How to begin to analyze information

LO3 How to prepare to take good notes

Skills to

LO4 Identify primary and secondary sources

LO5 Find electronic and print information

LO6 Use the Internet for research

LO7 Analyze sources

LO8 Write questions for surveys and interviews

LO9 Prepare to take good notes

MODULE OUTLINE

- How do I begin my research?
- How can I find information?
- How can I search efficiently?
- How should I analyze the information I find?
- How do I decide whom to survey or interview?
- How do I create surveys and write questions for interviews?
- How should I analyze the data I collect?

Module Summary

Assignments for Module 14

Polishing Your Prose: Combining Sentences

Employability Skills 2000+ Checklist

Module content builds these Conference Board of Canada Employability Skills 2000+

Communicate

Be Adaptable

Manage Information

Learn Continuously

Think and Solve Problems

Participate in Projects and Tasks

LO4 Researching includes finding and analyzing information. Research methods can be as simple as observing others' behaviours or getting a computer printout of sales for the last month; it may involve finding online material, or interviewing people. Whatever your methods, however, your information is only as valuable as your ability to analyze and apply it.

Secondary research retrieves information that someone else has gathered: library research and online searches are well-known kinds of secondary research. **Primary research** gathers new information. Personal observations, experiences and experiments, and interviews and surveys are common methods for gathering and analyzing new information.

To research effectively, you need to know

- Where and how to find information

- How to evaluate and analyze the information you find

- How to use that information professionally and ethically

This module covers how to research and evaluate primary and secondary research. Module 15 describes how to synthesize the information and credit your sources.

LO1 How Do I Begin My Research?

Focus your search: Identify your objective and draft a purpose statement.

To narrow your search for relevant information, identify your objective: What are you looking for, and why? Use PAIBOC analysis (Figure 14.1) to identify your objective.

Next, draft a thesis or **working purpose statement** to clarify your objective. Your working purpose statement

- Narrows your research parameters: you search for and find the right information more efficiently
- Structures your document or presentation
- Becomes part of your document or presentation introduction

In your working purpose statement, include the situation and your rhetorical purposes. Figure 14.2 gives examples of working purpose statements. For more details on writing working purpose statements, see Module 16.

FIGURE 14.1   PAIBOC Questions for Analysis

P	What's the **purpose** of the research? Why are you looking for information? Are you reporting or updating information? Justifying a request for funding to attend a conference? Writing a proposal to sell a product or service? Creating a business plan to attract investors? Describing a problem and recommending solutions? Are you making a decision? Exploring possibilities? Preparing for a test?
	Your purposes come from you and your organization; however, you must identify your purpose(s) before you can begin to research efficiently.
A	Who is your **audience**? Who will read/view/hear your plan, request, report, or idea? What are your audience's expectations? What proof or evidence does your audience value? What proof will convince them? What kind of information would maximize your audience's understanding? Why?
I	What **information** will achieve your purpose(s) by meeting your audience's needs? What information will cause your readers to think or act as you want them to? Where can you find the relevant information? What information is available, online and in print? What about primary sources: Can you use your own experiences and observations? Whom can you interview to get answers?
B	What reasons or reader **benefits** can you find to meet your purpose(s)? What kind of information will emphasize those benefits?
O	What audience **objections** do you anticipate? What information will overcome or de-emphasize audience objections?
C	What **context** will affect your research? What environmental, economic, organizational, professional, and personal factors will influence why, where, and how you collect information and the impact of your findings on your audience?

FIGURE 14.2   Working Purpose Statements

I need to

- Inform my manager and colleagues about the most relevant information I learned at the conference
- Explain why we should review our report templates
- Describe how we can increase productivity by moving Human Resources upstairs
- Examine the property's soil for contamination and report the results
- Prove that we need to hire another salesperson to improve customer service
- Demonstrate that our current window display is ineffective and describe improvements
- Convince my professor that I can find the information to write a good research report

You might change your thesis or purpose statement when you have gathered and analyzed your information. However, with a working thesis and your PAIBOC analysis, you can begin your search.

LO1 LO5 How Can I Find Information?

Learn what resources are available and how to use them

Ex.
14.6
14.7

Employability Skills

Libraries and the Internet offer billions of bytes of electronic information. Searchable databases of journals, periodicals, magazines, and newspapers are free online through your public library and university or college library. (See Tables 14.1 and 15.1 for examples.) College and university libraries encourage faculty and students to ask their research questions online in real time. Ask your reference librarian about the free resources available.

TABLE 14.1   Examples of Searchable Online Databases

ABI Inform
Information about most aspects of doing business in the global economy, including company backgrounds, competitive information, and new product development.

Business Source Premier
Full-text journals on business, marketing, accounting, economics, finance, and management. Includes *Harvard Business Review* and country economic reports. Resources include industry and company information, and SWOT and trends analysis.

Canadian Business and Current Affairs Complete
Collection of journals, magazines, newspapers, and newsletters searchable in full text, including *Canadian Business* and *Maclean's*.

Canadian Business Online
Directory information on more than 1.5 million Canadian businesses, primarily in the wholesale, retail, and manufacturing sectors. Great for market research and sales prospecting.

Canadian Periodical Index Quarterly
Many full-text Canadian magazines and newspapers, including selected articles from the *Globe and Mail*.

Countries and Cultures eBooks
Encyclopedias devoted to the world's countries: their history, geography, peoples, and cultures.

Euromonitor
Reports and databases on international market research information

Factiva
An excellent resource that offers a collection of information and tools on a wide range of subjects, including communications, technology, linguistics, and political science.

Gale's Canada in Context
Regional and national resources, including biographies, scholarly articles and "original essays... created especially for researchers and educators studying Canada, its people and its history."[1]

InfoTrac Student Edition
A great resource for students that includes databases, respected reference materials, over 1200 periodicals, and nearly nine million articles. Updated daily.

LexisNexis Canada
Information resource designed particularly to meet the needs of academic institutions, corporations, law firms, and government.

Print Measurement Bureau
An important source of marketing data.

WARC
An important source of marketing data.

Source: Interview and email conversation with Shelley Woods, Librarian, Sheridan Institute, January 17, 2012.

LO6 How Can I Search Efficiently?

Use keyword searches.   Keywords are the terms the computer looks for in a database or on the Web. The ABI/Inform Thesaurus lists synonyms and the hierarchies that index information in various databases.

At the beginning of a search, you might use all the synonyms and keywords you can think of. Skim several of the first sources you find; if they use additional or different terms, search for these new terms as well. You're looking for the keyword or phrase that will yield the specific information you need.

Refine your search:

- Use root words to find variations. A root word such as *stock* followed by the plus sign (*stock+*) will yield *stock, stocks, stockmarket*, and so forth.
- Use quotation marks for multi-word terms. If you want only sites that use the term "business communication," put quotes around the term.

- Use a Boolean search to get more specific hits. For example, to study the effect of the minimum wage on employment in the restaurant industry, you might specify (minimum wage) *and* (restaurant *or* fast food) *and* (employment rate *or* unemployment).

Without *and*, you'd get articles that discuss the minimum wage in general, articles about every aspect of restaurants, and every article that refers to unemployment, although many of these would not be relevant to your topic. The *or* calls up articles that use the term *fast food* but not *restaurant*, and vice versa. An article that used the phrase *fast food industry* would be eliminated unless it also used the term *restaurant*. Figure 14.3 illustrates this Boolean search technique.

- Use a variety of search engines. Check www.thesearchenginelist.com/ for a list of current and defunct search engines, or use Google, still the world's most popular search engine, to search for "search engine directories."
- Use others' research. Sharing/networking sites like del.ic.ious and digg let you browse for information other researchers have found, and to bookmark sites for yourself and other people.
- Use all available resources. Search engines and databases, and college, university, and public libraries offer search tips, topic browsing, advanced searches, and refined search topic phrases to help you navigate and focus your search. Databases also provide citation styles, with examples, and pop-ups that format the citation for you (Module 15).

Employability Skills

FIGURE 14.3   Example of a Boolean Search Result

FIGURE 14.4   Example of a Database Article from Boolean Search

Appears with the permission of Labour/ Le Travail and originally appeared in Issue # Spring 2007, p.59.

- Make the information come to you. Create an **RSS (really simple syndication) Feed** for the most current information available. RSS sends subscribers up-to-date news articles:

  > [Y]ou get all the latest news right away without having to search the Web. You set up your preferences once and the content comes to your desktop. Your subscription is anonymous.[1] Many feeds are free, and you can subscribe immediately on databases and search engines.[2]

LO2 LO7 How Should I Analyze the Information I Find?

Ex. 14.4 14.5 14.9

Find the best assessment tools available, and use them to examine every site critically.

As electronic information sources and access have increased, so has the need for critical assessment. A number of sites offer tutorials on how to use and evaluate Web sources. You can also find excellent online assessment tools on your public, college, and university library sites.

To begin your critical analysis,

- *Use reputable sources.* Start with sites produced by universities and established companies or organizations. Be aware, however, that such organizations are not going to post information that makes them look bad. To get the other side of the story, monitor blogs, bulletin boards, and email lists, or access pages critical of the organization. (Search for "consumer opinion" and the name of the organization.)

- *Look for an author.* Do individuals take "ownership" of the information? What are their credentials? Are they subject experts? Where do they work? How can you contact them with questions? Remember that ".edu" sites might be owned by students not yet experts on a subject.
- *Look for the date.* How current is the information?
- *Check the source.* Is the information adapted from other sources? If so, try to get the original.
- *Compare the information with other sources.* Internet sources should complement print sources. When facts are correct, you'll likely find them recorded elsewhere.

Evaluating online sources, especially Web pages, is absolutely vital, since anyone can post pages on the Web, create a blog, tweet, or contribute to Wikipedia. Can you find at least one credible online or print source that agrees with the Web information?

If you want to use citizen journalism, social networking, and community sites like Wikipedia,

- First check with your professor or supervisor; many organizations do not accept information from Wikipedia, How Stuff Works, or any encyclopaedia or ".com" (commercial) websites.
- If you do get approval, find other reliable sources that support the information.

By contrast, many online and print sources, especially academic and peer-reviewed articles, periodicals, and journals, have an editorial board that reviews material for accuracy and truthfulness. Peer experts often review these sources before they are accepted. The review process helps ensure that information meets high standards.

Where Else Can I Find Information?

Powerful as it is, the Internet is just one search tool. Ask your reference librarian for research ideas, including print sources. And remember that textbooks and on-file company information, such as annual reports, are useful sources.

You can also do primary research to get new information. You can use your own observations and experiences, and consult topic experts and colleagues for information through interviews and surveys.

LO2 How Do I Decide Whom to Survey or Interview?

Use a random sample for surveys, if time and money permit. Use a judgment sample for interviews.

Defining your population correctly is crucial to getting useful information. For example, suppose you wanted to research and report on why people use social networking sites. First, you would have to define your parameters. What do you mean by "use"? Are you considering frequency of visits? The number of hours spent on such sites? The number of contacts? The amount of shared information?

Next, you would have to identify the demographic you want to interview: Facebook and MySpace attract very different users from LinkedIn, ZoomInfo, and XpressBook.

Random Sample   Because it is not feasible to survey everyone, you select a **sample**. If you take a true random sample, you can generalize your findings to the whole population from which your sample comes. In a **random sample**, each person in the population theoretically has an equal chance of being chosen. When people say they did something *randomly,* they often mean *without conscious bias.* However, unconscious bias always exists. Someone passing out surveys in front of the library will be more likely to approach people who seem friendly and less likely to ask people who seem intimidating, in a hurry, much older or younger, or of a different race, class, or sex. True random samples rely on random-digit tables generated by computers and published in statistics texts and books such as *A Million Random Digits*.

Convenience Sample   A **convenience sample** is a group of respondents who are easy to reach: students who walk through the student centre, people at a shopping mall, workers in your own unit. Convenience samples are useful for a rough pre-test of a questionnaire. However, you cannot generalize from a convenience sample to a larger group.

Judgment Sample   A **judgment sample** is a group of people whose views seem useful. Someone interested in surveying the kinds of writing done on campus might ask each department for the name of a faculty member who cares about writing and then send surveys to those people. Judgment samples are often good for interviews, where your purpose is to talk to someone whose views are worth hearing.

LO8 How Do I Create Surveys and Write Questions for Interviews?

Test your questions to make sure they're clear and neutral.

A **survey** questions a large group of people, called **respondents** or subjects. The easiest way to ask many questions is to create a **questionnaire**, a written list of questions that people respond to.

An interview is a structured conversation with someone able to give you useful information. However, surveys and interviews are useful only if the questions are well designed.

Although survey and interview queries are based on your ideas and a theory—or *working purpose statement*—it's important to phrase questions in a way that won't lead the respondent to the answer you want, or bias the response. Remember that *people tend to answer the questions they are asked*. Poor questions yield poor data.

Phrase questions clearly. Use words that mean the same thing to your respondents as they do to you. Whenever you can, use concrete, quantitative, measurable language. Words like *important* and *often* are open to anyone's interpretation.

> **Vague:**   Do you use the Web to research often?
>
> **Better:**   How many hours a week do you spend researching on the Web?

Avoid questions that make assumptions about your subjects, unless you are seeking to qualify your respondents. The question "Does your spouse have a job outside the home?" assumes that the respondent is married.

Closed questions—those questions to which people can answer only *yes* or *no*—limit information. **Open questions**—the journalism or "W" questions (*who, what, when, where, why, how*)—encourage information and do not lock the subject into any sort of response. Closed questions are faster for subjects to answer and easier for researchers to score. However, since all answers must fit into chosen categories, closed questions cannot probe the complexities of a subject. You can improve the quality of closed questions by conducting a pre-test with open questions to find categories that matter to respondents.

When you use multiple-choice questions, make sure that only one answer fits in any one category. In the following example of overlapping categories, a person who worked for a company with exactly 25 employees could check either *a* or *b*. The resulting data would be unreliable.

Overlapping categories:	Indicate the number of full-time employees in your company on May 16:

__ a. 0–25

__ b. 25–100

__ c. 100–500

__ d. more than 500

Discrete categories:	Indicate the number of full-time employees in your company on May 16:

__ a. 0–25

__ b. 26–100

__ c. 101–500

__ d. more than 500

Branching questions direct different respondents to different parts of the questionnaire based on their answers to earlier questions.

10. Have you purchased an espresso coffee machine in the last three months?

Yes _____ No _____

(If "no," skip to question 14.)

Use closed, multiple-choice questions for potentially embarrassing topics; for example: What is your level of formal education? a) high school, b) college diploma, c) university undergraduate degree, d) graduate degree. Seeing their own situation listed as one response can help respondents feel that it is acceptable. However, very sensitive issues are perhaps better asked in an interview, where interviewers can build trust and reveal information about themselves to encourage the interviewee to answer.

Poor questions yield poor data.

Put questions that will be easy to answer (like gender or program of study) early in the questionnaire. Put questions that are harder to answer, or that people may be less willing to answer (e.g., age and income) near the end of the questionnaire. Even if people choose not to answer such questions, you'll still have the rest of the survey filled out.

How Should I Design the Questionnaire?

Pay careful attention to the physical design of the document. Use indentations and white space effectively; make it easy to mark and score the answers. Include a brief statement of purpose if you (or someone else) will not be available to explain the questionnaire, or answer questions. Pre-test the questionnaire to make sure the directions are clear. When a training facilitator handed out a double-sided questionnaire without mentioning it was double-sided, thirty percent of respondents answered only the questions on the first side.

L07 How Should I Analyze the Data I Collect?

Evaluate your sources; understand your sources; look for patterns and emerging stories.

Look for answers to your research questions and for interesting nuggets that may not have been part of your original focus that emerge from the data. Such stories can be more convincing in reports and oral presentations than pages of computer printouts.

Look for patterns.

- On which points do respondents agree? Which disagreements can be explained by early theories or numbers that have now changed? By different interpretations of the same data? By different values and criteria? In your interviews and surveys, what patterns do you see?
- Have things changed over time?
- Do geography, gender, or education account for differences?
- What similarities do you see?
- What differences do you see?
- What confirms your hunches?
- What surprises you?

Checking Your Logic

As you analyze your data, differentiate between causation and correlation. **Causation** means that one thing causes or produces another. **Correlation** means that two things happen at the same time. One might cause the other, but both might be caused by a third.

For example, suppose that you're writing a report to justify the purchase of a smartphone for every salesperson in your company. Your survey results indicate that employees who currently have smartphones are more productive than people who don't. Does having a smartphone lead to higher productivity? Perhaps. But perhaps productive people are more likely to push to get smartphones from company funds, while less productive people are more passive. Perhaps productive people earn more and are more likely to be able to buy their own smartphones if the organization doesn't provide them.

A Question of Ethics

What ethical considerations could face researchers collecting primary information?

Consciously search for at least three possible causes for each phenomenon you've observed and at least three possible solutions for each problem. The more possibilities you brainstorm, the more likely you are to find good options. In your report, mention all the possibilities; discuss in detail only those that will occur to readers and that you think are the real reasons and the best solutions.

When you have identified patterns that seem to represent the causes of the problem or the best solutions, check these ideas against reality. Can you find support in the quotes or in the numbers? Can you answer counterclaims? If you can, you will be able to present evidence for your argument in a convincing way.

If you can't prove the claim you originally hoped to make, you will need to revisit your working thesis or modify your conclusions to fit your data. Even when your market test is a failure, you can still write a useful report.

- Identify changes that might yield a different result (e.g., selling the product at a lower price might enable the company to sell more units).
- Discuss circumstances that may have affected the results.
- Summarize your negative findings in progress reports to let readers down gradually and to give them a chance to modify the research design.
- Remember that negative results are not always disappointing to the audience. A report demonstrating that an idea isn't feasible can save people time and money.

LO3 LO9   EXPANDING A CRITICAL SKILL

Preparing to Make Notes

Recording information efficiently and effectively enables you remember, understand, and retrieve your research. Creating useful notes is a critical information-processing skill.

To begin the process, and save time and energy with good preparation:

- *Define your purpose.* We take different notes for different purposes. Why are you making notes? How are you going to use the notes? How is the information important? What is valuable, and why?

- *Listen.* Defining your purpose helps you focus on what you need to listen to. What do you want to take away? What's the situation? Will you be writing a report? Taking an exam? What will you make notes about? What do you want to remember?
  - Listen for understanding: What ideas does the speaker emphasize? If you're listening to a prepared lecture or presentation, what ideas does the speaker highlight in the introduction? What does the speaker repeat or stress in the conclusion? What examples and details are relevant to your purpose?

- *Pre-read.* What are you reading? Will it be relevant to your purpose? Save time and energy by browsing the material to ensure that it's going to be useful. Look for the
  - Information context or medium: Is it an Intranet Web page? Newspaper? Magazine article? Textbook? Reference book?

- Organizational pattern: Information is organized (Module 17) according to the expectations of the discourse community (Module 2). Newspapers and well-written Web pages use the inverse pyramid pattern: all the important information is up front, in the first paragraph; details follow. Scan that paragraph to see if you need or want to read further.

- Summaries, overviews, abstracts, headings, and subheadings: These synthesize key ideas.

- Illustrations and visuals: These can condense and clarify text (Module 19). Scan to increase understanding and retention.

- Level of technical difficulty: If the material is incomprehensible, making notes won't do you much good. Scan for references to other texts. Pre-read these first.

- *Read to understand.* With your purpose in mind, focus only on relevant information.
  - Look for the main ideas in the topic sentences in each paragraph (usually the first or second sentence).
  - Look carefully at visuals: What information can you use?

- Decide what you're going to record.

Module 15 describes how to create useful notes.

MODULE SUMMARY

- **Primary research** gathers new information: personal observations, interviews, and surveys are common methods for gathering new information for business documents.

- **Secondary research** retrieves information that someone else has gathered. Library research and online searches are well-known kinds of secondary research.

- Begin your research by narrowing your focus. What are you looking for, and why?

- Draft a **working purpose statement** to clarify your objectives. This purpose statement

- Narrows your research parameters
  - Structures your document or presentation
  - Becomes part of your document or presentation introduction

- Next, ask your reference librarian about the free resources available in your library.

- To research efficiently online, use
  - Keyword and Boolean searches
  - Suggested topics searches
  - Advanced searches
  - A variety of search engines
  - RSS feeds
  - Online tools, topics, and tutorials to navigate, and narrow your quest

- A **survey** questions a large group of people, called **respondents** or **subjects. A questionnaire** is a written list of questions people fill out. An **interview** is a

structured conversation with someone who can give you useful information.

- When creating a questionnaire or interview questions, define your terms, and phrase questions clearly. Use words that mean the same thing to your respondents as they do to you. Use concrete, quantitative, measurable language.

- Closed questions limit answers to yes or no. Open questions encourage more information. Branching questions direct different respondents to different parts of the questionnaire based on their answers to earlier questions.

- To find credible information sources
  - Check the source: look for an author.
  - Look for credentials.
  - Look for the date.
  - Is the information adapted from other sources? If so, try to get the original.
  - Compare the information with other sources. Internet sources should complement print sources. When facts are correct, you'll likely find them recorded elsewhere.

- To take and create good notes, prepare beforehand:
  - Define your purpose.
  - Listen actively.
  - Pre-read materials.
  - Focus on the material you want to record.

ASSIGNMENTS FOR MODULE 14

Questions for Critical Thinking

14.1 What two variables must your working statement contain? Why?

14.2 Why look for alternative explanations for your research findings?

14.3 Why should you know the exact way a question was phrased before using results from the study as evidence?

14.4 How should users assess the credibility of a website? What methods would you use for critical evaluation?

14.5 How do you review and evaluate what you learn through your research? What systems or practices do you apply to assess how useful the information is?

Exercises and Problems

14.6 Finding and Using Search Engine Directories

Research "search engine directories" to find a directory you believe would be useful for students to know about. Explore the search engine's offerings.

As your instructor directs,

   a. Prepare a slide presentation describing the search engine's advantages and disadvantages

   b. Write a memo to your instructor and fellow students describing the search engine's advantages and disadvantages.

14.7 Finding and Using Web Resources

Visit the Web resources listed below. Evaluate each resource based on the following questions:

   1. What information does the site offer?

   2. How can you use this information?

   3. How reliable is the site, and the information? How do you know?

   4. How accessible is the site? Is it easy to navigate? Moderately difficult? Difficult?

Create an annotated bibliography for five (5) of these sites. Refer to www.writing.utoronto.ca/advice/specific-types-of-writing/annotated-bibliography for examples.

Based on questions 1 to 4 above, which sites were helpful to you? Why? Which were not helpful? Why not?

Web Sources Analysis

http://help.library.ubc.ca/researching/evaluating-internet-sources/

http://library.queensu.ca/inforef/tutorials/qcat/evalint.htm

www.ryerson.ca/library/ref/web_resources.html

http://bcs.bedfordstmartins.com/resdoc5e/tips-for-evaluating-sources.htm

www.vuw.ac.nz/staff/alastair_smith/evaln/evaln.htm

http://owl.english.purdue.edu/handouts/research/r_evalsource4.html

Web Tutorials

www.internettutorials.net/finding-scholarly-content.asp

www.internettutorials.net/best-bet-search.asp

www.internettutorials.net/choose.asp

www.lib.berkeley.edu/Help/tutorials.php

Alternative Search Engines

www.virtualprivatelibrary.com

http://ca.yahoo.com/

www.stumbleupon.com

www.bing.com/

www.lycos.com/

As your instructor directs,

   a. Post your results to the class on a blog or file-sharing application.

   b. Present your results in a memo to your instructor.

   c. Present your results to the class orally.

14.8 Evaluating Survey Questions

Evaluate each of the following questions. How acceptable are they? How can you improve them?

   a. Questionnaire on grocery purchases:

      1. Do you usually shop at the same grocery store?

         a. Yes

         b. No

      2. Do you buy locally?

         a. Yes

         b. No

      3. Do you buy organic produce?

         a. Yes

         b. No

      4. Do you buy organic meat?

         a. Yes

         b. No

      5. How much is your average grocery bill?

         a. Under $25

         b. $25–50

         c. $50–100

         d. $100–150

         e. More than $150

   b. Survey on technology:

      1. Would you generally welcome any technological advancement that allowed information to be sent and received more quickly and in greater quantities than ever before?

      2. Do you think that all people should have free access to all information, or do you think that information should somehow be regulated and monitored?

c. Survey on job skills:

How important are the following skills for getting and keeping a professional-level job in Canadian business and industry today?

	Low				High
Ability to communicate	1	2	3	4	5
Leadership ability	1	2	3	4	5
Public presentation skills	1	2	3	4	5
Selling ability	1	2	3	4	5
Teamwork capability	1	2	3	4	5
Writing ability	1	2	3	4	5

14.9 Evaluating Websites

Choose a report topic you would be interested in researching. Find and evaluate seven websites related to the topic of your report. For each, consider

- Author(s)
- Objectivity
- Information
- Revision date

Based on these criteria, which sites are best for your report? Which are unacceptable? Why?

As your instructor directs,

a. Share your results with a small group of students.
b. Present your results in a memo to your instructor.
c. Present your results to the class orally.

14.10 Designing Questions for an Interview or Survey

Submit either a one-to-three-page questionnaire or questions for a 20-to-30-minute interview and the information listed below for the method you choose.

Questionnaire

1. Purpose(s), goal(s)
2. Subjects (who, why, how many)
3. How and where to be distributed
4. Rationale for order of questions, kinds of questions, wording of questions

Interview

1. Purpose(s), goal(s)
2. Subject (who and why)
3. Proposed site, length of interview
4. Rationale for order of questions, kinds of questions, wording of questions, choice of branching or follow-up questions

As your instructor directs,

a. Create questions for a survey on one of the following topics:

- Survey students on your campus about their knowledge of, and interest in the programs and activities sponsored by a student organization.
- Survey students about their knowledge and use of campus services, such as the counselling, health, career, or tutoring centres.
- Survey workers at a company about what they like and dislike about their jobs.
- Survey people in your community about their willingness to pay more to buy products that use recycled materials and to buy products packaged with a minimum of waste.
- Survey students and faculty on your campus about their environmental awareness, habits, and concerns.
- Survey two groups on a topic that interests you.

b. Create questions for an interview on one of the following topics:

- Interview an international student about the form of greetings and farewells, topics of small talk, forms of politeness, festivals and holidays, meals at home, size of families, and roles of family members in his or her county.
- Interview the owner of a small business about the strategies the owner has used to increase sales and profits and the success of these strategies, and the owner's attitudes toward possible changes in product line, decor, marketing, hiring, advertising, and money management.
- Interview someone who has information you need for a report you're writing.

14.11 Reporting your Survey Results *

Together with three of your peers,

- Form a research team and decide on a relevant investigation topic.
- Choose a topic related to your audience's interests and that will elicit interesting and varied responses (tuition fees, transportation to school, part-time work, dating trends, career plans, hobbies, gender miscommunication, post-secondary choices, quality of teaching).
- Create a survey questionnaire (minimum five questions: see Exercises 14.8 and 14.10) to interview 20 people who would have the information or opinions you seek.
- Use closed, open, and probing questions to provide you with enough data for analysis.

As your instructor directs,

a. Using your findings, prepare a short oral report for the class, with headings and topic sentences; arrange your information to reflect the way you want your readers to think about the data:
   Introduction: *topic/purpose, scope, method (number of people interviewed, who)*

b. Create PowerPoint™ slides to summarize your data.

c. Draw conclusions based on your information. You might want to use your questions as headings throughout the report.
   Conclusion: What did you discover? Why might your audience care?

d. Use APA in-text citations and end with a Reference page (Module 15) indicating your sources.

* Thanks to Professor Kathryn Voltan, University of Toronto, for this exercise.

POLISHING YOUR PROSE

Combining Sentences

Combining sentences is a powerful tool to make your writing more concise and more forceful.

When too many sentences in a paragraph have fewer than 10 words and follow the same basic pattern, prose is *choppy*. Choppy prose seems less unified and either robotic or frenzied in tone.

Combining short sentences to create longer flowing ones can eliminate this problem.

Choppy: I went to the office supply store. I purchased a computer, a fax machine, and a laser printer. I went to my office. I installed the equipment. I am more efficient.

Better: At the office supply store, I purchased a computer, a fax machine, and a laser printer. After installing the equipment in my office, I am more efficient.

There are several ways to combine sentences.

1. Use **transitions**: words and phrases that signal connections between ideas. Common transitions are *first, second, third, finally, in addition, likewise, for example, however, on the other hand, nevertheless, because, therefore, before, after, while,* and *in conclusion*.

   Choppy: Neil drove the truck to the warehouse. Charlie loaded it with cement. Phil supervised the work.

   Better: First, Neil drove the truck to the warehouse. Then Charlie loaded it with cement, while Phil supervised the work.

2. Rewrite sentences using **subordinate clauses**. A clause with one of the following words will be subordinate: *after, although, though, because,* or *since*.

   Better: After Neil drove the truck to the warehouse, Charlie loaded it with cement. Phil supervised the work.

3. Join simple sentences together with *coordinating conjunctions*, such as *and, but,* and *or*. These conjunctions can also function as transitional words. Be sure to use the comma before the conjunction when combining two independent clauses.

   Better: Neil drove the truck to the warehouse, Charlie loaded it with cement, and Phil supervised the work.

4. Create a list using commas and coordinating conjunctions.

   Choppy: Sam put our old files in the storeroom. Sam placed extra copies of the company telephone directory in the storeroom. Sam put boxes of three-ring binders in the storeroom.

   Better: Sam put old files, extra copies of the telephone directory, and boxes of three-ring binders in the storeroom.

Exercises

Combine the following sentences to make them easier to read.

1. You can get promoted quickly at our company. Being organized and on time will help. Not meeting deadlines will not help.

2. There are many reasons to choose Canadian Human Resource Planners as your human resources consulting firm. Our organization has more than 20 years in the business. We have regional offices in Calgary and Toronto. Canadian Human Resource Planners has an international membership of members from industry, government, non-profit groups, educational institutions, and consulting firms.

3. Changing the toner cartridge on the photocopier is simple. Open the front panel. Find the green tabs. Depress the green tabs with your thumbs. Pull the black toner cartridge out. Put the toner cartridge in the recycling box. Slide a new toner cartridge into the compartment. The green tabs will snap back into place. Close the panel.

4. The development team members took a plane to Victoria. That was on Friday. They attended a conference. That was on Saturday. They came home. That was on Sunday. On Friday it rained. The team members used umbrellas. The other two days it did not rain. They did not need umbrellas on those days.

5. The tornado plan for our building has five parts. One part is to go to your designated shelter area in the basement of the building. One part is to listen for the tornado alert siren. One part is to sit down on the floor. One part is to take the stairs and not the elevator. One part is to cover your head with your arms.

Check your answers to the odd-numbered exercises in the Polishing Your Prose Answer Key.

Synthesizing and Documenting Information

Learning Objectives

After reading and applying the information in Module 15, you'll be able to demonstrate

Knowledge of

LO1 How to summarize and paraphrase information

LO2 How to create good notes

LO3 Why researchers document their sources of information

LO4 How to cite and document sources correctly

Skills to

LO5 Begin to write summaries and précis

LO6 Begin to take useful notes

LO7 Document sources legally, ethically, and correctly

MODULE OUTLINE

- How do I summarize information?
- How do I use my research effectively?
- Why must I document my sources?
- How should I document my sources?

Module Summary

Assignments for Module 15

Polishing Your Prose: Using APA and MLA Style

Employability Skills

Employability Skills 2000+ Checklist

Module content builds these Conference Board of Canada Employability Skills 2000+

Communicate	**Be Adaptable**
Manage Information	**Learn Continuously**
Think and Solve Problems	**Participate in Projects and Tasks**

This module describes how to note and synthesize information, how to use in-text citations for business reports, and how to document sources using APA and MLA styles. Throughout this module, APA style in-text citations credit both primary and secondary sources.

LO1 LO5 How Do I Summarize Information?

Read and listen for meaning, then write a synopsis, paraphrase, or précis.

We process information by sorting it into meaningful patterns. This pattern-making includes summarizing and paraphrasing. When you **summarize**, you condense the data you're hearing or reading. You omit all details except those that capture and compress the meaning.

Ex.
15.5
15.7
15.9

Summarizing Documents

To summarize text, use active reading strategies

- Pre-read, skim and scan the article, document, or visual (Module 14).
- Identify and analyze the context; use PAIBOC analysis to answer:
  - What's the medium? Research report? Scholarly journal? Newspaper? Magazine? Blog? University Web page? Intranet page? Social network page? The medium frames the meaning: every discourse community (Module 2) has its own language rules, dependent on purpose and audience. Academic writing, for example, is often longer, denser, and more formal than business writing. Scientific and technical report writers often use the passive voice (see the Revising and Editing Resources) to meet audience expectations.
  - What's the purpose of the document, and who is the intended audience?
  - Who wrote it? What are the author's credentials? What's the evidence of expertise?
  - How does the writer develop the argument or thesis? What is the pattern of organization? Comparison/contrast? Problem/solution? Elimination of alternatives? (Module 17)
  - When was it published? How current is it?
  - What's the language level?
- Find the thesis, or main idea in the abstract or in the introduction.
- Read the concluding paragraph: Does it sum up the information? What does it suggest the reader think or do?

- Find the topic sentences that control each paragraph. How are they related to the thesis?
- Look for proof. How does the author support his or her thesis? What's the evidence? Examples? Statistics? Studies? Experiments? Personal experience? Interviews?
- Set the text aside, and jot down or cluster (Module 4) an overview of the material: note (1) the main idea, (2) the medium, (3) the author's name, (4) an example or proof, (5) your questions about the material. Figure 15.1 illustrates a cluster summary of these points.
- Reread the document to ensure your summary information is accurate.
- Find the answers to your questions. If it suits your purpose, add them to your summary.
- Record all biographic data if you are using the summary in your report or presentation.
- Ask a peer or friend to check your summary against the original text.
- Add anything relevant.

Table 15.2 lists additional Internet information resources you can research and summarize.

FIGURE 15.1   Clustering Information

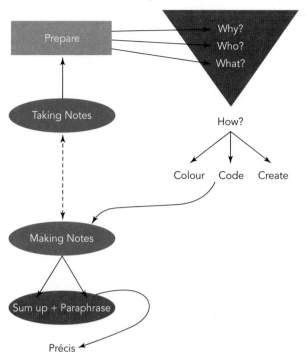

LO1 LO5 Summarizing Oral Communications

To summarize a lecture, presentation, interview, or speech,

- Listen for understanding; identify and analyze the context (Module 20):
  - Whenever possible, pre-read on the topic.
  - Listen for an overview. Use PAIBOC analysis: What? Why? Who? When? Where?
  - Identify the speaker's purpose. Note it.
  - Identify the speaker's expectations of his or her audience. Note them.
  - Listen for the thesis. Note it.
  - Identify and analyze the organizational pattern. How does the speaker develop the argument, or thesis (Module 21)?
  - Listen for the proof. Note examples, statistics, evidence.
  - Listen for points of emphasis. Note them.
  - Listen for the close: How does the speaker sum up? What does the speaker want the audience to think, or do? Note that.
  - Read the handouts or supplementary material if provided.
  - Note your questions. What is unclear? What else do you need to know to understand?
  - Ask your questions, if appropriate to the situation
- Jot down or cluster (Figure 15.1) an overview of the material: (1) the thesis or main idea, (2) the speaker's name, if relevant to your purpose, (3) evidence and examples, (4) points of emphasis, (5) the conclusion.
- Check your summary for accuracy.
  - If possible, ask the speaker to confirm that you have heard and understood all relevant information.
  - Read related documents.
  - If possible, compare your summary with that of another audience member.
- Add any relevant information.

Paraphrasing

Ex.
15.5
15.7–
15.9

When you **paraphrase**, you put information you're recording or reporting *into your own words* while maintaining the meaning.

You write a **précis** when you both paraphrase and summarize information. A précis interprets, summarizes, and translates information
- while listening actively (Module 20) during a presentation, lecture or interview
- while listening actively to provide feedback
- when reading material you want to learn
- when translating research data to incorporate the ideas into your reports

When you paraphrase or précis another person's words to include them in your oral and written reports, you don't use quotation marks because the ideas are now in your own words. However, you must credit the original source of the information with in-text citation or footnotes and in your references.

TABLE 15.1   Sources for Web Research, Analysis, and Synthesis

Canadian Government Information

Statistics Canada
http://www.statcan.ca

Most recent five years of data, constantly updated
http://www40.statcan.ca/ol/esto1

Profile of Canadian communities, tables for more than 5000 Canadian communities from most recent census, with the ability to create local base maps
www12.statcan.ca/english/census01/home/index.cfm

Canada Business Service Centres
www.cbsc.org

Canada's Business and Consumer Site
www.strategis.ic.gc.ca

Environment Canada
www.ec.gc.ca

Subject Matter Directories

AccountingNet
www.acountingnet.com

The Computer User High Tech Dictionary
www.computeruser.com/resources/dictionary/Dictionary.html

Education Index
www.educationindex.com

International Business Kiosk
www.calintel.org/kiosk

Management and Entrepreneurship
www.lib.lsu.edu/bus/management/html

The WWW Virtual Library: Marketing
www.knowthis.com

Reference Collections

Britannica Online
www.eb.com

CEO Express
www.ceoexpress.com

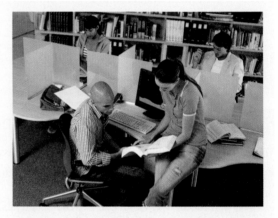

Your library offers billions of bytes of information.

Hoover's Online (information on more than 13 000 public and private companies worldwide)
www.hoovers.com/free

Reference Desk
www.refdesk.com

Interactive Atlas of Canada
http://atlas.nrcan.gc.ca/site/english/maps/topo/map

News Sites

Most Popular Business Websites EBizMBA
www.ebizmba.com/articles/business-sites

CBC News
www.cbc.ca/news

CBC Radio
http://cbc.ca/programguide

***Business Week* Online**
www.businessweek.com

Canadian Business Online
www.canadianbusiness.com

The *Globe and Mail* Online
www.globeandmail.com

***Maclean's* Online**
www.macleans.ca

The *National Post* Online
www.nationalpost.com

The *New York Times* on the Web
www.nyt.com

The *Wall Street Journal* Interactive Edition
www.wsj.com

Language FOCUS

Paraphrasing means that you are condensing the information you have and putting it *all* in your own words. You cannot just use synonyms for a few words and call it a précis or paraphrase. A paraphrase is also shorter than the original piece, so you leave out examples and illustrations that the original writer or speaker used.

When you paraphrase information, you are still using another person's ideas; therefore, you must always identify your source: who wrote it, what is the title and date of information, and where did it come from?

LO1 LO5 How Do I Use My Research Effectively?

Ex. 15.1– 15.5

Use sources strategically; integrate them seamlessly; credit them correctly.

Seeking information to clarify, verify, or develop your ideas, to find expert advice or inspiration, or to suggest topics for further development is part of the research process. Equally important parts of the process are to integrate the information smoothly into your document or presentation, and document your sources correctly.

Citation means attributing an idea or fact to its source in the body of the report:

"According to the 2012 Census..."

"Jane Bryant Quinn argues that..."

Documentation means providing the biographic information (in an APA References page or a MLA Works Cited page) your readers need to find the original source.

Whether you choose to paraphrase the information or quote others' work directly, incorporate the material seamlessly, and give your source credit.

Ex.
15.5
15.7–
15.9

EXPANDING A CRITICAL SKILL

LO2 LO6 Taking Great Notes

Note-taking is not duplicating information verbatim, but translating and recording information in a way *that informs you*. The best notes encode and encapsulate meaning.

This interpreting and synthesizing process uses both critical and creative thinking skills. First, you have to know *why* you are recording the information; then you have to focus on, filter, analyze, organize, and interpret the information to understand *what* you should record (Module 14).

You use your creative thinking skills to note the information in a way that is both meaningful and memorable for you.

Once you have identified your purpose, the context, and the content you want to record, experiment to find the most efficient note-taking system for you. Try the following strategies:

- Test all available tools: don't assume that creating e-notes is the best method for you. Try
  - Taking notes in longhand
  - Recording information on small note cards—one idea, quotation, summary, or paraphrase, with bibliographic information, per card; you can then organize your report information by rearranging the cards
  - Creating doodle notes, jot-dots, clusters

- Use an alphabetic shorthand: spell words phonetically; omit capitals, punctuation, and all unnecessary letters (Grossman, 1976, pp. 1–13; Jensen, 2003, p. 119). For example, you might write "You cite your sources even when you use your own words" as

u cte yr srcs evn whn u uz yr wn wrds

Use common symbols: use symbols that let you "write rapidly and interpret easily" (Jensen, 2003, p. 119):

TABLE 15.2 Note-Taking Symbols

>	greater than	(+)	positive, good
<	less than	(-)	negative, against
=	the same, equals	w/o	without
≠	different	↓	down, under, decreasing
X	times, cross	↑	above, up, increasing
→	toward, going	w/	with
←	from	$	dollars, money
∴	therefore, because	Q	question
∞	infinity		

- Create your own code. Make your own symbols to summarize, organize, and emphasize information.
  - Use mind mapping (Module 4) to note patterns, sequences, hierarchies, and relationships.
  - Use spacing, different-size fonts, and different colours to highlight information you want to emphasize.
  - Keep a separate section to note what you want to follow up: questions, unclear information, and additional resources.

Creating purposeful notes is an acquired skill that depends on your understanding of both content and context. Learning to take great notes is easier when you practise daily, read widely and frequently, and have an extensive vocabulary. Competent note-takers use PAIBOC to analyze purpose and audience, and to understand the pattern the writer or speaker is using to organize the information.

> ### *Language* FOCUS
>
> When taking notes, it is best to record them in the language they are given in. If the lecturer is using English, record your notes in English. Do not try to translate into your own language while taking notes, as this might lead to mistakes later when you are studying or writing a report. For example, if you have incorrectly translated a word during a lecture or in a meeting, it will affect the accuracy of your report when you are writing it later and not able to double-check on your translation accuracy.

Using Précis

When you paraphrase and summarize other's ideas or words, make sure that your précis

- fits seamlessly into the sentence,
- demonstrates, reinforces or proves the point you are making, and
- gives credit to the originator (St. Francis Xavier University, 2012a)

Using Quotations

When you quote words and phrases, "integrate them [into your text] as smoothly as possible" to ensure consistency (St. Francis Xavier University, 2012b).

Introduce a full sentence quote with a colon:

> Journalist and professor Leslie Butler is adamant about the ethical ramifications of plagiarism: "It's a personal violation" (L. Butler, July 8, 2012).

Introduce a word or phrase with a comma:

> Plagiarism, as journalist and professor Leslie Butler insists, "is a personal violation" (L. Butler, July 8, 2012).

Indent long quotations on the left and right to set them off from your text. Indented quotations do not need quotation marks; the indentation shows the reader that the passage is a quotation. Since many readers skip quotations, always summarize the main point of the quotation in a single sentence before the quotation. If the last sentence before the quotation is a complete sentence, end the sentence with a colon, not a period, since it introduces the quotation.

> Create an **RSS** Feed for the most current information available. **Really Simple Syndication** sends subscribers up-to-date news articles:
>
> > RSS (Rich Site Summary) is a format for delivering regularly changing web content. Many news-related sites, weblogs and other online publishers syndicate their content as an RSS Feed to whoever wants it. (http://www.whatisrss.com/)

You can also interrupt a quotation to analyze, clarify, or question it. When you add or change words to clarify the quotation, or to make the quotation fit the grammar of your sentence, use square brackets [ ] around the new or changed words. Omit any words in the original source that are not essential for your purposes. Use an ellipsis (…) to indicate omissions.

Why Must I Document My Sources?

Citing your sources of information protects you from charges of plagiarism, demonstrates your honesty, and enhances your credibility.

Copyright laws protect people's creative output: "Copyright applies to all original literary, dramatic, musical and artistic works" (Industry Canada, 2011). Ideas can't be owned, but the expression of those ideas can be. For example: "There have been many movies about Pirates, but only one Jack Sparrow" (Click & Copyright, 2012).

Legally, therefore, researchers are required to identify the source of information that they do not originate. **You must credit the source even when you put that information into your own words, or recreate a visual with your own software.** Not doing so—intentionally or unintentionally—means you are plagiarizing. Stealing someone else's work has serious legal, academic, and personal consequences (PlagiarismdotOrg, 2012). Academic penalties can include a grade failure or expulsion. In business, you can be sued for damages and lost revenue.

Furthermore, since our laws express our social values (L. Butler, personal communication, July 8, 2012), you are also **ethically responsible for crediting the ideas, facts, figures, symbols, and words of others.** Using someone else's work without giving him or her credit violates the individual's personal and professional rights. Doing so, even unintentionally, can damage your reputation.

Correctly documenting your sources also **makes you look good**. Investigating and citing a wide range of sources on your topic demonstrate your competence and your analytical and critical thinking skills. Using a variety of authoritative sources can suggest alternative points of view that lead to new insights and provide you with the evidence you need to develop and prove your thesis. Documenting this research ethically proves your professionalism.

How Should I Document My Sources?

Use APA or MLA format.

The two most widely used formats for endnotes and bibliographies are those of the **American Psychological Association** (APA) and the **Modern Language Association** (MLA). (This module uses APA in-text citations.) Figure 15.2 shows both APA and MLA models.

Formatting styles, like language itself, constantly evolve; you can find MLA (www.mla.org) and APA (www.apa.org) updates on their respective home pages. Moreover, you can use free APA and MLA formatting software such as RefWorks or Son of Citation to create your documentation material.

Cultural FOCUS

In some cultures, perhaps your own, repeating word for word what a scholar has said is considered the best way to show you have understood and agree with certain points. It is also considered the best way to show respect for that scholar. However, for documents to be acceptable in North America (and many other Western cultures), you have to cite the source and also integrate the points into your own writing. This is how respect for the original writer or thinker is shown; it also demonstrates your own understanding of the ideas. By following the expected rules here, you are showing respect for and understanding of the cultural norms, just as you would expect others to show the same respect while working in your culture.

Although citation software, like all technology, is always evolving, it still cannot think for itself. Be aware that the software creates errors (like not capitalizing proper names); if you use it, be prepared to edit thoroughly.

APA style is used to cite and document sources in business, technology, and social sciences. APA in-text citations give authors' last names and the date of the work in parentheses in the text. Put an ampersand for two authors (Paiz & Angeli, 2012) or commas and an ampersand for multiple authors (Paiz, Angeli, Wagner, Lawrick, Moore, & Anderson, 2012), then a comma and the date. If there are more than six authors, use the name of the first author followed by the abbreviation et al., which means and others (Paiz et al., 2012) Only give the page number for a direct quotation (Paiz et al., p. 74). If you use the author's name(s) in the sentence, give only the date in parentheses. The **References** page provides the full bibliographic citations, arranged alphabetically by the first author's last name.

FIGURE 15.2A   **APA Format for Documenting Sources**

References

American Psychological Association. (2012). *APA style*. Retrieved from www.apastyle.org

British Science Association. (n.d.). Welcome to the honesty lab. *Dishonestylab.com*. Retrieved from www.britishscienceassociation.org/web

Click & Copyright (2012). Copyright infringement. Retrieved from www.clickandcopyright.com/copyright-resources/copyright-infringement.aspx

Grossman, J. (1976). *Quickhand™*. New York: John Wiley & Sons, Inc.

Industry Canada (2011). A guide to copyrights. Ottawa: Canadian Intellectual Property Office. Retrieved from www.cipo.ic.gc.ca/eic/site/cipointernet-internetopic.nsf/eng/wr02394.html

Industry Canada. (2012). The copyright modernization act. Ottawa: Canadian Intellectual Property Office. Retrieved from http://balancedcopyright.gc.ca/eic/site/crp-prda.nsf/eng/home

iParadigms. (2012). What is plagiarism? Retrieved from www.plagiarism.org/learning_center/what_is_plagiarism.html

Jensen, E. (2003). *Student success secrets*. New York: Barron's Educational Series, Inc.

Mind Tools Ltd. (1995–2009). Mind maps, a powerful approach to note taking. Retrieved from www.mindtools.com/pages/article/newISS_01.htm

Modern Language Association of America. (2009). *MLA handbook for writers of research papers*. (7th ed.). New York: The Modern Language Association of America.

Paiz, J. M., Angeli, E., Wagner, J., Lawrick, E., Moore, K., Anderson, M., Soderlund, L., Brizee, A., and Keck, R. (2012a). Reference list: Electronic sources (web publications). *Purdue Online Writing Lab*. Retrieved from http://owl.english.purdue.edu/owl/resource/560/10/

Paiz, J. M., Angeli, E., Wagner, J., Lawrick, E., Moore, K., Anderson, M., Soderlund, L., Brizee, A., and Keck, R. (2012b). APA general format. *Purdue Online Writing Lab*. Retrieved from http://owl.english.purdue.edu/owl/resource/560/01/

PlagiarismdotOrg. (2009) What is plagiarism? Retrieved from http://plagiarism.org/

RefWorks (2009) Home page. Retrieved from www.refworks.com

St. Francis Xavier University. (2012a). Plagiarism. Angus L. Macdonald Library. Retrieved from http://library.stfx.ca/help/plagiarism.php

St. Francis Xavier University. (2012b). Quoting and paraphrasing. The Writing Centre. Retrieved from http://sites.stfx.ca/writingcentre/Quoting_and_Paraphrasing

University of Ottawa. (2012). Study skills—Note taking. *Student Academic Success Service*. Retrieved from www.sass.uottawa.ca/mentoring/undergraduate/note-taking.php

What is RSS? RSS explained. (n.d.). Retrieved from www.whatisrss.com

York University. (2009, Nov. 4). Note taking at university. *Learning Skills Services*. Retrieved from www.yorku.ca/cds/lss/skillbuilding/notetaking.html

Note: Emails and interviews by researcher are not listed in References. Identify emails and your interviews in the text as personal communications. Give name of author or interviewee and as specific a date as possible. Example: (L. Butler, personal communication, July 8, 2012).

FIGURE 15.2B   **MLA Format for Documenting Sources**

Works Cited

American Psychological Association. "APA Style." 2012. Web. 20 Aug. 2012.

British Science Association. "Welcome to the Honesty Lab." *Dishonestylab.com.* n.d. Web. 20 Aug. 2012.

Butler, Lorraine. Personal Communication, 8 July 2012.

Click & Copyright. "Copyright Infringement." Web. 10 Oct. 2012

Grossman, Jeremy. *Quickhand™.* New York: John Wiley & Sons, Inc., 1976. Print.

Industry Canada. Canadian Intellectual Property Office. "A Guide to Copyrights." 6 Dec. 2011. Web. 20 Aug. 2012.

---. Canadian Intellectual Property Office. "*The Copyright Modernization Act.*" 18 July 2012. Web. 20 Aug. 2012.

iParadigms. "What is Plagiarism?" 2012. Web. 20 Aug. 2012.

Jensen, Eric. *Student Success Secrets.* New York: Barron's Educational Series, Inc., 2003. Print.

Mind Tools Ltd. "Mind Maps, a Powerful Approach to Note Taking." *Mind Tools™,* 1996–2012. Web. 20 Aug. 2012.

Modern Language Association of America. *MLA Handbook for Writers of Research Papers.* 7th ed. New York: The Modern Language Association of America, 2009. Print.

PlagiarismdotOrg. "What Is Plagiarism?" 2009. Web. 20 Aug. 2012.

Paiz, J. M., Angeli, E., Wagner, J., Lawrick, E., Moore, K., Anderson, M., Soderlund, L., Brizee, A., and Keck, R. "APA General Format." *Purdue Online Writing Lab.* 2012. Web. 20 Aug. 2012.

---. "Reference List: Electronic Sources (Web Publications)." *Purdue Online Writing Lab.* 2012. Web. 20 Aug. 2012.

RefWorks. Home Page. 2009. Web. 20 Aug. 2012.

St. Francis Xavier University. "Plagiarism." Angus L. Macdonald Library. 2012. Web. 20 Aug. 2012.

---. "Quoting and paraphrasing." The Writing Centre. 2012. Web. 20 Aug. 2012.

University of Ottawa. "Study Skills—Note Taking." *Student Academic Success Service.* 2012. Web. 20 Aug. 2012.

"What Is RSS? RSS Explained." n.d. Web. 20 Aug. 2012.

York University. "Note Taking at University" *Learning Skills Services,* 4 Nov. 2009. Web. 20 Aug. 2012.

"MLA…style is most commonly used to write papers and cite sources within the liberal arts and humanities" (Paiz et al., 2012b). MLA in-text citations give the author's last name and page number in parentheses in the text. Example: (Paiz and Angeli 74). If you use the author's name in the sentence, give only the page number (74). The **Works Cited** provides the full bibliographic citation, arranged alphabetically by author's last name.

MODULE SUMMARY

- To summarize and/or paraphrase information effectively,
  - Prepare: Identify your purposes; pre-read; clarify the context.
  - Listen or read for a broad overview. Look for meaning.
  - Make sure you understand the material; if you don't, keep reading, read other sources, and ask questions until you do.
  - Create your own memorable and meaningful notes.
- To summarize and/or paraphrase information legitimately, ethically, and professionally, document your sources.
- Identifying your sources of information demonstrates your honesty, enhances your credibility, and protects you from charges of **plagiarism**—the conscious or unconscious theft of others' work.
- **Copyright laws** protect people's creative output; you are legally responsible for attributing intellectual property to its owner.

- Using someone else's work without giving credit is also unethical, since it violates the author's personal and professional rights.
- Academic penalties can include a grade failure or expulsion; in business, you can be sued for damages and revenue.
- As you research, document your sources immediately; this habit will save you hours of time and labour when composing your final copy.
- **Citation** means providing the source in the body of the report. When citing sources,
  - Pay attention to the order of the words and the punctuation. When you use a short quotation that is part of the main body of the text, the sentence period goes after the in-text citation. In a long indented quotation (about 30 words or more), the page number, in parentheses, follows the period at the end of the sentence. For example, for a short

quote, RefWorks is "an online research management, writing and collaboration tool" (RefWorks, 2009). And for a long, indented quote:

> RefWorks an online research management, writing and collaboration tool is designed to help researchers easily gather, manage, store and share all types of information, as well as generate citations and bibliographies. (RefWorks, 2009)

- **Documentation** means giving the bibliographic information readers need to find the original source.
  - ○ **APA** and **MLA** are the most commonly used formats for documenting references and endnotes.
  - ○ Free online software automatically formats your bibliographic information.

ASSIGNMENTS FOR MODULE 15

Questions for Critical Thinking

15.1   What kind of information would you find most difficult to summarize or paraphrase? Why?

15.2   What is unintentional plagiarism? What three strategies can you use to avoid it?

15.3   During a casual lunch conversation, a person at your table makes a comment that gives you a brilliant idea you can use in your report. Should you credit the person? Why or why not?

15.4   How can a researcher using only secondary sources come up with original material?

Exercises and Problems

15.5 Researching Plagiarism

Got to www.plagiarism.org and assess the site. What is the purpose of the site, and who are the audiences for the information?

Choose a research area from one of the six topic headings (What is plagiarism? Education tips on plagiarism prevention, Types of plagiarism, Plagiarism FAQ, How do I cite sources? What is citation?), or the Solutions topics on the right-hand side of the page. Read about and make notes on your topic.

As your instructor directs,

- a. Discuss your findings and your notes with two or three peers who chose the same research area as you. What information did you find surprising? What did you already know? What did your team members all agree was the most important information?
- b. Together with your two peers, use the most important information to create
  1. A three-minute slide presentation on your topic for your instructor and the class
  2. A ten-question quiz on your topic for your instructor and the class

15.6 Participating in an International Ethics Assessment

Together with the Brunel University Law School, the British Science Association (www.britishscienceassociation.org) has initiated a global "study to explore public concepts of honesty" (www.honestylab.com).

Go to www.honestylab.com, open the tab "More about dishonesty," and click on the link "Take the Honesty Test today" near the end of the text to participate in the study. Watch the videos, answer the questions, and participate in the activities. Create whatever notes you will need to summarize your responses and reactions to the questions and activities.

As your instructor directs,

- a. Together with two peers, discuss the experience: What surprised you? How similar were your answers? Where were the differences? How do you and your peers account for these differences?
- b. Together with your two peers, draft an email memo to your instructor and the class. In your memo
  1. Sum up some of the similarities and differences in responses among the members of your triad.
  2. Offer explanations for the differences.
  3. In your final paragraph, summarize your team members' individual reactions to the honesty study, and the questions and activities. Do you think the study will provide relevant, reliable data? Why or why not?

15.7 Creating Notes on a Document Resource

Create notes on any of the following resources:

www.sass.uottawa.ca/mentoring/undergraduate/note-taking.php

www.academicintegrity.uoguelph.ca/plagiarism_avoiding.cfm

www.cipo.ic.gc.ca/eic/site/cipointernet-internetopic.nsf/
eng/wr02394.html

www.alysion.org/handy/althandwriting.htm

http://owl.english.purdue.edu/owl/resource/619/1/

www.bridgewater.edu/WritingCenter/Workshops/summariztips.
htm

www.ic.gc.ca/eic/site/ippd-dppi.nsf/eng/home

http://lifehacker.com/software/note-taking/a-beginners-
guide-to-mind-mapping-meetings-288763.php

www.writingcentre.uottawa.ca/hypergrammar/grammar.html

www.socialresearchmethods.net/kb/ethics.php

www.utoronto.ca/ucwriting/paraphrase.html

www.yorku.ca/cds/lss/skillbuilding/notetaking.html

Before you begin, be sure to

1. Know your purpose: You are making notes to *write a
   précis* of the information (see Exercise 15.8).
2. Know your audiences: You are creating notes *for your
   peers, your instructor, and yourself.*
3. *Read all these directions* and all of the document
   material *before* making your notes.
4. *Pre-read the document.* Skim and scan for context and
   meaning: skim the material; scan headings,
   subheadings, and visuals; note white space, bold,
   italics, and underlining.
5. *Read the document again* as you make your notes.

Identify and note the most important information:

- The author, his or her credentials, evidence of expertise
- The purpose of and audiences for the document
- The organizational pattern: How does the author
  develop the argument: Direct or indirect pattern?
  Chronological? Problem/solution? Functional? Spatial?
  Elimination of alternatives? (Module 17)
- The controlling idea or thesis of the document
- Three different ways the author proves or demonstrates
  his or her argument
- The level of difficulty: Is the document easy to
  understand? Moderately easy? Difficult? Impossible?
  Note why you think so.
- The most significant idea you learned by reading the
  document
- One way you will apply what you learned
- Your questions or information you want to follow up

Now create notes, manually or digitally, on any one of the
resources.

As your instructor directs,

a. Use APA or MLA style to credit the source you chose.
b. Exchange notes with at least one peer (more is better)
   who has created notes on a different source. Read his
   or her notes. Provide feedback: 1) Do you understand
   the information based on reading the notes? What
   information is unclear? Why? 2) What note-taking
   strategies strike you as unusual, innovative, or

particularly useful? Why? Then listen to the other
person's feedback about your notes.
c. Reread and revise your notes based on the feedback,
   if necessary.
d. If you created electronic notes, send these as an email
   attachment to your instructor and the rest of the class.
   Be sure to include your APA or MLA documentation.
e. If you created handwritten notes, scan and send these
   as an email attachment to your instructor and the rest
   of the class. Be sure to include your APA or MLA
   documentation.

15.8 Writing a Précis on a Document

Précis the original document you chose in Exercise 15.7,
using only the notes you created and revised.

- Use a word processor to draft a summary of the text in
  your own words.
- Summarize in sentences and paragraphs.
- Rewrite the summary until it is one-third the length of
  the original material.

As your instructor directs,

a. Use APA or MLA style to credit the source.
b. Exchange your précis with at least one peer (more is
   better) who has made a précis of a different source.
   Read his or her précis. Read the original source.
   Provide feedback: 1) How clear is the précis? Does the
   précis capture the meaning of the original? What
   information is missing? Does the précis writer use his or
   her own words? If not, what words or phrases would
   have to be put in quotations? Why? 2) How concise is
   the précis? Is it a third of the original? If not, does the
   précis writer have good reasons for the length? What
   are the reasons? Now listen to the other person's
   feedback on your précis.
c. Reread and revise your précis based on the feedback,
   if necessary.
d. Send your précis as an email attachment to your
   instructor and the rest of the class. Be sure to include
   your APA or MLA documentation.
e. In the email itself, describe what you found most
   difficult about writing the précis. Identify one specific
   way you can apply précis writing.

15.9 Creating Notes and a Précis on
a Multimedia Source

Find a multimedia or interactive Web tutorial on any of the
topics mentioned in Modules 14 and 15. (Possibilities include
copyright; the legal, ethical, or professional implications of
research; academic versus business research; and how to
add in-text citations, choose a document style, paraphrase,
avoid plagiarism, use quotations, write a précis, take notes,
write summaries, or synopsize.)

1. Prepare to take handwritten or digital notes on the material.
2. Watch, listen to, and read the resource at least three times. Take notes.
3. Using only your notes, précis the material for the class, your instructor, and yourself.

As your instructor directs,

a. Use APA or MLA style to credit the source.

b. Send your précis as an email attachment to your instructor and the rest of the class. Be sure to include your APA or MLA documentation.

c. In the email itself, write a paragraph describing any differences between writing a précis of a written document and writing a précis of a multimedia source. How was it different? Was the difference due to content? To the medium? To your experience of having already done summaries and paraphrases? Explain.

POLISHING YOUR PROSE

Using APA and MLA Style

For examples of APA and MLA style, see Figure 15.2. Quick reference tips are available online at www.apastyle.org/faqs.html (APA) and http://owl.english.purdue.edu/owl/resource/557/01/ (MLA).

Identify and correct the errors in APA format in the following Reference items:

1. Trivers, Robert, The Folly of Fools, New York: Basic Books. 2011.
2. Altered States Self-experiments in chemistry. Oliver Sacks August 27, 2012, p. 40 -- 48. Retrieved August 24, 2012, from http://www.newyorker.com/reporting/2012/08/27/120827fa_fact_sacks#ixzz24Txi9fvC
3. Flavelle, Dana. Toronto Star, Canadian debt loads getting heavier, Friday, August 24, 2012, SECTION B, p. BE-2.
4. Study: Economic downturn and educational attainment, 2008 to 2011. Stats Can, The Daily, Thursday, June 21, 2012, retrieved June 26, 2012, from http://www.statcan.gc.ca/daily-quotidien/120621/dq120621c-eng.htm
5. John Loomis, telephone conversation with author, June 20, 2012.
6. Four dramatic ways retirement has changed since '08, By Kevin Press, BrighterLife.ca. Retrieved from http://brighterlife.ca/2012/08/13/four-dramatic-ways-retirement-has-changed-since-08/

Identify and correct the errors in MLA format in the following Works Cited items:

1. Trivers, Robert, The Folly of Fools, New York: Basic Books. 2011.
2. Altered States Self-experiments in chemistry. Oliver Sacks August 27, 2012, p. 40 -- 48. Retrieved August 24, 2012, from http://www.newyorker.com/reporting/2012/08/27/120827fa_fact_sacks#ixzz24Txi9fvC
3. Flavelle, Dana. Toronto Star, Canadian debt loads getting heavier, Friday, August 24, 2012, SECTION B, p. B1-2.
4. Study: Economic downturn and educational attainment, 2008 to 2011. Stats Can, The Daily, Thursday, June 21, 2012, retrieved June 26, 2012, from http://www.statcan.gc.ca/daily-quotidien/120621/dq120621c-eng.htm
5. John Loomis, telephone conversation with author, June 20, 2012.
6. Four dramatic ways retirement has changed since '08, By Kevin Press, BrighterLife.ca. Retrieved from http://brighterlife.ca/2012/08/13/four-dramatic-ways-retirement-has-changed-since-08/

Check your answers to the odd-numbered exercises in the Polishing Your Prose Answer Key.

connect

Practise and learn online with Connect. Connect allows you to practise important skills at your own pace and on your own schedule, with 24/7 online access to an eBook, practise quizzes, interactives, videos, study tools, and additional resources.

Writing Information Reports

MODULE OUTLINE

- What is a report?
- What should I do before I write any report?
- What types of short reports will I write?

Module Summary

Assignments for Module 16

Polishing Your Prose: *Who/Whom* and *I/Me*

Learning Objectives

After reading and applying the information in Module 16, you'll be able to demonstrate

Knowledge of

LO1 Types of reports

LO2 Specific kinds of information reports

LO3 The importance of writing good purpose statements

LO4 Informal report writing style

Skills to

LO5 Begin to write purpose statements

LO6 Compose information reports

LO7 Begin to develop a good writing style

Employability Skills 2000+ Checklist

Module content builds these Conference Board of Canada Employability Skills 2000+

Communicate

Manage Information

Think and Solve Problems

Be Adaptable

Learn Continuously

Participate in Projects and Tasks

Reports provide the information that people in organizations need to record information, and to plan, make decisions, and solve problems. Usually, reports are written *up* in an organization: supervisors and managers assign report topics and timelines to subordinates.

Your workplace may have report templates. However, these templates may include audience-inappropriate language and redundant sections.[1] Whenever you can, use clear language and a report style format that meets the needs of your audiences and achieves the report's purposes. Whether you follow a template or create your own, being able to write effective reports gets rewards: recognition for your competence, promotions, and pay increases.[2]

What Is a Report?

Many different kinds of documents can be reports.

In some organizations, one- and two-page memos are called *reports*. In other organizations, a report is a long document with illustrations and numerical data. Still other companies produce PowerPoint slides as a report. **Informal reports** may be letters and memos, slide presentations, website summaries, business cases, or even computer printouts of production or sales figures. **Formal reports** contain formal elements such as a title page, a letter or memo transmittal page, a table of contents, and a list of illustrations (see Module 18). Reports can provide information, provide information and analyze it, and/or provide information and analysis to support a recommendation (see Table 16.1).

Writers decide on the type of report, its format, organizational pattern, and information, its length, language, level of formality, and channel of distribution based on PAIBOC analysis, and of the expectations of their organization and intended audiences (Module 2).

Ex. 16.1– 16.3

What Do Reports Have in Common?

To orient readers, reports usually contain an **introduction**, **body**, and **conclusion**:

- The *introduction* section puts the report in context for readers; it includes
  - ✔ A lead-in sentence: "This report describes…"
  - ✔ A purpose statement: "The purpose of this report is to…"
  - ✔ The scope of the report: "In this report, I explain the need for the program, and its structure and costs."
  - ✔ A summary of findings or results: "Employee feedback for the program was overwhelmingly positive."

LO1   TABLE 16.1   **Types of Reports**

Reports Can Provide:

Information only

- **Progress, conference, trip, and periodic reports** provide information and summaries.
- **Incident reports** describe health and safety transgressions.
- **Sales reports** give sales figures for the week or month.
- **Quarterly reports** show productivity and profits for the quarter.

Information plus analysis

- **Annual reports** detail financial data and an organization's accomplishments over the past year.
- **Audit reports** interpret facts revealed during an audit.
- **Make-good or payback reports** calculate the point at which a new capital investment will pay for itself.
- **Technical reports** describe scientific/technical processes.
- **Business plans** describe and analyze business, market, and financial projections.

Information plus analysis plus a recommendation

- **Feasibility and yardstick reports** analyze and evaluate possibilities, and recommend what the organization should do.
- **Justification reports** justify the need for a purchase, an investment, a new personnel line, or a change in procedure.
- **Problem-solving reports** identify the causes of an organizational problem and recommend a solution.
- **Proposals** analyze a need and recommend a solution.

FIGURE 16.1   **PAIBOC Questions for Analysis**

P	Why are you writing the report? What is the report's **purpose**? What is the situation? What results do you want? Are you updating your supervisor on your progress? Introducing a new initiative? Reporting a health and safety issue? Asking for time and money to attend a conference? Justifying buying an expensive piece of equipment? Analyzing the feasibility of an idea?
A	Who is your **audience**? What are your audience's expectations? Does your audience want/need updates? Information? Analysis? Justification? What does your audience value? What is important to your audience? What evidence will convince them?
I	What **information** must your message include? What does your audience already know? What do they need to know? What kind of information will your audience find most persuasive?
B	What reasons or reader **benefits** can you use to support your position? If your solution will cost the reader (in time or money), what benefits—to the organization, the audience, your colleagues—can you use to rationalize or outweigh those costs?
O	What **objections** can you expect your readers to have? What negative elements of your message must you de-emphasize or overcome? *One important objection is time*: how long will it take your audience to read your report? To overcome that objection, revise your report for clarity and conciseness, edit it for correctness, and use a reader (a friend, colleague, or family member) to proof it.
C	How will the **context** affect the reader's response? Think about your relationship to the reader, the organizational culture and morale, the current economic situation, the time of year, and any special circumstances.

- The *body* section presents specifics (facts, figures, statistics, examples, visuals) the audience needs to understand a situation, and, in some cases, to make a decision.
- The *conclusion* section summarizes the most important information covered in the body, and can include
  - ✔ Recommendations, if the report's purpose is to effect change or solve a problem
  - ✔ Supplementary material the audience may want (appendices, questionnaires)
  - ✔ References, when the report uses secondary sources of information (Modules 14 and 15)

What Should I Do Before I Write Any Report?

Do your research. Define the situation. Draft a purpose statement.

Creating a report includes

- Defining the situation
- Gathering and analyzing the necessary information
- Organizing the information
- Drafting the report
- Revising and editing the report
- Submitting the report

Before you begin to draft your report, you'll need to analyze your purposes and audiences. You also need to complete part of your research, in order to define the situation your report will discuss, and to identify the topics you will cover.

Your supervisor's direction and your analysis will help you to define the situation or problem. However, you may need to narrow your focus. For example, the topic "using social media to improve business" is far too broad. Instead, use the following example to narrow the perspective and find your purpose:

- Choose one type of social media.
- Identify the specific situation or problem: what do you want the report to accomplish?
- Identify the specific audience with a stake in the situation, or with the power to support or implement your suggestions.

Your purpose statement might then be "Our company can use Twitter to build business." Your audience might be your boss, colleagues, or aspiring entrepreneurs.

Remember that *how you define the problem shapes the solutions you find*. For example, suppose that a manufacturer of frozen foods isn't making money. If the researcher defines the situation as a marketing problem, he or she may analyze the product's price, image, advertising, and position in the market. But perhaps the real problem is that overhead costs are too high due to poor inventory management, or that an inadequate distribution system does not get the product to its target market. Defining the problem accurately is essential to finding an effective solution.

LO3 LO5 Writing Purpose Statements

Once you've defined your problem or situation, you're ready to write a purpose statement. The purpose statement goes in the introduction, and is the organizing principle of every report. A good **purpose statement** makes three things clear:

- The situation or problem
- The specific information that must be explored, or questions that must be answered, to resolve the situation or solve the problem
- The rhetorical purpose (to explain, to inform, to recommend, to propose, to request) the report is to achieve

The following purpose statements have all three elements.

Scope: Information report explores

Current management methods keep the elk population within the carrying capacity of the habitat but require frequent human intervention. Both wildlife conservation specialists and the public would prefer methods that controlled the elk population naturally.

This report will compare the current short-term management techniques (hunting, trapping and transporting, and winter feeding) with two long-term management techniques, habitat modification and the reintroduction of predators. The purpose of this report is to recommend which techniques or combination of techniques would best satisfy the needs of conservationists, hunters, and the public.

Report Audience: Parks Canada Agency, responsible for Alberta's Elk Island National Park

Situation or problem

Organization pattern, method of development

Purpose: To recommend

When banner ads on Web pages first appeared in 1994, the initial response, or "click-through" rate, was about 10%. However, as ads have increased on Web pages, the click-through rate has dropped sharply. Rather than assuming that any banner ad will be successful, we need to ask, "What characteristics do successful banner ads share? Are ads for certain kinds of products and services, or for certain kinds of audiences, more likely to be successful on the Web?" The purpose of this report is to summarize the available research and anecdotal evidence and to recommend what Leo Burnett should tell its clients about whether and how to use banner ads.

Report Audience: Leo Burnett Advertising Agency

Situation

Questions report examines and answers

Purpose: To summarize research and make recommendation(s)

Situation and purpose: Proposal written in response to a request

Your request for a communications audit proposal reflects the City of Fredericton's commitment to its employees. A recent article in *The Globe and Mail* ("What Employees Care About," February 27, 2010, p. C1) details how poor communications cost organizations time and money. Good communication practices, however, have a proven 100 percent return on investment—in employee and customer satisfaction, employee retention, and improved productivity. My colleagues and I welcome the opportunity to work with you in identifying, developing, and implementing your communications' best-practices tools.

Report Audience: City of Fredericton HR Director

Focus of proposal: Vendor's proposal describes what vendor will do

To write a good purpose statement, you have to understand the basic situation, or problem, and have some idea of the questions that your report will answer. You can (and should) write a working purpose statement (Module 14) to help focus your research; expect to change your purpose statement as a result of your research findings.

LO2 LO6 What Types of Short Reports Will I Write?

You will write summary reports, documenting information.

Supervisors expect employees to report information using short, informal documents. These internal reports summarize work, conferences, and sales trips, and describe work progress and health and safety incidents, using memo format (Modules 6 and 7).

Information and Closure Reports

An **information report** summarizes your work or research to date. Similarly, a **closure report** summarizes a project and assesses the results.

Information and closure reports include

- An *introduction paragraph*, summarizing the report topic, purposes, and most important outcomes, from the reader's perspective
- A *chronological account* (Module 17) of problem identification, actions, and results
- A *concluding paragraph* assessing the success of the project or work

Depending on the writer's mandate, the conclusion might include suggestions for further action.

See Figures 16.2 and 16.3 for examples of these two types of reports.

FIGURE 16.2 Information Report, Memo Format

From:	Shobana Kunella, Dennis MacDonald
Date:	April 20, 2013
To:	Doug Perrin, Operations Manager
Subject:	Employee Writing Needs Assessment

Hi Doug,

Over the last month, Dennis and I collected and assessed the information you requested about employees' writing concerns. We created a two-page, online survey and sent it to all employees. We held eight interdepartmental focus groups and interviewed managers of five departments: Accounting, Engineering, Human Resources, Sales and Marketing, and Research and Development. Altogether, we spoke to 76 people and received 383 surveys.

In this report, I summarize the findings and suggest next steps.

What We Write

The survey results and interviews indicate that every employee writes emails.

Additionally, employees write any or all of

- Letters
- Reports, including project and final project reports, proposals, RFPs, technical descriptions, feasibility, audits, studies, and formal technical reports
- Contracts
- Research papers
- Articles
- Manuals
- Meeting minutes

What We Want

People were consistent in their concerns. Everyone wanted support in grammar, proofreading, editing, and tone. Additionally, employees said they wanted help with

- Formatting, consistency, and unity
- Writing concisely
- Writing clearly
- Organizing information
- Using appropriate language

Employees had very different opinions about how to learn these skills. The majority liked the idea of onsite training. Others would prefer to take a course or get individual coaching.

We need more information to make a decision. Dennis and I need to research the costs for people's preferences. Please let me if we should go ahead and when you would like the information.

FIGURE 16.3   Closure Report, Memo Format, Email Attachment

Date: March 15, 2012

To: Rob Dhillon, Human Resource Director

From: Irene Kaushansky, Staff Training and Development

Subject: Coaching Elisa Roberts

During our meeting of January 11, Elisa, you, and I agreed that Elisa would receive training in how to make successful accounts receivable calls. We agreed to hire a professional coach to help Elisa with the skills she needed to be successful in her new role. Further, we agreed that Elisa would identify the coach she felt she could work well with, and begin the training as soon as possible.

The purpose of this report is to describe the coaching program, and assess the results so far.

Coaching Elisa in Accounts Receivable Calls

In the week of January 18, Elisa and I interviewed three consultants about the coaching. We agreed that Mara Brady, of Brady and Associates, would be the right person to work with Elisa. Mara offered suggestions, and together she and Elisa decided on the program.

Coaching Parameters

Elisa, Mara, and I agreed on the training objectives:

1. To build Elisa's competence in AR calling
2. To identify AR calling best practices so that Elisa can train two other employees in successful AR calls

Mara recommended three coaching sessions of three hours each, a week apart, to begin January 25. In the first session, Elisa and Mara agreed to

- Analyze the current AR calling process
- Identify Elisa's telephone communication strengths
- Create SMART goals to build on those strengths

Coaching Methods

Mara suggested she observe Elisa making AR calls, and note (in writing) communication strengths and challenges. Together they would identify strategies (including active listening and negotiating techniques) to increase AR calling productivity, measured in

- Elisa's increased confidence
- Increased collection rate; amount to be determined after initial session
- Tips and techniques sheet

Further, they agreed that Elisa would keep a journal reflecting her learning experiences.

At the end of each session, Elisa and Mara would create a list of strategies for a best practices tip sheet. At the end of the three sessions, Elisa would evaluate the coaching experience and decide if she needed additional training.

Coaching Results

By the end of the second coaching session, I saw noticeable improvement in Elisa's AR calls. A week after the third session, I sat with Elisa during her AR calls and saw that she could

- Identify which clients would be motivated by AR calls
- Script a variety of calls
- Be courteous, calm, and confident throughout the call
- Listen to get results
- Control the tone and time of the call
- Ask for a commitment
- Produce written results, including suggestions for follow-up

Elisa has increased her collection rate by 30 percent and is developing the tip sheet and a coaching program for Janine and Armand. She feels she doesn't need more coaching sessions right now, but would like the option of calling Mara in for a follow-up session in a few months.

The cost of the coaching sessions was $1,800 plus HST. Based on Elisa's feedback and her increased productivity, we are very pleased with the results.

Conference and Trip Reports

Conference reports update your supervisor on industry trends, and justify the organizational expenditure (in your time and travel costs) by explaining the benefits to the audience. If your organization does not use templates, put the most significant information (for the audience) up front, and try to keep your report to a page or less. An example of a conference report appears in Figure 16.4.

Managers may accompany novice salespeople on client calls and record their observations about the representative's performance. These follow-up **trip reports** are kept in the rep's file for reference and may be copied to sales directors. Figure 16.5 shows an example of a trip report.

FIGURE 16.4   **Sample Conference Report, Email Attachment**

Conference Report: Fuel Cell Seminar and Exposition

Vancouver, B.C., November 16 to 19, 2013

This conference focused on high-temperature fuel cell research and development, and fuel processing and hydrogen development. Approximately 1,500 people attended, with international participants from Ireland, Denmark, Korea, Japan, and Germany.

The exhibition ran for four days, and was very well attended; ten fuel cell cars were available for test drives. After the plenary session and short technical presentations on Monday, participants could choose any of six parallel sessions, both mornings and afternoons, over the next three days.

The conference provided me with client networking opportunities and industry updates. I will be making use of both during client visits over the next month.

Highlights

Despite the recession, fuel cell shipments have increased globally, with greatest demand in Denmark, Europe, the Middle East, and Southeast Asia.

- Fuel cell power is now a recognized alternative energy source with universal applications.
- Greenhouse gas emission reductions are significant (up to 65% in large vehicles).
- The U.S., British, German, Korean, and Danish governments are committed to investing a billion dollars in funding for hydrogen and fuel cell R&D over the next two years.
- Canadian government support has increased since last year; the federal government has promised $3 million in R&D investment over the next five years.
- Hydrogen fuelling stations continue to be built in the United States—eight were built in 2012 alone. The American presenter said that poor infrastructure continues to plague the industry and suggested that governments and the private sector needed to be encouraged to understand the importance of hydrogen as the alternative energy source.
- One session examined alternative hydrogen sources production. Denmark is leading the world in biomass experimentation in this field.
- Cost reduction remains the priority: two sessions were devoted to panel discussions on possibilities. Since last year's conference, the emphasis has shifted from reducing material costs to improving manufacturing processes.

Approximately 110 more Canadian representatives attended than last year. Canada was also a significant presence in the exhibition. Perhaps the renewed enthusiasm is a result of the government's growing recognition of the importance of fuel cell technology.

FIGURE 16.5   **Sample Trip Report, Email Attachment**

Hi Lewis,

This email is long overdue; in future, I'll get my follow-up email to you in a timelier manner!

I had a great two days calling with you. You have made a very positive impact on your clients in such a short time.

I notice that you are very prompt with follow-up emails. This is excellent—it's one of the ways you can make yourself stand out as a sales rep. And you are making a good effort to meet as many people as possible when you are on campus, which is also great, especially at your travel schools.

As we discussed on Wednesday, one way to determine how important service is to instructors is to ask, "What do you look for in a sales rep?" It's another great question to set you apart. I am impressed that you are incorporating this line of questioning in your calls.

You were very strong in the presentation: you hit all the points you wanted to get across, and you took control of the room. You checked for questions, interest, and understanding, with challenges like "How do you see yourself using this in your course?" Your questions made the presentation very engaging. I know you were a little nervous leading up to it, but I suspect that as you get more practice, you'll feel more confident. And as always, the more you prep, the more confident you'll feel.

I'd like to see you continue to dig in your departments and get into areas where you haven't yet spent a lot of time. You'll pick up many units with a lot less work than in those big committee situations. Working both big and small will ensure you have a solid year. Push yourself out of your comfort zone, and you'll increase your sales.

I'd also like to see you get really comfortable questioning around technology and demonstrating on the fly. Let's talk after Closers to see where your comfort level is with the technologies for B&E and HSSL, and make plans accordingly.

I hope you found Closers helpful in developing strategies in all the different disciplines. Since you are the lead HSSL/B&E rep, I am going to arrange some extra product training for you. Let me know the areas where you would like more help.

Thanks again, Lewis. It's great to know I have such a strong rep in place in Man/Sask!

Ex.
16.5

Incident Report

To protect employees, and themselves, most Canadian organizations comply with federal and provincial health and safety regulations. These regulations include WHMIS training and incident reporting. Usually, your organization will have a template you follow for an **incident report**. When you record an incident, use bullets or brief sentences to describe exactly what happened. Put the information in chronological order, note only observable behaviours, and do not record your inferences, assumptions, or feelings. See Figure 16.6 for an example.

Language FOCUS

WHMIS stands for **Workplace Hazardous Materials Information System**. WHMIS is a Canadian standard that companies must follow for the use, storage, handling, and disposing of controlled substances and hazardous materials, such as cancer-causing chemicals. See www.hc-sc.gc.ca/ewh-semt/occup-travail/whmis-simdut/index-eng.php for more information.

FIGURE 16.6   Incident Report

MediGroup Centre
945 Bradshaw Place
Prince Albert, SK S6V 2P5
306.566.5555

Accident/Incident Report

Date of Incident: *Mar. 13, 2012*   Time: *2:13* AM/(PM)

Name of Injured Person: *Delphanie Hess*

Male: ____ Female: *✓*

Date of Birth: *November 19, 1985*

Address: *22 Longboat Ave., Prince Albert, ON*

Contact Phone Number: *416.232.1093*

Type of injury: *Verbal abuse*

Describe Incident: *Patient F. Baum arrived for app't 37 mins. late. When I explained he had missed his app't, he began yelling and swearing at me. He leaned over reception desk and said he would "punch" me. I apologized and asked "May I give you another app't?" Client turned and walked out door, still yelling. Slammed door.*

Required physician/hospital?   Yes___ No *✓*

Name of physician/hospital: *N/A*

Address: *N/A*

Physician/hospital phone number: *N/A*

Follow-up: *Written incident report; reported to Dr. Phillips*

Signature of injured person/parent/guardian: *D. Hess*   Date: *March 13, 2012*

Witness's signature: *Joanne Tuebot*   (patient)   Date: *March 13, 2012*

Reporter's signature: *D. Hess*   Date: *March 13, 2012*

Progress Reports

In **progress reports**, you report on what you've done, why it's important, and what you will do next.

When you're assigned to a single project that will take a month or more, you may be asked to file one or more progress reports. A progress report assures the employer or funding agency that you're making progress, and allows you and the employer or agency to resolve problems as they arise.

Different readers may have different concerns. An instructor may want to know whether you'll have your report in by the due date. A client may be more interested in what you're learning about the problem. Adapt your progress report to meet the needs of the audience.

Employability Skills

You can use progress reports to do more than just report progress:

- *Suggest alternatives*. Explain, "I could continue to do X (what you approved); I could do Y instead (what I'd like to do now)." The detail in the progress report can help back up your claim. Even if the idea is rejected, you don't lose face because you haven't made a separate issue of the alternative.
- *Minimize potential problems*. As you do the work, you may find that implementing your recommendations will be difficult. In your regular progress reports, you can alert your boss or the funding agency to the challenges, preparing your audience psychologically to act on your recommendations.

A study of the progress reports in a large research and development organization found that less successful writers tended to focus on what they had done and said very little about the value of their work. Good writers, in contrast, spent less space writing about the details of what they'd done but much more space explaining the value of their work for the organization.[3]

Subject lines for progress reports are straightforward. Specify the project on which you are reporting your progress.

    Subject: Progress on Developing a Marketing Plan for Compact Hybrids

    Subject: Progress on Organizing IABC Toronto Chapter Annual Conference

If you are submitting weekly or monthly progress reports on a long project, number your progress reports, or include the time period in your subject line. Include dates for the work completed since the last report, and the work to be completed before the next report.

Report as positively as you honestly can. You build a better image of yourself when you show that you can take minor problems in stride, and that you're confident of your own abilities.

    Negative: I have not deviated markedly from my schedule, and I feel that I will have very little trouble completing this report by the due date.

    Positive: I am back on schedule and expect to complete my report by the due date.

Progress reports can be organized in three ways: by chronology, by task, and by supporting a recommendation.

Chronological Progress Reports

Chronological progress reports focus on what the writer has done and what work remains. Organize the report this way:

1. *Summarize your progress in terms of your goals and your original schedule*. Use measurable statements.

    Poor: My progress has been slow.

    Better: The research for my report is about one-third complete.

2. *Under the heading "Work Completed," describe what you have already done*. Be specific, both to support your claims in the first paragraph, and to allow the reader to appreciate your hard work. Acknowledge the people who have helped you. Describe any serious obstacles you've encountered and tell how you've dealt with them.

    Poor: I have found many articles about Procter & Gamble on the Web. I have had a few problems finding how the company keeps employees safe from chemical fumes.

    Better: On the Web, I found Procter & Gamble's home page, its annual report, and its mission statement. No one whom I interviewed could tell me about safety programs specifically at P&G. I have found seven articles about ways to protect workers against pollution in factories, but none mentions P&G.

3. *Under the heading "Work to Be Completed," or "Next Steps," describe the work that remains*. If you're more than three days late (for school projects) or two weeks late (for business proj-

ects), submit a new schedule, showing how you will be able to meet the original deadline. You may want to discuss "Observations" or "Preliminary Conclusions" if you want feedback before writing the final report or if your reader has asked for substantive interim reports.

4. *Either express your confidence that you'll have the report ready by the due date or request a conference to discuss extending the due date or limiting the project.* If you are behind your original schedule, show why you think you can still finish the project on time.

Figure 16.7 shows a chronological progress report.

Task Progress Reports

In a task progress report, organize information under the various tasks you have worked on during the period. For example, a task progress report for a group report project might use the following headings:

> Finding Background Information on the Web and in Print
>
> Analyzing Our Survey Data
>
> Working on the Introduction of the Report and the Appendices

Under each heading, the group might discuss the tasks it has completed and those that remain.

FIGURE 16.7   Sample Chronological Progress Report

Date: November 2, 2012

To: Kathryn Hughes

From: Sheema Khan

Subject: Formal Report Progress

As you requested, this report summarizes the work I have completed on my formal report topic. I have found several excellent sources for current information on the status of women working in the building trades. Therefore, I have met the timelines stated in my proposal and anticipate submitting the report on the required due date.

Work Completed

Because I was able to access so many sound resources, I finished writing the first draft of the body of the report yesterday. A *Toronto Star* article about the lack of women in the trades helped focus my topic. This article provides information on Canada's current labour shortage, on apprentices and journeymen, and on the many construction jobs available that are not "in the field." The article includes a self-assessment quiz to help people recognize if they might want to work in construction trades. All of this information proved invaluable in drafting the text.

Through Internet research, I found the National Association of Women in Construction (NAWIC) and StatsCan, with relevant data on jobs and women's representation in the skilled trades.

By far the most important resource, however, has been my sister Maria, who graduated in engineering but now works as a superintendent for Schell Construction Canada. Through interviewing Maria, I learned about the barriers women face in the construction industry, and about the roles education, legislation, and restructuring can play in favourably transforming the industry.

Work in Progress

For the next six days, while revising the first draft, I will be inserting in-text citations and preparing the References page, using the *APA Formatting and Style Guide*. Then I will draft the Conclusions and Summary sections of the report.

Final Steps

By March 18, I will have drafted the first and last parts of the report. I have allotted another ten days for revising and editing. Maria will read the second draft to ensure my facts and citations are correct. And two friends have agreed to read this draft for unity and organization. All three will also be reading for correct grammar and punctuation. I intend finishing the final draft by March 31, for submission April 3.

All the information I have gathered while researching has proven to me that my topic is both personally and socially relevant. Thank you for providing this opportunity.

Recommendation Progress Reports

Recommendation progress reports recommend action: resourcing a new idea, increasing the funding for a project or changing its direction, cancelling a project that isn't working out. When the recommendation will be easy for the reader to accept, use the direct request pattern of organization from Module 8. If your recommendation is likely to meet strong resistance, the problem-solving pattern (Module 9) might be more effective.

LO4 LO7   EXPANDING A CRITICAL SKILL

Writing with Style

People's writing style conveys their attitudes about the subject and their audience. Good business writing is natural, polite, concise, and correct, indicating respect for readers. You develop your own writing style through knowledge and practice.

Make Your Writing Natural

Natural style is not spontaneous, but the result of critical thinking and revision.

- Use PAIBOC to analyze your purpose and your audience's expectations. In informal reports,
  - Use first person (*I*) and second person (*you*).
  - Put your readers in your sentences ("Thank you for…" "As you requested.…"
  - Keep your paragraphs short.
  - Vary sentence structure and length. Remember, however, that the most readable sentences are between 14 and 20 words, and structured subject+verb+object.
  - Use active, action verbs (Writing and Editing Resources).
  - Use concrete nouns.
  - Avoid jargon and technical language.
  - Use parallel structure (Writing and Editing Resources).

Make Your Writing Polite

- Address your audience by name: people want to be recognized and treated as individuals.

- Research the names and preferred courtesy titles (Module 6) of the people whom you write to and for, and use them.
- Include the information your audience needs to know (purpose, scope, results) up front, in your introduction.
- Use neutral or positive language; avoid the negative.
- Rewrite as the reader: reader-centred writing uses an organization pattern, sentence structure, and language that meet the audience's needs for clarity and understanding (Module 13).

Make Your Writing Concise and Correct

- Compose drafts and sections of longer documents as soon you can; make notes on your research; summarize; paraphrase (Module 15).
- Save most of your time for revision; use proven revision strategies:
  - Apply WIRMI (What I Really Mean Is…) as you read your sentences and paragraphs.
  - Eliminate every unnecessary word.
  - Use readers: Ask colleagues or friends to read your writing; ask for specific feedback; revise.
- Edit for correct spelling, grammar, and punctuation.
- Ask a friend to proof your final copy.

MODULE SUMMARY

- Any kind of document or slide show can be a report. Usually, supervisors assign report topics and timelines to subordinates.
- **Information reports** collect data for the reader; **analytical reports** present and interpret data; **recommendation reports** recommend action or a solution.
- Creating a report includes
  - Defining the situation
  - Gathering and analyzing the necessary information
  - Organizing the information

  - Drafting the report
  - Revising and editing the report
  - Submitting the report
- Before you write any report,
  - Do your research
  - Define the situation
  - Draft a good purpose statement
- A good **purpose statement** frames your message for the reader. A good purpose statement clarifies
  - The organizational situation or problem

○ The specific questions that must be answered to resolve the situation or solve the problem

○ The rhetorical purposes (to describe, to explain, to request, to propose, to recommend) the report is written to achieve

● In information, closure, conference, and incident reports, provide the information chronologically.

● In progress reports, focus the reader on what you have done, and what work remains:

○ Summarize your progress in terms of your goals and original work schedule.

○ Use headings "Work Completed," "Next Steps"—describe what you have done and will do.

○ Express your confidence in meeting the due date, or request a meeting to discuss extending the due date or limiting the project.

● Use **positive emphasis** in progress reports to demonstrate confidence and competence.

● Good business writing style is natural, polite, concise, and correct. You develop your own style through knowledge and practice.

ASSIGNMENTS FOR MODULE 16

Questions for Critical Thinking

16.1 What do you have to know to identify the kind of report you are writing? Why?

16.2 How do you decide what kind of language—formal, informal, technical, jargon—to use when writing a report?

16.3 How can you create a reader-friendly report? Identify three ways you can make your report more readable for your audience(s).

Exercises and Problems

16.4 Writing a Summary and Evaluation Report

Find a new or recently established business social networking site. Write an information report describing the site to the director of your college/university Employment Placement Office. Evaluate the site based on the following criteria

● Appearance
● Navigability
● Accessibility
● Community
● Business support
● Job search support

As your instructor directs

Attach the completed report to an email. Send the email to

a. The Employment Placement Office director
b. Your instructor

16.5 Writing an Incident Report

Write an incident report to your supervisor describing a recent organizational or workplace accident, or health and safety transgression that you observed. If your organization has a template, use it; if not, create your own. For ideas, go to the McGill University Services Environmental Health and Safety site at www.mcgill.ca/ehs/forms/forms/accidentincidentreport.

As your instructor directs

Attach the completed report to an email. Send the email to

a. Your supervisor
b. Your instructor

16.6 Writing an Investigation Report

Write a short report on the co-op placement opportunities available for graduates in your field of study. Begin your research by interviewing students with co-op experience, alumni, recent program graduates, and your teachers. Visit your campus placement office and the library for suggestions on how to research and contact industries and companies that hire co-op students.

In your report, include feedback from co-op students and their salaries/wages, as well as ideas for organizations that your college/university could approach for co-op placements.

As your instructor directs

Write the report to

a. Your instructor and class members
b. Your campus placement/co-op office

16.7 Writing a Chronological Progress Report

Write a memo report summarizing your progress on a major report that you have to write.

In the introductory paragraph, summarize your progress in terms of your schedule and your goals. Under a heading titled "Work Completed," list what you have already done. (This is a chance to toot your own horn: if you have solved problems creatively, say so! You can also describe obstacles you've encountered that you have not yet solved.) Under "Work to Be Completed," list what you still have to do. If you are more than two days behind your original schedule, include a revised schedule, listing the completion dates for the activities that remain.

In your last paragraph, either indicate your confidence in completing the report by the due date or ask for a conference to resolve the problems you are encountering.

As your instructor directs

Send the email or paper progress report to

a. The other members of your group
b. Your instructor

16.8 Writing a Task Progress Report

Write a memo report summarizing your progress on your report in terms of its tasks.

As your instructor directs

Send the email or paper progress report to

a. The other members of your group
b. Your instructor

POLISHING YOUR PROSE

Who/Whom and I/Me

Even established writers sometimes get confused about when to use *who* versus *whom* and *I* versus *me*. These pronouns serve different functions in a sentence or part of a sentence.

Use *who* or *I* as the subject of a sentence or clause.

Correct: Who put the file on my desk?

(*Who* did the action, *put*.)

Correct: Keisha and I gave the presentation at our annual meeting.

(Both *Keisha* and *I* did the action, *gave*.)

Correct: Ai-Lan, who just received a PhD in management science, was promoted to vice-president.

(*Who* is the subject of the clause "who just received a PhD in management science.")

Use *whom* and *me* as the object of a verb or a preposition.

Correct: Whom did you write the report for?

(*Whom* is the object of the preposition *for*.)

Correct: She recommended Thuy and me for promotions.

(*Me* is an object of the verb *recommended*.)

Though some print sources may use *who* and *whom* interchangeably, stick to the rules until this practice becomes widely acceptable.

If you're not sure whether a pronoun is being used as a subject or object, try substituting *he* or *him*. If *he* would work, the pronoun is a subject. If *him* sounds right, the pronoun is an object.

Correct: He wrote the report.

Correct: I wrote the report for him.

Exercises

Choose the correct word in each set of brackets.

1. Karen and [I/me] visited St. Francis Xavier University last week.
2. For [who/whom] is this letter intended?
3. Dr. Jacobsen, [who/whom] serves on the board of directors, is retiring.
4. Take it from Les and [I/me]: it pays to be prepared in business.
5. [Who/Whom] is the most experienced person on your staff?
6. There was only about an hour for Kelly, Maria, and [I/me] to get to the airport.
7. Between you and [I/me], my supervisor told me the committee will decide [who/whom] gets the promotion.
8. It is the customer for [who/whom] we make our product.
9. Three people at the firm [who/whom] can speak a second language are Van, Chang, and [I/me].
10. Trust [I/me]: it's not a good idea to begin a letter with "To [who/whom] it may concern," even if people frequently do.

Check your answers to the odd-numbered exercises in the Polishing Your Prose Answer Key.

McGraw Hill **connect**™

Writing Proposals and Analytical Reports

Learning Objectives

After reading and applying the information in Module 17, you'll be able to demonstrate

Knowledge of

LO1 How to compose more complex reports

LO2 How to organize report information

LO3 How to choose a pattern of organization

LO4 How to increase document readability

Skills to

LO5 Draft and revise analytical reports

LO6 Choose an appropriate organizing pattern

LO7 Increase document readability

MODULE OUTLINE

- What other kinds of reports will I be asked to write?
- What should go into a proposal?
- How should I organize reports?

Module Summary

Assignments for Module 17

Polishing Your Prose: Writing Subject Lines and Headings

Employability Skills 2000+ Checklist

Module content builds these Conference Board of Canada Employability Skills 2000+

Communicate

Manage Information

Think and Solve Problems

Be Adaptable

Learn Continuously

Participate in Projects and Tasks

Ex.
17.1–
17.8

Easy-to-read messages motivate people to do as you ask. When you write reports, organize the information to meet readers' expectations. Audiences usually want answers up front: Is the soil contaminated or not? Is the plan going to work? How and why? Should we expand or not?

LO5 As you revise, use PAIBOC analysis to 1) include only the information your reader needs, and 2) organize that information to influence your readers positively.

What Other Kinds of Reports Will I Be Asked to Write?

You'll be asked to write reports that analyze and justify information.

Analytical reports—including feasibility, yardstick, and justification reports, as well as proposals—organize and analyze information to persuade readers to accept the suggestions or recommendations of the writer.

These reports may be brief and use letter or memo format, depending on their purpose and audience expectations.

LO1 All reports, regardless of length, include an *introduction paragraph* stating the report's purpose and scope, and summarizing the problems or successes of the project (Module 16). And all reports *conclude* with a summary of the writer's key findings: this summary suggests next steps or *recommends* action, depending on the writer's purpose and audience expectations (Module 16).

Ex.
17.4
17.7–
17.8

LO1 LO2 Feasibility Reports

Feasibility or **yardstick reports** assess a plan or idea based on a set of criteria established by the organization or the writer. (Doing nothing or delaying action can be one of the conclusions of a feasibility report.) As an example, toy companies use feasibility studies to evaluate new toy designs, according to Peter Pook, Vice-President, Research and Development for Fisher-Price Toys.[1]

Feasibility and yardstick reports normally open by explaining the decision to be made, listing available alternatives, and explaining the criteria. In the body of the report, evaluate each alternative according to the criteria:

- Discuss each alternative separately when one alternative is clearly superior, when the criteria interact, and when each alternative is indivisible.
- Discuss each alternative under each criterion when the choice depends on the weight given to each criterion.

LO1
LO2 Business plans are developed in feasibility reports: the goal is to prove that the business idea is so sound that the audience—banks, angel investors, or venture capitalists—should invest in it (see Figure 17.1).

FIGURE 17.1 Criteria Discussed in a New Business Venture Feasibility Study

A. Business Description (Summary)

The Company
- Mission Statement
- Vision
- Values
- Brand Personality
- Location
- The Market
- Strategic Positioning

B. Products and Services
- Products
- Services

C. Location
- Test Market
- Channels

D. Market Analysis
- Economic Factors
- Environmental Factors
- Political/Legal Factors
- Social/Cultural Factors
- Demographic Factors
- Primary Customers
- Secondary Customers

E. Competitive Analysis
- Direct Competitors
- Indirect Competitors

F. Financials

G. Conclusions
- Summary of Business, Market, and Potential Returns

H. Appendix

I. References

Whether recommendations should come at the beginning or the end of the report, or be repeated in both sections, depends on company culture and the reader's expectations. Most readers want the "bottom line" up front. However, if your proposed solution will cost time or money, you may want to provide all your evidence before giving the recommendation (Modules 9 and 10).

LO1
LO2 Justification Reports

Ex.
17.5

Justification reports recommend or justify a purchase, investment, hire, or change in policy. If your organization has a standard format for justification reports, follow that format. If you can choose your headings and organization, use the *direct, deductive,* or *good news* pattern (Module 8) when your recommendation is easy for your reader to accept:

1. *Indicate what you're asking for and why it's needed.* When the reader has not asked for the report, you must link your request to organizational goals.
2. *Briefly give the background of the problem or need.*
3. *Explain each of the possible solutions.* For each, give the cost, and the advantages and disadvantages.
4. *Summarize the action needed to implement your recommendation.* If several people will be involved, indicate who will do what and how long each step will take.
5. *Ask for the action you want.*
6. *Conclude with a short paragraph linking the recommended solution to a benefit outcome.*

Language FOCUS

Angel investors are people who are usually wealthy and invest in new companies, often in exchange for benefits from the company.

Venture capitalists are people who invest in new companies, or in companies that are experiencing financial difficulties but have potential to make great profits.

When the reader is reluctant to grant your request because action will cost time or money, use the *indirect, inductive,* or *bad news* variation of the problem-solving pattern described in Modules 9 and 10:

1. *Describe the organizational problem that your request will solve.* Provide specific examples (results) to demonstrate the seriousness of the problem.
2. *Prove that easier or less expensive solutions will not solve the problem.*
3. *Present your solution impersonally.*
4. *Show that the advantages of your solution outweigh the disadvantages.*
5. *Summarize the action needed to implement your recommendation.* If several people will be involved, indicate who will do what and how long each step will take.
6. *Ask for the action you want.*
7. *Conclude with a short paragraph linking the recommended solution to benefit outcomes.*

The amount of detail you need to give in a justification report depends on your reader's knowledge of and attitude toward your recommendation, and on the corporate culture. Many organizations expect justification reports to be short—only one or two pages. Other organizations may expect longer reports with much more detailed budgets and a full discussion of the problem and each possible solution.

Language FOCUS

A **mission statement** explains the purpose of the company or organization.

A **vision statement** describes the goals and objectives your company tries to meet or exceed.

Values are a written list of the goals and objectives your company tries to meet or exceed.

LO1 LO2 What Should Go into a Proposal?

What you're going to do, how and when you'll do it, and evidence that you'll do it well.

Proposals are reports that describe a method for finding information or solving a problem. Proposals have two goals: to get the project accepted, and to obtain support for the writer to do the job. *Proposals must stress reader benefits and provide specific supporting details.*

Ex. 17.6 17.8

TABLE 17.1   **Relationships Between Situation, Proposal, and Final Report**

Company's Current Situation	The Proposal Offers To:	The Final Report Will Provide:
We don't know whether we should change	Assess whether change is a good idea	Insight, recommending whether change is desirable
We need to/want to change, but we don't know exactly what we need to do	Develop a plan to achieve the desired goal	A plan for achieving the desired change
We need to/want to change, and we know what to do, but we need help doing it	Implement the plan, increase (or decrease) measurable outcomes	A record of the implementation and evaluation process

Source: Adapted from Richard C. Freed, Shervin Freed, and Joseph D. Romano (1995), *Writing winning proposals: Your guide to landing the client, making the sale, persuading the boss* (New York: McGraw-Hill): 21.

FIGURE 17.2   Proposal for Services (Indirect Pattern of Development, Modules 9 and 10)

November 12, 2013
Sen Lee Chang, President
Tel-Direct Systems Inc.
1011 Bloor Street West
Oshawa, ON L1H 7K6

Dear Sen Lee Chang

Thank you for considering **communicore** for your training needs. Based on our conversation last Friday, I am pleased to propose this preliminary outline of the customer service workshop and to suggest ways to maximize your return on investment.

Workshop Overview

The two-day Customer Service Strategies workshop encourages participants to define and refine the criteria for superior customer service. During the workshop, participants will

- Begin with an ice-breaker, followed by self-assessment and goal-setting exercises
- Role-play active listening, questioning, and problem-solving strategies
- Analyze and identify excellent customer service attitudes and behaviours
- Identify and apply two conflict negotiating models
- Articulate best-practices behaviours as the organizational standard
- Set a goal for further development

Depending on participants' preference, we can begin at 8 or 8:30 a.m., and finish at 4 or 4:30 p.m. I've attached a proposed agenda for your approval.

Methods

Using a variety of interactive exercises—including case analysis, taped role-play, peer feedback, and peer and self-assessment—your employees will review, describe, and apply behaviours that build customer relationships.

Since customized content contributes to learning transfer, I would like to visit your locations for a few hours to observe your service representatives before the training dates. This complimentary needs assessment will allow me to gather information about current practices and to see your training facilities.

Resources

As we discussed, your employees will need uninterrupted time to review and practise customer service techniques. Because participants will be working together and moving around, they will need group seating, four to a table, and enough room to comfortably accommodate 16 people.

You mentioned that the room is equipped with a laptop, projector, and screen; participants will need writing materials, a USB key, and one flip chart per table. We will be bringing our own camera.

Qualifications

Our facilitators offer over 20 years' training experience, as well as expertise and accreditation in adult education principles, business, and interpersonal communications skills. As we agreed, I am attaching client reviews of our most recent training in customer service skills. Please visit our website: http://www.communicore.on.ca for more reviews.

Costs

The needs assessment is free. The cost for the training, including tailoring materials and exercises to participants' experiences, material printing and copying, two-day interactive facilitation, workshop evaluation sheet and summary, and written best-practices recommendations specific to your organization is $6 000, plus HST.

Again, thank you for your interest and consideration. At your convenience, please call or email me about your proposed employee training.

Sincerely

Kathryn Hughes

Kathryn Hughes
President

Psychology major Susan Ngo launched her successful business Bright Ideas Summer Adventure Camp with a $1,500 Ministry of Economic Development and Trade Grant, garnered through her winning business plan.

To write a good proposal, you need to have a clear view of the problem you hope to solve and the kind of research or other action needed to solve it. A proposal must answer the following questions convincingly:

Employability Skills

- What problem are you going to solve?
- How are you going to solve it?
- What exactly will you provide?
- How can you deliver what you promise?
- What benefits can you offer?
- When will you complete the work?
- How much will you charge?

Figure 17.2 shows a sample proposal selling services.

LO1 LO2 Sales Proposals, Requests for Proposals (RFPs), and Grants

Decision makers routinely ask for proposals when purchasing expensive goods or services. For everything you offer, show the reader benefits (Module 11) using you-attitude (Module 13). Use content and language appropriate for your audience. Even if buyers want a state-of-the-art system, they may not appreciate or understand minute details or technical jargon.

Attention to details—including good visual impact and proofreading—helps establish your professional image and suggests that you'll give the same care to the project if your proposal is accepted (see Figures 17.2 and 17.3).

Provide a one-page cover letter with long proposals. Organize the cover letter this way:

1. Catch the reader's attention and summarize up to three major benefits you offer.
2. Discuss each of the major benefits in the order in which you mention them in the first paragraph.
3. Deal with any objections or concerns the reader may have.
4. Mention other benefits briefly.
5. Ask the reader to approve your proposal. Provide a reason for acting promptly.

Government agencies and companies issue **Requests for Proposals**, known as **RFPs**, when contracting out work. The RFP details the project and vendor requirements in "a formal document describing...how the contract companies should respond, how the proposals will be reviewed, and contact information."[2]

You follow the RFP exactly when you respond. Competitive proposals are often scored by giving points in each category. Evaluators look only under the headings specified in the RFP. If information isn't there, the proposal gets no points in that category.

Proposals for Funding

If you need money for a new or continuing public service project, you may want to submit a proposal for funding to a foundation, a corporation, a government agency, or a religious agency. In a proposal for funding, stress the needs your project will meet, and show how your project helps fulfill the goals of the organization you are asking to fund it. Every funding source has certain priorities; most post lists of the projects they have funded in the past.

FIGURE 17.3   **Proposal for Foundation Repair (Indirect Pattern, Modules 9 and 10)**

Contract/EST#: 7565

Bowen Foundation Repair Inc.
2486 Kingston Rd.; Scarborough, ON M1N 1V3
Tel: 555-866-0547 Fax: 555-866-1275 www.bfr.ca
LIC# B-19658

Date: November 19, 2013

Client Name: Judy Green   **Cell Phone No:** _____   **Home Phone No:** 555-321-5267
Work Phone No: _____   **Email:** _____
Jobsite: 24 Queen Mary Rd.

The undersigned proposes to furnish all materials and provide all material and labour necessary to complete all repairs described below.

Exterior Waterproofing Repair:

Trench 51' linear ft from 1' to 2' deep, sloping toward rear of property. Place filter-cloth in bottom of trenched area. Install 4" perforated weeping tile with nylon sock. Pour ¾" gravel over weeping tile system. Remove and dispose of all soil. Clean up work area. Remove and dump all debris. All material and labour included.

20-year transferable warranty against leakage in repaired area.
(Please retain this contract for warranty purposes.)

No deposit required. Payment due in full upon completion of work.

All of the above work to be completed in a good and workmanlike manner for the sum of:

_____ ($990.00) DOLLARS

GST# 85151766 RT0001 _____ ($128.70) HST

_____ ($1,118.70) TOTAL

All changes in the work to be charged for same shall be made in writing.
  This estimate is made on the basis of current material and labour costs. This estimate is valid for 90 days from date above. Any delay in acceptance of this estimate beyond 90 days shall void this estimate, and a review of this estimate shall be performed before any agreement between the Client and Bowen Foundation Repair Inc. becomes binding.
  All warranties are based on normal weather conditions.
  BFR is not responsible for ground settlement.
  BFR is not responsible for leakage due to grade change and or acts of God, i.e., tornadoes, flooding, hurricane, and the like.

ACCEPTANCE

You are hereby authorized to furnish all materials and labour to complete the work mentioned in the above proposal, for which the undersigned agrees to pay the amount mentioned in said proposal, and according to the terms thereof.

Date: _____

_____   *Collen Bowen*
_____   _____
INDIVIDUAL/COMPANY NAME   BOWEN FOUNDATION REPAIR INC.

Estimating the Budget

A good budget is crucial to making the winning bid. Ask for everything you need to do a quality job. Asking for too little may backfire, leading the decision maker to assume you don't understand the scope of the project.

Read the RFP to find out what is and isn't fundable. Talk to the program officer and read successful past proposals to find out three things:

● What size projects will the organization fund in theory?

- Does the funder prefer making a few big grants or many smaller grants?
- Does the funder expect you to provide in-kind or matching funds from other sources?

Think about exactly what will be done and who will do it. What will it cost to get that person? What supplies or materials will he or she need? Also, think about indirect costs for office space, retirement and health benefits and salaries, office supplies, administration, and infrastructure.

Detail the specifics of your estimates.

Weak: 75 hours of transcribing interviews $1,500

Better: 25 hours of interviews; a skilled transcriber can complete an hour of interviews in 3 hours; 75 hours @ $20/hour $1,500

Without inflating your costs, give yourself a cushion. For example, if the going rate for skilled transcribers is $20 an hour, but you think you might be able to train someone and pay only $17 an hour, use the higher figure. Then, even if your grant is cut, you'll still be able to do the project well.

Proposals for Class Reports

A proposal for a student report usually has the following sections:

1. **Purpose statement**: In your first paragraph (no heading), summarize in a sentence or two the topic and purpose(s) of your report.
2. **Problem**: What organizational problem exists? What is the situation? What needs to change? Why? What background or history is relevant?
3. **Feasibility**: Can a solution be found in the time available? How do you know?
4. **Audience**: Who in the organization has the power to implement your recommendation? What secondary audiences might be asked to evaluate your report? What audiences would be affected by your recommendation? Will anyone serve as a gatekeeper, determining whether your report is sent to decision makers? What watchdog audiences might read the report? (Module 2)
   For each of these audiences and for your initial audience (your instructor), give the person's name, job title, and business address, and answer the following questions:

   - What is the audience's major concern or priority?
   - What will the audience see as the advantages of your proposal?
   - What objections, if any, is the reader likely to have?
   - How interested is the audience in the topic of your report?
   - How much does the audience know about the topic of your report?
   - What terms, concepts, equations, or assumptions might one or more of your audiences need to have explained? Briefly identify ways in which your audiences may affect the content, organization, or style of the report.

5. **Topics to investigate**: List the questions and sub-questions you will answer in your report, the topics or concepts you will explain, and the aspects of the problem you will discuss. Indicate how deeply you will examine each aspect you plan to treat. Explain your rationale for choosing to discuss some aspects of the problem and not others.
6. **Methods/procedure**: How will you get answers to your questions? Whom will you interview or survey? What published sources will you use? What websites will you consult? (Module 14) Give the full bibliographic references (Module 15). Your methods section should clearly indicate where and how you will get the information you need to answer the questions in the Topics to Investigate section.
7. **Qualifications/facilities/resources**: What attitudes, knowledge, and skills qualify you to conduct this study? Do you work in the organization? Do you have a contact or source for information? What's your professional or personal interest? Do you have access to the resources you will need to conduct your research (computer, books, etc.)? Where will you turn for help if you hit an unexpected snag? You'll be more convincing if you have already scheduled an interview, checked out books, or identified online sources.

8. **Work schedule**: Create a timeline to plan your work. (See Figure 17.4 for an example.) List both the total time you plan to spend on each of the following activities, and the date when you expect to finish:

- Gathering information
- Analyzing information
- Preparing the progress report
- Organizing information
- Writing the draft
- Revising the draft
- Preparing the visuals
- Editing the draft
- Proofreading the report

Put your timeline into a work schedule either in a chart or on a calendar. A good schedule provides realistic estimates for each activity, allows time for unexpected problems, and indicates that you can manage a project and complete the work on time.

9. **Close/call to action**: In your final paragraph, indicate that you'd welcome any suggestions that your instructor may have for improving the research plan. Ask your instructor to approve your proposal so that you can begin work on your report. Provide a contact number or email address for confirmation.

Figure 17.5 shows a draft student proposal for writing a research report using primary and secondary sources.

FIGURE 17.4   **Create a Timeline to Plan Your Schedule**

Jan. 19	Feb. 9	Feb. 18	Mar. 1	Mar. 10	Mar. 15	Mar. 20	Mar. 23	Apr. 5	Apr. 17
Choose report topic; start research; draft proposal	Revise and submit proposal	Get approval; research	Begin first draft of body	Finish draft of body; draft conclusions	Have peer read; revise	Draft summary	Have peer read; revise	Edit and proof	Submit report

FIGURE 17.5   **Draft Proposal for a Student Report Using Primary and Secondary Sources (Direct Pattern, Module 8)**

Date: January 20, 2013

To: Professor Marcus Stawski

From: Teresa Amirud

Re: My Formal Report Topic

Costing is possibly the most vital aspect of the manufacturing process, since companies must use the most effective system in order to reduce costs and increase profits. In the manufacturing sector, different variations on costing systems can be tailored to suit the needs of any specific company. In my formal report, I plan to research the costing system used by EcoSound Inc. in its paint manufacturing process. I will research the strengths and weaknesses of the costing system used during the paint manufacturing process, up to the completion of each unit. Using this research, I will analyze the company's cost system to determine if this system is suitable for the product line.

Topic Rationale

In deciding what to research and analyze for my formal report, I tried to incorporate what I already know, what I would like to learn more about, and what interests me. I decided to focus on EcoSound operation paint production costing for two reasons:

- Having worked part-time at Rona in Milton for several years, I have the contacts needed to get primary information about the manufacturing of EcoSound's paint products.

FIGURE 17.5   Draft Proposal for a Student Report Using Primary and Secondary Sources (Direct Pattern, Module 8), cont.

- I mix and sell this paint to my customers daily; I thought it would be interesting to learn more about the manufacturing side of the products I am selling. Furthermore, the more knowledge I have about a product, the easier it is to sell the product and answer any questions customers have.

Operations costing also appeals to me as a formal report topic because the research and writing will help me with my Cost and Budgets course. Not only will I learn how to write a formal report, but I will also be applying a real world example to the Cost and Budgets curriculum. Learning more about the actual application of operation costing within a real company will increase my understanding of the concepts being discussed in Cost and Budgets.

Formal Report Focus

In my preliminary research, I was able to learn some of the basics of EcoSound paint production, which I will use to formulate research questions. In my report I will

- Examine where costs are added to the product, for example:
  - ○ Overhead costs added to each product based on the time spent at each work centre
  - ○ Labour costs added by working out the number of employees at each work centre and their salary to get a labour rate at each work centre
- Create a flow chart of the production process, listing the "work stations" that each unit goes through before completion
- Analyze why there is such a large retail profit margin (40–45%) on EcoSound name-brand paints
- Discuss whether EcoSound's costing system is effective

Through my research and analysis, I will determine the effectiveness and any weaknesses of the EcoSound system manufacturing process.

Research Sources

Primary Sources

- Josef Usdan—EcoSound sales representative
- Mario Eccles—EcoSound marketing representative
- Katrina Glausiusz—EcoSound accountant (Brampton plant)
- Myself
- Marian Feierabend—Cost and Budget instructor
- The knowledge I have gained about EcoSound paint products through my employment at Rona

Secondary Sources

- Internet—www.ecosound.ca; www.highbeam.com/doc/1G1-146498025.html; http://ezinearticles.com/?Activity-Based-Costing---Part-I&id=3984203
- *Managerial Accounting—Cost and Budget* textbook

Tentative Research and Writing Schedule

To remain on schedule in researching and writing my formal report, I have created a tentative work schedule:

- February 18   Get approval for my proposal; begin research
- March 1   Complete research; begin first draft of report body
- March 10   Finish draft of body; draft conclusions
- March 15   Have peer read drafts; make necessary changes
- March 20   Begin draft of summary
- March 23   Have peer read summary; make necessary changes
- April 5   Edit report
- April 10   Proofread report

As you can see, I have selected an appropriate formal report topic for which I will be able to find relevant information. Please let me know at tamirud@ryerson.ca if my plan meets with your approval.

LO3 LO6 How Should I Organize Reports?

You can organize information in any of seven patterns. Use PAIBOC analysis to determine the pattern that best achieves your purposes, and meets your audience's needs.

Any of these patterns can be used for all or part of a report:

1. General-to-particular or particular-to-general
2. Chronological
3. Comparison or contrast
4. Problem–solution
5. Elimination of alternatives
6. Geographic or spatial
7. Functional

1. General-to-Particular or Particular-to-General

General-to-particular starts with the situation as it affects the organization, or as it exists in general, and then moves to a discussion of the parts of the situation and solutions to each of these parts.

Particular-to-general starts with the problem as the audience defines it and moves to larger issues of which the problem is a part. Both are useful patterns when you need to redefine the reader's perception of the problem to solve it effectively.

For example, the directors of a student volunteer organization, Students Mentoring Students (SMS), have defined their problem as "not enough volunteers." After doing their research, the writers are convinced that poor training, an inadequate structure, and low campus awareness are responsible for both a high dropout rate and low recruitment rate. The general-to-particular pattern helps the audience see the problem in a new way:

Why Students Helping Students (SMS) Needs More Volunteers
Why Some SMS Volunteers Drop Out

    Inadequate Training
    Feeling that SMS Takes Too Much Time
    Feeling that the Work is Too Emotionally Demanding

Why Some Students Do Not Volunteer

    Feeling that SMS Takes Too Much Time
    Feeling that the Work is Too Emotionally Demanding
    Preference for Volunteering with another Organization
    Lack of Knowledge about SMS Operations

How SMS Volunteers Are Trained
Emotional Demands on SMS Volunteers
Ways to Increase Volunteer Commitment and Motivation

    Improving Training
    Improving the Flexibility of Volunteer Hours
    Providing Emotional Support to Volunteers
    Providing More Information about Community Needs and SMS Services

2. Chronological

A chronological report records events in the order in which they happened or are planned to happen. Many information and progress reports use a chronological pattern:

> Revisions Completed in October
> Revisions Completed In November
> Work Planned for December

3. Comparison or Contrast

Comparison or contrast examines each alternative in turn, discussing strengths and weaknesses. Feasibility studies and yardstick reports usually use this pattern.

A variation of the divided pattern is the **pro–con pattern**. In this pattern, under each specific heading, give the arguments for and against that alternative.

Whatever information comes second will carry more psychological weight. This pattern is least effective when you want to de-emphasize the disadvantages of a proposed solution, for it does not permit you to bury the disadvantages between neutral or positive material.

A report recommending new plantings for a garden over an expressway, for example, uses the pro–con pattern:

> Advantages of Ornamental Grasses
>   High Productivity
>   Visual Symmetry
> Disadvantages of Ornamental Grasses
>   Investments and Replacement Costs
>   Visual Monotony

4. Problem–Solution

Identify the problem; explain its background or history; discuss its extent and seriousness; identify its causes. Discuss the factors (criteria) that affect the decision. Analyze the advantages and disadvantages of possible solutions. Conclusions and recommendations can go either first or last, depending on the length of the report, and preferences of your reader. This pattern works well when the reader is neutral.

A report recommending ways to eliminate solidification of granular bleach during production, for example, uses the problem–solution pattern:

> Reformulation for Alpha Bleach
> Problems in Maintaining Alpha's Granular Structure
>   Solidifying During Storage and Transportation
>   Customer Complaints about "Blocks" of Alpha in Boxes
> Why Alpha Bleach "Cakes"
>   Alpha's Formula
>   The Manufacturing Process
>   The Chemical Process
>
> Modifications Needed to Keep Alpha Flowing Freely

5. Elimination of Alternatives

After discussing the problem and its causes, discuss the *impractical* solutions first, showing why they will not work. End with the most practical solution. This pattern works well when the solutions the reader is likely to favour will not work, while the solution you recommend is likely to be perceived as expensive, intrusive, or radical.

A report on toy commercials, for example, eliminates the alternatives before concluding with the recommended solution:

Effect of TV Ads on Children
Camera Techniques Used in TV Advertisements
Alternative Solutions to Problems in TV Toy Ads
 Leave Ads Unchanged
 Mandate Ad Blockers on All TV Production
 Ask the Industry to Self-Regulate
 Give CRTC Authority to Regulate TV Ads Directed at Children

6. Geographic or Spatial

In a geographic or spatial pattern, you discuss problems and solutions in units by their physical arrangement. Move from office to office, building to building, factory to factory, province to province, region to region, and so on.

Sales and market research reports, for example, may use a geographic pattern of organization:

Sales Have Risen in the European Economic Community
Sales Have Fallen Slightly in Asia
Sales Have Fallen in North America

7. Functional

Functional patterns discuss the problems and solutions of each functional unit. For example, a report on a new plant might divide data into sections on the costs of land and building, on the availability of personnel, on the convenience of raw materials, and so on. A government report might divide data into the different functions an office performed, taking each in turn.

PST Plant Move
- Manufacturing
 Equipment
 Offices
- Sales and Marketing
 Furniture
 Filing Cabinets
- Executive Offices
 Furniture
 Filing Cabinets

Increasing Readability

Readers do not want to read every word in a business document. They want instantaneous meaning; they want to skim and scan for the information they need. They want business documents to be as eye-easy as the best Web writing.[3]

What Makes Documents Easy to Read?

Increase readability with blueprints, transitions, topic sentences, white space, and headings that "talk."

Blueprints forecast what you will discuss in a section or in the entire report. In an overview paragraph, blueprints tell the reader how many points there are and number them. This overview paragraph establishes **repetition for reinforcement**: the blueprint establishes a contract with readers, who now know what they are going to read and in what order:

Paragraph without blueprint

Employee Stock Ownership Programs (ESOPs) have several advantages. They provide tax benefits for the company. ESOPs also create tax benefits for employees and for lenders. They provide a defence against takeovers. In some organizations, productivity increases because workers now have a financial stake in the company's profits. ESOPs help the company hire and retain good employees.

Revised paragraph with blueprint

Employee Stock Ownership Programs (ESOPs) provide four benefits. First, ESOPs provide tax benefits for the company, its employees, and lenders to the plan. Second, ESOPs help create a defence against takeovers. Third, ESOPs may increase productivity by giving workers a stake in the company's profits. Fourth, as an attractive employee benefit, ESOPs help the company hire and retain good employees.

Transitions are words, phrases, and sentences that tell the reader the discussion is continuing on the same point or is shifting points.

There are economic benefits, too.

(Tells the reader that the discussion is still on advantages, and now moving to economic advantages.)

An alternative plan is…

(Tells the reader that a second option is coming up.)

These advantages, however, only apply in the case of short-term patients and not to those in long-term care.

(Prepares reader for a shift from short-term patients to those in long-term care.)

The **topic sentence** introduces or summarizes the main idea of a paragraph. Competent readers skim documents by searching for topic sentences at the beginning of paragraphs, because that's where competent writers put them.

Revised paragraph without summarizing topic sentence

Another main use of ice is to keep the fish fresh. Each of the seven different kinds of fish served at the restaurant requires almost 3.78 litres twice a day, for a total of 52.9 litres. An additional 22.7 litres a day are required for the salad bar.

Revised paragraph with summarizing topic sentence

Seventy-six litres of ice a day are needed to keep food fresh. Of this, the largest portion (52.9 litres) is used to keep the fish fresh. Each of the seven varieties requires almost four litres twice a day (7 x 7.56 = 52.9 litres). The salad bar requires an additional 22.7 litres a day.

White space increases reading ease because it separates and emphasizes ideas (Modules 5 and 6). To create white space, use

- Headings and subheadings
- Short paragraphs
- Tabs or indents
- Lists—with numbers or bullets

Headings are signposts that divide your letter, memo, or report into sections. **Subheadings** signal a subsection: the writer is providing specifics within the section. The best headings and subheadings "talk" to the reader; they

- Are short and specific
- Use highlighting: bold or italics
- Are differentiated: subheadings use a smaller or different font

- Summarize what the reader is about to read
- Cover all the material until the next heading
- Are parallel (i.e., use the same grammatical structure)

The following suggestions can help employers avoid bias in job interviews:

1. Base questions on the job description.
2. Ask the same questions of all applicants.
3. Select and train interviewers carefully.

Revising for readability (using blueprints, transitions, topic sentences, white space, and "talking" headings and subheadings) creates a story line your readers can readily follow.

MODULE SUMMARY

- **Feasibility**, **yardstick**, and **justification** reports analyze and evaluate information readers need to make decisions.
- **Proposals** are reports that describe a method for finding information, or solving a problem.
- PAIBOC analysis will help you choose the **content** and **organizational pattern** that best meets your audience's needs and expectations, and serves your purpose(s). You can organize your information using any of seven patterns:
  - ○ **General-to-particular** or **particular-to-general**. **General-to-particular** begins with the situation as it affects the organization or manifests itself in general. Then the report discusses the parts of the problem and offers solutions to each of these parts. **Particular-to-general** starts with specifics and then discusses the larger implications for the organization.
  - ○ **Chronological** records events in the order in which they happened or are planned to happen.
  - ○ **Comparison or contrast** examines each alternative in turn; the **pro–con pattern**, a variation of the pattern, gives the arguments for and against that alternative under each specific heading.
  - ○ The **problem–solution** pattern identifies the situation, explains causes, and analyzes the advantages and disadvantages of possible solutions.
  - ○ **Elimination of alternatives** identifies the situation, explains causes, and discusses the least practical solution first, ending with the solution the writer favours.
  - ○ **Geographic or spatial** patterns discuss the problems and solutions by units.
  - ○ **Functional pattern** examines the problems and solutions of each functional unit.
- Revising for readability (using blueprints, transitions, topic sentences, white space, and "talking" headings and subheadings) makes your writing reader-friendly.

ASSIGNMENTS FOR MODULE 17

Questions for Critical Thinking

17.1 When would you include visuals in your report?

17.2 How can you write headings in reports that are actually useful to readers?

17.3 How do you decide how to organize sections in your report?

Exercises and Problems

17.4 Writing a Yardstick Report

Write a two-page yardstick report to your instructor and peers suggesting how users can protect themselves from cyber-crime on social networking sites. Choose a specific site (Facebook, MySpace, etc.) and research specific examples (fraud, identity theft, scams). Using primary and secondary sources (your own observation and experience as well as expert advice), identify three possible solutions. Establish specific criteria by which to measure the solutions. Evaluate each based on your criteria. Conclude your report by identifying the best way users can protect themselves.

17.5 Writing a Justification Report

Write a two-page report to your supervisor justifying a change in policy, or a purchase, investment, or hire. Choose a topic that you can cover in two pages, and use an organizational pattern that your reader will find convincing. Possible topics include

- Introducing flex hours
- Extending breaks
- Funding a course you would like to take
- Purchasing a new coffee machine
- Bringing pets to work
- Hiring an new employee

17.6 Explaining "Best Practices"

Write a report describing the "best practices" of a unit or team of which you are a member. Convince your reader that other teams in your organization/college/university should adopt these practices.

17.7 Writing a Feasibility or Yardstick Report Recommending Action

Write a report identifying alternative actions your unit or organization could take, evaluating each solution, and recommending the best choice. Address your report to the person who has the power to approve your recommendation. Possibilities are

- Making your organization more eco-friendly
- Finding an additional worker for your department
- Making your organization more employee-friendly
- Making a change to improve efficiency
- Making changes to improve accessibility for customers or employees with disabilities

17.8 Writing a Proposal for a Student Report

Write a proposal to your instructor to do the research for a formal or informal report. The headings and questions in the section "Proposals for Class Reports" are your RFP; be sure to answer every question and to use the headings exactly as stated in the RFP.

Exception: Where alternative headings are given, combine them (Qualifications and Facilities) or use them as separate headings.

POLISHING YOUR PROSE

Writing Subject Lines and Headings

Subject lines are the title of a letter, memo, or email message. Headings within a document tell the reader what information you will discuss in that section. Good subject lines are specific, concise, and appropriate for your purposes and the response you expect from the reader. Subject lines are required in memos, optional in letters.

- Put in good news if you have it.
- If information is neutral, summarize it.
- Use negative subject lines if the reader may not read the message or needs the information to act, or if the negative is your error.
- In a request that is easy for the reader to grant, put the subject of that request, or a direct question, in the subject line.
- When you must persuade a reluctant reader, use a common ground, a reader benefit, or a directed subject line that makes your stance on the issue clear.

Headings are single words, short phrases, or complete sentences that indicate the topic in a document section. Headings must be *parallel*—that is, they must use the same grammatical structure—and must cover all the information until the next heading.

The most useful headings are **informative** or **talking heads**, which sum up the content of the section.

Weak:	*Problem:*
	Cause 1
	Cause 2
	Cause 3
Better:	*Communication Problems Between Air Traffic Controllers and Pilots:*
	Selective Listening
	Indirect Conversational Style
	Limitations of Short-Term Memory

LO4 FIGURE 18.3 **Plan Your Report**

May 4	May 12	May 20	May 25	May 27	May 28	May 31	June 4
Report assigned; write working thesis and begin research	Do PAIBOC analysis; draft body	Draft visuals	Have peer read body; start revisions; begin Conclusions and Recommendations	Finish Conclusions, Recommendations, and References	Start Summary	Have peer read Summary, Conclusions, and Recommendations; revise and proof	Report due

To use your time efficiently, think about the parts of the report and jot down draft headings. Mark those that are most important to your reader and to your proof; spend most of your researching and writing time on them. Draft the important sections early so you won't spend all your time on the background or history of the problem. Instead, you'll get to the meat of your report.

How Do I Draft the Report?

Start in the middle: write the body first, then draft the ending sections, then write the beginning parts of the formal report: the summary and the transmittal.

You may want to start by composing the report body, because every other part of the report depends your findings, backed by research. Draft the Conclusions and Recommendations next, because these sections flow naturally out of your research and findings.

As you revise for clarity and conciseness, organize the different report sections to serve your purposes and meet your audience's needs. For example, you might organize the proof in your body section using a comparison/contrast, problem–solution, or elimination of alternatives pattern. However, in your beginning and ending report sections (Transmittal, Summary, Introduction, Conclusions, and Recommendations) you will probably find a chronological development most useful to your purposes and readers (Module 17).

LO1
LO4 As you read about the content in each section below, you might want to turn to the corresponding pages of the long report in Figure 18.5 to see how each section is organized, and how it relates to the total report.

Report Body

Introduction

The Introduction pulls the reader into the situation, and previews the body; the Introduction contains a statement of purpose and scope, and may include other parameters:

- **Purpose**: Identify the organizational problem the report addresses, the technical investigations it summarizes, and the rhetorical purposes of the report: to explain, to analyze, to evaluate, to solve, to recommend.
- **Scope**: Identify the topics the report covers. For example, Company TSC is losing money on its line of customized, home-cooked meals. Does the report investigate the quality of the meals? The advertising campaign? The cost of cooking? The market for home-cooked meals? When you define the scope, you *contain* the content of the report: if the report is to examine only advertising, then readers cannot fault the report for not considering other factors.

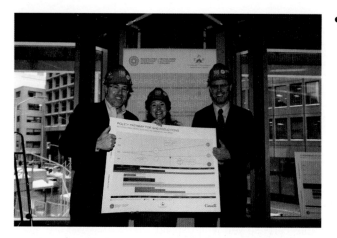

As policy advisor for the National Round Table on the Environment and the Economy (NRTEE: www.nrtee-trnee.com), Annika Tamlyn researches and writes formal reports that may take up to a year to complete.

- **Limitations**: Limitations usually arise because time or money constraints don't permit full research, and such limitations make the recommendations less valid, or valid only under certain conditions. For example, a campus pizza restaurant considering expanding its menu might not have enough money to take a random sample of students and non-students. Without a random sample, the writer cannot generalize from the sample to the larger population.

  Many feasibility studies and report recommendations remain valid only for a limited time. For example, in a business plan, the business location might be ideal at the time of writing, but economic or demographic changes may cause the location to lose its lustre. Or a store may want to investigate the kinds of clothing that will appeal to university students. The recommendations will remain in force only for a short time: a year from now, styles and tastes may change.

- **Assumptions**: Assumptions are statements whose truth you assume and that you use to support your conclusions and recommendations. If they are wrong, the conclusion will be wrong, too. For example, recommendations about what cars appeal to drivers aged 18 to 34 would be based on assumptions about the economy and gas prices. In a major recession, people wouldn't buy new cars. When gas prices radically rise or fall, young adults want different kinds of cars.

- **Methods**: Here writers describe how they found the report data: what they observed, whom they chose to survey and interview, and how, when, and where respondents were interviewed. Omit methods if your report is based solely on library and online research. Instead, simply cite your sources in the text and document them in the References or Works Cited section. See Module 15 on how to cite and document sources.

Background or History

Although the current audience for the report probably knows the situation, reports are filed and then consulted years later. These later audiences will probably not know the background, although it may be crucial for understanding the options possible.

In some cases, the history section might cover many years. For example, a report recommending that a Quebec consortium purchase an Ontario-based newspaper will probably provide the history of the newspaper's ownership, readership, and any editorial changes. In other cases, the background or history is much briefer, covering just the immediate situation.

Findings

The Findings section of the report provides the proof of your position. Here you present the facts, gathered through primary and secondary research (Modules 14 and 15), to demonstrate that your conclusions are accurate and your recommendations inevitable.

Spend most of your time composing, rewriting, and revising this section. Pay particular attention to the organization: you want to frame the situation and your solutions to influence your readers to your point of view. Through your PAIBOC analysis, you identify reader benefits and objections. Use this information to structure your argument: emphasize benefits through placement of text and headings (Module 17); de-emphasize negatives by offering alternatives (Module 12). Use *talking heads*—headings that describe what is coming next in the text to preview the subsequent content for the reader and contribute to clarity and understanding.

In the sample report (Figure 18.5), the writer's purpose is to provide information to the publisher of GreenZine about what articles her readers will find interesting.

The Report Ending

Conclusions and Recommendations

All communication is an act of creation: after all, when we make meaning, we create order out of chaos. Reports, too, can be creative. However, unlike fiction writing, your report should not contain any surprises for your intended audiences.

Because formal reports are so lengthy, they use a great deal of *repetition for reinforcement*. The ending sections do not introduce any new information; your conclusions and recommendations concisely and clearly summarize information covered in the body.

The Conclusions section sums up the key ideas proven by the facts in the body of the report. Note that you may present your conclusions in paragraphs or single sentences, depending on how full an explanation you have offered in the body, and on your reader's expectations. Use "should" throughout ("Ardene should hire one more full-time staff for the holiday season") because the writer and reader share the assumption that the points have been proven.

The Recommendations section identifies action items that will solve or partially solve the problem. Again, you have already explained these actions in the body, where your skill in finding, organizing, and presenting the relevant facts lead the reader to the inevitability of your recommendations.

Be sure to number the recommendations to make them easy to discuss. If your readers might find your recommendations expensive, difficult, or controversial, give a brief rationale paragraph after each recommendation. If your recommendations are easy for the audience to accept, simply list them without comments or reasons.

Depending on audience expectations, some recommendations use the imperative verb tense. "Do this."

1. *Choose* Positions for Co-op Students
2. *Set* Salaries
3. *Choose* Supervisors and Mentors
4. *Publicize* the Program
5. *Recruit* Students

Formal reports contain a great deal of repetition because of their length and because repeated information increases readability and retention. Therefore, your recommendations also go in the Summary, and if possible, in the Title and the Transmittal.

Appendixes and References or Works Cited

Place supplemental information, including visuals, questionnaires, scientific and survey data, historical documents, and even glossaries in appendixes at the end of the report, before your bibliography. When deciding if you need an appendix, follow the norms of your discourse community: if your readers expect plenty of supporting documentation, provide it.

If you are undecided about where to place such documentation, assess its value to the reader and to your proof. If the data are necessary to prove your point of view, place them in the body. If the information provides useful background to your argument, place it in an appendix. If the information is superfluous to your argument, omit it.

Your report's credibility and your own reputation depend on your careful documentation of sources and resources (Module 15). Again, follow the norms of your discourse community when deciding whether to use endnotes or in-text citations, and APA or MLA formats for your bibliography.

The Report Beginning

Title Page

The title page of a report contains four items: the title of the report, for whom the report is prepared, by whom it is prepared, and the release date. The title of the report should be as informative as possible:

Poor title: New Office Site

Better title: Why St. John's Newfoundland is the Best Site for the New Info.com Office

In many cases, the title states the recommendation in the report: "Improving Productivity at Cambridge International: Updating Communications Policies." However, omit the recommendations in the title when

- The reader will find the recommendations hard to accept
- The recommendations in the title would make the title too long
- The report is not supposed to offer recommendations

If the title does not contain the recommendation, it usually indicates the problem that the report solves: "Best-Practices Analysis, City of Montreal: The Communications Audit."

Letter or Memo of Transmittal

The Transmittal has several purposes: to send the report, to orient the reader to the report, and to influence the reader favourably toward the report and the writer. Use a *memo of transmittal* if you are a regular employee of the organization for which you prepare the report; use a *letter of transmittal* if you are not.

Organize the transmittal in this way:

1. State the report's purpose as well as when and by whom the report was authorized.
2. Summarize your conclusions and recommendations.
3. Indicate minor problems you encountered in your investigation and show how you overcame them.
4. Thank people who helped you.
5. Point out additional research required (if any).
6. Thank the reader for the opportunity to do the work and offer to answer questions. Even if you did not enjoy writing the report, readers expect some positive acknowledgment about the experience. An example of a transmittal memo is included in the long report, Figure 18.5.

Table of Contents

In the Contents, list the headings exactly as they appear in the body of the report. If the report is shorter than 25 pages, list all the headings. In a very long report, list the two or three highest levels of headings. Include your List of Illustrations in your Table of Contents.

List of Illustrations

Report visuals comprise both tables and figures. **Tables** are words or numbers arranged in rows and columns. **Figures** are everything else: bar graphs, pie graphs, maps, drawings, photographs, computer printouts, and so forth (Module 19). Number tables and figures independently, so you may have both a "Table 1" and a "Figure 1." In a report with maps and graphs but no other visuals, the visuals are sometimes called "Map 1" and "Graph 1." Whatever you call the illustrations, list them in the order in which they appear in the report; give the name of each visual as well as its number. See Module 19 for information about how to design and label visuals.

LO2 LO5 Executive Summary

The Executive Summary provides a précis (Module 15) of the whole report. For many readers, the Summary is the most important part of the report; here audiences find immediate answers to their questions.[1]

Although the Summary goes first, you create it last, because to write the Summary, you must know the report's methods, findings, and recommendations. Write and revise the Summary last, as a stand-alone document.

1. In the first paragraph, identify the report's recommendations or main point (purpose). State the situation briefly.
2. In the Summary body, identify the major supporting points for your argument. Include all the information decision makers will need.
3. Briefly describe your research methods.
4. If your report ends with conclusions, provide the conclusions section in the Summary.
5. If your report includes recommendations, provide the recommendations in the Summary.

FIGURE 18.4   Excerpt from an Executive Summary

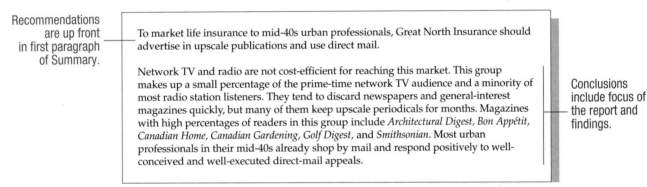

Recommendations are up front in first paragraph of Summary.

To market life insurance to mid-40s urban professionals, Great North Insurance should advertise in upscale publications and use direct mail.

Network TV and radio are not cost-efficient for reaching this market. This group makes up a small percentage of the prime-time network TV audience and a minority of most radio station listeners. They tend to discard newspapers and general-interest magazines quickly, but many of them keep upscale periodicals for months. Magazines with high percentages of readers in this group include *Architectural Digest, Bon Appétit, Canadian Home, Canadian Gardening, Golf Digest*, and *Smithsonian*. Most urban professionals in their mid-40s already shop by mail and respond positively to well-conceived and well-executed direct-mail appeals.

Conclusions include focus of the report and findings.

How Should I Submit the Report?

Follow instructions carefully. If you don't know, ask.

Pay attention to the receiver's instructions whenever you send any documents. If you don't, your material may not be read. Many organizations, for example, accept only job applications and resumés sent electronically. Government RFPs define not only the format, content, and organization of vendors' responses, but also the method, date, and cut-off time of submission. The RFP might specify that the vendors' pricing description must be submitted in a separate envelope from that containing the work proposal. Proposals that do not conform to the submission specifications, like those submitted after the designated deadline, are not accepted.

Your organizational culture may have very clearly defined specifications about how to send reports to internal and external audiences. If you don't know the expectations of your discourse community, ask a colleague or your supervisor.

Language FOCUS

RFP means **request for proposal**. Many organizations will ask for proposals from companies to complete necessary work, such as the construction or repair of city roads.

FIGURE 18.5 **Formal Report**

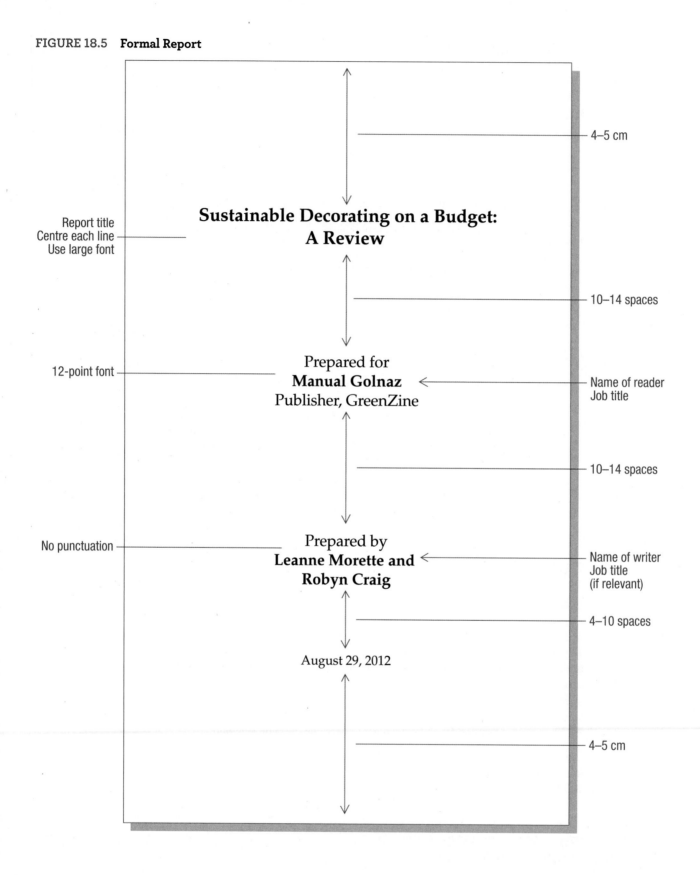

FIGURE 18.5   Formal Report (continued)

Date: August 29, 2012
To: Manual Golnaz
From: Leanne Morette and Robyn Craig
Subject: Sustainable Decorating on a Budget: A Review

Thank you for the opportunity to report on sustainable decorating on a budget. The purpose of this report is to identify eco-decorating trends in the design and renovation industries, suggest resources that allow people to decorate sustainably on a budget, and provide your magazine with ideas for future articles on the topic of sustainable living.

People have become more environmentally conscious and are searching for eco-responsible ways to renovate and decorate. Experts in design and environmental conservation agree that a few simple steps can lead to a more environmentally friendly and sustainable life:

1. Buy recycled and eco-friendly products
2. Shop second-hand whenever possible
3. Use as many energy-efficient products as possible in the home to reduce overall consumption

Through researching and writing this report, we learned that homeowners can make decorating decisions that save money and contribute to sustainability. We also learned that the architecture and design industries are leaders in promoting sustainable living choices, and creating environmentally sound and aesthetically pleasing products.

The information in our report came from our own experiences, from online sources, and from interviews with designer Harvaad Olsen, and Derek Mletzko, Manager, Marketing & Communications, Habitat for Humanity. Their insights were especially helpful.

Please let us know your comments and questions, and thank you again.

FIGURE 18.5   Formal Report (continued)

Writer chooses to position Executive Summary before Table of Contents

Executive Summary of whole report includes purpose, focus and findings, and recommendations. All information in Executive Summary comes from the report.

Executive Summary

This report:
1. Describes sustainable living and its benefits
2. Reviews experts' tips on renovating and decorating the home as a "green" space
3. Suggests available resources for someone living within a budget to create a more sustainable home

The report discusses:
- Benefits of sustainable living and sustainable products on the environment
- Quality and price efficiency of recycled goods
- Choices available through second-hand shops and organizations

Findings

Experts agree that reducing our overall consumption will help mitigate environmental damage. Moreover, the contributions of design and renovation experts to increasing consumer awareness—and access to a surfeit of consumer goods—has begun to make it financially as well as ethically attractive to go green in our homes.

Recommendations

For the future, GreenZine should focus on articles that provide readers with specific articles on:
1. How to make informed choices about eco-friendly products and services
2. Where to find—online or at "bricks and mortar" stores—budget-conscious products and services for home and office
3. How to decorate in economically and aesthetically pleasing ways

Information in this report is based on our own experiences, online sources, and interviews with Harvaad Olsen, designer, and Derek Mletzko, Manager, Marketing & Communications, Habitat for Humanity.

iii

FIGURE 18.5   Formal Report (continued)

Table of Contents does not list itself

Headings are parallel.

Indent subheads

Subheads within each section are parallel

Use lowercase roman numerals for frontmatter.

Report body Introduction begins on page 1.

Table of Contents

Transmittal ii
Executive Summary iii
Introduction 1
　　　　Background...1
Sustainable Living..1
　　Sustainable Production 1
　　Sustainable Living by Design...2
Sustainable Choices: A Beginning 4
　　Sustainable Shopping 4
　　Sustainable Knowledge 5
Conclusions and Recommendations...6
References 7

List of Illustrations

Figure 1: Reused furniture stores offers gently used and
　　　　　refinished furniture at budget-conscious prices..1
Figure 2: Recycled fibres create handsome new carpets 2
Figure 3: The hardy and beautiful EcoTop countertop is bamboo-based...............2
Figure 4: Water-saving showerheads are becoming increasingly
　　　　　more attractive and economical..3
Figure 5: These barstools and a refurbished old factory cart table,
　　　　　located through Kijiji, contribute to this homeowner's overall
　　　　　home decor concept...4
Figure 6: Habitat for Humanity's ReStore offers new building
　　　　　materials for a fraction of their retail cost 4

ii

FIGURE 18.5   **Formal Report (continued)**

Introduction

Intro paragraph summarizes all the content in this section.

This report explores the practices and benefits of sustainable living—"going green"—and the possibilities of renovating and decorating on a budget. The purpose of this report is to identify eco-decorating trends in the design and renovation industries, suggest resources that allow people to decorate sustainable on a budget, and provide your magazine with ideas for future articles on the topic of sustainable living.

The report describes sustainable living and provides resources for choosing to renovate and decorate in a sustainable way. The report considers the benefits of sustainable living, describes trends in the manufacture of recycled goods and materials, offers tips from designers and renovators for going green, and provides specific resources—both new and used—that consumers can use to renovate and decorate in an environmentally responsible and aesthetically pleasing way.

Background

To reverse the damage done to our environment, and in response to increasingly precarious global economic realities, people are making a conscious effort to live in an environmentally conscious way: to "go green" in their everyday lives. In its sustainable living resource guide, the Middletown Thrall Library defined going green as "pursuing knowledge and practices that can lead to more environmentally friendly and ecologically responsible decisions and life styles, which can help protect the environment and sustain its natural resources for current and future generations" (2010). Happily, the act of going green can also be cost effective, making sustainable renovating and decorating affordable even for those on a budget. This report provides information on sustainable renovating and decorating on a budget, and suggests resources to do so.

Sustainable Living

Sustainability is at the core of an environmentally conscious lifestyle. Post-consumer waste is the largest contributor to environmental degradation—worse than most post-industrial waste (Tilford, 2000). Therefore, any product that minimizes post-consumer waste by recycling or repurposing, especially while incorporating great design elements, is both an excellent sustainable choice and a sensible budgetary one. People who buy products made from rapidly renewable resources, durable products that will not need replacing, and reused products are helping to protect the environment and sustain our natural resources for current and future generations (Middletown Thrall Library, 2010).

Figure 1: Reused furniture stores offer gently used and refinished furniture at budget-conscious prices

Source: Supertrooper/Dreamstime.com

Sustainable Production

Not only individuals are embracing sustainable living choices; the engineering, manufacturing, architecture, and design industries are leading the way in educating consumers about making responsible and stylish interior design choices, and in creating ecologically responsible products (Harvaad Olsen, personal communication, January 2, 2012). As an example, *Interiors & Sources* magazine and the American Society of Interior Decorators (ASID) have introduced an annual awards program, the Bloom Awards, to honour companies that produce products that reflect both aesthetics and environmental responsibility (*Interiors & Sources*, 2009).

Talking head

Document sources

APA uses in-text citations for personal communications. These are not listed in the References.

Report introduction begins on page 1

1

FIGURE 18.5   Formal Report (continued)

The Bloom Awards reviews entries in the categories of furniture, flooring, lighting, textiles, and innovative products that, for consideration, must meet specific criteria: "environmental innovation, aesthetics, promotion of sustainability, and recycling and waste management within the manufacturing process and at the end of the products' life-cycle, to name a few" (*Interiors & Sources*, 2009). A recent Bloom Awards winner is "Refresh Fiber," by Universal Fibers; the "Refresh Fiber" is a carpet recycled from carpet fibres, "a breakthrough in recycling nylon 6-6 fibers, a method that was previously impossible and can prevent thousands of yards of carpet from being dumped into landfills" (*Interiors & Sources*, 2009).

Yet another Bloom Award winner is Klip Biotechnologies for its "EcoTop" countertop that focuses on sustainability by using materials such as bamboo (a tall grass that grows quickly and in abundance) and recycled paper fibres. EcoTop can last for decades and can be used as bio-fuel at the end of its life cycle, unlike many other countertops on the market. Most countertops must be disposed of in a landfill at the end of their life cycle. They can't be recycled because of the chemicals involved in the manufacturing process and cost, on average, $35/sq. foot (Klip Biotechnologies, 2009).

These Bloom Award winners are just two examples of products designed to promote sustainable living in the home at a manageable cost.

re*fresh*fiber

Figure 2: Recycled fibres create handsome new carpets.

Source: Universal Fibers

Figure 3: The hardy and beautiful EcoTop countertop is bamboo based.

Source: www.KlipTech.com

Sustainable Living by Design

[Topic sentences begin each paragraph.]

With today's attention on sustainable living, designers and renovators now focus on creating green spaces. These designers and renovation experts provide tips on creating healthy and sustainable environments by 1) adopting a few simple changes in personal habits and 2) choosing eco-friendly products and appliances for our homes.

Television host, author, and columnist Sara Snow shares her tips for green living in the article *Going Green with Sara Snow:*

> [Buy] eco-friendly materials like organic cotton for sheets and towels, and bamboo for flooring and countertops, [choose] second hand furniture (which saves the environment and your money), [hang] your clothes to dry (inside or outside), and [cut] down home energy usage by fitting your home with energy-efficient light bulbs. (Berggoetz, 2009, p. 3)

HGTV designer Linda Woodrum, on HGTV's website (2011), also offers similar suggestions for sustainable in-home materials. Woodrum suggests using sustainable woods such as bamboo or eucalyptus for floors and cabinets, shopping for recycled hardware like cupboard handles at flea markets, using natural stone for countertops, using carpet made of natural fibres like organic cotton and wool or recycled materials, and using Energy-Star rated appliances (Woodrum, 2011). Woodrum specifically suggests replacing shower heads and faucets with water-saving attachments, switching to a low-flow toilet, and investing in an energy efficient water heater, such as a instant tankless hot water heater, which heats water when needed rather than constantly heating a tank of water and thus wasting electricity (Woodrum, 2011).

Figure 4: Water-saving showerheads are becoming increasingly more attractive and economical.

Source: David Buffington/Getty Images

FIGURE 18.5   Formal Report (continued)

Sustainable Choices: A Beginning

Start major headings on a new page for emphasis

Obviously, newer, eco-friendly products can dramatically decrease the impact that we all personally make daily on the environment. In many cases, however, cutting back our consumption is a first and very important step in adopting a sustainable lifestyle. Josh Dorfman, host of The Sundance Channel's *The Lazy Environmentalist*, affirms that "whether people realize it or not, cutting back has made them accidental environmentalists." Dorfman goes on to identify the prime motivator in people's decision to embrace sustainability: "saving money is more important to most people than going green" (Judkis, 2010). Increasingly, therefore, designers, builders, renovators, and manufacturers must source and choose sustainable materials and methods that do not cost the conservationist consumer more, while emphasizing the global benefits of these choices: diverting waste from landfills, preserving our natural resources, and reducing the damage already done to our planet.

Sustainable Shopping

Create sub-headings to increase readability when introducing more specific information

Shopping for second-hand renovating and decorating materials and furnishings is a first, economical step in choosing an environmentally responsible lifestyle. To find second-hand or gently used products, consumers can venture to flea markets, rummage sales, garage sales, thrift stores such as The Salvation Army, Goodwill, or Value Village, or a Habitat for Humanity ReStore location. Consumers can also source decor finds through Craigslist or Kijiji.

Figure 5: These barstools and a refurbished old factory cart table, located through Kijiji, contribute to this homeowner's overall home decor concept.

Source: Robyn Craig

Habitat for Humanity's ReStore is one of the best options for a one-stop shop to meet renovators' green and budget decorating needs. Consumers not only save money and the environment by shopping at the ReStore; a large portion of the money consumers spend there goes towards funding for Habitat for Humanity projects in local communities (Habitat for Humanity, 2011).

Commonly found items available at the ReStore include sinks, windows, doors, paint, hardware, lumber, tools, lighting fixtures, and appliances, all at a fraction of their original cost. Much of what is sold is new, gently used, or retail customer returns that would otherwise end up in a landfill (Habitat for Humanity, 2011). In fact, in 2010 alone "ReStore locations across Canada kept 20,000 tonnes of materials out of landfills through taking donations from the public and re-selling them at ReStore locations" (Habitat for Humanity, 2011).

Figure 6: Habitat for Humanity's ReStore offers new building materials for a fraction of their retail cost

Source: Habitat for Humanity

FIGURE 18.5 Formal Report (continued)

Furthermore, Habitat for Humanity uses its ReStores to model sustainable building as well as waste management processes: ←

Longer quotations are introduced with colons

> [A] lot of our product is new end-of-line that comes directly from retailers. While encouraging many customers to visit our stores, this is also a green practice, as retailers would often otherwise dispose of this product in a landfill.
>
> Many of our homes are also built to recognized green building standards (making the green impact exponential!). In 2012, we expect 90% of our homes to be constructed to recognized green building standards, and for 75% of these to be certified. (Derek Mletzko, Manager, Marketing & Communications, Habitat for Humanity Canada, personal communication, August 24, 2012)

Longer quotations are indented.

Clearly the environmental and community benefits—and the choices and potential savings—of shopping for used and recycled goods from stores such as the Habitat for Humanity's ReStore make a strong case for choosing sustainable decorating.

Sustainable Knowledge

Subheadings within each section are parallel.

Consumers need to be aware, however, that some used building materials and appliances may not be the best environmental choice, although they may be budget friendly. Used older appliances are not energy efficient. Repurposed furniture may also contain lead paint or other health hazards. Eco-decorators need to be knowledgeable buyers, according to renovation expert and sustainable building advocate Mike Holmes:

> You need to be aware of the real differences between surplus new, used, and antique before you start shopping…[I]f you are buying an antique, you definitely won't have windows or doors with high thermal value. That's probably not a sensible idea, given the ever-climbing cost of energy….An old window might be framed in wood that's rotten. And older glass is typically single-glazed and much less energy-efficient than newer designs. So I'd use an antique window as an interior accent, or in non-heated space like a shed or porch. (Holmes, 2008)

Holmes goes on to suggest that a *knowledgeable*, budget-conscious eco-shopper can make informed sustainable choices: "A better idea, if you are looking to save on windows, would be to search the re-use centre for surplus new models that still might be perfect for your renovation needs" (Holmes, 2008).

4

Conclusions and Recommendations

Faced with harsh environmental and economic realities, people are becoming more eco-conscious in their lifestyle, renovating, and decorating choices. Experts in environmental conservation, renovation, and design all agree on a few simple key steps to begin to adopt an inexpensive approach to living a sustainable life:

Use bullets for readability

- Buy recycled and eco-friendly products
- Shop second-hand, whenever possible
- Fit homes with as many energy efficient products as possible

This reduction in overall consumption will help reverse the human-generated damage to our planet. Design and renovation experts have helped to increase consumer awareness. This awareness, combined with access to a surfeit of consumer goods, has begun to make it financially as well as ethically attractive to go green in our homes.

It is the recommendation of this report that, to ensure topicality and relevance, GreenZine should focus on articles that provide readers with specific articles on:

1. How to make informed choices about eco-friendly products and services
2. Where to find—online or at bricks-and-mortar stores—budget-conscious products and services for home and office
3. How to decorate in economically and ascetically pleasing ways

5

FIGURE 18.5   **Formal Report (continued)**

References

Berggoetz, B. (2009). Going green with Sara Snow. *Saturday Evening Post, 281*(2), pp. 56–59. Retrieved from http://search.ebscohost.com/login.aspx?direct=true&db=a9h&AN=36611455&site=ehost-live&scope=site

Habitat for Humanity (2011). *ReStore building supplies*, Habitat for Humanity Canada. Retrieved October 11, 2011, from www.habitat.ca/en/community/restores

Holmes, M. (2008, October 3). How green is your reno? *Globe and Mail*, G10.

Holmes, M. (2011, March 15). Using salvaged materials makes sense. *Globe and Mail*. Retrieved from http://m.theglobeandmail.com/life/home-and-garden/renovations/renovations-green/using-salvaged-materials-makes-sense/article44274/?service=mobile

Interiors & Sources (2009). The bloom awards. 16(4), pp. 71–76. Retrieved from Full Text HTMLWilson-Link HTML: http://vnweb.hwwilsonweb.com/hww/jumpstart.jhtml?recid=0bc05f7a67b1790e841a46ab33283c14bde461c4288200bdc7035f2d296f36c69eb183133fcd2904&fmt=H

Judkis, M. (2010). 10 ways to save by going green. *U.S. News & World Report, 147*(3), pp. 34–35. Retrieved from http://search.ebscohost.com/login.aspx?direct=true&db=a9h&AN=48174339&site=ehost-live&scope=site

Klip Biotechnologies. (2009). *Interiors & Sources* (2009), 16(2), p. 37. Retrieved from Full Text HTML-WilsonLink HTML: http://vnweb.hwwilsonweb.com/hww/jumpstart.jhtml?recid=0bc05f7a67b1790e841a46ab33283c14bde461c4288200bdaaf1e06837196cfd227652fe9410fe37&fmt=H

McAllister, C., & Ryan, J. (2011). It's worth a walk around the block. *yourhome.ca*, Retrieved August 12, 2012, from www.yourhome.ca/homes/article/1080803

Middletown Thrall Library (2010). *Going green: Sustainable living resource guide*. (2010), Retrieved October 16, 2011, from www.thrall.org/special/goinggreen.html

Tilford, D. (2000). Sustainable consumption: Why consumption matters. *Sierra Club*, www.sierraclub.org/sustainable_consumption/tilford.asp

Woodrum, L. (2011). Green decorating basics from Linda Woodrum. HGTV. Retrieved October 11, 2011, from www.hgtv.com/green-home/green-decorating-basics-from-linda-woodrum/index.html

6

EXPANDING A CRITICAL SKILL

LO3 Choosing a Long Report Format and Style

Ex.
18.1–
18.3

Many types of long reports exist in the workplace. Their formats and styles vary according to purpose, audience expectations, organization, and context.

Corporate annual reports are typically printed on glossy stock, filled with colour photos, charts, and graphs, and focused on information, like financial statistics, that is important to investors. These reports may have dozens of pages and be bound like a magazine or paperback book. Other organizations choose to use fewer colours and pages, and inexpensive binding. Still other organizations put their reports online only, saving money and paper.

Reports on scientific and engineering projects, like soil contamination remediation, highway repair efforts, or technology research and development, are frequently text-heavy, including jargon, but relatively light on visuals, which may be only the most technical of diagrams. They may have hundreds of pages and be bound in three-ring binders. A government report on the bereavement industry or tax law revisions might also be dense with text. Plain covers and paper stock closer to copy bond are typical.

Text in reports may be arranged in single or multiple columns, and feature a "drop cap"—an enlarged letter at the beginning of an opening paragraph—and "pull quotes"—portions of the body text repeated and set apart graphically from the rest. Online reports routinely include hypertext links to other documents.

Long reports are written formally. They

- Use the third person (*employees, waste management services, the retail sales team, finance graduates*).

- Are impersonal: long reports avoid *I* and *you* because the data are more important than the writer; the facts are supposedly objective; in a document to multiple, even global audiences, it is not clear who "you" is.
- Avoid contractions: use *they will* instead of *they'll*; *it is* instead of *it's*.

Use your resources to decide on the appropriate format and style:

- Start with PAIBOC analysis.
- Review organizational models. Many organizations have a databank of reports and generic report templates. Writers customize these for their purposes and audiences.
- Many organizations publish reports online, and some public and post-secondary libraries keep copies of government and annual reports. Use your research techniques to find these.
- Look at the report templates online: Microsoft Office Online provides a variety of templates; BDC offers templates and user guides to help writers prepare a business plan (www.bdc.ca/en/business_tools/business_plan/default.htm).
- Consult texts on writing reports, experts in your organization, or professional writers and graphic designers.
- Test your drafts with colleagues, and where possible, with audiences similar to ones that will read your report.

The more specialized the report, the more likely experienced employees will write it. However, many organizations expect novice writers to participate. Use this opportunity to begin to learn a valuable transferable skill.

MODULE SUMMARY

- Long formal reports might include a Transmittal, Executive Summary, Table of Contents with List of Illustrations, the body of the report itself, and Conclusions and Recommendations.
- Writing a long report takes time and organization:
  - ○ Create a timeline for parts of the report.
  - ○ Write the report in sections, starting with the body, where you present facts that prove your position.
  - ○ Jot down potential headings, both for the whole report, and for the sections in the body (The Problem, The Results, The Solution, The Benefits).
  - ○ When you revise the report, reshape the headings into talking heads to preview the subsequent content for the reader and contribute to clarity and understanding.
  - ○ As you research and analyze your information, prepare a bibliography of your sources. Use APA or MLA documentation according to the standards of your discourse community (Module 15).
- All reports should include an overview, to preview the report's contents for the reader. In a formal report, this overview is called a **Summary** or **Executive Summary**. The Summary
  - ○ Sums up the whole report and includes conclusions and recommendations
  - ○ Goes first, on a separate page
  - ○ Is about one-tenth the length of the whole report

- **Introduction**: statement of Purpose and Scope. The **Purpose** statement includes the situation the report addresses, the investigations it summarizes, and the rhetorical purposes (to explain, to describe, to recommend). The **Scope** statement identifies the topics the report covers. The Introduction may also include the following:
- **Limitations**: factors or problems that limit the scope of the report or the validity of the recommendations
- **Assumptions**: statements whose truth you assume, and that you use to prove your ideas
- **Methods**: explanations of how you gathered your data
- **Background** or **History**: this section is information for audiences who may need to read the report years later.
- **Conclusions**: a summary of the main ideas you make in the report body. All reports offer Conclusions.
- **Recommendations**: action items that would solve, or partially solve, the problem.
- Add additional appendixes, responses to questionnaires, figures and tables, and background information only if they are useful to the reader.
- Your choice of report format, style, and method of submission are as important as your content. Pay attention to the rules and norms of your discourse community. If you are unsure, ask someone who knows.

ASSIGNMENTS FOR MODULE 18

Questions for Critical Thinking

18.1 How do you decide on the length and formality of a report?

18.2 How do you decide how much background information to provide in a report?

18.3 How much evidence do you need to provide for each recommendation you make?

Exercises and Problems

As your instructor directs

Submit the following documents for Problems 18.4 through 18.8:

a. The approved proposal
b. Two copies of the report, including
  - Cover
  - Letter or Memo of Transmittal

- Title Page
- Table of Contents
- List of Illustrations
- Executive Summary
- Body (Introduction, all information). Your instructor may specify a minimum length, a minimum number or kind of sources, and a minimum number of visuals.

- Conclusions and Recommendations
- Appendixes, if useful or relevant
- References or Works Cited

c. Your notes and rough drafts

18.4 Writing a Feasibility Study

Write an individual or group report evaluating the feasibility of a plan or idea. Explain your criteria clearly, evaluate each alternative, and recommend the best course of action. Possible topics include the following:

1. What is the feasibility of your business idea? Write a business plan evaluating the opportunity for the start-up of an entrepreneurial business.
2. What is the feasibility of the electric car for common use in your province?
3. What is the feasibility of high-speed commuter trains in your province? If such trains already exist, what is the feasibility of increasing their use, so that they become the primary mode of transportation throughout your province?
4. What is the feasibility of starting a blog for students in your program or for employees in your organization?
5. What is the feasibility of starting a mentorship affiliation in your organization, or in your college/university program? What businesses or non-profits might you affiliate with? What benefits would the mentors enjoy?
6. With your instructor's permission, choose your own topic.

18.5 Writing a Research Report

Write an individual or group library research report. Possible topics include the value of Wikipedia, social networking, your province's healthcare policies, your city's strategies for providing homeless shelters, Canadian copyright or defamation legislation related to Internet material, your province's small business support resources, or your province's welfare strategies. Or, with your professor's permission, choose your own topic.

Start the project by finding the most current information available online and in print.

18.6 Writing a Recommendation Report

Write an individual or group recommendation report. Possible topics are the following:

1. *Recommending courses*: What skills are in demand in your community? What courses at what levels should the local college or university offer? What accreditation courses should graduates in your programs pursue to increase their marketability and salaries?

2. *Improving sales and profits*: Recommend ways a small business in your community can increase sales and profits. Focus on one or more of the following: the products or services it offers, its advertising, its decor, its location, its accounting methods, its cash management, or anything else that may be keeping the company from achieving its potential. Address your report to the owner of the business.
3. *Increasing student involvement*: How might an organization on campus persuade more of the students who are eligible to join or to become active in its programs? Do students know that it exists? Is it offering programs that interest students? Is it retaining current members? What changes should the organization make? Address your report to the officers of the organization.
4. *Evaluating a potential employer*: What training is available to new employees? How soon is the average entry-level person promoted? How much travel and weekend work are expected? Is there a "busy season," or is the workload consistent year-round? What fringe benefits are offered? What is the corporate culture? Is the climate open, friendly, and encouraging? Non-discriminatory? How economically strong is the company? How is it affected by current economic, demographic, and political trends?

Address your report to your college or university placement office; recommend whether the placement office should encourage students to work at this company.

Or, with your professor's permission, choose your own topic. Start the project by finding the most current information available online and in print.

18.7 Writing Up a Survey

Survey two groups of people on a topic that interests you. (For help in creating your survey, go to http://ezinearticles.com/?20-Top-Tips-To-Writing-Effective-Surveys&id=2622.) Possible groups are men and women, people in business and in English programs, younger and older students, students and non-students. Non-random samples are acceptable.

As your instructor directs

a. Survey 40 to 50 people.
b. Team up with your classmates. Survey 50 to 80 people if your group has two members, 75 to 120 people if it has three members, 100 to 150 people if it has four members, and 125 to 200 people if it has five members.
c. Keep a journal during your group meetings and submit it to your instructor.
d. Write a memo to your instructor. (See Module 21, Working and Writing in Teams.)

As you conduct your survey, make careful notes about what you do so that you can use this information when you write your report. If you work with a group, record who does what. Use a memo format. Your subject line should be clear. Omit unnecessary words such as "Survey of." Your first paragraph serves as an introduction, but it needs no heading. The rest of the body of your memo might be divided into four sections with the following headings: Purpose, Procedure, Results, and Discussion. Alternatively, make your survey report more interesting by using talking headings.

In your first paragraph, briefly summarize (not necessarily in this order) who conducted the experiment or survey, when it was conducted, where it was conducted, who the subjects were, what your purpose was, and what you found out.

In your **Purpose** section, explain why you conducted the survey. What were you trying to learn? Why did this subject seem interesting or important? In your **Procedure** section, describe in detail exactly what you did. In your **Results** section, first indicate whether or not your results supported your hypothesis. Use both visuals and words to explain what your numbers show. (See Module 19 on how to design visuals.) Process your raw data in a way that will be useful to your reader. In your **Discussion** section, evaluate your survey and discuss the implications of your results. Consider these questions:

1. Do you think a scientifically valid survey would have produced the same results? Why or why not?
2. Were there any sources of bias either in the way the questions were phrased or in the way the subjects were chosen? If you were running the survey again, what changes would you make to eliminate or reduce these sources of bias?

3. Do you think your subjects answered honestly and completely? What factors may have intruded? Is the fact that you did or didn't know them, or that they were or weren't of the same gender, relevant?
4. What causes the phenomenon your results reveal? If several causes together account for the phenomenon, or if it is impossible to be sure of the cause, admit this. Identify possible causes and assess the likelihood of each.
5. What action should the reader take?

The discussion section gives you the opportunity to analyze the significance of your survey. Its insight and originality lift the otherwise well-written memo from merely satisfactory to the ranks of the above average and the excellent.

18.8 Writing Summaries

Go to www.transcanada.com/keystone.html to view the TransCanada Corporation's overview of the Keystone Pipeline Project. Read any of the following sections: *Keystone Pipeline Project, Energy Security, Pipeline Safety, Environmental Responsibility,* or *Landowner Relations.* Create a one-paragraph Executive Summary for the section you chose.

As your instructor directs

1. Form a team with two other students who chose the same section to create their Summary.
2. Read and discuss your versions of the Executive Summary.
3. Together, rewrite and revise to create your team's version of the Executive Summary.
4. Hand in for grading.

POLISHING YOUR PROSE

Improving Paragraphs

Good paragraphs demonstrate unity, detail, and variety. The following paragraph from a sales letter illustrates these three qualities:

> The best reason to consider a Schroen Heat Pump is its low cost. Schroen Heat Pumps cost 25 percent less than the cheapest competitor's. Moreover, unlike the competition, the Schroen Heat Pump will pay for itself in less than a year in energy savings. That's just 12 months. All this value comes with a 10-year unlimited warranty—if anything goes wrong, we'll repair or replace the pump at no cost to you. That means no expensive repair bills and no dollars out of your pocket.

A paragraph is **unified** when all its sentences focus on a single central idea. As long as a paragraph is about just one idea, a topic sentence expressing that idea is not required. However, using a topic sentence makes it easier for the reader to skim the document. (Essays use a *thesis statement* for the central idea of the entire document.) Sentences throughout the paragraph should support the topic sentence, or offer relevant examples.

Transitions connect ideas from one point to another. Common transitions are *and, also, first, second, third, in addition, likewise, similarly, for example (e.g.), for instance, indeed, to illustrate, namely, specifically, in contrast,* and *on the other hand.*

Detail makes your points clearer and more vivid. Good details express clearly and completely what you mean. Use concrete words, especially strong nouns, verbs, adjectives, and adverbs that paint a picture in the reader's mind and say what you mean. Avoid unnecessary repetition.

Variety is expressed first in sentence length and patterns and second in the number of sentences in each paragraph. Most sentences in business writing should be 14 to 20 words, but an occasional longer or very short sentence gives punch to your writing.

The basic pattern for sentences is subject+verb+object (SVO): *Our building supervisor sent the forms*. Vary the SVO pattern by changing the order, using transitions and clauses, and combining sentences.

Also, vary paragraph length. First and last paragraphs can be quite short. Body paragraphs will be longer. Whenever a paragraph runs eight typed lines or more, think about dividing it into two paragraphs.

Exercises

Rewrite the following paragraphs to improve unity, detail, and variety.

1. I used to work for McCandless Realty as a receptionist. My many experiences in the accounting field make me an ideal candidate for a position as senior administrative assistant with Graham, Chang, and Associates. I answered phones at McCandless. I typed there. I worked at Dufresne Plastics as a secretary. At McCandless, I also handled payroll. There are a lot of reasons why I liked Dufresne. These included the opportunity for training in data entry and Microsoft Word. I learned to type 70 wpm with no mistakes.

2. Mr. Walter Pruitt visited our business communication class yesterday. He spoke about the importance of co-op placements. Mr. Pruitt works for Global Energy. Global Energy provides network and service management to companies around the world. Mr. Pruitt, who works for Global Energy, told us he got his first job because of a co-op. A co-op is an opportunity for students to work with a company for a period of time to get business experience. Mr. Pruitt went to university and worked at a co-op placement for Global Energy. At first, Global Energy only wanted him to work for 10 weeks. Mr. Pruitt did such a good job, they kept him on another 10 weeks and another. Mr. Pruitt was offered a job by Global Energy when he graduated.

Check your answers to the odd-numbered exercises in the Polishing Your Prose Answer Key.

MODULE 19

Using Visuals

MODULE OUTLINE

- Why use visuals?
- What are stories, and how do I find them?
- Does it matter what kind of visual I use?
- What design conventions should I follow?
- Can I use colour and clip art?
- What else do I need to check for?
- Can I use the same visual in my document and in my presentation?

Module Summary

Assignments for Module 19

Polishing Your Prose: Being Concise

Learning Objectives

After reading and applying the information in Module 19, you'll be able to demonstrate

Knowledge of

LO1 How visuals create stories

LO2 How to choose appropriate visuals

Skills to

LO3 Choose visuals to tell a story

LO4 Match the visual to your story

LO5 Choose ethical visuals

LO6 Use visuals in your documents and presentations

Employability Skills 2000+ Checklist

Module content builds these Conference Board of Canada Employability Skills 2000+

Communicate   **Think & Solve Problems**

Manage Information   **Participate in Projects & Tasks**

Pictures tell stories: charts and graphs make numbers meaningful; mall maps tell us where we are; your graduation photos document a rite of passage. Using visuals and text together "as tools to increase understanding" can "get our message across with great efficiency."[1]

LO1 **LO3** Why Use Visuals?

Appropriate, attractive visuals create immediate stories: they are faster and easier to understand and remember.

Visuals condense and clarify data; visuals are a reader-friendly way to communicate your points.

Ex. 19.5

Formal visuals are divided into tables and figures. **Tables** are numbers or words arranged in rows and columns; **figures** are everything else. In a document, formal visuals have both numbers and titles: Figure 1, The Falling Cost of Computer Memory, 2004–2012. In an oral presentation, the title is usually used without the number: The Falling Cost of Computer Memory, 2004–2012. The title puts the story in context, indicating what your audience should look for in the visual, and why it is important. Informal or spot visuals are inserted directly into the text; they do not have numbers or titles.

In your rough draft, use visuals

- *To see that ideas are presented completely.* A table, for example, can show you whether you've included all the items in a comparison.
- *To find relationships.* For example, charting sales on a map may show that the sales representatives who made their quotas all have territories on the west coast or in the Atlantic provinces. Is the product one that appeals to coastal lifestyles? Is advertising reaching the coasts but not the prairie provinces, Ontario, or Quebec? Even if you don't use the visual in your final document, creating the map may lead you to questions you wouldn't otherwise ask.

In the final presentation or document, use visuals

Ex. 19.6

- *To make points vivid.* Readers skim memos and reports; a visual catches the eye. The brain processes visuals immediately. Understanding words—written or oral—takes more time.
- *To emphasize material* that might be skipped if it were buried in a paragraph.
- *To present material more compactly and with less repetition* than words alone can.

The number and type of visuals you need depend on your purposes, your information, and the audience. You'll use more visuals when you want to show relationships, to persuade when the information is complex or contains extensive numerical data, and when the audience values visuals.

Your visual is only as good as the underlying data. Check to be sure that your data come from a reliable source (Module 14).

Ex. 19.5

FIGURE 19.1 **PAIBOC Questions for Analysis**

P	What are your **purposes** in communicating with visuals? Why are you using illustrations? Your purposes come from you, your organization, and the information you intend to convey.
A	Who is your **audience**? Who will read your message? What do they need to know? How will they use your visuals? Will they use them to follow instructions? to understand directions? to assemble something? to understand how a machine, a department or a process works? to see the future if they act a certain way now? What graphics/illustrations would most appeal to your audience? Why? What visuals would maximize your audience's understanding? Why?
I	What **information** must your visual include? What visual will cause your readers to think or do as you want them to? What images could tell your story dramatically and immediately? What numerical or quantitative data are you representing? What visuals would best convey that information?
B	What reasons or reader **benefits** support your position? What visuals would emphasize those benefits?
O	What audience **objections** do you anticipate? How can you use visuals to de-emphasize or overcome audience objections?
C	What **context** will affect reader response? Consider your relationship to your readers, organizational culture, the economy, recent organizational developments, current morale, and the time of year. When choosing your illustrations, consider also your audience demographic, cultural values, and norms.

Ex. 19.7

What Are Stories, and How Do I Find Them?

A story interprets something that is happening or will happen. Look for relationships, patterns, and changes.

Stories are made up of symbols—words, images, colours, and icons—that enable us to create and translate meaning. The garbage-can icon by the words "Recycle Bin" translates the computer's binary code into a story about what happens when we hit Delete. An organization's brand tells the story of its purposes and values.

Every visual should tell a story that is meaningful to your audience. Use the title of the visual to give your story context and emphasis.

Not a story:	Asian Exports, 2007–2012
Possible stories:	China and India Rule Export Trade
	Chinese Garlic Exports Flood Canadian Market

Stories that tell us what we already know are rarely interesting. Instead, good stories do at least one of several things:

- Support a hunch you have
- Surprise or challenge so-called common knowledge
- Show trends or changes you didn't know existed
- Have commercial, cultural, or social significance
- Provide information needed for action
- Have personal relevance to you and the audience

You can find stories in three ways:

1. *Focus on a topic* (starting salaries, alternative music choices, Twitter demographics).
2. *Simplify the data* on that topic and convert the numbers to simple, easy-to-understand units.

3. *Look for relationships and changes.* For example, compare two or more groups: Do men and women have the same attitudes? Look for changes over time. Look for items that can be seen as part of the same group; for example, to find stories about Internet ads, you might group ads in the same product category—ads for cars, for food, for beverages.

When you think you have a story, test it against all the data to be sure it's accurate.

Some stories are simple straight lines: "Workweek Comparison," as illustrated in Figure 19.2. But other stories are more complex, with exceptions or outlying cases. Such stories will need more vivid illustration to do them justice. And sometimes the best story arises from the juxtaposition of two or more stories. In Figure 19.3, for example, the bar graphs compare Canadians' feelings about the influence of social networking sites on their reputations with the attitudes of teachers. Whatever the story, your audience should be able to see what the visual says:

Does the chart support the title, and does the title reinforce the chart? So if I say in my title "sales have increased significantly," I want to see a trend moving up at a sharp angle. If not, if the trend parallels the baseline, it's an instant clue that the chart needs more thinking.[2]

Checkpoint

The Six Components of Every Visual

1. A title that tells the story that the visual shows
2. A clear indication of what the data are
3. Clearly labelled units
4. Labels or legends identifying axes, colours, symbols, and so forth
5. The source of the data, if you created the visual from data someone else gathered and compiled
6. The source of the visual, if you reproduce a visual that someone else created

---

FIGURE 19.2   EU Countries' Workweek Comparison ⟵— Title tells the story

Average usual hours worked, full-time workers, April to June 2011, selected European countries ⟵— Clear description of data

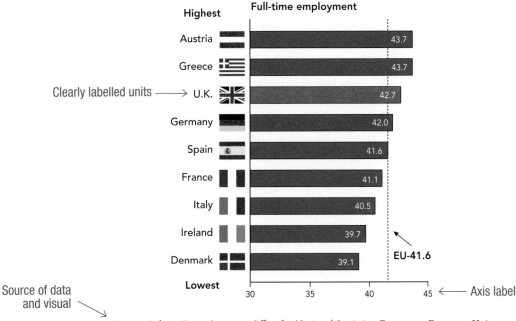

Source of data and visual

Source: Labour Force Survey — Office for National Statistics, Eurostat. © European Union, 1995-2012.

FIGURE 19.3   Bar Graphs Tell a Story

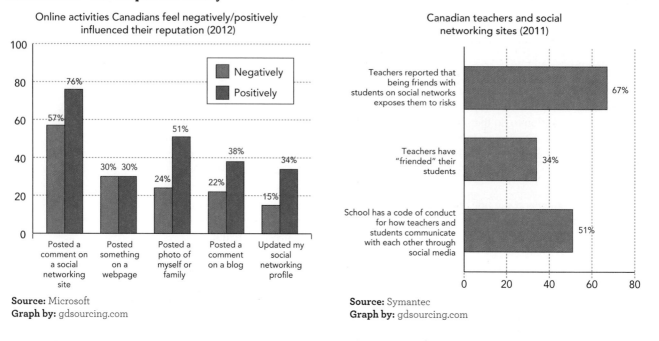

Source: Microsoft
Graph by: gdsourcing.com

Source: Symantec
Graph by: gdsourcing.com

For optimum audience impact, use the "tell, show, tell" rule:

- first, *tell* your readers or listeners what they are about to see
- next, *show* your audience what you promised to show them
- finally, *tell* them the significance of the visual

And, of course, the visual must depict exactly what you said it would.

Almost every data set allows you to tell several stories. Choose the story you want to tell based on your PAIBOC analysis.

LO2 LO4 Does It Matter What Kind of Visual I Use?

Yes! The visual must match the kind of story.

Visuals are not interchangeable. Use visuals that best present the data.

Whenever possible, create your own, original visuals. Use software to make charts, graphs, tables, and figures; use a digital camera to capture stories.

- Use **maps**, **diagrams**, and **graphics** to convey complex information (see Figure 19.3).
- Use **images** and **artwork** to reinforce themes (see Figure 19.4).
- Use **tables** when the reader needs to be able to identify exact values (see Figure 19.5a).
- Use a chart or graph when you want the reader to focus on relationships.[3]
  - To compare a part to the whole, use a **pie graph** (see Figure 19.5b).
  - To compare one item to another item, or items over time, use a bar graph or a line graph (see Figures 19.5c and 19.5d).

Language FOCUS

The word **data** is the plural form of the Latin word datum, which is related to the verb "to give."

FIGURE 19.4   Visual Imagery That Tells the Story of Data Management

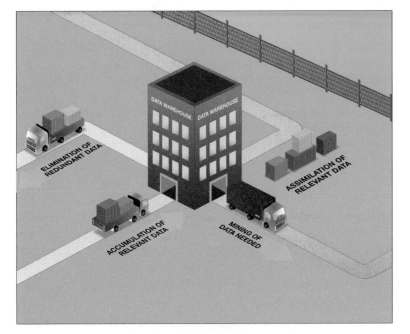

FIGURE 19.5   Choose the Visual to Fit the Story

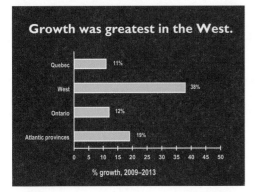

a. Tables show exact values.

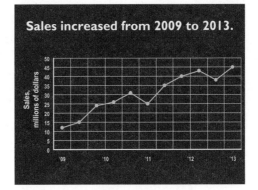

b. Pie graphs compare a component to the whole.

c. Bar graphs compare items or show distribution or correlation.

d. Line charts compare items over time or show distribution or correlation.

Tables

Use tables only when you want the audience to focus on specific numbers.

- Round off to simplify the data (e.g., 35 percent rather than 35.27 percent; 34 000 rather than 33 942). Provide column and row totals or averages when they're relevant.
- Put the items you want readers to compare in columns rather than in rows to facilitate mental subtraction and division.
- When you have many rows, screen alternate entries or double-space after every five entries to help readers line up items accurately.

Pie Graphs

Graphs convey less specific information but are always more memorable.

Pie graphs force the audience to measure area. Research shows that people can judge position or length (which a bar graph uses) much more accurately than they can judge area. The data in any pie graph can be put in a bar graph.[4] Therefore, *use a pie graph only when you are comparing one segment* to the whole. When you are comparing one segment to another, use a bar graph, a line graph, or a map—even though the data may be expressed in percentages.

- Start at 12 o'clock with the largest percentage or the percentage you want to focus on. Go clockwise to each smaller percentage or to each percentage in some other logical order.
- Make the graph chart a perfect circle. Perspective circles distort the data.
- Limit the number of segments to five or seven. If your data have more divisions, combine the smallest or the least important into a single "miscellaneous" or "other" category.
- Label the segments outside the circle. Internal labels are hard to read.

Bar Graphs

Bar graphs are easy to interpret, because they ask people to compare distance along a common scale, which most people judge accurately. Bar graphs are useful in a variety of situations: to compare one item to another, to compare items over time, and to show correlations.

FIGURE 19.6   A Grouped Bar Graph Allows You to Compare Several Items over Time

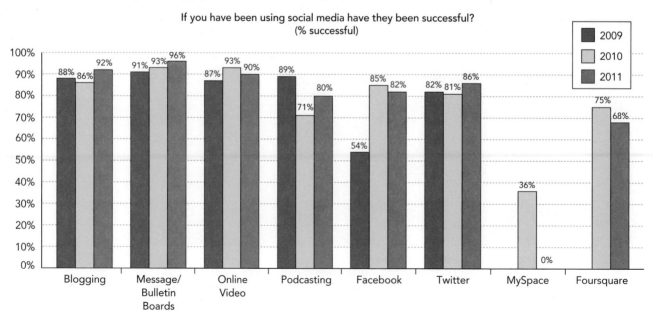

Source: University of Massachusetts, Dartmouth Centre for Marketing Research.

Use horizontal bars when your labels are long; when the labels are short, either horizontal or vertical bars will work.

- Order the bars in a logical or chronological order.
- Put the bars close enough together to make comparisons easy.
- Label both horizontal and vertical axes.
- Put all labels inside the bars or outside them. When some labels are inside and some are outside, the labels carry the visual weight of longer bars, distorting the data.
- Make all the bars the same width.
- Use different colours for different bars only when their meanings are different: estimates as opposed to known numbers, negative as opposed to positive numbers.
- Avoid using perspective. Perspective makes the values harder to read and can make comparison difficult.

Several varieties of bar graphs exist:

- **Grouped bar graphs** allow you to compare several aspects of each item or several items over time.
- **Segmented, subdivided, or stacked bars** sum the components of an item. It's hard to identify the values in specific segments; grouped bar charts are almost always easier to use.
- **Deviation bar graphs** identify positive and negative values, or winners and losers.
- **Paired bar graphs** show the correlation between two items.
- **Histograms** or **pictographs** use images to create the bars.

Line Graphs

Line graphs are also easy to interpret. Use line graphs to compare items over time, to show frequency or distribution, and to show correlations.

- Label both horizontal and vertical axes.
- When time is a variable, put it on the horizontal axis.
- Avoid using more than three different lines on one graph. Even three lines may be too many if they cross each other.
- Avoid using perspective. Perspective makes the values harder to read and can make comparison difficult.

> ### Checkpoint
>
> **Tables** are numbers or words arranged in rows and columns; **figures** are everything else. In a document, formal visuals have both numbers ("Figure 1") and titles. In an oral presentation, the title is usually used without the number.

LO2 LO3 LO6 What Design Conventions Should I Follow?

Ex.
19.4
19.5

Tell your story effectively and ethically. Provide the context. Cite your sources.

Tell Your Story Effectively

Plan your visuals to achieve your purposes, and meet audience needs (Modules 5 and 17). The best visuals

- Use clear, simple, and relevant images
- Use metaphors and pictures that make connections and patterns obvious
- Put people in the picture: show people working well in teams, using the new software, driving further and cleaner in the hybrid
- Blend seamlessly and are balanced with the text[5]

Provide the Context

Every visual should

1. Give a title that tells the story the visual shows
2. Clearly indicate the data
3. Clearly label units
4. Provide labels or legends identifying axes, colours, symbols, and so forth
5. Give the source of the data, if you create the visual from data someone else gathered and compiled
6. Give the source of the visual, if you reproduce a visual that someone else created

Cite Your Sources   Like all intellectual property, visuals are protected by copyright. Whenever you use secondary sources, you must credit the author. Information on how to cite images correctly is available online, in style guide sites, and on your local and university and college library sites (Modules 14 and 15).

> Ex.
> 19.5

Can I Use Colour and Clip Art?

Use colour and clip art carefully.

Colour makes visuals more dramatic, but creates at least two problems. First, readers try to interpret colour, an interpretation that may not be appropriate. Second, meanings assigned to colours differ depending on the audience's culture and profession.

Connotations for colour vary from culture to culture and within cultures (Module 3). Blue suggests masculinity in North America, criminality in France, strength or fertility in Egypt, and villainy in Japan. Red is sometimes used to suggest danger or stop in North American culture; it means go in China and is associated with festivities. Yellow suggests caution or cowardice in North America, prosperity in Egypt, grace in Japan, and femininity in many parts of the world.[6]

Corporate, national, or professional associations may override these general cultural associations. Some people associate blue with IBM or Hewlett-Packard and red with Coca-Cola, communism, or Japan. People in specific professions learn other meanings for colours. Blue suggests *reliability* to financial managers, *water* or coldness to engineers, and *death* to healthcare professionals. Red means *losing money* to financial managers, *danger* to engineers, but *healthy* to healthcare professionals. Green usually means *safe* to engineers, but infected to healthcare professionals.[7]

These various associations suggest that colour is safest with a homogenous audience that you know well. In an increasingly multicultural workforce, colour may send signals you do not intend.

When you do use colour in visuals, experts suggest the following guidelines:[8]

- Use no more than five colours when colours have meanings.
- Use glossy paper to make colours more vivid.
- Be aware that colours always look brighter on a computer screen than on paper, because the screen sends out light.

In any visual, use as little shading and as few lines as are necessary for clarity. Don't clutter up the visual with extra marks. When you design black-and-white graphs, use shades of grey rather than stripes, wavy lines, and checks to indicate different segments or items. Test print to ensure your chosen shades of grey make your story obvious to the reader.

Clip Art

In memos and reports, resist the temptation to make your visual "artistic" by turning it into a picture or adding clip art. A small drawing of a car in the corner of a line graph showing the number of kilometres driven might be acceptable in an oral presentation or a newsletter, but is out of place in a written report. Indeed, because of its blandness and ubiquity, clip art can diminish and trivialize content.

Statistician and visual design expert Edward Tufte uses the term **chartjunk** for visual details—"the encoded legends, the meaningless color[,] the logo-type branding"—that at best are irrelevant to

EXPANDING A CRITICAL SKILL

Integrating Visuals into Your Text

To keep your reader in your story, tell, show, tell: refer to every visual in your text.

ING Direct Canada ranks first in mid-size retail banks for customer satisfaction, as Figure 1, below, indicates.

FIGURE 1   ING Direct Canada Customer Satisfaction Standing

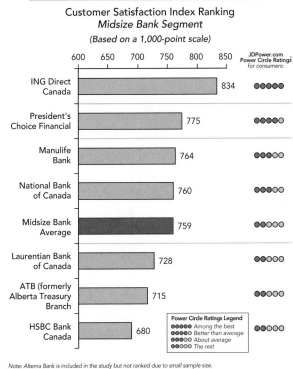

J.D. Power and Associates
2012 Canadian Retail Banking Customer Satisfaction StudySM

Customer Satisfaction Index Ranking
Midsize Bank Segment
(Based on a 1,000-point scale)

Bank	Score
ING Direct Canada	834
President's Choice Financial	775
Manulife Bank	764
National Bank of Canada	760
Midsize Bank Average	759
Laurentian Bank of Canada	728
ATB (formerly Alberta Treasury Branch)	715
HSBC Bank Canada	680

Power Circle Ratings Legend
●●●●● Among the best
●●●●○ Better than average
●●●○○ About average
●●○○○ The rest

Note: Alterna Bank is included in the study but not ranked due to small sample size.

Charts and graphs extracted from this press release must be accompanied by a statement identifying J.D. Power and Associates as the publisher and the J.D. Power and Associates 2012 Canadian Retail Banking Customer Satisfaction StudySM as the source. Rankings are based on numerical scores, and not necessarily on statistical significance. JDPower.com Power Circle RatingsTM are derived from consumer ratings in J.D. Power studies. For more information on Power Circle Ratings, visit jdpower.com/faqs. No advertising or other promotional use can be made of the information in this release or J.D. Power and Associates survey results without the express prior written consent of J.D. Power and Associates.

Source: J.D. Power and Associates 2012 Canadian Retail Banking Customer Satisfaction StudySM

Normally give the table or figure number in the text but not the title. Put the visual as soon after your reference as space and page design permit. If the visual must go on another page, tell the reader where to find it:

As Figure 3 shows (p. 10)...

(See Table 2 on page 3.)

Summarize the main point of a visual before you present the visual itself. Then when readers get to it, they'll see it as confirmation of your point.

Weak: Listed below are the results.

Better: As Figure 4 shows, sales doubled in the last decade.

How much discussion a visual needs depends on the audience, the complexity of the visual, and the importance of the point it makes. If the material is new to the audience, you'll need a fuller explanation than if similar material is presented to this audience every week or month. Help the reader find key data points in complex visuals. If the point is important, discuss its implications in some detail.

In contrast, one sentence about a visual may be enough when

- the audience is already familiar with the topic and data
- the visual is simple and well designed
- the information in the visual is a minor part of your proof

When you discuss visuals, spell out numbers that fall at the beginning of a sentence. If spelling out the number or year is cumbersome, revise the sentence so that it does not begin with a number.

Correct: Forty-five percent of the cost goes to pay wages and salaries.

Correct: The year 2011 marked the EU economic crisis.

the visual, and at worst mislead the reader.[9] Turning a line graph into a highway to show kilometres driven makes it more difficult to read: it's hard to separate the data line from lines that are merely decorative. Similarly, MS Office charts can create distortion—especially the 3D options for pie charts and the shadowing options for bar charts.

If you use clip art, do so ethically: make it relevant to your content, be sensitive to your audience's pluralistic interpretations, and be sure that the images of people show a good mix of both sexes, various races and ages, and various physical conditions (Module 3).

Ex. 19.5

LO5 What Else Do I Need to Check For?

Be sure that the visual is accurate and ethical.

Always double-check your visuals to be sure that the information is accurate. Be aware, however, that many visuals have accurate labels but misleading visual shapes. Visuals communicate quickly; audiences remember the shape, not the labels. If the reader has to study the labels to get the right picture, the visual is unethical even if the labels are accurate.

People manipulate images for a variety of reasons, some artistic, many commercial. Only the informed person qualifies for citizenship in the global marketplace. Be prepared to question the validity of all data; your personal and professional well-being depend on these critical thinking skills.

Even simple bar and line graphs may be misleading if part of the **scale** is missing, or **truncated**. Truncated graphs are most acceptable when the audience knows the basic data set well. For example, graphs of the stock market almost never start at zero; they are routinely truncated. This omission is acceptable for audiences who follow the market closely.

Data can also be distorted when the context is omitted. For example, a drop may be part of a regular cycle, a correction after an atypical increase, or a permanent drop to a new, lower plateau.

You can do several things to make your visuals more accurate:

- Differentiate between actual and estimated or projected values.
- When you must truncate a scale, do so clearly with a break in the bars or in the background.
- Avoid perspective and three-dimensional graphs.
- Avoid combining graphs with different scales.
- Use images of people carefully in histograms to avoid sexist, racist, or other exclusionary visual statements.

LO6 Can I Use the Same Visual in My Document and in My Presentation?

Use it in both only if the table or graph is simple.

For presentations, simplify paper visuals. To simplify a complex table, cut some information, round off the data even more, or present the material in a chart rather than in a table.

Visuals for presentations should have titles but don't need figure numbers. Know where each visual is so that you can return to one if someone asks about it during the question period. Use clip art only if it's relevant, and does not obscure the story you're telling with the visual.

MODULE SUMMARY

- Appropriate, attractive visuals tell stories concisely and immediately: visuals are faster and easier to understand, and more memorable.

- In your rough draft, use visuals to see that ideas are presented completely, and to identify patterns and relationships. In your reports and presentations, use visuals to make points vivid, to emphasize material the audience might overlook, and to present material more efficiently and more compactly than words alone can do.

- Use more visuals when you want to show relationships, when the information is complex, or contains extensive numerical data, and when the audience values visuals.

- Pick data to tell a story, to make your point. To find stories, look for relationships and changes. Writers and illustrators create worthy stories through research: they
  - ❍ Follow up on hunches
  - ❍ Find data that challenge accepted wisdom, have commercial, cultural or social significance, or indicate new trends
  - ❍ Identify information that requires immediate action, or has personal relevance for them and their audiences

- When you think you have a story, test it against all the data to be sure it's accurate.

- Formal visuals are divided into tables and figures. Tables are numbers or words arranged in rows and columns; figures are everything else, including clip art and photographs.

- Choosing the best visual depends on the kind of data and the point you want to make with the data.

- Visuals represent a point of view; they are never neutral. You are legally and ethically responsible for creating and using visuals that
  - ❍ Represent data accurately, both literally and by implication
  - ❍ Avoid chartjunk: decorations and details that are irrelevant or misleading
  - ❍ Give the source of the data

- Appropriate visuals are both accurate and ethical. They
  - ❍ Give a title that tells the story the visual shows
  - ❍ Clearly indicate the data
  - ❍ Clearly label units
  - ❍ Provide labels or legends identifying axes, colours, symbols, and so forth
  - ❍ Give the source of the data, if you created the visual from data someone else gathered and compiled
  - ❍ Give the source of the visual, if you reproduce a visual someone else created

ASSIGNMENTS FOR MODULE 19

Questions for Critical Thinking

19.1 Identify three specific types of reports that rely heavily on visuals.

19.2 How do MS chart styles create distortion? Find an example of a ready-made chart that distorts the data.

19.3 How could you take a photograph to tell a story?

19.4 Is it ethical to use dramatic pictures and visual metaphors to motivate people to give to charity? Why or why not?

Exercises and Problems

19.5 Reviewing Expert Advice on Creating Visuals

Review Tufte's Rules—Professor Tuft's compendium for creating the best visuals—at www.sealthreinhold.com/class_sites/tuftes_rules/rule_one.php.

On the basis of your review, create a summary of the rules.

Apply your summary to Exercises 19.6 through 19.9.

19.6 Evaluating Text and Images

Evaluate the following student report excerpt using these criteria:

1. The visuals tell a story.
2. The writer has used the best visuals to convey the story.
3. The visuals use clear, simple, and relevant images.
4. The writer balances visuals and text.
5. The writer integrates visuals and text.
6. The visuals and text together communicate the message compactly.

The Career Centre's brochures and information sheets are helpful for students.						
	Total		**Male**		**Female**	
	Number	**Percentage**	**Number**	**Percentage**	**Number**	**Percentage**
Agree strongly	25	25%	14	28%	11	22%
Agree somewhat	56	56%	27	54%	29	58%
Disagree somewhat	11	11%	5	10%	6	12%
Disagree strongly	8	8%	4	8%	4	8%
Total	**100**	**100%**	**50**	**100%**	**50**	**100%**

Source: Reprinted by permission of Lindsay Hopton-Piché, Sheridan Graduate and Silver Medallist, Business Administration Finance.

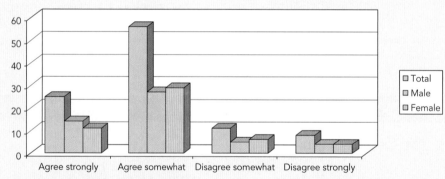

Source: Reprinted by permission of Lindsay Hopton-Piché, Sheridan Graduate and Silver Medallist, Business Administration Finance.

When asked to indicate if they felt that the Career Centre's brochures and information sheets are helpful for students, 56 percent of respondents agreed somewhat with this statement; of these respondents, 27 were male and 29 female. Twenty-five percent of respondents agreed strongly that the Career Centre's brochures and information sheets are helpful for students; of these respondents, 14 were male and 11 female. Eleven percent of respondents somewhat disagreed that the Career Centre's brochures and information sheets are helpful for students; of these respondents, 5 were male and 6 female. Eight percent of respondents strongly disagreed that the Career Centre's brochures and information sheets are helpful for students; of these respondents, 4 were male and 4 female. This data suggests that the large majority of respondents believe that the Career Centre's brochures and information sheets are helpful for students, and that the same number of males and of females feel this way.

How likely are you to use the Career Centre in the future?						
	Total		**Male**		**Female**	
	Number	**Percentage**	**Number**	**Percentage**	**Number**	**Percentage**
Very likely	37	37%	18	36%	19	38%
Somewhat likely	55	55%	29	58%	26	52%
Not likely	8	8%	3	6%	5	10%
Total	**100**	**100%**	**50**	**100%**	**50**	**100%**

Source: Reprinted by permission of Lindsay Hopton-Piché, Sheridan Graduate and Silver Medallist, Business Administration Finance.

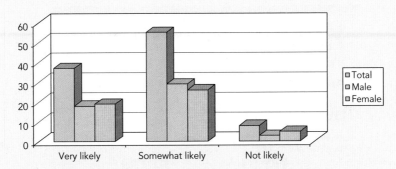

Source: Reprinted by permission of Lindsay Hopton-Piché, Sheridan Graduate and Silver Medallist, Business Administration Finance.

When asked to indicate how likely they are to use the Career Centre in the future, 55 percent of respondents indicated that they are somewhat likely to use the Career Centre in the future; of these respondents, 29 were male and 26 female. Thirty-seven percent of respondents indicated that they will be very likely to use the Career Centre in the future; of these respondents, 18 were male and 19 female. Eight percent of respondents indicated that they will not likely use the Career Centre in the future; of these respondents, 3 were male and 5 female. These data suggest that most students are likely to use the Career Centre in the future, and that males and females are almost equally likely to use the Career Centre in the future.

19.7 Matching Visuals with Stories

What visual(s) would make it easiest to see each of the following stories?

1. In Canada, the gap between rich and poor is widening.
2. An increasing number of young adults (ages 7 to 24) are politically active.
3. The Facebook Nation: Canadians are the largest population on Facebook.
4. Vegetarianism is becoming a lifestyle choice among young adults.
5. Canada's population is aging.
6. Number of years of postsecondary education correspond to employment success.

19.8 Evaluating Visuals

Evaluate each of the following visuals using Tufte's rules and these questions:

- Is the visual's message clear?
- Is it the right visual for the story?
- Is the visual designed appropriately? Is colour, if any, used appropriately?
- Is the visual free from chartjunk?
- Does the visual distort data or mislead the reader in any way?

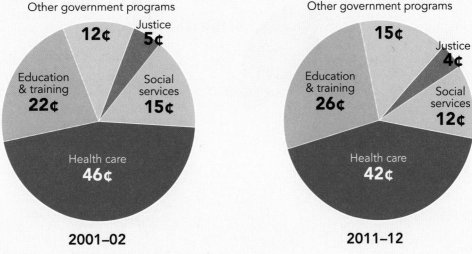

Source: Reprinted with permission. Torstar Syndication Services.

HOW CANADA'S CEOs SEE 2012

EXCLUSIVE CEO POLL

What will happen to Canada's economy in the next six to 12 months? Will it get...

6 MONTHS

1 1 14 42 42

12 MONTHS

8 1 16 51 24

| A lot worse | Somewhat worse | Remain about the same | Somewhat better | A lot better |

Thinking of the business you know best, will their fortunes...

Contract somewhat
16

Contract a lot
1

Stay the same
44

Grow somewhat
38

Source: COMPAS Research www.compas.ca. *Canadian Business,* February 20, 2012 p. 13.

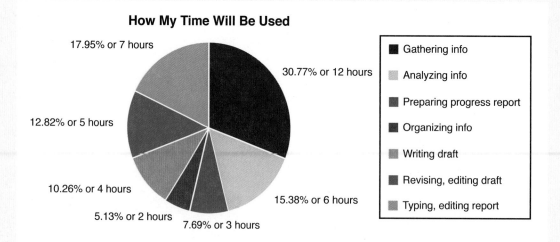

How My Time Will Be Used

17.95% or 7 hours

30.77% or 12 hours

12.82% or 5 hours

10.26% or 4 hours

5.13% or 2 hours

7.69% or 3 hours

15.38% or 6 hours

- Gathering info
- Analyzing info
- Preparing progress report
- Organizing info
- Writing draft
- Revising, editing draft
- Typing, editing report

A Year of Soda: 44.7 Gallons

Here's what carbonated soft drink consumption — sugared and diet sodas — looked like in 2010. The average American chugged the equivalent of 48 two-liter bottles and 206 12-ounce cans of soft drinks (one of many possible container combinations that add up to about 44.7 gallons):

Soda Is Cheap, and Staying Cheap

THE PRICE of carbonated drinks in the U.S. has crept up, but more slowly than overall prices — in effect, making them ever cheaper relative to other goods. Fruits and vegetables have become more expensive at a much faster rate.

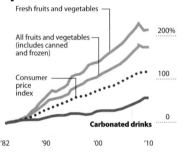

Fresh fruits and vegetables
All fruits and vegetables (includes canned and frozen)
Consumer price index
Carbonated drinks

200%
100
0

'82   '90   '00   '10

What a Small Federal Tax Could Do

Her is the revenue from a levy on sugar-sweetened beverages, in effect next year, according to Yale University's Rudd Center for Food Policy and Obesity.

If a 20-ounce bottle of soda costs $1.50 **+** it carries a one-cent tax per ounce

= **$1.70 total costs per bottle**
$13.2 billion in total tax revenue
from this and other sugar-sweetened beverages in 2012

Sources: Beverage Marketing Corporation, Advertising Age (consumption); U.S. Dept. of Agriculture (food inflation): Rudd Center for Food Policy and Obesity, Yale University (federal tax)

The iPhone: Designed in the U.S. ...		...Made Overseas...		...Assembled in China

	DISPLAYS	SEMICONDUCTOR (CHIPS)	BATTERIES	ASSEMBLY
27,300	**5,000 – 10,000**	**7,000 – 20,000**	**300 – 1,000**	**200,000**
non retail jobs in the U.S.	jobs in South Korea and other Asian countries	jobs in Taiwan, Singapore, Malaysia, Japan, Europe and elsewhere	jobs in China	jobs in China

Dreamed up in California	**An Industry lost**	**An industry outsourced**	**No catching up**	**It's not just cheap labor**
Apple once boasted that its products were manufactured in the United States. No longer. Specifics differ between versions, but an estimated 90 percent of iPhone components are manufactured overseas, by workers in Germany, Singapore, Korea, Taiwan China and elsewhere.	America was once a leader in television and other display manufacturing. Today, virtually no displays are made in the United States. They mostly come from Asia, especially South Korea and Japan, where wages are not much cheaper but technical manufacturing has outpaced American capabilities.	The semiconductor was essentially invent in the United States. Then foreign nations discovered that semiconductor manufacturing could jump-start technology industries. In the 1960s, assembly was outsourced to Asia. higher-skilled jobs soon followed. Although the latest iPhone processor is made in Texas, most of its other chips are made abroad.	Sony helped develop the lithium-ion battery in the early 1980s for use in its consumer electronics devices, including the Walkman. Japan came to dominate the manufacturing of these batteries. Energizer tried to open a battery factory in Florida in the 1990s, but raw material costs and labor rates made it unable to compete with Japan and other Asian countries.	The iPhone is assembled in China by Foxconn, the largest electronics assembler in the world. U.S. executives say they cannot function without companies like Foxconn. The Taiwanese company has a million workers, many willing to live in company dorms, work midnight shifts and spend 12 hours in a factory, six days a week. Chinese workers are cheaper they their American Counterparts — but just as important, they are more flexible and plentiful, and thousands can be hired overnight.

Thousands languish on wait lists

The number of people receiving transplants or waiting for a donor has not changed much since 2001.

■ People waiting
■ Transplants performed

3,500 THE NUMBER OF CASES

2001

2010

Kidney Liver Heart Lung Pancreas

THE NUMBER OF PEOPLE:

	WAITING	TRANSPLANTS
For Kidney:	3,014	1,062
For liver:	454	394
For heart:	125	161
For lung	163	126
For pancreas:	204	47

THE NUMBER OF PEOPLE:

	WAITING	TRANSPLANTS
	3,362	1,248
	501	442
	135	167
	310	179
	175	74

Source: Reprinted with permission. Torstar Syndication Services.

CMA gains/losses

Biggest and smallest percentage population changes among Canada's 33 census metropolitan areas:

Rank	Metropolitan area	Population	% change since previous census
1.	Calgary	1,214,839	+12.6%
2.	Edmonton	1,159,869	+12.1%
3.	Saskatoon	260,600	+11.4%
4.	Kelowna, B.C.	179,839	+10.8%
5.	Moncton, N.B.	138,644	+9.7%
6.	Vancouver	2,313,328	+9.3%
7.	Toronto	5,583,064	+9.2%
29.	Sudbury	160,770	+1.6%
30.	Saguenay, Que.	157,790	+1.0%
31.	St. Catharines, Ont.	392,184	+0.5%
32.	Thunder Bay	121,596	−1.1%
33.	Windsor	319,246	−1.3%

Fastest growing provincial populations

PER CENT CHANGE IN POPULATION BETWEEN 2006/2011 CENSUSES

■ 9% to 12%
■ 6% to 9%
□ 3% to 6%
□ less than 3%

Canadian communities

Canadian communities with highest and lowest percentage growth rates, 2006–2011:

GAINERS	Population	% change since previous census
Milton, Ont.	84,362	+56.5%
Martensville, Sask.	7,716	+55%
Whitchurch-Stouffville	37,628	+54.3%
Sainte-Brigitte-de-Laval	5,696	+50.35
Chestermere, Alta	14,824	+49.4%

LOSERS		
Thunder Bay, Ont.	5,909	−10.3%
Inverness, N.S.	5,280	−9.9%
Hearst, Ont.	5,090	−9.4%
Lac la Biche, Alta.	8,402	−7.9%
Kitmat, B.C.	8,335	−7.3%

Canada's population history

35 Population/millions

2011: **33,476,688**

1851 71 91 1901 11 31 51 71 81 91 01 11

	2001	2006	% increase since 2001	2011	% increase since 2006
Nfld./Labrador	512,930	505,469	−1.5%	514,536	1.8%
P.E.I.	135,294	135,851	0.4	140,204	3.2
Nova Scotia	908,007	913,462	0.6	921,727	0.9
New Brunswick	729,498	729,997	0.1	751,171	2.9
Quebec	7,237,479	7,546,131	4.3	7,903,001	4.7
Ontario	11,410,046	12,160,282	6.6	12,851,821	5.7
Manitoba	1,119,583	1,148,401	2.6	1,208,268	5.2
Saskatchewan	978,933	968,157	−1.1	1,033,381	6.7
Alberta	2,974,807	3,290,350	10.6	3,645,257	10.8
British Columbia	3,907,738	4,113,487	5.3	4,400,057	7.0
Yukon	28,674	30,372	5.9	33,897	11.6
Northwest Territories	37,360	41,464	11	41,462	0.0
Nunavut	26,745	29,474	10.2	31,906	8.3
CANADA	**30,007,094**	**31,612,897**	**5.4**	**33,476,688**	**5.9**

Source: Reprinted with permission. Torstar Syndication Services.

T.O. is the tops

Vibrant labour market and lower bankruptcy rates helped city outscore 25 other major metropolitan areas in economic growth, CIBC says.

■ Toronto
■ Canada

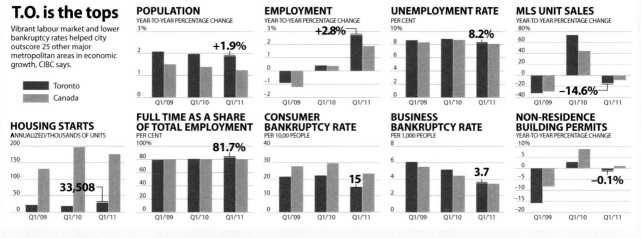

POPULATION
YEAR-TO-YEAR PERCENTAGE CHANGE
3%
+1.9%
Q1/'09 Q1/'10 Q1/'11

EMPLOYMENT
YEAR-TO-YEAR PERCENTAGE CHANGE
3%
+2.8%
Q1/'09 Q1/'10 Q1/'11

UNEMPLOYMENT RATE
PER CENT
10%
8.2%
Q1/'09 Q1/'10 Q1/'11

MLS UNIT SALES
YEAR-TO-YEAR PERCENTAGE CHANGE
80%
−14.6%
Q1/'09 Q1/'10 Q1/'11

HOUSING STARTS
ANNUALIZED/THOUSANDS OF UNITS
200
33,508
Q1/'09 Q1/'10 Q1/'11

FULL TIME AS A SHARE OF TOTAL EMPLOYMENT
PER CENT
100%
81.7%
Q1/'09 Q1/'10 Q1/'11

CONSUMER BANKRUPTCY RATE
PER 10,00 PEOPLE
40
15
Q1/'09 Q1/'10 Q1/'11

BUSINESS BANKRUPTCY RATE
PER 1,000 PEOPLE
8
3.7
Q1/'09 Q1/'10 Q1/'11

NON-RESIDENCE BUILDING PERMITS
YEAR-TO-YEAR PERCENTAGE CHANGE
10%
−0.1%
Q1/'09 Q1/'10 Q1/'11

Source: Reprinted with permission. Torstar Syndication Services.

Wave chamber

Waves cause a column of water to rise and fall, acting like a piston, forcing air to flow through a turbine.

Waves

Sealed inner chamber

Air flow to/from turbine

Rising and falling water column

Seabed

Wave bob

A wavebob converts the energy of heaving motion of waves into high pressure oil via a piston pump.

Waves

Float

Piston arm

Piston pump

High pressure oil line

Source: Reprinted with permission. Torstar Syndication Services.

Table 2
The contribution of background family characteristics

	Median number of months between high school graduation and start of first postsecondary education program number
Parents' highest level of educational attainment	
High school or less	14
Some postsecondary	13
Postsecondary graduate	3
Importance to parents that child obtains a postsecondary education	
Not important at all / slightly important	27
Fairly important	15
Very important	3
Frequency with which youth and parent talked about future education and career options	
Never	14
Less than once a year	15
A few times a year	4
A few times a month	3
A few times a week / daily	7

Source: Statistics Canada. Youth in Transition Survey. Cohort B.

Cumulative proportion of high school graduates who started postsecondary education by age 28

Proportion starting PSE by month

Note: Restricted to youth who graduated high school.
Source: Statistics Canada. Youth in Transition Survey. Cohort B. Cycle 5.

19.9 Graphing Data from the Web

Find data on the Web about a topic that interests you. Sites that provide data include

- www.canoe.ca
- www.statcan.ca
- www.findarticles.com
- Graphic, Visualization, & Usability Center's WWW surveys: www.cc.gatech.edu/gvu/user_surveys/

As your instructor directs,

a. Identify at least seven stories in the data.
b. Create visuals for three of the stories.
c. Write a memo to your instructor explaining why you chose these stories and why you chose these visuals to display them.
d. Write a short report to some group that might be interested in your findings, presenting your visuals as part of the short report.
e. Print out the data and include it with a copy of your memo or report.

POLISHING YOUR PROSE

Being Concise

Being concise in business writing means using only necessary words to make your point, without sacrificing courtesy or clarity. Wordy sentences may confuse or slow readers:

Wordy: All of our employees at Haddenfield and Dunne should make themselves available for a seminar meeting on the 5th of August 2012, at 10 o'clock in the morning. Please make sure you come to the conference room on the 2nd Floor of the Main Complex.

Concise: Please plan to attend a seminar at 10 a.m., August 5, 2012, in the Main Complex 2nd Floor conference room.

Being concise does not mean eliminating necessary information. Sometimes you'll have to write longer sentences to be clear.

Nor does being concise mean using short, choppy sentences.

Choppy: We have a new copier. It is in the supply room. Use it during regular hours. After 5 p.m., it will be shut down.

Concise: A new copier is available in the supply room for use before 5 p.m.

Use concrete words. Instead of vague nouns and verbs with strings of modifiers, use specifics.

Vague: The person who drops off packages talked about the subject of how much to charge.

Concrete: The delivery person discussed fees.

Avoid vague or empty modifiers. Words like *very, some, many, few, much, kind of/sort of,* and so forth, usually can be cut.

Cut redundant words or phrases. Don't say the same thing twice. *Cease and desist, first and foremost, the newest and latest, official company policy, 24 storeys tall, said out loud,* and *return back* are all redundant.

Avoid unnecessarily complex constructions. Instead of *the bid that won the contract,* use *the winning bid.*

Stick to simple verb tenses. Standard edited English prefers them. Instead of "I *have been attending* Royal Roads University" use "I *attend* Royal Roads University." Instead of "By 2013, I *will have completed my degree*" use "I *will graduate* by 2013."

Exercises

Rewrite the following sentences to make them concise.

1. It would be in your best interest to return the order form to us as quickly as possible.
2. Our official records show that you are a very responsible person.
3. The automobile that is blue belongs to the woman in charge of legal affairs.
4. The mainframe computer is located in our subterranean basement.
5. Call us on the telephone if you want to confirm your order.
6. We faxed a reproduced copy of the application on the fax machine.
7. Enclosed along with the rest of this job application letter is a list of references who can talk about my job qualifications because I used to work for them.
8. I enjoyed the presentation very much.
9. To begin with, let me start by telling you some stories about our guest of honour.
10. The guy that runs our advertising department yelled loudly across the parking lot that a delivery truck had left its two headlights on.

Check your answers to the odd-numbered exercises in the Polishing Your Prose Answer Key.

Listening Actively

Learning Objectives

After reading and applying the information in Module 20, you'll be able to demonstrate

Knowledge of

LO1 The fundamentals of good listening practice

LO2 Active listening as a core communication skill

Skills to

LO3 Begin to listen actively

LO4 Begin to listen for understanding

LO5 Continue to learn how to influence others positively

MODULE OUTLINE

- What do good listeners do?
- What Is the difference between good listening and active listening?
- How do I show people that I'm listening to them?
- Can I use these techniques if I really disagree with someone?

Module Summary

Assignments for Module 20

Polishing Your Prose: Using Colons and Semicolons

Employability Skills 2000+ Checklist

Module content builds these Conference Board of Canada Employability Skills 2000+

Communicate

Think and Solve Problems

Be Adaptable

Learn Continuously

Work with Others

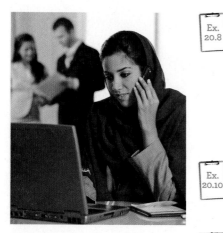

Good listening takes energy and practice.

Ex. 20.8

Listening means decoding and interpreting both verbal and non-verbal symbols, as the speaker intends them. In study after study, employers rank listening skills first among the most critical communication skills.[1] Yet we rarely receive formal training in this key skill.

In our digital, surround-sound world, good listening is more difficult and more important than ever.

Good listening is active, and takes energy and practice. Good listening is active because you must

Ex. 20.10

- Focus on accurately interpreting the speaker's words, gestures, and tone *in the moment*
- Reduce physical, emotional, and psychological distractions
- Clear your mind of your own preoccupations and biases

Ex. 20.1 20.3

Obviously, good listening demands practice because focusing on another person in an open, uncritical way does not come naturally to any of us.

LO1 What Do Good Listeners Do?

They prepare by analyzing (PAIBOC) the situation. Then they consciously follow four practices.

Ex. 20.5

After analyzing the listening situation, good listeners pay attention, focus on the other speaker(s) in a generous way, avoid making assumptions, and listen for feelings as well as for facts.

1. Good Listeners Pay Attention

Ex. 20.6

Good listening requires energy. You have to resist distractions and tune out noise (Module 2), whether it's another conversation nearby or worry about your parking meter expiring.

You can do several things to avoid listening errors caused by not paying attention:

- Before the conversation, use your PAIBOC analysis to anticipate the information you need. Make a list of your questions. When is the project due? What resources do you have? What is the most important aspect of this project from the other person's point of view? During a conversation, listen for answers to your questions.

FIGURE 20.1   **Use PAIBOC to Activate Your Listening**

P	What is the **purpose** of my listening? What do I want or need?
A	What is my role as **audience**? What is my relationship to the speaker? What are the expectations, values, and needs of the speaker?
I	What **information** do I want or need? What do I already know? What do I need to know?
B	What can I get out of listening? What **benefits**? What's in it for me?
O	What **objections** to the speaker, or the content, do I need to ignore or overcome until I hear the entire message?
C	What is the **context** of my listening? Am I listening for information only? Trying to establish or build a relationship? Trying to convince the speaker of my interest and enthusiasm? Trying to find out more about a prospective job?

- At the end of the conversation, check your understanding with the other person. Especially check who does what next.
- During or after the conversation, write down key points that affect deadlines or work assessment.

Ex.
20.5
20.9
21.10 ## 2. Good Listeners Focus on the Other Speaker(s) in a Generous Way

Often we miss meaning because we attend to our own internal monologues.[2] We focus on factors incidental to the topic, or look for flaws: "What an ugly tie." "She sounds like a little girl." "There's a typo in that slide." Often we listen only for the pause that signifies it's our turn to speak, or, as if the discussion were a competition, collect weapons to attack the other speaker. "Ah-ha! You're wrong about *that*!"

Good listeners, in contrast, use enlightened self-interest to block out the noise inside their heads. They focus on the message, not on the messenger's shortcomings. They concentrate on what's in the message for themselves: *What's going on here?*

Good listeners know that even people who are poor speakers may have something worthwhile to say. They realize that they can learn and use something even from people they do not like, or do not agree with. Good listeners

- Focus on the content, on what the speaker says, not his or her appearance or delivery
- Spend time evaluating what the speaker says, not just planning a rebuttal
- Consciously work to learn something from every speaker

3. Good Listeners Avoid Making Assumptions

Each of us brings our own perceptions to the communication process. Many listening errors, therefore, come from making faulty assumptions, based on a natural tendency to focus on our own ego needs and to interpret the speaker's meaning according to our own experiences. Furthermore, we perceive experience through our own cultural biases.

We are socialized to communicate the way we do. People from different cultures speak and listen very differently (Modules 2 and 3). The most adept listeners strive to listen for understanding without making assumptions.[3]

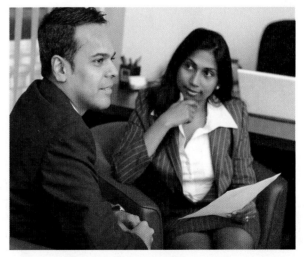

Good listeners pay attention and listen for feelings as well as for facts.

The Chinese character for listening; includes references to the eyes, the ears, and the heart.

Indeed, good listeners wait to ask questions to get and clarify information. Superb salespeople, for example, listen closely to client questions and objections to better identify and respond to the sticking points of a sale. You can avoid listening errors caused by faulty assumptions by doing the following:

- Focus on the other person's background and experiences. Why is this point important to the speaker? What might he or she mean by it? How can its importance to the speaker benefit you?
- Politely query instructions you think are unnecessary. Before you do something else, check with the order giver to see if there is a reason for the instruction.
- Paraphrase what the speaker has said, giving him or her a chance to correct your understanding.

4. Good Listeners Listen for Feelings *and* Facts

Ex. 20.8– 20.10

Sometimes, someone just needs to blow off steam, to vent. Sometimes, people just want to have a chance to express themselves fully: "winning" or "losing" does not matter. Sometimes, people may have objections that they can't quite put into words.

You can learn to avoid listening errors caused by focusing solely on facts by

- Consciously listening for feelings
- Paying attention to tone of voice, facial expression, and body language
- Paraphrasing what the speaker has said and acknowledging the feelings you are observing
- Inviting the other person to speak rather than assuming that silence means consent

LO2 What Is the Difference between Good Listening and Active Listening?

Active listening involves feeding back the literal meaning, or the emotional content, or both.

In **active listening**, receivers actively demonstrate that they've heard and understood by feeding back to the speaker either the literal meaning, or the emotional content, or both. Other techniques in active listening include asking for more information and stating your own feelings.

LO3 After listening without interrupting, use these five strategies to create active responses:

1. Paraphrase the content. Feed back the meaning, as you understand it, in your own words.
2. Mirror the speaker's feelings. Identify the feelings you think you hear.
3. State your own feelings. This strategy works especially well when you are angry (Module 21).

Ex. 20.9 20.10

4. Ask for information or clarification.
5. Ask how you can help.

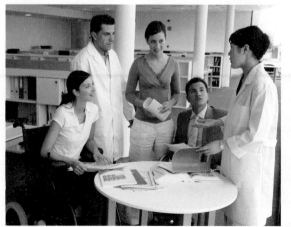

Active listening includes giving feedback.

Instead of mirroring what the other person says, many of us respond to our own needs by attempting to analyze, solve, or dismiss the problem. People with problems need to know, above all, that we hear that they're having a rough time. Table 20.1 lists some of the responses that block communication. Ordering others around or interrogating them tells speakers that the listener doesn't want to hear what they have to say.

TABLE 20.1   **Blocking Responses versus Active Listening**

Blocking Response	Possible Active Response
Ordering, threatening	**Paraphrasing content**
"I don't care how you do it. Just get that report on my desk by Friday."	"You're saying that you don't have time to finish the report by Friday."
Preaching, criticizing	**Mirroring feelings**
"You should know better than to air the department's problems in a general meeting."	"It sounds like the department's problems really bother you."
Interrogating	**Stating one's own feelings**
"Why didn't you tell me that you didn't understand the instructions?"	"I'm frustrated that the job isn't completed yet, and I'm worried about getting it done on time."
Minimizing the problem	**Asking for information or clarification**
"You think that's bad. You should see what I have to do this week."	"What parts of the problem seem most difficult to solve?"
Advising	**Offering to help solve the problem together**
"Well, why don't you try listing everything you have to do and seeing which items are most important?"	"What can I do to help?"

Source: The five responses that block communication are based on a list of twelve in Thomas Gordon and Judith Gordon Sands (1976), *P.E.T. in action* (New York: Wyden): 117–18.

Preaching attacks the other person. Minimizing the problem suggests that the other person's concern is misplaced. Even advising shuts off discussion. Giving a quick answer minimizes what the person feels and puts him or her down for not seeing (what is to us, because it's not our problem) the obvious answer. Even if it is a good answer from an objective point of view, the other person might not be ready to hear it. And sometimes, the off-the-top-of-the-head solution doesn't address the real problem.

Clearly, active listening takes time and energy. Even people who are skilled listeners can't do it all the time, because the listener's feelings interfere with open reception. Furthermore, as experts have pointed out, active listening works only if you genuinely accept the other person's ideas and feelings. Active listening can reduce the conflict that results from miscommunication, but active listening alone cannot reduce the conflict that comes when two people want apparently inconsistent things or when one person wants to change someone else.

The payback (PAIBOC), however, is well worth the effort: active listening is essential to providing the feedback necessary for true meaning exchange (Module 2). Active listening enables you to identify and solve problems. And since you must really pay attention to understand someone else's point of view, active listening helps you identify what motivates the speaker. Active listening, therefore, provides clues to how to influence others and is essential in successful negotiating.[4]

Ex. 20.2

Demonstrating that you are actively listening to customers is part of doing business in our wired world. Today's customers are better informed, and shop with high expectations of both products and services. Most important, customers use the Internet to "control the conversation." They "expect to be heard," and want "individual treatment."[5] And when they feel mistreated, they don't just go elsewhere; they post their negative experiences for a global audience.

Employability Skills

In response, savvy organizations use the Web to welcome conversations with their customers, and to demonstrate that they are listening. Home Depot has "a dedicated team to reply to every message sent to wearelistening@homedepot.com."[6] The CEO of Calgary's Memory Express computer products encourages customers to post comments about his products directly on his website.[7]

LO4 LO5 How Do I Show People That I'm Listening to Them?

Ex. 20.5 20.8– 21.10

Acknowledge their comments in words, in non-verbal symbols, and in actions.

Active listening is a good way to show people that you are listening. Referring to another person's comment is another way: "I agree with Diana that…"

Acknowledgment responses or **conversation regulators**—nods, uh-huhs, smiles, frowns— also help carry the message that you're listening. Remember, however, that listening responses vary from culture to culture.

European Canadians indicate attention and involvement by making eye contact, leaning forward, and making acknowledgment responses. However, as Module 3 shows, some cultures show respect by looking down. In a multicultural workforce, you won't always know whether a colleague who listens silently agrees with what you say or disagrees but is too polite to say so. The best thing to do is to observe the behaviour, without assigning a meaning to it: "You aren't saying much." Then let the other person speak.

Of course, if you go through the motions of active listening but then act with disrespect, people will feel that you have not heard them. When you act on what people say, you reassure them that they have been completely heard.

Can I Use These Techniques If I Really Disagree with Someone?

Ex. 20.5 20.8– 21.10

Most of us do our worst listening when we are in highly charged emotional situations, such as talking with someone with whom we really disagree, getting bad news, or being criticized. But at work, you need to listen even to people with whom you have major conflicts.

At a minimum, good listening enables you to find out why the speaker objects to the programs or ideas you support. Understanding the objections to your ideas is essential if you are to create a persuasive campaign to overcome those objections.

Good listening is crucial when you are being criticized, especially by your boss. You need to know which areas are most important and exactly what kind of improvement counts. Otherwise, you might spend your time and energy changing your behaviour, but changing it in a way not valued by your organization.

Listening can accomplish even more. Listening to people is an indication that you're taking them seriously. If you really listen to the people you disagree with, you show that you respect them. And taking that step may encourage them to respect you and listen to you.

EXPANDING A CRITICAL SKILL

Learning by Listening

The most effective managers lead by listening. Listening for understanding creates environments where people flourish. Indeed, listening to and meeting the needs of their employees distinguishes the cultures of the Greater Toronto Area's best 75 organizations.

Enormous energy, stamina, and curiosity characterize the habits of the best managers. And they draw on these skills ceaselessly, since at least 90 percent of their day is spent communicating. Canadian, American, British, and Swedish managers demonstrate a marked preference for gathering information by word of mouth, and through conversations, telephone calls, and meetings, rather than by reading documents. These managers lead by putting themselves in the centre of the organization's information flow. Listening to "soft" data, including opinions and gossip, allows them to recognize problems and opportunities, make decisions, motivate, and negotiate. To accumulate and disseminate the information necessary to do their jobs, these leaders spend most of their day listening.

You don't have to be in business to start to develop listening skills. While studying for a Business Accounting degree, University of Waterloo student Kim Aitken found it difficult to simultaneously listen to lectures and take notes. Kim began listening to understand the lecturer; instead of taking verbatim notes, Kim started writing down the key ideas so that they made sense to her.

Fortunately, Kim has had plenty of listening practice. In her accounting firm co-op job, Kim had learned that it was important to listen and remember what "partners and seniors would tell me [about] a client or file so as not to have to ask them to repeat themselves later." Kim started to take a note pad with her everywhere, "so that I can not only listen but write down notes for later."

In her third year, Kim applied for and won a coveted place in Waterloo University's School of Accounting and

When I am tutoring, I must listen closely

Finance Fellowship program. As ambassadors for Waterloo and the School of Accounting and Finance program, fellows receive leadership training and opportunities. They must maintain an 80 percent average while tutoring and coaching other students. "When I am tutoring, I must listen closely. We are not there to give students answers; instead, I must encourage students to tell me what they think and then figure out what they know so I can help them discover the answer. I must listen to their questions and pay attention to their thought processes, so as not to confuse them with an explanation they do not understand."

Fellowship Program participants receive a $2000 scholarship for their third and fourth years. Kim's place in the program will be a fine addition to her resumé. Her listening habits will prove a lifetime benefit.

Sources: The honour roll, *Toronto Star*, October 18, 2008 pp. R8-11; Henry Mintzberg, The manager's job: Folklore and fact, http://www.uu.edu/personal/bnance/318/mintz.html, retrieved August 14, 2006: Alex Gillis, BatMan, *National Post*, October 1999, pp.60–69.

MODULE SUMMARY

- Hearing means having the physical ability to perceive sounds. Listening means decoding these sounds and interpreting them the way the speaker intended.

- Good listeners pay attention, focus on the speaker rather than themselves, avoid making assumptions, and listen for feelings as well as facts.

- To avoid listening errors caused by inattention
  - Be conscious of the points you need to know, and listen for them.
  - At the end of the conversation, check your understanding with the speaker.
  - During or after the conversation, make notes: write down key points, deadlines, and evaluation procedures.

- To avoid listening errors caused by self-absorption
  - Focus on what the speaker says, not on his/her appearance or delivery.
  - Focus on understanding and assessing what the speaker says, not on your rebuttal.
  - Consciously work to learn something from every speaker.

- To reduce errors caused by misinterpretation
  - Pay attention to instructions.
  - Assess the speaker's background and experiences: Why is this point important to the speaker?
  - Paraphrase what the speaker's has said, giving him/her a chance to correct your understanding.

- To avoid listening errors caused by focusing solely on the facts
  - Consciously listen for feelings.
  - Pay attention to tone of voice, pauses, facial expression, and body language.
  - Don't ever assume that silence means agreement; invite the other person to speak.

- In active listening, you demonstrate that you have heard and understood a speaker by feeding back the literal meaning, or the emotional meaning, or both. To do this, you can
  - Paraphrase the content
  - Mirror the speaker's feelings
  - State your own feelings
  - Ask for information or clarification
  - Ask how you can help solve the problem

ASSIGNMENTS FOR MODULE 20

Questions for Critical Thinking

20.1 Think about someone who is a good listener. Why do you think this person is a good listener? List all the other qualities this person possesses. How does being a good listener enhance this person's other qualities?

20.2 Based on your own experience(s) describe some of the real-life effects of not listening. Describe what happened when you weren't listening in a work, relationship, or social situation.

20.3 Think about a time when you really felt that another person listened to you and a time when you felt unheard. How did you know the other person was listening? What behaviours and words caused you to feel unheard? What was different in each situation?

20.4 How well do you listen when on the telephone or on Skype? What strategies do you use to help you listen to others when technology enables the conversation?

Exercises and Problems

20.5 Reflecting on Your Own Listening

Keep a listening log for a week. Note how you listened, for how long, what barriers you encountered, and what strategies you used to listen more actively and more effectively. What situations were easiest? Which were most difficult? What cultural assumptions affected how and when you listened? What discourse communities have influenced your listening habits? Which parts of listening do you need to work hardest on?

After you analyze your listening behaviours, create a plan—with specific strategies—to improve your listening skills by 35 percent.

As your instructor directs

a. Share your plan with a small group of fellow students.
b. Present your findings orally to the class.
c. Present your findings in a memo to your instructor.
d. Join with other students to present your findings in a group report or presentation.

20.6 Diagramming Your Active Listening

Choose a class lecture or peer presentation that requires you to listen. Instead of taking linear notes of the speaker's ideas, cluster or mind-map (Module 4) the content.

As your instructor directs

a. Present your findings orally to the class.
b. Share your information with a small group of students in your class.
c. Present your findings in a memo to your instructor, with your cluster diagram.
d. Join with other students to present your findings in a group report or presentation.

20.7 Responding to Expert Opinion

Entrepreneur, author, and business expert Seth Godin gives his opinion of the value of social networking at www.youtube.com/watch?v=r0h0LlCu8Ks. Watch and listen, then summarize Godin's main idea in a single sentence.

Write a response (two to three paragraphs), either supporting or refuting Godin's ideas, and post it on his blog: http://sethgodin.typepad.com. In your argument, include specific examples from your own experience and research.

As your instructor directs

a. Share your writing with a small group of students in your class.
b. Present your opinion in a memo to your instructor.
c. Present your opinions in a group report to the class.

20.8 Interviewing Workers About Listening

Interview an employee or employer (choose an organization where you would like to work) about his or her on-the-job listening. Possible questions include:

- Whom do you listen to as part of your job? Subordinates? Managers? Peers? Customers or clients? Who else?
- How much time a day do you spend listening? What people do you talk to as part of your job? How do you tell whether they are listening?
- What strategies do you use to encourage others to listen to you?

- What strategies do you use to listen effectively?
- What prevents people from listening effectively? What advice do you have on how to listen more accurately?

As your instructor directs

a. Share your information with a small group of students in the class.
b. Present your findings orally to the class.
c. Present your findings in a memo to your teacher.
d. Present your findings in a group report to the class.

20.9 Reflecting on Acknowledgment Responses

Try to be part of at least three conversations involving people from more than one culture. What acknowledgment responses do you observe? Which seem to yield the most positive results? If possible, talk to the other participants about what verbal and non-verbal cues show attentive listening in their cultures.

As your instructor directs

a. Share your information with a small group of students in your class.
b. Present your findings orally to the class.
c. Present your findings in a memo to your instructor.
d. Present your findings in a group report to the class.

20.10 Listening for Understanding

Do this exercise as a class. Let each student complain about something (large or small) that really bothers him or her. Then the next student(s) will

a. Check his or her understanding of what the speaker said
b. Paraphrase the statement
c. Check for feelings that might lie behind the statement
d. Ask questions to clarify the problem

Note: The instructor should choose a group of student "assessors" (four or five) to note and comment on the accuracy of the paraphrasing and questioning responses.

POLISHING YOUR PROSE

Using Colons and Semicolons

Using colons and semicolons can help you to combine sentences efficiently. Indeed, colons and semicolons contribute to a sophisticated writing style. The trick is to learn to use them correctly.

Colons introduce lists, explanations, or qualifications.

> Think of it this way: only the informed citizen can be part of a democracy.

> His best feature was his fairness: all encompassing, just, and charitable.

> CA, CPA, or CMA: after your work placement, you'll have a better idea of which certification would be best for you.

Note that when you use a colon, you need only one complete thought: either before or after the colon.

Semicolons have the same emphasis as periods; however, you can use them only between two complete thoughts. Using a semicolon suggests that the thoughts are connected. Often writers use a transitional word after the colon to emphasize this connection further. The result: the semicolon contributes to the unity and flow of the sentence and allows the reader to write longer sentences without losing readers.

> Jasmine just spent two hours searching for the bill; she's reviewed the customer's last six months, checked for incorrect entries, and done a manual search.

> Toyota cannot keep up with the demand for its hybrid cars; apparently, Canadians have finally woken up and smelled the gas fumes.

> Most people appear delighted to use online banking services; for example, they pay bills, make deposits, and even invest electronically.

Facebook holds plenty of problems for the uninformed: you can be the object of bullying; you can be taken off someone's list; perhaps most important, your past is globally open to any potential employer.

Exercises

Use appropriate punctuation to combine the following sentences:

1. That file on the Richman proposal. Can you send me a copy by tomorrow, please?
2. Ms. Amarotti will arrive tomorrow. Nevertheless, we have enough time to find her a great space.
3. Watch out. Some people think there's a certain "ick" factor to social networking.
4. Take a moment to read the instructions before completing the form. Then bring it to the processing desk
5. Strange. I thought I had already signed up for another six months.
6. Darcy got the promotion he's been working for. Now he's human resources assistant manager.
7. Remember. When we turn on the break room lights, everyone is to yell, "Happy Birthday, Susharita,"
8. You have to make three copies for three different departments. Accounting, legal, and sales.
9. The best gig he ever had was his ten-month posting in Amsterdam. The nightlife is spectacular. Everything's open. Museums, pubs, shops. He was sad to come home.
10. Here's another effective career search question. What do you most enjoy doing?

Check your answers to the odd-numbered exercises in the Polishing Your Prose Answer Key.

Working and Writing in Teams

Learning Objectives

After reading and applying the information in Module 21, you'll be able to demonstrate

Knowledge of

LO1 The ground rules for working well with others

LO2 Roles people play in groups

LO3 The characteristics of successful work teams

Skills to

LO4 Work productively in a team

LO5 Begin to resolve conflicts constructively

LO6 Write collaboratively

MODULE OUTLINE

- What kinds of communication happen in groups?
- What roles do people play in groups?
- How can team members handle conflict?
- How can teams co-author good documents?

Module Summary

Assignments for Module 21

Polishing Your Prose: Delivering Criticism

Employability Skills 2000+ Checklist

Module content builds these Conference Board of Canada Employability Skills 2000+

Communicate

Think and Solve Problems

Demonstrate Positive Attitudes and Behaviours

Be Adaptable

Work with Others

Participate in Projects and Tasks

Teamwork is fundamental to doing business today. People work in teams to create new products, streamline processes, hire employees, identify and solve problems, and brainstorm, articulate, and implement strategic organizational goals. Increasingly, people also work in teams to produce documents.

In an ideal world, we get to work in teams whose members share our values. In reality, we often work with people who hold very different ideas from ours and who believe in the rightness of these ideas as insistently as we do in our own.

LO1 The most effective teams agree on and adopt explicit ground rules and outcomes. Team members operate on two basic behavioural principles: *What gets rewarded gets repeated; what gets measured gets done.*

Table 21.1 lists some of the most common behavioural ground rules used by teams collaborating in the workplace. Table 21.2 lists some of the most common task-focused outcomes for workplace teams.

LO1 **TABLE 21.1   Possible Group Ground Rules**

Start on time; end on time.	Practise NOSTUESO ("No one speaks twice until everyone speaks once").
Come to the meeting prepared.	If you have a problem with another person, tell that person, not everyone else.
Focus comments on the issues.	Communicate immediately if you think you may not be able to fulfil an agreement.
Avoid personal attacks.	If you agree to do something, do it.
Listen to and respect members' opinions.	Everyone must be 70 percent comfortable with the decision and 100 percent committed to implementing it.

Sources: Nancy Schullery and Beth Hoger (1998), *Business advocacy for students in small groups*, Association for Business Communication Annual Convention, San Antonio, November 9–11; An antidote to chronic cantankerousness (1998, February/March), *Fast Company*, 176; John Grossmann (1998, April), We've got to start meeting like this, *Inc.*, 70; Gary Dessler (1998, September), Winning commitment, quoted in *Team Management Briefings*, preview issue, 5; 3M Meeting Network, Groundrules and Agreements, http://www.3M.com/meetingnetwork/readingroom/meetingguide_grndrules.html, retrieved October 25, 2006.

LO1 **TABLE 21.2   Group Task Outcomes**

- Define, articulate, and agree on the goal(s) of the project.
- Describe the goal(s) in writing.
- Create time-management guidelines (**who** does **what, when**) to reach desired goal(s).
- Create measurements that describe both 1) successful products (proposals, interviews, visuals) that work toward the goal and 2) the successful final product (an A+ on the report, the sales contract).
- Ensure every team member has a copy of the goals, the timeline, individual responsibilities, and the criteria for success.

What Kinds of Communication Happen in Groups?

Employability Skills

Different messages occur at different points in a group's development.

Group messages fall into three categories: both *informational* messages and *procedural* messages relate to getting the task done; *interpersonal* messages focus on maintaining group norms and fostering group cohesion.

1. **Informational messages** focus on content: the problem or challenge, data, and possible solutions.
2. **Procedural messages** focus on method and process. How will the group make decisions? Who will do what? When will assignments be due?
3. **Interpersonal messages** focus on people, promoting friendliness, cooperation, and group loyalty.

Different messages dominate during the various stages of group development.

During **orientation**, when members meet and begin to define their task, people who want to work well together consciously communicate in ways that foster mutuality and interdependence. Group members work toward some sort of social cohesiveness and develop procedures for meeting and acting. Interpersonal and procedural messages reduce the tension that exists in a new group. Insisting on information at this stage of the process can impede the group's productivity.

LO4 Conflicts almost always arise when the group chooses a leader and defines the problem. In this **formation** phase, people use interpersonal communication to resolve the conflicts that surface. Good leaders clarify procedures and roles, so that each person understands what he or she is supposed to do. Successful groups define, analyze, and agree on the problem carefully before they begin to search for solutions.

Coordination is the longest phase, during which most of the group's work is done. Procedural and interpersonal communications maintain the trust necessary to gather and focus on the task information. Creative conflict reoccurs as the group members debate alternative solutions.

In **formalization,** the group seeks consensus. In this stage, the group tries to forget earlier conflicts as members focus on agreeing to the solution. The success of this phase determines how well the group's decision will be implemented.

Developing team unity depends on understanding different cultural values. Collective (high-context) cultures (Module 3) focus more strongly on relationship building (the formation and coordination stages) to ensure mutual understanding and respect among team members. Establishing and fostering this respect are vital processes for team productivity.

Indeed, businesses that incorporate the group dynamics of collective cultures enjoy higher employee retention and productivity rates. The "network group" adapts "Aboriginal community-building concepts such as talking circles, collective decision making, holistic approaches to life, cooperation, and respect for others and respect of self" to retain valuable Aboriginal employees. In our increasingly diverse and complex workplace, building relationships must be the first order of team business.[1]

Eagle's Flight® provides experiential training for the global business community. Here, participants work in a map-based adventure designed to teach the critical roles of team planning and fluid execution.

Talking circles help to build the relationships that make teams work.

Technology also contributes to building workplace relationships, as interactive media replace traditional communication methods. Company-managed social networking sites and blogs foster a sense of community, and let even the most reticent employee voice his or her concerns. The success of McDonald's Station M., created as "an online meeting place for…staff…feedback and engagement" has surpassed management's expectations: "more than 14,000" crew members "from all over North America" log in daily to chat, ask questions, or give/get peer advice.[2] More and more organizations are using digital media as a team-building tool.

LO2 What Roles Do People Play in Groups?

Ex. 21.4 21.5 21.12

People play both group maintenance and task roles, and every role can be positive or negative.

Employability Skills

Positive *maintenance* roles and actions that help the group build loyalty, resolve conflicts, and function smoothly to achieve task goals include:[3]

- *Listening actively*: Showing group members that they have been heard and that their ideas are being taken seriously (Module 20)
- *Encouraging participation*: Demonstrating openness and acceptance, recognizing the contributions of members, calling on quieter group members
- *Relieving tensions*: Joking and suggesting breaks and activities
- *Checking feelings*: Asking members how they feel about group activities and sharing one's own feelings with others
- *Solving interpersonal problems*: Opening discussion of interpersonal problems in the group and suggesting ways to solve them

Positive roles and actions that help the group achieve its *task* goals include:

- *Seeking information and opinions*: Asking questions, identifying gaps in the group's knowledge
- *Giving information and opinions*: Answering questions, providing relevant information
- *Summarizing*: Restating major points, pulling ideas together, summarizing decisions
- *Evaluating*: Comparing group processes and products to standards and goals
- *Coordinating*: Planning work, giving directions, and fitting together contributions of group members

Negative roles and actions that hurt the group's *products* and *processes* include:

- *Blocking*: Disagreeing with everything proposed. Criticizing ideas is necessary if the group is to produce the best solution, but criticizing every single idea without suggesting possible solutions blocks a group.
- *Dominating*: Trying to run the group by ordering, shutting out others, and insisting on one's own way. Active listening strategies (Module 20) build relationships, defuse conflict, and encourage participation. Authoritarian, tyrannical people don't just alienate others; they reduce or eliminate productivity.
- *Clowning*: Making unproductive jokes and diverting the group from the task. Jokes can defuse tension and make the group more creative, but too many or inappropriate jokes can frustrate or offend team members, or impede progress.
- *Withdrawing*: Being silent in meetings, not contributing, not helping with the work, not attending meetings. Silently listening encourages others to contribute; passive-aggressive behaviours can create a dysfunctional team.

Leadership in Groups

You may have noted that "leader" was not one of the roles listed above. Leadership is based on communication and interpersonal effectiveness. Several studies have shown that people who talk a lot, listen effectively, and respond non-verbally to other members in the group are considered leaders.[4]

Being a leader, however, does not mean doing all the work yourself. Indeed, someone who implies that he or she has the best ideas and can do the best work is likely playing the negative roles of blocking and dominating.

Effective groups balance three kinds of leadership, which parallel the three group development dimensions:

1. **Informational leaders** generate and evaluate ideas and text.
2. **Interpersonal leaders** monitor the group's process, check people's feelings, and resolve conflicts.
3. **Procedural leaders** set the agenda, make sure that everyone knows what's due for the next meeting, communicate with absent group members, and check to be sure that assignments are carried out.

Although it's possible for one person to take on all these responsibilities, in many groups, three (or more) different people take on the three kinds of leadership. Some groups formally or informally rotate or share these responsibilities, so that everyone—and no one—is a leader. Groups that rotate or share leadership roles are more productive, because more members assume responsibility for the group's success.

LO3 Characteristics of Successful Student Groups

Ex.
21.1
21.3
21.6
21.12

A case study of six student groups completing class projects found that students in successful groups were not necessarily more skilled or more experienced than students in less successful groups. Instead, successful and less successful groups communicated differently in three ways:[5]

1. In the successful groups, the leader set clear deadlines, scheduled frequent meetings, and dealt directly with conflict that emerged in the group. In less successful groups, members had to ask the leader what they were supposed to be doing. The less successful groups met less often, and they tried to pretend that conflicts didn't exist.
2. The successful groups listened to criticism and made important decisions together. Perhaps as a result, everyone in the group could articulate the group's goals. In the less successful groups, a subgroup made decisions and told other members what had been decided.
3. The successful groups had a higher proportion of members who worked actively on the project. The successful groups even found ways to use members who didn't like working in groups. For example, one student who didn't want to be a "team player" functioned as a "freelancer" for her group, completing assignments by herself and giving them to the leader. The less successful groups had a much smaller percentage of active members and each had some members who did very little on the final project.

A Question of Ethics

In the age of "citizen journalism," anyone with a cell phone can capture any incident, anytime, anywhere, and then post the record for the world to comment on.

What ethical concerns would you have before recording and posting an unflattering portrait of someone—a teacher, peer, or stranger?

Student groups produce better projects when they openly disagree over substantive issues of content and document design. The disagreement does not need to be angry: a group member can simply say, "Yes, and here's another way we could do it." Deciding between two (or more) alternative options forces the group member to explain the rationale for an idea. Even when the group adopts the original idea, considering alternatives rather than quickly accepting the first idea produces better writing.[6]

Writer Kimberly Freeman found that the students who spent the most time meeting with their groups had the highest grades—on individual as well as on group assignments.[7]

Peer Pressure and Groupthink

Groupthink is the tendency for groups to put such a high premium on agreement that they directly or indirectly punish dissent. Groups whose members never express conflict may be experiencing groupthink. Groups that "go along with the crowd" and suppress conflict ignore the full

EXPANDING A CRITICAL SKILL

Leading with Integrity

According to Harvard Business School professor Amy Edmondson, teams fail because: 1) some members don't believe their knowledge is interesting or relevant, 2) people are oblivious to others members' opposing interests, and 3) some members deliberately withhold information. Conversely, people who work together well tend to consult one another openly, honestly, and frequently. Members of successful teams act with integrity: they take responsibility for both task and maintenance functions; they tend to share power; and as team leaders or members, they act on the assumption that every person has a valuable contribution to make to the team.

In their book, *Integrity Works*, authors Adrian Telford and Dana Gostick identify ten behaviours that characterize leaders with integrity:

- You know that the little things count
- You find the white when others see the grey
- In a situation you mess up, you fess up
- You create a culture of trust
- You keep your word
- You care about the greater good
- You're honest but modest
- You act as if you're being watched
- You hire integrity
- You stay the course

You can begin to lead your team with integrity by putting some of these behaviours into action:

- *Smile*: Get to know the other members of your group as individuals. Invite members to say something about themselves, perhaps what job they're hoping to get and one fact about their lives outside schoolwork.
- *Share*: Tell people about your own work style and obligations, and ask others to share their styles and obligations. Savvy group members play to each other's strengths and devise strategies for dealing with differences. The earlier you know what those differences are, the easier it will be to deal with them.
- *Suggest*: "Could we talk about what we see as our purposes in this presentation?" "One of the things we need to do is…" "One idea I had for a project is…" Presenting your ideas as suggestions gets the group started without suggesting that you expect your views to prevail.
- *Think*: Leaders look at the goal and identify the steps needed to get there. "Our proposal is due in two weeks. Let's list the tasks we need to do in order to write a rough draft."
- *Volunteer*: Volunteer to take notes, to gather some of the data the group will need, or to prepare the charts after the data are in. Volunteer, not just for the interesting parts of the job (such as surfing the Web to find visuals for your presentation), but for some of the dull but essential work, such as proofreading.
- *Ask*: Bring other people into the conversation. Learn about their knowledge, interests, and skills so that you'll have as much as possible to draw on as you complete your group projects.

Sources: Amy C. Edmondson, James R. Dillon, and Kathryn S. Roloff (2006), *Three perspectives on team learning outcome improvement, task mastery, and group process*, Harvard Business School website, www.hbs.edu/research/pdf/07-029.pdf, retrieved September 13, 2012; Jared Sandberg (2004, October 1), Teamwork: When it's a bad idea, *Globe and Mail*, C7; Harvey Schachter (2005, June 15), Where integrity leads, and where it lags, *Globe and Mail*, C3.

range of alternatives, seek only information that supports the positions they already favour, and fail to prepare contingency plans to cope with foreseeable setbacks. A business suffering from groupthink may launch a new product that senior executives support but for which there is no demand. Student groups suffering from groupthink turn in inferior documents.

The best correctives to groupthink are the following:

- Brainstorm for additional alternatives.
- Test assumptions against those of a range of other people.
- Encourage disagreement, perhaps even assigning someone to be "devil's advocate."
- Protect the right of people in a group to disagree.

LO5 How Can Team Members Handle Conflict?

Ex.
21.1–
21.3
21.12

Listen actively to get at the real issue and repair bad feelings.

Conflicts will arise in any group of intelligent people who care about the task. Many of us feel so uncomfortable with conflict that we pretend it doesn't exist. However, unacknowledged conflicts rarely go away: they fester, impeding progress and productivity.

Try the following ways to reduce the number of conflicts in a group:

- Make responsibilities and ground rules clear at the beginning
- Acknowledge verbal and non-verbal messages of discomfort, anger, or hostility
- Discuss problems as they arise, rather than letting them fester until people explode
- Realize that group members are not responsible for each other's feelings

Table 21.3 suggests several possible solutions to frequent sources of group conflict. Often the symptom arises from a feeling of not being respected or appreciated by the group. Problems can be averted if people advocate for their ideas in a positive way. The best time to advocate for an idea is when the group has not yet identified all possible options, seems dominated by one view, or seems unable to choose among solutions. A tactful way to advocate for the position you favour is to recognize the contributions others have made, to summarize, and then to hypothesize: "What if…?" "Let's look six months down the road." "Let's think about this."[8]

Groups whose members take the time necessary to analyze and agree on the task, objectives, and group norms (expected, acceptable, and unacceptable behaviours) have less destructive conflict. Many groups articulate these objectives and behaviours in a contract, with defined rewards and penalties, which all members sign.

Steps in Conflict Resolution

Negotiating and resolving conflict start with active listening (Module 20). Dealing successfully with conflict requires attention to both the issues and to people's feelings, which you cannot understand unless you stop talking and listen. Taking notes helps you focus your listening.[9] Then follow this five-step procedure to help you resolve conflicts constructively:

1. Make Sure That the People Involved Really Disagree

Sometimes someone who's under a lot of pressure may appear upset. But the speaker may just be **venting** anger and frustration; he or she may not in fact be angry with the person who receives the explosion. One way to find out whether a person is just venting is to ask, "Is there something you'd like me to do?"

2. Check to See That Everyone's Information Is Correct

Sometimes different conversational styles (Module 3) or cultural differences create apparent conflicts when no real disagreement exists. Similarly, misunderstanding can arise from faulty assumptions. Ask open questions (*Who? What? Why? When? Where? How?*) to clarify concerns.

TABLE 21.3   Troubleshooting Group Problems

Behaviour	Possible Solutions
We can't find a time to meet that works for all of us.	a. Find out why people can't meet at certain times. Some reasons suggest their own solutions. For example, if someone has to stay home with small children, perhaps the group could meet at that person's home. b. Assign out-of-class work to "committees" to work on parts of the project. c. Meet virtually to share, discuss, and revise drafts.
One person isn't doing his or her fair share.	a. Ask for information. Is the person overcommitted? Does he or she feel unappreciated? You'd solve those different problems in different ways. b. Early on, do things to build group loyalty. Get to know each other as writers and as people. Sometimes, do something interesting together. c. Encourage the person to contribute. "Maria, what do you think?" "Savio, which part of this would you like to draft?" Then find something to praise in the work. "Thanks for getting us started." d. If someone misses a meeting, assign someone else to bring the person up to speed. People who miss meetings for legitimate reasons (job interviews, illness) but don't find out what happened may become less committed to the group. e. Consider whether strict equality is the most important criterion. On a given project, some people may have more knowledge or time than others. Sometimes the best group product results from letting people do different amounts of "work." f. Even if you divide the work, make all decisions as a group: what to write about, which evidence to include, what graphs to use, what revisions to make. People excluded from decisions become less committed to the group.
I seem to be the only one in the group who cares about quality.	a. Find out why other members "don't care." If they received low grades on early assignments, stress that good ideas and attention to detail can raise grades. Perhaps the group should meet with the instructor to discuss what kinds of work will pay the highest dividends. b. Volunteer to do extra work. Sometimes people settle for something that's "just OK" because they don't have the time or resources to do excellent work. They might be happy for the work to be done—if they didn't have to do it themselves. c. Be sure that you're respecting what each person can contribute. Group members sometimes withdraw when one person dominates and suggests that he or she is "better" than other members.
People in the group don't seem willing to disagree. We end up going with the first idea suggested.	a. Appoint someone as "devil's advocate." b. Brainstorm so you have several possibilities to consider. c. After an idea is suggested, have each person in the group suggest a way it could be improved. d. Have each person in the group write a draft. It's likely the drafts will be different, and you'll have several options to mix and match. e. Talk about ways to offer positive and constructive feedback. Sometimes people don't disagree because they're afraid other group members won't tolerate disagreement.
One person just criticizes everything.	a. Ask the person to follow up the criticism with a suggestion for improvement. b. Talk about ways to express criticism tactfully. "I think we need to think about X" is more tactful than "You're wrong." c. If the criticism is about ideas and writing (not about people), value it. Ideas and documents need criticism to improve them.

3. Discover the Needs Each Person Is Trying to Meet

Sometimes identifying the real need makes it possible to see a new solution. The **presenting problem** (the subject of the conflict) may or may not be the real problem. For example, a worker who complains about the hours he's putting in may in fact be complaining not about the hours themselves but about not feeling appreciated. A supervisor who complains that the other supervisors don't invite her to meetings may really feel that the other managers don't accept her as a peer.

Sometimes people have trouble seeing beyond the problem because they've been taught to suppress their anger, especially toward powerful people. One way to tell whether the presenting problem is the real problem is to ask, "If this were solved, would I be satisfied?" If the answer is no, then the problem that presents itself is not, in fact, the real problem. Solving the presenting problem won't solve the conflict. Keep probing until you get to the real conflict.

4. Search for Alternatives

Sometimes people get into conflict because they see too few alternatives. Indeed, people often see only two polarized choices—known as the *either–or logical fallacy*.

Creative people train themselves to think in terms of possibilities—the more the better. This technique, known as **brainstorming**, is an essential part of every step in the problem-solving process!

5. Repair Bad Feelings

Conflict can emerge without anger and without escalating the disagreement, as the next section shows. But if people's feelings have been hurt, the group needs to deal with those feelings to resolve the conflict constructively. Only when people feel respected and taken seriously can they take the next step of trusting others in the group.

Responding to Criticism

Conflict is particularly difficult to resolve when someone else criticizes or attacks us directly. When we are criticized, our natural reaction is to defend ourselves—perhaps by counterattacking. The counterattack prompts the critic to defend him or herself. The conflict escalates, feelings are hurt, and issues get muddied and more difficult to resolve.

Just as resolving conflict depends on identifying the needs each person is trying to meet, dealing with criticism depends on understanding the real concern of the critic. Constructive ways to respond to criticism and get closer to the real concern include:

- Paraphrasing
- Checking for feelings
- Checking for inferences
- Buying time with limited agreement

Paraphrasing

To **paraphrase**, repeat in your own words, in a neutral tone, the verbal content of the critic's message. The purposes of paraphrasing are: 1) to be sure that you have heard the critic accurately, 2) to let the critic know what his or her statement means to you, and 3) to communicate the feeling that you are taking the critic and his or her feelings seriously.

Criticism:	You people are stonewalling my requests for information.
Paraphrase:	You're saying that we don't give you the information you need quickly enough.

Checking for Feelings

When you **check the speaker's feelings**, you identify the emotions that the critic seems to be expressing verbally or non-verbally. The purposes of checking feelings are to try to understand: 1) the critic's emotions, 2) the importance of the criticism for the critic, and 3) the unspoken ideas and feelings that may actually be more important than the voiced criticism.

Criticism:	You people are stonewalling my requests for information.
Feeling check:	You sound pretty angry. Are you angry?

Always *ask* the other person if you are right in your perception. Even the best reader of non-verbal cues is sometimes wrong.

Checking for Inferences

When you **check the inferences** you draw from criticism, you identify the implied meaning of the verbal and non-verbal content of the criticism. You take the statement a step further than the words of the speaker, to try to understand why the person is bothered by the action or attitude under discussion. The purposes of checking inferences are: 1) to identify the real (as opposed to the presenting) problem, and 2) to communicate the feeling that you care about resolving the conflict.

Criticism: You people are stonewalling my requests for information.

Inference: Are you saying that you need more information from our group?

Inferences can be faulty. In the above interchange, the critic might respond, "I don't need more information. I just think you should give it to me without my having to send you three emails every time I want some data."

Buying Time with Limited Agreement

Buying time is a useful strategy for dealing with criticisms that really sting. When you buy time with limited agreement, you avoid escalating the conflict (as an angry statement might do) but also avoid yielding to the critic's point of view. To buy time, restate the part of the criticism that you agree is true. (This is often a fact, rather than the interpretation or evaluation the critic has made of that fact.) *Then let the critic respond, before you say anything else.* The purposes of buying time are: 1) to allow you time to think when a criticism really hits home and threatens you, so that you can respond to the criticism rather than simply reacting defensively, and 2) to suggest to the critic that you are genuinely listening to what he or she is saying.

Criticism: You people are stonewalling my requests for information.

Limited agreement: It's true that the cost projections you asked for last week still aren't ready.

Do *not* go on to justify or explain. A "Yes, but…" statement is not a time-buyer.

You-Attitude in Conflict Resolution

You-attitude (Module 13) means looking at the situation from the audience's point of view, respecting the audience, and protecting the audience's ego. The critical *you* statements that many of us use when we are upset do not illustrate respect for the audience. These statements make recipients feel attacked and defensive, destroying any possibility for dialogue.

In conflict resolution, **I-based** statements **about your own feelings and perceptions** can initiate positive conversation. I-based statements show good you-attitude.

Inflammatory (Lacks positive you-attitude):   You never do your share of the work.

I-based statement: I feel that I'm doing more than my share of the work on this project.

Inflammatory (Lacks positive you-attitude):   Even you should be able to run the report through a spell checker.

I-based statement: I'm not willing to have my name on a report with so many spelling errors. I did lots of the writing, and I don't think I should have to do the proofreading and spell checking, too.

As you answer the questions

- *Be honest*: You won't lose points for reporting that your group had problems or did something "wrong."
- *Show your knowledge of good group dynamics*: That is, if your group did something poorly, show that you know what should have been done. Similarly, if your group worked well, show that you know why it worked well.
- *Be specific*: Give examples or anecdotes to support your claims.

As your instructor directs

a. Discuss these questions with the other group members.

b. Present your findings orally to the class.

c. Present your findings in an individual memo to your instructor.

d. Join with the other group members to write a collaborative memo to your instructor.

POLISHING YOUR PROSE

Delivering Criticism

No one likes to be told that his or her work isn't good. But criticism is necessary if people and documents are to improve.

Depending on the situation, you may be able to use one of these strategies:

1. Notice what's good as well as what needs work.

   The charts are great. We need to make the text as good as they are.

   I really like the ideas you've used in the slides. We need to edit the bulleted points so they're parallel.

2. Ask questions.

   Were you able to find any books and articles, in addition to sources on the Internet?

   What do you see as the most important revisions to make for the next draft?

3. Refer to the textbook or another authority.

   The module on design says that italic type is hard to read.

   Our instructor told us that presentations should have just three main points.

4. Make statements about your own reaction.

   I'm not sure what you're getting at in this section.

   I wouldn't be convinced by the arguments here.

5. Criticize what's wrong, without making global attacks on the entire document or on the writer as a person.

   There are many typos in this draft.

   You begin almost every sentence with "um."

Exercises

Rewrite each criticism to make it less hurtful. You may add or omit information as needed.

1. This is the worst report I've ever seen.
2. My 10-year-old can spell better than you do.
3. I can't believe that you didn't go to the library to get any sources.
4. You've used four different fonts in this report. Didn't you read the book? Don't you know that we're not supposed to use more than two?
5. This design is really lame. It looks like every other brochure I've ever seen.
6. There's no way we'll get a passing grade if we turn this in.
7. Were you asleep? Didn't you hear our instructor say that we had to use at least five sources?
8. This is really creative. You've written the perfect illustration for "How to Fail This Course."
9. This proposal makes no sense.
10. This clip art is sexist. There's no way we should use it.

Check your answers to the odd-numbered exercises in the Polishing Your Prose Answer Key.

Mc Graw Hill connect™

MODULE
22

Planning, Managing, and Recording Meetings

MODULE OUTLINE

- What planning should precede a meeting?
- When I'm in charge, how do I keep the meeting on track?
- What decision-making strategies work well in meetings?
- How can I be an effective meeting participant?
- What should be in meeting minutes?
- What should I know about virtual meetings?

Module Summary

Assignments for Module 22

Polishing Your Prose: Using Hyphens and Dashes

Learning Objectives

After reading and applying the information in Module 22, you'll be able to demonstrate

Knowledge of

LO1 Meeting management

LO2 Opportunities and challenges of virtual meetings

Skills to

LO3 Plan a meeting

LO4 Lead a meeting

LO5 Participate in meetings

LO6 Take good meeting minutes

LO7 Participate in virtual meetings

Employability Skills

2○○+

Employability Skills 2000+ Checklist

Module content builds these Conference Board of Canada Employability Skills 2000+

Communicate

Manage Information

Demonstrate Positive Attitudes and Behaviours

Be Responsible

Be Adaptable

Work with Others

Participate in Projects and Tasks

Although meetings have always made up the largest proportion of the average manager's day, emphasis on teamwork and collaboration (Module 21) translates into even more frequent meetings for all employees. Furthermore, technological innovation, environmental concerns, and fossil fuel depletion will increase people's time in virtual, rather than face-to-face meetings. Regardless of the meeting medium, when people perceive their meetings as organized, with productive results, they feel their time is well spent.[1]

Business, non-profit, and government organizations hold several types of meetings:

- **Informal**, **one-on-one**, or **town hall meetings** are the most significant meetings; people see them as an opportunity to exchange meaningful information. Employees talk by the photocopier or the refrigerator. One person walks into a colleague's office or cubicle to ask a question. A supervisor stops to chat with an employee, to ask how things are going and thereby manages by "walking around." These informal meetings create or reinforce company culture, support networking, and can facilitate career advancement.

  Indeed, according to experts, informal meetings that include gossip serve as vital organizational arteries; gossip "can be a powerful way to spread information, boost bonding and morale, and release stress… [G]ossip in the office, over the Internet or on the phone … causes us to relax … and tell[s] [us] something about the underlying" organizational culture.[2]

- **Team meetings** bring people together to manage projects, solve problems, and collaborate on documents (Module 21). Recorded agendas and minutes formalize these meetings.
- **Regular staff meetings** provide information, announce new policies and products, answer questions, share ideas, and motivate people. Recorded agendas and minutes formalize these meetings.
- Other frequent **organizational** meetings include **sales meetings**, **staff training sessions**, **conventions**, and **retreats**. These sessions allow people to develop themselves professionally, to team-build, and/or to do long-range planning.
- **Parliamentary proceedings** are the most formal types of meetings, run according to strict rules, like those summarized in *Robert's Rules of Order*. These meetings are common only for boards of directors and legislative bodies.

Meetings today are usually supported by technology. Some organizations display proceedings for all the participants to

Many important meetings are informal.

see. "People literally see themselves being heard. Related comments are identified, linked, and edited on screen. The digressions and tangents quickly become apparent." The resulting document can be posted on the company intranet for further discussion and comments.[3]

Other organizations use group support software, such as Google Docs or Dropbox. Speakerphones, conference calls, and VoIP software like Skype allow people in different, even remote locations to participate in the same conversation; Google Voice's hangout lets eight to ten people "meet" virtually and simultaneously. And blogging allows a "chairperson" to initiate a worldwide cyber-meeting, and air his or her opinion without interruption.

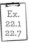
Ex.
22.1
22.7

Regardless of the sophistication of the technology, meetings are about content: the meeting's purposes, people, place, and timing affect outcomes. As either initiator or attendee, you can arrange more productive meetings.

LO1 LO3 What Planning Should Precede a Meeting?

Identify your purpose(s), and create an agenda.

Employability Skills

Identify Your Purpose

Meetings can have at least six purposes:

- To share information
- To brainstorm ideas
- To evaluate ideas
- To make decisions
- To create a document
- To motivate members

When meetings combine two or more purposes, it's important to make the purposes explicit. For example, in the meeting of a university student government, some items are presented for information. Discussion is possible, but the group will not be asked to make a decision. Other items are presented for action; the group will be asked to vote.

A business meeting might specify that the first half-hour will be allotted for brainstorming, with the second half-hour devoted to evaluation. Telling participants how their input will be used clarifies expectations and focuses the conversation.

FIGURE 22.1 **Use PAIBOC Analysis to Plan Successful Meetings**

P	Why are you holding/attending the meeting? What is the **purpose**? What specific outcomes do you want/need?
A	Who is **attending**? Why? What is your relationship to attendees? What are their expectations, values, and needs? What action(s) do you want/expect from attendees? How can you expect them to react? If it's a virtual meeting, what technology will maximize participation?
I	What **information** do people already know? What do they need to know for you to achieve your intended purpose(s)? What's the best way to prepare them?
B	How can participating in the meeting **benefit** your attendees? What's in it for them? Who else will benefit from the meeting, should you realize your purpose(s)?
O	What **objections** might attendees have to the meeting content, time, length, medium, outcome(s), or to you? How can you overcome or reduce these objections?
C	What is the meeting **context**? How long is the meeting? What time is the meeting? How will the meeting length and time of day affect attendees and outcome? What economic, environmental, political, and organizational realities will influence attendees' attitudes, feelings, and beliefs? How can you use technology to realize your intended outcomes?

Intel's agendas also specify *how* decisions will be made. The company uses four different decision-making processes:

- **Authoritative**: The leader makes the decision alone
- **Consultative**: The leader hears group comments but then makes the decision alone
- **Voting**: The majority wins
- **Consensual**: Discussion continues until everyone can "buy into" the decision[4]

The most successful peer-group team meetings use consensual decision making and share leadership roles (Module 21).

LO3 Create an Agenda

Ex. 22.5 22.7

Once you've identified your purposes, think about how you can make them happen. Your meeting **agenda** should be a blueprint of your expectations and objectives.

If you want a participatory meeting

1. Make sure attendees receive all the necessary information before the meeting
2. Make your expectations clear: ask people to read materials in advance
3. Ask people to bring required materials and information to the meeting

Distribute your agenda several days before the meeting. (*Agenda* is Latin for "to be done.") If possible, give participants a chance to comment; then revise the agenda in response to those comments. A good agenda answers five questions:

- **Where and when**: Time and place of the meeting
- **What**: Agenda items
- **Why**: Each item flagged for purpose—information, discussion, or decision
- **Who**: Participants and individuals sponsoring or introducing each item
- **How**: Meeting duration and time allotted for each item

Figure 22.2 shows an example of a meeting agenda.

Many groups put routine items first because getting agreement will be easy. Schedule controversial items early in the meeting for two important reasons: 1) people's energy levels are high, and 2) people have enough time for full discussion. Giving a controversial item only half an hour at the end of the meeting leads people to suspect that the leaders are trying to manipulate them.

FIGURE 22.2 **Sample Meeting Agenda**

Agenda

September 9, 2013
3 to 5 p.m. Conference Room

3:00–3:15	Budget report	MV
3:15–4:00	Project updates	All
4:15–4:20	New hire update	MV
4:20–4:40	Marketing/promotion ideas	All
4:40–5:00	New business	All

LO3 The best meetings encourage participation, creativity, and fun. If you are organizing a long meeting, a training session or conference, for example, make time for networking and socializing. These activities are vital to participants' perceptions of the value of the meeting. Allow for short breaks at least every two hours and generous breaks twice a day so participants can chat informally with each other. Include some social functions so people can get to know each other.

You might want to leave five minutes at the end of the meeting to evaluate it. What went well? What could be better? What do you want to change next time?

LO4 When I'm in Charge, How Do I Keep the Meeting on Track?

Pay attention both to task and to process.

Your goal as chair is to clarify the meeting's significance and goals, and help participants deal with agenda items adequately and in a timely manner.

- When people are new to the group, make the ground rules explicit (Module 21). Ground rules might cover whether it is acceptable to check email, send messages, or answer cell phones during the meeting, and whether people must stay for the whole meeting or may drop in and out.
- Introduce newcomers and each person as he or she covers an agenda item.
- Use positive reinforcements—seeking opinions, giving information, summarizing, evaluating, and coordinating (Module 21)—to remind the group of its progress: "We're a bit behind schedule. Let's try to get through the committee reports quickly."
- Acknowledge and negotiate conflict; shape the discussion or summarize issues when the issues are complex, or when members have major disagreements: "We're really talking about two things: whether the change would save money and whether our customers would like it. Does it make sense to keep those two together, or could we talk about customer reaction first and then deal with the financial issues?"
- If the issue is contentious, ask speakers for and against a recommendation to take turns speaking. If no one remains on one side, you can stop the discussion.
- Pay attention to people and process. In small groups, invite everyone to speak.
- If conflict escalates, focus on ways the group could deal with the conflict (Module 21) before getting back to the issue.
- If the group doesn't formally vote, summarize the group consensus after each point so that everyone knows what the decision is, who is responsible for implementing it or following up, and what the deadlines are.

LO1 What Decision-Making Strategies Work Well in Meetings?

Try the standard agenda or dot planning.

Probably the least effective decision-making strategy is to let the person who talks first, last, loudest, or most make the decision. Voting is quick but may leave people in the minority unhappy with and uncommitted to the majority's plan.

Coming to consensus takes time but results in speedier implementation of ideas. Two strategies that are often useful in organizational groups are the standard agenda and dot planning.

The **standard agenda** is a seven-step decision-making process for solving problems:

1. Clarify and reach agreement on the task: what the group has to deliver, in what form, by what due date. Identify available resources.
2. Identify and reach agreement on the problem or the situation: What question is the group trying to answer? What exactly is the issue?
3. Gather information, share it with all group members, and examine it critically.
4. Establish criteria: What would the ideal solution include? Which elements of that solution would be part of a less-than-ideal but still acceptable solution? What legal, financial, ethical, or other limitations might keep a solution from being implemented?
5. Generate alternative solutions: Brainstorm and record ideas for the next step.
6. Measure the alternatives against the criteria.
7. Choose the best solution.[5]

You can apply the standard agenda decision-making process in any personal and professional decision-making situation.

Dot planning offers a way for large groups to choose priorities quickly.

1. First, the group brainstorms ideas, recording each on pages that are put on the wall.
2. Each individual gets three to five adhesive dots in two colours. One colour represents high priority, the other lower priority.
3. People walk up to the pages and place dots beside the points they care most about. Some groups allow only one dot from one person on any one item; others allow someone who is passionate about an idea to put all of his or her dots on it.

As Figure 22.3 shows, the dots make it easy to see which items the group believes are most important.

FIGURE 22.3   Dot Planning Allows Groups to Set Priorities Quickly

Here, green dots mean "high priority"; blue dots mean "low priority." Group members can see at a glance which items have widespread support, which are controversial, and which are low priority.

Source: Christopher Caggiano, The color-coded priority setter, *Inc.*, June 1, 1995, pp. 70–71. Retrieved September 18, 2009 from http://www.inc.com/magazine/19950601/2300.html.

LO5 How Can I Be an Effective Meeting Participant?

Be prepared.

In a small meeting, you'll probably get several chances to speak. Research indicates that the most influential people in a meeting are those who say something in the first five minutes of the meeting (even just to ask a question), who talk most often, and who talk at greatest length.[7]

Prepare for meetings:

- Read the materials distributed before the meeting; think about the discussion topics.
- Bring those materials to the meeting, along with note-taking tools. (Taking notes enhances recall, and your notes may capture important nuances that meeting minutes do not).
- Arrive on time: five to ten minutes early. Your timely attendance shows respect for other participants, and for the meeting content. And you get your choice of seats; the best place is directly opposite the meeting chairperson because 1) you can make direct eye contact, and 2) you can observe subtle non-verbal messages.

Ex. 22.6

In a large meeting, you may get just one chance to speak. Make notes of what you want to say so that you can be concise, correct, and complete.

LO6 What Should Be in Meeting Minutes?

Minutes should include attendees' names, discussion topics, and action items: lists of who does what next.

Meeting expert Michael Begeman suggests recording three kinds of information:

1. Decisions reached
2. Action items, where someone needs to implement or follow up on something
3. Open issues—issues raised but not resolved[8]

EXPANDING A CRITICAL SKILL

Building an Online Community

People spend more time meeting virtually than on any other Internet activity. Social media sites are now "the number one platform for creating and sharing content";[6] and as blogs and Wikis become even more sophisticated digital applications, users' demand for participation in online communities will increase. And for employee communication, that's a good thing.

Organizations can use digital media to build an online community of interdependent teams. As is true of all team building, however, success depends on careful planning. The project managers must consider their purposes, and prospective audiences, content, and culture. When they have decided why they want to encourage virtual networking, companies have to consider how to encourage employees to engage, what content will keep people coming back, what guidelines will communicate appropriate behaviours, who will manage the technological and staffing logistics, and how they will measure success.

Online communities can truly democratize the workplace, facilitate interdisciplinary knowledge sharing, and foster team building. But the community can only be as good as its blueprint and its members.

Sources: Jason Falls, Seven questions to ask before starting an online community; Dave Wilkins and Drew Darnbrough, Developing an online community; Michael Wilson, Best practices for building successful online communities, *IABC CW Bulletin*, 7(4) (April 2009). Retrieved September 18, 2009 from http://www.iabc.com/cwb/archive/2009/0409/#feature1.

Minutes of formal meetings include who was present and absent, the wording of motions and amendments, and the votes. Committee reports are often attached for later reference. For less formal meetings, brief minutes are fine.

The most important items are the decisions and action assignments. Long minutes are most helpful when assignments are set off visually from the narrative:

> We discussed whether we should initiate an online company social network.
>
> **Action:**   Menhua will research options and best practices for next month's meeting.
>
> **Action:**   Sophie will survey employees online to get their opinions.

Most people, however, file meeting minutes under "G" for garbage. If you want to write meeting minutes to be read, keep them to a page or less, write in the active voice, and highlight the most important information (**who** *does* **what, next**).

FIGURE 22.4   **Sample Meeting Minutes**

Finance Team Presentation Meeting, Course FIN 2103: Reports and Presentations	**Agreed**
Tuesday, October 29, 2013, 8–11 a.m., Room C122	Anita introduces speaker.
Present: C. Cardiff, A. Borne, L. Monahan, M. Sidwath	Guest speaks for 3 minutes.
Regrets: None	Anita thanks speaker, does icebreaker, introduces us, gives overview.
Acting Chair: Martina Sidwath	
Acting Secretary: Lawrence Monahan	We give guest bottle of wine, end of presentation.
1. Martina called the meeting to order, and we approved last week's minutes.	In intro, Anita stresses quiz and prizes.
2. New business.	Lawrence introduces short video for his part.
Mohammed asked about the guest speaker: when should the guest speak, for how long, who was taking responsibility for introducing the guest, and what gift would we be giving the speaker. We discussed.	We will all find at least two relevant videos; bring to next week's meeting.
	We rehearse twice after next week's meeting.
3. Old business: a. We discussed how to involve the class. b. We discussed rehearsal dates and times.	Lawrence will to send a copy of the minutes to everyone by 5 p.m. today.
4. We adjourned the meeting at 11 a.m.	

LO2 LO7 What Should I Know About Virtual Meetings?

Be aware of the limitations of your communication medium. For important projects, build in some real meetings as well as some virtual ones. People still prefer to meet face to face.

When you meet technologically, you lose the informal interaction: going to lunch or chatting during a break. These personal meetings create bonds, so that people are more willing to work together. Face-time also gives people a chance to work out many small misunderstandings. However, global environmental and budget concerns mean you'll spend more time in virtual meetings. In response, meeting technology will continue to evolve.[9]

Virtual meetings have their limitations. With email, you lose both tone of voice and body language. In addition, email messages are often more brusque than comments in person (Module 7).

Employability Skills

Audio messages provide tone of voice but not the non-verbal signals that tell you whether someone wants to make a comment or understands what you're saying. Videoconferencing and Skype give you only the picture in the camera's lens. With all of these technologies, you'll need to attend specifically to your interpersonal skills: active listening, encouraging participation, positive team roles, and negotiating conflict.

Differences among national cultures create "significant challenges" for global virtual teams.[10] Culture and management consultants Salvador Apud and Talis Apud-Martinez maintain that team success depends not only on "a knowledgeable multicultural leader…assessment and alignment of both national and organizational cultures, and the proper use of the technology available" but also on an "[i]nitial face-to-face teambuilding meeting."[11]

MODULE SUMMARY

- People in private- and public-sector, for-profit and not-for-profit, and small, medium, and large organizations meet frequently as part of their routine responsibilities.
- If you are calling the meeting, plan carefully to make the meeting productive.
  - Analyze your purpose(s).
  - Consider how you can best engage participants.
  - Determine what meeting medium, what time of day, and what meeting duration would make the meeting most effective.
  - Distribute an agenda ahead of time.
  - State the purpose of the meeting at the beginning.
  - Attend to people and to process as well as to the task.
  - Allow enough time for people to discuss controversial items.
- A good agenda indicates
  - The meeting date, time, and place
  - Items for information, discussion, and decision, and the time allotted for each
  - The person introducing or sponsoring each item

- If you don't take formal votes, summarize the group's consensus after each point. At the end of the meeting, summarize all decisions and action items, and remind the group who is responsible for doing what, when.
- The **standard agenda** is a seven-step process for solving problems. In **dot planning**, group members brainstorm ideas, then each person puts adhesive dots beside the points or proposals he or she cares most about.
- Minutes should record
  - People present
  - Decisions reached
  - Action items, in which someone needs to do something
  - Open issues—topics raised but not resolved
- Participants in virtual meetings have to pay particular attention to their interpersonal skills in order to compensate for the limitations of the technology.

ASSIGNMENTS FOR MODULE 22

Questions for Critical Thinking

22.1 Consider virtual meetings you have been part of: how does the "virtual" aspect affect task and maintenance roles? What additional emphasis, if any, is on your interpersonal skills? What skills must you pay particular attention to, and why?

22.2 Describe the decision-making strategies used in the meetings you attend most frequently. How well do these strategies work?

22.3 In the groups of which you're a member (at school, at work, and in volunteer organizations), what kinds of comments are most valued in meetings?

22.4 What online communities do you belong to? What criteria do you use to decide to join a social network? What career benefits do social networks offer you?

Exercises and Problems

22.5 Writing an Agenda

Write an agenda for your next collaborative group meeting.

As your instructor directs

a. Write a memo to your instructor, explaining the choices you made.
b. Use Google Docs, or any other collaborative software to share your draft agenda with those developed by two other groups.
c. After your group has given and gotten feedback, revise your agenda and present it orally to the rest of the class.

22.6 Taking Minutes

As your instructor directs

Have two or more people take minutes of each class or collaborative group meeting for a week. Using collaborative software, compare the accounts of the same meeting.

- To what extent do they agree on what happened?
- Does one contain information missing in other accounts?
- Do any accounts disagree on a particular fact?
- How do you account for the differences you find?

22.7 Writing a Meeting Manual*

Create a procedures manual for students next term. Describe how to have effective meetings while they work on collaborative projects.

*Adapted from Miles McCall, Beth Stewart, and Timothy Clipson (1998), Teaching communication skills for meeting management, Refereed Proceedings, Association for Business Communication Southwestern United States, Marsha L. Bayless (Nacogdoches, TX), p. 68.

22.8 Planning Scripts for Informal Meetings

Create a script for a 90-second statement to your boss for each of the following:

1. Describe the progress on a project you're working on.
2. Provide an update on a problem the boss already knows about.
3. Tell about a success or achievement.
4. Tell about a problem and ask approval for the action you recommend.
5. Ask for resources you need for a project.
6. Ask for training you'd like to receive.
7. Lay the groundwork for a major request you need to make.

As your instructor directs

a. Discuss your scripts with a small group of students.
b. Present your script to the class.
c. Write a memo to your instructor explaining the choices you have made in terms of content, arrangement, and word choice.

POLISHING YOUR PROSE

Using Hyphens and Dashes

Hyphens and dashes are forms of punctuation used within sentences. Use a hyphen to do the following:

1. Indicate that a word has been divided between two lines.

   Correct: Our biggest competitor announced plans to introduce new models of computers into the European market.

   Divide words only at syllable breaks. If you aren't sure where the syllables break, look up the word in a dictionary. When a word has several syllables, divide it after a vowel or between two consonants.

   Although many word-processing programs automatically hyphenate for you, knowing where and when to divide words is important for words the program may not recognize or for special cases. For instance, don't divide words of one syllable (e.g., *used*), and don't divide a two-syllable word if one of the syllables is only one letter long (e.g., *acre*).

2. Join two or more words used as a single adjective.

   Correct: After a flurry of requests, we are marketing new lines of specialty dinners for Asian- and Jamaican-Canadian customers.

   Order five 10- or 12-metre lengths.

   Here, hyphens prevent misreading. Without the hyphen, readers might interpret *Asian-Canadian* incorrectly as Asian. (Typically, compound adjectives such as *Asian-Canadian* and *Jamaican-Canadian* are not hyphenated when used as nouns.) In the second sentence, five lengths are needed, not lengths of 5, 10, or 12 metres.

3. Use a dash to emphasize a break in thought.

   Correct: Despite our best efforts—which included sending a design team to Paris and increasing our promotional budget—sales are lagging.

Create a dash by typing the hyphen key twice. With some word processors, if you set up the Options that way, this double hyphen will automatically be replaced with a longer, single dash (called an "em dash"), which is used in typesetting. (See it above in the example.)

Exercises

Supply necessary dashes or hyphens in the following sentences. If no punctuation is needed—if a space is correct—leave the parentheses blank.

1. Our biggest competitors( )including those in the Asian and European markets( )introduced more product models during the fourth quarter.
2. Our cutting( )edge fashions sell best in French( ) Canadian cities like Montreal.
3. Please pick up three( )2( )by( )4 posts at the lumberyard.
4. Next Monday, *The Aboriginal Times* magazine will do a cover story on a thriving new business created by Native( )Canadians.
5. Painters from the building( )services department plan to give Tarik's office two( )coats of paint.
6. Our gift certificates come in 5( ), 10( ), and 15( )dollar denominations.
7. The latest weather reports suggest that travel over South( ) and Latin( )America may be interrupted by storms.
8. We need to work on more cost( )effective versions of our best( )selling software( )programs.
9. You can email the results to my office in the early( ) morning.
10. Katrina gave us four( )options during the sales( ) meeting on Friday afternoon.

Check your answers to the odd-numbered exercises in the Polishing Your Prose Answer Key.

Making Oral Presentations

Learning Objectives

After reading and applying the information in Module 23, you'll be able to demonstrate

Knowledge of

LO1 The differences between written and oral messages

LO2 Types of presentations

LO3 The criteria for effective presentations

Skills to

LO4 Reframe written material into an oral presentation

LO5 Plan and deliver oral presentations

LO6 Develop a good speaking voice

LO7 Prepare and deliver group presentations

MODULE OUTLINE

- What kinds of presentations are there?
- What decisions must I make as I plan a presentation?
- How should I organize a presentation?
- How can I create a strong opening and closing?
- How should I use visuals?
- What are the keys to delivering an effective presentation?
- How should I handle questions from the audience?
- What are the guidelines for group presentations?

Module Summary

Assignments for Module 23

Polishing Your Prose: Choosing Levels of Formality

Employability Skills 2000+ Checklist

Module content builds these Conference Board of Canada Employability Skills 2000+

Communicate

Think and Solve Problems

Demonstrate Positive Attitudes and Behaviours

Be Adaptable

Work with Others

Participate in Projects and Tasks

In every new communication situation, you have fewer than 90 seconds to make that first—and lasting—impression. How are you going to make that a positive one? Effective presenters make that 90 seconds work for them.

Most presentations serve more than one purpose, and every presentation contains an element of persuasion: you must know how to attract and hold your audience's attention if you want to achieve your purposes. The best oral presentations inform and influence people positively.

LO2 What Kinds of Presentations Are There?

Ex.
23.6
23.9

Informative presentations inform or teach the audience. For example, health and safety training sessions are primarily informative. Secondary purposes may be to conform to legislation, to meet ISO standards, to persuade employees to follow organizational procedures, and to orient new employees (Module 2).

The goal of most presentations is to get to *yes*.

Persuasive and **sales presentations** motivate the audience to act or to believe. Giving information and evidence persuades through appeals to credibility and reason (Module 10). The speaker must also build goodwill by appearing trustworthy and sensitive to the audience's needs.

In business presentations, speakers want to persuade the audience to buy their product, proposal, or idea. Sometimes the goal is to change attitudes and behaviours, or to reinforce existing attitudes. Thus, a speaker at a workers' compensation and benefits information meeting might stress the importance of following safety procedures; a speaker at a city council meeting might talk about the problem of homelessness in the community to try to build support for homeless shelters.

As Thornhill, Ontario, brothers Craig and Marc Kielburger—founders of Me to We and Free the Children—know, all successful presentations are persuasive.

Goodwill presentations entertain and validate the audience. In an after-dinner speech, the audience wants to be entertained. Presentations at sales meetings may be designed to stroke the audience members' egos and to validate their commitment to organizational goals.

Regardless of the presentation purpose, the best presenters work the three Ps: plan, prepare, and practise:

1. **Plan** a strategy by analyzing the situation (PAIBOC analysis, Figure 23.1)
2. **Prepare** stories and examples relevant to your audience
3. **Practise** until you are completely comfortable with the content

All this preparation increases confidence and reduces the anxiety most speakers feel.

FIGURE 23.1   PAIBOC Questions to Plan Powerful Presentations

P	What is the **purpose** of your presentation? What do you want to happen because of your presentation? What do you want your audience to think, say, or do?
A	Who is your **audience**? What do they already know? What do they need to know? What do they care about? What will motivate them to do as you want? How do members of your audience differ? What cultural/corporate values and norms shape their perceptions? How can you grab your audience's attention positively? What's in it for them?
I	What is your key message? What idea do you want the audience members to take away with them? What do you have to say that is important to them? How can you make the **information** relevant and achieve your purpose(s)? How long is your presentation? What information can you omit?
B	What **benefits** does your message offer the audience? How can you highlight these benefits?
O	What **objections** will your audience have to your message? How will you overcome those objections? What are the negative aspects of your message? How can you de-emphasize, compensate for, or overcome these negatives?
C	What is the **context** of your message? What economic, environmental, professional, and/or personal realities will affect how your audience perceives your message? What time of day is your presentation? In what kind of room is it? How can you make your presentation interactive, engaging, and stimulating? What technology will you use, and why?

LO1 LO4 What Decisions Do I Need to Make as I Plan a Presentation?

Choose your main point, the kind of presentation, and ways to involve your audience.

An oral presentation needs to be simpler than a written message to the same audience. Identify the one idea—or critical takeaway—you want the audience to remember. Then phrase your idea so that it offers a specific benefit to the audience.

Employability Skills

Weak:	The purpose of my presentation is to discuss saving for retirement.
Better:	The purpose of my presentation is to persuade my audience to put their retirement funds in stocks and bonds, not in money market accounts and GICs.
Or:	The purpose of my presentation is to explain how to calculate how much money someone needs to save in order to maintain a specific lifestyle after retirement.

Note: Your purpose is *not* the introduction of your talk; it is the principle that guides your decisions as you plan your presentation.

Ex.
23.5
23.6
23.9

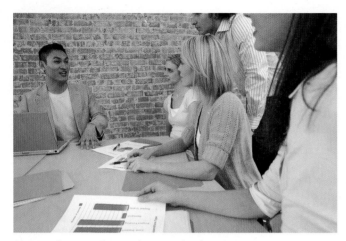

Always tell your audience what's in it for them.

Now reinforce that idea through clarity, repetition, and emphasis:

- Simplify your supporting detail so it's easy to follow
- Use visuals that can be taken in at a glance
- Choose concrete words and brief sentences that are easy to understand

Analyze your audience for an oral presentation just as you do for a written message. If you'll be speaking to co-workers, talk to them about your topic or proposal to find out what questions or objections they have. For audiences inside the organization, the biggest questions are often practical ones: Will it work? How much will it cost? How long will it take?[1]

And always answer for your audience: What's in it for them?

Before you begin planning your presentation, you need to know *for how long*, *where*, and *when* you will be speaking. Your time and the audience's expectations shape both the content and the kind of presentation you will give. The size and comfort of the room will affect the success of your presentation, as will the time of day.

What size is the room? What equipment will be available? Will the audience be tired at the end of a long day of listening? Sleepy after a big meal? Will the group be large or small? The more you know about your audience and your environment, the better you can shape your presentation for maximum persuasive impact. And that knowledge is power: the more you know, the more in control you will feel.

LO2 Choosing the Kind of Presentation

When you have identified your *purpose*, including the results you want to achieve, analyzed your audience's needs, and considered your time, you can decide on the kind of presentation you will give. Table 23.1 identifies the speaker's role in three kinds of presentations: monologue, guided discussion, and sales.

TABLE 23.1   Guidelines for Choosing Your Presentation Role

Chair When You Want To:	Facilitate When You Want To:
Exchange information	Increase participation
Get informal feedback	Deal with group dynamics
Hear members report back	Have members problem solve
Review the current agenda	Have members make decisions
Set the parameters of the discussion	Have members create action plans
Review meeting objectives with members	Shift ownership and commitment levels

Source: Michael Goldman (2001, January/February), To chair or to facilitate, that is the question, *The Training Report*, 13.

A Question of Ethics

Politicians do it. Movie stars do it. Why shouldn't you do it? You can pay to pad your Twitter follower numbers to impress real friends and clients. What ethical considerations might make you hesitate to do so?

LO5 How Should I Organize a Presentation?

As always, you organize your message based on the results of your PAIBOC analysis. To meet audience needs, you often start with the main point, then use one of five standard organizational patterns.

Most presentations use a direct pattern of organization, even when the goal is to persuade a reluctant audience. Audience members know that you want to persuade them. Be honest about your goals, and prepare your opening to demonstrate that your goal dovetails with the audience's needs. Start with your strongest point, your best reason. If you're making more than one point, put the weakest one in the middle. End on a strong note, and if time permits:

- Give additional reasons
- Anticipate and respond to possible objections

Based on your purpose and audience analysis, use one of five standard patterns of organization:

- **Chronological**: Start with the past, move to the present, and end by looking ahead.
- **Problem/causes/solution**: Explain the symptoms of the problem, identify its causes, and suggest a solution. This pattern works best when the audience will find your solution easy to accept.
- **Exclude alternatives**. Explain the symptoms of the problem. Explain the obvious solutions first and show why they won't solve the problem. End by discussing a solution that will work. This pattern may be necessary when the audience will find the solution hard to accept.
- **Pro/con**: Give all the reasons in favour of something, then those against it. This pattern works well when you want the audience to see the weaknesses in its position.
- **1-2-3**. Discuss three aspects of a topic. This pattern works well to organize short informative briefings. "Today I'll review our sales, production, and profits for the last quarter."

Because people have limited attention spans, the best presentations use **repetition for reinforcement**: tell 'em, tell 'em, and tell 'em again. Early in your talk—perhaps immediately after your opener—provide an agenda or overview of the main points you will make. Include a presentation duration time, and end when you promised you would:

> In the next 20 minutes, I'm going to describe how you can make our city a safer, saner place. First, I'd like to talk about the people who are homeless on Vancouver's East Side. Second, I'll talk about the services the Open Shelter provides. Finally, I'll talk about what you—either individually or as a group—can do to help.

An overview provides a mental peg that hearers can hang each point on. It can also prevent someone missing what you are saying because he or she wonders why you aren't covering a major point that you've saved for later.[2]

Offer a clear signpost or **transition** as you come to each new point. A signpost is an explicit statement of the point you have reached. Choose wording that fits your style. The following statements provide four different ways that a speaker could introduce the last of three points:

> Now we come to the third point: what you can do as a group or as individuals to help homeless people in Vancouver.
> So much for what we're doing. Now let's talk about what you can do to help.
> You might be wondering, what can I do to help?
> As you can see, the shelter is trying to do many things. We could do more with your help.

Employability Skills

LO4 LO5 How Do I Adapt My Ideas to the Audience?

Remember that *people can take in only so much information before they shut down!* If you want people to listen, tell them a meaningful story. If your audience is indifferent, skeptical, or hostile, focus on the part of your message the audience will find most interesting and easiest to accept. Here's an example of a story from a speech about world hunger to an audience of college students:

> When was the last time you were hungry? Maybe you remember being hungry while you were on a diet, or maybe you had to work late at a lab and didn't get back to the dorm in time for dinner.

Remember to make your ideas relevant to your audience by

1. Linking what you have to say to the audience's experiences, interests, and needs
2. Showing your audience members that the topic affects them directly
3. Using language the audience knows and understands
4. Relating your purposes to some everyday experience

LO3 LO5 How Can I Create a Strong Opening and Closing?

Use your introduction and your conclusion as points of emphasis.

Employability Skills

The beginning and the end of a presentation, like the beginning and end of a written document, are positions of emphasis. Use those key positions to interest the audience and emphasize your main point. You'll sound more natural and more effective if you write out your opening and closing in advance and memorize them. Keep them short: just a sentence or two.

Begin with…

Your introduction is particularly important. To catch and hold audience attention, try these strategies:

- Stand still
- Focus on your audience
- Attract their interest with a **dramatic statement**, **story**, **question**, or **quotation**
- Make the hook or grabber relevant to them

The more you can do to personalize your opener for your audience, the better. Recent events are better than things that happened long ago; local events are better than events at a distance; people they know are better than people who are only names.

Dramatic Statement

> Twelve of our customers have cancelled orders in the past month.

This presentation to a company's executive committee went on to show that the company's distribution system was inadequate and to recommend an additional warehouse located in the Prairies.

Story

A mother was having difficulty getting her son up for school. He pulled the covers over his head.

"I'm not going to school," he said. "I'm not ever going again."

"Are you sick?" his mother asked.

"No," he answered. "I'm sick of school. They hate me. They call me names. They make fun of me. Why should I go?"

"I can give you two good reasons," the mother replied. "The first is that you're 42 years old. And the second is you're the school principal."[3]

This speech given at a seminar for educators went on to discuss "the three knottiest problems in education today." Educators had to face those problems; they couldn't hide under the covers.

Question

Are you going to have enough money to do the things you want to when you retire?

This presentation to a group of potential clients discusses the value of using the services of a professional financial planner to achieve retirement goals.

Quotation

According to Towers Perrin, the profits of Fortune 100 companies would be 25 percent lower—they'd go down $17 billion—if their earnings statements listed the future costs companies are obligated to pay for retirees' health care.

This presentation on options for health care for retired employees urges executives to start now to investigate options to cut the future cost.

Your opener must interest the audience and establish rapport. Some speakers use humour to achieve those goals. However, an inappropriate joke can turn the audience against the speaker. Never use humour directed against the audience. In contrast, speakers who make fun of themselves usually succeed:

It's both a privilege and a pressure to be here.[4]

Humour isn't the only way to put an audience at ease and establish a positive emotional connection. Smile at your audience before you begin; let them see that you're a real person and a pleasant one.

Close with...

The end of your presentation should be as strong as the opener. For your close, create a mental image of your critical message:

- Refer to your opener to create a frame for your presentation
- End with a vivid, positive picture
- Tell the audience exactly what to do to resolve the situation or solve the problem you've discussed

The following close from a fundraising speech combines a restatement of the main point with a call for action, telling the audience what to do:

> Plain and simple, we need money to run the foundation, just as you need money to develop new products. We need money to make this work. We need money from you. Pick up that pledge card. Fill it out. Turn it in at the door as you leave. Make it a statement about your commitment…make it a big statement.[5]

LO4 When you write out your opening and closing, remember that listeners can take in only so much information; then they disengage and tune out. Use the *KISS* formula: *Keep it short and simple*. As you can see in the example above, speaking style uses shorter sentences and shorter, simpler words than writing does. Oral style can even sound a bit choppy when it is read. Oral style uses more personal pronouns, a less varied vocabulary, and much more repetition.

Ex. 23.2

LO3 LO5 How Should I Use Visuals?

Use a variety of visuals to emphasize your main points. Keep them simple and specific.

People understand and retain information better when they both *see* and *hear* the facts; they understand and remember best when they *see*, *hear*, and *do*. However, your topic or your time may preclude having your audience practise what you're preaching.

Whatever your topic, your choice of visual support can add emphasis and excitement. You can use dramatizations, demonstrations, questionnaires, quizzes, video clips, and role-plays.

The best presentations, however, depend on the speaker's preparedness and rapport with the audience. For North American audiences, your face is your number-one visual aid. Making eye contact with audience members is vital. And audience rapport comes from creating stories that speak to people's values and beliefs.

The best visuals are simple, clear, and specific. Illustrations should reinforce your message honestly and ethically (Module 19). Whenever possible, put people in the picture—doing or using whatever you're selling (Module 19). Keep text to a minimum. Use images and graphics immediately familiar to your audience. And when in doubt…leave it out.[6]

Ex. 23.3

What About PowerPoint?

Design and rhetoric experts agree that PowerPoint™ slides—once attention-grabbers— are now misused and overused in presentations.[7]

When using slides, prepare well-designed visuals only as memory devices for your audience. With complicated material, provide handouts.

PowerPoint slides aren't the only way to involve the audience. Dan Leebar persuaded UPS to switch to Valeo clutches by disassembling the competitor's clutch and showing part by part why Valeo's product was better.

To create effective presentation visuals, use these guidelines:

- Use a sans-serif font (e.g., Arial, Helvetica, Technical) to maximize text readability.
- Use a minimum 24-point type to maximize readability (Module 5).
- Keep it simple.
- Use clear illustrations—charts, graphs, tables—whenever possible.
- Make only one point with each visual. Break a complicated point down into several visuals.
- Give each visual a title that makes a point connected to your presentation's main point.
- Limit the amount of text: no more than five lines per slide or five words per line.

To present your visuals effectively, use these guidelines:

- Have a friend/colleague manage the visuals for you, so you can concentrate on your ideas and your delivery.
- Use your visuals as enhancement, not competition.
- Use no more than one visual or slide per minute.
- Put up your visual (or have your friend/colleague put up the visual) only when you are ready to talk about it.
- Leave the visual up until your next point.

See Module 19 for information on how to present numerical data through visuals and see Figure 23.2 for more information on using PowerPoint.

Visuals work only if the technology they depend on works. When you give presentations in your own office, check the equipment in advance. When you make a presentation in another location or for another organization, arrive early so that you'll have time not only to check the equipment but also to track down a service worker if the equipment isn't working. Be prepared with a backup plan if you're unable to show your slides or videotape.

And because PowerPoint presentations have become commonplace, you must engage your audience in a variety of other ways:

- Students presenting on intercultural business communications demonstrated the way Chinese, Japanese, and Canadians exchange business cards by asking audience members to role-play the differences.
- Another student discussing the need for low-salt products brought in a container of salt, a measuring cup, a measuring spoon, and two plates. As he discussed the body's need for salt, he measured out three teaspoons onto one plate: the amount the body needs in a month.

FIGURE 23.2 PowerPoint Slides for an Informative Presentation

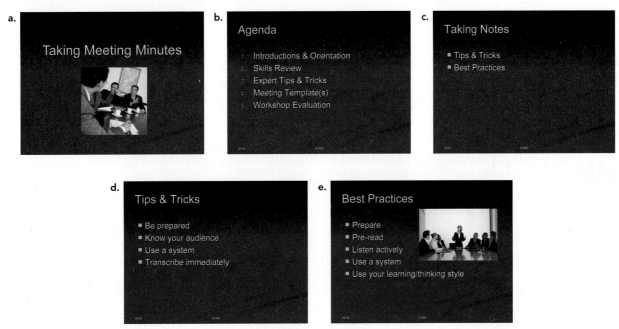

As he discussed the amount of salt the average diet provides, he continued to measure out salt onto the other plate, stopping only when he had 500 grams of salt—the amount in the average North American diet. The demonstration made the discrepancy clear in a way words or even a chart could not have done.[8]

- Some presenters use quizzes, game formats, and dramatizations to encourage audience members to share their expertise with others.
    - ✔ To make sure that his employees understood where money went, the CEO of a specialty printing shop printed up $2 million in play money and handed out big cards to employees marked "Labour," "Depreciation," "Interest," and so forth. Then he asked each "category" to come up and take its share of the revenues. The action was more dramatic than a colour pie chart could ever have been.[9]
    - ✔ Another speaker trying to raise funds used the simple act of asking people to stand to involve them, to create emotional appeal, and to make a statistic vivid:

"[A speaker] was talking to a luncheon club about contributing to the relief of an area that had been hit by a tsunami. The news report said that 70 percent of the people had been killed or disabled. The room was set up with ten people at each round table. He asked three persons at each table to stand. Then he said, "You people sitting are dead or disabled. You three standing have to take care of the mess. You'd need help, wouldn't you?"[10]

LO6 EXPANDING A CRITICAL SKILL

Finding Your Best Voice

Paralanguage—*how* we say what we say—accounts for more than 30 percent of the meaning in our messages. Next to your face, therefore, your voice is your most important presentation aid! Effective speakers use their voices to support and enhance content. Your best voice will vary pitch, intonation, tempo, and volume to express energy and enthusiasm.

Pitch

Pitch measures whether a voice uses sounds that are low (like the bass notes on a piano) or high. Voices that are low-pitched project more credibility than do high-pitched voices. Low-pitched presenters are perceived as being more authoritative and more pleasant to listen to. Most voices go up in pitch when the speaker is angry or excited; some people raise pitch when they increase volume. People whose normal speaking voices are high might need to practise projecting their voices to avoid becoming shrill when they speak to large groups.

To find your best pitch, try humming. The pitch at which the hum sounds loudest and most resonant is your best voice.

Intonation

Intonation marks variation in pitch, stress, or tone. Speakers who use many changes in pitch, stress, and

tone usually seem more enthusiastic; often they also seem more energetic and more intelligent. Someone who speaks in a monotone may seem apathetic or unintelligent. Speakers whose first language does not use tone, pitch, and stress to convey meaning and attitude may need to practise varying these voice qualities.

Avoid raising your voice at the end of a sentence, since in English a rising intonation signals a question. Therefore, speakers who end sentences on a questioning or high tone—known as *uptalk*—sound immature or uncertain of what they're saying.

Tempo

Tempo is a measure of speed. In a conversation, match your tempo to the other speaker's to build rapport. In a formal presentation, vary your tempo. Speakers who speak quickly and who vary their volume during the talk are more likely to be perceived as competent.

Volume

Volume is a measure of loudness or softness. Very soft voices, especially if they are also breathy and high-pitched, give the impression of youth and inexperience. People who do a lot of speaking to large groups need to practise projecting their voices so they can increase their volume without shouting.

Sources: George B. Ray (1986), Vocally cued personality prototypes: An implicit personality theory approach, *Communication Monographs*, 53(3), 266–76; Jacklyn Boice (2000, March), "Verbal impressions," *Selling Power*, 69.

[LO3] What Are the Keys to Delivering an Effective Presentation?

Turn your nervousness into energy, look at the audience, and use natural gestures.

Audience members want you to succeed in your presentation out of a vested self-interest: they don't want to feel uncomfortable for you. They also want the sense that you're talking directly to them, that you've taken the time and trouble to prepare, that you're interested in your subject, and that you care about their interest.

They'll forgive you if you get tangled up in a sentence and end it ungrammatically. They won't forgive you if you seem to have a "canned" talk that you're going to deliver no matter who the listeners are or how they respond. You convey a sense of caring to your audience by making direct eye contact and by using a conversational style.

Putting Your Nervousness to Work

Feeling nervous is normal. Indeed, we are genetically programmed to feel anxious about speaking in public: being aware of other community members' perceptions was an essential survival mechanism for our ancestors.[11]

But you can harness that nervous energy to do your best work. As one student said, you don't need to get rid of your butterflies. All you need to do is make them fly in formation.

To calm your nerves as you prepare to give an oral presentation, try the following:

- Be prepared: analyze your audience, organize your thoughts, prepare visual aids, practise your opening and closing, check out the arrangements.
- Practise, practise, practise.
- Use positive emphasis to reframe what you're feeling. Instead of saying, "I'm scared," try saying, "My adrenaline is up." Adrenaline sharpens our reflexes and helps us do our best.
- Visualize your success: see yourself moving naturally and confidently around the room; see people jumping up, smiling and clapping, as you end your presentation.
- Focus on what you know you have done to succeed. "I've practised the presentation; I know it really well; I've checked out the room, know where to put the screen; I've prepared for most questions."
- Use only the amount of caffeine you normally use. More or less may make you jumpy.
- Avoid alcoholic beverages.

Just before your presentation, use relaxation techniques:

- Consciously contract and then relax your muscles, starting with your feet and calves and going up to your shoulders, arms, and hands.
- Take several deep breaths from your diaphragm.

During your presentation, be sure to do the following:

- Pause and look at the audience before you begin speaking.
- Concentrate on communicating well.
- Channel your body energy into emphatic gestures and movement.

Using Eye Contact

Look directly at the people you're talking to. Speakers who looked the most at the audience during a seven-minute informative speech were judged to be better informed, more experienced, more honest, and friendlier than speakers who delivered the same information with less eye contact.[12] An earlier study found that speakers judged sincere looked at the audience 63 percent of the time, while those judged insincere looked at the audience only 21 percent of the time.[13]

The point in making eye contact is to establish one-on-one contact with the individual members of your audience. People want to feel that you're talking to them. Looking directly at individuals also enables you to be more conscious of feedback from the audience, so that you can modify your approach if necessary.

Standing and Gesturing

Stand with your feet far enough apart for good balance, with your knees flexed. Unless the presentation is very formal or you're on camera, you can walk if you want to. Some speakers like to come out from the lectern to remove that barrier between themselves and the audience.

Build on your natural style for gestures. Gestures usually work best when they're big and confident.

Using Notes and Visuals

Unless you're giving a very short presentation, you'll probably want to use notes. Even experts use notes. The more you know about the subject, the greater the temptation to add relevant points that occur to you as you talk. Adding an occasional point can help to clarify something for the audience, but adding too many points will overwhelm the audience, destroy your outline, and put you over the time limit.

Put your notes on cards or on sturdy pieces of paper. Use prompts (opening and closing sentences, then your points, large font, highlighting, reference to visuals) that work for you. Practise your presentation using your notes, and make whatever changes increase your comfort level.

During your presentation, look at your notes infrequently. Direct your eyes to members of the audience. Hold your notes high enough so that your head doesn't bob up and down like a yo-yo as you look from the audience to your notes and back again.

If you know your topic well, you won't need to look at your notes, and you'll feel more confident. You can focus on being yourself and establishing rapport with your audience.

Get out of the way of your visuals: stand to the side of the screen, and *face the audience, not the screen*. Never read your visuals; the audience members can read for themselves. If your talk is lengthy, and the topic complicated, prepare handouts for your audience. Many people expect speakers to provide a copy of their slides at the end of the presentation.

Keep the room lights on if possible; turning them off makes it easier for people to fall asleep and harder for them to concentrate on you.

LO3 LO5 How Should I Handle Questions from the Audience?

Use PAIBOC to anticipate audience questions. Be honest. Rephrase biased or hostile questions.

Prepare for questions by listing every fact or opinion you can think of that challenges your position. Treat every objection seriously and try to think of a way to deal with it. If you're talking about a controversial issue, you may want to save one point for the question period, rather than making it during the presentation. Speakers who have visuals to answer questions seem especially well prepared.

During your presentation, tell the audience how you'll handle questions. If you have a choice, save questions for the end. In your talk, answer the questions or objections that you expect your audience to have.

During the question period, acknowledge questions by looking directly at the questioner. As you answer the question, expand your focus to take in the entire group.

If the audience may not have heard the question, or if you want more time to think, repeat the question before you answer it. Link your answers to the points you made in your presentation. Keep the purpose of your presentation in mind, and select information that advances your goals.

If a question is hostile or biased, rephrase it before you answer it. "You're asking whether…" Or suggest an alternative question: "I think there are problems with both the positions you describe. It seems to me that a third possibility is…"

If someone asks about something that you already explained in your presentation, simply answer the question without embarrassing the questioner. Even when actively participating, audiences remember only about 70 percent of what you say.

If you don't know the answer to a question, say so and promise to get the information and respond as soon as possible. Write down the question so that you can look up the answer before the next session. You may want to refer the question to your audience, which both involves and flatters them. If it's a question to which you think there is no answer, ask whether anyone in the room knows. When no one does, your "ignorance" is vindicated.

At the end of the question period, take two minutes to summarize your main point once more. (This can be a restatement of your close.) Questions may or may not focus on the key point of your talk. Take advantage of having the floor to repeat your message briefly and forcefully.

LO7 What Are the Guidelines for Group Presentations?

In the best presentations, voices take turns within each point.

Plan carefully to involve as many members of the group as possible in speaking roles. The easiest way to make a group presentation is to outline the presentation and then divide the topics, giving one to each group member. Another member can be responsible for the opener and the close. During the question period, each member answers questions that relate to his or her topic.

In this kind of divided presentation, be sure to do the following:

- Plan transitions.
- Strictly enforce time limits.
- Coordinate your visuals so that the presentation seems a coherent whole.
- Choreograph the presentation: plan each member's movement and seating arrangements as the group transfers from speaker to speaker. Take turns managing the visual support so that each speaker can focus on content and delivery without worrying about changing slides or transparencies.
- Practise the presentation as a group at least once; more is better.

The best group presentations appear fully integrated; together, the members of the group complete the important tasks:

- Writing a very detailed outline
- Choosing points and examples
- Creating visuals
- Identifying and answering possible objections and questions

Then, *within* each point, speakers take turns, and different speakers field the questions they have prepared for.

This presentation is most effective because each voice speaks only a minute or two before a new voice comes in. However, it works only when all group members know the subject well, and when the group plans carefully and practises extensively.

Whatever form of group presentation you use, introduce each member of the team to the audience at the beginning of the presentation and at each transition: use the next person's name when you change speakers: "Now, Jason will explain how we evaluated the Web pages."

As a team member, pay close attention to your fellow speakers; don't ever have sidebar conversations with others in the group. If other members of the team seem uninterested in the speaker, the audience gets the sense that that speaker isn't worth listening to.

MODULE SUMMARY

- Most oral presentations have more than one purpose. People present to inform, persuade, and build goodwill.

- Oral presentations need to be simpler than written messages.

- In a **monologue presentation**, the speaker delivers the content without deviation.

- In a **guided discussion**, the speaker presents the questions or topics that both speaker and audience have agreed on in advance. The speaker serves as facilitator to help the audience tap its members' own knowledge.

- A **sales presentation** is a conversation using questions to determine the buyer's needs, probe objections, and gain commitment to the purchase.

- Adapt your message to your audience's experiences, beliefs, and interests.

- Use the beginning and end of your presentation as points of emphasis.

- Use visuals to reinforce your main idea; make the visuals clear, simple, and relevant.

- Use a direct pattern of organization: put your strongest reason first.

- Limit your talk to three main points. After your opener, **provide an overview of the main points** you will make. Give a clear signpost as you transition to each new point. This verbal signal is an explicit statement of the point you have reached.

- Even the most seasoned speakers feel nervous when giving a presentation. Such anxiety is natural and normal. To reduce apprehension about presenting,

  o Be prepared: analyze your audience, plan your content, prepare visuals, practise, create notes, check out the presentation room and arrangements.
  o Drink your usual amount of coffee; avoid alcohol.
  o Visualize scenarios of your presentation success.
  o Reframe your nervousness into positive affirmations.

- Just before your presentation
  o Consciously contract and then relax your muscles, starting with your feet and calves and moving up to your shoulders, arms, and hands.
  o Take several deep breaths from your diaphragm.

- During your presentation
  o Pause and look at your audience before you begin to speak.
  o Concentrate on communicating confidently.
  o Use your energy in strong gestures and movement.

- Establish rapport with the audience members by making direct eye contact, and using a conversational style.

- Treat questions as opportunities to give more detailed information. Connect your answers to the points you made in your presentation.

- Repeat the question before answering it if you think that the audience may not have heard it, or you want more time to think. Rephrase hostile or biased questions before you answer them.

- The most effective group presentations result when the group writes a very detailed outline, chooses points and examples, creates visuals collaboratively, and, within each point, allows members' voices to trade off one another.

ASSIGNMENTS FOR MODULE 23

Questions for Critical Thinking

23.1 What strategies do you use to overcome presentation anxiety?

23.2 When and how would you use images or a video clip in a brief presentation? What copyright laws apply to such use?

23.3 How do you create interesting PowerPoint slides? How do you test for audience reaction?

23.4 Think of a public speaker/orator you find impressive. What specific strategies does this person use to design and deliver effective presentations?

23.5 How would you begin to outline your presentation? What questions would you ask yourself to decide on your organizational pattern?

Exercises and Problems

23.6 Evaluating Monroe's Motivated Sequence as a Presentation Guide

Watch any of the many videos (for example, at www.youtube.com/watch?v=k0ED3PckYaM) on Monroe's Motivated Sequence, a five-step pattern of persuasion.

As your instructor directs

Create a short (two-to-five-minute) presentation, supported by appropriate visuals, on your opinion of the quality of the video and the usefulness of the pattern.

23.7 Making a Short Oral Presentation

As your instructor directs

Make a short (two-to-five-minute) presentation, supported by appropriate visual aids, on one of the following topics:

a. Explain how what you've learned in classes, in campus activities, or at work will be useful to the employer who hires you after graduation.

b. Profile someone who is successful in the field you hope to enter and explain what makes him or her successful.

c. Describe a specific situation in an organization in which communication was handled well or badly.

d. Make a short presentation based on another problem in this book, such as the following:

- Explain a "best practice" in your organization.
- Tell your boss about a problem in your unit and recommend a solution.
- Explain one of the challenges (e.g., technology, ethics, international competition) that the field you hope to enter is facing.
- Profile a company you would like to work for and explain why you think it would be a good employer.
- Explain your interview strategy.

23.8 Making a Longer Oral Presentation

As your instructor directs

Create a five-to-twelve-minute individual or group presentation on one of the following. Use any appropriate visual communication, *excluding slides*, to make your talk powerful.

a. Show why your unit is important to the organization and either should be exempt from downsizing or should receive additional resources.

b. Persuade your supervisor to make a change that will benefit the organization.

c. Persuade your organization to make a change that will improve its image in the community.

d. Persuade classmates to donate time or money to a charitable organization (Module 10).

e. Persuade an employer that you are the best person for the job.

f. Use another problem in this book as the basis for your presentation.

23.9 Making a Group Oral Presentation

As your instructor directs

Make a five-to-twelve-minute presentation using communication visuals on one of these topics:

a. Show how cultural differences can lead to miscommunication.

b. Evaluate the design of a Web page.

c. Recommend an investment for your instructor.

d. Recommend ways to retain workers.

e. Present brochures you have designed to the class.

f. Share the advice of students currently in the job market.

23.10 Presenting to Global Audiences

What tips can you give your peers about presenting to pluralistic audiences?

As your instructor directs

Create a twelve-to-fifteen-minute group presentation with communication visuals on presenting to a global audience:

- What specifically should presenters be aware of/sensitive to?
- How can presenters compensate for cultural diversity?
- What North American presentation norms should presenters particularly avoid?

23.11 Creating a Presentation Skills Evaluation Matrix

As your instructor directs

Together with four peers, create an evaluation guide to assess your class presentations. Begin by brainstorming the components of a presentation, such as content, delivery, visuals, time, organization, audience relevance, and so on. Create a table with headings (e.g., *Excellent, Good, Needs Improvement*) and beside the criteria describe the behaviours you would expect to see.

Use collaborative software to show your evaluation guide to the rest of the class.

POLISHING YOUR PROSE

Choosing Levels of Formality

Some words are more formal than others. Generally, business messages call for a middle-of-the-road formality, not too formal, but not so casual as to seem sloppy.

Formal and Stuffy	Short and Simple
ameliorate	improve
commence	begin, start
enumerate	list
finalize	finish, complete
prioritize	rank
utilize	use
viable option	choice

Sloppy	Casual
befuddled	confused
diss	criticize
guess	assume
haggle	negotiate
nosy	curious
wishy-washy	indecisive, flexible

What makes choosing words so challenging is that the level of formality depends on your purposes, the audience, and the situation. What's just right for a written report will be too formal for an oral presentation or an advertisement. The level of formality that works in one discourse community might be inappropriate for another.

Listen to the language that people in your discourse community use. What words seem to have positive connotations? What words persuade? As you identify these terms, use them in your own messages.

Exercises

In each sentence, choose the better word or phrase. Justify your choice.

1. On Monday, I [took a look at/inspected] our [stuff/inventory].
2. [Starting/commencing] at 5 p.m., all qualifying employees may [commence/begin] their [leave times/vacations].
3. Though their [guy/representative] was [firm/stubborn], we eventually [hashed out/negotiated] a settlement.
4. Call to schedule [some time/a meeting] with me to [talk about/deliberate on the issues in] your memo.
5. The manager [postponed making/waited until she had more information before making] a decision.
6. Rick has [done his job/performed] well as [top dog/manager] of our sales department.
7. In my last job, I [ran many errands/worked as a gofer] for the marketing manager.
8. Please [contact/communicate with] [me/the undersigned] if you [have questions/desire further information or knowledge].
9. This report [has problems/stinks].
10. In this report, I have [guessed/assumed] that the economy will continue to grow.

Check your answers to the odd-numbered exercises in the Polishing Your Prose Answer Key.

Researching Jobs

Learning Objectives

After reading and applying the information in Module 24, you'll be able to demonstrate

Knowledge of

LO1 Job search strategies

LO2 Information interviews

LO3 The hidden job market

LO4 New job interview practices

Skills to

LO5 Begin to self-assess realistically

LO6 Find information about employers

LO7 Use the Internet in your job search

LO8 Find posted jobs and explore the hidden job market

LO9 Present your non-traditional experience positively

LO10 Prepare for job interviews

MODULE OUTLINE

- What do I need to know about myself to job-hunt?

- What do I need to know about companies that might hire me?

- How should I use social networking sites?

- What is the information interview?

- What is the "hidden job market"? How do I tap into it?

- How do I present my non-traditional experiences?

Module Summary

Assignments for Module 24

Polishing Your Prose: Using Details

Employability Skills 2000+ Checklist

Module content builds these Conference Board of Canada Employability Skills 2000+

Communicate

Think and Solve Problems

Demonstrate Positive Attitudes and Behaviours

Be Adaptable

Work with Others

Participate in Projects and Tasks

Ex.
24.1
24.2
24.4
24.6
24.7
24.10

The first step in any job search is to analyze and identify your own abilities and interests.[1] The second step is to establish and nourish contacts—online, and through friends, friends of friends, and family.

Ex.
24.5

LO1 LO5 What Do I Need to Know About Myself to Job-Hunt?

Your need to self-assess realistically: identify your knowledge, skills, abilities, interests, and values.

Each person could happily do several jobs. Personality and aptitude tests can tell you what your strengths are, but they won't say, "You should be X." In preparation for the job search, and for the interview, you need to answer specific questions like these:

- What achievements have given you the most satisfaction? Why did you enjoy them?
- Would you rather have firm deadlines or a flexible schedule? Do you prefer working alone or with other people? Do you prefer specific instructions and standards for evaluation, or freedom and uncertainty? How comfortable are you with pressure? How do you manage multiple deadlines? How much challenge do you want?
- Are you willing to take work home? Are you prepared to travel? How important is recognition to you? How important is money compared to having time to spend with family and friends?
- Where do you want to live? What features in terms of weather, geography, and cultural and social life do you see as ideal?
- What do you want from your work? Do you work to achieve certain purposes or values, or is work "just a way to make a living"? How important are the organization's culture and ethical standards to you?

Once you have identified in writing what is most important to you, look at the job market to find what you want. For example, your greatest interest is athletics, but you aren't good enough for the pros. Your job market analysis might suggest several alternatives. You might

- Teach sports and physical fitness as a high school coach or a corporate fitness director
- Cover sports for a newspaper, magazine, TV station, or new digital medium
- Go into management or sales for a professional sports team, a health club, or a company that sells sports equipment
- Create or manage a sports website

What Do I Need to Know About Companies That Might Hire Me?

LO6
LO7
LO8

Ex.
24.3
24.8
24.9

You need to know as much as you can.

Organizations always have room for people who demonstrate motivation, energy, and critical thinking. Preparation through research demonstrates all these skills. Moreover, to adapt your letter and resumé to a specific organization, and to shine at the interview, you need information both about the employer and about the job itself. You can find this information free through numerous resources (see Figure 24.1).

Employability Skills

You'll need to know

- *Jobs available:* Start your research online, at the library or the college or university career centre. Libraries' research databases provide resources for every part of your job hunt: the best local and national companies to work for (www.canadastop100.com/fp10); postings on Workopolis, Monster.ca, and Working.com; trade and professional websites, crucial for knowledge of industry regulations, developments and conferences; municipal, provincial, and national labour market, apprenticeship, and skilled trades information—even salary averages and negotiation tips.

Social networking sites like Facebook, LinkedIn, and Twitter do not offer free job search tips, but are increasingly popular for networking itself: use them to connect with mentors and prospective employers.[2]

Notebooks at campus placement offices often have fuller job descriptions than appear in ads. Talk to friends who have graduated recently to learn what their jobs involve. Request information interviews to learn more about opportunities that interest you.

- *Contact information:* Check the ad or the organization's website, or call the company. An advantage of calling is that you can find out whether your contact prefers a courtesy title (Mr., Ms., or Mrs.).
- *At least four or five facts about the organization and what it does:* Knowing the organization's products and services enables you to describe how you can contribute. Understanding the

FIGURE 24.1   Websites Covering the Job Search Process

Human Resources and Skills Development Canada **www.hrsdc.gc.ca/eng/home.shtml**	The Rockport Institute **www.rockportinstitute.com**
Career Builder **www.careerbuilder.ca**	Simply Hired **www.simplyhired.ca**
Fast Company **www.fastcompany.com/guides/reinvent.html**	WetFeet.com **www.wetfeet.com**
The Five O'Clock Club **www.fiveoclockclub.com**	Workopolis **www.workopolis.com**
Job Search by Indeed **www.indeed.ca**	Vault **www.vault.com**
Monster **www.monster.ca**	Working in Canada **www.workingincanada.gc.ca**
Job Hunter's Bible (Dick Bolles) **www.jobhuntersbible.com**	Spherion Career Centre **www.spherion.com**
Eluta.ca **www.eluta.ca**	

Laura Archer, who completed her degree in nursing at the University of P.E.I., has spent her career in the United States and Africa, where she is regularly deployed with Medecins Sans Frontiers. When she is not overseas, Laura works as a visual artist in Canada.

organization's values, goals, market, and competition allows you to define specifically how your skills outshine those of other candidates

Useful facts include the following:

- Market share
- Competitive position
- New products, services, or promotions
- Technology or manufacturing equipment applications
- Plans for growth or downsizing
- Challenges the organization faces
- The corporate culture (Module 2)

You can find these facts on the Internet, including information about corporate culture and even anonymous statements from employees. Check blogs, professional electronic mailing lists, and electronic bulletin boards. Employers sometimes post specialized jobs online; they're always a good way to get information about the industry you hope to enter.

Industry Canada's free, searchable Canadian Company Capabilities database (CCC, at https://www.ic.gc.ca/eic/site/ccc-rec.nsf/eng/home) provides full data, including contact names, for over 60,000 national businesses.[3]

The directories listed in Table 24.1 provide information such as net worth, market share, principal products, and the names of officers and directors. Ask your librarian to identify additional directories. To get specific financial data (and to see how the organization presents itself to the public), get the company's annual report on the Web (www.orderannualreports.com). (*Note:* Only companies whose stock is publicly traded are required to issue annual reports. In this day of mergers and buyouts, many companies are owned by other companies. The parent company may be the only one to issue an annual report.)

Many company websites provide information about training programs and career paths for new hires. To learn about new products, plans for growth, or solutions to industry challenges, read business newspapers such as the *Globe and Mail*, *National Post*, *Wall Street Journal*, or *Financial Post*; business magazines such as *Report on Business*, *Canadian Business*, *Strategy Magazine*, *Fortune*, *Business Week*, and *Forbes*; and trade journals. Each of these has indices listing which companies are discussed in a specific issue. A few of the trade journals available are listed in Table 24.2.

TABLE 24.1   Where to Get Addresses and Facts about Companies

General Directories

Canadian Business Directory
www.canadianbusinessdirectory.ca

Canadian Federation of Independent Business
www.cfib-fcei.ca

Directory of Corporate Affiliations

Dun's Million Dollar Directory

Standard & Poor's Register of Corporations, Directors, and Executives

Thomas Register of American Manufacturers

Specialized Directories and Resource Books

Accounting Firms and Practitioners

Directory of Hotel and Motel Systems

Dun and Bradstreet

Franchise Annual: Directory

Hoover's Handbook of American Business

O'Dwyer's Directory of Public Relations Firms

The Rand McNally Bankers' Directory

Scott's Business Directory

Standard Directory of Advertisers ("Red Book")

Television Factbook

Traders

"I'm a Lot Older Than the Other Employees"

Mature workers remain in demand for their sophisticated interpersonal and communications abilities. Uninformed employers are concerned that older people won't be flexible, up to date, or willing to be supervised by someone younger. You can counter these fears:

- Keep up to date. Read trade journals; attend professional meetings.
- Learn the computer programs your field uses. Refer to technology in the resumé, job letter, and interview: "Yes, I saw the specifications for your new product on your website."
- Work with younger people, in classroom teams, in volunteer work, or on the job. Be able to cite specific cases where you've learned from young people and worked well with them.
- Use positive emphasis (Module 12). Talk about your ability to relate to mature customers, the valuable perspective you bring. Focus on recent events, not ones from twenty years ago.
- Show energy and enthusiasm to counter the stereotype that older people are tired and ill.

MODULE SUMMARY

- Begin your job search by assessing your priorities, abilities, and interests. Do this assessment in writing, to make it real, and to note the information that might go on your resumé.

- Use directories, annual reports, recruiting literature, business periodicals, trade journals, and websites to get information about employers, and job search tips.

- The most effective way to find the job you want is to self-recruit. The second most effective way is through a referral. Both these methods depend on your ability to network.

- Information and referral interviews can help you tap into the **hidden job market**—jobs that are not advertised. Collect contact names by networking: talk to friends, relatives, salespeople, and suppliers; do volunteer and community work. Ask for an **information interview** to find out what the daily work involves, and how you can best prepare to enter the field. Or schedule brief **referral interviews** to learn about current job opportunities in your field.

- Prepare carefully for these interviews: these people know other people, and can offer suggestions and other referrals.

- Use social networking sites discreetly. Join business/industry-related sites, get involved in online discussions, update your profile frequently, and use the site's technology to showcase your skills.

ASSIGNMENTS FOR MODULE 24

Questions for Critical Thinking

24.1 What networking sites would be most relevant for a career in your field? Why?

24.2 Identify three community and/or volunteer activities that would expand your networking opportunities.

24.3 Suggest three reasons how knowing the corporate culture of a potential employer can make your job search much more successful.

24.4 What strategies can you use to build a compelling digital dossier?

Exercises and Problems

24.5 Beginning Your Self-Inventory

Initiate the job-hunting process on the nextSteps.org Job Search site (www.nextsteps.ca/career/start.php) by completing the inventory questionnaire. Note the results as part of the process of knowing yourself.

24.6 Assessing your Digital Identity

Research your digital tattoo to discover what employers can readily find online about you.

As your instructor directs

   a. Share your findings with a small group of students.

   b. Summarize your findings in a memo to your instructor.

24.7 Networking

Contact a friend, family member, or acquaintance who is already in the workforce, asking about one or more of the following topics:

- What jobs in your field are available in your contact's organization?
- If a job is available, can your contact provide information, beyond the job listing, that will help you write a more detailed, persuasive letter? (Specify the kind of information you'd like to have.)
- Who else can your contact suggest who might be useful to you in your job search? (Ask about any organizations you're especially interested in.)

24.8 Networking with Social Media

Social media experts suggest specific strategies for online job networking. Read Dave Fleet's blog post "13 Ways Social Media Can Improve Your Career," or find your own expert advice on using social media for your job search.

As your instructor directs

- **a.** Establish or revise your professional online presence according to your expert's advice.
- **b.** Present your new or revised professional presence to other members of the class.
- **c.** Based on class feedback, revise your professional social media profile.
- **d.** Write an email to your instructor summarizing the results.

24.9 Gathering Information about an Industry

Use six recent issues of a trade journal to report on three to five trends, developments, or issues that are important in an industry.

As your instructor directs

- **a.** Share your findings with a small group of students.
- **b.** Summarize your findings in a memo to your instructor.
- **c.** Present your findings orally to the class.
- **d.** Email your findings to the other members of the class.
- **e.** Form a group with two other students to write a blog summarizing the results of this research.

24.10 Gathering Information about a Specific Organization

Gather printed information about a specific organization, using several of the following methods:

- Use the most current edition of *The Career Directory*.
- Check the company's website.
- Read the company's annual report.
- Talk to someone who works there.
- Pick up relevant information at your local board of trade or chamber of commerce.
- Read articles in trade publications and online at the *Globe and Mail*, *National Post*, *Wall Street Journal*, or *Financial Post* that mention the organization (check the indices).
- Get the names and addresses of its officers (from a directory or from the Web).
- Read recruiting literature provided by the company.

As your instructor directs

- **a.** Share your findings with a small group of students.
- **b.** Summarize your findings in a memo to your instructor.
- **c.** Present your findings orally to the class.
- **d.** Email your findings to the other members of the class.
- **e.** Form a group with two other students to write a blog summarizing the results of this research.

24.11   Conducting an Information Interview

Interview someone working in a field you're interested in. Use the questions listed in the module or the shorter list here:

- How did you get started in this field?
- What do you like about your job?
- What do you dislike about your job?
- What three other people could give me additional information about this job?

As your instructor directs

- **a.** Share the results of your interview with a small group of students.
- **b.** Write up your interview in a memo to your instructor.
- **c.** Present the results of your interview orally to the class.
- **d.** Email a summary of your interview to other members of your class.
- **e.** Write to the interviewee thanking him or her for taking the time to talk to you.

POLISHING YOUR PROSE

Using Details

Details are especially important in reader benefits (Module 11), reports, resumés, job applications, and sales letters. Customers or potential employers look for specific details to help them make decisions, such as what makes your product better than the competition's or how your experience would help the reader. Here's an example:

I can offer you more than ten years of advertising experience, including five years of broadcast sales in Ottawa, where I generated more than $19 million in revenue, as well as three years with J. Walter Thompson, Toronto's leading advertising company. For the first four years of my career, I also wrote advertising copy, including hundreds of local and regional radio spots for such diverse products as cookies, cat food, fishing tackle, and children's toys. I also wrote print pieces, including the entire 15-month campaign for Vancouver-based "Uncle Bill's Electronic Bazaar," which increased sales by nearly 37 percent during that period.

Reader Benefits

What features or experiences make your product or service unique? Useful? Cost-effective?

Weak: With the Stereobooster, your car will sound great.

Better: The Stereobooster safely gives your car audio system a full 30 watts per channel of sheer sound excitement—double that of other systems on the market—all for under $50.

The Five Senses

Describe sight, sound, taste, touch, and smell. Some sensations are so powerful that they immediately conjure up thoughts or emotions—the smell of fresh coffee, the sound of ocean waves, the feeling of sunlight against the skin.

Concrete Nouns and Verbs

Concrete nouns and verbs are better than more general nouns and verbs combined with adjectives and adverbs. For instance, *manager* and *15 months* are more concrete than *the person in charge* or *a while*. Concrete words make meaning clear and vivid:

Weak: At my last job, I typed stuff.

Better: As a clerk typist II for Hughes and Associates, I typed hundreds of memos, letters, and reports.

Increase your vocabulary by reading a variety of materials. Keep a dictionary and thesaurus handy. Do crossword puzzles or computer word games to practise what you know.

Adjectives and Adverbs That Count

Omit or replace vague or overused adjectives and adverbs: *basically, some, very, many, a lot, kind of, sort of, partly, eventually*. Increasingly, novice writers are using *so* as an adjective, as in "He was so happy about the promotion." Exactly how happy is this?

Conversational English, Not Jargon or Obscure Words

In general, choose the more conversational option over jargon or obscure words: *exit*, *typical*, or *second to last* rather than *egress*, *quintessential*, or *penultimate*.

Exercises

Add details to the following sentences.

1. I work for a company.
2. The person in charge of our department wants some files.
3. Sometime in the future I will get a job in my field.
4. It's been a while since I went there.
5. Our product will help you.
6. There are lots of reasons why you should hire me.
7. This product is so much better than its competitors.
8. We will have a meeting in the afternoon.
9. My experience makes me a good candidate for this job.
10. We plan to travel to a couple of provinces sometime next month.

Check your answers to the odd-numbered exercises in the Polishing Your Prose Answer Key.

MODULE
25

Creating Persuasive Resumés

MODULE OUTLINE

- How do employers read resumés?
- How can I encourage the employer to pay attention to my resumé?
- What kind of resumé should I use?
- How do resumé formats differ?
- What parts of resumé formats are the same?
- What should I do if the standard categories don't fit?
- Should I limit my resumé length?
- How do I create a scannable resumé?
- How should I prepare an online resumé?

Module Summary

Assignments for Module 25

Polishing Your Prose: Proofreading

Learning Objectives

After reading and applying the information in Module 25, you'll be able to demonstrate

Knowledge of

LO1 Current resumé-writing practices

Skills to

LO2 Create the resumé that best showcases your qualifications

LO3 Make your experience relevant to employers

LO4 Increase the number of "hits" your resumé receives

Employability Skills

2000+

Employability Skills 2000+ Checklist

Module content builds these Conference Board of Canada Employability Skills 2000+

Communicate

Learn Continuously

Manage Information

Demonstrate Positive Attitudes and Behaviours

A **resumé** summarizes your qualifications so persuasively that you get an interview. When you're in the job market, having a resumé prepares you for every opportunity. When you're employed, having a current resumé allows you to assess your skills' improvement; this ongoing inventory makes it easier for you to take advantage of other job opportunities that come up.

Even if you're several years away from job hunting, preparing a resumé now will make you more conscious of what to do in the next two or three years to make yourself a more attractive candidate. Writing a resumé is also an ego-building experience: the person who looks so good on paper is *you*!

FIGURE 25.1 PAIBOC Questions for Analysis

P	What are your *purposes* in creating a resumé? The resumé must display your knowledge, skills, and analytical abilities: you are recording your interpersonal and vocational aptitudes and shaping a persuasive story. Your ultimate purpose is to get the interview.
A	Who is your **audience**? Who will scan/read your resumé? What does your audience value, and how do you know? How can you create a resumé that will attract and hold your audience's attention?
I	What **information** should you include in your resumé? What information is the employer looking for? What do you know about the industry? The employer? What life/work experiences will make you stand out from other candidates? What keywords should you use to frame that information for immediate and maximum positive emphasis?
B	What communication and technical skills can you offer to **benefit** the potential employer immediately?
O	What audience **objections** do you anticipate? How can you create a resumé that stands out positively among all those others?
C	What **context** will affect your reader's response? Consider your relationship to the reader, the reader's values and expectations, the economy, recent organizational developments, current morale, and the time of year.

How Do Employers Read Resumés?

Your resumé can be screened in two ways: electronically or by a person.

If people do the reading, employers may skim the resumés quickly, putting them into two piles: "reject" and "maybe." In the first round, each resumé may get as little as 2.9 seconds of the reader's attention. Then the reader goes through the "maybe" pile again, weeding out more documents. If there are many resumés (and some companies get 2,000 a week), resumés may get only 10 to 30 seconds at this stage. After the initial pile has been culled, whether it's to one-half or one-hundredth of the initial pile, the remaining documents will be read more carefully to choose the people invited for interviews.

Alternatively, your resumé may be electronically scanned into a job-applicant tracking system. Then a computer does the first set of cuts. The employer specifies the keywords from the job description, listing the knowledge, skills, and abilities that the ideal applicant would have. Sometimes personal characteristics (e.g., *hard worker, good writer, willing to travel*) are included. The employer receives the resumés that match the keywords, arranged with the most "hits" first. The employer then chooses the interviewees.

How Can I Encourage the Employer to Pay Attention to My Resumé?

Show how your qualifications fit the job and the company.

You need both a paper resumé that's attractive to the human eye and an electronic resumé that serves your purposes in a job-applicant tracking system. You can do several things to increase the chances that a human being will pay attention to your resumé:

- Begin with a Skills or Summary statement: specifically describe your value to the organization (see Figure 25.3, Summary of Qualifications).
- Frame your skills and activities in measurable terms: "increased sales 10 percent"; "supervised five people"; "implemented a data entry system that saved the company $5,000."
- Emphasize achievements that
  - Are most relevant to the position for which you're applying
  - Demonstrate your superiority to other applicants
  - Are recent
- Use the keywords and technical terms of the industry and the organization; find these in the ad, in trade journals, and from job descriptions.
- Make your paper resumé attractive and readable by using
  - **Plenty of white space:** Don't squeeze the margins to get more information onto a page.
  - **A serif font:** Times New Roman, Century Schoolbook, or Bookman Old Style, for example.
- Left justify and bold the major headings.
- Include transferable skills: the ability to write and speak well, to identify and solve problems, to think critically and creatively, to work well independently and with others, to speak other languages, and to use a variety of computer programs.
- Design one resumé to appeal to the human eye and the second to be easily processed by an electronic scanner.
- Revise and edit your resumé to ensure it's error-free: grammar and spelling mistakes will cost you the interview.

The best resumés convey relevant details as concisely and attractively as possible. Most resumés use bullet points, omit *I*, and use sentence fragments that may be punctuated as complete sentences. Complete sentences are acceptable, as are *me* and *my*, if they are the briefest way to present information.

You may need to create several different resumés. But the more carefully you customize your resumé to a specific employer, the greater your chances for getting an interview.

Ex. 25.4

LO3 What Kind of Resumé Should I Use?

Use the format that makes you look best.

Depending on their experience and the audience, people use one of three kinds of resumés: **chronological**, **functional**, or **combination**.

The chronological resumé summarizes what you have accomplished, starting with the most recent events and going backward: that is, using **reverse chronology**. It emphasizes dates. Figure 25.2 shows a chronological resumé. Use a chronological resumé when you have limited relevant work experience and your education and experience show

- A logical preparation for the position for which you're applying
- A steady progression leading to the present

EXPANDING A CRITICAL SKILL

Creating Attention-Getting Resumés

Keep your resumé simple and specific: you have only a few minutes to attract and hold a recruiter's attention. Follow these strategies to create a resumé that gets you the job interview:

Play with Layout and Design

If submitting a hard copy

- Use a laser printer to print your resumé on high-quality letter-sized paper. White paper is standard for business resumés; cream, pale grey, and parchment colours are also acceptable.
- Make your resumé readable and attractive:
  - Use the Tables tool to create invisible columns.
  - Use the same font throughout: Arial and Times New Roman are business standards.
  - Vary font size: use 12-point for headings, and 11-point type for the text to get more on a page.
  - Bold and italicize for emphasis; use bullets in lists.
  - Highlight your desktop publishing skills: try smaller margins; use lines or borders.
  - Use enough white space to make your resumé easy to read.
- Explore resumé templates to expand your range of options.

If emailing your resumé

- Attach it as a Word or PDF document.

- Save the document with your name included in the filename so that the recruiter can easily retrieve it among others.

Consider the Content

Employers want to interview eligible candidates. Ensure your resumé emphasizes your eligibility.

- Highlight skills relevant to the position and the organization.
- Be specific: reframe experiences into skills; provide facts and numbers.
- Be clear: use short, concrete nouns, and active verbs to describe your skills.
- Be honest. Even if potential employers don't check—and increasingly they do—lies and exaggerations are often glaringly obvious.

Proofread

Employers assume that the resumé represents your best work. Proofread, and then have at least two other people proofread for you, to ensure the document is perfect. Especially check

- Spelling of your college, university, and your employers
- Parallelism (Module 8)
- Consistency: headings, bullets, abbreviations
- Dates
- Phone numbers, email addresses, and URLs

FIGURE 25.2   **A Chronological Resumé**

Mohammed Shafer
210 Steeles Avenue West, Brampton, ON L6Y 2K3
905.555.3828 mshafe@bell.live

Objective

To find a challenging information technology position where my communication and technical
skills can make a contribution

Profile

Detail-oriented, analytical problem-solver
Experienced in customer service and negotiating skills
Experienced LAN, Internet, and Intranet user
Hardware certified: IBM and MAC
Trained in WHMIS and MSDS
Work well with others, without supervision, and to deadlines

Education

2013	Diploma	Chemical Engineering Technology Co-op Program
		Sheridan Institute, Brampton, ON

Graduated with a GPA of 3.96/4.0

Work Experience

2009–2013 Summers	Assembly Line	FAN Personnel Solutions Brampton, ON
2008–2013 Summers	Property maintenance	Self-employed

Hobbies and Interests

Carpentry, electrical wiring, plumbing, canoeing, hiking, hockey

References

Upon request

Resumé
emphasizes
skills to
compensate
for limited
work
experience

The **functional resumé** emphasizes the applicant's most important (to the reader) job titles and
responsibilities, or functions, regardless of chronology. Use the functional/combination resumé if

- Your work experiences match the position responsibilities.
- Your skills and expertise match the position requirements.

- Your education and experience are not the usual route to the position for which you're applying.
- You want to de-emphasize your formal education.

FIGURE 25.3   **A Functional Resumé**

Dennis Crawford
65 Dunnet Drive
Barrie, ON L4N 0J6
705.555.4807
dcrawford@address.ca

Summary of Qualifications

- A highly skilled executive sales professional specializing in the CCTV/Video Surveillance marketplace
- Inducted into the company's President's Club four times for exceeding sales by 115% to 149%

Recognized for achievements in

- Regional & National Account Management
- Sales & Marketing Strategies
- Consultative Sales
- Product Management & Promotion

- Project Management
- Technical Sales Training
- Systems Design & Implementation
- Forecasting & Budgets

Professional Experience

Panasonic Canada Inc., Mississauga, ON
A global leader in consumer and industrial electronics manufacturing and sales

National Account Manager, Professional Imaging & Display Solutions Group *(2012–2013)*
Identified and managed high-profile national re-seller accounts while developing new growth opportunities through strategic networking with large national end-user accounts within Canada

- Developed a new national sales and marketing strategy while managing the Panasonic sales activities of 3 high-profile national re-seller accounts with over 35 sales professionals between them
- Identified, engaged, and closed new business opportunities with national re-seller accounts for a projected increase in sales of $500K within year one
- Successfully presented B2B strategies to high-profile end-user accounts securing net new business in excess of $1.5 million for select re-seller accounts
- Consultant to professional engineers, architects, sales professionals, and end users for the design and implementation of complex video solutions that exceed customer expectations
- Key liaison and consultant to product manager for industry trade shows and national marketing initiatives, often collaborating on booth design, marketing concepts, and product presentations for large industry trade shows, national technical sales seminars, and new product launches

Regional Account Manager, Central Division
Professional Imaging & Display Solutions Group *(2004–2012)*
Identified and managed regional re-seller accounts while developing new growth opportunities through strategic networking with Ontario regional and national end user accounts

- Developed sales and marketing strategies that successfully managed the Panasonic sales activities of 14 regional re-seller accounts with over 80 sales professionals
- Increased sales and market share within a territory that represented 40% of the department's annual sales forecast and budget
- Presented B2B strategies to several high-profile end-user and regional accounts resulting in a P.O. for over $1 million, setting a new record within the department
- Successfully organized, managed, and led an offsite national sales meeting on behalf of National Sales & Marketing Manager, opening channels of communication to a new level within the department; still considered by my peers to be the most effective and constructive sales meeting of record for the department
- Created and led successful product and sales training seminars, presenting at industry trade shows and technical product launches across Canada. Educated over 100 sales personnel and several hundred end users and consultants on the benefits of technology and products offered by Panasonic Canada Inc.

FIGURE 25.3 **A Functional Resumé** (continued)

Dennis Crawford
65 Dunnet Drive
Barrie, ON L4N 0J6
705.555.4807
dcrawford@address.ca

Product Manager, Professional Imaging & Display Solutions Group (2003–2004)
Technical product sales liaison among Panasonic factories, internal sales, service, and upper management representatives, external sales, and end-user clientele

- Redesigned, developed, and deployed a struggling national product training program targeted at over 35 Panasonic re-sellers with sales representatives in excess of 150 people; several hundred end users, consultants, and engineers; and over a dozen internal sales, service, and management staff across Canada
- Developed and presented strategies to factory representatives based on competitive product and market data, resulting in a more focused approach to product development for the North American market
- Managed product promotion and Regional Account Manager's involvement at industry trade shows both locally and nationally, aiding in the increase of product awareness and knowledge of our sales and customer base
- Successfully provided pre- and post-technical sales and system design support to over 35 re-sellers and three distribution accounts with a combined sales force of over 200 people, and over a dozen Panasonic internal sales, marketing, and technical service support people

KM Video & Security, Mississauga, ON (2000–2004)
An industry leader in the design and implementation of complex video surveillance systems for medium and large businesses

Service Technician, CCTV Products (2002–2004)
Technical service representative responsible for maintaining complex video solutions for KM clientele

- Maintained a high level of customer service support by successfully diagnosing and repairing complex system/product faults, effectively reducing system downtime and maintaining the integrity of security solution
- Facilitated open communication between sales and customer service departments, resulting in more efficient customer service for our key clientele
- Designed, developed, and maintained weekly/monthly/yearly service contract schedule for key customers and successfully delegated work orders to service technicians for service contract clientele, increasing productivity by over 25%, which increased sales

Installation Technician, CCTV Products (2000–2002)
Installed complex video surveillance solutions

- Team lead, responsible for the installation and commissioning of complex video surveillance solutions
- Consultant to sales staff regarding installation estimates and project management, ensuring efficient use of installer's time and meeting strict deadlines to ensure project profitability
- Trainer of end users, internal sales people, and service staff on the operation of complex video solutions

Education

York University, Schulich School of Business

Sheridan College, School of Applied Arts & Technology
Architectural Technician Diploma (2001–2003)

Panasonic Canada Inc.

Canadian Professional Sales Association

FIGURE 25.4   **A Combination/Skills Resumé for Changing Jobs**

On the first page of a skills resumé, put skills directly related to the job for which you're applying.

The centred format is eye-catching but it can be hard to read. Here, bold headings draw the reader's eye.

Marcella G. Cope

370 Mahon Avenue
Vancouver, B.C. V7M 3E1
250-555-1997
mcope@postbox.com

Objective

To help create high-quality CD-ROM products in Metatec's New Media Solutions Division

Put company's name in objective.

Editing and Proofreading Experience

- **Edited** a textbook published by Simon & Schuster, revising with attention to format, consistency, coherence, document integrity, and document design.
- **Proofed** training and instructor manuals, policy statements, student essays and research papers, internal documents, and promotional materials.
- **Worked with authors** in a variety of fields including English, communication, business, marketing, economics, education, history, sociology, biology, agriculture, computer science, law, and medicine to revise their prose and improve their writing skills by giving them oral and written feedback.

Writing Experience

- **Wrote** training and instructor manuals, professional papers, and letters, memos, and reports.
- **Co-authored** the foreword to a forthcoming textbook (Fall 2012) from NCTE press.
- **Contributed** to a textbook forthcoming (Fall 2012) from Bedford Books/St. Martin's Press.

Computer Experience

Computer experience is crucial for almost every job. Specify the software and hardware you've worked with.

- **Designed** a Web page using Microsoft Front Page
  (www.cohums.ohio-state.edu/english/People/Bracken.1/Sedgwick/)
- **Learned and used** a variety of programs on both Macintosh and PC platforms:
  Word processing and spreadsheets
  Microsoft Project
  FrontPage
  PageMaker
  Aspects (a form for online synchronous discussion)
  Storyspace (a hypertext writing environment)
  PowerPoint
  Email

Other Business and Management Experience

- **Developed** policies, procedures, and vision statements.
- **Supervised** new staff members in a mentoring program.
- **Coordinated** program and individual schedules, planned work and estimated costs, set goals, and evaluated progress and results.
- **Member of team that directed** the nation's largest first-year writing program.

FIGURE 25.4   A Combination/Skills Resumé for Changing Jobs (continued)

Marcella G. Cope

Page 2

Employment History

- **Graduate Teaching Associate,** Department of English, University of Victoria,
  September 2008–Present. Taught Intermediate and First-Year Composition.
- **Writing Consultant,** University Writing Centre, Simon Fraser University, January–April 2007
- **Program Administrator,** First-Year Writing Program, University of Victoria,
  September 2008–January 2012

Honours

- **Phi Kappa Phi Honour Society,** inducted 2008. Membership based on performance
  in top 10 percent of graduate students nationwide.
- **Letters of Commendation,** 2003. Issued by the Director of Graduate Studies in recognition of
  outstanding achievement.
- **Dean's List**

Education

- **Master of Arts,** June 2013, the University of Victoria, Victoria, B.C.
  Cumulative GPA: 4.0/4.0
- **Bachelor of Arts,** June 2012, Simon Fraser University, Burnaby, B.C.
  Graduated with Honours

The **combination/skills resumé** (Figure 25.4) emphasizes skills you've acquired through work experience. Use a skills resumé when

- You want to combine experience from paid jobs, activities or volunteer work, and courses to show the extent of your experience in transferable and technical skills: administration, finance, public speaking, and so on.
- Your education and experience do not provide the usual route to the position for which you're applying.
- You're changing fields.
- Your recent work history might create the wrong impression (e.g., it has gaps, shows a demotion, shows job-hopping, etc.).

How Do Resumé Formats Differ?

They highlight you differently, depending on your experiences, your purpose (the job you're applying for), and your audience.

A chronological resumé, such as the one in Figure 25.2, focuses on *when*, then *what*, and emphasizes academic qualifications. Experience is organized by date, with the most recent job first. The functional resumé (Figure 25.3) highlights the applicant's qualifications according to relevant job functions or responsibilities. Extensive experience, not dates or academic degrees, is the focus. Seasoned and highly qualified applicants use this format.

A combination/skills resumé, such as the one in Figure 25.4, summarizes experience and acquired skills needed for the job. Under each heading, the resumé lists, in order of importance, paid and unpaid work (in classes, activities, and community groups). An Employment History section lists job titles (or functions), employers, city, and province.

Chronological Resumés

In a chronological resumé, start with the heading most relevant to the reader. Under Work Experience or Employment History, include employment dates, position or job title, organization, city, province, and other details: seasonal, full- or part-time status, job duties, special responsibilities, and promotions within companies. Include unpaid jobs and self-employment if they provided relevant skills (e.g., supervising people, budgeting, planning, persuading). If you've held co-op or intern placements (very significant to employers), include these under a separate heading such as Co-operative Placement Experience.

Normally, go back as far as the summer after high school. Include earlier jobs if you started working somewhere before graduating from high school but continued working there after graduation. However, give minimal detail about high school jobs. If you worked full-time after high school, make that clear.

If, as an undergraduate, you've earned a substantial portion of your college or university expenses, say so, either under Experience or in the Interpersonal or Skills Profile section with which you can begin the resumé (graduate students are expected to support themselves):

- These jobs paid 40 percent of my university expenses.
- Paid for 65 percent of expenses with jobs, scholarships, and loans.

Omit information about low-level jobs, unless they illustrate experience important to your reader.

Use details to display your attitudes, abilities, or talents. Tell how many people you trained or supervised, how much money you budgeted or raised. Describe the aspects of the job you did.

Too vague: 2010–2013 Sales Manager, the *Daily Collegian*, Mount Royal University, AB. Supervised staff; promoted ad sales.

Good details: 2010–2013 Sales Manager, the *Daily Collegian*, Mount Royal University, AB. Supervised 22-member sales staff; helped recruit, interview, and select staff; assigned duties and scheduled work; recommended best performer for promotion. Motivated staff to increase paid ad sales 10 percent over previous year's sales.

Verbs or gerunds (the *-ing* form of verbs) always create a more dynamic image than do nouns, so use them on resumés that will be read by people rather than computers. (Rules for scannable resumés to be read by computers come later in this module.) In the revisions below, nouns, verbs, and gerunds are in bold type.

Nouns: 2010–2013 Chair, Income Tax Assistance Committee, Winnipeg, MB. Responsibilities: **recruitment** of volunteers; flyer **design**, **writing**, and **distribution** for **promotion** of program; **speeches** to various community groups and nursing homes to advertise the service.

Verbs: 2010–2013 Chair, Income Tax Assistance Committee, Winnipeg, MB. **Recruited** volunteers for the program. **Designed**, **wrote**, and **distributed** a flyer to promote the program; **made presentations** to various community groups and nursing homes to advertise the service.

Gerunds: 2010–2013 Chair, Income Tax Assistance Committee, Winnipeg, MB. Responsibilities included **recruiting** volunteers for the program; **designing**, **writing**, and **distributing** a flyer to promote the program; and **presenting** to various community groups and nursing homes to advertise the service.

Note that the items in the list must be in parallel structure. Table 25.1 lists action verbs that work well in resumés.

TABLE 25.1 **Action Verbs for Resumés**

accomplished	calibrated	debugged	entertained	incorporated
achieved	canvassed	decided	equipped	induced
acted	carried out	decreased	estimated	inducted
adapted	categorized	dedicated	evaluated	influenced
addressed	caused	defined	examined	informed
acquired	changed	delegated	exchanged	initiated
activated	charted	delineated	expanded	inquired
adjusted	clarified	delivered	expedited	inspected
administered	classified	demonstrated	experimented	instituted
adopted	collaborated	depicted	explained	instructed
advised	collected	derived	explored	insured
advanced	combined	described	extracted	integrated
aided	communicated	designed	fabricated	interfaced
allocated	compiled	detailed	facilitated	interpreted
altered	completed	detected	filed	interviewed
analyzed	composed	determined	filled	introduced
announced	computed	developed	financed	invented
answered	conceived	devised	finalized	investigated
appointed	conducted	diagnosed	formed	justified
appraised	concluded	differentiated	forwarded	labelled
approved	condensed	directed	founded	licensed
arranged	conferred	discharged	furnished	located
ascertained	constructed	discussed	gathered	maintained
assembled	consulted	dispensed	generated	managed
assessed	contracted	displayed	graded	manipulated
assigned	contributed	disseminated	graduated	manufactured
assisted	controlled	documented	granted	mapped
assured	converted	drafted	guarded	marketed
attended	cooperated	earned	guided	maximized
audited	co-ordinated	edited	handled	measured
authorized	corresponded	educated	helped	mechanized
automated	corrected	elected	identified	mediated
began	costed	eliminated	illustrated	minimized
billed	counselled	employed	implemented	mobilized
budgeted	created	engaged	imported	modelled
built	cultivated	engineered	improved	modified
calculated	customized	ensured	improvised	monitored

TABLE 25.1   Action Verbs for Resumés (continued)

motivated	preserved	regulated	served	transferred
negotiated	presided	related	set	transformed
observed	prevented	released	set up	translated
obtained	priced	removed	settled	transmitted
officiated	printed	reorganized	sold	transported
operated	produced	repaired	solicited	transposed
orchestrated	programmed	reported	started	treated
organized	projected	represented	stimulated	tutored
oversaw	protected	researched	studied	updated
packaged	provided	responded	strengthened	upgraded
paid	published	restored	submitted	used
participated	purchased	retained	summarized	utilized
performed	qualified	retrieved	supervised	validated
persuaded	questioned	reviewed	supplied	valued
planned	rated	revised	supported	verified
positioned	received	sampled	surveyed	visited
practised	recommended	saved	taught	worked
precipitated	recorded	scheduled	tested	wrote
predicted	rectified	screened	theorized	
prepared	reduced	searched	timed	
prescribed	referred	secured	traced	
presented	refined	selected	trained	

Functional Resumés

The functional resumé focuses on the *what*; this format provides the flexibility to highlight relevant job responsibilities or functions, and to include a variety of experiences. Mature, highly skilled people with the right job credentials use the functional resumé to describe their extensive skills.

Begin with Career Achievements or Career Highlights, where you summarize your primary professional accomplishments. The Employment History is most important: describe your work responsibilities and subsequent skills as they relate to the position for which you are applying. Later in the resumé, identify conferences, clubs, and professional associations in reverse chronology to demonstrate your industry currency. Unless applying for a job for which your education credentials are paramount (like an academic position) and you have those credentials, place Education near the end of this format.

Combination and Skills Resumés

Combination/skills resumés use the *skills* or *aspects* of the job you are applying for as headings, rather than the category title or the dates of the jobs you've held (as in a chronological resumé). For entries under each skill, combine experience from paid jobs, unpaid work, classes, activities, and community service.

Use headings that reflect the jargon of the job for which you're applying: *logistics* rather than *planning* for a technical job; *procurement* rather than *purchasing* for a civilian job with the military. Figure 25.4 shows a skills resumé for someone who is changing fields. Marcella suggests that she already knows a lot about the field she hopes to enter by using its jargon for the headings.

Try to have least three headings related to the job in a combination resumé. Give enough detail to convince the reader that you have developed the requisite skill sets through a variety of experience. Put the most important category—**from the reader's perspective**—first.

A job description can give you ideas for headings. Possible headings and subheadings for skills resumés include

Administration

Alternatives or subheadings:

    Coordinating

    Evaluating

    Implementing

    Negotiating

    Planning

    Keeping Records

    Scheduling

    Solving Problems

    Budgeting

    Supervising

Communication

Alternatives or subheadings:

    Conducting Meetings

    Editing

    Fundraising

    Interviewing

    Speaking

    Negotiating

    Persuading

    Proposal Writing

    Report Writing

Many jobs require a mix of skills. Include the skills that you know will be needed in the job you want.

In a combination resumé, list your paid jobs under Employment History near the end of the resumé (see Figure 25.4). List only job title, employer, city, province, and dates. Omit details about what you did, since you will have already used them under Experience.

Checkpoint

A **chronological resumé** summarizes what you did in a timeline, starting with the most recent events and going backward (**reverse chronology**). Use a chronological resumé when your education and experience

- Are logical preparations for the position for which you're applying
- Show a steady progression leading to the present

Use a **functional** or **combination resumé** in these cases:

- Your education and experience are not the usual route to the position.
- You're changing fields.
- You want to combine experience from paid jobs, activities, volunteer work, and courses.
- Your recent work history might create the wrong impression.

What Parts of Resumé Formats Are the Same?

Increasingly all resumés begin with an attention-grabbing heading, such as Career Achievements, Career Highlights, Communication and Technical Skills, or Interpersonal Profile.

Every resumé should have an overview of your communication skills and an Education section. Career Objective, Honours and Awards, and References are optional.

Career Objective

Some job coaches and recruiters consider Career Objective statements irrelevant, and a waste of valuable space and placement.[1]

However, if you want to include a career objective statement, write it like the job description the employer might use in a job listing. Keep your statement brief—two or three lines at most. Tell what you want to do and what level of responsibility you want to hold.

Ineffective career objective:	To offer a company my excellent academic foundation in hospital technology and my outstanding skills in oral and written communication.
Better career objective:	Selling state-of-the-art Siemens medical equipment.

Including the employer's name in the objective is a nice touch.

As an alternative to writing a career objective statement, put the job title or field under your name:

Joan Larson Ooyen	Terence Garvey	David R. Lunde
Marketing	Technical Writer	Corporate Fitness Director

Career Achievements

Highlight proficiency in foreign and computer languages, and identify your outstanding communication skills, in order of importance to the reader:

- Excellent researcher, writer, and editor
- Conversant in all software applications
- Multilingual: speak, read, and write English, Arabic, and Punjabi
- Proficient in Internet, Intranet, and LAN usage

The functional or combination resumé uses career achievements to highlight measurable accomplishments:

- Started seasonal landscaping business Spring 2009; by Spring 2012 employed six full-time employees, generating revenues of $300,000
- Generated revenue of $2.5 million over quota as Western Division Sales Manager
- Implemented employee-mentoring program resulting in a 40% increase in retention
- Created new assembly procedure that cut production costs by 25%
- Developed procedures manual now used in every national and international office

Education

Education can be your first major category if you've just earned (or are about to earn) a degree, if you have a degree that is essential or desirable for the position you're seeking, or if you lack relevant work experience. Put Education later if you need all of page one to emphasize your skills and experience, or if you lack a degree that other applicants may have.

Include summer school if you took optional courses or extra electives to graduate early. Include study abroad, even if you didn't earn college credits. If you got a certificate for international study, give the name of the program and explain the significance of the certificate.

Professional certifications can be listed under Education, under or after your name, or in a separate category.

Include your GPA only if it's good. Because grade point systems vary, specify what your GPA is based on: "3.4/4.0" means 3.4 on a 4.0 scale. If your GPA is under 3.0 on a 4.0 scale, use words rather than numbers: "B average." If your GPA isn't impressive, calculate your average in your major and your average for your last 60 hours. If these are higher than your overall GPA, consider using them.

List the following in reverse chronological order: each degree earned; field of study; date; school, city, province, or state of any graduate work; short courses and professional certification courses; university, college, community college, or school from which you transferred.

> B.S. in personnel management, June 2012, University of Waterloo, Waterloo, ON
>
> A.S. in office management, June 2012, Georgian College, Barrie, ON

To fill a page, you can also list selected courses, using short descriptive titles rather than course numbers. Use a subhead such as "Courses Related to Major" or "Courses Related to Financial Management" that will allow you to list all the courses (including psychology, speech, and business communication) that will help you in the job for which you're applying.

> Bachelor of Science in management, May 2012, University of Guelph, Guelph, ON
>
> GPA: 3.8/4.0
>
> Courses Related to Management:

Personnel Administration	Business Decision-Making
Finance	International Business
Management I and II	Marketing
Accounting I and II	Legal Environment of Business
Business Report Writing	Business Speaking

> Salutatorian, Eastview High School, June 2008, Toronto, ON

A third option is to list the number of hours in various subjects, especially if the combination of courses qualifies you for the position for which you're applying.

> B.Sc. in marketing, May 2012, St. Francis Xavier University, Nova Scotia
>
> 30 hours in Marketing
>
> 15 hours in Spanish
>
> 9 hours in Human Resources Management

Honours and Awards

The Honours and Awards heading creates a positive impression even when the reader skims the resumé. Include this category for all awards that reflect your drive for achievement and recognition.

Include the following kinds of entries in this category:

- Listings in recognition books (e.g., *Who's Who in Web Design*)
- Academic honour societies (Specify the nature of Greek-letter honour societies so the reader understands that these are more than social clubs.)
- Fellowships and scholarships
- Awards given by professional societies and community associations
- Major awards given by civic groups
- Music accreditation and awards; varsity letters; selection to provincial or national sports teams; finishes in provincial, national, or Olympic meets (These might also go under Activities but may look more impressive under Honours. Put them under one category or the other—not both.)

Build your praise portfolio: keep a file of letters, emails, thank-you cards, and notes praising your job performance.

Omit honours such as "Miss Congeniality" that work against the professional image you want your resumé to create.

As a new graduate, you should try to put Honours on page one. In a skills and functional or combination resumé, place Honours and Awards on page two or three, depending on the space your Work Experience takes.

References

Ex. 25.3

Including references on a separate page anticipates the employer's needs and removes a potential barrier to your getting the job. You can omit this category on your resumé, however, since prospective employers now take it for granted that applicants will supply references when required.

When you list references, use three to five. Include at least one professor and at least one employer or advisor—someone who can comment on your work habits and leadership skills.

Always ask the person's permission to list him or her as a reference. Don't say, "May I list you as a reference?" Instead, say, "Can you speak specifically and positively about my work?" Jog the person's mind by taking along copies of work you did for him or her and a copy of your current resumé. Tell your references what points you'd like them to stress in a letter.

Keep your list of references up to date. If it's been a year or more since you asked someone, ask again—and tell the person about your recent achievements.

References the reader knows are by far the most impressive. In a functional and skills resumé, choose people to recommend you who can testify to your abilities in the most important skills areas.

What Should I Do If the Standard Categories Don't Fit?

Ex. 25.4–25.10

Employability Skills

Create new ones.

Create headings that match your qualifications: Computer Skills, Military Experience, Foreign Languages, Summer and Part-Time Jobs, Marketing Experience, Publications, Exhibitions, Professional Associations.

The items Education and Experience (if you use the latter term) always stand as separate categories, even if you have only one item under each heading. Combine other headings so that you have at least two long or three short items under each heading. For example, if you're in one honour society, two social clubs, and on one athletic team, combine them all under Activities and Honours.

If you have more than seven items under a heading, consider using subheadings. For example, a student who had a great many activities might divide them into Student Government, Other Campus or Extracurricular Activities, and Community Service.

Put your strongest categories near the top and at the bottom of the first page. If you have impressive work experience, you might want to put that category first after your name, Education in the middle of the page, and your address at the bottom.

Should I Limit My Resumé Length?

Don't limit the length if you have many qualifications.

The average resumé is now two pages, unless you need more space to emphasize your qualifications. Executive search firm founder Michael Stern (Michael Stern Associates, Toronto) says readability always trumps conciseness: "Someone with a lot of experience and expertise is better going to three pages than trying to fit everything on two pages of tiny, hard-to-read type."[2]

If you do use more than one page, the second page should have at least 10 to 12 lines. Use a second sheet stapled to the first so that readers who skim know that there's more. Leave less important information for the second page. Put your name and "Page 2" or "Cont." on the second page. If the pages become separated, you want the reader to know whom the qualifications belong to and that the second page is not your whole resumé.

Ex. 25.9

LO1 LO4 # How Do I Create a Scannable Resumé?

Take out all the formatting.

Employability Skills

Figure 25.5 shows an example of a scannable resumé. To increase the chances that the resumé is scanned correctly

- Use a standard typeface: Helvetica, Futura, Optima, Times Roman, New Century Schoolbook, Courier, Univers, or Bookman.[3]
- Use 12- or 14-point type.
- Use the "ragged right" style—that is, do not use *justification* (which stretches each line out to the same length). Scanners can't always handle the extra spaces between words and letters that justification creates.
- Don't italicize or underline words—even for titles of books or newspapers that grammatically require such treatment.

FIGURE 25.5   A Scannable Resumé

Jerry A. Jackson

Keywords: family financial management; financial planning; retirement planning; investment sales; computer modelling; competitive; self-starter; hard worker; responsible; self-managing; collegiate athletics; sales experience

Campus Address
St. Mary's Road
Winnipeg, SK R2H 1J2
(306) 555-5718
Email address: jjackson@ccw.sk.ca
Created a Web page on saving for life goals, such as a home, children's education, and retirement: http://hotmail.com/jackson.2495/home.htm

Permanent Address
2105 East Hill Avenue
Saskatoon, SK S7J 3C8
(306) 555-4108

Summary of Qualifications
High energy. Played sports during two years of college. Started two businesses.
Sales experience. Sold both clothing and investments successfully.
Presentation skills. In individual and group presentations, spoke to groups ranging from 2 to 75 people. Gave informative, persuasive, and inspirational talks.
Financial experience. Knowledgeable about stocks and bonds, especially energy and telecommunication companies.
Computer experience. Microsoft Word, Excel, SPSS, PowerPoint, and Dreamweaver.
Experience creating Web pages.

Education
A.A.S. in Finance, May 2012, Community College of Winnipeg, Winnipeg, MB
B Average
Comprehensive courses related to program provide not only the basics of family financial management but also skills in communication, writing, speaking, small groups, and computer modelling
Intermediate Accounting I and II
Business Writing
Consumer Finance
Financial Management
Interpersonal Communication
Investments
Microeconomics
Presentation Skills
Public Speaking
Report and Technical Writing
Sociology of Marriage and Family
Statistics

Sports Experience
Intramural Hockey Team (Champions, Winter 2011)
Two-Year Varsity Letterman, Community College of Winnipeg
Men's NCAA Division II Basketball

Use 12- or 14-point type in a standard typeface. Here, Times Roman is used.

In keywords, use labels and terms that employers might include in job listings.

Give as much information as you like. The computer doesn't care how long the document is.

Don't use columns. Scanners can't handle them.

FIGURE 25.5   A Scannable Resumé (continued)

Experience
Financial Sales Representative, Primerica Company, Winnipeg, MB, February 2010–present. Work
with clients to plan investment strategies; recommend specific investments, including stocks,
bonds, mutual funds, and annuities.

Entrepreneur, Winnipeg, MB, and Saskatoon, SK, September 2005–January 2010. Created a saleable
product, secured financial backing, found a manufacturer, supervised production, and sold
product—12 dozen T-shirts at a $5.25 profit each—to help pay for school expenses.

Landscape Maintenance Supervisor, Saskatoon, SK, Summers 2003–2008. Formed a company to
cut lawns, put up fences, fertilize, garden, and paint houses. Hired, fired, trained, motivated, and
paid friends to complete jobs. Managerial experience.

Collector and Repairman, ACN Inc., Saskatoon, SK, Summer 2008. Collected and counted up to
$10 000 a day. Worked with technicians to troubleshoot and repair electronic and coin mechanisms
of video and pinball games, cigarette machines, and jukeboxes. Drove company cars and trucks
throughout Saskatoon metro area to collect cash, and move and repair machines.

Willing to relocate
Willing to travel
Canadian citizen

> Don't justify margins.
> Doing so creates extra
> spaces that confuse
> scanners.

- Put the text in bold to make sure letters don't touch each other. Then remove the bold.
- Don't use lines, boxes, script, leader dots, or borders.
- Don't use two-column format, indents, or centred text.
- Put each phone number on a separate line.
- Use plenty of white space.
- Don't fold or staple the pages.
- Don't write anything by hand on your resumé.
- Send a laser copy. Stray marks defeat scanners.
- To increase the number of matches or "hits"
  - Use a Keywords section under your name, address, and phone numbers. Put the following in this section:
    - Degrees, job field or title, accomplishments
    - Interpersonal strengths and attitudes: *dependable, skilled in time management, leadership, sense of responsibility.*[4]
- Use industry buzzwords and jargon, even if redundant. For example, "Web page design and HTML coding" will "match" either "Web" or "HTML" as a keyword.
  - Use nouns. Some systems don't handle verbs well.
  - Use common headings such as Summary of Qualifications, Strengths, Certifications, as well as Education, Experience, and so on.
- Use as many pages as necessary.
- Mention specific software programs (e.g., Adobe Dreamweaver, Microsoft FrontPage) that you've used.
- Be specific and quantifiable. "Managed $2 million building materials account" will generate more hits than "manager" or "managerial experience." Listing Microsoft FrontPage as a skill won't help as much as "Used Microsoft FrontPage to design an interactive website for a national fashion retailer, with links to information about style trends, current store promotions, employment opportunities, and an online video fashion show."
- Join honour societies, and professional and trade organizations, since they're often used as keywords.[5]

- Spell out Greek-letter societies (the scanner will mangle Greek characters, even if your computer has them): "Pi Sigma Alpha Honour Society." For English words, spell out the organization name; follow it with the abbreviation in parentheses: "Canadian University Press (CUP)." That way, the resumé will be tagged whether the recruiter searches for the full name or the acronym.
- Put everything in the resumé, rather than "saving" some material for the cover letter. Although some applicant tracking systems can search for keywords in cover letters and other application materials, most only extract information from the resumé, even though they store the other papers. The length of the resumé doesn't matter.

LO1 LO4 How Should I Prepare an Online Resumé?

Follow these guidelines.

In your Web resumé,

Employability Skills

- Include an email link at the top of the resumé under your name.
- Omit your street addresses and phone numbers. (A post office box is okay.) Employers who find your resumé on the Web will have the technology to email you.
- Consider having links under your name and email address to the various parts of your resumé. Use keywords and phrases that tell the viewer what you offer: *Marketing Experience.*
- Link to other pages that provide more information about you (a list of courses, a report you have written) but not to organizations (your university, an employer) that shift emphasis away from your credentials.
- Be businesslike: link to other pages only if they highlight or demonstrate your abilities, and convey the same professional image as your resumé.
- Put your strongest qualification immediately after your name and email address. If the first screen doesn't interest readers, they won't scroll through the rest of the resumé.
- Specify the job you want.
- Specify city and province for educational institutions and employers.
- Use lists, indentations, and white space to create visual variety.
- Proofread the resumé carefully.

MODULE SUMMARY

- Your resumé should fill at least one page. Use two or more pages if you have extensive experience and activities.
- Make the resumé attractive and readable: use plenty of white space, bold headings, and revise and edit to perfection.
- Emphasize your key points:
  - ○ Put them in headings
  - ○ Use keywords
  - ○ List them vertically
  - ○ Provide details
- Emphasize information that is
  - ○ Relevant to the job you want
  - ○ Expressed in industry- and ad-related language
  - ○ Specific about how you can contribute to the job

- Resumés use sentence fragments. Make items concise and parallel. Emphasize action verbs and gerunds.
- The **chronological** resumé summarizes your experiences and activities in a timeline, starting with the most recent events and going backward. It emphasizes degrees, dates, and job titles. Use a chronological resumé when your education and experience
  - ○ Provide a logical preparation for the position
  - ○ Show a steady progression leading to the present
- **Functional** and **skills** resumés emphasize your experiences and applied skills. Use a skills resumé when
  - ○ Your education and experience are not the usual route to the position for which you are applying
  - ○ You are changing fields

○ You want to highlight the extent of your experience from a combination of paid jobs and community and volunteer work

○ Your recent work history may create the wrong impression (has gaps, indicates a demotion, shows job-hopping, etc.)

• To create a scannable resumé, create a plain text using industry jargon, buzzwords, and acronyms.

• In a Web resumé, put your strongest qualification(s) first, and specify the position you want. Omit street addresses and phone numbers, consider having links to parts of the resumé, and proofread carefully.

ASSIGNMENTS FOR MODULE 25

Questions for Critical Thinking

25.1 How would you create a Skills Statement for Mohammed Shaffer's resumé (Figure 25.2)?

25.2 How would you quantify an important transferable skill you have developed? Choose one transferable skill you know would benefit any employer and describe it in measurable terms.

25.3 When would you consider creating a video resumé?

Exercises and Problems

25.4 Analyzing Job Postings

1. Find three job postings (print or electronic) for an entry-level position you are interested in.
2. For each job posting, identify the keyword descriptors, including those for interpersonal, intrapersonal, communication, technological, and technical skills.
3. Create a list of these keywords to use for your headings and information for Exercises 25.5 though 25.10.

25.5 Analyzing Your Accomplishments

1. List the 10 accomplishments that give you the most personal satisfaction—perhaps achievements that other people wouldn't notice. They can be accomplishments or things you did years ago.

   Use jot notes or clustering to answer the following questions for each accomplishment:
   a. What skills or knowledge did you use?
   b. What personal traits did you exhibit?
   c. What about this accomplishment makes it personally satisfying for you?
2. Find a print or Web ad for a company or industry that appeals to you.
3. Create skills statements about each of your accomplishments:
   a. Use the language of the advertised position and the industry.
   b. Start with your accomplishments that appear most relevant to the position.
   c. Quantify your accomplishments when possible.

As your instructor directs
   a. Share your answers with a small group of students.
   b. Summarize your answers in a memo to your instructor.
   c. List the most significant of these on your resumé.

25.6 Remembering What You've Done

Use the following list to jog your memory about what you've done. For each, give three or four details as well as a general statement.

Describe a time when you

1. Used research to gain agreement on an important point
2. Made a presentation or a speech to a group
3. Identified a problem faced by a group or organization and developed a plan for solving the problem
4. Responded to criticism
5. Interested other people in something that was important to you and persuaded them to take the actions you wanted
6. Helped a group deal constructively with conflict
7. Demonstrated creativity

As your instructor directs
   a. Identify which job(s) each detail is relevant for.
   b. Identify which details would work well on a resumé.
   c. Identify which details, further developed, would work well in a job letter.

25.7 Evaluating Career Objective Statements

None of the following career objective statements is effective. What is wrong with each as it stands? Which might be revised to be satisfactory? Which should be dropped?

1. To use my acquired knowledge of accounting to eventually own my own business
2. A progressively responsible position as a MARKETING MANAGER where education and ability would have valuable application and lead to advancement
3. To work with people responsibly and creatively, helping them develop personal and professional skills
4. A position in international marketing that makes use of my specialization in marketing and my knowledge of foreign markets
5. To design and maintain websites

25.8 Writing a Paper Resumé

Write a resumé on paper that you could mail to an employer or hand to an interviewer at an interview.

As your instructor directs

a. Write a resumé for the field in which you hope to find a job.
b. Write two different resumés for two different job paths you are interested in pursuing.
c. Adapt your resumé to a specific company you hope to work for.

25.9 Writing a Scannable Resumé

Create a scannable, electronic version of one of the resumés you created for Exercise 25.7. Post your resumé on three industry-specific websites.

25.10 Creating a Video Resumé

Create a video resumé.

As your instructor directs

a. Share your video with three peers and get feedback.
b. Reshoot your video based on peer feedback.
c. Upload your video and request class and viewer feedback.
d. Upload your final version.

POLISHING YOUR PROSE

Proofreading

Wait until the final draft is complete to edit and proofread. There is no point in proofreading words and passages that might change. (Some writers claim to proofread documents while they're composing; this practice is like trying to mow the lawn and trim the hedges at the same time.)

Editing includes checking for you-attitude and positive emphasis, fixing any sexist or biased language, and correcting grammatical errors.

Proofreading means making sure that the document is free from typos. Check each of the following aspects:

- **Spelling:** Scan for misspelled or misused words that spell checkers don't catch: *not* instead of *now*, *you* instead of *your*, *its* instead of *it's*, *their* instead of *there* or *they're*, *one* instead of *won*, and so forth.
- **Consistency:** Check abbreviations and special terms.
- **Names:** Double-check the reader's name.
- **Punctuation:** Make sure that parentheses and quotation marks come in pairs. Be on the lookout for missing or extra commas and periods.

- **Format:** Look for errors in spacing, margins, and document design, especially if you compose your document on one computer and print it out at another. Use the correct format for citations—MLA, APA, *Chicago Manual of Style*, and so on.
- **Numbers and dates:** Double-check all numbers to make sure they add up. Make sure page numbers appear where they should and are sequential. Do the same for tables of contents or appendices. Check dates.

Proofreading is as individual as writing style. Try these methods or invent your own:

- *Read the document from the last word to the first* to catch spelling errors.
- *Read the document in stages*—first page, second page, third page—with plenty of "rest" in between so you are fresh for each page.
- *Read pages out of sequence* so you can concentrate on the characters on the page rather than the meaning.
- *Read the document aloud*, listening for awkward or incorrect phrasing.
- *Ask a friend to read the document aloud*, with punctuation, while you follow along with the original.

Whatever your approach, build time into the composing process for proofreading. If possible, finish the document a day or two before it's due to allow enough time. (If the document is a 100-page report, allow even more time.) If you're in a hurry, use a spell checker, proof the document yourself, and ask a friend or colleague to proof it as well.

Exercises

Proofread the following passages:

1. Ours are a company worth doing business with. Your can count on our promiss to provide not only the best service but, also the finest in materials, fit, and, finish. All of are products our made to exacting specifications meaning that you received the best product for the best prices. If you aren't satisfied for any reason, simply call the toll-free hotline at 1-800-555-1212 to get a promp refund. Or you can right us at: The John Doe Company, 123 Main Street Anytown Canada M6V 2B4. Remember; our moto is "the customers is always's right?

2. Resumee for Kathy Jones
   332 West Long Strt.
   Moncton, New Brunswick E4Z 1Z8
   614-555-8188

Objection

A management position in fullfilament services where my skills, expereince can be best be used to help your company acheeve it's goals.

Relevent Experience:

2010 to Present Day: Ass. Manager for high-end sports equipment distributor. Responsible for checking new customers out.

2005–2010: Owned and Operated Jones, Inc., a telephone order procesing company for lady's apparel.

2008: Received a plague for Must Promising Executive of the Year" from *Monthly* Magazine.

2010: Delivery address to local high school seniors on why accuracy is important in business.

Special Skills
Type 7 or more words per minute
Studied English all my life. Fluent in French.
Shot at local gun club.

Check your answers to the odd-numbered exercises in the Polishing Your Prose Answer Key.

Creating Persuasive Application Letters

Learning Objectives

After reading and applying the information in Module 26, you'll be able to demonstrate

Knowledge of

LO1 The two types of application letter formats

Skills to

LO2 Organize the solicited application letter

LO3 Organize the prospecting application letter

LO4 Catch the reader's interest even when the company isn't planning to hire

LO5 Show that you have the qualifications for the job

LO6 Persuade the employer that you're in the very top group of applicants

LO7 Use information about the company effectively in your letter

MODULE OUTLINE

- What kind of letter should I use?
- How are the two letters different?
- What parts of the two letters are the same?
- How long should my letter be?
- How do I create the right tone?
- How should I write an email application?

Module Summary

Assignments for Module 26

Polishing Your Prose: Using *You* and *I*

Employability Skills 2000+ Checklist

Module content builds these Conference Board of Canada Employability Skills 2000+

Communicate

Manage Information

Think and Solve Problems

Participate in Projects and Tasks

Demonstrate Positive Attitudes and Behaviours

A well-written application letter captures the recruiter's interest, ensuring he or she will read your resumé. The letter is also your first step in showing a specific company what you have to offer.

The best application letters are customized for their audiences. Use the cover letter to provide a brief preview of your resumé, focusing on

- Key requirements of the job for which you're applying, using the language in the job posting
- Skills and knowledge that differentiate you from other applicants
- Language and information that demonstrates your knowledge of the organization and the industry
- Experiences expressed in transferable, marketable skills

Note that the advice in this book applies to job-hunting in Canada. Conventions, expectations, and criteria differ from culture to culture: different norms apply in different countries. Even within Canada, different discourse communities (Module 2) may have different preferences. Whether you're seeking employment in your home province, nationally, or internationally, however, PAIBOC analysis (see Figure 26.1) is vital to your success.

FIGURE 26.1   PAIBOC Questions for Analysis

P	What are your **purposes** in writing? As usual, you have several: to attract and hold attention, to stand out favourably from other candidates, to demonstrate you have researched the organization and the position, and to preview your resumé.
A	Who is your **audience**? What audience characteristics are relevant to this particular message? What does your audience want to know? How much time will your audience give your message? What can you do to influence your audience favourably to continue reading?
I	What **information** must your message include? In a cover letter, highlight 1) the superiority of your skills, and 2) the fit between the organization's needs and your qualifications.
B	What reasons or reader **benefits** can you use to support your position? Use the application letter to summarize briefly the qualifications you bring to the position and their value to the organization.
O	What **objections** can you expect your readers to have? What elements of your message will your audience perceive as negative? How can you write to overcome audience objections or de-emphasize negative elements?
C	How will the **context** affect reader response? Consider your relationship to the reader, the reader's values and expectations, recent organizational history and current morale, the economy, the time of year, and any special circumstances surrounding the message exchange. *Here is the overriding cultural context: recruiters want to interview only those prospects whose application letter and resumé demonstrate their value to the organization.*

LO5 Every employer wants businesslike employees who understand professionalism. Follow these guidelines to make your application letter professional:

- Create your letter on a computer. Use the same font style and size as in your resumé.
- Whenever possible, address your letter to a specific person; if you do not know the person's name, address your letter to Human Resources.
- Use the language of the organization and the industry.
- Use contact or employee names if the reader knows them and thinks well of them, if they think well of you and will say good things about you, and if you have permission to use their names.
- Always connect an experience (course work, co-op placement, community involvement) with a resultant skill that you know the prospective employer wants.
- Unless you're applying for a creative job, use business stationery and a conservative style: few contractions, and no sentence fragments, clichés, or slang.
- Edit the letter carefully and proof it several times to make sure it's perfect.

LO1 LO2 What Kind of Letter Should I Use?

It depends on whether or not the company has asked for applications.

Two different hiring situations call for two different kinds of application letters. Write a **solicited letter** when you know that the company is hiring:

- You've seen an ad
- You've been advised to apply by a professor or friend
- You've read online or in a trade publication that the company is expanding

Sometimes, however, the advertised positions may not be what you want, or you may want to work for an organization that has not announced that it has openings in your area. Then the situation calls for an **unsolicited** or **prospecting letter**.

A prospecting letter will help you tap into the hidden job market (Module 24). In some cases, your prospecting letter may arrive at a company that has decided to hire but has not yet announced the job. In other cases, companies create positions to get a good person who is on the market.

LO1 LO2 How Are the Two Letters Different?

They begin and end differently.

When you know the company is hiring, organize your letter in this way:

1. State that you're applying for the job (phrase the job title as your source phrased it). Tell where you learned about the job (Web, referral, ad). Briefly show that you have the major qualifications required by the ad: a degree, professional certification, job experience, and so forth. Summarize your other qualifications briefly in the same order in which you plan to discuss them in the letter. This **summary sentence** or **paragraph** covers everything you will talk about and serves as an organizing device for your letter.

> I have a good background in standard accounting principles and procedures, and a working knowledge of some of the special accounting practices of the oil industry. This knowledge is based on practical experience in the oil fields: I've pumped, tailed rods, and worked as a roustabout.
>
> Let me put my oil industry experience and accounting knowledge to work for Standard Oil.

2. Develop your major qualifications in detail. Be specific about what you've done; relate your achievements to the work you'd be doing in this new job. This is not the place for modesty!

3. Develop your other qualifications, even if the ad doesn't ask for them. (If the position description states numerous qualifications, pick the most important three or four.) Show what separates you from the other prospects who will also apply. Demonstrate your knowledge of the organization.

4. Ask for an interview; tell when you'll be available to be interviewed. End on a positive note.

Figures 26.2 and 26.3 are examples of solicited letters.

FIGURE 26.2   A Solicited Letter (1)

210 Steeles Avenue West	Phone: 905.555.3828
Brampton, ON L6Y 2K3	Email: mshafe@bell.live

February 1, 2013

Region of Peel
1126 Fewster Drive
Mississauga, ON L4W 2A4

Open punctuation

Attention Human Resources

Subject: Job/95423-134317
                HHW Facility Operator (Co-op)

As a second-year Chemical Engineering Technology Co-op student at Sheridan Institute, I have the skills and knowledge to contribute to the operation of your Hazardous Waste facility. Through practical application, I understand the Occupational Health and Safety Act WHMIS. Furthermore, in my summer jobs I learned how to handle and store hazardous materials.

Letter uses short sentences, clear language and language of the industry and job posting throughout

At Sheridan I have also developed excellent written and oral communication skills which enable me to communicate information about hazardous waste and depot services to the public clearly and helpfully.

I have my Class G driver's license, a clean driving record, and my own vehicle. I am very flexible and am able to work rotating shifts and weekends. I am used to hard physical shift work. For the past two summers, I worked rotating shifts at an auto parts factory to pay my college tuition. You can count on me to be at work on time and complete tasks to the best of my ability. I take initiative and work well in a team environment.

My Grade Point Average of 3.96 (out of 4.0) illustrates that I am diligent and a quick learner. I will quickly adapt to the Region of Peel's system of receiving, categorizing, storing, and co-coordinating waste shipment.

Letter asks for the interview

Please contact me to arrange an interview to further discuss how I can contribute to your organization.

Sincerely

Mohammed Shafer

Mohammed Shafer

Encl.

FIGURE 26.3   A Solicited Letter (2)

638 Changery Court
Lethbridge, AB T1J 2A5
May 21, 2012

Shelley Aquina
Human Resources Manager
Home Outfitters
425 18 Avenue Northwest
Calgary, AB T2N 2G6

Dear Shelley Aquina:
RE: File # 7664566-F

Please consider me for the position of sales manager, advertised in the *Calgary Sun*, Saturday, May 20. I possess the educational background, work experience, and exceptional organizational and communication skills for which you have advertised.

In June I will graduate with a business administration diploma from Mount Royal University, Calgary, Alberta. Throughout my college career I worked with peers on a variety of projects, including sales proposals, formal reports, and sales presentations. In my third year I was chosen team captain for our marketing project, a year-long analysis, and oral and written report of possible marketing initiatives for a Calgary client, MediaWaves. My responsibilities included identifying time lines, delegating tasks, negotiating conflicts among group members, reporting to the client and our Marketing professor, and revising and editing the final 30-page report. Our team project not only secured the top grade in the class, but the client also accepted our recommendations, resulting in an immediate 10 percent sales increase for MediaWaves.

Since Grade 11, I have worked part-time and summers at Canadian Tire in Lethbridge, Alberta. Starting as a stock clerk, I worked my way up to sales associate. My supervisor has commented on my excellent sales skills, particularly my product knowledge and ability to up-sell. During my employment with Canadian Tire—a high-energy, fast-paced environment—I learned to focus calmly on clients' concerns and to communicate confidently. As a result of my performance, I was promoted to assistant manager. While working part-time, attending school, and participating in varsity basketball, I learned to juggle multiple priorities, to manage my time, and to problem-solve.

Please see my resumé for further details.

The market for home decorations and furnishings has become increasingly competitive, and with the entry of American big-box stores like Heritage Homes, it promises to become even more so. I would welcome an opportunity to apply my skills to increase your market share. Please call me at 403-555-4339 to arrange an interview time and date at your convenience.

Sincerely,

[signature]
Carlos DeLeon
ENC: Resumé

Annotations (left margin):
- Addresses reader as ad indicates
- Repeats words of the ad
- Specifics directly connect the experience with the resultant skill
- Demonstrates research and industry awareness

Annotations (right margin):
- Quotes file number as ad requests
- Thesis or controlling paragraph tells the reader what's going to be proven in the letter
- Jargon of the marketing industry
- Skills would have been identified in the ad as necessary for the position
- Asks for the interview

LO3 Prospecting Letters

When you don't have any evidence that the company is hiring, organize your letter this way:

1. Catch the reader's interest.
2. Create a **bridge** between the attention-getter and your qualifications. Focus on what you know and can do. Since the employer is not planning to hire, he or she won't be impressed

with the fact that you're graduating. Summarize your qualifications briefly in the same order in which you plan to discuss them in the letter.

3. Develop your strong points in detail. Be specific. Relate what you've done in the past to what you could do for this company. Show that you know something about the company. Identify the niche you want to fill.

4. Ask for an interview and tell when you'll be available for interviews. (Don't tell when you can begin work.) End on a positive, forward-looking note.

Figure 26.4 shows an example of a prospecting letter.

FIGURE 26.4   A Prospecting Letter

Kristine Manalili
2 Inverary Court
Porters Lake, Nova Scotia B3E 1M8
902-555-6488 kmanalili@hotmail.com

Kristine creates a boxed "letterhead"

2012-06-25

Mr. John Harrobin
HealthRhab Inc.
2653 Dublin Street
Halifax, NS B3K 3J7

Dear Mr. Harrobin:

Providing an athlete with physiotherapy can assist with a debilitating injury in the short term. However, treatment alone does not provide the long-term product and therapy information necessary for complete recovery. It can be a real challenge finding employees who are conversant with the latest injury-management modalities, who are familiar with the most current injury-management support equipment, and who also work well with rehabilitating clients. However, you will see from my enclosed resumé that I have this useful combination of skills.

In an unsolicited or prospecting letter, open with a sentence that creates reader interest and provides a natural bridge to talking about yourself

Refers to her enclosed resumé

Rita Haralabidis tells me that HealthRhab needs people to identify injury-management therapy and equipment for your clients. My education and work experience have provided me with the injury evaluation and product knowledge that you require. While studying in Nunavut Arctic College's Sports Injury Management program, for example, I provided more than 200 hours of successful client care at the college clinic.

Refers to mutual acquaintance

Shows knowledge of the company

Moreover, I was able to apply the most current therapy modalities and learn about sophisticated sports injury products and equipment while serving my four-month co-op term at Wu's Sports Clinic in Victoria, British Columbia. Wu's Clinic is renowned for its progressive therapy options. My co-op placement provided me with practical experience in injury prevention and treatment. Equally important, I learned about the latest equipment, products, and techniques available to maximize client rehabilitation and recovery.

Demonstrates knowledge and skills she promised in first paragraph

Relates what she's done to what she could do for this company

My communication skills and product knowledge would enable me to adapt immediately to clients' specific needs and to develop programs for your clients. I am flexible, a quick study, and committed to proactive health care. I will call you next week to arrange a mutually convenient time when we can discuss putting my talents to work for HealthRhab.

Promises action

Sincerely,

Kristine Manalili
Enclosed: Resumé

LO2 The First Paragraph of a Solicited Letter

When you know that the firm is hiring, refer to the specific position in your first sentence. Your letter can then be routed to the appropriate person, thus speeding up consideration of your application. Identify where you learned about the job: "the position of junior accountant announced in Sunday's *Vancouver Sun*," "Kadji Kado, our placement director, told me that you are looking for…"

Note how the following paragraph picks up several of the characteristics of the ad:

Ad:	Business Education Instructor at University of New Brunswick. Candidate must possess a bachelor's degree in Business Education. Will be responsible for providing in-house training to business and government leaders… Candidate should have at least six months' office experience. Prior teaching experience not required.
Letter:	Please consider me for the position of **Business Education Instructor**, advertised on Workopolis.com. My Business Education degree, knowledge of adult education principles, and previous office experience make me the ideal candidate for the position.

LO6 Good word choices can help set your letter apart from the hundreds of letters the company is likely to get in response to an ad. The following first paragraph of a letter in response to an ad by Allstate Insurance Company shows knowledge of the firm's advertising slogan and sets itself apart from the dozens of letters that start with "I would like to apply for..."

The Allstate Insurance Company is famous for its "Good Hands" policy. I would like to lend a helping hand to Allstate as a financial analyst, as advertised in yesterday's *National Post*. I have an Accounting Co-op diploma from Georgian College and I have worked with figures, computers, and people.

Note that the last sentence forecasts the organization of the letter, preparing for paragraphs about the student's academic background and (in this order) experience with "figures, computers, and people."

LO4 First Paragraphs of Prospecting Letters

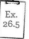
Ex.
26.5

In a prospecting letter, asking for a job in the first paragraph is dangerous; unless the company plans to hire but has not yet announced openings, the reader is likely to throw the letter away. Instead, catch the reader's interest. Then in the second paragraph shift the focus to your skills and experience, showing how they can be useful to the employer.

Here are effective first and second paragraphs of a letter applying to be a computer programmer for an insurance company:

Computers alone aren't the answer to demands for higher productivity in the competitive insurance business. Merging a poorly written letter with a database of customers just sends out bad letters more quickly. But you know how hard it is to find people who can both program computers and write well.

My education and training have given me this useful combination of skills. I'd like to put my degree in computer technology and my business writing experience to work in Sun Canada's service approach to insurance.

Last Paragraphs

In the last paragraph, indicate when you'd be available for an interview. If you're free any time, say so. But it's likely that you have responsibilities in class and work. If you'd have to go out of town for an interview, there may be only certain days of the week or certain weeks that you could leave town for several days. Use a sentence that fits your situation.

> I could come to Thunder Bay for an interview anytime between March 17 and 21.
>
> Please call me at 519-555-4229 for an interview time and date at your convenience.

Should you wait for the employer to call you, or should you call the employer to request an interview? In a solicited letter, you may want to wait to be contacted: you know the employer wants to hire someone, and if your letter and resumé show that you're one of the top applicants, you'll get an interview.

In a prospecting letter, definitely call the employer. Because the employer is not planning to hire, you'll get a higher percentage of interviews if you're assertive. When you do call, be polite to the person who answers the phone.

If you're writing a prospecting letter to a firm that's more than a few hours away by car, say that you'll be in the area the week of such-and-such and could stop by for an interview. Some companies pay for follow-up visits, but not for first interviews. A company may be reluctant to ask you to make an expensive trip when it isn't yet sure it wants to hire you.

End the letter on a positive note that suggests you look forward to the interview and that you see yourself as a person who has something to contribute, not as someone who just needs a job.

> On Wednesday, April 25, I will call you between 9:00 and 9:30 a.m. to schedule a time when we can discuss how my skills can contribute to ISM Canada's continued growth.

LO2 LO3 What Parts of the Two Letters Are the Same?

The body paragraphs discussing your qualifications are the same.

In both solicited and prospecting letters, you should follow these guidelines:

- Address the letter to a specific person.
- Indicate the specific position for which you're applying.
- Be specific about your qualifications.
- Show what separates you from other applicants.
- Demonstrate knowledge of the company and the position.
- Refer to your resumé (which you would enclose with the letter).
- Ask for an interview.

LO4 Showing Knowledge of the Position and the Company

Employability Skills

If you can substitute another inside address and salutation, and send out the letter without any further changes, it isn't specific enough. Use your knowledge of the position and the company to choose relevant evidence from what you've done to support your claims that you could help the company.

One or two specific details are usually enough to demonstrate your knowledge. Be sure to use the knowledge, not just repeat it. Never present the information as though it will be news to the reader. After all, the reader works for the company and presumably knows much more about it than you do.

Separating Yourself from Other Applicants

Your knowledge of the company separates you from other applicants. You can also use course work, an understanding of the field, and experience in jobs and extracurricular events to show that you're unique.

This student uses summer jobs and course work to set herself apart from other applicants:

> A company as diverse as Desjardins Credit Union requires extensive record keeping as well as numerous internal and external communications. Both my summer jobs and my course work have prepared me for these responsibilities. As office manager for Safety Express Limited, I was in charge of most of the bookkeeping and letter writing for the company. I kept accurate records for each workday, and I often entered more than 100 transactions in a single day. In business and technical writing courses, I learned how to write persuasive letters and memos and how to present extensive data in clear and concise reports.

How Long Should My Letter Be?

Highlight the fit between the position and your qualifications clearly and concisely.

Your cover letter and resumé may be one of hundreds under review. The more readable your application letter, the more likely you will attract the favourable attention of those responsible for deciding whom to interview. Keep your letter as concise and clear as possible. Try to keep it to one page.

Without eliminating content, make each sentence concise to be sure that you're using space as efficiently as possible. If your letter is still slightly over a page, use smaller margins, a type size that's one point smaller, or justified proportional type to get more on the page.

If you really need more than one page, though, use it. The extra space gives you room to be more specific about what you've done and to add details about your experience that separate you from other applicants. Employers don't want longer letters, but they will read them *if* the letter is well written and *if* you establish early in the letter that you have the credentials and skills the company needs.

How Do I Create the Right Tone?

Ex.
26.6

Use you-attitude and positive emphasis.

You-attitude and positive emphasis help you sound assertive without being arrogant.

You-Attitude

Unsupported claims may sound overconfident, selfish, or arrogant. Create you-attitude (Module 13) by describing exactly what you have done and showing how that relates to what you could do for this employer.

Lacks you-attitude:	An inventive and improvising individual like me is a necessity in your business.
You-attitude:	Building a summer house-painting business gave me the opportunity to find creative solutions to challenges.

Remember that the word *you* refers to your reader. Using *you* when you really mean yourself or "all people" can insult your reader by implying that he or she still has a lot to learn about business.

Since you're talking about yourself, you'll use *I* in your letter. Do so sparingly. Reduce the number of *I*'s by revising some sentences to use *me* or *my*.

> Under my presidency, the Agronomy Club…
>
> Courses in media and advertising management gave me a chance to…
>
> My responsibilities as a co-op student included…

In particular, avoid beginning every paragraph with *I*. Begin sentences with adverbs (*presently, currently*), prepositional phrases, or introductory clauses.

LO7 EXPANDING A CRITICAL SKILL

Targeting a Specific Company in Your Letter

If your combination of skills is in high demand, a one-size-fits-all letter may get you an interview. But when you must compete against dozens—perhaps hundreds or even thousands—of applicants for an interview slot, you need to target your letter to the specific company. Targeting a specific company also helps you prepare for the job interview.

The Web makes it easy to find information about a company. The example below shows how applicants could use available information about Sleeman Breweries.

Check for Facts About the Company

Like most corporate websites, Sleeman offers dozens of facts about the company. A computer network administrator might talk about helping to keep the 3500 LANs working well. A Web weaver might talk about supporting a new investor relations site or about developing even more interactive content for both national and international customers. Someone in corporate communications, advertising, marketing, or multimedia programs might write a prospecting letter about Sleeman's recent media campaign. An interviewee with experience in international business might pitch the company on the expertise necessary to do business in Boston, Germany, and South Africa. And someone in human resources management might talk about the electronic processing of HR data benefits for the thousands of employees joining this expanding company, or about current recruitment and retention strategies for the company that CIBC World Markets Inc. calls "a well-managed, creative company."

Check News Releases and Speeches

Recent press releases have covered everything from the company's national expansion—across the Maritimes, into Quebec, and Western Canada—to its international partnerships with U.S., German, and South African breweries. Anyone in international business might talk about helping Sleeman expand its base into China—and beyond.

In May 2009, in recognition of its "commitment to the environment and its sustainable packaging practices," the company received a Certificate of Environmental Sustainability from corrugated container supplier Atlantic Packaging Products Ltd. Students about to complete environmental studies, marketing, finance, and management programs might demonstrate how their course work and experience prepare them to expand community-focused programs, or students might offer technical or managerial expertise on the best way for Sleeman Breweries to adopt e-business strategies to support its continuing growth.

Check the Corporate Culture

In his interviews, Chair and CEO John Sleeman emphasizes that his family-owned business produces a quality product based on his great-great-grandfather's recipe. The company's website material also refers to the family beer-making tradition and the site's design reinforces this commitment to traditional values. These promotional strategies appeal to the mature consumers who buy Sleeman beers. Yet Sleeman's partnership arrangements and media advertisements indicate the company's enthusiasm for creativity and flexibility. Prospective job applicants would do well to stress their creative abilities and their support of community arts activities.

Sources: Ontario Brewing Awards Winners List, (2011, May 10) retrieved from http://www.canadianbeernews.com/2011/05/10/ontario-brewing-awards-2011-winners-list/; Cheers to Sleeman, (2009, June 12) *Canadian Packaging*, retrieved from http://www.canadianmanufacturing.com/packaging/sustainability/cheers-to-sleeman-2465; 2009 CBS Interactive Inc., Sleeman Breweries Ltd., *BNET Industries*, retrieved from http://resources.bnet.com/topic/sleeman+breweries+ltd.html; Michael Van Aelst, quoted in Oliver Bertin (2001, June 20), Sleeman brew balance of risk and caution, *Globe and Mail*, M1.

Positive Emphasis

Be positive. Don't plead ("Please give me a chance") or hedge ("I cannot promise that I am substantially different from everyone else").

Avoid word choices with negative connotations (Module 12). Note how the following revisions make the writer sound more confident.

Negative: I have learned an excessive amount about writing through courses in journalism and advertising.

Excessive suggests that you think the courses covered too much—hardly an opinion likely to endear you to an employer.

Positive: Courses in journalism and advertising have taught me to recognize and to write good copy. My profile of a professor was published in the campus newspaper; I earned an A on my direct mail campaign for the Canadian Dental Association to persuade young adults to see their dentists more often.

How Should I Write an Email Application?

Compose a document using a word-processing program. Then attach it to a courteous email message.

Employability Skills 2000+

When you submit an email letter (see Figure 26.5) with an attached resumé, you need to

- Use a plain, professional-sounding email address, such as your own name (Module 25).
- Tell in what word-processing program your scannable resumé is saved.

FIGURE 26.5   An Email Application Letter

Attach your scannable resumé.

Omit salutation.

Choose details that use words from job ad and interest reader.

Repeat name and email address at the end.

Put job number in the subject line and the first paragraph.

Tell what program it's in.

If you have a Web page, list it to show that you're technologically savvy. Keeping the "http://" in the URL creates a hotlink in many email programs.

To: r_h_catanga@ibm.com
From: Tracey McKenna <mckenna.74@rogers.ca>
Subject: Application for jof17747
Cc:
Bcc:
Attached: D:\Jobhunt\resume.scan;

Attached is a scannable resumé in WordPerfect for the accounting position announced on IBM's website (jof17747). I will receive a B.Sc. in accountancy from McMaster University in Hamilton, ON this August and plan to take the CPA exam in December.

As a result of my studies, I've learned to identify the best measures for fixed assets and property controls, and to figure inter-company/intra-company and travel expenses. I can analyze expenditures and compare them to past statements to identify trends and recommend ways to reduce costs.

Furthermore, I can use Excel to create computer graphics to provide the clear, reliable accounting data that IBM needs to continue growing each year. Please visit my Web page to see the report I wrote on choosing the best method to accelerate depreciation.

My three years of experience at Allstate have given me the opportunity to take leadership and show responsibility. I developed a procedure for making out arbitration reports that saved so much time I was asked to teach it to the other employees in my department.

At your convenience, I could come to Toronto for an interview any Tuesday or Thursday afternoon.

Tracey McKenna
mckenna.74@rogers.ca
http://www.mcmaster/business/students/mckenna/report.htm

- Put the job number or title for which you're applying in your subject line and in the first paragraph.
- Prepare your letter in a word-processing program with a spell checker to make it easier to edit and proof the document.
- Don't send anything in all capital letters.
- Don't use smiley faces or other emoticons.
- Put your name and email address at the end of the message. Most email programs send along the "sender" information on the screen, but a few don't, and you want the employer to know whose letter this is!

MODULE SUMMARY

- When you know the company is hiring, send a solicited application letter. When self-recruiting, send a prospecting or unsolicited cover letter.
- Organize your solicited letter this way:
  - State that you are applying for the job, and tell where you learned about the job (ad, referral, etc). Briefly show that you have the major qualifications for the position. In your opening paragraph, summarize your qualifications in the order in which you discuss them in the letter.
  - Develop your major qualifications in detail.
  - Develop your other qualifications. Show what separates you from the other candidates who will apply.
  - Demonstrate your knowledge of the organization.
  - Ask for an interview; say when you are available to be interviewed and to begin work. End on a positive note.
- Organize your prospecting letter this way:
  - Catch the reader's interest.
  - Create a bridge between the opening and your qualifications. Summarize your qualifications in the order in which you discuss them in the letter.
  - Develop your strong points in detail. Relate what you've done in the past to what you could do for this company. Demonstrate your knowledge of

the company. Identify the specific position you are interested in.
  - Ask for an interview and state when you are available for interviews. End on a positive note.
- In both letters
  - Address the letter to a specific person.
  - Indicate the specific position for which you are applying.
  - Be specific about your qualifications.
  - Show what separates you from the other applicants.
  - Demonstrate your knowledge about the company and the position.
  - Refer to your resumé (which you enclose or send with the letter).
  - Ask for an interview.
  - Use your knowledge of the company, your course work, your understanding of the field, and your experience in jobs and extracurricular activities to show that you're unique.
  - Use you-attitude by providing specific details and by relating what you have done with the knowledge or experience the employer needs. Use positive emphasis to sound confident.

ASSIGNMENTS FOR MODULE 26

Questions for Critical Thinking

26.1 How could you write a cover letter that differentiates you positively from other applicants?

26.2 What techniques can you use in the first paragraph to catch the reader's positive interest immediately?

26.3 Identify four methods you can use to create you-attitude throughout your letter.

26.4 When you submit your application letter and resumé by email, what should you write in the email itself?

Exercises and Problems

26.5 Analyzing First Paragraphs of Prospecting Letters

The following are first paragraphs in prospecting letters written by new graduates. Evaluate the paragraphs on these criteria:

- Is the paragraph likely to interest the reader and motivate him or her to read the rest of the letter?
- Does the paragraph have some content that the student can use to create a transition to talking about his or her qualifications?
- Does the paragraph avoid asking for a job?

1. Ann Gibbs suggested that I contact you.

2. Each year, the holiday shopping rush makes more work for everyone at the Bay, especially for the Credit Department. While working for the Bays' Credit Department for three holiday seasons and summer vacations, I became aware of many credit situations.

3. Whether to plate a five-centimetre eyebolt with cadmium for a tough, brilliant shine or with zinc for a rust-resistant, less-expensive finish is a tough question. But your salespeople must answer similar questions daily. With my experience in the electroplating industry, I can contribute greatly to your customer growth.

4. Prudential Insurance Company did much to help my university career, as the sponsor of my National Merit Scholarship. Now I think I can give something back to Prudential. I'd like to put my education, including a degree in finance from university, to work in your investment department.

5. Since the beginning of Delta Electric Construction Co. in 1997, the size and profits have grown steadily. My father, who is a stockholder and vice-president, often discusses company dealings with me. Although the company has prospered, I understand there have been a few problems of mismanagement. I feel with my present and future qualifications, I could help ease these problems.

26.6 Improving You-Attitude and Positive Emphasis in Job Letters

Revise each of these sentences to improve you-attitude and positive emphasis. You may need to add information.

1. I understand that your company has had problems due to the mistranslation of documents for international ad campaigns.
2. Included in my resumé are the courses in finance that earned me a fairly attractive grade average.
3. I am looking for a position that gives me a chance to advance quickly.

4. Although short on experience, I am long on effort and enthusiasm.
5. I have been with the company from its beginning to its present unfortunate state of bankruptcy.

26.7 Writing a Solicited Letter

Write a letter of application in response to an announced opening for a full-time job that a new graduate could hold.

Turn in a copy of the listing. If you use option (a), (b), or (d) below, your listing will be a copy of an actual listing. If you choose option (c), you will write the listing and can design your ideal job.

a. Respond to an ad that you find in a newspaper, in a professional journal, in the placement office, or on the Web. Use an ad that specifies the company, not a blind ad. Be sure that you are fully qualified for the job.

b. Find a job description and assume that it represents a current opening. Use a directory to get the name of the person to whom the letter should be addressed.

c. If you have already worked somewhere, assume that your employer is asking you to apply for full-time work after graduation. Be sure to write a fully persuasive letter.

d. Respond to one of the listings below. Use a directory or the Web to get the name and address of the person to whom you should write.

1. Cotts Beverages is hiring an **assistant auditor**. Minimum 12 years of accounting experience. Work includes analysis and evaluation of operating and financial controls and requires contact with many levels of company management. Extensive travel (50 percent of job hours) required through the Canadian West, along with some international work. Effective written and oral communication skills a must, along with sound decision-making abilities. Locations: Edmonton, Toronto, Halifax, New York, Los Angeles, Dallas, Atlanta, Philadelphia, Denver, Chicago. Refer to job FA-2534.

2. Roxy Systems (Roxy.com) seeks **Internet marketing coordinators** to analyze online campaigns and put together detailed reports, covering ad impressions and click-through rates. Must have basic understanding of marketing; be organized, creative, and detail-oriented; know Microsoft Excel; have excellent communication skills; and be familiar with the Internet. Send letter and resumé to mike@roxy.com.

3. Bose Corporation seeks **public relations/communications administrative associate** (Job Code 117BD). Write, edit, and produce the in-house newsletter using desktop publishing software. Represent the company

to external contacts (including the press). Provide administrative support to the manager of PR by scheduling meetings, preparing presentations, tabulating and analyzing surveys, and processing financial requests. Excellent organizational, interpersonal, and communication skills (both written and oral) required. Must be proficient in MS Office and FileMaker Pro.

4. The Gap is hiring **executive development program trainees**. After completing 10-week training programs, trainees will become assistant buyers. Prefer people with strong interest and experience in retailing. Apply directly to the store for which you want to work.

5. A local non-profit seeks a **coordinator of volunteer services**. Responsibilities for this full-time position include coordinating volunteer schedules, recruiting and training new volunteers, and evaluating existing programs. Excellent listening and communication skills required.

26.8 Writing a Prospecting Letter

1. Look in the business sections of your local and national newspapers for stories that suggest an organization is expanding and may be hiring for positions in various areas. Identify an area or department (accounting, finance, human resources, information technology, marketing, publicity and promotion, research and development, etc.) in which you would like to work.
2. Apply for a specific position. The position can be one that already exists, or one that you would create, if you could, to match your unique blend of talents. Be sure that you are fully qualified for the job.
3. Use the Web or directories to get the name and address of the person with the power to create a job for you.

POLISHING YOUR PROSE

Using *You* and *I*

You-attitude (Module 13) means that you'll use lots of *you*s in business messages. However, use *you* only when it refers to your reader. When you mean "people in general," use another term.

Incorrect:	When I visited your office, I learned that you need to find a way to manage your email.
Correct:	When I visited your office, I saw the importance of managing one's email.
Incorrect:	Older customers may not like it if you call them by their first names.
Correct:	Older customers may prefer being called by courtesy titles and their last names.

Omit *you* when it criticizes or attacks the reader.

Not you-attitude:	You didn't turn your expense report in by the deadline.
You-attitude:	Expense reports are due by the fifth of each month. We have no record of receiving your report.

When you talk about what you've done, use *I*.

Correct:	In the past month, I have completed three audits.

In general, keep *I*'s to a minimum. They make you sound less confident and more self-centred.

Weak:	I think that we would save money if we bought a copier instead of leasing it.
Better:	We would save money by buying a copier instead of leasing it.
Weak:	I want to be sure that I understand how I will be affected by this project.
Better:	How will this project affect our unit?

When you write a document that focuses on you (such as a progress report or a job application letter), vary sentence structure so that you don't begin every sentence with *I*.

Correct:	This job gave me the opportunity to…
Correct:	As an intern, I…
Correct:	Working with a team, I

When you use a first-person pronoun as part of a compound subject or object, put the first-person pronoun last.

Correct:	She asked you and me to make the presentation.
Correct:	You, Mohammed, and I will have a chance to talk to members of the audience before the dinner.

Be sure to use the right case. For the above two examples, you might omit the other part(s) of the compound to see the case you should use, as follows:

She asked me…

I will have a chance…

These are grammatically correct, so you would use the same form when you restore the other words.

Exercises

Revise the following sentences to eliminate errors and improve the use of *you* and *I*.

1. I worked with a team to create a class website. I was responsible for much of the initial design and some of the HTML coding. I also tested the page with three people to see how easily they could navigate it. I and the other team members presented the page to a committee of local businesspeople.
2. I have taken a lot of time and trouble to get a copy of *Using Excel* for each of you.
3. If you offend someone in the team, you need to resolve the conflict you have created.
4. Please return the draft to me and Mehtap.
5. I think that it would be a good idea for us to distribute an agenda before the meeting.
6. I have asked each department head if he or she had information to announce at the meeting, collated the responses, and arranged the topics to cover in an agenda. I have indicated how much time each topic will take. I am herewith distributing the agenda for Friday's meeting.
7. You haven't made the website accessible to users with impaired vision.
8. My last job showed me that you have to be able to solve problems quickly.
9. I observed department meetings during my co-op. I also sat in on client meetings. I designed PowerPoint slides for client presentations. I participated in strategy sessions. Finally, I drafted brochures.
10. The client asked me and my supervisor to explain our strategy more fully.

Check your answers to the odd-numbered exercises in the Polishing Your Prose Answer Key.

Managing the Interview Process

MODULE OUTLINE

- What's the best interview strategy?
- What details should I think about?
- What should I practise before the interview?
- How should I answer traditional interview questions?
- How can I prepare for behavioural and situational interviews?
- How can I prepare for phone or Skype interviews?
- How should I follow up the interview?
- What if my first offer isn't for the job I most want?

Module Summary

Assignments for Module 27

Polishing Your Prose: Matters on Which Experts Disagree

Learning Objectives

After reading and applying the information in Module 27, you'll be able to demonstrate

Knowledge of

LO1 Job interview best practices

LO2 The attitudes and behaviours employers seek

Skills to

LO3 Be your best self at a job interview

LO4 Plan and practise for the interview

LO5 Answer traditional interview questions

LO6 Prepare for behavioural and situational interviews

LO7 Participate in phone or video interviews

LO8 Make a good impression in follow-up letters and emails

Employability Skills 2000+ Checklist

Module content builds these Conference Board of Canada Employability Skills 2000+

Communicate

Manage Information

Think and Solve Problems

Demonstrate Positive Attitudes and Behaviours

Be Adaptable

Learn Continuously

Work with Others

Participate in Projects and Tasks

Today many employers expect job candidates to

- Follow instructions to the letter. The owner of a delivery company tells candidates to phone at a precise hour. Failing to do so means that the person can't be trusted to deliver packages on time.[1]
- Participate in many interviews, including a panel or group interview. In these interview situations, several people in the organization are present throughout the interview. Each person is assigned a question to ask the candidate, and the whole team assesses the applicant's interview performance.
- Have one or more interviews by phone, computer, or video.
- Take one or more tests, including psychological/personality assessments, aptitude tests, computer simulations, and essay exams where you're asked to explain what you'd do in a specific situation.
- Be approved by the team you'll be joining. In companies with self-managed work teams, the team has a say in who is hired.
- Provide—at the interview or right after it—a sample of the work you're applying to do. You may be asked to write a memo or a proposal, calculate a budget on a spreadsheet, make a presentation, or do a mini-teach.

Successful job applicants prepare an interview strategy tailored to their audience.

LO1 What's the Best Interview Strategy?

Prepare so that you get what you want.

Develop an overall strategy based on your answers to these three questions:

1. *What do you want the interviewer to know about you?* Pick two to five points that represent your strengths for that particular job. These facts may be achievements, positive character traits (such as enthusiasm, attention to detail, creativity), and experiences that qualify you for the job and separate you from other applicants.

   Identify and write down a specific action or accomplishment to support each strength (Module 25). For example, be ready to give an example to prove that you're "hardworking." Show how you have saved money, served customers better, or led the team in other organizations where you've worked.

In Nelvana's creative environment, employees are hired because they possess both the skills to do the job and the creativity to imagine original ideas. Applicants' portfolios are expected to contain evidence of both.

At the interview, listen to every question to see how you can make one of your key points part of your answer. If the questions don't allow you to make your points, bring them up at the end of the interview.

2. *What disadvantages or weaknesses do you need to minimize?* Expect to be asked to explain apparent weaknesses in your record: lack of experience, so-so grades, or gaps in your record.

3. *What do you need to know about the job and the organization to decide whether to accept this job if it is offered to you?* Do research to ensure the organization is the right fit for you. Analyze the company website: its language, colours, and navigation can tell you plenty about organizational values. Read blogs, bulletins, and associated industry journals.

Network. Use information interviews (Module 24) as opportunities to scope out the reception area, the way visitors are greeted and treated, congruence between mission statement and morale. Talk to as many employees and friends of employees as you can.

Keep a list of topics you want to research further. Before the interview, prioritize these, and reframe them as questions to ask during the interview.

Checkpoint

Interview Strategy

Plan an interview strategy based on these three questions:

1. What two to five facts about yourself do you want the interviewer to know?
2. What disadvantages or weaknesses do you need to overcome or minimize?
3. What do you need to know about the job and the organization to decide whether or not you want to accept this job if it is offered to you?

LO3 LO4 What Details Should I Think About?

Decide what you'll wear, how to get there, and what you'll take with you.

What to Wear

Employability Skills

Your interview clothing should be at least as formal as the clothing of the person likely to interview you. When the interview is scheduled, ask the person who invites you whether the company has a dress policy. Even if the dress is "casual," wear a dressy shirt and a good-quality skirt or pants, not jeans.

If you're interviewing for a management or office job, wear a business suit in a conservative colour (black, grey, or navy) and a season-appropriate fabric. If you have good taste and a good eye for colour, follow your instincts.

If fashion isn't your strong point, thumb through newspapers and magazines for ideas, or visit stores, noting details—the exact shade of blue in a suit, the number of buttons on the sleeve, the placement of pockets, the width of lapels. You can find quality clothes at bargain prices in second-hand and vintage clothing shops in your town or city.

If you're interviewing for a position that involves working, visiting, or supervising muddy or dirty sites, wear sturdy clothes that suggest you're willing to get dirty.[2] In this case, looking "good" is less important than looking businesslike.

Consider the corporate culture. A woman interviewing for a job at Gap wore a matching linen skirt and blouse that were similar to Gap clothing. Her clothing was evidence that she'd researched the job.[3]

Choose comfortable shoes. The last thing you want to be thinking about during an important interview is how much your feet hurt! You may also do a fair amount of walking during the office visit or plant trip.

Take care of all the details. Check your heels to make sure they aren't run-down; make sure your shoes are shined. Have your hair cut or styled conservatively. Keep jewellery and makeup understated. Personal hygiene must be impeccable. If you wear cologne or perfume, keep it to a minimum. More and more workplaces have "scent-free" policies to accommodate people with allergies.

How to Get There

If you're going to a place you haven't been to before, do a practice run at the same time of day your interview is scheduled for. Check out bus transfers or parking fees. On the day of the interview, leave early enough so that you'll get to the interview 15 minutes early.

Use the extra time to check your appearance in the restroom mirror and to look through the company publications in the waiting room. If an accident does delay you, call to say you'll be late.

What to Take to the Interview

Take extra copies of your resumé. If your campus placement office has already given the interviewer a data sheet, present the resumé at the beginning of the interview: "I thought you might like a little more information about me."

Bring something to write on, something to write with, and a typed list of the questions you want to ask.

Bring copies of your work or a portfolio: an engineering design, a copy of a report you wrote on a job or in a business writing class, an article you wrote for the campus paper. You don't need to present these unless the interview calls for them, but they can be very effective.

Bring the names, addresses, and phone numbers of your references if you haven't already provided them.

Bring complete details about your work history and education, including dates and street addresses, in case you're asked to fill out an application form.

If you can afford it, buy a briefcase to carry these items. An inexpensive briefcase is fine.

What Notes to Take

During or immediately after the interview, write down the details:

- The name of the interviewer, or all the people you talked to, if it's a group interview or an office visit. (The easiest way to get the interviewer's name is to ask for his or her card.)
- The traits/facts the interviewer seemed to like best about you.
- Any negative points or concerns that came up that you need to counter in your follow-up letter or phone calls.
- Answers to your questions about the company.
- The date you'll hear from the company.
- Details you'll want to include in your follow-up thank-you letter.

LO3 LO4 What Should I Practise Before the Interview?

Practise everything, and often; practice builds confidence.

Your interviewing skills will improve with practice. Rehearse everything you can: put on the clothes you'll wear and practise entering a room, shaking hands, sitting down, and answering questions. Ask a friend to interview you, and video record the interview. Saying answers aloud is surprisingly harder than saying them in your head. Recording is more valuable if you can do it at least twice, so you can modify your behaviour the second time and check to see if the modification works.

How to Act

Should you "be yourself"? There's no point in assuming a radically different persona. If you do, you run the risk of getting into a job that you'll hate (though the persona you assumed might have loved it). On the other hand, we all have several selves: we can be lazy, insensitive, bored, slow-witted, and tongue-tied, but we can also be energetic, perceptive, interested, intelligent, and articulate. Be your best self at the interview.

To increase your confidence, review your positive personality traits and accomplishments—the things you're especially proud of having done—in writing (Module 25). You'll make a better impression if you have a firm sense of your own self-worth.

Every interviewer repeats the advice that parents often give: Sit up straight, don't mumble, and look at people when you talk. It's good advice for interviews. Be aware that many people respond negatively to smoking.

Office visits that involve meals and semi-social occasions call for sensible choices. When you order, choose something that's easy and not messy to eat. Watch your table manners. Eat a light lunch, with no alcohol, so that you'll be alert during the afternoon. At dinner or an evening party, decline alcohol if you don't drink or are underage. If you do drink, accept just one drink: you're still being evaluated. Be aware that some people respond negatively to applicants who drink hard liquor.

Parts of the Interview

Every interview has an opening, a body, and a close.

In the **opening** (two to five minutes), good interviewers will try to put you at ease. Some interviewers will open with easy questions about your major or interests. Others open by telling you about the job or the company. If this happens, listen so you can answer later questions to show that you can do the job and contribute to the company that's being described.

The **body** of the interview (10 minutes to an hour) is an all-too-brief time for you to highlight your qualifications and find out what you need to know to decide if you want to accept a second interview. Expect questions that allow you to highlight your strong points, and questions that probe any weaknesses evident from your resumé. (You were neither in school nor working last fall. What were you doing?) Normally the interviewer will also try to sell you on the company and give you an opportunity to ask questions.

Be aware of time so that you can make sure to get to your key points and questions: "We haven't covered it yet, but I want you to know that I…" "I'm aware that it's almost 10:30. I do have some more questions that I'd like to ask about the company."

In the **close** of the interview (two to five minutes), the interviewer will usually tell you what happens next: "We'll be bringing our top candidates to the office in February. You should hear from us in three weeks." One interviewer reports that he gives applicants his card and tells them to call him. "It's a test to see if they are committed, how long it takes for them to call, and whether they even call at all."[4]

Close with an assertive statement. Depending on the circumstances, you could say, "I've enjoyed learning more about ITracks; I'd really like to see the new system you talked about." Or, "This job seems to be a good match with my qualifications and expertise."

Cultural FOCUS

In many cultures, smoking is acceptable and normal; in Canada, smoking is becoming less acceptable. If you are a smoker, try not to smoke at all before the interview. Tobacco smoke clings to fabric and a non-smoker will be able to smell it. If you do need to smoke before the interview, try not to smoke for at least 30 minutes before the interview. Never smoke as soon as you leave the interview. Wait until you are away from the property, as you never know who may be watching you leave.

LO2 LO5 How Should I Answer Traditional Interview Questions?

Choose answers that fit your qualifications and your interview strategy.

As Table 27.1 shows, successful applicants use different communication behaviours than do unsuccessful applicants. Successful applicants are more likely to

- Use the company name during the interview
- Support their claims with specific details
- Ask specific questions about the company and the industry

In addition to practising the content of questions, try to incorporate tactics recommended in column three of Table 27.1.

TABLE 27.1   The Communication Behaviours of Successful Interviewees

Behaviour	Unsuccessful Interviewees	Successful Interviewees
Statements about the position	Had only vague ideas of what they wanted to do; changed "ideal job" up to six times during the interview.	Were specific and consistent about the position they wanted; were able to tell why they wanted the position.
Use of company name	Rarely used the company name.	Referred to the company by name four times as often as unsuccessful interviewees.
Knowledge about company and position	Made it clear that they were using the interview to learn about the company and what it offered.	Made it clear that they had researched the company; referred to specific brochures, journals, or people who had given them information.
Level of interest, enthusiasm	Responded neutrally to interviewer's statements: "OK," "I see." Indicated reservations about company or location.	Expressed approval of information verbally and non-verbally; explicitly indicated desire to work for this particular company.
Non-verbal behaviour	Made little eye contact; smiled infrequently.	Made eye contact often; smiled.
Picking up on interviewer's cues	Gave vague or negative answers even when a positive answer was clearly desired ("How are your math skills?").	Answered positively and confidently—and backed up the claim with a specific example of "problem solving" or "toughness."
Response to topic shift by interviewer	Resisted topic shift.	Accepted topic shift.
Use of industry terms and technical jargon	Used almost no technical jargon.	Used technical jargon: "point of purchase display," "NCR charge," "two-column approach," "direct mail," "big pharma."
Use of specifics in answers	Gave short answers—10 words or fewer, sometimes only one word; did not elaborate. Gave general responses: "fairly well."	Supported claims with specific personal experiences, comparisons, statistics, statements of teachers and employers.
Questions asked by interviewee	Asked a small number of general questions.	Asked specific questions based on knowledge of the industry and the company. Personalized questions: "What would my duties be?"
Control of time and topics	Interviewee talked 37 percent of the interview time; initiated 36 percent of the comments.	Interviewee talked 55 percent of the total time, initiated subjects 56 percent of the time.

Source: Based on research reported by Lois J. Einhorn (1981, July), An inner view of the job interview: An investigation of successful communicative behaviors, *Communication Education*, 30, 217–28; Robert W. Elder and Michael M. Harris, Eds. (1999), *The employment interview handbook* (Thousand Oaks, CA: Sage): 300, 303, 327–28.

> ## Checkpoint
>
> ### Successful Interviewees
> - Know what they want to do
> - Have researched the company in advance
> - Use the company name in the interview
> - Support skills and knowledge claims with specifics
> - Use industry language
> - Ask specific questions
> - Talk more of the time

Interviewers frequently ask the following questions during interviews. Prepare on paper before the interview so that you'll be able to come up with answers that are responsive, honest, and paint a positive picture of you.

Choose answers that fit your qualifications and your interview strategy.

1. *Tell me about yourself.*

   Don't launch into an autobiography. Instead, talk about your achievements as they relate to the organization's culture and goals. Give specific examples to prove each of your strengths.

2. *What makes you think you're qualified to work for this company? Or: I'm interviewing 120 people for two jobs. Why should I hire you?*

   This question might feel like an attack. Use it as an opportunity to state your strong points: your qualifications for the job, the skills, knowledge, and character traits that separate you from other applicants.

3. *What two or three accomplishments have given you the greatest satisfaction?*

   Pick accomplishments that you're proud of, that create the image you want to project, and that enable you to share one of the things you want the interviewer to know about you (Module 25, Exercise 25.4). Focus not just on the desired result, but also on the transferable skills—teamwork, problem solving, and critical thinking—that made the achievement possible.

4. *Why do you want to work for us? What is your ideal job?*

   Even if you're interviewing just for practice, make sure you have a good answer—preferably two or three reasons you'd like to work for that company. Do your homework; know everything possible about the company and the job. If you don't seem to be taking the interview seriously, the interviewer won't take you seriously, and you won't even get good practice.

5. *What college or university courses did you like best and least? Why?*

   This question may be an icebreaker; it may be designed to discover the kind of applicant the organization is looking for. If your favourite class was something outside your program, prepare an answer that shows that you have qualities that can help you in the job you're applying for: "My favourite class was Canadian Literature. We got a chance to think on our own, rather than just regurgitate facts; we made presentations to the class every week. I found I really like sharing my ideas with other people and presenting reasons for my conclusions about something."

6. *Why are your grades so low?*

   If possible, show that the cause of low grades has now been solved or isn't relevant to the job you're applying for: "My father almost died last year, and my schoolwork really suffered."

"When I started, I didn't have any firm goals. Since I discovered the program that is right for me, my grades have all been B's or better." "I'm not good at multiple-choice tests. But you need someone who can work with people, not someone who can take tests."

7. *What have you read recently? What movies have you seen recently?*

   These questions may be icebreakers; they may be designed to probe your intellectual depth. Be prepared: read at least one book or magazine (regularly) and see at least one movie that you could discuss at an interview.

8. *Show me some samples of your writing.*

   The year you're interviewing, go through your old papers and select the best ones, editing and reformatting them, if necessary, so that you'll have samples if you're asked for them. Show interviewers essays, reports, or business documents, not poetry or song lyrics.

   If you don't have samples at the interview, mail them to the interviewer immediately after the interview.

9. *Where do you see yourself in five years?*

   Employers ask this question to find out if you are a self-starter or if you passively respond to what happens. You may want to have several scenarios for five years from now to use in different kinds of interviews. Or you may want to say, "Well, my goals may change as opportunities arise. But right now, I want to…"

10. *What are your interests outside of work? What campus or community activities have you been involved in?*

    Although it's desirable to be well rounded, naming 10 interests might work against you: the interviewer might wonder when you'll have time to work. If you mention your fiancé(e), spouse, or children in response to this question ("Well, my fiancé and I like to go sailing"), it is perfectly legal for the interviewer to ask follow-up questions ("What would you do if your spouse got a job offer in another town?"), even though the same question would be illegal if the interviewer brought up the subject first.

11. *What have you done to learn about this company?*

    An employer may ask this to see what you already know about the company (if you've read the recruiting literature, the interviewer doesn't need to repeat it). This question may also be used to see how active a role you're taking in the job search and how interested you are in this job.

12. *What adjectives would you use to describe yourself?*

    Use only positive ones. Be ready to illustrate each with a specific example of something you've done.

13. *What is your greatest strength?*

    Employers ask this question to give you a chance to sell yourself and to learn something about your values. Pick a strength related to work, school, or activities: "I'm good at working with people." "I can really sell things." "I'm good at solving problems." "I learn quickly." "I'm reliable. When I say I'll do something, I do it." Be ready to illustrate each with a specific example of something you've done.

14. *What is your greatest weakness?*

    Employers ask this question to get a sense of your values and self-awareness. Use a work-related negative, and emphasize what you're doing about it. Interviewers won't let you get away with a "weakness" like being a workaholic or just not having any experience yet. Instead, use one of the following three strategies:

a. Discuss a weakness that is not related to the job you're being considered for, and that will not be needed even when you're promoted. End your answer with a positive related to the job:

For a creative job in advertising: I don't like accounting. I know it's important, but I don't like it. I even hire someone to do my taxes. I'm much more interested in being creative and working with people, which is why I find this position interesting.

For a job in administration: I don't like selling products. I hated selling cookies when I was a Girl Guide. I'd much rather work with ideas—and I really like selling the ideas that I believe in.

b. Discuss a weakness that you are working to improve:

In the past, I wasn't a strong writer. But last term I took a course in business writing that taught me how to organize my ideas and how to revise. Now I'm a lot more confident that I can write effective reports and memos.

c. Discuss a work-related weakness:

Sometimes I procrastinate. Fortunately, I work well under pressure, but a couple of times I've really put myself in a bind.

15. *Why are you looking for another job?*

Stress what you're looking for in a new job, not why you want to get away from your old one.

If you were fired, say so. There are four acceptable ways to explain why you were fired:

a. You lost your job, along with many others, when the company downsized for economic reasons.
b. It wasn't a good match. Add what you now know you need in a job, and ask what the employer can offer in this area.
c. You and your supervisor had a personality conflict. Make sure you show that this was an isolated incident and that you normally get along well with people.
d. You made mistakes, but you've learned from them and are now ready to work well. Be ready to offer a specific anecdote proving that you have indeed changed.

16. *What questions do you have?*

Employability Skills

This gives you a chance to cover things the interviewer hasn't brought up; it also gives the interviewer a sense of your priorities and values. Don't focus on salary or fringe benefits. Instead, prepare a typed list of specific questions such as

- What would I be doing on a day-to-day basis?
- What kind of training programs do you have? If, as I'm rotating among departments, I find that I prefer one area, can I specialize in it when the training program is over?
- How do you evaluate employees? How often do you review them? Where would you expect a new trainee (banker, staff accountant, salesperson) to be three years from now?
- What happened to the last person who had this job?
- How are interest rates (a new product from competitors, imports, demographic trends, government regulation, etc.) affecting your company?
- How would you describe the company's culture?

- This sounds like a great job. What are the drawbacks?

Increasingly, candidates are asking about work–life balance and about the control they'll have over their own work:

- Do people who work for you have a life off the job?
- If my job requires too much travel, can I change jobs without doing serious damage to my career?
- Do you offer flextime?
- How much pressure do you have to achieve your projects? How much freedom is there to extend a deadline?[5]

You won't be able to anticipate every question you may get. (One interviewer asked applicants, "What vegetable would you like to be?" Another asked, "If you were a cookie, what kind of cookie would you be?")[6] Check with other people who have interviewed recently to find out what questions are being asked in your field.

[LO6] How Can I Prepare for Behavioural and Situational Interviews?

Think about skills you've used that could transfer to other jobs. Learn as much as you can about the culture of the company you hope to join.

Many companies are now using behavioural or situational interviews. **Behavioural interviews** ask the applicant to describe actual behaviours, rather than plans or general principles. Thus, instead of asking, "How would you motivate people?" the interviewer might ask, "Tell me what happened the last time you wanted to get other people to do something." Follow-up questions might include, "What exactly did you do to handle the situation? How did you feel about the results? How did the other people feel? How did your superior feel about the results?"

In your answer

- Describe the situation
- Tell what you did
- Describe the outcome
- Show that you understand the implications of what you did and suggest how you might modify your behaviour in other situations

For example, if you did the extra work yourself when a team member didn't do his or her share, does that fact suggest that you do not handle conflict well or prefer to work alone? You might go on to demonstrate that doing the extra work was appropriate in that situation, but that you could respond differently in other situations.

Since behavioural questions require applicants to tell what they actually did—rather than to say what ought to be done—interviewers feel they offer better insight into how someone will actually function as an employee. Figure 27.1 lists common behavioural questions.

Situational interviews put you in a situation that allows the interviewer to see whether you have the qualities the company is seeking.

Situational interviews may also be conducted using traditional questions but evaluating behaviours other than the answers. For its customer assistance centre, Greyhound hired applicants who made eye contact with the interviewer and smiled at least five times during a 15-minute interview.[7]

Increasingly common is the situational interview that asks you to do—on the spot—the kind of thing the job would require. An interviewer for a sales job handed applicants a ballpoint pen and said, "Sell me this pen." (It's OK to ask who the target market is and whether this is a repeat or a new customer.)

FIGURE 27.1   **Behavioural Interview Questions**

Describe a situation in which you

1. Created an opportunity for yourself in a job or volunteer position.
2. Used writing to achieve your goal.
3. Went beyond the call of duty to get a job done.
4. Communicated successfully with someone you disliked.
5. Had to make a decision quickly.
6. Overcame a major obstacle.
7. Took a project from start to finish.
8. Were unable to complete a project on time.
9. Used good judgment and logic in solving a problem.
10. Worked under a tight deadline.
11. Worked with a tough boss.
12. Handled a difficult situation with a co-worker.
13. Made an unpopular decision.
14. Gave a presentation.
15. Worked with someone who wasn't doing his or her share of the work.

Candidates who make it through the first two rounds of interviews for sales jobs at Dataflex are invited to participate in a week's worth of sales meetings, which start at 7 a.m. four times a week. The people who participate—not merely attend—are the people who get hired.[8] Other interview requests include asking applicants to participate in role-plays, to make presentations, or to lead meetings.

[LO7] How Can I Prepare for Phone or Skype Interviews?

Practise short answers. Practise until you feel comfortable.

Employability Skills

Try to schedule phone interviews for home, not work, and for a time when things will be quiet. If a company wants to interview you on the spot, accept only if the timing is good. If it isn't, say so: "We just sat down to dinner. Could you call back in 30 minutes?" Then get your information about the company, ask your roommates to be quiet, and get your thoughts in order. Use a landline, not a cell phone, to ensure good reception.

Three strategies are important when preparing for a phone interview:

- Research the company information, and identify in writing how your qualifications can contribute.
- Record yourself so you can make any adjustments in pronunciation and voice qualities.
- Practise short answers to questions. After giving a short answer in the interview, say, "Would you like more information?" Without a visual channel, you can't see the body language that tells you someone else wants to speak.

During the interview, listen closely to the questions; speak slowly; do the interview standing up: "an erect and confident poise will help you come across more confidently."[9]

For Skype interviews, use the same guidelines as for a phone interview.

As technology changes, many companies are altering their interview practices. If the company sends a list of questions, asking you to pre-record the responses

- Practise your answers.
- Record the interview as many times as necessary to present yourself at your best.
- Be specific. Since the employer can't ask follow-up questions, you need to be detailed about how your credentials could help the employer.

For phone, Skype, or pre-recorded interviews, smile when you talk to put more energy into your voice.

L08 How Should I Follow Up the Interview?

Send a letter that reinforces positives and overcomes any negatives. Use PAIBOC analysis to clarify your message content.

Following up after the interview is a multi-step process. Immediately after the interview, make notes on any questions and ideas that impressed you. These notes can help focus your first letter.

Then, based on your PAIBOC analysis, send an email or hard copy letter to reinforce positives from the first interview, to overcome any negatives, and to get information you can use to persuade the interviewer to hire you (see Figure 27.2).

FIGURE 27.2 **PAIBOC Questions for Analysis**

P	What are your **purposes** in writing? You have several: to demonstrate your emotional intelligence, to emphasize your interest in the job, to reinforce the fit between the organization and you, and to influence the recruiter's opinion positively.
A	Who is your **audience**? What do they value? What do they need? How can you further demonstrate to your audiences that you have the qualifications and interpersonal skills they seek?
I	What **information** must your message include? What information—about the company and the position—did the interviewers emphasize? What further information can you provide to impress your readers favourably?
B	What reasons or reader **benefits** can you use to support your position?
O	What **objections** can you expect your readers to have? What negative elements of your message must you de-emphasize or overcome?
C	How will the **context** affect the reader's response? Think about your relationship to the reader, the economy, the goals of the organization, the time of year, and any special circumstances.

Career coach Kate Weldon suggests asking the following questions in a follow-up phone call:

- "What additional information can I give you?"
- "I've been giving a lot of thought to your project and have some new ideas. Can we meet to go over them?"
- "Where do I stand? How does my work compare with the work others presented?"[10]

A letter (whether a hard copy or an email attachment) is a more formal follow-up message than an email. Base your decision on which to send on your audience analysis. A letter thanking your hosts is essential, however, when your interview includes an office visit or other forms of

Take notes during and immediately after the interview: they're the source of your follow-up letters.

hospitality. A well-written letter can be the deciding factor that gets you the job.[11] In your letter, be sure to do the following:

- Thank the interviewer for his or her time and hospitality.
- Reinforce the interviewer's positive impressions.
- Counter any negative impressions that may have come up at the interview.
- Use the language of the company, and refer to specific things you learned during your interview or saw during your visit.
- Be enthusiastic.
- Refer to the next step: whether you'll wait to hear from the employer or you will call to learn about the status of your application.

Be sure that the letter is well written and error-free. One employer reports

> I often interviewed people whom I liked…but their follow-up letters were filled with misspelled words and names, and other inaccuracies. They blew their chance with the follow-up letter.[12]

Career coaches and recruiters concur. Sending poorly written emails, using shorthand language and/or emoticons, texting: all can reflect sloppy work habits and poor judgment.[13]

Figures 27.3 and 27.4 offer examples of follow-up messages.

FIGURE 27.3   **A Follow-Up Email**

From:	Ahmed Dhanray <adhanray@address.ca>
To:	dland@notime.ca
Sent:	Monday, August 11, 2013, 5:45 PM
Subject:	Thank you

Dear Delmarie Land:

Acknowledges hospitality and reinforces interest in the position — Thank you for your hospitality during my interview last Thursday. After visiting Notime International and speaking with you and your team, I am convinced that a career in logistics is the right choice for me.

Seeing Kelly, Gene, and Leah work together to coordinate an international client's shipment gave me a sense of the deadlines you have to meet and of the collaboration required for customer service success. As we discussed, I learned to meet deadlines and work collaboratively during my summer co-op placement with Crowley Logistics. As I mentioned during the interview, my team at Crowley suggested a computerized warehouse system that saved the company more than $30 000 in its first year of implementation. I welcome the opportunity to make a similar contribution at Notime. — *Reminds the reader of strengths*

Follow-up makes it easy for the reader — Please call me at 416-555-4567 if you have additional questions, or if I can provide you with more information.

Sincerely,
Ahmed Dhanray

FIGURE 27.4   **A Follow-Up Letter**

71 Autumn Ridge Road
Kitchener, ON N2P 2J6

March 23, 2013

Mr. Gino Focasio
Human Resources Department
Perlmutter Canada
8069 Lawson Road
Milton, ON L9T 5C4

Dear Mr. Focasio:

Thank you for interviewing me for the industrial engineering technician position, available in your Milton plant. I appreciate the time that Ms. Rossiter, Mr. Alverez, Mr. Storino, and you gave me.

Refers to important items he saw and heard during the interview →

My expertise in jig and fixture design, and in AutoCAD software, would contribute to your commitment to continuous improvement, as described by Mr. Storino during the interview. Seeing your machining and assembly processes assured me that I would be able to apply my CNC programming experience to benefit the company.

← *Reminds interviewer of his strong points*

Provides positive confirmation of interest in the position →

Again, thank you for your time and for the plant tour. I am very excited at the prospect of working with Perlmutter Canada. Please call me at 519-555-5912, or email me at zhang@address.com if you have any additional questions.

← *Makes it easy for the reader to respond*

Sincerely,

Zhang Huang
Zhang Huang

As part of the process, some career coaches suggest writing additional letters developing a discussion, or answering a question that came up in the interview. These notes indicate your interest in the job, and keep you uppermost in the minds of the interviewers.[14]

Checkpoint

Follow-Up Letters

A letter after an office visit should

- Remind the interviewer of what he or she liked about you
- Counter any negative impressions
- Use the jargon of the company and refer to specifics from the visit
- Be enthusiastic
- Refer to the next move

The skilled trades continue to be underemployed, despite their multiple attractions: excellent remuneration, numerous opportunities, and work flexibility. York Region's Apprenticeship project, supported by the Ontario Youth Apprenticeship Program, offers high school students a semester of technical apprenticeship, under the tutelage of skilled co-op teachers. Licensed skilled trades workers, including plumbers, electricians, and construction workers, can make over $100,000 annually. Yet a recent Manpower Inc. survey found that "according to employers [skilled trades] still are the most difficult-to-fill roles in Canada and the U.S." (Manpower Group (2012). 2012 talent shortage survey research results. Retrieved from http://www.manpowergroup.us/campaigns/talent-shortage-2012/pdf/2012_Talent_Shortage_Survey_Results_US_FINALFINAL.pdf)

What If My First Offer Isn't for the Job I Most Want?

Phone your first-choice employer to find out where you are on that list.

Some employers offer jobs at the end of the office visit. In other cases, you may wait for weeks or even months to hear. Employers usually offer jobs orally. You must say something in response immediately, so plan some strategies.

If your first offer is not from your first choice, express your pleasure at being offered the job, but do not accept it on the phone. "That's great! May I let you know?" Most firms will give you a week to decide.

Then call the other companies you're interested in. Explain, "I've just gotten a job offer, but I'd rather work for you. Can you tell me what the status of my application is?" Nobody will put that information in writing, but almost everyone will tell you over the phone. With this information, you're in a better position to decide whether to accept the original offer.

Make your acceptance contingent on a written job offer confirming the terms. That letter should spell out not only salary but also fringe benefits and any special provisions you have negotiated. If something is missing, call the interviewer for clarification: "We agreed that I'd be reviewed for a promotion and higher salary in six months, but I don't see that in the letter." You have more power to resolve misunderstandings now than you will after six months or a year on the job.

When you've accepted one job, let the other places you visited know that you're no longer interested. Then they can go to their second choices. If you're second on someone else's list, you'll appreciate other candidates' removing themselves so the way is clear for you. Because the world is a small place, because everyone is the customer, and because you may someday want to work for the company you're currently turning down, follow the *KISS* formula: *Keep it short and simple.*

Dear Jackson Phillips:

Thank you for offering me the sales position in your electronics division.

Since Allied Signal enjoys an international reputation for innovative quality products, I'm pleased to be considered as part of the Allied team.

After a great deal of thought, however, I have decided to look for employment opportunities closer to home while investigating courses for an advanced degree. I must, therefore, decline your offer.

Again, thank you for your consideration.

Sincerely,

EXPANDING A CRITICAL SKILL

Projecting Professional Attitude

As more Canadians use clothing to reflect their personalities and/or ethnicities, organizations are adopting more flexible dress codes.

Even on dress-down or casual Fridays, however, organizations still expect employees to take care of business. Attention to detail, organization, accuracy, economy, and courtesy are the norm. According to Max Messruer, chair of Accountemps and author of the best-selling *Job Hunting for Dummies*® (IDG Books Worldwide), what you wear determines others' perceptions of you and directly affects your career advancement.

On casual days, wear clothes in good condition that are one or two "notches" below what you'd wear on other days. If suits are the norm, choose blazers and slacks or skirts. If blazers and slacks or skirts are the norm, choose sweaters or knit sport shirts; khakis, simple skirts, or dressier jeans; or simple dresses. Wear good shoes and always be well groomed. Avoid anything that's ill fitting or revealing.

Other symbols also convey professionalism. Your work area, for instance, says a lot about you. If your organization allows employees to personalize their desks or offices with photographs, knickknacks, and posters, don't display so much that you seem frivolous. And never display offensive photos or slogans, even in an attempt to be funny. The same caution goes for screen savers and radio stations.

It isn't professional to play a morning "shock jock" who uses coarse language and offensive stereotypes.

If your organization allows employees to listen to music, keep the volume at a reasonable level. If your organization allows, consider wearing headphones.

Avoid playing computer games, surfing the Web inappropriately, or ordering personal items on company time. These activities are fine on your own clock, but unethical, and in some cases illegal, on the organization's clock. You can be fired for browsing for inappropriate material online.

Keep your voicemail messages succinct and professional—find out what co-workers say in theirs.

Keep your desk organized. File papers; keep stacks to a minimum. Throw away anything you don't need. Don't store food in your office. Clean periodically. Water your plants.

The volume of your voice can also disturb others. Although most people wouldn't shout across an office, many of us don't realize how loud our voices can be when we're excited or happy. Keep personal conversations to a minimum, in person and on the phone.

Learn the culture of your organization and fit into it as much as you can. When in doubt, model your dress and behaviour on someone the organization respects.

MODULE SUMMARY

- To be your best self at the interview,
  - Develop an overall interview management strategy based on your answers to these three questions:
    1. What two to five personal or professional characteristics do you want the interviewer to know about you?
    2. What disadvantages or weaknesses do you want to overcome or minimize?
    3. What do you need to know about the organization and the job to decide whether you want to accept this job if it is offered to you?
  - Plan the interview logistics—what to wear, how to get there, what to bring—so that you can concentrate on rehearsing a confident interview session.

1. Wear clothes appropriate for the position.
2. Bring an extra copy of your resumé, something to write on and with, copies of your best work, and a list of typed questions you want to ask.
  - Rehearse: ask a friend to interview you; watch a recording of yourself so that you can evaluate and modify your behaviour.
  - During and immediately after the interview, note the name of the interviewer, positives and negatives, answers to your questions, and the date you will hear from the company.
- Successful applicants are prepared; they
  - Know what they want to do
  - Use the company name throughout the interview

○ Demonstrate that they have researched the company

○ Support claims with specific examples and stories

○ Use industry and company jargon

○ Ask specific questions

○ Talk more of the time

- In behavioural interviews, recruiters ask applicants to describe actual behaviours and outcomes.

  ○ To answer a behavioural question, describe the situation, tell what you did, describe the outcome, show that you understand the implications of your behaviour, and describe how you might modify your behaviour in other situations.

- Situational interviews put you in a position that allows the interviewer to see if you have the qualities the company is seeking.

- For a phone interview, ensure you have no distractions, do the interview standing up, and listen carefully to each question before giving concise answers.

- If you make a recording, make sure to re-record to show your best self.

- Use follow-up phone calls to reinforce positives from the first interview, to overcome any negatives, and to get information you can use to persuade the interviewer to hire you.

- Use a follow-up letter to

  ○ Remind the reviewer of your qualities

  ○ Counter any negative impressions

  ○ Use the language of the industry and company to refer to specifics that came up in the interview, or that you saw in your visit

  ○ Be enthusiastic

  ○ Refer to next steps

ASSIGNMENTS FOR MODULE 27

Questions for Critical Thinking

27.1 How can you demonstrate your greatest strengths during an interview?

27.2 How can you deal with your weaknesses if they come up during an interview?

27.3 What are your options if you are asked what you believe is an illegal interview question? Which option seems best to you? Why?

27.4 Why is "mirroring" an interviewer's communication style a good interview tactic?

Exercises and Problems

27.5 Interviewing Job Hunters

Talk to students at your school who are interviewing for jobs this term. Possible questions to ask them include the following:

- What field are you in? How good is the job market in that field this year?
- What questions have you been asked at job interviews? Were you asked any illegal or sexist questions? Any really oddball questions?
- What answers seemed to go over well? What answers bombed?
- Were you asked to take any tests (skills, physical, drugs)?
- How long did you have to wait after a first interview to learn whether you were being invited for an office visit? How long after an office visit did it take to learn whether you were being offered a job? How much time did the company give you to decide?
- What advice would you have for someone who will be interviewing next term or next year?

As your instructor directs

  a. Summarize your findings in a memo to your instructor.
  b. Report your findings orally to the class.
  c. Join a group of two or three other students to write a blog describing the results of your survey.

27.6 Interviewing an Interviewer

Talk to someone who regularly interviews candidates for entry-level jobs. Possible questions to ask are

- How long have you been interviewing for your organization? Does everyone on the management ladder at your company do some interviewing, or do people specialize in it?
- Do you follow a set structure for interviews? What are some of the standard questions you ask?
- What are you looking for? How important are 1) good grades, 2) leadership roles in extracurricular groups, or 3) relevant work experience? What advice would you give

to someone who doesn't have one or more of these?

- What behaviours do students exhibit that create a poor impression? Think about the worst candidate you've interviewed. What did he or she do (or not do) to create such a negative impression?
- What behaviours make a good impression? Recall the best student you've ever interviewed. Why did he or she impress you so much?
- How does your employer evaluate and reward your success as an interviewer?
- What advice would you give to someone who still has a year or so before the job hunt begins?

As your instructor directs

- **a.** Summarize your findings in a memo to your instructor.
- **b.** Report your findings orally to the class.
- **c.** Team up with a small group of students to write a group report describing the results of your survey.
- **d.** Write to the interviewer thanking him or her for taking the time to talk to you.

27.7 Preparing an Interview Strategy

Based on your analysis for Problems 27.5 and 27.6, prepare an interview strategy.

1. List two to five things about yourself that you want the interviewer to know before you leave the interview.
2. Identify any weaknesses or apparent weaknesses in your record and plan ways to explain them or minimize them.
3. List the points you need to learn about an employer to decide whether to accept an office visit or plant trip.

As your instructor directs

- **a.** Share your strategy with a small group of students.
- **b.** Describe your strategy in a memo to your instructor.
- **c.** Present your strategy orally to the class.

27.8 Preparing Answers to Behavioural Interview Questions

Think about

1. A conflict you have been part of and your role in resolving it
2. A team you have worked on and the role you played
3. A time you were asked to behave in a way you thought was unethical
4. A time you were unable to complete a project by the due date

5. A time you handled a difficult situation with a co-worker
6. A time you overcame a major obstacle
7. A time you adapted to a difficult situation

As your instructor directs

- **a.** Share your answers with a small group of students.
- **b.** Present your answers in a memo to your instructor, and explain why you've chosen the examples you describe.
- **c.** Present your answers orally to the class.

27.9 Preparing Questions to Ask Employers

Prepare a list of questions to ask at job interviews.

1. Prepare a list of three to five general questions that apply to most employers in your field.
2. Prepare two to five specific questions for each of the three companies you are most interested in.

As your instructor directs

- **a.** Share the questions with a small group of students.
- **b.** List the questions in a memo to your instructor.
- **c.** Present your questions orally to the class.

27.10 Writing a Follow-Up Letter After an Office Visit or Plant Trip

Write a follow-up email message or letter after an office visit or plant trip. Thank your hosts for their hospitality, relate your strong points to things you learned about the company during the visit, overcome any negatives that may remain, be enthusiastic about the company, and submit receipts for your expenses so you can be reimbursed, if the company has indicated they will do so.

27.11 Clarifying the Terms of a Job Offer

Last week, you got a job offer from your first-choice company, and you accepted it over the phone. Today, the written confirmation arrived. The letter specifies the starting salary and fringe benefits you had negotiated. However, during the office visit, you were promised a 5 percent raise after six months on the job. The job offer says nothing about the raise. You do want the job, but you want it on the terms you thought you had negotiated.

Write to your contact at the company, Damon Winters.

POLISHING YOUR PROSE

Matters on Which Experts Disagree

Any living language changes. New usages appear first in speaking. Here are five issues on which experts currently disagree:

1. Plural pronouns to refer to *everybody*, *everyone*, and *each*. Standard grammar says these words require singular pronouns: *his* or *her* rather than *their*.
2. Split infinitives. An infinitive is the form of a verb that contains *to*: to understand. An infinitive is "split" when another word separates the *to* from the rest of an infinitive: *to easily understand, to boldly go*. The most recent edition of the *Oxford English Dictionary* allows split infinitives.
3. *Hopefully* to mean *I hope that*. *Hopefully* means "in a hopeful manner." However, a speaker who says, "Hopefully, the rain will stop" is talking about the speaker's hope, not the rain's.
4. *Verbal* to mean *oral*. *Verbal* means "using words." Therefore, both writing and speaking are verbal communication. Non-verbal communication (e.g., body language) does not use words.
5. Comma before *and* (the serial or series comma). In a series of three or more items, some experts require a comma after the next to last item (the item before the *and*); others don't. This book uses serial commas.

Ask your instructor and your boss if they are willing to accept the less formal usage. When you write to someone you don't know, use standard grammar and usage.

Exercises

Each of the following sentences illustrates informal usage. (a) Which would your instructor or your boss accept? (b) Rewrite each of the sentences using standard grammar and usage.

1. Everyone should bring their laptops to the sales meeting.
2. The schedule includes new product information, role-plays with common selling situations, and awards to the top salespeople.
3. To really take advantage of the meeting, you need to bring all of your new product info.
4. Prepare to make a brief verbal report on a challenging sales situation.
5. Think of a time when it was hard to even get in the door to see a potential customer.
6. Hopefully, we will have time to work through many of these situations in our role-plays.
7. Awards include best rookie sales representative, the most improved region, everyone who beat their quota, and sales representative of the year.
8. We'll feature verbal quotes from customers in our radio ads.
9. Our website will let people listen to each customer summarizing verbally what they like best about our products.
10. Hopefully, the website will be live so that we can access it during the meeting.

Check your answers to the odd-numbered exercises in the Polishing Your Prose Answer Key.

Revising Sentences and Paragraphs

Writing *style* is the result of the conscious choices that writers make to convey meaning. Style elements include every symbol the writer uses, including

- Page layout and design
- Typeface and size
- White space, bullets, headings, and subheadings
- Format and organizational pattern
- Paragraph and sentence length
- Word choice

Style describes the way writers choose to use these elements.

Good business style creates messages that are easy for the audience to read and understand. Effective writers work on their individual styles through revision and editing, consciously shaping the style of each document to meet the needs of their audiences and to achieve their purposes.

What Is Good Business Writing Style?

Good business style is polite, friendly, and natural.

Good business writing sounds like one person talking to another. Although academic writing is traditionally more formal than business writing (see Table A.1), professors also like essays that are lively, engaging, and grammatically correct.

Most people have several styles of talking, which they vary *depending on the audience*. Good writers have several styles, too. A memo to your boss complaining about the delays from a supplier may be informal, perhaps even chatty, depending on your relationship; a letter to the supplier demanding better service will be more formal.

Keep the following points in mind when you choose a level of formality for a specific document:

- Always err on the side of courtesy: use a friendly, informal style for someone you've talked with.
- Avoid contractions, slang, and even minor grammatical lapses in messages and texts you write to people you don't know. Abbreviations are only acceptable in email messages if they're part of the group's culture.
- Avoid *business-speak* and clichés that obscure meaning and add clutter.
- Pay particular attention to your style when you have to write uncomfortable messages, such as when you write to people in power or when you must give bad news.

TABLE A.1 Different Types of Style

	Conversational Style	Good Business Style	Traditional Term-Paper Style
Formality	Highly informal	Conversational; sounds like a real person talking	More formal than conversation would be, but retains a human voice
Use of contractions	Many contractions	OK to use occasional contractions	Few contractions, if any
Pronouns	Uses *I*, first- and second-person pronouns	Uses *I*, first- and second-person pronouns	First- and second-person pronouns kept to a minimum
Level of friendliness	Friendly	Friendly	No effort to make style friendly
Personal	Personal; refers to specific circumstances of conversation	Personal; may refer to reader by name; refers to specific circumstances of readers	Impersonal; may generally refer to "readers" but does not name them or refer to their circumstances
Word choice	Short, simple words; slang	Short, simple words but avoids slang	Many abstract words; scholarly, technical terms
Sentence and paragraph length	Incomplete sentences; no paragraphs	Short sentences and paragraphs	Sentences and paragraphs usually long
Grammar	Can be ungrammatical	Uses standard edited English	Uses standard edited English
Visual impact	Not applicable	Attention to visual impact of document	No particular attention to visual impact

Good business style allows for individual variation. Your writing style contributes to your narrative voice (see Polishing Your Prose, Module 9) and expresses how you feel about both your audience and your topic.

What Style Rules Should I Follow?

In writing, as in design, less is more: keep it short and specific.

Readers rate writers who use clear, simple language and easy-to-read fonts as more intelligent than those who choose to express themselves in a more complicated style.[1]

You can do several things to create your own, readable style:

- Read and write every day. Reading not only expands your vocabulary; regular reading also improves syntax (the way you put words together to make sentences), and your grammar, punctuation, and usage. Furthermore, research proves that reading fiction makes you smarter. Psychology professor, novelist, and Toronto team leader Keith Oatley proved that reading fiction improved people's social intelligence.[2]
- Start with a clean page or screen, so that you aren't locked into old sentence structures.
- Try WIRMI: What I Really Mean Is.[3] Then revise accordingly.
- Try reading your draft aloud to someone sitting nearby. If the words sound stiff, they'll seem stiff to a reader, too.
- Ask someone else to read your draft aloud. Readers stumble if the words on the page aren't what they expect to see. Revise for clarity in the places readers stumble.

What Should I Look for When I Revise Sentences?

Try these six techniques to make your writing readable.

1. Use active verbs whenever possible.
2. Use strong action verbs to carry the weight of your sentences.
3. Make your writing concise.
4. Vary sentence length and sentence structure.
5. Use parallel structure.
6. Put your readers in your sentences.

1. Use Active Verbs Whenever Possible

"Who does what" sentences emphasize the action that creates clear and interesting writing.

A verb is **active** if the subject of the sentence does the action the verb describes. Business communication favours the use of active verbs. A verb is **passive** if the subject is acted on. Passives are usually made up of a form of the verb *to be* plus a past participle. Passive has nothing to do with the past tense. Passives can be past, present, or future:

> were received (passive past)
> is recommended (passive present)
> will be implemented (passive future)

To identify a passive verb, find the verb. If the verb describes something that the subject is doing, the verb is active. If the verb describes something that is being done to the subject, the verb is passive.

Active

The ⟨customer⟩ received 500 widgets.

⟨I⟩ recommend this method.

The ⟨provincial agencies⟩ will implement the program.

Passive

Five hundred ⟨widgets⟩ were received by the customer.

This ⟨method⟩ is recommended by me.

The ⟨program⟩ will be implemented by the provincial agencies.

To change a passive verb to an active one, you must make the agent ("by _____" in < >) the new subject. If no agent is specified in the sentence, you must supply one to make the sentence active.

Passive

The ⟨request⟩ was approved by the <plant manager>.

A decision will be made next month. No agent in sentence.

A ⟨letter⟩ will be sent informing the customer of the change. No agent in sentence.

Active

The ⟨plant manager⟩ approved the ⟨request⟩.

The ⟨committee⟩ will decide next month.

[You] Send the customer a ⟨letter⟩ informing her about the change.

If the active sentence does not have a direct object, no passive equivalent exists.

Active   **(No Passive Exists)**

I would like to go to the conference.

The freight charge will be $1,400.

The phone rang.

Passive verbs have at least three disadvantages:

1. If all the information in the original sentence is retained, passive verbs make the sentence longer. Passives take more time to understand.[4]
2. If the agent is omitted, it's not clear who is responsible for doing the action.
3. When many passive verbs are used, or when passives are used in material with many big words, the writing can be boring and pompous.

However, passive verbs are desirable in some situations:

- Use passives to **emphasize** the object receiving the action, not the agent.

   Your order was shipped November 15.

The customer's order, not the shipping clerk, is important.

- Use passives to provide coherence within a paragraph. A sentence is easier to read if "old" information comes at the beginning of a sentence. When you have been discussing a topic, use the word again as your subject even if that requires a passive verb.

   The bank made several risky loans in 2008. These loans were written off as "uncollectable" in 2011.

Using loans as the subject of the second sentence provides a link between the two sentences, making the paragraph as a whole easier to read.

● Use passives to avoid assigning blame.

The order was damaged during shipment.

An active verb would require the writer to specify who damaged the order. The passive here is more tactful.

2. Use Strong Action Verbs to Carry the Weight of Your Sentence

The verb is the most important word in an English sentence, and active words (*send, met, see, ask, reply, tell, start, end, fall, rise*) create word pictures for clarity that linking verbs (*is, are, was, were, seem, appear, become, became*) cannot. Since the verb is the most important word in any sentence, put the weight of your sentence in the verb. When the verb is a form of *to be*, revise the sentence to use a more forceful verb.

Weak: The financial advantage of owning this equipment, instead of leasing it, is 10 percent after taxes.

Better: Owning this equipment rather than leasing it will save us 10 percent after taxes.

Nouns ending in *-ment*, *-ion*, and *-al* often hide verbs.

make an adjustment	adjust
make a payment	pay
make a decision	decide
reach a conclusion	conclude
take into consideration	consider
make a referral	refer
provide assistance	assist

Use verbs to present the information more forcefully.

Weak: We will perform an investigation of the problem.

Better: We will investigate the problem.

Weak: Selection of a program should be based on the client's needs.

Better: Select the program that best fits the client's needs.

3. Make Your Writing Concise

Writing is **wordy** if the same idea can be expressed in fewer words. Unnecessary words bore your reader, and make your meaning more difficult to follow, since the reader has to keep all the extra words in mind while trying to understand your meaning.

Good writing is concise. Sometimes you may be able to look at a draft and see immediately how to tighten it. When wordiness isn't obvious, try the following strategies to make your writing more concise:

a. Eliminate words that say nothing.

b. Use gerunds (the *-ing* form of verbs) and infinitives to make sentences shorter and smoother.

c. Combine sentences to eliminate unnecessary words.

d. Put the meaning of your sentence into the subject and verb to use fewer words.

The following examples show how to use these four techniques.

Eliminate Words That Say Nothing

Cut words that are already clear from other words in the sentence. Substitute single words for wordy phrases.

Wordy:	Keep this information on file for future reference.
More Concise:	Keep this information for reference.
	File this information.
Wordy:	Ideally, it would be best to put the billing ticket just below the screen and above the keyboard.
More Concise:	If possible, put the billing ticket between the screen and the keyboard.

Phrases beginning with *of*, *which*, and *that* can often be shortened.

Wordy:	the question of most importance
More Concise:	the most important question
Wordy:	the estimate that is enclosed
More Concise:	the enclosed estimate

Sentences beginning with *There is / are* or *It is* delay important information and bore the reader. Tighten these sentences for readability.

Wordy:	There are three reasons for the success of the project.
More Concise:	Three reasons explain the project's success.
Wordy:	It is the case that college and university graduates make more money.
More Concise:	College and university graduates make more money.

Check your draft. If you find these phrases or any unnecessary words, eliminate them.

Use Gerunds and Infinitives to Make Sentences Shorter and Smoother

A **gerund** is the *-ing* form of a verb; grammatically, it is a verb used as a noun. In the sentence, "Running is my favourite activity," *running* is the subject of the sentence. An **infinitive** is the form of the verb that is preceded by *to*: *to run* is the infinitive.

In the revision below, a gerund (*purchasing*) and an infinitive (*to transmit*) tighten the sentence.

Wordy:	A plant suggestion has been made where they would purchase a fax machine for the purpose of transmitting test reports between plants.
More Concise:	The plant suggests purchasing a fax machine to transmit test reports between plants.

Even when gerunds and infinitives do not greatly affect length, they often make sentences smoother and more conversational.

Combine Sentences to Eliminate Unnecessary Words

In addition to saving words, combining sentences focuses the reader's attention on key points, makes your writing sound more sophisticated, and sharpens the relationship between ideas, thus making your writing more coherent.

Wordy:	I conducted this survey by telephone on March 22. I questioned two groups of third-year and fourth-year students—male and female—who, according to the Student Directory, were still living in the dorms. The purpose of this survey was to find out why some third-year and fourth-year students continue to live in the dorms even though they are no longer required by the university to do so. I also wanted to find out if there were any differences between male and female third-year and fourth-year students in their reasons for choosing to remain in the dorms.
More Concise:	On March 22, I phoned male and female third-year and fourth-year students living in the dorms to find out 1) why they continue to live in the dorms even though they are no longer required to do so and 2) whether men and women had the same reasons for staying in the dorms.

Put the Meaning of Your Sentence into the Subject and Verb to Use Fewer Words

Put the core of your meaning into the subject and verb of your main clause. Think about what you mean and try saying the same thing in several different ways. Some alternatives will be more concise than others. Choose the most concise one.

Wordy:	The reason we are recommending the computerization of this process is because it will reduce the time required to obtain data and will give us more accurate data.
Better:	We are recommending the computerization of this process because it will save time and give us more accurate data.
Concise:	Computerizing the process will give us more accurate data, faster.
Wordy:	The purpose of this letter is to indicate that if we are unable to mutually benefit from our seller–buyer relationship, with satisfactory material and satisfactory payment, then we have no alternative other than to sever the relationship. In other words, unless the account is handled in 45 days, we will have to change our terms to a permanent COD basis.
Better:	A good buyer–seller relationship depends on satisfactory material and satisfactory payment. You can continue to charge your purchases from us only if you clear your present balance within 45 days.

4. Vary Sentence Length and Sentence Structure

Readable prose mixes sentence lengths and varies sentence structure. Most sentences should be between 14 and 20 words. A really short sentence (fewer than 10 words) can add punch to your prose. Really long sentences (more than 30 words) are danger signs.

You can vary sentence patterns in several ways. First, you can mix simple, compound, and complex sentences. **Simple sentences** have one main clause:

We will open a new store this month.

Compound sentences have two main clauses joined with *and*, *but*, *or*, or another conjunction. Compound sentences work best when the ideas in the two clauses are closely related.

We have hired staff, and they will complete their training next week.

We wanted to have a local radio station broadcast from the store during its grand opening, but the DJs were already booked.

Complex sentences have at least one main and one subordinate clause; they are good for showing logical relationships:

> When the stores open, we will have balloons and specials in every department.
>
> Because we already have a strong customer base in the north, we expect the new store to be just as successful as the store in the City Centre Mall.

Compound-complex sentences have two or more main clauses with one or more subordinate clauses; these sentences combine interdependent, complex ideas:

> Although we have a strong customer base in the north, we expect the new store to attract younger, urban professionals, and, therefore, we'll be focusing our promotional efforts on this particular demographic.

You can also vary sentences by changing the order of elements. Normally the subject comes first:

> We will survey customers later in the year to see if demand warrants a third store on campus.

To create variety, begin some sentences with a phrase or a dependent clause:

> Later in the year, we will survey customers to see if demand warrants a third store on campus.
>
> To see if demand warrants a third store on campus, we will survey customers later in the year.

Use these guidelines for sentence length and structure:

- Always edit sentences for conciseness. Even a 15-word sentence can be wordy.
- When your subject matter is complicated or full of numbers, make a special effort to keep sentences short.
- Use longer sentences
  - To show how ideas are linked to each other
  - To avoid a series of short, choppy sentences
  - To reduce repetition
- Group the words in long and medium-length sentences into chunks that the reader can process quickly.[5]
- When you use a long sentence, keep the subject and verb close together.

Let's see how to apply the last three principles.

Try for an Average Sentence Length of 14 to 20 Words

The sentence below is hard to read, not simply because it is long but because it is shapeless. Just cutting it into a series of short, choppy sentences doesn't help. The best revision uses medium-length sentences (between 15 and 20 words) to show the relationship between ideas.

Too long: It should also be noted in the historical patterns presented in the summary that though there were delays in January and February, which we realized were occurring, we are now back where we were about a year ago, and although we are not off line in our collect receivables as compared to last year at this time, we do show a considerable over-budget figure because of an ultraconservative goal on the receivable investment.

Choppy: There were delays in January and February. We knew about them at the time. We are now back to where we were about a year ago. The summary shows this. Our present collect receivables are in line with last year's. However, they exceed the budget. The reason they exceed the budget is that our goal for receivable investment was very conservative.

Better: As the summary shows, we have now regained our position of a year ago, although there were delays in January and February (of which we were aware). Because our receivable investment goal was conservative, our present collectables exceed the budget and are in line with last year's.

Group Words in Sentences into Chunks

The "better" revision above has seven chunks. In the list below, the chunks starting immediately after the numbers are main clauses. The indented chunks indicate subordinate clauses and parenthetical phrases.

1.   As the summary shows,
2.   we have now regained our position of a year ago,
3.   although there were delays in January and February
4.   (of which we were aware).
5.   Because our receivable investment goal was very conservative,
6.   our present collectables exceed the budget,
7.   and are in line with last year's.

The first sentence has four chunks: 1) a subordinate clause, 2) the main clause of the first sentence, 3) and another subordinate clause followed by 4) a parenthetical phrase. The second sentence begins with 5) a subordinate clause explaining the reason for the reversal. The sentence's 6) main clause, followed by the conjunction *and*, shows that a further explanation is coming. Another main clause 7) completes the sentence. At 27 and 20 words, respectively, these sentences aren't short, but they're readable because no chunk is longer than 10 words.

Any sentence pattern will become boring if it is repeated sentence after sentence. Use different sentence patterns—different kinds and lengths of chunks—to keep your prose interesting.

Keep the Subject and Verb Close Together

Often you can move the subject and verb closer together if you put the modifying material in a list at the end of the sentence. For maximum readability, present the list vertically.

Hard to read: Movements resulting from termination, layoffs and leaves, recalls and reinstatements, transfers in, transfers out, promotions in, promotions out, and promotions within are presently documented through the Payroll Authorization Form.

Smoother: The following movements are documented on the Payroll Authorization Form: termination, layoffs and leaves, recalls and reinstatements, transfers in and out, and promotions in, out, and within.

Still better: The following movements are documented on the Payroll Authorization Form:
   - Termination
   - Layoffs and leaves
   - Recalls and reinstatements
   - Transfers in and out
   - Promotions in, out, and within

Sometimes you will need to change the verb and revise the word order to put the modifying material at the end of the sentence.

Hard to read: The size sequence code, which is currently used for sorting the items in the NOSROP lists and the composite stock list, is not part of the online file.

Smoother: The online file does not contain the size sequence code, which is currently used for sorting the items in the composite stock lists and the NOSROP lists.

5. Use Parallel Structure

Words or ideas that share the same logical role in your sentence must also be in the same grammatical form. Whatever part of speech (noun or verb; verb recommended) you choose to begin your list must start every other part of the list; otherwise, your reader has to work harder to understand your meaning.

Parallelism is a powerful device for making your writing smoother and more forceful. Note the **parallel structure** in the following examples:

Faulty: Errors can be checked by reviewing the daily exception report or note the number of errors you uncover when you match the lading copy with the file copy of the invoice.

Parallel: Errors can be checked by reviewing the daily exception report or by noting the number of errors you uncover when you match the lading copy with the file copy of the invoice.

Also parallel: Check errors, by noting
1. The number of items on the daily exception report
2. The number of errors discovered when the lading copy and the file copy are matched

Note that a list in parallel structure has to fit grammatically into the umbrella sentence (or stem) that introduces the list. (See Figure A.1.)

6. Put Your Readers in Your Sentences

Use second-person pronouns (*you*) rather than third-person (*he, she, one*) to give your writing more impact. *You* is both singular and plural; it can refer to a single person or to every member of your organization.

Third person: Funds in a participating employee's account at the end of each six months will automatically be used to buy more stock unless a "Notice of Election Not to Exercise Purchase Rights" form is received from the employee.

FIGURE A.1   Use Parallelism to Make Your Writing More Concise

These are the benefits the customer gets.
- Use tracking information.
- Our products let them scale the software to their needs.
- The customer can always rely on us.

Customer Benefits
- Tracking information
- Scalability
- Reliability

Second person: Once you begin to participate, funds in your account at the end of each six months will automatically be used to buy more stock unless *you* submit a "Notice of Election Not to Exercise Purchase Rights" form.

Be careful to use *you* only when it refers to *your reader*.

Incorrect: My visit with the outside sales rep showed me that your schedule can change quickly.

Correct: My visit with the outside sales rep showed me that schedules can change quickly.

Checkpoint

Revise for Readability

- Use active verbs.
- Use action verbs.
- Use as few words as possible.
- Vary sentence length and sentence structure.
- Use parallel structure.
- Put your readers in your sentences.

What Should I Look for When I Revise Paragraphs?

Check for topic sentences and transitions.

Paragraphs are visual and logical units. Use them to chunk your sentences.

1. Begin Most Paragraphs with Topic Sentences

A good paragraph has **unity**: it develops only one idea or topic. The **topic sentence** states the main idea and provides a base on which to structure your document. Your writing will be easier to read if you make the topic sentence explicit and put it near the beginning of the paragraph.[6]

Hard to read
(no topic sentence):   In fiscal 2012, the company filed claims for refund of federal income taxes of $3,199,000 and interest of $969,000 paid as a result of an examination of the company's federal income tax returns by the Canada Revenue Agency for the years 2008 through 2012. It is uncertain what amount, if any, may ultimately be recovered.

Better
(paragraph starts with topic sentence):   The company and the Canada Revenue Agency disagree about whether the company is liable for back taxes. In fiscal 2012, the company filed claims for a refund of federal income taxes of $3,199,000 and interest of $969,000, paid as a result of an examination of the company's federal income tax returns by the Canada Revenue Agency for the years 2008 through 2012. It is uncertain what amount, if any, may ultimately be recovered.

A good topic sentence provides *reader redundancy*: it forecasts the structure and content of the paragraph.

Plan B has economic advantages.

(Prepares the reader for a discussion of B's economic advantages.)

We had several personnel changes in June.

(Prepares the reader for a list of the month's terminations and hires.)

Employees have complained about one part of our new policy on parental leaves.

(Prepares the reader for a discussion of the problem.)

When the first sentence of a paragraph is not the topic sentence, readers who skim may miss the main point. Move the topic sentence to the beginning of the paragraph. If the paragraph does not have a topic sentence, you will need to write one. Without a single sentence that serves as an "umbrella" to cover every sentence, the paragraph lacks unity. To solve the problem, either split the paragraph into two, or eliminate the sentence that digresses from the main point.

2. Use Transitions to Link Ideas

Transition words and sentences signal connections between ideas.

Transitions tell whether the next sentence continues the previous thought or starts a new idea; they tell whether the idea that comes next is more or less important than the previous thought. Table A.2 lists some of the most common transition words and phrases.

How Does Corporate Culture Affect Style?

Different cultures may prefer different styles.

Different organizations and bosses may have different ideas about what constitutes good writing. If the style the company prefers seems reasonable, use it.

If the style doesn't seem reasonable—if you work for someone who likes flowery language or wordy paragraphs, for example—you have several choices.

- Use the proven techniques discussed in this text. Sometimes seeing good writing changes people's minds about the style they prefer.

TABLE A.2   Transition Words and Phrases

To Show Addition or Continuation of the Same Idea	To Introduce an Example	To Show That the Contrast Is More Important Than the Previous Idea	To Show Time
and	for example (e.g.)	but	after
also	for instance (i.e.)	however	as
first, second, third	indeed	nevertheless	before
in addition	to illustrate	on the contrary	**To Indicate Time Relations**
likewise	namely		next
similarly	specifically	**To Show Cause and Effect**	then
To Introduce the Last or Most Important Item	**To Contrast**	as a result	until
	in contrast	because	when
	on the other hand	consequently	while
finally	or	for this reason	**To Summarize or End**
furthermore		therefore	in conclusion
moreover			in summary
			finally

- Help your organization learn about writing. Add up-to-date writing reference texts to the company library. (If your company doesn't already offer employees a reference library, start one online.)
- Recognize that a style serves many communication purposes. An abstract, hard-to read style may forge group identity or emphasize exclusivity. For example, government, medical, and legal writing reflect highly specialized knowledge accessible only to the initiated. When big words, jargon, and wordiness are central to a group's self-image, change will be difficult, since changing style will mean changing the corporate culture.
- Ask. Often the documents that end up in files aren't especially good. Later, other workers may find these documents and imitate them, thinking they represent a corporate standard. Bosses may prefer better writing.

Building your own writing style takes energy and effort, but it's well worth the work. Good style makes every document more effective; moreover, developing a good style builds confidence, critical thinking, and competence, and makes you, the writer, valuable to every organization.

REVISING EXERCISES AND PROBLEMS

A.1 Changing Verbs from Passive to Active

Identify the passive verbs in the following sentences and convert them to active verbs. In some cases, you may need to add information to do so. You may use different words as long as you retain the basic meaning of the sentence. Remember that imperative verbs are active, too.

1. The marketing plan was prepared by Needra Smith.
2. With the assistance of computers, inventory records are updated and invoices are automatically issued when an order is entered by one of our customers.
3. When the Web page is finalized, it is recommended that it be routed to all managers for final approval.
4. As stated in my resumé, Polish is a language I speak fluently.
5. All employees being budgeted should be listed by name and position. Any employee whose name does not appear on the "September Listing of Salaried Employees" must be explained. If this employee is a planned replacement, indicate who will be replaced and when. If it is an addition, the reason must be explained.

A.2 Using Strong Verbs

Revise each of the following sentences to use stronger verbs.

1. The advantage of using colour is that the document is more memorable.
2. Customers who make payments in cash will receive a 1 percent rebate on all purchases.
3. When you make an evaluation of media buys, take into consideration the demographics of the group seeing the ad.

4. We provide assistance to clients who are in the process of reaching a decision about the purchase of hardware and software.
5. We maintain the belief that Web ads are a good investment.

A.3 Reducing Wordiness

1. Eliminate words that say nothing. You may use different words.
   a. It is necessary that we reach a decision about whether or not it is desirable to make a request that the office be allowed the opportunity and option of hiring additional workers.
   b. The purchase of a new computer will allow us to produce form letters quickly. In addition, return on investment could be calculated for proposed repairs. Another use is that the computer could check databases to make sure that claims are paid only once.
   c. There are many subjects that interest me.
2. Use gerunds and infinitives to make these sentences shorter and smoother.
   a. The completion of the project requires the collection and analysis of additional data.
   b. The purchase of MS Publisher will make possible the in-house production of the newsletter.
   c. The treasurer has the authority for the investment of assets for the gain of higher returns.
3. Combine sentences to show how ideas are related and to eliminate unnecessary words.
   a. Some buyers want low prices. Other buyers are willing to pay higher prices for convenience or service.

b. We projected sales of $34 million in the third quarter. Our actual sales have fallen short of that figure by $2.5 million.

c. We conducted this survey by handing out questionnaires on January 10, 11, and 12. Our office surveyed 100 customers. We wanted to see whether they would like to be able to leave voicemail messages for their representatives. We also wanted to find out whether our hours are convenient for them. Finally, we asked whether adequate parking was available.

A.4   Improving Parallel Structure

Revise each of the following sentences to create parallelism.

1. Training programs
   - Allow employees to build skills needed for current and future positions
   - Employees enjoy the break from routine work
   - Training programs are a "fringe benefit" that helps to attract and retain good employees

2. Newsletters enhance credibility, four times as many people read them as read standard ad formats, and allow soft-sell introduction to prospective customers.

3. When you leave a voicemail message, it gives the listener a poor impression when you start with a negative or an apology.
   - Summarize your main point in a sentence or two.
   - The name and phone number should be given slowly and distinctly.
   - The speaker should give enough information so that the recipient can act on the message.
   - Tell when you'll be available to receive the recipient's return call.

A.5   Editing Sentences to Improve Style

Revise these sentences to make them smoother, less wordy, and easier to read. Eliminate jargon and repetition. Keep the information; you may reword or reorganize it. If the original is not clear, you may need to add information to write a clear revision.

1. The table provided was unclear because of hard-to-understand headings.

2. By working a co-op or intern position, you may have to be in school an additional year to complete the requirements for graduation, but this extra year is paid for by the income you make in the co-op or intern position.

3. There is a seasonality factor in the workload, with the heaviest being immediately prior to quarterly due dates for estimated tax payments.

4. Informational meetings will be held during next month at different dates and times. These meetings will explain the health insurance options. Meeting times are as follows:
   October 17, 12:00 p.m.–1:00 p.m.
   October 20, 4:00 p.m.–5:00 p.m.
   October 23, 2:00 p.m.–3:00 p.m.

5. Listed below are some benefits you get with OHIP:
   1. Routine doctors' visits will be free.
   2. No hassle about where to get your prescriptions filled.
   3. Hospitalization is covered 100 percent.

A.6   Putting Readers in Your Sentences

Revise each of the following sentences to put readers in them. As you revise, use active verbs and simple words.

1. Mutual funds can be purchased from banks, brokers, financial planners, or from the fund itself.

2. Every employee will receive a copy of the new policy within 60 days after the labour agreement is signed.

3. Another aspect of the university is campus life, with an assortment of activities and student groups to participate in and lectures and sports events to attend.

A.7   Using Topic Sentences

Make each of the following paragraphs more readable by opening each paragraph with a topic sentence. You may be able to find a topic sentence in the paragraph and move it to the beginning. In other cases, you'll need to write a new sentence.

1. At Disney World, a lunch put on an expense account is "on the mouse." McDonald's employees "have ketchup in their veins." Business slang flourishes at companies with rich corporate cultures. Memos at Procter & Gamble are called "reco's" because the model P&G memo begins with a recommendation.

2. The first item on the agenda is the hiring for the coming year. Nicky has also asked that we review the agency goals for the next fiscal year. We should cover this early in the meeting since it may affect our hiring preferences. Finally, we need to announce the deadlines for grant proposals, decide which grants to apply for, and set up a committee to draft each proposal.

3. Separate materials that can be recycled from your regular trash. Pass along old clothing, toys, or appliances to someone else who can use them. When you purchase products, choose those with minimal packaging. If you have a yard, put your yard waste and kitchen scraps (excluding meat and fat) in a compost pile. You can reduce the amount of solid waste your household produces in four ways.

A.8 Writing Paragraphs

Write a paragraph on each of the following topics:

a. Discuss your current communication style. Include as evidence your use of e-devices and your use of space.

b. Visit BMO Bank of Montreal's Business Coach podcasts for small business owners at http://www.bmo.com/podcast/en/?businessCoach. Summarize one of the podcasts for your peers.

c. Explain how technology is affecting the field you plan to enter.

d. Explain why you have or have not decided to work while you attend college or university.

e. Write a profile of someone who is successful in the field you hope to enter.

As your instructor directs

a. Label topic sentences, active verbs, and parallel structure.

b. Edit a classmate's paragraphs to make the writing more concise and smoother.

c. Post your revised and edited paragraph on your blog.

Editing for Grammar and Punctuation

With the possible exception of spelling, grammar is the one aspect of writing that writers seem to find most troublesome. Your document represents you and your organization; it's a permanent record of your capability. Business messages with mechanical errors interfere with readability, reflect poorly on the quality of your work, and ultimately cost time and money.

What Grammatical Errors Should I Focus On?

Focus on editing for

- Subject–verb agreement
- Noun–pronoun agreement
- Pronoun case
- Dangling and misplaced modifiers
- Parallelism
- Predication
- Punctuation

Agreement

Singular subjects use singular verbs; plural subjects use plural verbs.

Incorrect: The accountants who conducted the audit was recommended highly.

Correct: The accountants who conducted the audit were recommended highly.

Subject–verb agreement errors often occur when other words come between the subject and the verb. Edit your draft by finding the subject and the verb of each sentence.

Canadian and American usage treats company names and the words *company* and *government* as singular nouns. British usage treats them as plural:

Correct (Canada):   Clarica Insurance trains its agents well.

Correct (U.S.):   Allstate Insurance trains its agents well.

Correct (U.K.):   Lloyd's of London train their agents well.

Use a plural verb when two or more singular subjects are joined by *and*.

Correct: Larry McGreevy and I are planning to visit the client.

Use a singular verb when two or more singular subjects are joined by *or*, *nor*, or *but*.

Correct: Either the shipping clerk or the superintendent has to sign the order.

When the sentence begins with *Here* or *There*, make the verb agree with the subject that follows the verb.

Correct: Here is the booklet you asked for.

Correct: There are the blueprints I wanted.

Note that some words that end in *s* are considered singular and require singular verbs.

Correct: A series of meetings is planned.

When a situation doesn't seem to fit the rules, or when following a rule produces an awkward sentence, revise the sentence to avoid the problem.

Problematic: The plant manager, in addition to the sales representative, (was, were?) pleased with the new system.

Better: The plant manager and the sales representative were pleased with the new system.

Problematic: None of us (is, are?) perfect.

Better: All of us have faults.

Errors in *noun–pronoun agreement* occur if a pronoun is of a different number (singular or plural) or person than the word it refers to.

Incorrect: All drivers of leased automobiles are billed $100 if damages to his automobile are caused by a collision.

Correct: All drivers of leased automobiles are billed $100 if damages to their automobiles are caused by collisions.

Incorrect: A manager has only yourself to blame if things go wrong.

Correct: As a manager, you have only yourself to blame if things go wrong.

The following words require a singular pronoun:

| anyone | each | everyone | nobody |
| everybody | either | neither | a person |

Correct: Everyone should bring his or her copy of the manual to the next session on changes in the law.

Because pronoun pairs (*his or hers*), necessary to avoid sexism, may seem cumbersome, substitute words that take plural pronouns (*people*, *employees*, *persons*) or use second-person *you*.

Each pronoun must refer to a specific word. If a pronoun does not refer to a specific term, add a word to correct the error.

Incorrect: We will open three new stores in the suburbs. This will bring us closer to our customers.

Correct: We will open three new stores in the suburbs. This strategy will bring us closer to our customers.

Hint: Make sure *this* and *it* refer to a specific noun in the previous sentence. If either refers to an idea, add a noun ("this strategy") to make the sentence grammatically correct.

Use *who* and *whom* to refer to people and *which* and *that* to refer to objects.

Correct: The new executive director, who moved here from St. John's, is already making friends.

Correct: The information that she wants will be available tomorrow.

Correct: This confirms the price, which I quoted you this morning, is correct.

Case

Case refers to the grammatical role a noun or pronoun plays in a sentence. Table B.1 identifies the case of each personal pronoun.

Use **subjective** or **nominative** pronouns for the **subject** of a clause.

Correct: Shannon Weaver and I talked to the customer, who was interested in learning more about integrated software.

TABLE B.1   The Case of the Personal Pronoun

	Nominative (subject of clause)	Possessive	Objective	Reflexive/Intensive
Singular				
1st person	I	my, mine	me	myself
2nd person	you	your, yours	you	yourself
3rd person	he/she/it one/who	his/her(s)/its one's/whose	him/her/it one/whom	himself/herself/itself oneself
Plural				
1st person	we	our, ours	us	ourselves
2nd person	you	your, yours	you	yourselves
3rd person	they	their, theirs	them	themselves

Use **possessive** pronouns to show who or what something belongs to.

Correct: Microsoft Office 2007 will exactly meet her needs.

Use **objective pronouns** as **objects** of verbs or prepositions.

Correct: When you send in the quote, thank her for the courtesy she showed Shannon and me.

Hint: Use *whom* when *him* or *her* would fit grammatically in the same place in your sentence.

> I am writing this letter to (who, whom?) it may concern.
> I am writing this letter to him.

Whom is correct.

> Have we decided (who, whom?) will take notes?
> Have we decided she will take notes?

Who is correct.

Reflexive pronouns emphasize a noun or pronoun that has already appeared in the sentence.

I **myself** think the call was a very productive one.

Reflexive pronouns are used very infrequently in English Canadian business practice, since they emphasize the writer or speaker unnecessarily.

Do not use reflexive pronouns as subjects of clauses, or as objects of verbs or propositions.

Incorrect: Elaine and myself will follow up on this order.

Correct: Elaine and I will follow up on this order.

Incorrect: He gave the order to Dan and myself.

Correct: He gave the order to Dan and me.

Note that the first-person pronoun comes *after* names or pronouns that refer to other people.

Dangling Modifier (DM)

Modifiers are words or phrases that give more information about the subject, verb, or object in a clause. A modifier dangles when the word it modifies is not actually in the sentence. The solution is to reword the modifier so that it is grammatically correct.

Incorrect: Confirming our conversation, the truck will leave Monday. (The speaker is doing the confirming. But the speaker isn't in the sentence.)

Incorrect: At the age of eight, I began teaching my children about business. (This sentence says that the author was eight when he or she had children who could understand business.)

Correct a dangling modifier in one of these ways:

1. Recast the modifier as a subordinate clause.

Correct: As I told you, the truck will leave Monday.

Correct: When they were eight, I began teaching my children about business.

2. Revise the main clause so its subject or object can be modified by the now-dangling phrase.

Correct: Confirming our conversation, I have scheduled the truck to leave Monday.

Correct: At the age of eight, my children began learning about business.

Hint: Whenever you use a verb or adjective that ends in *-ing*, make sure it modifies the grammatical subject of your sentence. If it doesn't, reword the sentence.

Misplaced Modifier (MM)

A *misplaced modifier* is a word, phrase, or clause that appears beside a different element of the sentence than the writer intended, causing confusion or misinterpretation.

Incorrect: Customers who complain often alert us to changes we need to make. (Does the sentence mean that customers must complain frequently to teach us something? Or is the meaning that frequently we learn from complaints?)

Correct a misplaced modifier by moving it closer to the word it modifies or by adding punctuation to clarify your meaning. If a modifier modifies the whole sentence, use it as an introductory phrase or clause; follow it with a comma.

Correct: Often, customers who complain alert us to changes we need to make.

Parallelism

Items in a series or list must have the same grammatical structure.

Not parallel: In the second month of your internship, you will

  1. Learn how to resolve customer complaints
  2. Supervision of desk staff
  3. Interns will help plan store displays

Parallel: In the second month of your internship, you will

  1. Learn how to resolve customer complaints
  2. Supervise desk staff
  3. Plan store displays

Also parallel: Duties in the second month of your internship include resolving customer complaints, supervising desk staff, and planning store displays.

Hint: When you have two or three items in a list (whether the list is horizontal or vertical), make sure the items are in the same grammatical form. Write lists vertically to make them easier to see.

Predication Errors

The predicate of a sentence must fit grammatically and logically with the subject to avoid **predication errors**. In sentences using *is* and other linking verbs, the complement must be a noun, an adjective, or a noun clause.

Incorrect: The reason for this change is because the OSC now requires fuller disclosure.

Correct: The reason for this change is that the OSC now requires fuller disclosure.

Make sure that the verb describes the action done by or done to the subject.

Incorrect: Our goals should begin immediately.

Correct: Implementing our goals should begin immediately.

How Can I Fix Sentence Errors?

Learn to recognize main clauses.

A **sentence** contains at least one main clause. A **main** or **independent clause** is a complete statement, with a subject and a verb. A **subordinate** or **dependent clause** contains both a subject and a verb, but is not a complete statement and cannot stand by itself; it depends on an independent clause (a sentence or complete thought) for meaning. A phrase is a group of words that does not contain a verb.

MAIN/INDEPENDENT CLAUSES

Your order will arrive Thursday.

He dreaded talking to his supplier.

I plan to enrol in summer-school classes.

SUBORDINATE/DEPENDENT CLAUSES

If you place your order by Monday

Because he was afraid the product would be out of stock

Since I want to graduate next spring

Although I was prepared for the test

PHRASES

With our current schedule

As a result

A clause with one of the following words will be subordinate:

after	if
although, though	since
because	when, whenever
before	until while, as

Using the correct punctuation will enable you to avoid three major sentence errors: comma splices, run-on sentences, and sentence fragments.

Comma Splices (CS)

A **comma splice** or **comma fault** occurs when writers join two main clauses with only a comma.

Incorrect: The contest will start in June, the date has not been set.

Correct a comma splice in one of the following four ways:

- If the ideas are closely related, use a semicolon rather than a comma.

Correct: The contest will start in June; the exact date has not been set.

- If they aren't closely related, start a new sentence.

Correct: The contest will start in June. We need to determine the exact date.

- Add a coordinating conjunction (*and, but, or, for, nor, yet*).

Correct: The contest will start in June, but the exact date has not been set.

- Subordinate one of the clauses.

Correct: Although the contest will start in June, the date has not been set.

Remember that you cannot use just a comma with the following transitional words when they begin an independent clause:

however	therefore	nevertheless	moreover

Instead, use a semicolon to separate the clauses, or start a new sentence.

Incorrect: Computerized grammar checkers do not catch every error, however, they may be useful as a first check before an editor reads the material.

Correct: Computerized grammar checkers do not catch every error; however, they may be useful as a first check before an editor reads the material.

Language FOCUS

Do not overgeneralize the rule about using a semicolon before **however**. If the word "however" begins a new thought, use a semicolon. If the word "however" is being used to add to a thought, as in "Julian thought that the movie was terrible. I, however, thought it was fantastic," use a comma.

Run-On Sentences (RO)

A **run-on sentence** strings together several main clauses using *and*, *but*, *or*, *so*, and *for*. Run-on sentences and comma splices are "mirror faults." A comma splice uses *only* the comma and omits the coordinating conjunction, while a run-on sentence uses *only* the conjunction and omits the comma. Correct a short run-on sentence by adding a comma. Separate a long run-on sentence into two or more sentences. Consider subordinating one or more of the clauses.

Incorrect: We will end up with a much smaller markup but they use a lot of this material so the volume would be high so try to sell them on fast delivery and tell them our quality is very high.

Correct: Although we will end up with a much smaller markup, volume will be high since they use a lot of this material. Try to sell them on fast delivery and high quality.

Sentence Fragments (Frag)

In a **sentence fragment**, a group of words that is not a complete sentence is punctuated as if it were a complete sentence. Sentence fragments often occur when a writer thinks of additional detail that the reader needs. Fragments are acceptable in resumés, advertising, and sales letters, but they're rarely acceptable in other business documents.

Incorrect: Observing these people, I have learned two things about the program. The time it takes. The rewards it brings.

To fix a sentence fragment, either add whatever parts of the sentence are missing or incorporate the fragment into the sentence before it or after it.

Correct: Observing these people, I have learned that the program is time-consuming but rewarding.

Remember that clauses with the following words are not complete sentences. Join them to a main clause.

after	if
although, though	since

because	when, whenever
before, until	while, as

Incorrect: We need to buy a new computer system. Because our current system is obsolete.

Correct: We need to buy a new computer system because our current system is obsolete.

When Should I Use Commas?

Use commas only to signal the reader.

Commas, like other punctuation marks, are road signs to help readers predict what comes next, thereby contributing to ease and speed of reading, or **readability**. The easier you make it for the reader to scan and understand the text, the more credible you appear, and the more likely it is that the reader will be persuaded to your point of view.

When you move from the subject to the verb, you're going in a straight line; no comma is needed. When you end an introductory phrase or clause, the comma tells readers the introduction is over and you're turning to the main clause. When words interrupt main clause, like this, commas tell the reader when to turn off the main clause for a short side route and when to return.

What Punctuation Should I Use Inside Sentences?

Use punctuation to clarify meaning for your reader.

A good writer knows how to use the following punctuation marks: apostrophes, colons, commas, dashes, hyphens, parentheses, periods, and semicolons. Table B.2 outlines what some of these marks tell the reader.

TABLE B.2   What Punctuation Tells the Reader

Mark	Tells the Reader
Period	We're stopping.
Semicolon	What comes next is another complete thought, closely related to what I just said.
Colon	What comes next is an illustration, an example, or a qualification of what I just said.
Dash	What comes next is a dramatic example of or a shift from what I just said.
Comma	What comes next is a slight turn, but we're going in the same direction.

Apostrophes

1. Use an apostrophe in a contraction to indicate that a letter has been omitted or to indicate a number has been omitted.

   We're trying to renegotiate the contract.

   The '90s were years of restructuring for our company.

2. To indicate possession, add an apostrophe and an *s* to the word.

   The corporation's home office is in Vancouver, British Columbia.

Apostrophes to indicate possession are especially important when one noun in a comparison is omitted.

> This year's sales will be higher than last year's.

When a word already ends in an *s*, you may add only an apostrophe to make it possessive.

> The meeting will be held at St. Johns' convention centre.

Adding an *s* and an apostrophe would not be incorrect, but doing that can make pronunciation difficult.

With many terms, the placement of the apostrophe indicates whether the noun is singular or plural.

Incorrect: The program should increase the participant's knowledge. (Implies that only one participant is in the program.)

Correct: The program should increase the participants' knowledge. (Many participants are in the program.)

Hint: Use *of* in the sentence to see where the apostrophe goes.

> The figures of last year = last year's figures
> The needs of our customers = our customers' needs

Possessive pronouns (e.g., *his, ours, its*) do not have apostrophes. The only exception is *one's*.

> The company needs the goodwill of its stockholders.
> His promotion was announced yesterday.
> One's greatest asset is the willingness to work hard.

3. Use an apostrophe to make plurals that could be confused for other words. However, other plurals do not use apostrophes.

> I earned A's in all my business courses.

Colons

1. Use a colon to separate the main clause (sentence) from a list, explanation, or qualification that explains the last element in the clause. The items in the list are specific examples of the word that appears immediately before the colon.

> Please order the following supplies:
> printer ribbons
> computer paper (20-lb. white bond)
> bond paper (25-lb., white, 25% cotton)
> company letterhead
> company envelopes

Because English is a living language, grammar, punctuation, and usage rules evolve over time; however, current contemporary Canadian usage indicates a preference for lowercase after the colon. Capitalize the first letter after the colon only if a complete sentence follows.

Please order the following supplies: printer ribbons, computer paper (20-lb. white bond), bond paper (25-lb., white, 25% cotton), company letterhead, and company envelopes.

Avoid using a colon when the list is grammatically part of the main clause.

Incorrect: The rooms will have coordinated decors in natural colours such as: eggplant, moss, and mushroom.

Correct: The rooms will have coordinated decors in natural colours such as eggplant, moss, and mushroom.

Correct: The rooms will have coordinated decors in a variety of natural colours: eggplant, moss, and mushroom.

Even if the list is presented vertically, there is no need to introduce the list with a colon if the words in the stem are not a complete sentence.

2. Use a colon to join two independent clauses when the second clause explains or restates the first clause.

Selling is simple: give people the service they need, and they'll come back with more orders.

Language FOCUS

Use a colon only if the sentence preceding it is a complete thought, such as in "I need the following supplies for camping: a tent, a sleeping bag, and a canteen." Do not use a colon if the list is part of the sentence, as in "I need a tent, a sleeping bag, and a canteen."

Commas

1. Use commas to separate the main clause from an introductory clause, the reader's name, or words that interrupt the main clause. Note that commas both precede and follow the interrupting information.

J. Camaya, the new sales manager, comes to us from the Saskatoon office.

A **non-essential clause** gives extra information that is not needed to identify the noun it modifies. Because non-essential clauses give extra information, they need extra commas.

Sue Decker, who wants to advance in the organization, has signed up for the company training program in sales techniques.

Do not use commas to set off information that restricts the meaning of a noun or pronoun. **Essential clauses** give essential, not extra, information.

Incorrect: Anyone who wants to advance in the organization, should take advantage of on-the-job training.

Correct: Anyone who wants to advance in the organization should take advantage of on-the-job training.

Do not use commas to separate the subject from the verb, even if you would take a breath after a long subject.

Incorrect: Laws regarding anyone collecting $5,000 or more on behalf of another person, apply to schools and private individuals as well to charitable groups and professional fundraisers.

Correct: Laws regarding anyone collecting $5,000 or more on behalf of another person apply to schools and private individuals as well to charitable groups and professional fundraisers.

2. Use a comma after the first clause in a compound sentence if the clauses are very long or if they have different subjects.

This policy eliminates all sick leave credit of the employee at the time of retirement, and payment will be made only once to any individual.

Do not use commas to join independent clauses without a conjunction. Doing so produces comma splices.

3. Use commas to separate items in a series. Using a comma before the *and* or *or* is not required by some authorities, but using a comma always adds clarity. The comma is essential if any of the items in the series themselves contain the word *and*.

The company contributes equally to full hospital coverage for eligible employees, spouses, and unmarried dependent children under age 21.

Language FOCUS

Many students are taught the pause rule for comma use. This rule states that if you were to pause when reading, add a comma. This is a broad overgeneralization and is not appropriate for this level of writing.

Dashes

Use dashes to emphasize an aside, or break in thought.

Ryertex comes in 30 grades—each with a special use.

To type a dash, use two hyphens with no space before or after.

Hyphens

1. Use a hyphen to indicate that a word has been divided between two lines.

Attach the original receipts for lodging, transportation, and registration fees.

Divide words at syllable breaks. If you aren't sure where the syllables divide, look up the word in a dictionary. When a word has several syllables, divide it after a vowel or between two consonants. Don't divide words of one syllable (e.g., *used*); don't divide a two-syllable word if one of the syllables is only one letter long (e.g., *acre*).

2. Use hyphens to join two or more words used as a single adjective.

> Order five 10- or 12-metre lengths.
>
> It's a 10-year-old plan.
>
> The computer-prepared Income and Expense statements will be ready next Friday.

The hyphen clarifies meaning. In the first example, five lengths are needed, not lengths of 5, 10, or 12 metres. In the third example, without the hyphen, the reader might think that *computer* was the subject and *prepared* was the verb.

Parentheses

1. Use parentheses to set off words, phrases, or sentences explaining or commenting on the main idea.

> For the thinnest Ryertex (1 mm) only a single layer of the base material may be used, while the thickest (10 cm) may contain more than 600 greatly compressed layers of fabric or paper. By varying the fabric used (cotton, asbestos, glass, or nylon) or the type of paper, and by changing the kind of resin (phenolic, melamine, silicone, or epoxy), we can produce 30 different grades.

Any additional punctuation goes outside the second parenthesis when the punctuation applies to the whole sentence. It goes inside when it applies only to the words in the parentheses.

> Please check the invoice to see whether credit should be issued. (A copy of the invoice is attached.)

2. Use parentheses for the second of two numbers presented both in words and in digits.

> Construction must be completed within two (2) years of the date of the contract.

Periods

1. Use a period at the end of a sentence. Leave only one space before the next sentence.
2. Use a period after some abbreviations. When a period replaces a person's name, leave one space after the period before the next word. In other abbreviations, no space is necessary.

> P. Chow has been named vice-president for marketing.
>
> The B.C. division plans to hire 10 new M.B.A.s in the next year.

The tendency today is to reduce the use of punctuation. It would also be correct to write

> The BC division plans to hire 10 new MBAs in the next year.

Language FOCUS

If you have been educated in a system that uses British English, you are probably familiar with the term **full stop**. Most North Americans refer to the full stop as a **period**.

Semicolons

1. Use semicolons to join two independent clauses when they are closely related.

> We'll do our best to fill your order promptly; however, we cannot guarantee a delivery date.

Using a semicolon suggests that the two ideas are very closely connected. Using a period and a new sentence is also correct but implies nothing about how closely related the two sentences are.

2. Use semicolons to separate items in a series when the items themselves contain commas.

> The final choices for the new plant are Edmonton, Alberta; Sydney, Nova Scotia; Mississauga, Ontario; Quebec City, Quebec; Winnipeg, Manitoba; Yellowknife, Northwest Territories; and Victoria, British Columbia.

> Hospital benefits are also provided for certain specialized care services such as diagnostic admissions directed toward a definite disease or injury; normal maternity delivery, Caesarean-section delivery, or complications of pregnancy; and inpatient admissions for dental procedures necessary to safeguard the patient's life or health.

Hint: A semicolon could be replaced by a period and the next word capitalized. It has a sentence on both sides.

What Do I Use When I Quote Sources?

Use quotation marks, square brackets, and ellipses when quoting sources.

Quotation marks, square brackets, ellipses, and underlining are necessary when you quote material.

Quotation Marks

1. Use quotation marks around the names of brochures, pamphlets, and magazine articles.

> Enclosed are 30 copies of our pamphlet "Saving Energy."

> You'll find articles like "How to Improve Your Golf Game" and "Can You Keep Your Eye on the Ball?" in every issue.

In Canada and the United States, periods, and commas go inside quotation marks. Colons and semicolons go outside. Question marks go inside if they are part of the material being quoted.

2. Use quotation marks around words to indicate that you think the term is misleading.

> These "pro-business" policies actually increase corporate taxes.

3. Use quotation marks around words that you are discussing as words.

> Forty percent of the respondents answered "yes" to the first question.

> Use "Ms." as a courtesy title for a woman unless you know she prefers another title.

It is also acceptable to use underlining or to italicize words instead of using quotation marks. Choose one method and use it consistently.

4. Use quotation marks around words or sentences that you quote from someone else.

"The Fog Index," says its inventor, Robert Gunning, is "an effective warning system against drifting into needless complexity."

Square Brackets

Use square brackets to add your own words to or make changes in quoted material.

MPP Smith's statement: "These measures will increase the deficit."

Your use of Smith's statement: According to MPP Smith, "These measures [in the new tax bill] will increase the deficit."

The square brackets show that Smith did not say these words; you add them only so that the quotation makes sense in your document.

Ellipses

Ellipses are made up of three spaced dots. In the days of typewriting, three spaced periods were used for an ellipsis; nowadays, if using a word processor, a true ellipsis (which is a single character) should be used.

When an ellipsis comes at the end of a sentence, use a period immediately after the last letter of the sentence. Then add the three spaced dots or true ellipsis. A space follows the last of the dots.

1. Use ellipses to indicate that one or more words have been omitted in the middle of quoted material. You do not need ellipses at the beginning or end of a quote.

The Wall Street Journal notes that Japanese magazines and newspapers include advertisements for a "$2.1 million home in New York's posh Riverdale section … 185 acres of farmland [and] … luxury condos on Manhattan's Upper East Side."

2. In advertising and direct mail, use ellipses to imply the pace of spoken comments.

If you've ever wanted to live on a tropical island … cruise to the Bahamas … or live in a castle in Spain … you can make your dreams come true with Vacations Extraordinaire.

Italics versus Underlining

1. Underlining causes the reader's eye to **fixate**, or stop unnecessarily, thereby interfering with both reading speed and retention. Unless you're typing or handwriting documents, it is preferable to use italics to indicate titles or emphasis:

Calgary Sun

Maclean's

Boom, Bust and Echo 2000

Titles of brochures and pamphlets are put in quotation marks rather than in italics.

2. Italicize words to emphasize them.

> Here's a bulletin that gives you, in handy chart form, *workable data* on more than 50 different types of tubing and pipe.

Note: You may alternatively use bold to emphasize words.

How Should I Write Numbers and Dates?

Spell out numbers under 10 and those used at the beginning of sentences.

Spell out numbers from one to nine. Use digits for numbers 10 and over in most cases. Always use digits for amounts of money.

Numbers (e.g., *19 percent*) should not begin sentences. Spell out any number that appears at the beginning of a sentence. If spelling it out is impractical, revise the sentence so that it does not begin with a number.

> Fifty students filled out the survey.
> The year 1992 marked the official beginning of the European Economic Community.

When two numbers follow each other, use words for the smaller number and digits for the larger number.

In dates, use digits for the day and year. The month is normally spelled out. Be sure to spell out the month in international business communication. Canadian usage often shows the day first: *10/01/13* means *January 10, 2013*. United States usage puts the month first, so *01/10/13* means *January 10, 2013*. European usage puts the day first, so *10/01/13* means *January 10, 2013*.

Modern punctuation uses a comma before the year only when you give both the month and the day of the month:

> May 1, 2012

but

> Summers 2010–12
> August 2012
> Fall 2012

No punctuation is needed in military or European usage, which puts the day of the month first: 13 July 2009. Do not use spaces before or after the slash used to separate parts of the date: 5/09–10/09.

Use a hyphen or short dash (en dash) to join inclusive dates.

> March–August 2012 (or write out: March to August 2012)
> '98–'08
> 1996–2012

Note: You do not need to repeat the century in the date that follows the hyphen or dash: 2000–12. But do give the century when it changes: 1999–2012.

How Do I Mark Errors I Find When Proofreading?

Use these standard proofreading symbols.

Use the proofreading symbols in Figure B.1 to make corrections when you don't have access to a computer. Figure B.2 shows how the symbols can be used to correct a typed text.

FIGURE B.1   **Proofreading Symbols**

ℰ	delete	⌐	move to left
ℰ	insert a letter	⌐	move to right
¶	start a new paragraph here	⊓	move up
(stet)	stet (leave as it was before the marked change)	⊔	move down
(tr) ∿	transpose (reverse)	#	leave a space
(lc)	lowercase (don't capitalize)	⌒	close up
☰	capitalize	∥	align vertically

FIGURE B.2   **Marked Text**

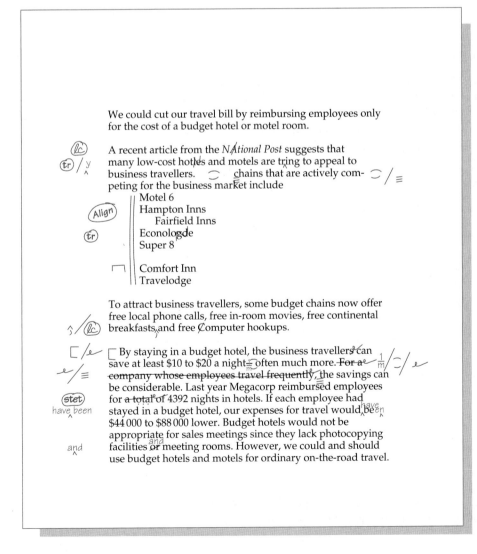

EDITING EXERCISES AND PROBLEMS

B.1   Making Subjects and Verbs Agree

Identify and correct the errors in the following sentences.

1. My education and training has prepared me to contribute to your company.
2. I know from my business experience that good communication among people and departments are essential in running a successful corporation.
3. A team of people from marketing, finance, and production are preparing the proposal.
4. The present solutions that has been suggested are not adequate.
5. There has also been suggestions for improving the airflow in the building.

B.2   Using the Right Pronoun

Identify and correct the errors in the following sentences.

1. A new employee should try to read verbal and nonverbal signals to see which aspects of your job are most important.
2. With people like yourself giving gifts, the Habitat for Humanity program will be able to grow.
3. If a group member doesn't complete their assigned work, it slows down the whole project.
4. Todd drew the graphs after him and I discussed the ideas for them.
5. Thank you for the help you gave Joanne Jackson and myself.

B.3   Fixing Dangling and Misplaced Modifiers

Identify and correct the errors in the following sentences.

1. As one of the students in a good program, our company is interested in interviewing you.
2. By making an early reservation, it will give us more time to coordinate our trucks to better serve your needs.
3. Children are referred to the Big Brother or Big Sister program by their school social workers, often from underprivileged homes.
4. At times while typing and editing, the text on your screen may not look correct.
5. All employees are asked to cut back on energy waste by the manager.

B.4   Creating Parallel Structure

Identify and correct the errors in the following sentences.

1. We help clients
   - Manage change
   - Marketing/promotion
   - Developing better billing systems
2. Volunteers need a better orientation to Planned Parenthood as a whole, to the overall clinic function, and to the staff there is also a need to clarify volunteer responsibilities.
3. The benefits of an online catalogue are
   1. We will be able to keep records up to date
   2. Broad access to the catalogue system from any networked terminal on campus
   3. The consolidation of the main catalogue and the catalogues in the departmental and branch libraries
   4. Cost savings
4. You can get a reduced rate on your life insurance if you have an annual medical exam. Another rebate is available to employees who do not use tobacco. Exercising for 30 minutes a day three times a week also entitles employees to an insurance rebate.
5. The ideal job candidate will be able to
   - Create and maintain Web pages
   - The ability to create PowerPoint slides is expected
   - It would be best if the candidate could speak a second language

B.5   Correcting Sentence Errors

Identify and correct the errors in the following sentences.

1. Videoconferencing can be frustrating. Simply because little time is available for casual conversation.
2. Not everyone is promoted after six months some people might remain in the training program a year before being moved to a permanent assignment.
3. Pay yourself with the Automatic Savings Account, with this account any amount you choose will be transferred automatically from your chequing account to your savings account each month.
4. You can take advantage of several banking services. Such as automatic withdrawal of a house or car payment and direct deposit of your paycheque.
5. Our group met seven times outside class, we would have met even more if we could have found times when we could all get together.

B.6 Providing Punctuation Within Sentences

Provide the necessary punctuation in the following sentences. Note that not every box requires punctuation.

1. The system □ s □ user □ friendly design □ provides screen displays of work codes □ rates □ and client information.
2. Many other factors also shape the organization □ s □ image □ advertising □ brochures □ proposals □ stationery □ calling cards □ and so on.
3. Miss Manners □ author of □ *Miss Manners'* □ *Book of Modern Manners* □□ says □□ Try to mention specifics of the conversation to fix the interview permanently in the interviewer □ s □ mind and be sure to mail the letter the same day □ before the hiring decision is made □□
4. What are your room rates and charges for food service □
5. We will need accommodations for 150 people □ five meeting rooms □ one large room and four small ones □□ coffee served during morning and afternoon breaks □ and lunches and dinners.
6. The Operational Readiness Inspection □ which occurs once every three years □ is a realistic exercise □ that evaluates the □ Royal Canadian Air Cadet □ s □ ability to mobilize □ deploy □ and fight.
7. Most computer packages will calculate three different sets of percentages □ row percentages □ column percentages □ and table percentages □
8. In today □ s □ economy □ it □ s almost impossible for a firm to extend credit beyond it □ s □ regular terms.
9. The Ministry of Transportation does not have statutory authority to grant easements □ however □ we do have authority to lease unused areas of highway right □ of □ way.
10. The program has two goals □ to identify employees with promise □ and to see that they get the training they need to advance.

B.7 Providing Punctuation

Provide the necessary punctuation in the following sentences. Note that not every box requires punctuation.

1. To reduce executive assistants □ overtime hours □ the office should hire part □ time secretaries to work from 5:00 to 9:00 p.m.
2. Since memberships can begin at any time during the year □ all member □ s □ dues are recognized on a cash basis □ when they are received.

3. I would be interested in working on the committee □ however □ I have decided to do less community work □ so that I have more time to spend with my family.
4. One of the insurance companies □ Allstate Insurance □ □ Fredericton □□ NB □ said it hopes to persuade the provincial government to reconsider the rule.
5. The city already has five □ two □ hundred □ bed hospitals.
6. Students □ run the whole organization □ and are advised by a board of directors from the community.
7. I suggest putting a bulletin board in the rear hallway with all the interviewer □ s □ pictures on it.
8. □ Most small businesses just get enough money to open the doors □□ says Mr. Quinn □ adding □ that the $10 000 or so of savings he used to start up simply wasn □ t enough □□
9. Otis Conward Jr □□ who grew up in this area □ now heads the Council for Economic Development.
10. Volunteers also participate in a one □ on □ one pal program.

B.8 Fixing Errors in Grammar and Punctuation

Identify and correct the errors in the following passages.

a. Company's are finding it to their advantage to cultivate their suppliers. Partnerships between a company and its suppliers can yield hefty payoffs for both company and supplier. One example is Bombardier, a Montreal headquartered company. Bombardier makes airplanes, subway cars and control systems. They treat suppliers almost like departments of their own company. When a Bombardier employee passes a laser scanner over a bins bar code the supplier is instantly alerted to send more parts.
b. Entrepreneur Trip Hawkins appears in Japanese ads for the video game system his company designed. It plugs into the future! he says in one ad, in a cameo spliced into shots of U.S kids playing the games. Hawkins is one of several U.S. celebrities and business people whom plug products on Japanese TV.
c. Between 1989 and 2009 the number of self-employed grew by more than 40 percent to 2.4 million; but this growth includes a huge increase of one person operations. "The self-employed sector now accounts for more than 16 percent of all workers; an increase from 13 percent in 1989. According to bizSmarts report Self-Employment in Canada, Trend's and Prospect's, over the next ten years, self-employment will become even more dominant in the Canadian labour market

B.9   Identifying Audience Concerns About Grammar

Most readers care passionately about only a few points of grammar. Survey one or more readers (including your boss, if you have a job) to find out which kinds of errors concern them. Use a separate copy of this survey for each reader.

Directions: Each of the following sentences contains an error. Please circle Y if the error bothers you significantly, S if the error bothers you slightly, and N if you would not be bothered by the error (or perhaps even notice it).

Y S N   1. She brung her secretary with her.

Y S N   2. Him and Richard were the last ones hired.

Y S N   3. Wanted to tell you that the meeting will be November 10.

Y S N   4. Each representative should bring a list of their clients to the meeting.

Y S N   5. A team of people from administration, human services, and animal control are preparing the proposal.

Y S N   6. We cannot predict, how high the number of clients may rise.

Y S N   7. He treats his clients bad.

Y S N   8. She asked Eva and I to give a presentation.

Y S N   9. Update the directory by reviewing each record in the database and note any discrepancies.

Y S N   10. He has went to a lot of trouble to meet our needs.

Y S N   11. She gave the report to Davlic and myself.

Y S N   12. I was unable to complete the report. Because I had a very busy week.

Y S N   13. The benefits of an online directory are
a. We will be able to keep records up-to-date
b. Access to the directory from any terminal with a modem in the county
c. Cost savings

Y S N   14. By making an early reservation, it will give us more time to plan the session to meet your needs.

Y S N   15. She doesn't have no idea how to use the computer.

Y S N   16. The change will not effect our service to customers.

Y S N   17. Confirming our conversation, the truck will leave Monday.

Y S N   18. The sessions will begin January 4 we will pass around a sign-up sheet early in December.

Y S N   19. I will be unable to attend the meeting, however I will send someone else from my office.

Y S N   20. Its too soon to tell how many proposals we will receive.

Compare your responses with those of a small group of students.

- Which errors were most annoying to the largest number of readers?
- How much variation do you find in a single workplace? in a single type of business?

As your instructor directs

a. Present your findings to the class in a short group report.

b. Present your findings to the class in an oral presentation.

Credits

PASSIM

Employability Skills text and icons: *Employability Skills 2000+ Brochure 2000 E/F* (Ottawa: The Conference Board of Canada, 2000). Reprinted with permission.

FIGURES, TABLES AND TEXT:

Figure 1.4, page 6: Daphne A. Jameson

Box 1.6, page 10: Mathew Ingram (2008, March 26), Stuff white people like, the book, *Globe and Mail*, http://v1.theglobeandmail.com/servlet/story/ RTGAM.20080326.WBmingram20080326111531/WBStory/WBmingram/; Mathew Ingram, (2008, March 14), Stuff white people in Toronto like, Torontoist, http://torontoist.com/2008/03/stuff_white_peo.php; Allan Salkin (2008, April 6), Why blog? Reason no. 92: Book deal, New York Times, www.nytimes.com/2008/03/30/fashion/30web.html?ref=style.

Table 2.2, page 27: Modified and reproduced by special permission of the Publisher, CPP, Inc., Mountainview, CA 94043 from Introduction to Type®, Sixth Edition by Isabel Briggs Myers. Copyright 1998 by Peter B. Myers and Katharine D. Myers. All rights reserved. Further reproduction is prohibited without the Publisher's written consent.

Figure 3.1, page 43: Adapted from Farid Elashmawi and Philip R. Harris (1998), Multicultural Management 2000: Essential Cultural Insights for Global Business Success (Houston: Gulf), 169.

Table 3.2, page 44: Geert Hofstede, Gert Jan Hofstede, Michael Minkov, "Cultures and Organizations, Software of the Mind," Third Revised Edition, McGraw-Hill 2010, ISBN 0-07-166418-1. ©Geert Hofstede B. V. quoted with permission.

Box 3.2, page 45: Daniel Goleman, Emotional Intelligence (New York: Bantam Books, 1995); Joan Vinall Cox, statement to Kathryn Braun, April 9, 2009; "Richard Boyatzis/Anita Howard Career Success Through Emotional Intelligence: Developing EI Competencies," www.careertrainer.com; Cary Chernis, "The Business Case for Emotional Intelligence," www.eiconsortium.org/reports/business; Michael E. Rock, "The 90% Factor: EQ (Emotional Intelligence) and the New Workplace," www.canadaone.com/magazine/eq050198.html; "Emotional Intelligence May Be Good Predictor of Success in Computing Studies," *Science Daily*, October 5, 2005, www.sciencedaily.com/releases/2005/10/051005072152.htm

Figure 4.3, page 67: Email and proposal guides based on Fred Reynolds (1995), *What adult work-world writers have taught me about adult work-world writing, Professional writing in context: Lessons from teaching and consulting in worlds of work* (Hillsdale, NJ: Lawrence Erlbaum Associates), 18, 20.

Table 4.1, page 69: *Oxford Companion to the English Language* edited by Tom McArthur (1992). Adapted "Interpreting Flesch Readability Scores," p. 407

Figure 5.2, page 79: Adapted from Elk and Deer Inventory Certificates with permission of Alberta Agriculture & Rural Development.

Box 7.4, page 114: Reprinted with permission–Torstar Syndication Services.

Figure 9.2, page 147: Sinclair Stewart and Richard Bloom (7 July 2005), BlackBerry battle chills Bay St. gossips, *Globe and Mail*, www.blackberryforums.com/blackberry-news/2169-2005-01-07-blackberry-battle-chills-bay-st-gossips.html; Javad Heydary (26

May 2005), Is your boss monitoring your BlackBerry? *E-Commerce Times*, www.ecommercetimes.com/story/43376.html; Elizabeth A. McCord (1991), The business writer, the law, and routine business communication: A legal and rhetorical analysis, *Journal of Business and Technical Communication* 5(2), 173–199.

Figure 10.1, page 161: Imagine Creative Communications Inc. ©2008 The Art of Marketing.

Box 12.2, page 202: Chris MacDonald (2004, August 4), Why act ethically? And does the answer a company gives matter?, http://businessethicsblog.com/; Carmella M. Padilla (1987, July 17), It's a … a … a … all-terrain vehicle, yeah, that's it, that's the ticket, *The Wall Street Journal*, p. 17; Donna S. Kienzler (1997), Visual ethics, *Journal of Business Communication* 34, 175–76.

Figure 13.1, page 210: Courtesy of The Salvation Army, Ontario Central Division. Reprinted with permission.

Box 13.4, page 216: Fabrice Taylor (2010, November 17), How to make money teaching english for free, Report on Business, *Globe and Mail*, www.theglobeandmail.com/report-on-business/how-to-make-money-teaching-english-for-free/article4344887/. Lingo Media, October 2012, www.lingomedia.com

Figure 14.4, p.224: Appears with the permission of Labour/LeTravail and originally appeared in issue #Spring 2007, p. 59

Table 17.1, p.266: Adapted from Richard C. Freed, Shervin Freed, and Joseph D. Romano, *Writing winning proposals: your guide to landing the client, making the sale, persuading the boss* (New York:McGraw-Hill 1995) p. 21

Figure 17.3, p. 269: Courtesy BFR Inc.

Figure 18.5, p. 288: Courtesy Leanne Morette

Figure 19.2, p. 305: Labour Force Survey—Office for National Statistics, Eurostat. ©European Union, 1995-2012

Figure 19.3, p. 306: Graphs by GDSourcing.com

Figure 19.6, p. 308: University of Massachusetts, Dartmouth Centre for Marketing Research.

Module 19, Figure 1, p. 311: J.D. Power and Associates 2012 Canadian Retail Banking Customer Satisfaction Study™

Box 19.5, 19.6 pp. 314–315 (top): Reprinted by permission of Lindsay Hopton-Piché, Sheridan Graduate and Silver Medallist, Business Administration Finance.

Module 19, Figure 4, p. 315 (bottom): Reprinted with permission. Torstar Syndication Services.

Module 19, Figure 5, p. 316 (top): COMPAS Research www.compas.ca, Canadian Business, February 20, 2012. p.13

Module 19, Figure 7, p. 31 (top): From the *New York Times*, 7/23/2011 ©2011 *The New York Times*. All rights reserved. Used by permission and protected by the Copyright Laws of the United States. The printing, copying, redistribution, or retransmission of the Content without express written permission is prohibited.

Module 19, Figure 8, p. 317 (bottom): Reprinted with permission. Torstar Syndication Services.

Module 19, Figure 9, p. 318 (top left): Reprinted with permission. Torstar Syndication Services.

Module 19, Figure 10, p. 318 (top right): Reprinted with permission. Torstar Syndication Services.

Module 19, Figure 11, p. 318 (bottom): Reprinted with permission. Torstar Syndication Services.

Module 19, Figure 12, p. 319 (top): Reprinted with permission. Torstar Syndication Services.

Module 19, Table 2, p. 319 (bottom): Statistics Canada, Youth in Transition Survey, Cohort B.

Module 19, Table 3, p. 320: Statistics Canada, Youth in Transition Survey, Cohort B. Cycle 5.

Module 19, Table 20.1 p. 327: Based on Thomas Gordon and Julia Gordon Sands, P.E.T. In Action (New York-Wyden 1976) pp.117-118

Box 20.2, p. 330: "The Honor Roll," Toronto Star, October 18, 2008, pp. R8–11; Henry Mintzberg, "The Manager's Job: Folklore and Fact," Alex Gilles, "Batman," *National Post*, October 1999, pp. 60–69

Table 21.1, p. 334: Nancy Schullery and Beth Hoger (1998), Business advocacy for students in small groups, Association for Business Communication Annual Convention, San Antonio, November 9–11; An Antidote to Chronic Cantankerousness (1998, February/March), *Fast Company*, 176; John Grossmann (1998, April), We've got to start meeting like this, *Inc.*, 70; Gary Dessler (1998, September), Winning commitment, quoted in Team Management Briefings, preview issue, 5; 3M Meeting Network, Groundrules and agreements, http://www.3M.com.

Box 21.2, p. 338: Amy C. Edmondson, James R. Dillon, and Kathryn S. Roloff (2006), Three perspectives on team learning outcome improvement, task mastery, and group process, Harvard Business School website, www.hbs.edu/research/pdf/07-029.pdf. Jared Sandberg (2004, October 1), Teamwork: When it's a bad idea, *Globe and Mail*, C7; Harvey Schachter (2005, June 15), Where integrity leads, and where it lags, *Globe and Mail*, C3.

Figure 21.1, p. 344: Paul Benjamin Lowry, Aaron Curtis, and Michelle Rene Lowry, "Building a Taxonomy and Nomenclature of Collaborative Writing to Improve Interdisciplinary Research and Practice," *Journal of Business Communications* 41 (1) (January 2004).

Figure 22.3, p.356: Christopher Caggiano, "The Colour-Coded Priority Setter," *Inc.*, June 1, 1995, pp. 70–71. http://www.inc.com

Box 22.2, p. 356: Jason Falls, "Seven Questions to Ask Before Starting an Oline Community"; Dave Wilkins and Drew Darnbrough, "Developing an Online Community"; Michael Wilson, "Best Practices for Building Successful Online Communities," IABC CW Bulletin 7 (4) (April 2009).

Table 23.1, p. 364: Michael Goldman, "To Chair or to Facilitate, That is the Question," *the training report*, January/February 2001, p.13

Box 23.2, p. 369: George B. Ray, "Vocally Cued Personality Prototypes: An Implicit Personality Theory Approach," Communication Monographs 53 (3) (1986): 266–76; and Jacklyn Boice, "Verbal Impressions" *Selling Power*, March 2000, p.69

Box 24.1, p. 385: Wallace Immen, "Job Hunting 101," *The Globe and Mail*, February 18. 2009, p. C1; Ron McGowan, "Forget a Job: Grads Must Sell Selves to New World of Work," *The Globe and Mail*, May 4, 2004, p. C1; Wallace Immen, "Thinking on Your Feet Gets a Foot in the Door," *The Globe and Mail*, September 16, 2005, p. C3; Andy Holloway, "Recruit Right: A Guide to Finding the Best Fit," *Canadian Business*, October, 10–23, 2005, p. 123; and Arlen H. Hirsch, "'Tell Me About Yourself' Response Is Trickier Than You Might Think," *The Globe and Mail*, November 10, 2004, p. C9.

Box 26.1, p. 422: Canadian Packaging staff, "Cheers to Sleeman," *Canadian Packaging*, June 12, 2009, http://www.canadian-manufacturing.com; CBS Interactive Inc., "Sleeman Breweries Ltd.," BNET Industries, http://resources.bnet.com; Michael Van Aelst, Quoted in Oliver Bertin, "Sleeman Brew Balance of Risk and Caution," *The Globe and Mail*, June 20, 2001, p. M1.

Table 27.1, p. 433: Source: Based on research reported by Lois J. Einhorn, "An Inner View of the Job Interview: An Investigation of Successful Communicative Behaviors," *Communication Education* 30 (July 1981): 217–28; and Robert W. Elder and Michael M. Harris, eds., *The Employment Interview Handbook* (Thousand Oaks, CA: Sage, 1999), pp. 300, 303, 327–28.

PHOTOS AND CARTOONS:

Page 4 (top): Digital Vision

Page 4 (bottom): Royalty–Free/Corbis

Page 7: Courtesy Imran Ahmed/Business of Fashion

Page 8: ©Blue Images/Corbis

Page 10: Jessica Lander

Page 22: Courtesy of Lee Scott, WoW Company

Page 28: The Canadian Press (Darryl Dyck)

Page 28: The Canadian Press/Associated Press (Anja Niedringhaus)

Page 29: Jason Halstead, Sun Media

Page 32: ©Nick Beecham

Page 41: ©Dick Hemingway

Page 42: The Canadian Press (Image Source)

Page 46: ©Rhiana Sneyd

Page 47: Digital Vision

Page 48: Digital Vision/ Getty Images

Page 64: ©Matthias Tunger/Corbis

Page 71: Comstock/PictureQuest

Page 104: Helen King/Corbis

Page 113: DILBERT©1998 Scott Adams. Used by permission of Universal Uclick. All rights reserved.

Page 114: Richard Lautens/Torstar Syndications Services

Page 125: Tetra Images/Getty Images

Page 126: Courtesy DuckDuckGo.com

Page 147: Non Sequitor ©1997 Wiley. Distributed by Universal Press Syndicate. All Rights Reserved.

Page 166: DILBERT ©1998 Scott Adams. Used by permission of Universal Uclick. All rights reserved.

Page 168: Courtesy of Halton-Peel Communications Association.

Page 168: Courtesy of 1-800-got-junk? Reprinted with permission.

Page 180: Courtesy of Staples Canada

Page 195: Comstock/Punchstock

Page 199: Courtesy Hewlett-Packard

Page 209: ©Dick Hemingway

Page 216: Rene Johnston/Getstock.com

Page 227: Tribune Media Services, Inc. All rights reserved. Printed with permission.

Page 238: ©Goodshoot/Punchstock

Page 268: Simon Hayter/Getstock.com

Page 284: Sean Kilpatrick

Page 292: Supertrooper/Dreamstime.com

Page 293 (top right): Courtesy Universal Fibres

Page 293 (center): www.KlipTech.com

Page 293 (bottom): David Buffington/Getty Images

Page 294 (Fig. 5): Robyn Craig

Page 294 (Fig. 6): Habitat for Humanity Canada

Page 324: Terry Vine/Blend Images/Getty Images

Page 325: ©Ruslan Dashinsky/iStock

Page 326: Pixtal/AGE Fotostock

Page 330: Courtesy Kim Aitken

Page 335: Copyright of Eagle's Flight, Creative Training Excellence Inc. Used with permission.

Page 336: Getstock.com/david hancock/Alamy

Page 351: Digital Vision/Getty Images

Page 362: ©Scott Ramsey

Page 364: ©Klaus Tiedge/Corbis

Page 368: Junebug Clark/Photo Researchers

Page 380: Courtesy Laura Archer

Page 384: ©BrandXPictures/Punchstock

Page 405: ©liquidlibrary/PictureQuest

Page 429: ©Masterfile/Royalty–Free

Page 430: ©Danny Shanahan/Riley Illustrations

Page 439: ©The Canadian Press/OJO Images/Rex Features

Page 442: ©Kelly Redinger/Design Pics/Corbis

Polishing Your Prose: Answer Key

Here are possible solutions to the odd-numbered Polishing Your Prose exercises. Check with your instructor about any other solutions you propose.

Module 1: Sentence Fragments

1. Because people are constantly fiddling with their smartphones, even during meetings and training sessions, we need to establish some ground rules about electronic etiquette. People also surf the Web on their laptops, and leave meetings to look at email and listen to voicemail messages. I am not convinced that our preoccupation with technology is really saving us time and money, or contributing to productivity.

Module 2: Comma Splices

1. The conference call came at 1 p.m., and we took it immediately.
3. After Janelle drafted her problem-solving report, she sent a copy to each committee member for review.
5. Katy called the hotel in Montreal for a reservation; the desk staff booked a room for her immediately.
7. I'll have Tina call the main office, and you ask Polsun to set up an appointment for the four of us tomorrow.
9. I like to make oral presentations; they're fun.

Module 3: Making Subjects and Verbs Agree

1. Each of us is entitled to company healthcare benefits.
3. The price of our stocks is increasing.
5. We order a dozen new toner cartridges each month.
7. Marina Schiff and her assistant are attending the conference in Halifax.
9. Professor Beauparlant, Mr. Kincaid, and Ms. Carolla are on the guest list and plan to sit at the same table.

Module 4: Commas in Lists

1. Please send me the "fruit of the month" in April, May, June, and July. (Last comma is optional.)
3. The special parts division is opening offices in Brampton, Ontario; Fredericton, New Brunswick; and Big Salmon, Yukon.
5. I need to telephone Mary, Frank, and Paul, to finish my report, and mail copies of it to Ted, Sam, and Latanya. (While semicolons might be used after *Paul* and *report*, commas are acceptable because the groupings of listed items are understandable with commas.)
7. The weather affects our offices in Montreal, New York City, and Philadelphia.
9. Elizabeth, Tyrone, Mark, and Sara presented the team's recommendations.

Module 5: Active and Passive Voice

1. Unless the context of the sentence is negative, change to active voice: The vice-president of finance signed the contract.
3. The visitors' arrival is more important than who is expecting them. Therefore, use passive voice.
5. Changing this sentence to active voice would cast blame. Therefore, use passive voice.
7. The human resources administrator returned phone calls.
9. Return phone calls within 24 hours.

Module 6: Making Pronouns Agree with Their Nouns

1. An administrative assistant should help his/her boss work efficiently. *Or:* Administrative assistants should help their bosses work efficiently.
3. The company announces its quarterly profits today.
5. A CEO's pay is often based on the performance of his/her company. *Or:* CEOs' pay is often based on the performance of their companies.
7. In my first month of work, I learned to check my email at least three times a day.
9. The team will present its recommendations to the Executive Committee. (Correct.)

Module 7: Correcting Dangling Modifiers

1. After working here a year, you are covered by dental insurance.
3. I bought my daughter her first share of stock when she was 10.
5. By calling ahead of time, you can make reservations efficiently.
7. Posting risqué material on Facebook shows poor judgment, because potential employers can access this material even years later.
9. If you share files with our legal department, our attorneys can work better with you

Module 8: Applying Parallel Structure

1. Last week, Alain and Rochelle flew to Toronto, Montreal, Quebec City, and Lansing.
3. To ship a package:
   1. Fill out an address form.
   2. Specify on the form how the package should be sent.
   3. Have your supervisor initial the appropriate box on the address form if you want the package shipped by overnight mail.
5. Appointments can be scheduled in 5-minute, 10-minute, 15-minute, or 20-minute intervals.
7. This report discusses Why We Should Upgrade Capital Equipment, Why We Should Increase Staff by 25 Percent, Why We Should Decrease Employee Turnover, and Why We Should Identify New Product Markets.
9. Use the telephone to answer customer questions, email to send order confirmations, and our Web page to take orders.

Module 9: Finding Your Narrative Voice

1. This voice sounds authoritative, perhaps even threatening due to the constant use of *will* commands and all caps in *no exception*.
3. Appropriate.
5. Wordiness and obsolete language ("It has been brought to our attention") make this voice seem contrived.
7. Obsolete and redundant language make this voice unintelligible.
9. Writer's emphasis on his/her time, choice of language and use of caps create rude, aggressive voice.
11. Numerous negatives reflect a domineering, negative voice.

Module 10: Correcting Run-On Sentences

1. The marketing department ordered new, four-colour brochures. They are really nice.
3. Let's schedule a meeting next week. We'll talk about your promotion so you can transition easily into the new job.
5. Employees may request benefits changes during the annual enrolment period. Supervisors should pass out the required forms, and employees should have them completed by the deadline on the form.
7. Mohammed should make sure he specifies 20-lb. rather than 15-lb. paper stock, Jenna should call the print shop and ask whether the employees need anything, and Bruce should tell Ms. Winans we appreciate her letting us know we originally ordered the wrong stock.
9. A few customers are concerned about the shipping date, but the mailroom is sure we can ship overnight. I think there's no reason to be concerned.

Module 11: Plurals and Possessives

1. Canadian companies are competing effectively in the global market.
3. Managers' ability to listen is more important than their technical knowledge.
5. The community social workers tell clients about services available in their neighbourhoods.
7. Information about the new community makes the family's move easier.
9. Memos are internal documents, sent to other workers in the same organization. Letters are for external readers.

Module 12: Using the Apostrophe to Show Possession

1. Research indicates most Canadians feel responsible for the world's global warming.
3. Canadians' views of the economy reflect their confidence in the stock market.
5. We meet the local, provincial, and federal governments' standards for quality control.
7. The committee's duties will be completed after it announces its decision.
9. We'll decide whether to have more computer training sessions on the basis of employees' feedback.

Module 13: Using the Apostrophe for Contractions and *It's/Its*

1. It's too bad that the team hasn't finished its presentation.
3. It's going to require overtime because the data centre needs its reports quickly.

5. The company will announce its new name at a press conference.
7. It's a good idea to keep your travel receipts in a separate file.
9. The Saskatoon office will share its findings with the other branch offices.

Module 14: Combining Sentences

1. To get promoted quickly at our company, be organized, be on time, and meet deadlines.
3. Changing the toner cartridge on the photocopier is simple. To begin, open the front panel. Find the green tabs and depress them with your thumbs. Next, pull the black toner cartridge out and put it in the recycling box. Slide a new toner cartridge into the compartment until the green tabs snap back into place. Finally, close the panel.
5. The tornado plan for our building has five parts: first, listen for the tornado alert siren; second, go to your designated shelter area in the basement of the building; third, be sure to take the stairs and not the elevator; fourth, sit down on the floor; fifth, cover your head with your arms.

Module 15: Using APA and MLA Style

APA format:

1. Trivers, R. (2011). *The folly of fools*. New York, NY: Basic Books.
2. Flavelle, D. (2012, August 24). Canadian debt loads getting heavier. *Toronto Star*, p. B1.
3. Do not list in references.

MLA format:

1. Robert Trivers, *The Folly of Fools*. New York: Basic Books, 2011.
3. Dana Flavelle, "Canadian Debt Loads Getting Heavier." *Toronto Star* 24 Aug. 2012: B1–B2.
5. John Loomis, Telephone interview. 20 June 2012.

Module 16: *Who/Whom* and *I/Me*

1. Karen and I visited Shawnee Community College last week.
3. Dr. Jacobsen, who serves on the Board of Directors, is retiring.
5. Who is the most experienced person on your staff?
7. Between you and me, my supervisor told me the committee will decide who gets the promotion.
9. Three people at the firm who can speak a second language are Van, Chang, and I.

Module 17: Writing Subject Lines and Headings

1. An Introduction from the New Customer Service Department Supervisor. (Better with actual name.)
3. Your donation of blood on Tuesday can save a life.
5. Insurance Rates Will Increase July 31.
7. Research; Logistics; Profit
9. Clemente Research Group's Five-Year Goals; Clemente Research Group's Ten-Year Goals; Clemente Research Group's Fifteen-Year Goals

Module 18: Improving Paragraphs

1. My experience in the secretarial field makes me an ideal candidate for a position as senior administrative assistant with Graham, Chang, and Associates. As a receptionist at McCandless Realty, I typed, answered phones, and handled payroll. Then, as a secretary at Dufresne Plastics, I took training courses in data entry and Microsoft Word, and learned to type 70 WPM with no mistakes.

Module 19: Being Concise

1. Please return the order form ASAP.
3. The blue car is the legal affairs director's.
5. Call to confirm your order.
7. The enclosed references can discuss my job qualifications further.
9. Let me start by sharing stories about our guest of honour.

Module 20: Using Colons and Semicolons

1. That file on the Richman proposal: can you send me a copy by tomorrow, please?
3. Watch out: some people think there's a certain "ick" factor to social networking.
5. Strange: I thought I already signed up for another six months.
7. Remember: when we turn on the break room lights, everyone is to yell, "Happy Birthday, Susharita."
9. The best gig he ever had was his ten-month posting in Amsterdam. The night life is spectacular; everything's open: museums, pubs, shops. He was sad to come home.

Module 21: Delivering Criticism

1. We need to make this report meet our company's standards.
3. This assignment must have library resources.
5. The information in this brochure is terrific. Let's work on making the design match the content.
7. Our instructor said that we have to use at least five sources.
9. Would you help me to better understand this proposal?

Module 22: Using Hyphens and Dashes

1. Our biggest competitors—including those in the Asian and European markets—introduced more product models during the fourth quarter.
3. Please pick up three 2-by-4 posts at the lumberyard.
5. Painters from the building services department plan to give Tarik's office two coats of paint.
7. The latest weather reports suggest that travel over South and Latin America may be interrupted by storms.
9. You can email the results to my office in the early morning.

Module 23: Choosing Levels of Formality

1. On Monday, I inspected our inventory.
3. Though the representative was firm, we eventually negotiated a settlement.
5. The manager postponed making a decision.
7. In my last job, I worked as a gofer for the marketing manager.
9. This report has problems.

Module 24: Using Details

1. I am the Webmaster for the Jessica London Company.
3. In June, I plan to graduate from Seneca Community College and start my career in respiratory therapy at St. Ann's Hospital.
5. Fortified with antioxidants and Vitamins D and K, EnVigorate Power Drink will make you feel healthy and energetic all day long.
7. The new Mark VII pool filter is 33 percent more energy-efficient than competitors' filters and features a 10-year warranty, the best on the market.
9. More than 17 years of experience and $7.9 million in real estate sales make me the ideal candidate for district sales manager.

Module 25: Proofreading

1. Ours is a company worth doing business with. You can count on our promise to provide not only the best service but also the finest in materials, fit, and finish. All of our products are made to exacting specifications, meaning that you receive the best product for the best prices. If you aren't satisfied for any reason, simply call the toll-free hotline at 1-800-555-1212 to get a prompt refund. Or you can write us at The John Doe Company, 123 Main Street, Anytown, Canada M6V 2B4. Remember, our motto is "The customer is always right."

Module 26: Using *You* and *I*

1. Our team created a class Web page. I was responsible for much of the initial design and some of the HTML coding. Four of us tested the page to see how easily we could navigate it. We presented the page to a committee of local businesspeople.
3. Team members should resolve any conflicts they have created with other team members.
5. Please distribute an agenda before the meeting.
7. Make the Web page accessible to users with impaired vision.
9. During my co-op placement, I observed department meetings, sat in on client meetings, designed PowerPoint slides for client presentations, participated in strategy sessions, and drafted brochures.

Module 27: Matters on Which Experts Disagree

1. Everyone should bring his or her laptop to the sales meeting.
3. To take advantage of the meeting fully, you need to bring all of your new product information.
5. Think of a time when it was hard even to get in the door to see a potential customer.
7. Awards include best rookie sales representative, the most improved region, everyone who beat his or her sales quota, and sales representative of the year.
9. Our Web page will let people listen to each customer summarizing orally what he or she likes best about our products.

Notes

Module 1

1. "Technical Training Ain't All It's Cracked Up to Be," *The Training Report*, January/February, 2000, p. 8.
2. Daniel H. Pink, "Revenge of the Right Brain," *Wired* 13(2) (February 2005), retrieved April 5, 2008, from http://www.wired.com/wired/archive/13.02/brain.html.
3. Heather Sokoloff, "Engineers Forced to Learn How to Write," *National Post*, May 28, 2003, p. A6.
4. "International Adult Literacy and Skills Survey: Building on Our Competencies," *The Daily*, November 30, 2005, retrieved April 10, 2009, from http://www.statcan.gc.ca/daily-quotidien/051130/dq051130b-eng.htm.
5. Terrence Belford, "Engineers Need 'Soft' Skills," *The Globe and Mail*, January 13, 2003, p. B10.
6. H. Wilkie, "Communicate Well and Prosper," *The Globe and Mail*, February 27, 2004.
7. Elizabeth Allen, "Excellence in Public Relations & Communication Management," IABC/Dayton Awards Banquet, Dayton, OH, July 12, 1990.
8. Watson Wyatt Worldwide, "Effective Communication: A Leading Indicator of Financial Performance," 2005/2006 Communication ROI Study™, retrieved April 10, 2009, from http://www.watsonwyatt.com/research/resrender.asp?id=w-868&page=1.

Module 2

1. "2006 Census: Labour Market Activities, Industry, Occupation, Education, Language of Work, Place of Work and Mode of Transportation," *The Daily*, March 4, 2008, http://www.statcan.ca/Daily/English/080304/d080304a.htm; "Canada's Changing Labour Force, 2006 Census: The Provinces and Territories—The Aging Workforce—Baby Boomers Edging Closer to Retirement," http://www12.statcan.ca/english/census06/analysis/labour/ov-cclf-23.cfm; and "Canada's Changing Labour Force, 2006 Census: The Provinces and Territories—Immigrants in the Workforce—Majority of Recent Immigrants Went to Ontario's Labour Market," http://www12.statcan.ca/english/census06/analysis/labour/ov-cclf-28.cfm.
2. Peter Urs Bender, "Identifying Your Personality Type," retrieved November 16, 2009, from http://www.peterursbender.com/quiz/index.html, retrieved July 26, 2006.
3. Isabel Briggs Myers, *Introduction to Type* (Palo Alto, CA: Consulting Psychologists Press, 1980).
4. Isabel Briggs Myers and Mary H. McCaulley, *Manual: A Guide to the Development and Use of the Myers-Briggs Type Indicator* (Palo Alta, CA: Consulting Psychologists Press, 1985), pp. 251, 248, respectively.
5. Keith McArthur, *The Globe and Mail*, June 6, 2005, retrieved July 26, 2006, from http://www.theglobeandmail.com/servlet/story/RTGAM.20050606.wxrbrand06/BNStory/Business.

6. Aldo Santin, "Canadian Tire's Catalogue Is History," *The Gazette*, March 26, 2008, retrieved April 13, 2009, from http://www2.canada.com/montrealgazette/news/business/story.html?id=c7febd59-933e-4ef7-ba59-8a2972ed88c5.
7. Erin Anderssen, "They Know When You Are Sleeping, They Know When You're Awake and Whether You Like Sushi," Globe Focus, *The Globe and Mail*, December 18, 2004, pp. F1 and F8, retrieved July 26, 2006, from http://www.theglobeandmail.com/servlet/story/RTGAM.20041220.gtcover20/BNStory/einsider/?pageRequested=all; http://www.tetrad.com/pricing/can/prizmce.html, retrieved July 26, 2006.
8. Ibid.
9. Craig Silverman, "The Traditional Job Interview: That's So Yesterday," *The Globe and Mail*, April 7, 2008, retrieved November 11, 2009, from http://www.theglobeandmail.com/servlet/story/RTGAM.20080407.wlintvu07/BNStory/lifeWork/home.
10. TD–Canada Trust Web site, http://www.tdcanadatrust.com, and Royal Bank Web site, http://www.royalbank.com, both retrieved August 25, 2006.
11. Matt Siegel, "The Perils of Culture Conflict," *Fortune*, November 9, 1998, p. 258.
12. "Top 10 Reasons to Work at Google," Google Jobs, 2009, retrieved April 13, 2009, from http://www.google.com/intl/en/jobs/lifeatgoogle/toptenreasons.html and http://www.google.com/intl/en/jobs/lifeatgoogle/toptenreasons.html.
13. Linda Driskill, "Negotiating Differences Among Readers and Writers," Conference on College Composition and Communication, San Diego, CA, March 31–April 3, 1993.

Module 3

1. "More Than 200 Different Ethnic Origins Reported," *The Daily*, April 28, 2008, retrieved April 15, 2009, from http://www.statcan.gc.ca/daily-quotidien/080402/dq080402a-eng.htm.
2. Statistics Canada, "Canada's Ethnocultural Mosaic, 2006 Census: National Picture," p. 1, retrieved April 15, 2009, from http://www12.statcan.ca/english/census06/analysis/ethnicorigin/more.cfm; Canadian Heritage site, retrieved April 15, 2009, from http://www.pch.gc.ca/progs/multi/respect_e.cfm.
3. "Canadian Cities & Provinces of the Future 2005/06," *FDI Magazine*, June 7, 2005, retrieved November 11, 2009, from http://www.fdimagazine.com/news/fullstory.php/aid/1250/CANADIAN_CITIES_PROVINCES_OF_THE_FUTURE_2005_06.html.
4. Statistics Canada, "Some Facts About the Demographic and Ethnocultural Composition of the Population," retrieved April 28, 2008, from http://www.statcan.gc.ca/pub/91-003-x/2007001/4129904-eng.htm#2.

5. Erin Anderssen, "People Deficit Gives Workers Upper Hand," *The Globe and Mail*, January 22, 2003, p. A6.

6. Ibid.

7. Statistics Canada, "Some Facts About the Demographic and Ethnocultural Composition of the Population," pp. 2–3, retrieved April 28, 2008, from http://www.statcan.ca/english/freepub/91-003-XIE/2007001/few-en.htm.

8. Ibid.

9. "CARP Announces 'It's the Zoomers, Stupid' Press Conference," CNW Group site, retrieved April 17, 2009, from http://www.newswire.ca/en/releases/archive/September2008/15/c4428.html.

10. Richard Sweeney, "Millennial Behaviors & Demographics," December 22, 2006, retrieved April 17, 2009, from http://74.125.95.132/search?q=cache:ZBXEFHEBypYJ:library1.njit.edu/staff-folders/sweeney/Millennials/Article-Millennial-Behaviors.doc+millennials+%2B+behaviours&cd=1&hl= en&ct=clnk&client=firefox-a.

11. Rob McMahon, "Millennials in the Workplace," *straight.com*, January 31, 2008 (Vancouver Free Press, 2009), retrieved April 18, 2009, from http://www.straight.com/article-130265/millennials-in-the-workplace.

12. "Multiculturalism," *Vive le Canada*, November 26, 2005, retrieved July 26, 2006, from Canadian Heritage site, http://www.pch.gc.ca/progs/multi/respect_e.cfm.

13. David A. Victor, *International Business Communication* (New York: HarperCollins, 1992), pp. 148–60.

14. John Webb and Michael Keene, "The Impact of Discourse Communities on International Professional Communication," in Carl R. Lovitt with Dixie Coswami, Eds., *Exploring the Rhetoric of International Professional Communication: An Agenda for Teachers and Researchers* (Amityville, NY: Baywood, 1999), pp. 81–109.

15. "Student Won't Be Expelled over Facebook Study Group," CBC.ca, March 18, 2008, retrieved May 1, 2008, from http://www.cbc.ca/canada/toronto/story/2008/03/18/facebook-avenir.html.

16. Christina Haas and Jeffrey L. Funk, "'Shared Information:' Some Observations of Communication in Japanese Technical Settings," *Technical Communication* 36(4) (November 1989): 365.

17. Laray M. Barna, "Stumbling Blocks in Intercultural Communication," in Larry A. Samovar and Richard E. Porter, Eds., *Intercultural Communication* (Belmont, CA: Wadsworth, 1985), p. 331.

18. Marjorie Fink Vargas, *Louder Than Words* (Ames: Iowa State University Press, 1986), p. 47.

19. Michael Argyle, *Bodily Communication* (New York: International University Press, 1975), p. 89.

20. Jerrold J. Merchant, "Korean Interpersonal Patterns: Implications for Korean/American Intercultural Communication," *Communication* 9 (October 1980): 65.

21. Ray L. Birdwhistell, *Kinesics and Context: Essays on Body Motion Communication* (Philadelphia: University of Philadelphia Press, 1970), p. 81.

22. Paul Ekman, Wallace V. Friesen, and John Bear, "The International Language of Gestures," *Psychology Today* 18(5) (May 1984): 64.

23. Brenda Major, "Gender Patterns in Touching Behavior," in Clara Mayo and Nancy M. Henley, Eds., *Gender and Nonverbal Behavior* (New York: Springer-Verlag, 1981), pp. 26, 28.

24. "Minor Memos," *The Wall Street Journal*, February 12, 1988, p. 1.

25. "Doing Business in India: 20 Cultural Norms You Need to Know," *Business Intelligence Lowdown*, March 6, 2007, p. 1, retrieved May 1, 2008, from http://www.businessintelligencelowdown.com/2007/03/doing_business_.html.

26. Natalie Porter and Florence Gies, "Women and Nonverbal Leadership Cues: When Seeing Is Not Believing," in *Gender and Nonverbal Behavior*, Clara Mayo and Nancy M. Henley, Eds., (New York: Springer-Verlag, 1981), pp. 48–49.

27. Lawrence B. Nadler, Marjorie Keeshan Nadler, and Benjamin J. Broome, "Culture and the Management of Conflict Situations," in William B. Gudykunst, Lea P. Stewart, and Stella Ting-Toomey, Eds., *Communication, Culture, and Organizational Processes* (Beverly Hills, CA: Sage, 1985), p. 103.

28. Argyle, *Bodily Communication*, p. 90.

29. Mary Ritchie Key, *Paralanguage and Kinesics* (Metuchen, NJ: Scarecrow, 1975), p. 23.

30. Fred Hitzhusen, conversation with Kitty Locker, January 31, 1998.

31. Lisa Davis, "The Height Report: A Look at Stature and Status," New York Times Special Features, *Columbus Dispatch*, January 19, 1988, p. E1.

32. Deborah Tannen, *That's Not What I Meant!* (New York: William Morrow, 1986).

33. Karen Ritchie, "Marketing to Generation X," *American Demographics*, April 1995, pp. 34–36.

34. Marina Jimenez, "The Linguistic Divide," *The Globe and Mail*, April 17, 2009, p. L1.

35. Daniel N. Maltz and Ruth A. Borker, "A Cultural Approach to Male–Female Miscommunication," in John J. Gumperz, Ed., *Language and Social Identity* (Cambridge: Cambridge University Press, 1982), p. 202.

36. Vincent O'Neill, "Training the Multi-Cultural Manager," Sixth Annual EMU Conference on Languages and Communication for World Business and the Professions, Ann Arbor, MI, May 7–9, 1987.

37. Akihisa Kumayama, comment during discussion, Sixth Annual EMU Conference on Languages and Communication for World Business and the Professions, Ann Arbor, MI, May 7–9, 1987.

38. Brenda Arbeláez, statement to Kitty Locker, December 12, 1996.

39. "Participation and Activity Limitation Survey," *The Daily*, December 3, 2007, retrieved May 9, 2008, from http://www.statcan.ca/Daily/English/071203/d071203a.htm.

Module 4

1. Leslie Butler, personal communication, November 26, 2005.

2. See especially Linda Flower and John R. Hayes, "The Cognition of Discovery: Defining a Rhetorical Problem," *College Composition and Communication* 31 (February 1980): 21–32; and the essays in two collections: Charles R. Cooper and Lee Odell, *Research on Composing: Points of Departure* (Urbana, IL: National Council of Teachers of

English, 1978), and Mike Rose, Ed., *When a Writer Can't Write: Studies in Writer's Block and Other Composing-Process Problems* (New York: Guilford Press, 1985).

3. Rebecca E. Burnett, "Content and Commas: How Attitudes Shape a Communication-Across-the-Curriculum Program," Association for Business Communication Convention, Orlando, FL, November 1–4, 1995.

4. Peter Elbow, *Writing with Power: Techniques for Mastering the Writing Process* (New York: Oxford University Press, 1981), pp. 15–20.

5. See Gabriela Lusser Rico, *Writing the Natural Way* (Los Angeles: J. P. Tarcher, 1983), p. 10.

6. Rachel Spilka, "Orality and Literacy in the Workplace: Process- and Text-Based Strategies for Multiple Audience Adaptation," *Journal of Business and Technical Communication* 4(1) (January 1990): 44–67.

7. Fred Reynolds, "What Adult Work-World Writers Have Taught Me About Adult Work-World Writing," *Professional Writing in Context: Lessons from Teaching and Consulting in Worlds of Work* (Hillsdale, NJ: Lawrence Erlbaum Associates, 1995), pp. 18–21.

8. Raymond W. Beswick, "Communicating in the Automated Office," American Business Communication Association International Convention, New Orleans, LA, October 20, 1982.

9. This three-step process is modelled on the one suggested by Barbara L. Shwom and Penny L. Hirsch, "Managing the Drafting Process: Creating a New Model for the Workplace," *Bulletin of the Association for Business Communication* 57(2) (June 1994): 10.

10. Glenn J. Broadhead and Richard C. Freed, "The Variables of Composition: Process and Product in a Business Setting," Conference on College Composition and Communication Studies in Writing and Rhetoric (Carbondale, IL: Southern Illinois University Press, 1986), p. 57.

11. Robert Boice, "Writing Blocks and Tacit Knowledge," *Journal of Higher Education* 64(1) (January/February 1993): 41–43.

Module 5

1. Once we know how to read English, the brain first looks to see whether an array of letters follows the rules of spelling. If it does, the brain then treats the array as a word (even if it isn't one, such as *tweal*). The shape is processed in individual letters only when the shape is not enough to suggest meaning. Jerry E. Bishop, "Word Processing: Research on Stroke Victims Yields Clues to the Brain's Capacity to Create Language," *The Wall Street Journal*, October 12, 1993, p. A6.

Module 7

1. Sinclair Stewart and Richard Bloom, "BlackBerry Battle Chills Bay St. Gossips," July 7, 2005, retrieved August 8, 2006, from http://www.theglobeandmail.com/servlet/ArticleNews/TPStory/LAC/20050107/BLACKBERRY07/TPNational/TopStories; Javad Heydary, "Is Your Boss Monitoring Your BlackBerry?," *E-Commerce Times*, May 26, 2005, retrieved August 8, 2006, from http://www.ecommercetimes.com/story/43376.

html; Jaikumar Vijayan Boston, "Lawsuit Reveals an Open BlackBerry," *Computerworld*, January 18, 2005, retrieved May 6, 2009, from http://computerworld.co.nz/news.nsf/0/A0DF45190F24C05BCC256F8C00018087?OpenDocument&pub=Computerworld.

2. H. Lotherington, and Yejun Xu, "How to Chat in English and Chinese: Emerging Digital Language Conventions," *ReCALL* 16(2): 308–329, retrieved August 8, 2006, from http://www.yorku.ca/foe/People/Faculty/ProfilesFac/file_Lothering_Xu_2004.pdf; Heather Lotherington, "NetSpeak Changes Offline Communication," G4TechTV.ca, retrieved November 16, 2009, from http://techtvcanada.ca/callforhelp/ guests/0148A.shtml.

3. Bettina A. Blair, "Teaching Technology," email to Kitty Locker, October 22, 1999.

Module 8

1. Richard C. Whitely, *The Customer-Driven Company* (Reading, MA: Addison-Wesley, 1991), pp. 39–40.

2. In a study of 483 subject lines written by managers and M.B.A. students, Priscilla S. Rogers found that the average subject line was five words; only 10 percent of the subject lines used 10 or more words; see Rogers, "A Taxonomy for Memorandum Subject Lines," *Journal of Business and Technical Communication* 4(2) (September 1990): 28–29.

3. An earlier version of this problem, the sample solutions, and the discussion appeared in Francis W. Weeks and Kitty O. Locker, *Business Writing Cases and Problems*, 1984 ed. (Champaign, IL: Stipes, 1984), pp. 64–68.

Module 9

1. John D. Pettit, "An Analysis of the Effects of Various Message Presentations on Communicatee Responses," Ph.D. dissertation, Louisiana State University, 1969; and Jack D. Eure, "Applicability of American Written Business Communication Principles Across Cultural Boundaries in Mexico," *Journal of Business Communication* 14 (1976): 51–63.

2. Lillian H. Chaney and Jeanette S. Martin, *Intercultural Business Communication* (Englewood Cliffs, NJ: Prentice Hall Career and Technology, 1995), p. 185; and Larry A. Samovar and Richard E. Porter, *Communication Between Cultures* (Belmont, CA: Wadsworth Publishing, 1990), pp. 234–44.

3. Jack W. Brehm, *A Theory of Psychological Reactance* (New York: Academic Press, 1966).

4. An earlier version of this problem, the sample solutions, and the discussion appeared in Francis W. Weeks and Kitty O. Locker, *Business Writing Cases and Problems* (Champaign, IL: Stipes, 1980), pp. 40–44.

Module 10

1. J. C. Mathes and Dwight W. Stevenson, *Designing Technical Reports: Writing for Audiences in Organizations* (Indianapolis: Bobbs-Merrill, 1979), pp. 18–19.

2. Karen Lowry Miller and David Woodruff, "The Man Who's Selling Japan on Jeeps," *Business Week*, July 19, 1993, pp. 56–57.

3. Priscilla S. Rogers, "A Taxonomy for the Composition of Memorandum Subject Lines: Facilitating Writer Choice in Managerial Contexts ," Journal of Business and Technical Communication 4, no.2 (September 1990): 21–43.

4. An earlier draft of this problem and analysis appeared in Francis W. Weeks and Kitty O. Locker, Business Writing Problems and Cases (Champaign, IL: Stipes, 1980), pp. 78–81.

Module 11

1. Wray Herbert, "A Recipe for Motivation: Easy to Read, Easy to Do," Scientific American, February 2009, retrieved May 2, 2009, from http://www.scientificamerican.com/ article.cfm? id=a-recipe-for-motivation.

2. See Tove Helland Hammer and H. Peter Dachler, "A Test of Some Assumptions Underlying the Path–Goal Model of Supervision: Some Suggested Conceptual Modifications," Organizational Behavior and Human Performance 14 (1975): 73.

3. Edward E. Lawler, III, Motivation in Work Organizations (Monterey, CA: Brooks/Cole, 1973), p. 59. Lawler also notes a third obstacle: people may settle for performance and rewards that are just OK. Offering reader benefits, however, does nothing to affect this obstacle.

4. Abraham H. Maslow, Motivation and Personality (New York: Harper & Row, 1954).

5. Stephen J. Stine, "Managing the Millennials: Part 1," HRHero.com, April 4, 2008, retrieved May 2, 2009, from http://www.hrhero.com/hl/040408-lead-millennials.html; Claire Raines, "Managing Millennials," 2002, retrieved January 1, 2010, from http://generationsatwork.com/ articles_millenials.php.

6. John J. Weger reports Herzberg's research in Motivating Supervisors (New York: American Management Association, 1971), pp. 53–54.

7. Diane L. Coutu, "Human Resources: The Wages of Stress," Harvard Business Review, November–December 1998, pp. 21–24; and Charles Fishman, "Sanity, Inc.," Fast Company, January 1999, pp. 85–99.

8. Susan Greco, "Hire the Best," Inc., June 1999, pp. 32–52.

Module 12

1. Steven Bradley (2010, June 7), The Framing Effect: Influence Your Audience by Setting the Context, Vanseo Design, http://www.vanseodesign.com/web-design/framing-expectation-exposure-effect.

2. Angus MacKenzie and Scott Evans (2010, January), the Toyota Recall Crisis: A Chronology of How the World's Largest and Most Profitable Automaker Drove into a PR Disaster, Motor Trend, http://www.motortrend.com/ features/auto_news/2010/112_1001_toyota_recall_crisis/ viewall.html.

3. Charles E. McCabe, edited and updated by Ryan P. Allis, "Motivating and Retaining Employees," 2004, retrieved August 8, 2006, from http://www.zeromillion.com/business/ employeemotivate.html.

4. Jill Lambert, "The Economics of Happiness," Canadian Business, Summer 2005, pp. 184–187.

5. Mayo Clinic, "Mayo Clinic Study Finds Optimistic People Live Longer," February 8, 2000, retrieved August 8, 2006, from http://www.mayoclinic.org/news2000-rst/603.html.

6. The Business Link, "The Makeup of a Successful Entrepreneur," 2005, retrieved August 8, 2006, from http:// www.cbsc.org/alberta/newsletter/February2005_1.html.

7. Annette N. Shelby and N. Lamar Reinsch, Jr., "Positive Emphasis and You-Attitude: An Empirical Study," Journal of Business Communication 32(4) (October 1995): 303–327.

8. Mark A. Sherman, "Adjectival Negation and the Comprehension of Multiply Negated Sentences," Journal of Verbal Learning and Verbal Behavior 15 (1976): 143–57.

9. Margaret Baker Graham and Carol David, "Power and Politeness: Administrative Writing in an 'Organized Anarchy,'" Journal of Business and Technical Communication 10(1) (January 1996): 5–27.

10. John Hagge and Charles Kostelnick, "Linguistic Politeness in Professional Prose: A Discourse Analysis of Auditors' Suggestion Letters, with Implications for Business Communication Pedagogy," Written Communication 6(3) (July 1989): 312–39.

Module 13

1. Lima Paul, "An On-line Concierge Service's Ticket to Success," Technology, Small & Medium Business, The Globe and Mail, July 14, 2005, p. B8, and Eservus Online Concierge Services, retrieved June 13, 2008, from http:// toronto.eservus.com.

2. Artwork produced in the Enrichment Program at the Salvation Army's Broadview Village, an adult residential program. Residents attend school, a day program, or work placement training in the Toronto area.

Module 14

1. "Welcome to Knowledge Ontario," Knowledge Ontario site, 2008, retrieved January 28, 2008, from http://www. knowledgeontario.ca.

2. "RSS Feeds—A Tutorial," PRESSfeed, 2009, retrieved July 9, 2009, from http://www.press-feed.com/howitworks/ rss_tutorial.php#whatarewebfeeds.

Module 15

Notes are given in the module, in the illustrations of APA and MLA bibliographies referring to in-text citations.

Module 16

1. Telephone interview with Lee-Anne E. Bell, B.Sc., Associate ENVIRON EC (Canada) Inc., June 30, 2009, and Franco Agar, B.A. Honours, KPMG Support, Global Applications, July 6, 2009.

2. Agar, ibid.

3. Christine Peterson Barabas, Technical Writing in a Corporate Culture: A Study of the Nature of Information (Norwood, NJ: Ablex Publishing, 1990), p. 327.

Module 17

1. Peter Pook, Vice-President, Research and Development, Fisher-Price Toys, personal communication with author, July 15, 2009.

2. Meryl K. Evans, "Writing an RFP (Request for Proposal)," *Ezine @rticles*, retrieved June 27, 2009, from http://ezinearticles.com/?Writing-an-RFP-(Request-for-Proposal)&id=1795; and "Writing a Request for a Proposal (RFP)," *meryl.net*, 2009, retrieved July 30, 2009, from http://www.meryl.net/tag/rfp.

3. Janice Redish, *Letting Go of the Words: Writing Web Content That Works* (San Francisco: Morgan Kaufmann Publishers, 2007); Jakob Nielsen, "Writing Style for Print vs. Web," *Jakob Nielsen's Alertbox*, June 9, 2008, retrieved June 28, 2009, from http://www.useit.com/alertbox/print-vs-online-content.html; and Mindy McAdams, "Tips for Writing for the Web," November 19, 2006, retrieved June 28, 2009, from http://www.macloo.com/webwriting/index.htm.

Module 18

1. Natalie Canavor and Claire Meirowitz, "Summaries: A Good Way to Make Life Easier for Your Readers," *CW Bulletin*, pp. 1–4, retrieved January 17, 2009, from http://www.iabc.com/cwb/archive/2009/0109/WorkingWords.htm.

Module 19

1. Brian O'Mara-Croft, "Every Picture Tells a Story," *Communication World*, September–October 2008. IABC. pp. 23–24.

2. Gene Zelazny, *Say It with Charts: The Executive's Guide to Successful Presentations*, 2nd ed. (Burr Ridge, IL: IPRO, 1981), p. 52.

3. Most of these guidelines are given in Zelazny, *Say It with Charts: The Executive's Guide to Successful Presentations*.

4. W. S. Cleveland and R. McGill, "Graphical Perception: Theory, Experiments, and Application to the Development of Graphic Methods," *Journal of the American Statistical Association* 79(3 & 7) (1984): 531–53, cited in Jeffry K. Cochran, Sheri A. Albrecht, and Yvonne A. Greene, "Guidelines for Evaluating Graphical Designs: A Framework Based on Human Perception Skills," *Technical Communication* 36(1) (February 1989): 27.

5. Brian O'Mara-Croft, pp. 22–25.

6. L. G. Thorell and W. J. Smith, *Using Computer Color Effectively: An Illustrated Reference* (Englewood Cliffs, NJ: Prentice Hall, 1990), pp. 12–13; William Horton, "The Almost Universal Language: Graphics for International Documents," *Technical Communication* 40(4) (1993): 687; and Thyra Rauch, "IBM Visual Interface Design," *STC Usability PIC Newsletter*, January 1996, p. 3.

7. Thorell and Smith, p. 13.

8. Ibid., pp. 49–51, 214–15.

9. Edward Tufte, "PowerPoint Is Evil," *Wired*, Issue 11.09 | September 2003, retrieved August 23, 2009 from http://www.wired.com/wired/archive/11.09/ppt2.html.

Module 20

1. "Listening," retrieved October 18, 2008, from http://accel-team.com/communications/busComms_02.html. © 2008 Accel-Team.

2. Deep Listening: Listening from Within the Heart, retrieved from http://www.martinasteiger.com/Deep-Listening.

html, and Stephen R. Covey, The Seven Habits of Highly Effective People (New York: Free Press, 2004).

3. "Listen Up and Sell," *Selling Power*, July/August 1999, p. 34.

4. Rich Whittle, "Improve Your Listening Skills," Dane Carlson's Business Opportunities Weblog, July 2, 2008, retrieved October 26, 2008, from http://www.business-opportunities.biz/2008/07/02/improve-your-listening-skills.

5. Kara Aaserud, "The 7 New Truths About Your Customers and Why You Need to Know Them," *Profit*, March 2009, pp. 34–40, retrieved November 11, 2009, from http://www.canadianbusiness.com/entrepreneur/sales_marketing/article.jsp?content=20090201_30010_30010.

6. Ibid.

7. Ibid.

Module 21

1. D. M. Zinni, Barry Wright, and Mark Julien, "Research Forum: Want to Retain Employees? Try a Networking Group," *HRProfessional*, July/August 2005, retrieved August 14, 2006, from http://www.yorku.ca/hrresall/frm2005~08.htm; and Olivia Li, "Top 90 Employers," *The Toronto Star*, October 17, 2009, pp. U1–6.

2. Bonita Summers, "Workplace Without Borders: Why Companies Are Using Social Networking as a Team Building Tool," *Your Workplace* 11(2) (March/April 2009): 32, 34.

3. For a fuller listing of roles in groups, see David W. Johnson and Frank P. Johnson, *Joining Together: Group Theory and Group Skills* (Englewood Cliffs, NJ: Prentice Hall, 1975), pp. 26–27.

4. Beatrice Schultz, "Argumentativeness: Its Effects in Group Decision-Making and Its Role in Leadership Perception," *Communication Quarterly* 30(4) (Fall 1982): 374–75; Dennis S. Gouran and B. Aubrey Fisher, "The Functions of Human Communication in the Formation, Maintenance, and Performance of Small Groups," in Carroll C. Arnold and John Waite Bowers, Eds., *Handbook of Rhetorical and Communication Theory* (Boston: Allyn and Bacon, 1984), p. 640; and Curt Bechler and Scott D. Johnson, "Leadership and Listening: A Study of Member Perceptions," *Small Group Research* 26(1) (February 1995): 77–85.

5. Nance L. Harper and Lawrence R. Askling, "Group Communication and Quality of Task Solution in a Media Production Organization," *Communication Monographs* 47(2) (June 1980): 77–100.

6. Rebecca E. Burnett, "Conflict in Collaborative Decision-Making," in Nancy Roundy Blyler and Charlotte Thralls, Eds., *Professional Communication: The Social Perspective* (Newbury Park, CA: Sage, 1993), pp. 144–62.

7. Kimberly A. Freeman, "Attitudes Toward Work in Project Groups as Predictors of Academic Performance," *Small Group Research* 27(2) (May 1996): 265–82.

8. Nancy Schullery and Beth Hoger, "Business Advocacy for Students in Small Groups," Association for Business Communication Annual Convention, San Antonio, TX, November 9–11, 1998.

9. Jim Camp, *Start with No* (New York: Crown Business, 2002), pp. 151–154.

10. Paul Benjamin Lowry, Aaron Curtis, Michelle René Lowry, "Building a Taxonomy and Nomenclature of Collaborative Writing to Improve Interdisciplinary Research and Practice," *Journal of Business Communication* 41(2004): 66, 67, DOI: 10.1177/0021943603259363, retrieved June 19, 2009, from http://job.sagepub.com/cgi/reprint/41/1/66.pdf.

11. Rebecca Burnett, "Characterizing Conflict in Collaborative Relationships: The Nature of Decision-Making During Coauthoring," Ph.D. dissertation, Carnegie-Mellon University, Pittsburgh, PA, 1991.

12. Kitty O. Locker, "What Makes a Collaborative Writing Team Successful? A Case Study of Lawyers and Social Service Workers in a State Agency," in Janis Forman, Ed., *New Visions in Collaborative Writing* (Portsmouth, NJ: Boynton, 1991), pp. 37–52.

13. Lisa Ede and Andrea Lunsford, *Singular Texts/Plural Authors: Perspectives on Collaborative Writing* (Carbondale, IL: Southern Illinois Press, 1990), p. 66.

14. Paul Benjamin Lowry, Aaron Curtis, Michelle René Lowry, "Building a Taxonomy and Nomenclature of Collaborative Writing to Improve Interdisciplinary Research and Practice," *Journal of Business Communication* 41(2004): 66–97, DOI: 10.1177/0021943603259363, retrieved June 19, 2009, from http://job.sagepub.com/cgi/reprint/41/1/66.pdf.

15. Meg Morgan, Nancy Allen, Teresa Moore, Dianne Atkinson, and Craig Snow, "Collaborative Writing in the Classroom," *Bulletin of the Association for Business Communication* 50(3) (September 1987): 22.

16 Based on John Case (1998), The Open-Book Experience: Lessons from Over 100 Companies Who Successfully Transformed Themselves (Reading, MA: Addison-Wesley): 129–201.

Module 22

1. "Scientific Study Finds Meetings at Work Decrease Employee Well-Being, But Not for Everyone," *ScienceDaily*, February 2006, retrieved August 24, 2006, from http://www.sciencedaily.com/releases/2006/02/060224192947.htm.

2. Kevin Voight, "Don't Mind Your Own Business at Work," *The Globe and Mail*, January 26, 2005, p. C10.

3. Michael Schrage, "Meetings Don't Have to Be Dull," *The Wall Street Journal*, April 29, 1996, p. A12.

4. Eric Matson and William R. Daniels, "The Seven Deadly Sins of Meetings," *Fast Company Handbook of the Business Revolution*, 1997, p. 29.

5. Ibid., p. 30.

6. Rich Young, "Social Media: How New Forms of Communications Are Changing Job Search and Career Management," *IABC Communicator*, January/February 2009, p. 3.

7. H. Lloyd Goodall, Jr., *Small Group Communications in Organizations* (Dubuque, IA: William C. Brown, 1985), pp. 39–40.

8. Roger K. Mosvick and Robert B. Nelson, *We've Got to Start Meeting Like This: A Guide to Successful Meeting Management*, rev. ed. (Indianapolis: Park Avenue, 1996), p. 177.

9. Gina Imperator, "You Have to Start Meeting Like This," *Fast Company*, December 19, 2007, retrieved June 24, 2009, from http://www.fastcompany.com/magazine/23/begeman.

10. Salvador Apud and Talis Apud-Martinez, "Global Teams: Communicating Across Time, Space and, Most Important, Cultures," *CW Bulletin*, 2006, retrieved June 23, 2009, from http://www.iabc.com/cwb/archive/2006/0306/apud.htm.

11. Ibid.

Module 23

1. Carol Hymowitz, "When You Tell the Boss, Plain Talk Counts," *The Wall Street Journal*, June 16, 1989, p. B1.

2. Linda Driskill, "How the Language of Presentations Can Encourage or Discourage Audience Participation," paper presented at the Conference on College Composition and Communication, Cincinnati, OH, March 18–21, 1992.

3. Ray Alexander, *Power Speech: Why It's Vital to You* (New York: AMACOM, 1986), p. 156; Wharton Applied Research Center, "A Study of the Effects of the Use of Overhead Transparencies on Business Meetings," reported in Martha Jewett and Rita Margolies, Eds., *How to Run Better Business Meetings: A Reference Guide for Managers* (New York: McGraw-Hill, 1987), pp. 109–110, 115.

4. Robert S. Mills, conversation with Kitty O. Locker, March 10, 1988.

5. Phil Thiebert, "Speechwriters of the World, Get Lost!" *The Wall Street Journal*, August 2, 1993, A10.

6. Brian Mara-Croft, "Every Picture Tells a Story," *IABC Communication World*, *Visual Appeal* 25(5) (September/October 2008): 22–25.

7. Edward Tufte, "PowerPoint Is Evil," *Wired*, September 2003, retrieved June 22, 2009, from http://www.wired.com/wired/archive/11.09/ppt2.html; Virginia Galt, "Glazed Eyes a Major Peril of Using PowerPoint," *The Globe and Mail*, June 4, 2005, p. B10; and Dave Paradi, "Slide Makeover Video Podcast," retrieved June 22, 2009, from http://www.youtube.com/watch?v=jArg6s4KARo&feature=related.

8. Stephen E. Lucas, *The Art of Public Speaking*, 2nd ed. (New York: Random House, 1986), p. 248.

9. John Case, "A Company of Businesspeople," *Inc.*, April 1993, p. 90.

10. Edward J. Hegarty, *Humor and Eloquence in Public Speaking* (West Nyack, NY: Packer, 1976), p. 204.

11. Carmine Gallo, "Manage Your Fear of Public Speaking," *BusinessWeek*, December 30, 2008, retrieved June 22, 2009, from http://www.businessweek.com/smallbiz/content/dec2008/sb20081230_141498.htm; and Daniel J. DeNoon, "Fear of Public Speaking Hardwired," *WebMD*, April 20, 2006, retrieved June 22, 2009, from http://www.webmd.com/anxiety-panic/guide/20061101/fear-public-speaking.

12. S. A. Beebe, "Eye Contact: A Nonverbal Determinant of Speaker Credibility," *Speech Teacher* 23 (1974): 21–25, cited in Marjorie Fink Vargas, *Louder Than Words* (Ames, IA: Iowa State University Press, 1986), pp. 61–62.

13. J. Wills, "An Empirical Study of the Behavioral Characteristics of Sincere and Insincere Speakers," Ph.D. dissertation, University of Southern California, 1961, cited in Marjorie Fink Vargas, *Louder Than Words* (Ames, IA: Iowa State University Press, 1986), p. 62.

Module 24

1. Richard Bolle, "Here's How to Pack Your Parachute," *Fast Company*, September 1999, p. 242.
2. Interview with Sherine Mansour, coordinator, Journalism New Media, Sheridan College, February 25, 2012, and Social Networking. (2012). About.com. Job Searching, Retrieved from http://jobsearch.about.com/od/onlinecareernetworking/Career_Social_Networking.htm]
3. Industry Canada, "Canadian Company Capabilities," January 2, 2008, retrieved March 3, 2009, from http://www.ic.gc.ca/eic/site/ccc-rec.nsf/eng/home.
4. Rich Young, "Social Media: How New Forms of Communications Are Changing Job Search and Career Management," *IABC Toronto, Communicator*, January/February 2009, pp. 1, 3; Omar El Akkad, "The Medium Is No Longer the Message," *The Globe and Mail*, March 10, 2009, p. A3; Wallace Immen, "Job Hunting 101…A Guide for the New Realities of These Tougher Times," *The Globe and Mail*, February 18, 2009, p. C1; Heather Havenstein, "One in Five Employers Uses Social Networks in Hiring Process," *ComputerWorld*, September 12, 2008, retrieved August 8, 2009, from http://www.computerworld.com/s/article/9114560/One_in_five_employers_uses_social_networks_in_hiring_process; Joan Vinall Cox, personal communication, June 8, 2009; Kathy Voltan, personal communication, March 14, 2008.
5. Ibid., all sources.
6. Be aware that your digital identity is accessible to anybody, anytime. "With options like Pipli or Persona or Spezify it's a breeze to look someone up. Persona is an interesting and frightening experience because it uses key words like character and sports and education and genealogy and management to create a character timeline of who you are. It's never too early to take control of your digital identity. [personal interview Sherine Mansour, February 24, 2012].
7. Heather Huhman, "Networking as a Job Search Tool (Part 5): Find a Mentor," *examiner.com*, September 10, 2009, retrieved August 15, 2009, from http://www.examiner.com/x-828-Entry-Level-Careers-Examiner~ y2008m9d10-Networking-as-a-job-search-tool-part-5-Find-a-mentor.
8. Carl Quintanilla, "Coming Back," *The Wall Street Journal*, February 22, 1996, p. R10; and Megan Malugani, "How to Re-enter the Health-Care Job Market," *Columbus Dispatch*, March 22, 2000, p. 13.
9. LeAne Rutherford, "Five Fatal Résumé Mistakes," *Business Week's Guide to Careers* 4(3) (Spring/Summer 1986): 60–62.
10. Phil Elder, "The Trade Secrets of Employment Interviews," Association for Business Communication Midwest Convention, Kansas City, MO, May 2, 1987.

Module 25

1. Allison Green, "7 Things to Leave Off Your Resume," *US News & World Report*, March 2, 2009, retrieved March 6, 2009, from http://www.usnews.com/blogs/outside-voices-careers/2009/03/02/7-things-to-leave-off-your-resume.html; and Kimberly Lankford, "A New Resume for a New Year," Your Money, *Kiplinger's Personal Finance Magazine* 59(1) (January 2005): 87, retrieved March 7, 2009, from http://find.galegroup.com/itx/infomark.do?contentSet=IAC-Documents&docType=IAC&type= retr ieve&tabID=T003&prodId=AONE&docId=A126207190&userGroupName=sols_oakvillerpa&version=1.0&searchType=BasicSearchForm&source=gale.
2. Wallace Immen, "How Did You Get to the Top with That Résumé?," *The Globe and Mail*, October 12, 2005, p. C3.
3. Beverly H. Nelson, William P. Gallé, and Donna W. Luse, "Electronic Job Search and Placement," Association for Business Communication Convention, Orlando FL, November 1–4, 1995.
4. Rebecca Smith, *Electronic Résumés & Online Networking: How to Use the Internet to Do a Better Job Search, Including a Complete, Up-to-Date Resource Guide* (Franklin Lakes, NJ: Career Press, 1999), pp. 191–96.
5. Taunee Besson, *The Wall Street Journal National Employment Business Weekly: Résumés* (New York: John Wiley and Sons, 1994), p. 245.

Module 27

1. Thomas Petzinger, Jr., "Lewis Roland's Knack for Finding Truckers Keeps Firm Rolling," *The Wall Street Journal*, December 1, 1995, p. B1.
2. Judith A. Swartley to Kitty Locker, March 20, 1989.
3. Sherri Eng, "Company Culture Dictates Attire for Interviews," *Columbus Dispatch*, August 25, 1996, p. 33J.
4. The Catalyst Staff, *Marketing Yourself* (New York: G. P. Putnam's Sons, 1980), p. 179.
5. Sue Shellenbarger, "New Job Hunters Ask Recruiters, 'Is There Life After Work?'" *The Wall Street Journal*, January 29, 1996, p. B1; and Sue Shellenbarger, "What Job Candidates Really Want to Know: Will I Have a Life?" *The Wall Street Journal*, November 17, 1999, p. B1.
6. Donna Stine Kienzler, letter to Ann Granacki, April 6, 1988.
7. Christopher Conte, "Labor Letter," *The Wall Street Journal*, October 19, 1993, p. A1.
8. Richard C. Rose and Echo Montgomery Garrett, "Guerrilla Interviewing," *Inc.*, December 1992, pp. 145–47.
9. "Job Application and Interview Advice," Job-Application-and-Interview-Advice.com, 2007–2009, retrieved November 16, 2009, from http://www.job-application-and-interview-advice.com/job-interview-article.html.
10. Kate Weldon, *Through the Brick Wall: How to Job-Hunt in a Tight Market* (New York: Villard Books, 1992), p. 244.
11. Carol A. Hacker, *Job Hunting in the 21st Century: Exploding the Myths, Exploring the Realities* (Boca Raton: St. Lucie Press, 1999), p. 154.
12. Ray Robinson, quoted in Dick Friedman, "The Interview as Mating Ritual," *Working Woman*, April 1987, p. 107.
13. Sarah E. Needleman, Thx 4 Cing me, Wud Luv a Job!" *The Globe and Mail*, August 15, 2008, p. C3; G. L. Hoffman, "How to Write the Perfect Thank-You Note After the Interview," *U.S.ANEWS*, February 10, 2009, retrieved March 15, 2009, from http://www.usnews.com/blogs/outside-voices-careers/2009/2/10/the-perfect-thank-you-note-after-the-interview.html; Katharine Hansen, Ph.D., "FAQs About Thank You Letters," QuintCareers.com, retrieved August 25, 2009, from http://www.quintcareers.com/thank_you_letters.html; and Jeramy Colvin, "How to Send a Thank You Note After a Job Interview," eHow.com, retrieved November 16, 2009, from http://www.ehow.com/how_4729287_thank-note-after-job-interview.html.

14. Wallace Immen, "Job Hunting 101: A Guide for the New Realities of These Tougher Times," *The Globe and Mail*, February 18, 2009, p. C1; Kathryn Lee Bazan, "The Art of the Follow Up After Job Interviews," QuintCareers.com, retrieved November 16, 2009, from http://www.quintcareers.com/job_interview_follow-up.html; David Nassief, "How to Follow Up After an Interview," About.com, retrieved August 25, 2009, from http://jobsearch.about.com/od/interviewsnetworking/a/intfollowup.htm; and Yana Parker, "Guide to Follow-Up Letters," The DamnGoodResume site, retrieved August 25, 2009, from http://www.damngood.com/ready/exmpl/follow-up.html.

Revising Sentences and Paragraphs

1. "The Secret of Impressive Writing? Keep It Plain and Simple," *ScienceDaily*, November 1, 2005, retrieved August 19, 2009, from http://www.sciencedaily.com/releases/2005/10/051031075447.htm.

2. Sam Kornell, "Read Novels, Be Smarter," TheStar.com, retrieved August 16, 2008, from http://www.thestar.com/article/475516.

3. Linda Flower, *Problem-Solving Strategies for Writing* (New York: Harcourt Brace Jovanovich, 1981), p. 39.

4. Harris B. Savin and Ellen Perchonock, "Grammatical Structure and the Immediate Recall of English Sentences," *Journal of Verbal Learning and Verbal Behavior* 4 (1965): 348–53; Pamela Layton and Adrian J. Simpson, "Deep Structure in Sentence Comprehension," *Journal of Verbal Learning and Verbal Behavior* 14 (1975): 658–64.

5. Arn Tibbetts, "Ten Rules for Writing Readably," *Journal of Business Communication* 18(4) (Fall 1981): 55–59.

6. Thomas N. Huckin, "A Cognitive Approach to Readability," *New Essays in Technical and Scientific Communication: Research, Theory, Practice*, Paul V. Anderson, R. John Brockmann, and Carolyn R. Miller, Eds. (Farmingdale, NY: Baywood, 1983), pp. 93–98.

Index

Aboriginal community-building, 335
accurate messages, 9, 312
acknowledgement, 328
acronym, 12
action verbs, 400–401, 451
active
  listening, 238, 254, 326–327
  reading, 236
  verbs, 449–451
  voice, 91–92
adjectives, 389
adjustments, 124–125
adverbs, 389
age diversity, 41–42, 48
ageism, 51
agendas, 353–355
agreement
  noun-pronoun, 106, 463–464
  subject-verb, 59–60, 463
all-capitals, 83
alternatives, 146–147
Amed, Imran, 7
American spelling, 476
analytical proposals, 102
analytical reports, 264–266
angel investors, 265
annual reports, 250
APA format, 242, 243, 247
apologies, 204
apostrophes, 207, 218, 469–470
appendices, 285
Apud, Salvador, 358
Apud-Martinez, Talis, 358
Arbeláez, Brenda, 51
Archer, Laura, 380
arrogant tone, 168
assumptions, 325–326
attachments
  managing, 115–116
  and viruses, 115
audience
  analysis, use of, 23, 30–32
  business messages, 23
  communication process, 21–22
  critical thinking, 24
  demographic factors, 25–26
  different needs, 32–33
  empathy, 24
  expectations, 4
  external, 5–6
  focus, 189, 209
  gatekeeper, 20, 21, 32
  group members as, 24–28
  identification, of, 11, 19–21
  importance of, 21–23
  individuals, 24–28
  initial, 19, 21

internal, 5–6
  letters, 94
  members of groups, 24–28
  memos, 94
  oral presentations, 364, 366, 372–373
  organizations, people in, 28–30
  PAIBOC, 23
  past behaviour, 28
  personality, 26–27
  primary, 19, 21, 32
  prior knowledge, 25
  psychographic characteristics, 27
  questions from, 372–373
  reaching your audience, 33–34
  reaction, analysis of, 31
  reader benefits, matching, 181–185, 186
  secondary, 20, 21
  subgroups, 185
  talking to, 66
  type analysis, 27
  understanding, 24
  values and beliefs, 27–28
  watchdog, 20, 21
audit reports, 250

background, 284
bad news messages. see negative messages
BallHype, 29
bar graphs, 306, 308–309
The Beer Store, 187
Begeman, Michael, 356
behavioural interviews, 28, 437–438
beliefs, 27–28, 43–44
Bender, Peter Urs, 26
benefits to readers. see reader benefits
Bertin, Oliver, 422
Best Buy, 32
better writing, benefits of, 12
bias-free illustrations, 55
bias-free language
  definition, 51
  negative terms, 55
  neutral language, 54
  non-ageist language, 54
  non-racist language, 54
  non-sexist language, 52–53
bias-free photos and illustrations, 55
Birdwhistell, Ray, 46
blind copies, 99
block format, 94–95, 97, 100

blocking responses, 327
blogs
  describing experience and goals, 16
  meetings, 352
Bloom, Richard, 147
blueprints, 276
body clocks, 48
body language, 46–47
body of report, 250, 283–284
Boice, Jacklyn, 370
Boice, Robert, 73
boilerplate, 72
bold, 86
Bolles, Richard, 379
Boolean search, 223
Boom, Bust and Echo (Foot), 25–26, 41
Boomers, 41, 49
Borker, Ruth A., 49
brainstorming, 11, 66, 181–185, 341
branching questions, 227
Braun, Kathryn, 45
Brehm, Jack W., 147
bridge, 417
Brown, Vincent J., 20
buffer
  definition, 144
  examples, 144–145
bulleting, 97
bullets, 86
Burnett, Rebecca, 343
business communication
  analysis of situations, 11–12, 13
  audience, 5–6, 23
  audience expectations, meeting of, 4
  conventions, 4
  cost of, 8–9
  culture, 22, 42–50
  purpose of, 4–6
  technology, impact of, 5
  writing, amount of, 7–8
business image, 104
business plans, 250, 265
business-speak, 448
buying time, 342
buzzwords, 7

Canadian Charter of Rights and Freedoms, 42
Canadian Council for Aboriginal Business, 114
Canadian culture, 40–42
  age diversity, 41–42
  cultural sensitivity, 42
  ethnic diversity, 41

Canadian government websites, 238
Canadian Human Rights Act, 42
Canadian spelling, 476
Canadian Tire, 28
Canadian values, 43–44
carbon copy, 99
career achievements, 403
career objective, 403
case, 464–465
causation, 228
chair's role in meetings, 354
channels
  communication process, 22
  large audiences, 34
  multiple, 33, 34
  overload, 22
chartjunk, 311
Chatman, Jennifer, 30
Chernis, Cary, 45
choice, details of, 32
Christianity, 44
chronological
  oral presentations, 365
  pattern, 274
  progress reports, 258–259
  resumés, 393, 394, 398, 399–400, 402
  short report, 253
Chrysler, 165
CIBC, 108
citation, 240, 310
citizen journalism, 225, 337
claim letter, sample, 143
class associations, 28
class reports
  proposals, 270–271
  sample using primary and secondary sources, 271–272
  sections to include, 270–271
clauses
  dependent, 454, 466–467
  essential, 471
  independent, 466, 467
  main, 466, 467
  non-essential, 471
  subordinate, 233, 466–467
clear messages, 9
clip art, 311–312
closed body positions, 46
closed questions, 226
closure report, 253–254
clothing, 48, 430
cluster, 63
  example of, 63
  information, 66
co-authored documents, 343–345
  activities, 344
  audience, 343

collaborative writing
    activities, 343, 344
    computer software, 344
    drafts, 344–345
    editing, 345
    group process, 345
    planning, 343–344
    proofreading, 345
    purposes, 343
    revisions, 345
collaborative writing, 343
collaborative writing projects.
    see co-authored documents
collection letters, 121, 161–162
collective culture, 335
colons, 332, 470–471
colour
    culture, 48, 310
    presentations, 85
    use of, 48, 310
combination resumés, 397–399,
    401–402
comma splices (CS), 38,
    467–468
commas, 471–472
    faults, 467–468
    general use, 471–472
    lists, in, 76
    readability, 469
    serial, 446
    splices, 38, 467–468
    use of, 469
common ground, 167
communication
    behaviours, 433
    context, 33
    cultural, 22
    definition, 21
    effective, 9
    ineffective, 8–9
    intercultural, 51
    international, 51
    interpersonal, 6, 7
    non-verbal (see non-verbal
        communication)
    oral (see oral
        communication)
    purpose of, 4
    successful, 4, 22
    written, 4, 7–8
communication process
    audience and, 21–22
    channel overload, 22
    definition, 21–22
    feedback, 22
    frames of reference, 22
    group, 335–336
    information overload, 22
    model, 21
    noise, 22
communication skills, 6–7, 403
    business success, 6–7
    importance of, 6–7
    listening, 237
company websites, 380
comparison or contrast pattern,
    274
complaints, 124–125

competence, 54
complete messages, 9
complex constructions, 321
complex sentences, 454
complimentary closes, 95
compliments, 50
compound sentences, 453
compound-complex sentences,
    454
comprehensive messages, 9
computer copy, 99
concise messages, 9
concise writing, 260, 321
conclusion, 250
Conclusions, 285
concrete nouns, 321, 389
concrete verbs, 321, 389
condescending, 209
conference report, 250, 255
confidence, 431–432
confirmations, 122
conflict resolution
    alternatives, 341
    bad feelings, repairing, 341
    brainstorming, 341
    buying time, 342
    criticism, 341
    feelings, checking, 341
    group, 339–342
    inferences, checking, 342
    information, checking, 339
    problem, presenting of, 340
    steps, 339–342
    venting, 339
    you-attitude, 342
congratulatory notes, 125
connotations, 198–200
content, 32, 215
context
    communication, 33
    format and, 94
    high, 42
    low, 42
    message, 10–12
    reader's response, 12
    visual, 310
continuation heading, 98, 100
contractions, 218
convenience sample, 226
conventions
    grammar, 4
    meetings, 351
conversation regulators, 328
    correspondence, cost of, 8–9
    courtesy titles, 99–101,
        202–203
    credibility, 167
conversation regulators, 328
conversational English, 389
conversational style, 49, 448
coordination, 335
corporate culture, 29–30, 422,
    430. see also organizational
    culture
    writing style, 458–459
correct messages, 9
correlation, 228
correspondence, cost of, 8–9

courtesy titles, 99–101, 202–203
cover letters. see also job
    application letters
    common components, 420
    components, 414–415
    knowledge of company/
        position, 420
    length of, 421
    PAIBOC, 414
    positive emphasis, 423
    proposals, included with, 268
    purpose of, 414–415
    you-attitude, 421–422
creative thinking, 10
credibility, 167
critical skills
    computer-created design, 86
    creating a business image, 104
    creative thinking, 10
    emotional intelligence, 45
    ethical implications, 147
    goodwill ending, 132
    integrity, 338
    job hunting, 385
    legal implications, 147
    listening, 329
    long reports, 297
    natural writing style, 260
    note-taking, 240
    note-taking, preparation for,
        229
    online community, building,
        356
    personal contact, 114
    persuasive messages, 167
    point of view, others', 216
    positive emphasis, ethical
        use of, 201
    professional image, 443
    readability, 276–277
    reader benefits and audience,
        186
    resumés, computer layout
        and design, 393
    revising after feedback, 72
    targeting specific companies,
        422
    visuals, integration into text,
        311
    voice, 370
    workplace rules, 25
critical thinking, 24, 242
criticism, 341, 349
cultural dimensions, 44
cultural discrimination, 51
cultural sensitivity, 42
culture. see also diversity
    age, 48
    beliefs, 43–44
    bias-free language, 51–55
    body language, 46–47
    business communication, 22,
        42–50
    clothing, 48, 430
    colours, 48
    communication, 22, 51
    compliments, 50
    corporate, 29–30, 458–459

courtesy titles, 99–101,
    202–203
definition, 40, 50
exaggeration, 50
eye contact, 46
gestures, 46–47
height, 48
high-context, 42–43
international audiences (see
    international audience)
low-context, 42–43
misunderstandings, 45–46
monochronic, 48
motivation, 42
non-verbal communication,
    45–46
non-verbal symbols, 48–49
oral communication, 49–50
organizational, 29–30,
    458–459
personal space, 47
persuasive writing, 50
polychronic, 48
practices, 43–44
religion, influences of, 44
silence, 50
smoking, 432
spatial arrangements, 47
stereotypes, avoidance of, 22
technology, 43
time, perception of, 48
touch, 47
understatement, 50
values, 43–44
cycling process, 8

Dambrough, Drew, 357
dangling modifiers (DM), 119,
    465
dashes, 360, 472
data, 306
dates, 411, 476
deaf people, 55
decision-making process, 353
decode, 22
defensive body positions, 46
demographics, 25–26
dependent clauses, 454, 466–467
design, 78–79, 309–310
    all-capitals, 83
    all-capitals, use of, 83
    bullets, 81
    colours, 85
    computers, using, 86
    fonts, 83–84
    form follows function, 125
    headings, 82–83
    importance of, 78–79
    letters, 86
    margins, justification of, 84
    memos, 86
    multiple fonts, 83
    paper pages, 80–84
    parallelism, 81
    persuasion, 87
    presentation slides, 84–85
    questionnaire, 228
    testing, 86

thinking about, 80, 87
visual impact, 80–84
visuals, 309–310
web pages, 86
white space, 80–81
Desjardins, Gabriel, 8
details, 388–389
Dillon, James R., 338
direct messages, 121
direct refusals, 146
direct request pattern, 163–164
direct request subject line, 169
direct requests, 163–164
    checklist, 173
    patterns, 163–164
directed subject line, 169
disabilities, 54
disabled people, 54–55
disagreement and active
  listening, 328
discourse communities, 28–30
discrimination
    ageism, 54
    bias-free language, 51–55
    bias-free photos and
      illustrations, 55
    Canada, 54
    cultural, 51
    disabilities, 54–55
    non-ageist language, 54
    non-racist language, 54
    non-sexist language, 52–53
    people-first language, 55
    racism, 51
diversity. *see also* culture
    bias-free language, 51–55
    bias-free photos and
      illustrations, 55
    disabilities, 54–55
    discrimination in Canada, 54
    legal recognition, 42
    non-ageist language, 54
    non-racist language, 54
    non-sexist language, 52–53
    people-first language, 55
    workplace, in the, 41–42
document design, 31
document literacy, 8
documentation, 240
documentation of sources,
  242–244
documents
    bias-free, 51–55
    costs of, 8–9
    cycle, 8
    summarizing, 236–237
dot jotting, 97
dot jots, 64
dot planning, 355
drafting, 64
dramatic statement, 366

Eagle's Flight, 335
Echos, 41
Ede, Lisa, 343
editing, 68–69, 462–477
    after revision, 64
    co-authored documents, 345

definition, 64, 68, 411
grammar checker, 69–70
grammatical errors, 462–466
punctuation rules, 68,
  469–474
for readability, 69
tips, 69
Edmondson, Amy C., 338
education heading, 404
effective messages
    criteria, 9
    multiple channels, use of, 33
Elashmawi, Farid, 43
Elder, Phil, 386
electronic communication
    discretion, 108, 116
    electronic trail, 108, 116
    netiquette, 115, 116
    responsibility, 110–111
    text messages, 108–109
elimination of alternatives
  pattern, 275
ellipses, 475
email code, 113
email letters, 13–14
email messages
    acronyms, 113
    attachments, 112, 115–116
    concise, 114
    content, 111, 113–115
    emoticons, 113
    etiquette, 115, 116
    examples, 110, 111, 112
    formats, 110
    guidelines, 108–109
    informative, 115, 123
    job application, 423–424
    legal implications, 114
    limitations, 114
    negative, 114
    organization, 110–112
    PAIBOC analysis, 109, 113
    persuasive, 114, 115
    positive, 115
    proofreading, 112
    salutation, 110
    signature block, 110
    subject lines, 109, 113
    templates, 13–14, 109–112
    time allocation, 114
    tone, 113–115
    viruses, 115–116
    when to avoid, 113
emoticons, 113
emotional appeal, 167
emotional intelligence, 45
Emotional Intelligence
  (Goleman), 45
empathy, 24
Employability Skills 2000+, 2–3
    apologizing, 203
    audience, adaptation of
      message to, 19
    audience analysis, 25, 30
    causation and correlation,
      228
    checklist, 2–3, 19, 40, 62,
      78, 94, 108, 121, 141, 160,

180, 195, 209, 220, 236,
  249, 264, 281, 303, 324,
  334, 351, 362, 378, 391,
  414, 429
closure reports, 252
co-authored documents, 343,
  345
communication channels, 33
communication process, and
  audience, 21
communications skills, 6
conflict resolution, 341
courtesy titles, 99
cover letters, 420, 421
critical thinking, 24
cultural assumptions, 42, 44
cultural sensitivity, 42, 51
culture, 40
design, 87
documenting sources, 242,
  243
email job applications, 422
email messages, 108, 111,
  113, 114, 116
empathy, 24
evaluation of sources, 228
feasibility reports, 250,
  264–265
form letters, 72
formal reports, 282, 283,
  285, 286
format letters and memos,
  94, 95
goodwill, 215
grammar editing, 69
group presentations, 373
information interview, 381
information reports, 252
informative messages, 121,
  129
job application letters, 414
job hunting, 379
job interview clothing, 430
job interviews, 384, 429,
  434, 436
listening, 50, 324, 327, 328
long reports, 281
margins, 84
meetings, 351, 352, 354,
  356, 357
negative messages, 140, 145,
  146, 150
neutral language, 54
non-sexist language, 52
non-verbal symbols, 46
note-taking, 431
online resumés, 408
online searching, 221
oral communication, 48
oral presentations, 363, 366
organizational patterns, 125,
  142
personality, 26
persuasive messages, 160,
  171
phone interviews, 438
planning, writing and
  revising, 66

positive emphasis, 195, 196,
  200, 203
positive messages, 125, 129
presentation slides, 85
presentations, organization
  of, 362, 371
progress reports, 257
proofreading, 70
proposals, 266, 267
purpose statements, 251
reader benefits, 181, 183,
  185, 188
reader's name, 101
reports, 248, 249, 250, 264, 272
research, 220, 223
resumés, 391, 393, 406
rewriting, 64
scannable resumés, 406
self-assessment, 378
social networking, 381
teamwork and writing, 334,
  335, 336, 337
traditional job interview
  questions, 433
visuals, 368
working purpose statement, 220
writing process, 65, 73
writing to international
  audiences, 50
yardstick reports, 264
you-attitude, 209, 213, 421
Employment Equity Act, 42
Employment Standards Act/
Code, 196
empty modifiers, 321
enclosures, 98
encoding, 21
end-date, 115
endings, 148, 285
Eservus.com Online Services
  Ltd., 209
essential clauses, 471
ethical implications, 147
ethics
    fundraising, and, 7
    positive emphasis, 201
    visuals, use of, 312
ethnic diversity, 41
ethnic groups, 41
exaggeration, 50
excluding alternatives, 365
Executive Summary, 287
experienced writers, 65
external audience, 5–6
extrinsic benefits, 187
extrovert, 26, 27
eye contact, 46, 371–372

Facebook, 29, 43, 225, 379
fairness, 43
Falls, Jason, 356
faulty logic, 188
feasibility reports, 250, 264–265
features vs. benefits, 184–185
feedback, 71
    communication process, 22
    obtaining, 71
    revision after, 72

feeling types, 26, 27
feelings
    conflict resolution, 341
    listening for, 326
    you-attitude, 211–212
figures, 286, 303, 309
findings section, 284
First Nations, 54
Fisher-Price Toys, 264
five senses, 389
fixed fonts, 83
Flesch-Kincaid Grade Level, 69
Flesch-Kincaid Readability
    Scores, 69
focus, 325
follow-up questions, 165
fonts
    business, 86
    fixed, 83
    proportional, 83
    sans serif, 84
    serif, 83–84
Foot, David, 26, 41
form letters, 72
formal reports. *see also* long
    reports
    appendixes, 285
    assumptions, 284
    background, 284
    beginning, 286–287
    body, 283–284
    citations, 285
    components of, 281–282
    conclusions, 285
    draft, 283–287
    ending, 285
    Executive Summary, 287
    figures, 286
    findings section, 284
    format, 297
    history, 284
    illustrations, list of, 286
    introduction, 283–284
    limitations, 284
    methods, 284
    PAIBOC, 282
    planning, 283
    purpose, 283
    recommendations, 285
    references, 285
    samples, 288–296
    scope, 283
    style, 297
    submission, 287
    table of contents, 286
    tables, 286
    time management,
        282–283
    title page, 286
    titles, 286
    transmittal, 286
    works cited, 285
formality, 376, 448
formalization, 335
format
    APA, 242–244
    block, 94–95, 97, 100
    email messages, 110

full block letters, 94–95
    letter (*see* letter format)
    long report, 297
    memo (*see* memo format)
    MLA, 242–244
    modified block letters, 94–95
    resumés, 398–402
formation, 335
frames of reference, 22
Free IQ, 29
Freeman. Kimberly, 338
freewrite, 66
frosh week, 80
full block letter format, 94–95
full justification, 84
functional pattern, 275
functional resumés, 394–396,
    398, 401, 402
fundamental skills, 2
funding proposals, 268
fundraising, politics of, 7
Future Shop, 32

gatekeeper, 20, 21, 32
gender
    bias-free photos and
        illustrations, 55
    non-sexist language, 52–53
    unknown letter recipient, 101
general-to-particular pattern,
    273
Generation X, 41, 49
Generation Y, 41
Genuity Capital Markets
    Technology, 108
GenX, 41, 49
GenY, 41
geodemographic data, 28
geographical pattern, 275
gerunds, 399, 452
gestures, 46–47, 372
Gillis, Alex, 329
global ethnography, 28
Goldman, Michael, 364
Goleman, Daniel, 45
good listening, 324–326
good news. *see* positive
    messages
good news messages. *see*
    positive messages
good writing style, 260, 448
goodwill
    apologies, 204
    building, through effective
        messages, 7, 9
    ending, 132
    informative messages, 126
    positive emphasis (*see*
        positive emphasis)
    positive messages, 126
    presentations, 362
    reader benefits (*see* reader
        benefits)
    subject line, 128
    you-attitude (*see* you-
        attitude)
Google, 30
Gostick, Dana, 338

grammar
    adjectives, 389
    adverbs, 389
    agreement, 463–464
    case, 464–465
    checker, 69–70
    clauses (*see* clauses)
    dangling modifiers, 465
    disagreement among experts,
        446
    formal usage, 376
    gerunds, 399, 452
    independent clauses, 466,
        467
    infinitives, 452
    main clauses, 466, 467
    misplaced modifiers, 466
    modifiers, 465
    nominative pronouns, 464
    noun-pronoun agreement,
        463–464
    nouns, concrete, 321, 389
    parallelism, 466
    personal pronouns, 464
    possessive pronouns, 464,
        465, 470
    predication errors, 466
    run-on sentences, 468
    sentence fragments (frag.),
        468–469
    split infinitives, 446
    subject-verb agreement, 463
    subjective pronoun, 464
    verbs (*see* verbs)
grapevine, 7
gripe, 124
group presentations, 373–374
grouped bar graphs, 309
groups. *see also* teams
    Aboriginal community-
        building, 335
    audience reaction in, 28–30
    co-authored documents,
        343–345
    collaborative writing, 343
    communication in, 335–336
    conflict in, 339–342
    conflict resolution, 339–341
    coordination, 335
    criticism, 341
    feelings, 341
    formalization, 335
    formation, 335
    ground rules, 334
    groupthink, 338–339
    inferences, 342
    leadership in, 337, 338
    limited agreement, 342
    maintenance roles, 336
    messages, 335–336
    negative roles, 336
    network, 335
    oral presentations, 373–374
    orientation, 335
    paraphrase, 341
    peer pressure, 338–339
    positive roles, 336
    preferences, 54

presenting problem, 340
    roles played in, 336–339
    student, 337
    task outcomes, 334
    technology, 336
    troubleshooting problems,
        340
    venting, 339
    you-attitude, 342
groupthink, 338–339
guided discussions, 364

Hagge, John, 204
hall meetings, 351
Hall, Edward T., 42, 48
Hamonic, Jesse, 29
Harris, Philip R., 43
headings
    all-capitals, 83
    bold, 86
    definition, 82
    design, 82–83, 86
    document, 278
    informative, 278
    parallelism, 81
    readability, 276
    resumés, 403–405, 406
    signposts, 32
    talking heads, 278
height, 49
Herzberg, Frederick, 187
Heydary, Javad, 147
hidden job market, 383–384
hidden negatives, 199
high-context cultures, 42–43
highlighting, 97
Hirsch, Arlen H., 385
histograms, 309
history, 284
Hofstede, Geert, 44
Holloway, Andy, 385
Holmstrom, Candice, 114
Home Depot, 327
honours and awards heading,
    405
hopefully, 446
however, 468
Human Rights Commission, 196
humour, 367
hyphens, 360, 472–473

I, 212, 426–427
I/me, 262, 422
IBM, 10
ideas, encouraging, 66–67
idioms, 7
illustrations, 55, 286
Immen, Wallace, 385
impersonal constructions, 448
implied refusals, 146
incident report, 250, 256–257
indents, 86
independent clauses, 466, 467
IndianPad, 29
indirect request messages, 164
    checklist, 174
individualism, 43, 44
individuals, analyzing, 24–28

Industry Canada's Canadian Company Capabilities (CCC), 380
inferences, 342
infinitives, 452
informal meetings, 351
information
　business communication, 12
　gathering, 63
　interviews, 381–383
　negative (*see* negative messages)
　organizational patterns, 142–144
　overload, 22
　reports, 253
　summarization of, 236–239
informational leader, 337
informational messages, 335
informative headings, 278
informative messages
　adjustments, 124–125
　audience needs, 122–123
　checklist, 129
　collection letters, 121
　complaints, 124
　complaints, responses to, 124–125
　confirmations, 122
　congratulatory note, 125
　definition, 121
　details, 125
　email, 115, 123
　examples of, 123, 127
　good news, 125
　goodwill, 126
　instructions, 121, 124
　negative elements, 126
　organization, 125–126
　PAIBOC, 12, 129–130
　primary purpose, 121, 123
　reader benefits, 126–127
　secondary purpose, 121, 123
　subject line, 127–129
　summaries, 122–123
　thank-you note, 125
　transmittals, 121
　types of, 121–125
informative presentations, 362
Ingram, Mathew, 10
initial audience, 19, 21
instructions, 121, 124
integrity, 338
Integrity Works, 338
intercultural communication, 51
internal audiences, 5–6
International Association of Business Communicators, 9
international audience
　bias-free language, 51–55
　bias-free photos and illustrations, 55
　disabilities, 54
　flexibility, 51
　negative messages, 55
　non-ageist language, 54
　non-racist language, 54
　non-sexist language, 52–53

organizational patterns, 50
people-first language, 55
sensitivity, 51
writing to, 50
international communication, 51
Internet
　Canadian government information, 238
　evaluation of information, 224–225
　job hunting, 379–381
　news sites, 238–239
　online research, 221–224
　reference collections, 238
　resumés, scannable, 406–409
　social websites, 379, 381
　subject matter directories, 238
　web research sources, 238
interpersonal communication
　importance of, 6, 7
　listening (*see* listening)
　virtual meetings, 357–358
interpersonal leader, 337
interpersonal messages, 336
interpersonal profile, 403
interviews
　behavioural, 28, 437–438
　defined, 226
　job (*see* job interviews)
　judgment samples, 226
　phone, 438–439
　questions, 226–228
　video, 439
intonation, 370
intrinsic benefits, 185
introduction, 249, 283–284
introverts, 26, 27
intuitive types, 26, 27
Inuit, 54
italics, 475–476
it's/its, 218

Japanese culture, 43
Javor, Nick, 114
Jewish communities, 44
job application letters. *see also* cover letters
　body paragraphs, 420
　bridge, 417
　email, 423–424
　guidelines for professional, 415
　knowledge of company/ position, 420
　length, 421
　PAIBOC, 414
　positive emphasis, 423
　prospecting letter (*see* prospecting letters)
　purpose of, 414
　separation from other applicants, 421
　solicited letters (*see* solicited letters)
　summary paragraphs, 415–416
　summary sentences, 415–416

targeting specific companies, 422
　tone, 421–423
　types of, 415
　unsolicited letters (*see* prospecting letters)
　you-attitude, 213, 421–422
job hunting
　absent from job market, 384–385
　change fields, 385
　cover letters, 414–424
　email, 440–441
　email letters, 423–424
　employer expectations, 429
　family business, 384
　fired, 386
　follow-up phone call/letter, 439–441
　hidden job market, 383–384
　information interviews, 381–383
　interviews (*see* job interviews)
　job application letters (*see* job application letters)
　job offers, 442
　job search websites, 379–380
　lack of experience, 386
　mature workers, 387
　non-traditional experiences, 384–387
　offers (*see* job offers)
　online information, 379–381
　prospecting letters, 417–418
　referral interviews, 383
　researching companies, 379–381
　resumés (*see* resumés)
　self-assessment, 378
　self-recruitment, 382
　selling yourself, 385
　social networking, 379, 381
　solicited letter, 415, 416–417
　targeting specific company, 422
　unsolicited letter, 417–418
　volunteer community involvement, 386
Job Hunting for Dummies (Messruer), 443
job interviews
　behavioural interviews, 437–438
　being yourself, 432
　body of, 432
　closing of, 432
　clothing, 430–431
　communication behaviours, 433
　confidence, 431, 432, 438
　follow up phone call/letter, 439–441
　group interviews, 429, 431
　how to act at, 432
　items to bring to, 431
　note taking, 431
　offers (*see* job offers)

opening of, 432
PAIBOC, 439
parts of interview, 432
phone interviews, 438–439
place of, 431
practice, 431–432
professional attitude, 443
questions, 433–437
situational interviews, 437
Skype interviews, 438
strategy, 429–430
thank you letters, 439–440
traditional interview questions, 433–437
video interviews, 439
work-life balance question, 437
job offers
　acceptance letters, 442
　contingent acceptances, 442
　second-choice jobs, 442
　turning down, 442
job titles, 52
jotting, 64
judgment sample, 226
judging types, 27
justification of margins, 84
justification reports, 250, 265–266

Keene, Michael, 43
keep it short and simple (KISS) formula, 368
keywords, 222
Kielburger, Craig, 362
Kielburger, Marc, 362
King, Samantha, 7
KISS formula, 368
Klenzler, Donna S., 201
Kostelnick, Charles, 204
Kraft, Michael, 216

ladylike posture, 46
Lander, Christian, 10
language
　bias-free, 51–55
　boilerplate, 72
　level, 32
　neutral, 54
　non-ageist, 54
　non-racist, 54
　non-sexist, 52–53
　people-first, 55
Layton, Kirk, 209
leadership
　groups, in, 337
　integrity, 338
　listening by, 329
Leadership from Within (Bender), 26
legal implications, 147, 204
letter format
　audience, 94
　blind copies, 99
　block, 94–95
　bolded attention/subject lines, 101
　complimentary closes, 95

copies, 99
courtesy titles, 99–101
date, 95
dear, use of, 95
definition, 94
difference between letters, 97
enclosures, 98
full block, 94–95
gender unknown, 101
indented format, 96
letterhead, 97
mixed punctuation, 96
modified block, 94–95
multiple pages, 98
name unknown, 101
open punctuation, 96
parallel courtesy titles, 99
reference line, 97
salutation, 99
semi-block, 94–95
subject line, 97
letterhead, 95, 96, 97
letters
  audience for, 94
  form letters, 72
  format (see letter format)
  job applications (see job
    application letters)
  sample (see sample letters)
  samples (see sample letters)
  thank you, 125, 439–441
  transmittal, of, 286
  vs. memos, 94
limitations, 284
limited agreement, 342
line graphs, 309
Lingo Media Corporation, 216
LinkedIn, 29, 225, 379
listening
  acknowledgement, 328
  active, 238, 254, 326–327
  blocking responses, 327
  conversation regulators, 328
  defined, 324, 328
  disagreement, and, 328
  faulty assumptions, 325–326
  feelings, for, 326
  focus, 325
  good, 324–326
  importance of, 6
  internal monologue, 325
  leading by, 329
  learning by, 329
  PAIBOC, 325
  paying attention, 324–325
  preaching, 327
lists
  commas in, 76
  parallelism, 81, 466
literacy and employment, 8
Little Mosque on the Prairie, 49
long reports, 297. see also
  formal reports
  appendixes, 285
  background, 284
  components, 281–282
  conclusions, 285
  drafting, 283–287

Executive Summary, 287
figures, 286
findings, 284
format, 297
history, 284
illustrations, list of, 286
introduction, 283–284
letter of transmittal, 286
memo of transmittal, 286
recommendations, 285
references, 285
style, 297
table of contents, 286
tables, 286
time management, 282–283
title page, 286
titles, 286
works cited, 285
Long-Term Orientation (LTO),
  44
Lotherington, Heather, 113
low-context cultures, 42–43
Lunsford, Andrea, 343

MacDonald, Chris, 201
main clause, 466, 467
maintenance roles, 336
make-good reports, 250
Maltz, Daniel N., 49
margin justification, 84
margins, 84, 86
masculinity, 44
Maslow's hierarchy, 142, 183
Maslow, Abraham H., 183
Mathieu, Emily, 114
McCain Foods, 30
McCord, Elizabeth A., 147
McDonald's Station M, 336
McGowan, Ron, 385
me/I, 262, 422
meetings
  agendas, 353–354
  chair's role, 354
  computer supported, 352
  controversial issues, 353
  conventions, 351
  decision-making strategies,
    354–355
  dot planning, 355
  hall, 351
  informal, 351
  maintenance functions, 336
  minutes, 356–357
  networking, 354
  one-on-one, 351
  online, 356
  organizational, 351
  PAIBOC, 352
  parliamentary proceedings,
    351
  participation, effective, 356
  pre-meeting planning,
    352–354
  purpose of, 352–353
  retreats, 351
  sales, 351
  socializing, 354
  staff, 351

standard agendas, 355
task functions, 354
technology, 351–352
team, 351
town hall, 351
types of, 351
virtual, 357–358
memo format
  block format, 101–103
  definition, 101
  letterhead, 103
  standard format, 103
Memory Express, 327
memos
  audience for, 94
  examples, 102, 103
  format (see memo format)
  introductory, 15
  multiple pages, 104
  samples (see sample memos)
  transmittal, of, 286
  vs. letters, 94
Mennonites, 44, 45
menu writing. see white space
Messruer, Max, 443
methods, 284
Métis, 54
Millennials, 41, 184
A Million Random Digits, 226
mind-mappers, 11
Mintzberg, Henry, 329
minutes, 356–357
miscommunication, 48
misplaced modifiers, 466
mission statement, 266
mixed punctuation, 96
MLA format, 242, 244, 247
modified block format, 94–95,
  97, 98
modifiers, 465
  dangling, 465
  empty, 321
  misplaced, 466
  vague, 321
monochronic cultures, 48
monologue presentation, 364
Monster.ca, 379
motivation
  culture, 42
  reader benefits, 180
Mowat, Dave, 195
multicultural perspective, 40–42
Multiculturalism Act, 42
multiple-choice questions,
  226–227
multi-tasking, 31
Muslim, 44
Myers-Briggs Type Indicator,
  26–27
MySpace, 225

names
  courtesy titles (see courtesy
    titles)
  gender unknown, 101
  parallel forms, 101
  unknown, 101
narrative voice, 157–158

natural writing style, 260
negative connotations, 198–200
negative messages
  alternatives, 146–147
  audience needs, 142–143
  bad news, 196
  bad news pattern, 143–144
  buffer, 144–145
  burial of, 202
  checklist, 153
  common types, 141–142
  compact presentation, 202
  compromises, 146–147
  endings, 148
  ethical implications, 147
  examples, 142, 143
  hedging your statements, 204
  justification of, 200–201
  legal implications, 147
  Maslow's hierarchy, 142
  omitting, 201
  organizational pattern,
    142–149
  PAIBOC, 142, 150–153
  passive verbs, 212
  peers, to, 148–149
  primary purposes, 141
  purpose of, 141
  reasons, 145–146
  refusals, 141–142, 146
  rejections, 141–142
  sample letter, 143
  sample memo to
    subordinates, 149
  sample refusal, 142
  secondary purposes, 141
  subject lines, 149–150
  subordinates, to, 148–149
  superiors, to, 148
  time, allocation of, 151
  types of, 141–142
negative roles, 336
negative terms
  bias-free language, 51–55
  double negatives, 200
  hidden negatives, 199
  unnecessary negatives, 201
  words to avoid, 198–200
negative words, 55, 196,
  198–200
negotiation, successful, 196
nervousness, 371
netiquette, 115, 116
netizen, 115
network groups, 335
networking, 7, 354, 430
neutral language, 54
new work world, 385
news sites, 238–239
noise, 22
nominative pronouns, 464
non-ageist language, 54
non-essential clauses, 471
non-racist language, 54
non-sexist language, 52–53
  job titles, 52
  phrases, 52
  pronouns, 52–53

vs. you-attitude, 99
words, 52
non-traditional job experiences, 384–387
non-verbal communication
  body language, 46–48
  closed body position, 46
  conventions, 4
  definition, 45
  eye contact, 46
  gestures, 46–47
  misunderstandings, 45–46
  open body position, 46
  personal space, 47
  spatial arrangements, 47
  symbols, 46
  time, perception of, 48
  touch, 47
non-verbal symbols
  clothing, 48
  colour, 48
  height, 49
North American Free Trade Agreement (NAFTA), 42
North American values, 43
note-taking, 229, 240
notes, 372, 431
noun-pronoun agreement, 106, 463–464
nouns, concrete, 321, 389
numbers, 228–229, 411, 476

Oatley, Keith, 449
objections, 12, 164–168
objective pronouns, 464, 465
Official Languages Act, 42
office scuttlebutt, 7
omission, 201
one-on-one meetings, 351
one-two-three organizational pattern, 365
online communities, 356
online news sites, 238–239
online research, 222–224, 379–381
online resumés, 409
Ontario Youth Apprenticeship Program, 442
open body positions, 46
open punctuation, 96
open questions, 164–165
oral communication
  advantages, 33
  compliments, 50
  conventions, 4
  conversational style, 49
  culture, 49–50
  disadvantages, 34
  exaggeration, 50
  Generation X, 49
  PowerPoint, 84–85
  presentation slides, design of, 84–85
  silence, 50
  summarizing, 237
  understatement, 50
oral presentations
  alternatives, excluding, 365

audience, 364, 365
audience, questions from, 372–373
chairperson role, 364
chronological, 365
close, 367–368
dramatic statement, 366
effective delivery, 371–372
eye contact, 371–372
facilitator role, 364
gesturing, 372
goodwill presentations, 362
group presentations, 373–374
guided discussions, 364
humour, 367
ideas for, 366
informative presentations, 362
keep it short and simple (KISS), 368
location of, 369
monologue presentation, 364
nervousness, 371
notes, 372
one-two-three, 365
opening, 366–367
organizational patterns, 365
overview, 365
PAIBOC, 237, 363
persuasive presentations, 362
planning, 363–364
PowerPoint, 368–370
presentation slides, 369, 372
pro/con, 365
problem/causes/solution, 365
purpose of, 363–364
question, 367
quotation, 367
repetition for reinforcement, 365
roles, 364
sales presentations, 362
signpost, 365
simplification, 364
standing, 372
story, 367
summarizing, 237
time of, 364
transition, 365
types of, 362–363, 364
visuals, 312, 368–370, 372
voice, 370
order of importance, 125
orders, 161
organization, 25
  analyzing people in, 28–30
  audience analysis, 31
  building goodwill with, 215
  different needs of audience, 32
  reports, 273–275
organizational culture, 29–30, 458–459. *see also* corporate culture
organizational meetings, 351
organizational patterns, 142
  audience analysis, 30

chronological, 365
direct requests, 163–164
exclude alternatives, 365
informative messages, 125–126
negative messages, 142–149
one-two-three, 365
oral presentations, 365–366
persuasive messages, 164
positive messages, 125–126
pro/con, 365
problem/causes/solution, 365
problem-solving messages, 164
subject lines, 128
orientation, 335
overstatement, 50
overview of presentation, 32

Padilla, Carmella M., 201
PAIBOC
  analysis, 11–12
  attachments, 115
  business communications, 11–12
  channels, 23
  communications context, 23
  compared to Maslow's hierarchy, 142
  cover letters, 414
  definition, 11–12
  design, 80
  email messages, 109
  follow up to job interviews, 439
  formal reports, 282
  informative messages, 129–132
  intercultural communication, 51
  job application letters, 414
  key questions, 11–12
  letter format, 94
  listening, 325
  meetings, 352
  negative messages, 142, 150–153
  oral presentations, 237, 363
  persuasive messages, 169–173
  positive messages, 129–132
  reader benefits, 181–182
  reports, 250
  research, 221
  resumés, 391
  summarization of text, 236
  synthesize information, 236–237
  visuals, 304
paired bar graphs, 309
paper pages, design of, 80–84
paragraph revision
  topic sentences, 457–458
  transitions, 458
  unity, 457
paragraphs
  detail, 301
  improvement of, 300–301

revision (*see* paragraph revision)
  topic sentences, 457–458
  transitions, 300, 458
  unified, 300, 457
  variety, 301
paralanguage, 370
parallel structure, 138–139, 456
parallelism, 81, 456, 466
  courtesy titles, 99
  forms for names, 101
  lists, 81, 466
  structure, 81
paraphrase, 238, 239, 341
parental tone, 168
parentheses, 473
parliamentary proceedings, 351
participation, 73, 356
particular-to-general pattern, 273
passive verbs, 212
  use of, 449–451
passive voice, 91–92
past behaviour, 28
patterns, 228
Pay Equity Act, 42
payback reports, 250
paying attention, 324–325
peer pressure, 338–339
peers, bad news to, 148–149
people-first language, 55
perceive, 22
perception, 22
perceptive types, 27
periodic reports, 250
periods, 473
personal groups, 28
personal management skills, 3
personal pronouns, 464
personal space, 47
personality, 26–27
persuasion
  direct requests, 163–164
  elements of, 160
  indirect, 164
  positive emphasis, 195
persuasive appeals, 160
persuasive messages
  appeals, 160
  checklist, 173–174
  collection letters, 161–162
  common ground, 167
  common types, 161–162
  credibility, 160, 167
  definition, 160
  direct requests, 163–164
  directed subject lines, 169
  email, 160, 171
  emotional appeal, 160, 167
  indirect requests, 164
  job application letters (*see* job application letters)
  logic, 160
  objections, identification and overcoming, 164–168
  orders, 161
  organizational pattern, 163–164
  PAIBOC, 169–173

primary purposes, 160
problem-solving messages, 169, 171, 174
problem-solving pattern, 164
prompt action, reasons for, 168
purpose of, 160
rational appeal, 164
request action, 168
secondary purposes, 160
strategies, 164–165
stories and psychological description, 167–168
subject line, 169
tone, 167
type analysis, 27
persuasive presentations, 362
phone interviews, 438–439
photocopy, 99
photographs, 31–32, 55
phrases, 467
pictographs, 309
pie graphs, 308
Pink Ribbons, Inc., 7
pitch, 370
planning
audience, talking to, 66
brainstorm, 66
career, 379–381
clustering, 63, 66
co-authored documents, 343–344
definition, 63
dot, 355
freewrite, 66
guide, 66–67
guidelines for documents, 67
oral presentations, 363–364
pre-meeting, 352–354
rewriting, 64
time spent on, 66
planning guides, 66–67
plural possessives, 193
plural pronouns, 53
plurals, 193
politeness, 203, 260
political groups, 28
polychronic cultures, 48
Pook, Peter, 264
Pool, Léa, 7
population, 225
positive connotations, 198–200
positive emphasis
apologies, 204
burial of negative information, 202
compact presentation of negatives, 202
creation of, 196–202
definition, 195–196
delivery of, 196
ethical use of, 201
hedging statements, 204
hidden negatives, 199
job application letters, 423
negative words to avoid, 198–200
omission, 201
point of, 195–196

politeness, 203
power, 202–203
presentation, 202
reader benefit, 200–201
reader's ability, 200
sensitive delivery, 196
strategic placement of negatives, 202
tone, 203–204
unnecessary negatives, 201
words with negative connotations, 198–200
you-attitude, checking for, 200
positive messages
adjustments, 124–125
audience needs, 125–126
checklist, 129
confirmations, 122
collection letter, 121
congratulatory notes, 125
email, 115
examples of, 127
good news, 125
goodwill ending, 126
instructions, 121, 124
negative elements, 126
organizational pattern, 125–126
PAIBOC, 129–132
primary purposes, 121
reader benefits, 126–127
responses to complaints, 124–125
sample memo, 127
secondary purposes, 121
subject line, 127–129
summaries, 122–123
thank-you notes, 125
transmittals, 121
types of, 121–125
positive roles, 336
possessive nouns, 193
possessive pronouns, 193, 464, 465, 470
power, 203
Power Distance Index (PDI), 44
PowerPoint, 84–85, 368–370
practices, 43–44
practising, 73, 431–432
preaching, 327
preachy tone, 168
précis, 238, 241
predication errors, 466
prejudice. *see* discrimination
pre-meeting planning, 352–354
preparation, 356
presentation slides, 84–85
presentations. *see* oral presentations
presenting problem, 340
primary audience, 19, 21, 32
primary purposes
business messages, 123
informative messages, 121
negative messages, 141
persuasive messages, 160
positive messages, 121

primary research, 220, 225
print sources for research, 225
prior knowledge, 25
pro/con pattern, 365
problem/causes/solution pattern, 365
problem-solution pattern, 274
problem-solving pattern, 164
problem-solving persuasive messages, 164–168
problem-solving reports, 250
procedural leader, 337
procedural messages, 336
procrastination, avoiding, 73
professional attitude, 443
professional image, 104
progress reports, 250, 257–258
chronological, 258–259
recommendation, 260
sample chronological, 259
subject lines, 258
task, 259
pronouns
nominative, 464
non-sexist, 52–53
nouns, agreement with, 106
objective, 464, 465
personal, 464
plural, 53
possessive, 193, 464, 465, 470
reflexive, 464, 465
second person, 456–457
singular, 464
subjective, 464
third person, 456
proofreading, 70, 411–412
co-authored documents, 345
consistency, 411
dates, 411
definition, 70, 411
email messages, 112
format, 411
names, 411
need for, 70
numbers, 411
punctuation, 411
spell checker, 70, 412
symbols, 477
tips, 70
proportional fonts, 83
proposals
budgets, 269–270
class reports, 270–271
definition, 266
funding, 268
purpose of, 266
reports, 250
requests for proposals (RFP), 268
sales, 268
sample, proposal for foundation repair, 269
sample, proposal for services, 267
sample, student report, 271–272
student reports, 270–271
timeline, 271

prospecting letters
body paragraphs, 420
bridge, 417
first paragraphs, 419
guidelines, 417–418
last paragraphs, 420
when to use, 415
psychographic characteristics, 27
psychological description, 167, 186
psychological noise, 22
psychological reactance, 147
punctuation
apostrophes, 207, 218, 469–470
colons, 332, 470–471
commas. *see* commas
dashes, 360, 472
ellipses, 475
hyphens, 360, 472–473
italics, 475–476
mixed, 96
open, 96
parentheses, 473
periods, 473
quotation marks, 474–475
semicolons, 332, 468, 474
square brackets, 475
two-point, 96
underlining, 475–476
Puritan work ethic, 45
purpose statement, 251–252
purposes
business communication, 4
co-authored documents, 343
communication, 4
cover letters, 414–415
formal report, 283
job application letters, 414
meetings, 352
oral presentations, 363–364
primary. *see* primary purposes
reader benefits, 180
secondary purposes. *see* secondary purposes
writing, 11
writing, of, 11

quarterly reports, 250
question, 367
questionnaires, 226, 228
questions
branching, 227
closed, 226
multiple-choice, 226–227
open, 226
quotation, 367
quotation marks, 222, 474–475
quotations, use of, 243–244
quotes
documentation of, 243–244
ellipses, 475
oral presentations, 367
quotation marks, 474–475
square brackets, 475

racism, 49, 51. *see also* discrimination
ragged right margins, 84
random sample, 225–226
rational appeal, 164
Ray, George B., 370
readability, 69, 276–277, 469
reader benefits
   appeal of, 180
   audience focus, 189
   audience, identification of, 181–185
   brainstorm, 181–185
   choice of, 185–189
   context, 183
   definition, 180
   detailed, 188–189, 389
   extrinsic benefits, 187
   features of product/service, 184–185
   identifying, 181–185
   informative messages, 182
   intrinsic benefits, 185
   motivation, 180
   objections, anticipation of, 183
   positive emphasis, 200–201
   positive messages, 126–127
   psychological description, 186
   purpose of, 180
   relevancy, 188–189
   subgroups, 185
   subject line, 169
   you-attitude, 188, 211
reader-centered documents, 9
reader redundancy, 457
reader's ability, 200
readers' needs, 183–184
reading, 6
really simple syndication (RSS), 224, 241
receive, 22
recommendation progress report, 260
recommendations, 285
redundant phrases, 321
reference collections, 238
reference line, 97
references, 285, 405
referral interviews, 383
referrals, 383
reflexive pronouns, 464, 465
refusals, 146
   direct, 146
   implied, 146
   reasons for, 145–146
rejections, 141–142
religious groups, 28
repetition for reinforcement, 365
reports
   analytical, 264–266
   annual, 250
   audit, 250
   body, 250, 283–284
   business plans, 250
   chronological progress, 258–259

closure, 253–254
conclusion, 250
conference, 250, 255
definition, 249
documentation of sources, 242–244
feasibility, 250, 264–265
formal. *see* formal reports
functional pattern, 275
incident, 250, 256–257
informal, 249
information, 253
introduction, 249
justification, 250, 265–266
long. *see* long reports
make-good, 250
organizational patterns, 273–275
payback, 250
periodic, 250
preparation for writing, 251–252
problem identification, 251
problem-solving, 250
progress. *see* progress reports
proposals, 250, 266–272
purpose statement, 251–252
quarterly, 250
recommendation, 260
sales, 250
short. *see* short reports
steps in writing, 251
task progress, 259
technical, 250
trip, 250, 255–256
types of, 250
yardstick, 250, 264
requests for proposals (RFP), 268, 287
research
   analysis of data, 228–229
   beginning, 220–221
   Boolean search, 223
   branching questions, 227
   Canadian government information, 238
   causation, 228
   closed questions, 226
   companies, for job search, 379–381
   convenience samples, 226
   correlation, 228
   data source, 228
   definition, 220
   documentation of sources, 242–244
   effective use of, 239–241
   evaluation of sources, 224–225
   finding information, 221–224
   identify objective, 220–221
   interview questions, 226–228
   judgment samples, 226
   keyword search, 222–223
   multiple-choice questions, 226–227
   news websites, 238–239

notes, making of, 229
online reference collections, 238–239
online sources, 222
open questions, 226
others', 223
PAIBOC, 221
population, 225
primary, 220, 225
print sources, 225
questionnaire, 226
questionnaire design, 228
random samples, 225–226
really simple syndication (RSS), 224
reference collections, 238
reports, 251
reputable resources, 224–225
resources, 221–222
samples, 225
search strategies, 222–224
secondary, 220
sources, evaluation of, 224–225
subject matter directories, 236
survey questions, 226–228
surveys, 226
working purpose statement, 220–221
respondents, 226
responses to complaints, 124–125
resumés
   action verbs, 399, 400–401
   attention getting, 392–393
   career achievements, 403
   career objective, 403
   chronological, 393, 394, 398, 399–400, 402
   combination, 397–399, 401–402
   communication skills, 403
   definition, 391
   design, 392
   detail, 399
   education, 404
   formats, 398–402
   functional, 394–396, 398, 401, 402
   gerunds, 399
   honours and awards, 405
   interpersonal profile, 403
   length, 406
   new headings, creation of, 406
   nouns, 399
   online, 409
   PAIBOC, 391
   reader's perspective, 392
   references, 405
   reverse chronology, 393
   scannable, 406–409
   skills, 397–399, 401–402
   websites, 379
retreats, 351
reverse chronological resumé, 393

revision, 67–68
   checklist, 68
   co-authored documents, 345
   definition, 67
   after feedback, 72
   light, 68
   paragraphs. *see* paragraph revision
   sentences. *see* sentence revision
   time for, 65
   tips, 67
rewriting, 62, 64
Reynolds, Fred, 67
Robert's Rules of Order, 351
Rock, Michael E., 45
Roloff, Kathryn S., 338
root words, 222
Royal Bank, 30
RSS (really simple syndication), 224, 241
rules of writing, 449
run-on sentences (RO), 177–178, 468

sales
   meetings, 351
   presentations, 362, 364
   proposals, 268
   reports, 250
Salkin, Allan, 10
salutation, 95
The Salvation Army, 210
sample, 225
sample emails, 110
   attachment, with an, 112
   follow-up, job interview, 440
   informative, 115, 123
   job application letter, 423
   job interviews, 440
   Outlook Express memo template, 109
   request for adjustment, 111
   response to complaint, 13–14
   sales letter, 111
sample formal reports, 288–296
sample letters
   block format on letterhead, 95
   block format without letterhead, 98
   claim letter, 143
   collection letter, 95, 162
   employee evaluation, 96
   follow-up to job interview, 440
   indented format on letterhead, 96
   informative, 100
   mixed punctuation, 95, 96, 100
   modified block format without letterhead, 98
   open punctuation, 98
   prospecting letters, 418
   refusal with alternative, 142
   solicited letters, 416–417
   two-page block format, 100

two-page modified block format, 100
two-point punctuation, 100
sample memos
    analytical proposal, 102
    announcement, 14–15
    bad news to subordinates, 149
    closure report, 254
    conference report, 255
    good news, 103, 127
    information report, 253
    informative, 127
    letterhead, 103
    negative to subordinates, 149
    persuasive, 181
    safety procedures, 124
    short report, 102
    simple request, 102
    trip report, 255
    two-page, 102
sample reports
    chronological progress report, 259
    conference report, 255
    incident report, 257
    information report, 253
    trip report, 256
Sandberg, Jared, 338
sans serif fonts, 84
Sato, Mitsuru, 165
scale, 312
scannable resumés, 406–409
Schachter, Harvey, 338
scope, 283
Scott, Lee, 22
search engines, 223
searchable online databases, 222
second person pronouns, 456–457
secondary audience, 20, 21
secondary purposes
    business messages, 123
    informative messages, 121
    negative messages, 141
    persuasive messages, 160
    positive messages, 121
secondary research, 220
Secrets of Powerful Presentations (Bender), 26
segmented bar graphs, 309
self-assessment, 378
self-recruitment, 382, 384
semi-block letter format, 94–95
semicolons, 332, 468, 474
sensing types, 26, 27
sentence fragments (Frag.), 16–17, 468–469
sentence revision
    active verbs, 449–451
    combining sentences, 452–453
    complex sentences, 454
    compound sentences, 453
    compound-complex sentences, 454
    gerunds, 452
    grouping into chunks, 455

infinitives, 452
medium length, 454–455
parallel structure, 456
readers in sentence, 456–457
sentence length, 454–455
sentence structure, 454–455
simple sentences, 453
strong action verbs, 451
subject/verb closeness, 453, 455–456
weight of sentence, 451
wordy phrases, elimination of, 452
sentences
    combining, 233–234, 452–453
    complex, 454
    compound, 453
    compound-complex, 454
    dependent clauses, 454, 466–467
    fragments (Frag.), 16–17, 468–469
    grouping words in, 455
    guidelines, 454
    independent clauses, 466, 467
    length of, 454–455
    long, 454
    main clauses, 466
    numbers at beginning of, 476
    parallel structure, 456
    parenthetical phrases, 455
    phrases, 454, 467
    revision. *see* sentence revision
    run-on (RO), 177–178, 468
    short, 451–452
    simple, 453
    smooth, 452
    structure, 454
    subordinate clauses, 466–467
    summary, 415
    topic, 276, 457
    weight of, 451
serial comma, 446
serif fonts, 83–84
sexist terms and phrases, 52
short reports
    analytical reports, 264–266
    blueprints, 276
    chronological progress reports, 258–259
    closure, 253–254
    conference reports, 255
    feasibility reports, 250, 264–265
    headings, 97
    incident reports, 256–257
    information reports, 253
    justification reports, 250, 265–266
    memos. *see* memos
    progress reports, 257–258
    recommendation progress reports, 260
    samples. *see* sample memos

style, 260
talking heads, 278
task progress reports, 259
topic sentences, 457–458
transitions, 458
trip reports, 255–256
yardstick reports, 250, 264
short words, 448
signpost, 365
silence, 550
simple sentences, 453
simple verb tenses, 321
singular possessives, 464
situational interviews, 437
skills resumés, 397–399, 401–402
Skype, 438
slang, 448
Sleeman Breweries, 30, 422
Sleeman, John, 422
smoking, 432
social groups, 28
social networking, and job hunting, 379, 381
socializing, 354
solicited letters
    body paragraphs, 420
    first paragraphs, 419
    guidelines, 415–416
    last paragraphs, 420
    summary paragraph, 415–416
    when to use, 415
sources
    citation of, 240, 310
    documenting, 240, 242–244
    evaluation, of, 228–229
    finding, 221–224
    strategic use of, 239–240
    understanding, of, 228–229
space, 47
spatial arrangement, 47
spatial pattern, 275
Speak2Me.cn, 216
speaking, 8, 11, 33
spell checkers, 70, 412
split infinitives, 446
square brackets, 475
stacked bar graphs, 309
staff meetings, 351
staff training sessions, 351
standing, 372
standard agenda, 355
Staples, 180
Statistics Canada, 41, 238
stereotypes, avoidance of, 22
Stewart, Sinclair, 147
stories, 167, 304–306, 309
story, 304–306, 367
strategy, 30–31
stream of consciousness, 64
student groups, 337–338
Student Harvest, 29
student reports, 271–272
Students Mentoring Students (SMS), 273
Stuff White People Like, 10
style, 31, 297, 447. *see also* writing style

subculture, 30
subdivided bar graphs, 309
subheadings, 276
subject, close to verb, 455–456
subject lines, 97
    appropriate, 128
    bolded, 101
    catchy, 113
    concise, 113, 128
    criteria, 128
    defined, 97, 127
    direct request, 169
    directed, 169
    email, 109, 113, 278
    highlighting good news, 128
    informative, 127–129
    informative messages, 127–129
    letters, 278
    memos, 278
    negative, 149
    negative messages, 149–150
    persuasive, 169
    persuasive messages, 169
    positive, 127
    positive messages, 127–129
    progress reports, 258
    reader benefit, 169
    specific, 113, 128
subject matter directories, 238
subject to verb proximity, 453, 455–456
subject-verb agreement, 59–60, 463
subjective pronouns, 464
subjunctive verbs, 186
subordinate clauses, 233, 466–467
subordinates, bad news to, 148–149
summaries, 122–123, 236–239
summarize, 236
summary paragraph, 415
summary sentence, 415
superiors, bad news to, 148
Supreme Court of Canada, 147
surveys
    convenience sample, 226
    defined, 226
    design, 228
    judgment sample, 226
    population sample, 225
    questions, 226–228
    random sample, 225–226
    types of questions, 226–228
synchronous messages, 113

tab settings, 86
table of contents, 286
tables, 286, 303, 308, 309
tabs, 86
Tagliamonte, Sali, 49
talking
    positive, 73
    writing, about, 73
talking heads, 278
Tannen, Deborah, 49
task progress report, 259

Taylor, Fabrice, 216
TD–Canada Trust, 30
team meetings, 351
teams. *see also* groups
    ground rules, 334
    importance of, 334
    task outcomes, 334
teamwork skills, 3
technical reports, 250
technical terms, 32–33
telegraphing, 97
Telford, Adrian, 338
tell-show-tell rule, 306
template, 72
tempo, 370
term-paper style, 448
testing designs, 86
text messages, 108–109
thank-you notes, 125
theory, use of, 32–33
think tank, 20
thinking types, 26
third person pronouns, 456
Tim Hortons, 27–28, 114
time
    cultural perception of, 4, 48
    good writing, and, 9
    management, 65
    writing process, 65
time is money, 4, 48
timeline
    report planning, 283
    writing process, 65
title page, 286
titles, 286
tone, 203–204, 421–423
topic sentences, 276, 457
touch, 47
town hall meetings, 351
Toyota, 195
transition words, 458
transitional phrases, 458
transitional words, 458
transitions, 233, 276, 300, 365,
    458
transmit, 22
transmittals, 121, 286
trip report, 250, 255–256
truncated graphs, 312
truncation, 312
Tufte, Edward, 311, 314
Tufte's Rules, 314
turnover, 188
Twitter, 29, 379
two-point punctuation, 96
type analysis, 27

Uncertainty Avoidance Index
    (UAI), 44
underlining, 475–476
understatement, 50
unity, 457
unsolicited letter. *see*
    prospecting letters

vague modifiers, 321
values, 27–28, 43–44, 266
Van Aelst, Michael, 422
VanCity Savings Credit Union,
    195
venting, 339
venture capitalists, 265
verbal, 446
verbs
    action, 400–401, 451
    active, 449–451
    close to subject,
        455–456
    concrete, 321, 389
    gerund, 399
    infinitive, 452
    passive, 449–451
    plural, 463
    singular, 463
    strong, 451
    subjunctive, 186
vested interest, 165
video interviews, 439
Vinall-Cox, Joan, 45
virtual meetings, 357–358
virus, computer, 115
vision statement, 266
visuals, 31–32, 286, 303–312
    accuracy, 312
    audience analysis, 31–32
    bar graphs, 306, 308–309
    chartjunk, 311
    citation, 310
    clip art, 311–312
    colour, use of, 310
    components of, 305
    context, 310
    design, 309–310
    ethical, 312
    figures, 286, 303, 309
    guidelines, 310
    histograms, 309
    integration into text, 311
    line graphs, 309
    oral presentations, 312, 368,
        372
    PAIBOC, 304
    pictographs, 309
    pie graphs, 308
    purpose of, 303
    reports, 286
    scale, 312
    stories, 304–306, 309
    tables, 286, 303, 308, 309
    truncated graphs, 312
    types of, 286, 306–309
voice
    active, 91–92
    intonation, 370
    oral presentations, 370
    passive, 91–92
    pitch, 370
    tempo, 370
    volume, 370

VoIP software, 352
volume, 370
volunteer community
    involvement, 386
        Wall Data, 196
        watchdog audience, 20, 21
        water cooler, 7
        Watson Wyatt Worldwide, 9
        we, 212
web logs. *see* blogs
web page design, 86
Webb, John, 43
Weldon, Kate, 439
white space, 80–81, 276
WHMIS, 256
who, 262, 465
whom, 262, 465
Wikipedia, 225
Wilkie, Helen, 8
Wilkins, Dave, 357
Wilson, Michael, 357
word choice
    slang, 448
    spell checkers, 70, 412
word elimination, 451–452
word processing, 86
words
    concrete, 321, 389
    negative, 198–200
    negative connotations,
        198–200
    non-sexist, 52
    obscure, 448
    positive connotations,
        198–200
    power implications, 203
    short, 448
    simple, 448
    unnecessary, 452–453
wordy writing, 451
working purpose statement,
    220–221, 226
working with others, 7, 334–345
Working.com, 379
Workopolis, 379
Workplace Hazardous Materials
    Information System (WHMIS),
    256
works cited, 285
WOW company, 22
writing
    actions, activities,
        encouragement, 73
    advantages, 9, 33
    amount of, 7–8
    concise, 451–453
    dates, 476
    definition, 62
    disadvantages, 8–9, 33
    editing, 64
    encouraging, 73
    good, 9
    importance of, 6, 7–8
    international audiences, 50

numbers, 476
poor, cost of, 8–9
proofreading, 64
revision, 64, 67–68
talking about, 73
you-attitude, 209–210
wordy, 451
writing process
    choosing, 65
    described, 63–64
    design, 87
    differences, 65
    drafting, 64
    getting started, 73
    planning, 63, 66–67
    rewriting, 64
    time management, 65
    timelines, 65
writing rules, 449
writing style, 260, 447, 448
    corporate culture, 458–459
    good, 260, 448
    levels of formality, 448
    long report, 297
    paragraph revision, 457–458
    rules, 449
    sentence revision, 449–457
    transition words and phrases,
        458
    types of, 448

XpressBook, 225

yardstick reports, 250, 264
you, 53, 212–213, 426–427, 456
you-attitude
    checklist, 214
    conflict resolution, 342
    content, 215
    creation of, 211–213
    definition, 209
    feelings, 211–212
    impersonal constructions,
        212
    in negative situations,
        212–213
    job application letters,
        421–422
    organization, 215
    passive verbs, 212
    positive situations, 212
    reader benefits, 211
    reader-focused, 211
    second person, use of,
        456–457
    third person, use of, 213
    we, 212
    words to use, 213
    in writing, 209–210
youth, 48

Zoomers, 41
ZoomInfo, 225